A Cruising Guide To
The Northwest Caribbean

From The Windward Passage to Guatemala

Second Edition

*Including
The Northern Coast of Jamaica,
The Cayman Islands,
The Bay Islands and mainland Honduras,
Guatemala and the Río Dulce.*

by
Stephen J. Pavlidis

Seaworthy Publications
Cocoa Beach, Florida

A Cruising Guide to the Northwest Caribbean
Second Edition

ISBN-13: 978-1-892399-38-0
7.0

Published in the USA by:
Seaworthy Publications, Inc.
2021 N. Atlantic Ave., #226
Cocoa Beach, Florida 32931
Phone 321-610-3634
email orders@seaworthy.com
www.seaworthy.com - Your Bahamas and Caribbean Cruising Advisory

CAUTION: Sketch charts are not to scale and are not to be used for navigational purposes. They are intended as supplements for NOAA, DMA, or British Admiralty charts and no warranties are either expressed or implied as to the usability of the information contained herein. The Author and Publisher take no responsibility for their misuse.

A publication like this is actually the result of a blending of many people's knowledge and experiences. First off, I would like to thank the following for their help with the updates to this guide: Annie Lewis; Bob and Trish Meredith on S/V *Barnacle;* Jimmy Peters; Captain Lee Bakewell of the S/V *Escape Cay*; Jack Boatwright; Bob, Margery, Alex, and Sweet of the S/V *Island Time*; Alicia Bonnet; Steve Bowden of *Sea Tech Systems*; John, Vivian, and the entire staff of *Bluewater Books and Charts* in Ft. Lauderdale; John Brandes of *Capt. John's Marina*; George and Helen Brown of the S/V *True Colors*; Valeria Cerezo; Marco Antonio Linares; Karen Carpenter of the S/V *Rasmus*; Nelson Christiana; Cherie and Sandy of the S/V *Namaste*; Captain Dale Westin; Julie and Michael Frick of the S/V *Surprize*; Jim Gibbs, *Pier 83*; Joyce and Roger Hill; *La Ceiba Shipyard*; Richard and Nancy Laub of the S/V *Cookie Monster*; Jim, Nikki, and everybody at *Mario's Marina*; Mike Payne; George Munro Sr., and George Munro Jr. of Port Antonio, Jamaica; Paul and Linda Petzold; Jimmy Peters; Randy and Sherry of the S/V *Procyon*; Roger Quigg of *Jolly Roger Cruises* in Roatán; Chris Parker of the *Caribbean Weather Center*; Mike and Karen Rhea of *Rhea of Hope*; Roady (ILMTB); Daniel Rouse of the S/V *Yankee*; Daryl and Cristal Simpson of the M/V *Izabal Queen*; Sharon Smith of the S/V *Beach House*: Kent Trompeter of the S/V *Southern Mist II*; Jack and Pat Tyler of the S/V *Whoosh*; Dave Waltz of the S/V *Victoria*; Bruce and Rosa Van Sant of the M/V *Tidak Apa*; and Tom Williams of the *Montego Bay Yacht Club*.

I would like to thank Bob Smith for his sketches that we use in this guide.
If there is anybody that I have neglected to mention here, rest assured that it is an oversight and I sincerely apologize.

All photos are by the author except where noted.
Cover Design by Ken Quant, *Broad Reach Marketing*, Milwaukee, WI

Library of Congress Cataloging-in-Publication Data

Pavlidis, Stephen J.
  A cruising guide to the northwest Caribbean : from the windward Passage to Guatemala : including the northern coast of Jamaica, the Cayman Islands, the Bay Islands and mainland Honduras, Guatemala and the Rio Dulce / by Stephen J. Pavlidis. -- Second Edition.
      pages cm
  Includes bibliographical references and indexes.
  ISBN-13: 978-1-892399-38-0 (alk. paper)
  ISBN-10: 1-892399-38-5 (alk. paper)
  1. Boats and boating--Caribbean Area--Guidebooks. 2. Nautical charts--Caribbean Area. 3. Caribbean Area--Guidebooks. 4. Boats and boating--Central America--Guidebooks. 5. Nautical charts--Central America. 6. Central America--Guidebooks. I. Title.
  GV776.23.P38 2014
  797.109163'65--dc23
                    2014003804

Introduction

I have a T-shirt that says "Panama City, Redneck Riviera." A catchy moniker I'm sure, but it's not the first place I've heard described in that regard. The first time I heard that description of an area the speaker directed his comment to the area of the Northwest Caribbean, from Mexico to Honduras, and I had to laugh. Perhaps the breed of cruiser attracted to this paradise is a bit different than those who spend their time in the Eastern Caribbean, but I'd hardly call them rednecks. I was born and raised in Georgia and I know what a redneck is and isn't, and these folks here are not rednecks, they're simply cruisers who have opted for the most enjoyment out of their allotted cruising time. The cruisers here don't need the hustle and bustle of Antigua Race Week, they don't need to spend their entire cruising kitty trying to re-provision their larder in the BVI (although the Cayman Islands can be nearly as expensive I'll grant you), and they've chosen to voyage in waters where the people are very open to cruisers.

When was the last time you saw a marina give you free phone calls to the U.S., free Internet access, and free rides to town? When was the last time you saw a resort on a tiny cay offer you free moorings, ice, water, and laundry service? When was the last time you saw a residence ashore with a huge "Welcome Cruisers" sign on their private dock? I've never seen all that in one place, except here in the Northwest Caribbean. But you know, it's not that we are looking for something free, it's just that when these people go out of their way like that it makes you feel welcome, down home sort of welcome, if that's redneck then call me Bubba!

Of course some of the more scholarly among us will say that there is no culture in the Northwest Caribbean; that you must go to Europe to find true culture. I beg to differ. The Mayans in Central America had a highly developed culture when barbarians were the only inhabitants of Europe. These same folks say that the Northwest Caribbean is nothing but a string of banana republics. One of these banana republics has established a marine free zone to allow yachts to import supplies duty free, let's see if I can remember where in the Eastern Caribbean that's available, and don't even get me started on a European VAT.

Probably the biggest draw for cruisers to the Northwest Caribbean is the Río Dulce in Guatemala. Probably the safest area in the Caribbean to enjoy hurricane season, the Río Dulce has seen a huge influx of hurricane season cruisers, especially since the devastation of the last few years in Florida and New Orleans. It's not that the Río Dulce is full of little hidey-holes, it does have several small bays in which shelter can be found with little fetch, the river's real value is that it is so difficult for a hurricane to hit the river full force without going over large areas of mountainous land. This does not mean that the Río Dulce is bulletproof, but the odds are in its favor. And even with a direct hit, most boats are so far upriver the tidal surge would be minimal.

It's a different kind of cruising here, mega-yachts are rarely seen on the Río Dulce, these vessels simply cannot make it over the bar at Livingston. And it's a different kind of cruiser here as well. The folks here are down to earth, friendly, the economy good, the prices fair, and the camaraderie as rich as anywhere.

I have just realized that I suffer from mixed emotions with the creation of this guide. I want to help my fellow cruisers make their way down here and enjoy this area to the fullest, yet I don't want to attract TOO many folks and spoil paradise. I seem to be caught between a rock and a hard place. Perhaps I'll just stop writing now…I think I've said too much…shhhhh…

Steve Pavlidis

Table of Contents

A Little Basic Jamaican........... 260

Dining... 262

Busing Around.......................... 271

References.................................. 275

References.................................. 276

Appendices............................... 277

The Basics

Anchoring

Just as important as getting your vessel moving and keeping her heading along your chosen courseline quickly and efficiently is the fine art of keeping your vessel from moving. Anchor choice is basically a personal preference. Some skippers prefer *CQRs*, while others swear by a *Bruce*, *Mantus*, *Rocna*, or a *Danforth*. Of the lot, you will find that a *Danforth* holds as well or better than a *CQR* or *Bruce* in sandy bottoms while the *CQR* or *Bruce* is preferred when anchoring in rocky bottoms. Whatever your choice of anchor, you must deploy your anchor correctly and with sufficient scope to hold you when the tide changes, if a front approaches, or if a squall should blow through at 2:00 a.m. (which seems to be the time they choose to blow through). Your anchor should have a length of chain (at least 15') shackled to your anchor to keep your rode from chafing against coral or rocks and to create a catenary curve that helps absorb shock loads while lowering the angle of pull on your anchor. Too high an angle may cause your anchor to pull up and out of the bottom. Some cruisers prefer all chain rodes with a nylon snubber to absorb the shock loads. This is an excellent arrangement but a windlass may be needed unless you prefer the workout involved with hauling in the chain and anchor every time you move.

In most of the lee side anchorages in the Northwest Caribbean you will find that you can lie quite comfortably to only one anchor. When setting your anchor, do not just drop it and let your rode run out, piling itself on top of your anchor. Lower your anchor to the bottom and deploy the rode as you fall back with the current or wind until you have a 7:1 scope out. When calculating the amount of scope required, be sure to allow for high tide as well as the height of your anchor roller or fairlead above the water. Without being precise, you can figure on a 1'-1½' tidal rise in the waters covered in this guide although occasionally you may find a 2' rise or more during Spring tides, a little more during a full moon and a little less at new moon. When you have secured your rode, back down with the engine at about ½ throttle to set the anchor. If you have not succeeded in securing your anchor, try again. To check the set it is best to dive on your anchors or at the very least, look at their set through a glass bottom bucket from your dinghy. You may find that you will have to set them by hand,

especially in rocky areas. If you are riding on one anchor and find that you are lying to the wind but that the swell is rolling you, position another anchor at an angle off the stern so as to align your bow into the swell making for a more comfortable night. A better idea is to set a bridle: run a line from your anchor rode, at least ½ your waterline length, from your bow and lead it back to a winch through a block near your stern. You can then winch in the line to change the angle your boat lies to the swells.

Many of the anchorages in this book are swept by swift tidal currents (sometimes up to 2.5 knots), such as *Dick Sesinger's Bay* on Cayman Brac, and two anchors, as in a Bahamian Moor are required. To avoid bumping into your neighbor in the middle of the night or putting your vessel on the rocks or a beach, two anchors, such as in a Bahamian Moor, are required. Although one anchor may be fine if you have the swinging room, when the tide changes it may pull out and fail to reset. Sometimes these anchorages can be crowded and while you may swing wide on your one anchor and not find yourself endangered by the rocks or the beach, you and your neighbor may go bump in the night because his two anchors have kept him in one spot. If unsure, the best thing to do is follow the lead of those boats that are there before you. Conversely, if you arrive at an anchorage and everyone is on one anchor and you choose to set two, do so outside the swing radius of the other boats.

To set a Bahamian Moor you must first decide where you wish for your vessel to settle. You will lay out two anchors, one up-current and one down-current of that spot, which will keep you swinging in a small circle. Head into the current to where you will drop your first anchor and set it properly. Let out as much rode as you need, setting your anchor on the way by snubbing it, until you are at the spot where you are to drop your down-current anchor. If the wind has pushed you to one side or the other of the tidal stream, you will have to power up to the position where you will set your second anchor. Lower your second anchor and pull your vessel back up-current on your first rode, paying out the rode for the second anchor and snubbing it as you maneuver back up-current to your chosen spot. You may want to dive on your anchors to check their set. Keeping your rodes tight will keep you swinging in a tighter circle. Check your anchor rodes daily as they will twist together and make it extremely difficult to undo them in an emergency. You can also set your up-current anchor and settle back to where you wish to lie, and then dinghy your second anchor out down-current. The only problem with this is that you must make sure your down-current anchor has set well before the tide changes.

In some tight anchorages you will be unable to set your anchors 180° apart. An alternative is to set them 90° apart in a "Y" configuration perpendicular to the wind. A skipper with a large swing radius in very tight quarters is apt to find out what his neighbors think of his anchoring technique as soon as the wind shifts. Responsible anchoring cannot be overstressed. Always set an anchor light. Some cruisers feel this is unimportant in some of the more isolated anchorages. What they probably do not understand is that many locals run these islands at all hours of the night, even on moonless nights, and an anchor light protects your vessel as well as theirs.

Never anchor in coral, even with your dinghy anchor. An anchor can do a great deal of damage to a very fragile ecosystem that will take years to recover if it is to recover at all. Besides, sand holds so much better.

In summer months and on into the early fall, or when there is no wind, you may wish to anchor a good distance from shore to keep away from the relentless biting insects. Cays with a lot of vegetation or mangroves will have a higher concentration of biting insects.

Proper anchoring etiquette should by practiced at all times. For instance, if the anchorage is wide and roomy and only one boat is at anchor, don't anchor right on top of them; give your neighbor a little breathing room and some solitude. You would probably appreciate the same consideration should the situation be reversed. All too often cruisers exhibit a herding instinct where they seek the comfort of other nearby cruisers, anchoring much too close at times. Many boaters, after a long, hard day in rough seas or bad weather, anxiously await the peace and tranquility of a calm anchorage. The last thing they want is noise and wake. If you have a dog aboard that loves to bark, be considerate of your neighbors who don't wish to hear him. They do have that right. Jet skis can be a lot of fun, but only when you're astride one. Many cruisers have little tolerance for the incessant buzzing back and forth of high-speed jet skis. It is a good show of manners to slowly leave the anchorage where you can have your high-speed

fun and games and not disturb anyone. If at all possible, try not to run your generators at sunset or after dark. At sunset, many cruisers are sitting in their cockpits enjoying cocktails and watching the sun go down and don't want a generator disturbing their soft conversations. Courtesy shown is usually courtesy returned.

Clothing-What to Bring

In a word...hot! Plan to wear what is comfortable for you in a tropical climate. You will most likely live in shorts and T-shirts (if that much). Long pants and sturdy, comfortable shoes are preferred when hiking for protection from the bush and the rugged terrain. Long sleeved shirts and long pants (or old cotton pajamas) and wide brimmed hats are important in keeping the sun and mosquitoes off you. Polarized sunglasses (extremely helpful for piloting) and suntan lotion (suntan oil tends to leave a long lasting greasy smear all over everything) should be included in your gear. In winter months it is advisable to bring something warm to wear, especially in the evenings. Long pants and sweaters are usually adequate and a light jacket would be a good idea as some frontal passages will occasionally drop the temperature to 60° F, not to mention the fact that the temperatures drop rapidly at night in the mountainous regions (as in COLD).

It is very important that all men and women dress appropriately when entering settlements. Skimpy bathing suits are excellent for the beach or boat but in town they are not apropos. Men should wear shirts in town as some local inhabitants are quick to remind you to cover up. Remember, you are a visitor here and that entails a certain responsibility.

Currency

In many places in Central America you'll run across black market money changers. Some will offer you a higher exchange rate than is given at banks and change booths, but they can also give you far less than the current rate. How? Sleight of hand. To begin with, you'll probably be dealing with a currency you haven't seen before and therefore are unfamiliar with the color and denomination of each bill. Often the changers will be counting and separating the bills into small piles so fast that you will have trouble keeping up and by the time you get to count your money you realize that you've been taken and the changer is long gone. A combination of the changer's speed and your unfamiliarity with the currency work against you, and the money changer knows that. By going slowly, keeping a sharp eye on the tally, and marking the piles as they are counted (don't let the changer touch them again after they've been counted), you can usually assure yourself of a fair exchange, but if you're not careful you'll find yourself being taken like a country bumpkin at a traveling carnival's shell game.

Another money changer's trick is offering "X" amount of pesos (I'm using this as an example because I ran across this trick on the Mexico/ Guatemala border, on the Mexican side) for "Y" amount of U.S. dollars, and then handing you less than the agreed on amount while showing you on a calculator that same amount. Don't let someone get away with this. If you're at the border threaten to call a policeman or soldier; there will be a few of those nearby, which should do the trick. But to be truthful, the best protection is to make currency arrangements in advance and avoid the black market money changers until you're adept at handling them. And on a final note, before leaving a country, make sure you have some of the local currency left in case there is a departure fee. Besides, having a little money left over is a good incentive to later return to the area if no other reason than to spend it.

Although prices are fixed for services and hotel rooms in the Northwest Caribbean, you're expected to bargain in the markets. I usually offer 25% of the initial asking price and after a period of back and forth banter settle at around 50%-75% of the starting price (bear in mind that what I just wrote is NOT set in concrete, be flexible and don't forget that you can always raise your offer, but you can't lower it so start LOW). Remember to keep your sense of humor and good luck with your bargaining. And for a final note let me remind you that the exchange rates quoted here are current at the time of this writing and may change at any time without notice unless the currency rates are fixed such as in Belize and the Cayman Islands.

You'll also find the following information in each chapter under the heading of *The Local Currency*. If you need to get the latest quotes you can go online to http://www.xe.com/ucc/full.shtml for up to the minute currency exchange rates.

Belize
In Belize the standard is the *Belize Dollar* (BZ$), which has a fixed rate of exchange of BZ$2 (actually BZ$2.2) to US$1. Most hotels, resorts, restaurants,

and tour operators will accept U.S. currency, traveler's checks, or credit cards. When using your credit cards in Belize, most establishments will add a 5% service charge to your bill and many establishments will add a 10% service charge to your bill in lieu of a tip. Always make sure that you understand which dollar rate is being quoted, BZ$ or US$. Belize has an 8% sales tax which is applied to all goods and services except hotel accommodations. The current hotel tax is at 7% but that is expected to increase, and some hotels will add a service charge of 10-15% to your bill.

Cayman Islands
The currency in use in the Cayman Islands is the *Cayman Islands Dollar*, CI$, which is divided into 100 cents and valued at US$1=CI$1.21 as of this writing. The Cayman Islands mint coins in denominations of 1¢, 5¢, 10¢, and 25¢, and print bills in denominations of $1, $5, $10, $25, $50, and $100. U.S. dollars are widely accepted in the islands (in fact they're preferred in many establishments) as are the major credit cards, so there is really no need to change U.S. dollars into CI dollars. Most restaurants, but not all, automatically add a 15% service charge to the bill and taxi drivers expect a 10%-15% tip. Hotels add a government levied 10% tax on all rooms, and there is also a departure tax of CI$10. You can exchange money at banks, *ATM*s (which will give you your money in CI or U.S. dollars), and many hotels. Although the standard of living is higher than any other place in the Caribbean, the cost of living is higher as well. Bear in mind that all goods must be imported into the Cayman Islands so the prices you pay will reflect this expense. Expect prices to range from 20%-30% higher than in the United States so it's best to provision for a long voyage elsewhere, however there are grocery items you'll find here that you won't find in places like Jamaica.

If you plan to arrive in the Cayman Islands from Cuba, bear in mind that you may not import ANY Cuban products, and that includes cigars, into the Cayman Islands.

Guatemala
In Guatemala the monetary unit is the *Quetzale* (called *Q*'s for short), approximately 7.579Q per US$1. It's almost a waste of time to change anything other than U.S. dollars; even currencies from Guatemala's neighbors can be difficult to exchange. If you do have change anything other than U.S. dollars try one of the change kiosks (*Casas de Cambios*) at the airport in Guatemala City or in Flores. You can pay for many

purchases with a debit card, *VISA*, or *MasterCard*, and even get cash advances from banks and *ATM's* in many places, but 6% will be tacked on to the price for using those cards. There is a 12% *IVA* (value added tax) applied to all purchases, and hotels charge a 22% tourist tax.

Honduras

In Honduras the currency in use is the *Lempira* (*L*), called *lemps* for short, which comes in L1, L5, L10, L20, L50, L100, L500, and L1,000 denominations. You can get a better exchange rate if you convert your dollars into *Lempiras* and pay for your purchases in *Lempiras*; the current exchange rate, at the time of this writing, is L19.91 per US$1. There is also a 12% sales tax applied to merchandise and services, a 15% sales tax on alcohol and tobacco products, a 4% tax on lodging, and tipping is customarily 10%-15%. Bear in mind that if you pay for your purchase in U.S. dollars that your change will be in *Lempiras*. It's a good idea to have a few *lempira* in your pocket when you clear in at Guanaja, either that or several U.S. dollars, enough to cover the US$3.00 *Immigration* fee (per person).

Jamaica

In Jamaica the currency in use is the *Jamaican dollar*, J$, which at the time of this writing was J$95.475 to US$1. If you clear in at Port Antonio there is a *Scotia Bank* with an *ATM* just outside the gate of the *Port Antonio Marina* that can supply you with all the change you need. Credit cards are accepted in most places, especially in the tourist areas. If you want the best deal possible, try to pay in Jamaican dollars, called "Js" (jays), you'll pay less in the long run. Bills come in J$50, $100, $500, and $1,000 denominations and coins can be found in denominations of $5, $1, $0.50, and $0.25.

In Jamaica you'll often find a 15% GCT (*General Consumption Tax*) applied to your bill of rooms, goods, and services, although in some instances it may already be figured in the price quoted. Tipping is from 10%-15% although route taxi drivers don't expect a tip. You'll need to keep any receipts you get for changing dollars or pounds into Js, you will need them when you try to change your Js to dollars or pounds before leaving (you're not allowed to take Js out of the country).

Mexico

In Mexico, although dollars are accepted everywhere, the standard currency is the *Peso* which floats against the U.S. dollar and can be exchanged for the current rate at banks or change booths called *Casitas de Cambio*. Sometimes called the *New Peso* after a hefty devaluation in 1994, the exchange rate today is P12.697 to US$1.00, but shop around as rates at different change booths may vary. The *Peso* is made up of 100 *centavos* and most prices in shops are quoted in *Pesos* and written as $, NP$, or N$, and sometimes it is shown as MN (*moneda nacional*), but make sure before you actually commit to purchasing any item. Peso bills come in P20, P50, P100, P200, P500, P1,000, P5,000, P10,000, P20,000, and P50,000 denominations while the coins are P.10, P.20, and P.50 centavos and P1, P2, P5, P10, P20, and 500 pesos. Most restaurants will add a 10%-15% gratuity to your bill and most will accept your credit card. When exchanging money U.S. dollars bring the highest exchange rate followed by U.S. dollar traveler's checks, and then the rates decrease for Canadian dollars, *British Pounds*, *Yen* and *Deutschmarks*, followed by all other foreign monies. There is little black market money changing activity in Mexico with the exception of the border towns along the Guatemala and Belizean borders.

Dinghy Safety

Most cruisers spent a considerable amount of time in their dinghies exploring the waters and islands in the vicinity of their anchorage. It is not unknown for a dinghy engine to fail or a skipper to run out of gas miles away from the mother vessel. For this reason I urge boaters to carry some simple survival gear in their dinghies. First, I would recommend a handheld VHF radio for obvious reasons. If there are any other boats around this may be your best chance for getting some assistance. A good anchor and plenty of line are also high on the list. I do not mean one of those small three-pound anchors with thirty feet of line that is only used on the beach to keep your dinghy from drifting away. It may pay to sacrifice the onboard room and use a substantial anchor with a few feet of chain and at least 100' of line. Just as you would go oversize on your mother vessel do the same with your dinghy. If you are being blown away from land a good anchor and plenty of line gives you a good chance of staying put where someone may find you. Next, a dinghy should have a supply of flares. In some places boaters carry a large coffee can with a rag soaked in oil lying in the bottom. If they get in trouble lighting the rag will produce an abundant amount of smoke that can be seen from a quite a distance.

A dinghy should be equipped with survival water, a bottle or some small packages manufactured by a company called *DATREX*. It would be a good idea to throw in a few MRE's. These are the modern, tastier version of K-Rations that our armed forces survived on for years. Each MRE also contains vital survival components such as matches and toilet paper. Another handy item that does not take up much room is a foil survival blanket. They really work and take up as much space as a couple of packs of cigarettes.

Please don't laugh at these suggestions. I have seen people forced to spend a night or two in a dinghy and these few items would have made their experience much more pleasant if not entirely unnecessary. I have run out of gas and used flares to attract some local attention even though one of my boat mates was ready to dive in and swim for the nearest island to fetch help. Now, I never leave in my dinghy without my little survival bag stashed away in the dink. It doesn't take much effort to prepare a small bag for your dinghy and it will be worth its weight in gold should you need it.

Flora and Fauna

In the Northwest Caribbean you will find flora and fauna that are certainly not found in the islands of the Bahamas or the Eastern Caribbean, or on the mainland of the United States and Canada. By far, the most diversity of plant and animal life will be found on the mainland of Central America, and it is here, especially along the Río Dulce in Guatemala, that we shall focus this brief primer on the plants and animals of the Northwestern Caribbean.

Flora
Much of Central America is covered by rainforests, unique eco-systems where all plants tend to have shallow roots due to the thin layer of topsoil available for nutrients. The trees you'll find here often have buttressed root systems and continuously shed their bark to throw off parasitic plants. Huge ceiba trees are common as are all manner of hardwoods such as mahogany and teak as well as palm trees and fruit trees that you will find growing everywhere.

Most of the plants you'll find here are flowering making for a very colorful backdrop to your strolling about (I love walking the paths at *Mario's Marina* on carpets of small yellow or purple flowers). Bromeliads are common as are vines, some of which grow up from the ground while others, such as strangler vines (*matapalos-tree killers*) take root among the upper branches of a tree and grow downwards eventually killing the host tree. Ask a local to show you a "gringo's nose" tree; it's the one with the peeling bark. Along the shores of the rivers and creeks mangroves reign offering a wide diversity of creatures that thrive in their environment. For those with a deeper interest in the flora of the area you'll find thousands of plant species from algae, fungi, lichens, mosses, and liverworts to grasses, vines and all manner of trees in the area, in fact, over 90 species of trees have been identified just on the *Hacienda Tijax* farm on the *Río Dulce*.

Fauna
The types of fauna found in the Northwestern Caribbean range from the harmless iguanas found on all the islands to deadly snakes and insects, most of which are found only on the mainland of Central America.

Fish
Since so many cruisers will be staying on the Río Dulce for hurricane season, I'll touch briefly on the fish you'll find there, some of which are so delicious that they'll likely become a favorite on your menu.

One of the most delicious fish in the river is the snook, or as it's better known locally, the *robalo* (you can often find Jennifer selling smoked *robalo* at the weekly nautical flea market in *Río Dulce*). But the most common food fish on the river is the *mojarra*, much like a perch, and as tasty as any grouper I've ever had. Everywhere on the river you'll find fishermen in their cayucos throwing out nets or setting seines as the sun goes down, hoping to catch *mojarra*, but often only bringing in *machaca*, a shad, that cruisers rarely eat since it is so bony but which is popular with the local population. At times you'll find tarpon on the river and even the occasional dolphin (not the *dorado*, the mammal dolphin) that swims up from the sea but rarely ventures past *El Golfete*.

One delicacy that you'll find for sale from the fishermen along the shores of *El Golfete* in *Guatemala* are blue crabs, fresh water blue crabs. These are quite tasty and very meaty and large, and the ones in El Golfete are much preferred over the blue crabs that you'll find upriver in Lago Izabal or Río Dulce.

Divers will be interested in knowing that Utila (Bay Islands of Honduras) is famed for the whale sharks that populate its waters while the Mosquito Coast of Honduras is equally as famous for its hammerhead sharks.

Insects

In the Northwestern Caribbean you'll find insects the likes of which you've only dreamt of back in North Dakota. One of the loveliest insects that you'll find on the *Río Dulce* is the blue morph butterfly which can grow to 5 inches. The tops of the blue morph's wings are an electric, vibrant blue while the undersides are colored to match the surrounding foliage. Although you'll find many other species of butterflies colored yellow, green, black, orange, and even one with red and silver wings, the blue morph earns the top prize for taking your breath away. Other winged creatures include a variety of moths that can grow to 6 inches.

Ants are everywhere in along the shores of the *Río Dulce* ranging from tiny household ants that will come aboard your boat at the dock to larger leaf-cutter ants that carry enormous loads long distances, to huge "bullet ants" that look as big as small beetles. Some ants will bite and leave a nice welt behind, some such as the household ants are harmless to humans.

There are certain bees along the *Río Dulce* that like to make their homes in people's masts. Bring along a can or two of wasp killer that will spray a good twenty or more feet. The sprays you find in the local stores don't work very well so bring something truly deadly from home, or you can pay a local exterminator US $35 to handle the problem for you. Not all boats have this problem, just a very few, the bees seem to be selective and I've not noticed a pattern to their habitations. More of physical nuisance are the yellow flies that love to land on you and bite, and they bite HARD! Mosquitoes, called *zancudos* in Spanish, are found throughout the Northwest Caribbean and carry the threat of Malaria and Dengue Fever, long sleeved shirts, long pants, and *DEET* go a long way in combating these creatures. The incidence of Malaria is slim along the river, more so inland, but Dengue Fever, although rare, can occur.

You'll find all manner of stinging insects in the Northwestern Caribbean, spiders and scorpions, most of the spiders are harmless, but some are extremely venomous. The tarantula, the *araña de caballo* (horse spider) is usually found more inland and like to make their homes in bunches of bananas, the reason they are also called banana spiders. Most tarantula bites are not fatal to humans but are very, very painful. Cattle ranchers and farmers are usually most affected by these creatures and their efforts in eradicating them has lowered the tarantula's overall numbers dramatically. Black widows are often seen, but by far the most worrisome spider is the brown recluse which is often found in dark places and whose bite can cause tremendous pain and tissue damage. If you find a small circular bite mark on your body with a bit of an infection spreading, it is past time to get to a doctor! Though usually not fatal, these bites can result in a loss of tissue in the immediate area of the bite.

Scorpions, locally called *alacran*, are often found in leaf piles and inhabiting thatched roofs, and everywhere you go you'll find thatched roofs. The male is large and black and has the worse sting, while the female, whose sting is a bit less painful, has yellow legs. To avoid a scorpion sting don't walk around in bare feet or put your hand into a dark place, box, or bag, without looking inside first. A scorpion sting is extremely painful but only lasts for about three hours and I'm told the best treatment is simply to lie down and rest. The locals tell me to eat sugar to combat the effects of a scorpion sting, I haven't tried this as I haven't been stung by a scorpion, but if I am you can bet I'll be gulping sugar by the spoonful.

Reptiles and Amphibians

Frogs and toads are found everywhere on the *Río Dulce*, walking back to your boat at night you'll find these harmless creatures hopping out of your way, your biggest concern being how to avoid stepping on one. I have to advise you not to touch the frogs, some of these creatures can secrete powerful toxins through the skin of their backs, and although the more dangerous types are found further south in Costa Rica and Panama, don't take a chance. It's also a good idea to keep an eye on your dog and keep them from eating one of the little critters as well; you'll notice that the local dogs won't touch them.

Iguanas are found throughout the Caribbean and are celebrated in places like Little Cayman Island and given the right of way over cars; and on Roatán where there is an iguana farm with over 2,000 iguanas in residence. But the lizard that you will most likely come across on the Río Dulce, as well as on some of the Bay Islands, is *basilisk* lizard, or the *Jesus Christ lizard* as it's sometimes called. The *basilisk* lizard has a brown body with a yellow stripe on each side and is usually about 12" long, though some have been reported to lengths of over 2'. It is quite harmless and more scared of you than you are of it. For this reason it will flee from you at a high rate of speed on its hind legs, a magnificent sight, especially if you can view them running across water in this manner.

Crocodiles and the smaller cousin, the caiman, can be found along the waters of the *Río Dulce* in the side streams and rivers, rarely in the areas around the marinas. Usually all you'll see of them are their eyes and nostrils sitting just above the water unless you quietly paddle up some side creek and find one sunning itself on the bank. If you care to view a crocodile up close and personal without daring a dinghy hunt, you can travel to the town of El Estor on *Lago Izabal* where you can view three of the creatures in a small pool in the town park. One thing to remember is that for the most part, the crocodiles prefer muddy water to clear water, that's why you'll rarely see a croc in places like *Bahía de Tejano* on the eastern shore of *El Golfete*, but you will find them on the western and northern side of *El Golfete*.

Now let's discuss the creatures that cause cruisers the most anxiety, snakes, particularly the poisonous snakes. If you spend any time at all on the *Río Dulce*, the chances are good that you will at least see a snake. Remember that most snakes are not venomous, but don't let that thought goad you into aggravating the snake, the poisonous snakes that are found here can be very aggressive and you will quickly rue the thought that caused you to irritate the creature. There are several varieties of boa constrictors around and all are harmless to humans, even the largest ones are far too small to do any real damage except scaring the beejeezus out of us.

One very poisonous snake you'll find on the *Río Dulce* is the coral snake with its brightly colored bands of red, black, and yellow. There is a snake that appears identical to the deadly coral snake but its bands are a bit different. If in doubt remember this little ditty: "Red touches black, friend of Jack, red touches yellow, kill a fellow." One of the most venomous and aggressive snakes you'll find is the bushmaster which can grow to over 6' in length and is the largest venomous snake in all of the Americas. The bushmaster is a VERY aggressive snake and is not scared of humans and has been known to chase those who have crossed its path. The good news is that the bushmaster is rarely seen on the Río Dulce, it prefers inland areas and mountains.

The most common poisonous snake on the *Río Dulce* is the fer de lance, sometimes called *barba amarilla, yellow beard*, due to the yellow coloration of its underside. Its head also has a slightly unusual shape, it is pointed, much like the tip of a lance, hence its name. These snakes are extremely dangerous, very aggressive, will attack and pursue without provocation, and are highly lethal. Now some cruisers will tell you tales of snakes climbing up their anchor chains at night, this has happened, I've known people at the docks who have come up on deck to find a 6' boa resting on their side decks, but this is rare. You should however avoid the huge floating islands of hyacinths that often find their way into *Lago Izabal, El Golfete*, and the *Río Dulce* as these are often home to snakes, all of whom are looking for a way off their tiny floating universe.

Mammals

As you travel upriver from Livingston, one of the first mammals you will encounter will likely be the howler monkeys, called *saraguates* by the Guatemalans, especially if you head upriver around dawn when they are most active. The howler monkey's roar, which is produced by its oversized vocal chords, sounds more like a gorilla and can be quite intimidating. Spider monkeys are also found everywhere in Central America and the Bay Islands and are a treat to see moving through the trees in packs, their long limbs grasping branches as their prehensile tail grasps larger limbs. Occasionally seen on the *Río Dulce* these days is the manatee, especially in northern part of El Golfete near the *Biotópo de Chocón Machacas*, a nature preserve designed to protect the habitat of the manatee.

Inland you will find all manner of mammals such as the tapir, a nocturnal herbivore that is the size of a very small donkey and looks like a pig with a long, flexible snout. You'll also find small anteaters, armadillos, sloths, kinkajous, and a creature locally called a *tazuerin* which looks like a large, black possum and carries its young on its back. Ocelots are found in the hills surrounding the *Río Dulce* but are rarely seen. Ocelots look like large housecats and they are sometimes kept as pets by those lucky enough to find one as a cub. Sacred to the Maya is the Jaguar, but their range, which once stretched from Mexico to Argentina has been severely reduced and today a sighting is extremely rare. Jaguars are not known to attack man and you can often hear one at night in the Petén and at Tikal.

Avian Life

The national symbol of Guatemala is the Quetzal bird which is rarely seen today, usually in and around the area of Cobán. However parrots and storks can be seen almost everywhere while deeper in the jungle you'll find toucans and brilliantly colored woodpeckers.

The deadly Fer de Lance, *Yellowbeard*

Fishing on the *Río Dulce*

Río Dulce crocodile with young on her head

Coatimundi

Lineated Woodpecker

Guatemalan Parrot

Health Concerns

I must advise cruisers planning a trip to the Northwest Caribbean to check the *Communicable Disease Center's* (*CDC*) web site for the latest information on health concerns in that part of Central America. Their address is http://www.cdc.gov/travel/camerica.htm. You can also telephone the *CDC* at 1-888-232-3299 for fax information. Please note that *Amoebic dysentery* is endemic while *Malaria* and *Dengue Fever* occur throughout the year.

The most common malady that you may encounter is *Montezuma's Revenge*, or in plain English, diarrhea. The best way to combat this problem is to watch what you eat and drink. Take it easy and slowly work your way into the local cuisine, don't go from the *Immigration* office to the local bar to down *habaneros* by the handful. Contaminated water is a major source of the problem, make sure you know the source of your drinking water and especially the ice in your drinks, something many people overlook, and another major factor in keeping you near the toilet for long periods of time. *Hydroclonozone* and *Halazone* are water purification additives that work and are fairly easy to acquire at most drug stores in the countries you are visiting (or bring them with you from home).

One of the biggest problems in this part of the world is malaria, in fact, I've heard it said that most of the people in the smaller villages have had malaria at one point in their lives, but of course this is hearsay and I've found nothing to back this up, however the threat of malaria is very real. It is estimated that worldwide there are some 300-500 million cases per year with about 1 million being fatal. If you think that the United States is excluded think again, there are over 1,200 cases of malaria occurring in the United States every year, although most cases in the U.S. are immigrants and travelers returning from malaria risk areas overseas.

Malaria is a serious and sometimes fatal disease caused by a parasite that is passed to a human when that person is bitten by an infected mosquito. The parasites enter the person's bloodstream and travel to the person's liver to enter the liver cells, grow, and multiply. During this period the person does not feel sick, and it is not until the parasites leave the liver and enter the red blood cells (usually from 8-days to months after the mosquito bite) that the illness comes upon the host. Red blood cells burst freeing the parasites to attack other blood cells and toxins are released into the blood that make the host human feel sick. At this point a mosquito biting that individual will receive these parasites and can pass them on to other humans after an incubation period of about one week.

Symptoms of malaria usually begin about 10-30 days after infection (although some people have exhibited symptoms from 8 days to one year after infection, with one type of malaria taking up to 4 years for the symptoms to manifest) and include fever and a flu-like illness including shaking chills, headaches, muscle aches, and fatigue; nausea, vomiting, and diarrhea may also occur. Malaria may also cause anemia, jaundice (yellow discoloration of the skin and eyes) because of the loss of red blood cells. There are four types of malaria that can affect humans, and if one type, *Plasmodium falciparum*, is not treated promptly it may cause kidney failure, seizures, mental confusion, coma, and even death.

Now don't panic fellow cruisers, malaria can be prevented, and simply traveling to the Northwest Caribbean does not insure infection. Prior to your departure for the Northwest Caribbean you can ask your physician for an anti-malarial drug such as *Chloroquine*, which is the recommended drug for Mexico, Belize, Guatemala, and Honduras, the same countries discussed in this cruising guide. If you decide to take this drug, do it religiously, exactly on schedule and without missing a dose, and upon leaving the area continue taking the drug for four weeks. You can also go far towards prevention by wearing long sleeves and long pants to avoid mosquito bites and using an insect repellent with *DEET* on exposed skin. *DEET* is toxic so don't breathe it in, swallow it, or get it in your eyes, and never use it on children under two months of age. Mosquito screens on hatches are a very good idea as well, and if you can spray a repellent or insecticide such as *permethrin* or *deltamethrin* on the screens, so much the better.

Other mosquito borne disease such as *Dengue Fever*, *filariasis*, *leishmaniasis*, *onchocerciasis*, and American *trypanosomiasis* (*Chagas Disease*) are also known to occur in Central America. Protecting yourself against insect bites is your best defense against these diseases.

Food and waterborne diseases are also a concern in the Northwest Caribbean. *Traveler's Diarrhea*, *E. coli*, *Salmonella*, *cholera*, and *hepatitis* are also found in the region with hepatitis being the most prevalent disease found. In Puerto Barrios, Guatemala, *hepatitis* is as rampant as aids in the town that is known for its 14 brothels. It is recommended that visitors to the Northwest Caribbean get a hepatitis shot before arriving in the Northwest Caribbean as well as following a few simple guidelines to keep you healthy and happy. Wash your hands often with soap and water and drink only bottled water or drinks in cans or bottles, avoiding tap water, fountain drinks, and ice cubes. Eat only thoroughly cooked foods and fruits or vegetables that you have washed and peeled yourself, the CDC suggests that you do not buy food from street vendors (I know a bit about this, I lost a good friend from a parasite he picked up in Costa Rica).

On the other hand if you don't buy from street vendors you may miss a good opportunity to really sample the local cuisine (see the chapter on Dining in the Northwest Caribbean). There's a little ditty to remind you of how to handle locally bought foods: *Boil it, cook it, peel it, or forget it!* And to prevent fungal and parasitic infections always wear shoes, don't go barefoot (that's a tough one for me, I love going barefoot).

Don't eat any dairy products unless you are sure they have been pasteurized, and don't handle animals such as monkeys to avoid animal bites. It is also suggest by the *CDC* to avoid swimming in fresh water, either swim in a pool or in salt water. Sometimes I think the *CDC* wants to take all the fun out of traveling.

Holidays

All of the countries and islands of the Northwest Caribbean celebrate the usual holidays such as Christmas, New Year's, and Easter, but there are several holidays unique to each nation.

Belize:
January 1: New Year's Day
March 9: Baron Bliss Day
Varies: Good Friday and Easter Monday
May 1: Labor Day
May 24: Commonwealth Day
September 10: Commemoration of the Battle of St. George's Cay (National Day)
September 21: Independence Day
October 12: Columbus Day
November 19: Garifuna Settlement Day
December: Christmas

December 26: Boxing Day

Cayman Islands:
January 1: New Year's Day
January 24: National Heroes' day
Varies: Ash Wednesday
Varies: Good Friday and Easter Monday
May, varies: Discovery Day
June, varies: Queen's Birthday
July, varies: Constitution Day
November, varies: Remembrance Day
December 25: Christmas
December 26: Boxing Day

Jamaica:
January 1: New Year's Day
Varies: Ash Wednesday
Varies: Good Friday and Easter Monday
May 11: Bob Marley Day
May 23: Labour Day
1st Monday in August: Independence Day
3rd Monday in October: National Heroes Day
December 25: Christmas
December 26: Boxing Day

Guatemala:
January 1: Año Nuevo (New Year's Day)
January 6: Epiphany
Varies: Semana Santa, Easter Week
May 1: Día del Trabajo (Labor Day)
June 30: Día del Ejército (Army Day-day of the 1871 revolution)
July 25: Día de Santiago, Antigua's big festival
August 15: Día de la Asunción-Patrona de Guatemala (Assumption of the Virgin Mary-Guatemala City)
September 15: Día de la Independencia (Independence Day)
October 20: Conmemoración de la Revolución (Revolution Day-commemorating the 1944 revolution)
November 1: Día de Todos Los Santos (All Saints' Day)
December 25: Navidad (Christmas)
December 31: Fin del Año (New Year's Eve)

Honduras:
January 1: Año Nuevo (New Year's Day)
Varies: Semana Santa, Easter Week
April 12: Garifuna Day
April 14: Día de las Américas (Day of the Americas)
May 1: Día del Trabajo (Labor Day)

September 15: Día de la Independencia
(Independence Day)
October 3: Nacimiento de Morazán (Francisco Morazán's Birthday)
October 12: Decubrimiento de América (Discovery of America)
October 21: Día de las Fuerzas Armadas (Armed Forces Day)
December 25: Navidad (Christmas)

Mexico:
January 1: Año Nuevo
January 6: Día de los Reyes Magos (Day of the Three Kings)
February 2: Candeleria
February 5: Aniversario de la Constitución de 1917 (Constitution Day-Flag Day)
February 24: Día de la Bandera
February/March-varies: Carnival
March 21: Natalicio de Benito Juárez (Benito Juarez Birthday and Vernal Spring Equinox when the shadow of a serpent appears to undulate down the steps of the pyramid of Kukulcán at Chichén Itzá)
March/April-varies: Jueves Santo
March/April-varies: Viernos Santo (Good Friday)
March/April-varies: Sábado de Gloria
April-varies: El Cedral Fair in Cozumel
May 1: Día del Trabajo (Labor Day)
May 5: Batalla de Puebla-Cinco de Mayo (The anniversary of the *Battle of Puebla* ,1862, when the Mexican Army defeated the French)
May-varies: Jazz Festival in Cancún
June through August-varies: Saints Peter and Paul festival in Cozumel
July 25: Saint James the Apostle
August 17: Cruz de la Bahía, the founding of Isla Mujeres in 1854
September 1: Informe de Gobierno
September 15-16: Aniversario de la Independencia (Independence Day-the celebration actually begins the evening before-September 15)
September 23: Autumnal Fall Equinox celebrated at Chichén Itzá
October 12: Día de la Raza (Columbus Day)
November 1: Día de Todos Los Santos
November 2: Los Fieles Difuntos (All Souls Day)
November 20: Aniversario de la Revolución
December 8: Immaculate Conception
December 12: Nuestra Señora de Guadalupe
December 25: Navidad (Christmas)

Hurricane Holes

Wherever you cruise during hurricane season, you should always keep a lookout for a safe hurricane hole and you should always know where the nearest protection lies and how long it will take for you to get there. With that in mind let me offer a few of the places I consider hurricane holes in the Northwestern Caribbean. Bear in mind that if you ask ten different skippers what they look for in a hurricane hole you're likely to get ten different answers. Some of the places that I mention may not meet your requirements. I offer them only for your consideration when seeking safety for your vessel. The final decision is yours and yours alone. If in doubt always check with the locals, they usually know the best spots.

To begin with, let me state that **THERE IS NO SUCH THING AS A HURRICANE HOLE**! There is no anchorage so secure that it cannot be decimated by a strong hurricane and a high storm surge. There are no guarantees; there is no Fort Knox to hide in when a named windstorm threatens. Now, with that of the way, we can discuss how to protect yourself in those special places that offer the best hurricane protection. Let's begin our discussion with what constitutes protection and pass along a few hints as to how to secure yourself as well as get along with your neighbors.

First, make sure your fuel is topped off and you have enough food and water for an extended period. Also, make sure you have enough cash to see you through as phone lines may be down for a while which would prohibit credit card usage. Once your tanks, lockers, and wallet are topped off, you can head for protection. Some skippers prefer to head to sea when a hurricane threatens. Some will take off at a ninety-degree angle from the hurricane's forecast path. I cannot advise you as to what course to take, but I for one, unless absolutely necessary, will not gamble with racing a storm that is unpredictable (no matter what the forecasters claim).

For protection, most of us would prefer a narrow creek that winds deep into the mangroves where we will be as snug as the proverbial bug-in-a-rug. These creeks are rare, and to be assured of space you must get there early. When a storm threatens, you can bet that everybody will soon be aware of it and the early birds will settle in the best places. Sure, those early birds might have to spend a night or two in the hot, buggy mangroves, but isn't that better than coming in too late and finding the best spots taken and your choices for protection down to anchoring in the middle of a pond with a bit of fetch and no mangroves to offer protection? Hint number one...get to safety early and secure your vessel.

So how do you secure your vessel? Easy! First, find a likely looking spot where you'll be safest from the oncoming winds. Try to figure out by the forecast path of the storm where the wind will be coming from as the storm passes and plan accordingly (remember that the winds blow counterclockwise around the center in the northern hemisphere). If your chosen spot is in a creek that is fine. Set out bow and stern anchors and tie off your vessel to the mangroves on each side with as many lines as you can, including lines off the bow and stern to assist the anchors. Use plenty of chafe gear (I like old fire-hose, leather, and towels) as the lines lead off your boat and rig your lines so that they don't work back and forth on the mangroves as well. If chain can be used to surround the mangroves that will help (not the mangroves of course). If other boats wish to proceed further up the creek past your position, remove your lines from one side of your boat to allow them to pass and then re-secure your vessel. Courtesy amongst endangered vessels will add to the safety factor of all involved, especially if somebody needs to come to somebody else's aid later on.

If your only choice is to head into the mangroves bow or stern first, always go in bow first; it stands to reason that if you place your stern into the mangroves serious rudder damage could result. I prefer to go bow-in as far as I can, until my boat settles her keel in the mud (trying to keep the bow just out of contact with the mangroves), tie off well, and set out at least two stern anchors. If other boats will be tying off into the mangroves in the same manner on each side of you, courtesy dictates each skipper assist the other in the setting of anchors (so that they don't snag on each other) and the securing of lines in the mangroves (and don't forget to put out fenders).

If you must anchor in the open, away from the mangroves, place your anchors to give you 360° protection. The greatest danger to your vessel will likely be the other boats around you, and in the Caribbean there's going to be a better than average chance that you'll be sharing your hole with several unattended boats, often times charter boats that are not secured in the best of manners. A good lookout is necessary for these added dangers.

Once secure, your next step is to strip everything off your boat and stow it below. Sails, bimini top, dodger, awnings, rail-mounted grill, wind-generators, solar panels, jerry cans, and anything small and loose that can become a dangerous object should it fly away at a hundred plus miles an hour. And, don't forget to secure your dinghy as well! Keep a mask and snorkel handy in the cockpit, you might need it to stand watch. Also, keep a sharp knife close at hand, you never know when you might need it. Pack all your important papers in a handy waterproof container, and in the most severe of circumstances, use duct tape to secure your passport, wallet, and/or purse to your body. Plan ahead as you secure your vessel so that you will not have to go on deck if you don't absolutely have to, it is most difficult to move about in 100-knot winds.

The Northern Coast of Jamaica

There is only one spot that I would even consider when seeking hurricane shelter on the northern coast of Jamaica, and that is at *Bogue Lagoon*, just south of *Montego Bay*. Enter the bay as shown on the chart (be sure to read the text first, it's tricky and the entrance channel can only take a 7' draft, and possibly an 8' draft with a very high tide, but then you'll need another very high tide to get out, but for now the problem is finding shelter, worry about getting out later). Once inside find a suitable spot in the mangroves and secure your vessel so as to allow the most protection from the expected wind directions.

The Cayman Islands

If I were in the Caymans and a hurricane was approaching, there is only one place I would dare to ride out a hurricane, in the confines of *North Sound* on Grand Cayman. My first choice for protection, depending on where the wind is forecast to come from, would be tucked in along the eastern shore of *North Sound*, past the *Kaibo Yacht Club* or in *Little Sound*. A second choice would be to find shelter in *Governor's Harbour* on the western shore of North Sound, it is very protected but that area was hit very hard by Hurricane Ivan a couple of years ago. There are some other canals on the southern shore of *North Sound* such as *North Sound Estates* that carry 7' at MLW. However this area is full of private homes and it's best to get permission before tying up in the canals.

Guatemala

As far as actual protection from hurricanes for cruisers in the Northwestern Caribbean, the finest protection is up the *Río Dulce* in Guatemala. In fact, the *Río Dulce* is probably the finest hole in the entire Caribbean offering excellent protection, economical prices, and an eclectic group of gregarious cruisers. The marinas are well upstream, miles from the coast and the worst of any hurricane surge, and the surrounding hills go a long way in lessening the strength of the wind. Arguably this may be the best hurricane hole in the entire Caribbean. Why you may ask? It's not because it abounds in narrow mangrove-lined creeks in which to hide. In fact, if every boat on the *Río Dulce* sought shelter at the same time, the few good hurricane holes would be overflowing. The river's saving grace is its location. It is very difficult for a hurricane to make a direct hit on the river without crossing a good bit of mountainous land that would do nothing for it except weaken it. Even if a Category 5 hurricane were to make a direct hit at the mouth of the river, the storm surge at the marinas twenty miles upstream would be minimal, a third perhaps of the surge at the mouth of the river. If you are seeking hurricane shelter on the river I advise you NOT to seek shelter in one of the smaller rivers that feed into the *Río Dulce*. These rives can rise 4' or more in no time when the rains from a hurricane begin falling and all the water rushes down to the *Río Dulce*. If you'd like to look for yourself, take a dinghy ride up any river, you'll see logs strewn about here and there, and bear in mind that on the next flood they will be moving downstream and aiming at your vessel should you tie up for shelter in these small rivers.

For hurricane protection on the *Río Dulce* there are several small coves you can access that offer protection from both wind and seas. In *El Golfete* you can work your way northwest past Cayo Grande to anchor in *Laguna Salvador* or *Laguna Calix*, or in the narrow waterway that leads to them. On the eastern shore of *El Golfete, Bahía de Tejano* (*Texan Bay*) offers great protection in the inner harbor off the marina. Here mangroves abound and the small cove is very protected from seas save those that build in the short fetch of the cove itself which would amount to very little.

South of the bridge is the small cove where *Suzana's Laguna Marina* used to be located and it is the best protected cove on this stretch of the river. At the extreme southwestern end of *Lago Izabal* is a small cove called *Puerto Refugio*, a very good place to secure your boat but it is open to some fetch from the southwest.

Honduras

On the mainland of Honduras only two places can give you any decent type of protection in the event of a hurricane, one being upriver of *Puerto de Cabotaje* at *La Ceiba Shipyard*, the other is *Laguna el Diamante* just southwest of Punta Sal. In La Ceiba you can count on the river at *Puerto de Cabotaje* to bring a lot of debris downstream as it did in *Hurricane Mitch* but in a pinch this shelter will suffice, especially if there is not a strong storm surge. *Laguna el Diamante* offers very good protection but a strong storm surge will make this harbor untenable (as would a direct hit). If nothing else is available in a reasonable amount of time, *Laguna el Diamante* might be an option to consider as long as the hurricane is forecast to miss this area.

In the Bay Islands you have a few choices, mostly on Roatán. Small, shallow-draft vessels can work their way up the small canal northwest of Bonacca Town on Guanaja, and also into the lagoon at East Harbour, Utila. On Roatán you can find good shelter at the extreme northern ends of the harbors at *Calabash Bight*, *Hog Pen Bight,* and *Jonesville Bight* (in *Bodden Bight*-just past the power lines), and possibly off the marinas at *Brick Bay* and *Old French Harbour,* however these two last harbors will be untenable with a strong storm surge. Bear in mind that if you plan to stay in any of the holes on Roatán for a hurricane that you'll likely be sharing your spot with a lot of local boats, many of them large, unattended, steel, shrimpers.

Language

Spanish is the primary language of the Northwestern Caribbean, however English is spoken in most places. English is the primary language of the Cayman Islands and Jamaica although you'll hear many Jamaicans speaking patois. In Honduras and Guatemala you'll hear Spanish but in the Mayan communities you'll find a variety of Amerindian languages such as K'iche, Cakchiquel, Kelchi, Mam, and Xinca, while in the Garifuna settlements on the mainland and in the Bay Islands you'll hear Creole and Garifuna spoken.

Guatemala is home to hundreds of Spanish schools, and Antigua is the focus for those wanting to learn the language. You can sign up for a one-on-one course costing US$70 and up per week (you'll have to supply your own hotel room), or you can try one of the popular immersion courses where you actually live in a Guatemalan family's home for weeks at a time and only Spanish is spoken.

Phoning Home

In the Northwestern Caribbean you will have no fears of being out of telephone contact with your home, family, and friends. Public phones are common and in some places you can purchase cheap cell phones, some of which can be used in Honduras, Guatemala, Belize, and Mexico simply by changing a chip (pick up one of the TIGO phones in Guatemala for this service).

A modern telephone system links the Cayman Islands to the world by submarine cable and satellite and card-phone service is available at select locations on all three islands. Pre-paid phone cards in values of CI$15 and CI$30 can be purchased at the Cable & Wireless main office in Anderson Square in George Town and at the Cayman Brac post office and gas stations. Unregistered roaming is available and visitors with TDMA handsets can make calls without registering, provided they can give a credit card number.

In Jamaica the phone system is handled by Jamaica International Telecommunications Limited, JAMINTEL, with their main office in Kingston (876-922-6031). Mariners in Kingston harbour can place collect calls via Kingston Radio by contacting them on VHF ch. 16 and then switching to a working frequency, either channel 26 or 27. Cable and Wireless Company, CAW, handles cellular communication in Jamaica and can be reached at 876-968-4000.

In Honduras the local phone company is Hondutel, and in all the major cities you'll find pay phones that work with L0.20 and L0.50 coins. AT&T USA Direct is accessible from Honduras by dialing #123.

The area code for Belize is 501; for the Cayman Islands the area code is 345; the area code for Guatemala is 502; the area code for Honduras is 504; and the area code for Jamaica is 876.

Radio Nets

The following is a list of SSB and Ham nets that may interest you while cruising in the waters of the Northwest Caribbean. By far the most popular net is the Northwest Caribbean Cruiser's Net, and their accompanying website, www.nwcaribbean.net, is a must for participation.

Caribbean M/M Net: Saint Croix. 7.230 MHz - 7.240 MHz. at 1100 Zulu

Central American Breakfast Club: 7.083 MHz at 1300 Zulu

Halo Net: 21.390 MHz at 2100 Zulu, covers the United States and South America.

Mississauga Net: 14.121MHz. at 1245 Zulu, covers Europe, the Med, the Atlantic, the Caribbean and Central America.

Northwest Caribbean Cruisers Net: 6.209 MHz or 6.212MHz at 1400 Zulu, covers from Mexico to San Andres Island and I've picked them up as far away as Jamaica and the Caymans. The *Northwest Caribbean Net* is a directed net. A weather report is given and check-ins are requested from boats in the waters of Belize, Guatemala, Honduras and Mexico. The net finishes with boat to boat contacts. Several boats anchored along the Río Dulce usually check in to this net every day and this would be an opportunity for you to talk directly with boaters who are currently on the river.

Panama Canal Connection Net: 8.107 MHz at 1330 Zulu, covers the Pacific from Mexico to Galapagos, and the Atlantic from Belize to Colombia with an emphasis on the southwestern Caribbean.

Trans-Atlantic Net: 21.400 MHz at 1300 Zulu, covers north Atlantic and Caribbean.

Waterway Net: 7.268 MHz at 0745 EST, covers east coast of the USA and the Bahamas primarily.

Safety and Security

To say there are not security issues in the Northwest Caribbean would be a lie. There are problem areas, some of which should be avoided completely, while others can be visited with proper precautions. In the Cayman Islands I know of no security issues, a haven for security conscious cruisers for sure. The northern coast of Jamaica on the other hand is one of the problem areas. With the exception of Port Antonio and the anchorages off Falmouth and the *Montego Bay Yacht Club*, I would not recommend leaving your boat unattended at anchor, especially at night. *San San Beach,* east of Port Antonio, is not a place to even consider anchoring at night! In the Bay Islands of Honduras *French Harbour* is known for having theft problems as is Coxen Hole while West End seems to be fine in that regard. However Utila is another story. In Puerto Este the anchorage is known as *Burglary Bay,* never, I repeat, NEVER, leave your boat unattended here! On the *Río Dulce* it is recommended to travel to the southwestern parts of L*ago Izabal* with a buddy boat although I do know of some cruisers that venture there alone with no problems. Here again, safety being the issue, it's better to be safe than sorry, so travel with a buddy boat south of *Denny's Beach* in *Lago Izabal* and in the northern end of *El Golfete* as well, except in *Bahía Buenavista (Gringo Bay)* or *Bahía de Tejano,* these are two safe havens for cruisers. One final word, never leave your boat unattended in Livingston.

Tides and Currents

Cruising in the Northwest Caribbean, and in general just getting to the Northwest Caribbean, you will encounter strong currents that, depending on your route, will be either with you or against you.

The currents that you encounter originate 93 million miles from Earth where our Sun generates the heat that warms the lower latitudes of our planet causing the air to expand creating trade winds that drag the ocean waters with them (thanks in part to the rotation of the Earth and the influence of the Moon). In the *Caribbean Sea* and the southern part of the *North Atlantic Ocean*, these currents flow westward at about .7 knot and originate off the western coast of Africa, just north of the Cape Verde Islands as the *North Equatorial Current.*

South of the equator the *South Equatorial Current* begins its westward flow with the trades like its cousin to the north. Somewhere off the coast of Brazil the current splits in two with the northern half running northward along the eastern coast of South America (as the *North Brazil* and *Guiana Currents*-the *Guiana Current* enters the Caribbean along the northern shore of South America and is influenced by the flow of the *Amazon River* and the *Río Orinoco*) where it joins with the *North Equatorial Current.* This combined current pushes into the Caribbean basin where the flow divides, the larger *Antilles Current* heads north through the islands while the second current enters the Caribbean basin through the *Grenada, St. Vincent,* and *St. Lucia Passages* and moves northwest in a poorly defined and highly variable stream called the *Caribbean Current.* In fact, the *Caribbean Current* begins as several westward flowing streams that are separated by eastward flowing countercurrents (in the extreme southwestern Caribbean a counterclockwise current called the *Columbia-Panama Gyre* is evident from Nicaragua through Panama and eastward to Columbia).

Eventually these westward flowing streams merge as the *Caribbean Current* and continue west past Jamaica and Cuba and then northward through the *Yucatán Channel* (where it is called the *Yucatán Current*) and into the *Gulf of Mexico* (where it is called the *Loop Current*). Flowing north the *Yucatán Current* begins experiencing a certain resistance from the waters already in the *Gulf of Mexico* and rarely is felt in the western *Gulf.* Along the main path of the clockwise rotation of the *Loop Current* in the *Gulf of Mexico* several eddies break off as the current turns towards the only exit, through the *Straits of Florida* between Florida and Cuba where it is technically called the *Florida Current,* though it's better known as the *Gulf Stream,* and is joined by the *Antilles Current* that flows west along Cuba's northern coast. At some point in the *Straits of Florida* the powerful *Gulf Stream* is born. Once past the Bahamas the *Gulf Stream* joins up again with a part of the *Antilles Current* that flowed northwest along the eastern edge of the Bahamas and begins its easterly trek across the *North Atlantic Ocean* to re-circulate and do it all over again.

What this all boils down to is this: if you intend to leave the Florida Keys to cross the *Yucatán Channel* and work your way south along the eastern coasts of Quintana Roo, Belize, and into the *Gulf of Honduras* and the *Río Dulce,* the current will be on the nose, at times up to 4 knots in the middle of the *Yucatán Channel,* and often 1-2 knots and more along the eastern coast of Quintana Roo, and a bit less in the lee of the *Belizean Reef.* If you are heading to the Northwest Caribbean from the *Windward Passage* or Jamaica the current will be on your quarter or beam, and if you're approaching from the Eastern Caribbean you'll have the current with you. For more information on how these currents affect your route planning, see the chapter *Heading to the Río Dulce.*

The tides in the Cayman Islands are primarily diurnal with one high and one low each day, though on some days the tides will be semi-diurnal with two highs and lows per day, and are generally in the range of 1'. The currents in and around the Cayman Islands generally set to the west, though a northward flowing current can be found south of Grand Cayman at times, and a southward and/or eastward flowing current can be found between Cuba and the Cayman Islands at times.

Tides in Jamaica are primarily diurnal, one high and one low each day, and are small, generally about 1 foot or less. There is a westward setting current off both the northern and southern coasts of Jamaica of about .7-1.0 knot with a reported current of up to 2-3 knots two miles off Morant Point. At times, the westward setting current has been reported to reverse its direction, especially during periods of westerly winds.

Weather Broadcasts

The wonderful cruising grounds of the Northwest Caribbean are blessed by easterly trade winds, generally northeast in the winter and more east and southeast in the summer. Along the coasts the sea breezes in the winter tend to blow from the northeast in the morning and usually strengthen and move to the east in the afternoon. During the winter the occasional *norther*, or frontal passage, will blow through bringing several days of strong winds and rain. These frontal passages are rarely are felt south of the Mosquito Coast of Honduras, although their strong winds will intensify the trades in the lower Caribbean from Columbia to Panama. Summertime weather is characterized by squally conditions in the late afternoon and evening, particularly in the *Río Dulce*.

A pretty good on-line source is Weather Caribe at http://www.weathercarib.com/.

The *United States Coast Guard* in Portsmouth, Virginia weather broadcasts can be received on 4428.7 KHz (ch. 409), 6506.4 KHz (ch. 601), 8765.4 (ch. 816), 13113.2 KHz (ch. 1205), and 17307.3 (ch. 1625). Times are 0600, 0800, 1400, and 2200.

Weather coverage is usually quite good in the Northwest Caribbean especially if you have an SSB or HF receiving capabilities. Ever since the passing of David Jones, Chris Parker has become the weatherman of note for cruisers and has proved his work countless times to thousands of cruisers over the years. Chris' summer schedule, April 1 to October 31, begins at 0630 AST/EDT, on 4.045 MHz; at 0700 AST/EDT, Chris moves to 8.137 MHz; at 0800 AST/EDT, you'll find Chris once again on 4.045 MHz; and

0830 AST/EDT Chris transmits on 8.104 MHz; and at 0900 AST/EDT, Chris can be found at 12.350 MHz; at 0915 AST/EDT, Chris transmits on 16.525 MHz, and at 0930 AST/EDT, Chris will be found on 6.221 MHz. Chris' winter schedule, which usually begins on or about November 1, is as follows: at 0630 EST, 0730 AST, Chris will broadcast on 4.045 MHz; at 0830 AST, 0730 EST, Chris can be found on 8.104 MHz; at 0930 AST, 0830 EST, Chris transmits on 12.350 MHz; at 0945 AST, 0845 EST, Chris is broadcasting on 16.525 MHz; and at 1000 AST, 0900 EST, Chris will be found on 6.221 MHz.

Quite often during the winter months Chris may be late in getting to the 12 meg and 16 meg frequencies. If 12.359 MHz is busy Chris will use either 12.356 MHz or 12.362 MHz. When severe weather or tropical weather systems threaten, and this will be during his summer schedule, Chris will also transmit in the evenings, usually on 8.137 MHz at 1900 AST/EDT, and he will usually announce this on the morning net. Chris begins the net with a 24-48 hour wind and sea summary followed by a synoptic analysis and tropical conditions during hurricane season. After this, Chris repeats the weather for those needing fills and finally he takes check-ins reporting local conditions from sponsoring vessels (those vessels who have paid an annual fee for this service). For those who seek more information about weather, weather patterns, and the forecasting of weather, should pick up a copy of Chris Parker's excellent publication: *Coastal and Offshore Weather, The Essential Handbook*. You can e-mail Chris at chris@mwxc.com. By the way, unless tropical weather is threatening, Chris does not broadcast on Sundays, everybody needs a day off.

Besides Herb and Chris, your primary source of weather on the SSB will likely be the *Northwest Caribbean Cruiser's Net* on 6.209MHz or 6.212MHz at 1400 Zulu. The net covers the entire Northwest Caribbean from Yucatán southward to San Andres Island and I've picked them up as far away as Jamaica and the Caymans. The *Northwest Caribbean Cruisers Net* is a directed net and a weather report is given and check-ins are requested from boaters in Belize, Guatemala, Honduras, and Mexico, as well as anywhere offshore.

For weather forecasts courtesy of the local ham nets, see the earlier section on *Radio Nets*. On a local level you can find weather forecasts on the *AM* and *FM* bands; although all the stations broadcast in Spanish, some offer English forecasts at certain times. In Mexico, *XFP* in Chetumal stands by on 2.182 MHz, *XFC* in Cozumel stands by on 2.182 MHz, and the *San Miguel de Cozumel Pilots* can be contacted on VHF ch. 16. On the AM and FM bands there are hundreds of stations up and down the dial.

In Belize you can pick up news and weather in English on *Radio Belize* at 830 KHz, 910 KHz, 930 KHz, and on the FM band at 88.9 MHz and 91.1 MHz at 0100, 0300, 1300, 1500, 1700, 1830, 2100, and 2300 UTC. *British Forces Broadcast Service* can be found on the FM band at 93.1 MHz and 99.1 MHz while the *Voice of America* relay station is on 1530 KHz and 1580 KHz. The *Belize Pilot Station* stands by on 2.182 MHz, *Belize Customs* stand by on 2.750 MHz, and the *Belize City Pilots* can be contacted on VHF ch. 16.

In Guatemala try *Radio Cultural* at 730 KHz which broadcasts in English daily from 0300-0430 UTC and on Sundays from 2345-0430 UTC. *Unión Radio* broadcasts in English daily from 0200-0400 UTC on 1330 KHz.

In Honduras you can contact the Puerto Cortés pilots on VFH ch. 6 or 16 for weather info. *La Vox Evangelica* is a religious station that broadcasts in English from 0300-0500 on Mondays at 810 KHz, 1310KHz, and 1390KHz, and on 4.8202 MHz. If you have access to the Internet you'll find an interesting website at http://63.245.92.231/weather.htm. Here you'll find several weather links for the Bay Islands and a live webcam of Roatán's north coast.

In Jamaica you can receive weather forecasts from *Radio Kingston* on 2.738 MHz, USB at 0830 and 1330 local time. *Radio Kingston* also broadcasts on VHF ch. 13 at 0930, 1430, and 2030 local time.

The Local Cultures

As you travel about the Northwestern Caribbean, you'll encounter four distinct local cultures unique to each area. You'll find the *Garifuna* who inhabit the Bay Islands of Honduras as well as parts of mainland Honduras, Guatemala, and Belize, the *Maya*, whose origins predate Christ by 2,000 years, the *Maroons*, escaped slaves who hid in the mountains of Jamaica and harassed the British soldiers and plantation owners for 150 years, and the *Rastafarians*, who sprang from Jamaica in the last century and who can be seen all over the Caribbean as well as the entire world.

The Garifuna

You will find many Garifuna settlements in the Northwest Caribbean, particularly along the coast between Belize and Honduras. The *Garifuna*, sometimes called the *Garínagu*, are the descendants of Black Caribs from St. Vincent and their name means *cassava eating people* in their language. The Garifuna culture is very strong with great emphasis being placed on music, dance and story-telling. The Garifuna practice their own brand of religion, a mix of Catholic, African, and Indian beliefs. Because of their independent nature, and perhaps just because they are different, over the years the Garifuna have been feared and discriminated against and variously accused of devil-worship, polygamy, voodoo and speaking a secret language.

The history of the Garifuna begins in 1675, when a Dutch ship carrying settlers and slaves wrecked in the waters between St. Vincent and Bequia. The slaves were the only survivors and were accepted by the indigenous Kalipuna Indians who arrived from the mainland of South America long before Columbus discovered St. Vincent in 1498. The Kalipuna, called the *Caribes* (*cannibals*) by the Spanish, eventually intermarried and were later joined by escaped slaves from St. Lucia and Grenada. They became known as the *Black Caribs* as opposed to the *Yellow Caribs*, those of pure Carib descent, and St. Vincent was divided between the two groups with the western side of St. Vincent being allocated to the Yellow Caribs and the eastern side to the Black Caribs.

Even with this sharing of the island, their differences eventually led to a civil war among the Yellow and Black Caribs in 1700. Fearing domination at the hands of the Black Caribs, the Yellow Caribs sought help from the French and allowed French settlers to build a small community on the island in 1719 where the settlers sought to live in harmony with both tribes of Caribs. In reality, the French considered St. Vincent theirs and wished only to remove the British from the island and in planning this course of action foresaw a way of acquiring new slaves through the conflict.

The British, had earlier moved into St. Vincent in 1627 by way of a series of royal grants and treaties when Charles I granted St. Vincent's rule to the Earl of Carlisle. However, the first real attempt at British colonization did not come until a century later, in 1722, when King George I gave St. Lucia and St. Vincent to the Duke of Montagu and a Captain Braitwaite was sent to St. Vincent to start a settlement at which point the series of private land treaties between the French and the Caribs were declared null and void.

Both the British and the French sought to use the tension between the Yellow and Black Caribs for their own causes by enlisting their help in battle. Seeing that the Black Caribs were the more successful soldiers, winning several battles with British settlers in the early 1700s, the French farmers provisioned the Black Carib leaders with wine, cognac, and weapons, which in turn encouraged more trade with the French and caused the Black Caribs to take up the French language, some of their customs, and even some of their names.

In 1748, the *Treaty of Aix-la-Chapelle* officially made St. Vincent a neutral territory. A few years later, in 1762, the *Treaty of Paris* allocated certain territories to the British, and in 1763, after the first Carib War, the British took control over the island and settlement began in earnest. In 1773, George II drafted a peace treaty with the Caribs and the two dozen Carib chiefs who signed the treaty could not read English so it was not until later that the true meaning of the treaty manifested itself as the Caribs were unknowingly restricted to smaller and smaller areas of the island.

Hostilities renewed and in 1779, the Black Caribs requested assistance from the French in Martinique. So it was that a French ship sailed to St. Vincent with 500 troops and the French took over St. Vincent with little resistance. The British soldiers were all at the northern end of the island working on the Governor's plantation, and no one could find the key to the battery. The French won in a matter of a few minutes and were able to keep the Black Caribs from massacring the British settlers, troops, and the Governor.

In 1783, the *Treaty of Versailles* restored St. Vincent to British control. In 1795, the Black Caribs, with the aid of the French, went on the offensive in what is called the *Second Carib War*, sometimes called the *Brigands War*. A French radical, Victor Hughes, after a successful uprising in Guadeloupe, incited two Black Carib chiefs, Chatoyer and Duvalier (sometimes spelled Duvallé), to attack the British and drive them from the island. Duvalier's forces burned British plantations along the eastern coast, often putting the owners themselves through the gears of their own sugar mills, while other Black Caribs under their great chief Chatoyer, killed many people without destroying property and forced British forces southward along the western coast to Kingstown. In short order, the two chiefs met in the hills above

Kingstown when Duvalier took Dorsetshire Hill, removed the British flag, and replaced it with the French Flag. British troops stormed Dorsetshire Hill and in a battle that lasted ten days, Chatoyer was finally killed in a swordfight with a British officer, Major Leith.

The Black Caribs, although deprived of their great leader, continued to fight for a year after Chatoyer's death. General Abercrombie had already taken St. Lucia where the Black Caribs, without the assistance of the French, were quickly overcome and surrendered. Abercrombie then moved his troops to St. Vincent where the British soldiers destroyed the Black Carib villages and crops, and a year later, delivered an ultimatum to the Black Carib chiefs that the Black Caribs would be shipped to the Bay Islands off Honduras. Only 280 Caribs surrendered for the

Garifuna drummers

shipping, arriving at Balliceaux where half of them died of yellow fever.

The British then hunted nearly 5,000 Black Caribs who were deported to Roatán, off the coast of Honduras. En route one of the British ships was taken by the Spanish and taken to Trujillo on the mainland of Honduras where the Black Caribs were put to work. When the Spanish later captured Roatán the 1,700 Caribs on the island were also brought to Trujillo and being skillful at farming, and the Spanish not, the Caribs got along well, some were even allowed to join the Spanish army.

The first Garifuna to arrive in Belize were brought there as woodcutters by the Spanish in 1802 in the *St. Ann Creek* area near Punta Gorda where they fished and farmed. By 1811, the Garifuna of Stann Creek were taking their produce to market in Belize Town which infuriated the local residents and merchants. At a public meeting, the city fathers passed a regulation stating that all "Caribs" who arrive in Belize Town must get a permit or they must leave within 48 hours Three years later the Garifuna of Stann Creek attempted to join the public meeting in Belize Town but were refused entry. When Central America achieved independence from Spain, the Garifuna suddenly found themselves unwelcome in places where the sentiments against Spain were strong.

In 1832, many Garifuna left Honduras after a civil war there, and led by Alejo Beni, headed to Belize where they arrived on November 19, 1832, now know as *Garifuna Settlement Day*. Locals were afraid that the Garifuna would help slaves to escape and so tried to instill a fear and distrust of the Garifuna into their slaves by branding the Garifuna as "devil worshippers" and "baby eaters." Then the locals began to see the Garifuna as a secondary source of labor and within a year of their arrival had them working in their mahogany camps. Finding that they now had a problem with runaway "Caribs," a public meeting in Stann Creek appointed a Constable in Stann Creek whose sole responsibility was to deal with runaway "Caribs." In the 1850s, many laws were passed that forbade Garifuna, as well as Maya, from owing land in Belize.

But all that is only history now. Over the years the Garifuna have spread along the coastal regions of Central America. The Garifuna that served in the Spanish Army served with distinction, and at one time, the fortress at San Felipe, *El Castillo de San Felipe*, was commanded by a Garifuna officer, and in more recent times, many Garifuna served in World War II. Today there are even Garifuna communities in Los Angeles, New Orleans, and New York City.

The Maroons

The history of the Maroons is the saga of Africans who refused to live in slavery, and it begins on the island of Jamaica with the fleeing of the Spanish in 1655. At that time the Spanish had a settlement west of present day Kingston at *St. Jago de la Vega, St. James of the Plain*, which is now known as Spanish Town. When some 8,000 British troops attempted to take the town on May 11, 1655, the Spaniards surrendered, but secretly prepared to flee. They freed some 1,500 slaves, emptied the town of anything of value, and fled into the hills before the British ever set foot in the town. When the British arrived in *St. Jago de la Vega* they found it empty and in anger destroyed most of the settlement. The freed slaves fled to the mountains and were organized into a fighting force by Don Cristóbal Amaldo de Ysassi, the Spanish Governor of Jamaica at the time.

De Ysassi's plan was for the freed slaves to harass the British troops until the Spanish could return and retake the island. These freed slaves, who would later become known as the *Maroons*, and settled primarily in two areas of Jamaica. Some settled in St. Catherine Parish and the Trelawney Cockpit Country, also known as the *Land of Look Behind*, in the south and central part of Jamaica, and became known as the *Leeward Maroons*. The Leeward Maroons always had a strong leader and their main settlement was located at Old Town, now called Accompong. Other Maroons settled in the northeastern part of Jamaica, in the *Blue Mountains* and the *John Crow Mountains* and are called the *Windward Maroons* and today can be found in places like Moore Town, Scott's Hall, and Charles Town. The *Windward Maroons* did not have a central leader, instead they formed into small groups in different communities with different leaders, each group cooperating with the other as the need arose.

The name *Maroon* is the British corruption of the Spanish *cimarrones*, meaning *wild* or *untamed*. Living in inaccessible regions of Jamaica, the numbers of the Maroons grew as more and more runaway slaves, this time from the new British plantations, flocked to their cause, and with their continual raiding of the British plantations, they rapidly became a thorn in the side of the British colonists. Unique among all Africans that were brought to the New World as slaves, the Maroons earned for themselves an autonomy that no other African slaves could.

In 1690, a large group of slaves from Clarendon, consisting mainly of *Coromantees*, an extremely brave and warlike people from Africa's Gold Coast, today's Ghana, rebelled and escaped into the interior of Jamaica. They aligned themselves with the Spanish-freed Maroons and a great leader emerged, Cudjoe. Legend tells us that Cudjoe was short, thick-necked and almost bear-like in appearance, as well as a fierce, cunning fighter, Cudjoe, his two brothers Accompong and Johnny, and his followers vowed to have freedom from British enslavement or death, reminiscent of Patrick Henry's "Give me liberty or give me death." Cudjoe, and his Windward Maroon compatriots Quao and Cuffee, fought the British to a standstill in what has been described as a decade long campaign of robbery and murder that began in 1729 and is now known as the *First Maroon War*.

The Maroons were bound by a sacred oath that all men had to take to show loyalty and to keep Maroon secrets. Any runaway slave who refused to take the oath was put to death, the Maroons could not afford security risks and the casual runaway was certainly that. Such runaways might stay a few days or a week or two and then wander off only to be captured, and in order to save their own hide would divulge the locations of the Maroon settlements. Women were not bound by the oath and most of the intelligence that the British troops received on the Maroons came from captured women.

The Maroons were highly dependent on nature to survive. The Maroons could not farm on a large scale, to farm one needed to clear and burn the land, and smoke would give away the Maroon positions to the British. But the Maroons would make do the best way they could, relying on the knowledge of nature that they brought with them from Africa. They managed to use the environment very efficiently to take care of all their basic needs, nourishment, shelter, and protection from the soldiers that hunted them. Most people are not aware that jerk pork, pork cooked over pimiento wood, began with the Maroons who invented it as a way of cooking and preserving meat with little or no smoke. Besides the supplies that nature provided, the Maroons needed guns, and they had precious few, so they took some from dead British soldiers, stole some, and traded for

some. The Maroons were very successful at raiding the British plantations, coming in out of the mist and taking whatever they needed, food, arms, or slave women (the Maroons were so successful in capturing slave women that by 1730, the number of women and children in Nanny Town and Guy's Town exceeded the number of men). It is said that during these raids some Maroons would kill any white man they met.

In their dealings with the British troops, nature also played a huge role in the success of the Maroon warriors. The Maroons developed camouflage and ambush techniques that took many an unwary British soldier's life. The *cacoon vine*, also called the *five finger wiss*, was a Maroon favorite for ambushing the British troops. The Maroons would peel strings off the vine, which also was used in the manufacturing of furniture, and stretched them over pitfalls like netting which was then covered with a layer of brush as camouflage. Pointed stakes were often set in the bottoms of these pits, much like the punji sticks that were used so effectively in Vietnam. Some of the Windward Maroons also used the white kernels hidden inside the seed pods of the cacoon vine in a stew they called *Rundown*.

The Maroons would also camouflage themselves, *bushing up* was the term they used, to make them impossible to spot against the trees and plants that surrounded them. The Maroons would also bathe in a mountain stream, scrubbing their bodies with the leaves of a certain plant that gave them a fresh lemon scent. Then they would lie in wait in the brush that emitted the same odor, camouflaging their scent. So good were the Maroons at camouflage that legends grew about them. It was said that the Maroons had the ability to appear and disappear at will, to stand so still in the evergreen that a party of soldiers could walk right past them and not see them. When they raided plantations it was said that the guard dogs could not even detect their approach. So successful were they that they could not be found by Carib Indian scouts (brought in from the Mosquito Coast of Honduras) and Cuban slave hunters who were recruited by the British to find the Maroons. So successful were the Maroons that the Trelawney Cockpit Country of Jamaica became the *Land of Look Behind* for the British always had to look behind their ranks for a sudden ambush.

Maroon settlements, Maroon towns as they were called, were constructed with security foremost. They were always set up in the mountains with the lower levels more easily accessible, and the upper levels almost inaccessible. Few if any British soldiers reached the upper levels. All Maroon towns were well supplied with food, and if the Maroons had to flee, they would escape to another equally secure town that was also amply supplied with food. The Maroons would maintain contact with one another by mimicking animal sounds such as birdcalls. So precise were they in this that they studied seasonal and mating calls so that they would make no errors that could be detected by a Carib Indian scout, who were also bush experts. Maroons also used a drum and the *abeng* horn, for more long-distance communications which were totally incomprehensible to the British. Maroon towns always had a commanding view of the neighboring countryside, and keen-eyed Maroon sentries who would signal by blowing on an *abeng* horn when search and raiding parties appeared headed in their direction. The *abeng*, made from a cow's horn, was able to produce many different sounds, each with its own meaning and able to be heard from great distances. The *abeng* blowers could relay information such as troop strengths, type of armaments, direction of travel, and even which paths the troops were taking. This gave the Maroons plenty of time to set up an ambush and before long British troops dreaded the sound of the *abeng* horn.

The British used many methods of tracking and fighting the Maroons. They imported Carib Indians from the Mosquito Coast of Honduras, but they were eventually wiped out. The British also had a certain number of renegade Maroons, those who had surrendered and had never really had the heart to fight the long fight. The British also had a unit of slave soldiers called the *Black Shots* who were nearly as good as the Maroons in the woods. One, a man who came to be known as Captain Sambo, was a great leader who often embarrassed white officers with his drive and determination. Sambo was so competent that he eventually was promoted to Captain, freed, and later on, oddly enough, settled around the Nanny Town area in 1739 with his wife and children who were also freed.

A number of heroes have arisen out of the Maroon's fight for freedom, and probably the best known is a lady known simply as Nanny. Nanny, who fought the British at the beginning of the 1700s, is often described as an almost supernatural Ashanti warrior Queen who could catch musket balls and fire them back. Nanny was Cudjoe's sister so it seems that courage and determination ran in their family.

Nanny possessed exceptional leadership ability and was excellent in directing guerilla warfare to keep the British out of the Blue Mountains where she and some other *Windward Maroons* lived in a stronghold called Nanny Town. Nanny also kept the African traditions alive, handing down stories and legends to the younger Maroons and by encouraging music and songs that her people brought from Africa.

Nanny led numerous brilliant hit and run attacks on British plantations and troops and she played a large part in treaty negotiations with the British (whom she did not trust, and believed their treaties were just another means of subjugation-the British offered land and full freedom to any *Maroon* who surrendered). When British troops tried to attack her almost inaccessible stronghold in the Blue Mountains (after six years of searching for it), Nanny and her followers would dump vats of boiling water onto the troops from the heights above.

In 1734, Nanny lost her life to British troops when a British Captain named Stoddart led a successful attack on Nanny Town aided by Mosquito Coast Carib Indians, the Black Shots, and tracking dogs.

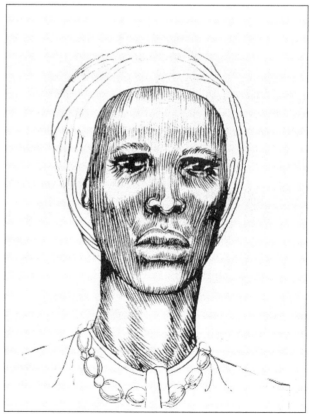

Nanny

The British soldiers managed to drag two cannons to the heights overlooking Nanny Town and Captain Stoddart leveled the town. The Maroon survivors fled deeper into the mountains, Nanny Town was reclaimed by the jungle, and the Warrior Queen Nanny was buried in Moore Town, just to the southeast of Nanny Town.

Today Nanny Town is a place of legend where it is said the ghosts (duppys) of those who died in the battle still haunt the hills and that none but a Maroon may enter Nanny Town and return alive. It is said that the white birds that roost in the trees around Nanny Town cannot be shot, the pellets go right through them for they are the ghosts of the Nanny Town dead.

The British held Nanny Town for a year before the Maroons recaptured the town and occupied it between May and August of 1735. The British once again succeeded in driving off the Maroons and retaking Nanny Town, the harassed Maroons being driven deeper and deeper into the interior, low on provisions and ammunition, and suffering from fatigue, hunger, and sickness.

The Windward Maroons separated into several smaller groups and began a long walk of some 150 miles to St. Elizabeth on the leeward side of Jamaica. Upon their arrival they were not greeted warmly by Cudjoe who said there were not enough provisions for his people much less the newcomers. Cudjoe blamed the Windward Maroons for provoking the white man when there was no need for such actions. He showed them graves of his own people that he had executed for murdering white men against his orders. Cudjoe told the Windward Maroons that their barbaric cruelty and insolence to the white man was the reason they were hunted like dogs and in time would be destroyed. Some historians suggest that this was a ploy and that the despotic Cudjoe simply did not want to share power with his eastern comrades.

After the loss of Nanny and Nanny Town, Cudjoe found himself less secure, so he moved deeper into the Trelawney Cockpits to establish a new settlement and resume fighting the British. The Maroons, even though they were very successful guerilla fighters, found their situation getting desperate as their provision grounds were being destroyed and they were being forced into smaller and smaller areas. Cudjoe masterminded a massacre of British soldiers from a hiding spot in a cave that later was to become known as the Peace Cave, and after this tragedy, the

British government sent a representative to Cudjoe to offer terms of peace. The Windward Maroons embraced Nanny's stance against any treaty with the British, but stood by it in the end.

On January 6, 1738, Cudjoe, and Colonel Guthrie of the British Army met and signed the peace treaty with an exchange of hats as a sign of friendship. Although historians claim that the treaty was signed under a huge tree called *Cudjoe's Tree* and today called the *Kinda One Family Tree*, Maroon historians claim different. Some say the *Peace Cave* was the site of the official signing with Colonel Guthrie and Cudjoe performing a blood brother ceremony instead of exchanging hats. The official document is even harder to discern, some day that it is in the care of a trusted Maroon elder and its location a secret of the highest priority. Cudjoe was appointed *Chief Commander* in Trelawney Town, a position now known as *Colonel*. The following year a similar treaty was signed by Quao, the chief of the Windward Maroons, in what is called Moore Town today. Cudjoe died and was buried in Old Town, now called Accompong after Cudjoe's brother who took over leadership of the Leeward Maroons after the passing of Cudjoe.

The treaty gave official recognition to the Maroons as a free people and deeded them 1,500 acres of land. It also allowed them to administer their own laws, gave them freedom from taxes, allowed the Maroons to hunt wild boar anywhere except within 3 miles of a town or plantation, and it bound the Maroons to fight with the British should any outside party attempt to invade Jamaica, such as the French from Haiti or the Spanish form Cuba. The Maroons were also bound to hand over any new runaway slaves and in later years some Maroons became slave hunters.

After the signing of the peace treaty to end the *First Maroon War*, Jamaica was blessed with over 50 years of peace. Two later conflicts broke out, none of which involved the Leeward Maroons who remained neutral. The Maroons assisted the British in controlling their slaves, but the British were not happy about dealing with free Africans on their slave island. In 1795, the *Second Maroon War* broke out when some 300 Maroons in Trelawney Town revolted because two Maroons had been flogged in Montego Bay instead of being handed over to their own people for punishment. This time however the British were on top of things. They employed 5,000 troops and quickly rounded up the Maroons using large hunting dogs to flush them from their hiding places in the mountains and forced them to sue for peace. A reward of 10 pounds was offered for every Maroon captured during this period.

After the signing of the peace treaty to end the *Second Maroon War*, the British thought it time to get rid of the Maroon problem entirely. The government captured some 543 Maroons and exiled them to Halifax, Nova Scotia, on June 26, 1796. The Maroons worked on the fortifications at Citadel Hill in Halifax, and later built a settlement called Preston while the Canadian government provided religious instruction and schooling, happy to be assisting in the civilization of these new settlers. The Canadians feared the French might attack and try to recapture Nova Scotia and organized the Maroons into semi-military units complete with vests, jackets, and metal buttons with the insignia of an alligator holding a wheat sheaf and an olive branch.

The Canadian winters of 1796-1798 took their toll on the Maroons, killing some, and shortening the tempers of those who survived. In the spring of 1799, a Canadian military unit arrived in Preston to maintain order and withheld valuable supplies to do so. The Canadian government was finding that the Maroons were not the fine settlers they first thought them to be and decided that the best course of action was to remove the Maroons from Canadian soil. After much negotiation with the government of Sierra Leone in West Africa, the Maroons were shipped off to Freetown Harbour, Sierra Leone, on October 1, 1880, completing a circle begun almost two centuries before when the Maroon's ancestors were stolen from their homelands in West Africa.

Today, in Jamaica, the descendants of the Leeward and Windward Maroons can still be found in Accompong, Moore Town, Scott's Hall, Trelawney Town, and a couple of other small settlements, all led by a Colonel who is elected to a five-year term (at one time it was a lifetime position). Today's Maroons are no different in appearance than any other Jamaican that you might see sipping rum or hunting wild boar, but they maintain that they are not part of independent Jamaica and don't mix with other people of the country, forever cautious of outsiders. Every January 6, the Maroons of Accompong celebrate the signing of the 1739 peace treaty with eating, drinking, singing and dancing to the beat of the Maroon drum and the blowing of the *abeng*, and the Maroons recall when their ancestors fought the mighty British army to a draw.

The Rastafarians

Everywhere you look in the Caribbean, and particularly on the island of Jamaica, you will see and meet Rastafarians. The man that sells you fruit and veggies, the boat boy that takes your line, or perhaps the man that is working on your boat in the yard, Rastafarians, Rastas for short, are as much a part of Jamaica as the trade winds and the Blue Mountains. A goodly number of cruisers on their first voyage to the Caribbean bring preconceived notions with them about these highly religious folks and I strongly urge visitors to these islands to come here with an open mind.

Mention the word Rasta and a vision of dreadlocks, ganja, and reggae music comes to mind, but there is a lot more to these people than that, remember, don't judge a book by its cover. Sure, there are many folks who you'll meet that sport the dreadlocked look of the Rastafarian, and who will claim to be a follower of Rastafari, but who are not what they seem. This book's cover is a false one. Sometimes it is difficult to tell the difference, but if you observe them, the speech, their diet (those that tend to be more Orthodox in their style of living adhere to certain dietary practices that are the hallmark of this religion), you will soon learn the difference. This is not to say that there is a clear line between true Rastas and false Rastas, there are all kinds of Rastafarians the same as there are all manner of Catholics, Protestants, or Jews. Some live a life with a strict adherence to their beliefs, while others live a life a bit more relaxed. Some uninformed persons fear all Rastafarians feeling that they are involved with drug smuggling and other assorted crimes. Not all are involved with illegal activities, one cannot indict an entire religion for the indiscretions of a few, what would happen to the Catholic faith if one indicted all Priests in the same manner?

Where lie the roots of the Rastafari? It is generally accepted that the movement began in Jamaica in the 1930s with Marcus Mosiah Garvey, a Jamaican born (1887) black nationalist leader who, in 1914, founded the *Universal Negro Improvement Association (UNIA)*, the most powerful black group of the 1920s, whose goal was to bring the black race to a higher prominence. Garvey, who is said to be of Maroon descent, immigrated to the United States in 1916 after a stint as a time-keeper on a banana plantation in Costa Rica and furthering his education at a college in England. Although Garvey was a Catholic, he encouraged his followers to view Jesus as

Black and organize their own church, neither Catholic nor Protestant, and adopt the name "Orthodox." Thus was born the *African Orthodox Church* which, although rejected by the *Russian Metropolia* when they applied for formal recognition as an Orthodox jurisdiction, the followers of Garvey were accepted by a group of "American Catholics," a loose group of worshipers who had rejected the Pope but in all other things remained Catholic. Garvey's church grew to thousands of members on three continents when discontent raised its ugly head. The *African Orthodox Church* in Kenya and Uganda broke off relations with their New York brethren and aligned themselves with the Greek Patriarchate of Alexandria and became fully Orthodox.

Today however, Garvey's church is for the most part defunct although the parish of *St. John Coltrane* in San Francisco remains active. In 1922, Garvey was indicted for mail fraud, serving 2½ years in the federal penitentiary in Atlanta before his sentence was commuted and he was deported back to Jamaica in 1927. Garvey had been listed as a "subversive" by the U.S. and many believe the charges against him were trumped up and racially motivated. Garvey moved the *UNIA* headquarters to London where, in 1940, he died in relative obscurity.

A true picture of Garvey shows a man who is somewhere between a prophet and a con man. Garvey wanted his black race to be economically equal to the whites and suggested an exodus of blacks from the Americas back to Africa and the establishment of a black nationality. In a church in Kingston in 1927, Garvey preached that Africans would someday rise again to their true stature and that a mighty black king would be crowned who would lead all blacks to freedom saying, "Look to Africa, for there a king will be crowned." In this Garvey appears as a John the Baptist figure for the eventual mighty king, Haile Selassie. The crowning of Haile Selassie I as Emperor of Ethiopia on November 2, 1930, became Garvey's prophecy fulfilled. Selassie, whose real name was Ras (Prince) Tafari Makonnen (upon his coronation he took the name Haile Selassie which means *Might of the Trinity*), is believed to be the 225th direct descendent of King Solomon and Queen Sheba and is said to be the second Messiah, Jesus in all his Kingly glory, the *Conquering Lion of the Tribe of Judah, Elect of God* and *King of the Kings of Ethiopia*. Many Jamaican's claimed Garvey's prophecy fulfilled and the *Ras Tafari* movement was born. Garvey was alive to see Selassie crowned, although his

religious movement had for the most part collapsed and he himself jailed on charges of business fraud. Garvey himself was not a fan of Selassie, admitting that slavery was still alive in Ethiopia and he attacked the new Rastafarians as being crazy fanatics even though several of Garvey's most trusted followers, men of his inner circle, had agreed that Selassie did indeed fulfill Garvey's prophecy.

From the 1930s until the mid-1960s, *Rastafari* was mainly a Jamaican religious movement with few if any outside influences, but the members could not develop a Jamaica-wide identity or agree on a basic doctrine or canon. The original Rastafarians did not consider themselves an organization or a philosophy, rather they only sought to discern the will of *Jah* (God) and keep true to it. Their meetings, *Reasonings*, were part theological debate and part prayer meeting, and at all times the Rastafarians sought only the Truth. Rastafarians sought an *overstanding* of the Truth, not an understanding since the term *under* has a negative connotation. Rastafarians often use their own language, removing many negative components in today's English. For instance, *sincere* becomes *I-cere* when the *sin* is removed, and *divine* becomes *I-vine* since *di* is too much like the word *die*. A popular phrase that you will often here is *I&I*, which can mean I, we, or you, all with *Jah* present.

Although no doctrine was formally compiled, one thing the early Rastafarians did agree on was that Haile Selassie was divine and that he intended to restore New World Blacks to Africa. Early Rastas wanted nothing more than to repatriate to Ethiopia and Jamaican authorities could not deal with the situation. It was one thing to live by a slogan like *power to the people*, it was quite another when the Rasta motto became *let my people go*. The government of Jamaica ignored the demands of the Rastas and the situation between the Rastas and the government became increasingly unstable until in 1954 the government overran a Rastafarian mini-state called *The Pinnacle*, ruled by a Rasta Elder named Leonard Howell who governed in the style of a traditional West African chief. Howell was arrested for preaching a revolutionary doctrine and his followers migrated to the slums of Kingston. With this, Rastafari went from a rural separatist movement to a ghetto separatist movement, and without a leader, the way the Rastas wanted it after all the harassment Howell had to endure. In the 1950s and 1960s, some Rastas rejected the non-violent teachings of their elders and mounted a series of violent uprisings which led to shootouts between Rastas and British troops, forever branding Rastafarians with a negative violent label.

In 1966, Jamaica was in the throes of a national crisis in which the Rastas were perceived as a revolutionary threat that needed to be defused. It was suggested that closer ties to Ethiopia might cool things down a bit and with that came the Lion of Judah. Emperor Haile Selassie flew into Kingston on April 21. 1966, *Groundation Day* to Rastas ever since, to meet with Rasta leadership, many of whom thought Selassie was no less than Jah Himself. Selassie stepped off the plane and thousands of white-robed Rastafarians chanting "Hosanna to the Son of David" and "Jah Rastafari" surged forward past police barricades, causing Selassie to retreat back to the safety of his plane. Later Selassie granted an audience to a delegation of Rasta elders, but the details of that meeting are sketchy. Some say that Selassie urged the Rastas to become Orthodox, while others say that Selassie suggested that Jamaica settlers might receive land grants in southern Ethiopia. But most agree that Selassie gave the elders a "secret" message, BUILD JAMAICA FIRST, in other words, don't even think about moving to Ethiopia until you have taken care of your home island.

From a historical point of view, it must be noted that Selassie is looked upon as a tyrant, a man who allowed 100,000 of his people to die from drought as charged by the military leaders who deposed Selassie in 1975. Selassie passed away in a small apartment in his palace in Addis Ababa on August 27, 1975, but many Rastafarians do not believe this. Some say his death was a fabrication, faked only to harm their movement, others say Selassie is still here in another plane of existence and that is death was inconsequential since he was a personification of God. Whatever he is or was, today Selassie lives on in each and every Rasta individual.

Rastafari is a religion full of ideals of purity, strength, and freedom from corruption and oppression that plagued black people for centuries. Rastas maintain that God is black, Ethiopia is the promised land, and that Rastas are one of the lost tribes of Israel. True Rastas are basically vegetarians, their diet is by *ital* rules, a dietary code based on the *Bible* and they cook only natural foods, fish less than a foot long, and they use no salt or oil. Rastas celebrate their Sabbath on Saturdays and view our modern society as "Babylon," an evil institution that is responsible for that same corruption and oppression. Most Rastas

tend to distance themselves from Babylon as much as possible, seeking independence from the evils associated with it. That is why so many Rastas that you meet are self-sufficient, many of them farming, or earning a living from their own talents, such as wood-carving and crafts, preferring to live peaceful, simple, healthy lives.

These people are very proud of who they are and are eager to educate others about their beliefs and way of life. During his reign, Haile Selassie stressed education as the way forward for his people, and as a result, Rastas seek knowledge from the Bible as well as academically. Many are well-educated and hold excellent positions. However, because of a lack of understanding, many Rastas are prevented from achieving levels of success they deserve. Without a doubt, a better understanding of the Rastafarian culture will assist in removing the barriers that prejudice has placed in their paths. One of those prejudices stems from the Rasta's use of ganga, marijuana, *wisdom weed*, for religious, meditational, medicinal, and culinary purposes and justified by several quotations from the Bible. Some Rastas do not smoke ganga recreationally, and others, those of the *Ethiopian Orthodox* sect (there are several different "types" of Rastas such as the *Bobo Dread*, a sect based on the teachings of Prince Emanuel Edwards, they are recognizable by their turban-like headgear and flowing white robes), don't use ganga at all. But the most obvious icon of the Rasta is the dreadlocks, the long locks that are seen as a symbol of strength that also has a basis in the Bible, in the story of Samson. And what discussion of Rastafari would be complete without the mention of Reggae music and especially the music of Bob Marley, who helped bring the message of Rastafari, of *Jah*, of Haile Selassie, to the world.

The Maya

The history of the peoples of Mesoamerica, the vast region that stretches from Central Mexico southward through Belize, Guatemala, Honduras, El Salvador, and Nicaragua, begins 60,000 years ago, during the *Fourth Ice Age*, when great glaciers stretched as far southward as the central United States and there was no tropical climate anywhere on our planet, today's tropics being only grasslands at that time. Sea level at that time was much lower and a thousand mile wide land bridge existed between Asia and North America where the Bering Strait is today. At first travel across the land bridge was impossible due to huge walls of ice, but during the *Paleo-Indian Period*, from about 20,000 B.C.-8,000 B.C. when the climate began to warm, the ice began to melt and people migrated southward into the Americas.

The Maya, the oldest civilization in the Northwestern Caribbean and the largest homogenous group of Indians north of Peru, are descendants of the early migrating peoples that crossed the Bering Sea land bridge and wandered south through Canada, the western United States, Central America, and into South America. Although not the oldest of the great Mesoamerican civilizations, the Maya are generally considered the most brilliant of the classic groups. The term *Maya* comes from their word for the Yucatán Peninsula area, the *Mayab*. However, similar terms are found throughout history and in various other cultures, perhaps it is just a popular word. *Maya* is a *Hindu* philosophical term meaning *origin of the world*, or *world of illusion*, it is also an ancient *Sanskrit* word with several meanings, *great*, *magic*, *mind*, and *mother*, and while we've touched the subject of mother, *Maya* was the name of the Buddha's mother. In the *Vedic* classic, *The Mahabharata*, *Maya* was the name of a noted astronomer/astrologer/magician/ architect, as well as the name of a wandering tribe of navigators. In ancient Egypt, *Maya* was the name of *King Tut's* treasurer and the term *Mayet* meant *universal world order*. And today, our month of May is named after the Roman goddess, *Maiea*, the *Goddess of Spring*.

The first settlers in Central America of which there is any physical proof were a group of hunter-gatherers known as the *Clovis*, named after the site of a find of stone spear tips at Clovis, New Mexico. The *Clovis* settled in the central highlands of Guatemala somewhere between 11,000-9,000 B.C. The physical proof, a collection of stone tools and spear tips, is dated to 10,000 B.C.-9,000 B.C., but it is speculated the *Clovis* had actually been residing in Guatemala for some 1,000-2,000 years prior to that. A recognizable pattern of settlements have been traced to the *Archaic Era* (8,000 B.C. – 2,000 B.C.), just as mankind was making the shift from hunting to a more agrarian way of life as the ice age was retreating and larger game was rapidly becoming scarce with the warming climate. This period saw the development and domestication of plants such as corn, peppers, beans, and squash at a time when the Petén, now a rainforest, was an area of savannahs and woodlands. It is during this period, around 2,000 B.C., that one of the staples of the Mayan diet was created, *nixtamil*,

a flour made from corn and white lime, a mineral enriched flour which would appear in tamales and tortillas throughout the history of Mesoamerica.

The end of the *Archaic Era* brought the birth of a tropical jungle climate to Mesoamerica as the Mayan civilization enters what is known as their *Pre-Classic Period*. The history of the Mayan civilization is broken down into several time periods, the first being the *Pre-Classic Period*, from about 2,500 B.C. - 250 A.D. There has been much discussion over the actual dates for the periods of Mayan history, and if you check several sources you will see different dates. And as scholars learn more about the Maya they are changing their ideas of the timeline of these periods. Some archeologists are calling the term *Pre-Classic* a misnomer suggesting that certain *Pre-Classic* Mayan societies have been found to have many features attributed to the *Classic Period*. Some scholars suggest calling the *Pre-Classic Period* the *Formative Period*, while others opt to add in a *Proto-Classic Period* prior to the *Classic Period*. But for the most part the periods are: the *Pre-Classic Period*, which is broken down into the *Early Pre-Classic Period* (2,000 B.C. to 1,000 B.C.), the *Middle Pre-Classic Period* (1,000 B.C.-300 B.C.), and the *Late Pre-Classic Period* (300 B.C.-250 A.D.). In 250 A.D. the Maya enter what is called the *Classic Period* which lasts from 250 A.D.-900 A.D. and is split into the *Early Classic Period* (250 A.D.-600 A.D.), and the *Late Classic Period* (600 A.D.-900 A.D.). *The Post Classic Period* begins in 900 A.D. and lasts until the arrival of the Spanish in 1521 A.D.

Early Pre-Classic Period
2,000 B.C. – 1000 B.C.

The *Early Pre-Classic Period* saw the birth of agriculture in Mesoamerica. Evidence of Mayan field burnings (found in lake core sediments) dating back over 2,000 years B.C. have been discovered in Guatemala's Petén region. By 2,000 B.C., fishing and farming villages were prevalent on Guatemala's Pacific coast and were the forerunners of the great Mayan civilization which dominated Central America for centuries. Between 1,500 B.C. - 1,000 B.C., the *Olmecs*, Mesoamerica's "mother culture" and the first true civilization in the region, began constructing ceremonial pyramid-like structures in Central America. The Olmecs, whose existence was not discovered until the 1920s, primarily settled along Mexico's Gulf Coast from Vera Cruz to Tabasco, where the remains of several ceremonial centers have been found. The earliest Olmec site, their greatest city, is located in the *Grijalva Depression* in Mexico's Chiapas state, and was populated sometime around 1,600-1,500 B.C. San Lorenzo was abandoned around 1,000 B.C. and the Olmec's principal city then became La Venta, an island on Mexico's Gulf Coast in western Tabasco which flourished from 900-400 B.C. The first Olmec settlements of record in the Yucatán Peninsula were founded between 1,000-300 B.C., although there is evidence of an earlier inhabitation in some caves in Loltún. Olmec art has been found along Guatemala's Pacific Coast as well as at Copán in Honduras, and as far south as El Salvador. Translated, *Olmec* means *rubber people*, and it is the Olmecs who are credited with creating the ball games the Maya so loved, as well as the rubber balls that were employed in those games.

The Olmecs considered the jaguar to be of supernatural origin and Olmec artifacts bearing images of a were-jaguar, a cross between a human and a jaguar, have been found scattered throughout Mexico. Between 1,200 B.C. – 900 B.C., the Olmecs maintained an important political and religious center in the basin of the Río Coatzacoalcos where the three sites known as San Lorenzo are found. Here the Olmecs constructed the first conduit drainage system in the Americas and carved six immense basalt heads, each measuring 8'-9' in height and weighing 20-40 tons. These colossal heads were carved from stones that were found over 50 miles from their present location. The heads are noted for their distinctly Negroid facial features and appear to be wearing helmets. Other massive stone heads are thought to have been moved by waterways to La Venta. As a side note, La Venta appears to have been deliberately destroyed around 400 B.C. - 300 B.C.

The Olmecs also developed a hieroglyphic writing system, the long-count calendar, a complex religion, and it is also believe that they also understood the concept of zero. They had considerable influence on the early Mayan culture as the Maya adopted and developed many of the Olmec's skills. Their myths and rituals are said to have influenced the Maya, Zapotec, Mixtec, and Aztec cultures.

The first Maya originated in Mexico's Yucatán Peninsula around 2500 B.C., migrating from the west led by their earliest leader and deified hero, Itzamná, considered a Sun-God to his people. It is said he led his people in their first migration from the Far East,

beyond the ocean, along a path that miraculously opened through the waters.

Middle Pre-Classic Period
1,000 B.C. – 300 B.C.

The *Middle Pre-Classic Period* is marked by the decline of the Olmecs and the growth and spread of the Mayan civilization, particularly in Guatemala's Petén. During these years the Maya expanded their commerce with the beginnings of widespread trade as they moved from coastal areas into the interior of Mesoamerica forming small communities with little public architecture. At this time Mayan farmers in the Petén began settling a series of low rainforest ridges at Tikal, and what may have been the first true Mayan city, Nakbé (meaning "by the road" in the Yucatec Mayan language), was constructed northwest of Tikal and south of El Mirador in the northern Petén. Tikal's prominence as a Mayan center did not come about until the *Early Classic Period* around the same time as Teotihuacan in Mexico, and it was one of several regional centers in the *Late Classic Period* along with Calakmul, Palenque, and Copán (where rich tombs were created during these years). Nakbé dominated the Mayan civilization until the focus shifted to El Mirador during the *Late Pre-Classic Period*, sometime around 100 B.C. (possibly because of El Mirador's richer supply of water and more defensible position). El Mirador's only competition was Kaminaljuyú, a city built where Guatemala City sits today. In Belize, the Maya built many powerful cities at Altun Ha, Lubaantun, Lamanai, Exuantunich, Nohmul, Cerros, and the most powerful of all, Caracol. With her coastline and numerous offshore islands, and her location midway between the Yucatán and Guatemala and Honduras, Belize was an important link in the Mayan economy with major trading centers at Moho Caye, Santa Rita, Ambergris Caye, and Wild Cane Caye.

Late Pre-Classic Period
300 B.C. – 250 A.D.

The *Late Pre-Classic Period* was a busy era of cultural development, the blossoming of writing, and calendrics, and a tremendous growth of the Mayan population. But the greatest advancements the Maya made were in the area of public architecture and monuments. The greatest of the Mayan cities, El Mirador, Kaminaljuyú, Río Azúl, El Pilar, and Tikal, all rose to prominence during these years as the Mayan population expanded resulting in greater competition for land. This led to larger communities, an increased settlement density, and the development of better strategies for organizing and feeding their growing populations. Mayan kingship came to the forefront in these years and shaped the social history of the Mayan people of the lowlands through the *Classic Period* and *Post Classic Periods.*

Towards the end of the *Late Pre-Classic Period*, around 250 A.D., El Mirador, the greatest city in the Mayan world was abandoned and conjecture as to why is all we have. Was it disease? Famine? Warfare? Nobody knows for certain but evidence points to a long, dry climatic period. To the south the *Ilopango* volcano in El Salvador erupted and covered much of the region in ash forcing the abandonment of Kaminaljuyú around the same time as the decline of El Mirador. Due to the eruption the Maya's Pacific trade routes were disrupted and the focus for trade shifted to the north bringing more of a Mexican influence to the cities of the Petén.

Classic Period
250 A.D. – 900 A.D.

As *Mesoamerica* enters the *Classic Period*, the Maya's greatest period of achievement, when art writing, calendrics, mathematics, astronomy, and religion reached their pinnacle, the Golden Age of Mesoamerica. This era is defined by the appearance and use of dated monuments (like the *stelae* that you find at places like Quiriguá) and the great temple pyramids that we see today at ancient cities like El Mirador and Tikal. This *Classic Period* architecture is, without a doubt, the most elegant and beautiful of the pre-Columbian world, especially the carvings and reliefs at Palenque in Mexico, and Copán in Honduras. And it wasn't until the finding of the key to the Mayan language in the 1970s that we learned that Mayan artists signed their works.

Either the Maya or the Olmec predecessors independently developed the concept of zero and used a base 20 numbering system occasionally working with sums into the hundreds of millions. Through their developed grasp of mathematics the Mayan calculation of the length of the solar year was superior to that of the Gregorian calendar and their highly accurate astronomical calculations, and their charts of the heavenly bodies, are more advanced than any other civilization using naked eye observations. The Mayan calendar began around 3114 B.C., even before the Mayan culture existed in its true form, and could measure time well into the future.

The Mayan system of writing, which is often called hieroglyphics for its superficial resemblance to the Egyptian writings (the two systems are NOT related), was actually a combination of phonetic symbols and ideograms, actually syllables rather than a strict alphabet and was able to express all types of thoughts. The glyphs are read from left to right and from top to bottom in paired columns.

The *Classic Period* begins with a second Mayan migration during the *Early Classic Period*, from 250-600 A.D. This migration, which originated in the west and made its way to the Yucatán around 200 A.D., was led by Kukulcán, a priest and teacher who was to become recognized as the founder of the Yucatec Mayan civilization. Under Kukulcán the people were divided into four tribes, ruled by as many kingly families: the Cocom, Tutul-xiu, Itzá and Chele. Kukulcán was a member of the Cocom tribe and he established his residence at Mayanspan, which thus became the capital of the Yucatec Mayan world. The Tutul-xiu ruled at Uxmal, the Itzá at Chichen-Itzá, and the Chelé at Izamal. To the Chele was appointed the hereditary high priesthood, and so their city became the sacred, holy city of the Mayans. Each provincial king was obliged to spend a part of each year with the monarch at Mayapan, which continued until the eleventh century, when, as the result of a successful revolt, Mayapan was destroyed, and the Yucatec Maya rule passed to the Tutul-xiu at Uxmal (pronounced oosh-mal). Mayapan was later rebuilt as the capital of the Yucatec Maya and reigned until about the middle of the fifteenth century, when, during a revolt, it was finally destroyed. The Mayapan monarchy split into nineteen small, independent states, of which eighteen still existed on the Yucatán Peninsula when the Spanish arrived. As a consequence of this revolt part of the Itzá moved south to the Petén, in Guatemala, where they established a kingdom with their capital and sacred city on Isla Flores in Lago Petén.

The major cities of the *Classic Period* were Tikal and Quiriguá in Guatemala, Chichen Itzá, Palenque and Yaxchilán in Mexico, and Copán in Honduras, the southernmost major Mayan city. For most of this period, the majority of the Mayans population lived in the central lowlands of Mexico and Belize. Cobá, Muyil, Tulum, Xel-Há, and Tankah on the coast of the Yucatán Peninsula became vital trading centers with links to other cities in the peninsula as well as other Mayan communities in Guatemala's Petén as well as Campeche on the *Gulf of Mexico.* Muyil was in fact linked to the coast by canals that wound their way through the wetlands. So strong were these links that the architectural styles of the Maya in Quintana Roo was influenced by the styles of the Petén as evidenced by the ruins of Dzibanché, Calakumul, and Tikal. At this time Northern Belize was part of the flourishing Mayan province of Chactemal, now known as Chetumal, with its capital located at Santa Rita, near Corozal. To the south was the Dzuluinicob, the *land of the foreigners* as it was known to the Chactemal Maya. This southern Mayan province, which controlled the upper *Belize River* valley, had its capital at Tipú, near Negroman on the *Macal River* south of San Ignacio.

The Maya were not a true urban culture, their urban centers, were primarily for religious use by the people surrounding them. The most complex centers were located in Guatemala's Petén, in fact, the Maya are only one of two civilizations to develop an urban culture in a tropical rainforest. In the highlands of Guatemala the Mayan culture developed less fully although the highlands are more temperate and the communities located their became the suppliers of the raw materials for the construction of the urban centers. A tropical rainforest is a difficult place to live and it can only support small groups of humans as a greater amount of area is required to support each person, this encourages population dispersal rather than the concentration necessary to build cities and temples.

To the north of the Petén, a city in the highlands of Mexico about thirty miles northeast of where Mexico City stands today, begins to exert her influence upon the Maya to her south. Teotihuacán, which originated around the time of Christ, was home to some 200,000 people with a dominant, and sometimes violent nature, who spread their influence from Mexico southward into Honduras and who even rebuilt Kaminaljuyú in Teotihuacán style. Teotihuacán had a well-defined class structure whose people possessed a knowledge of writing and books, used a bar and dot number system, and had a 260-day sacred calendar

In 400 A.D., Teotihuacán was the sixth largest city in the world, and 300 years later was deserted. In 650 A.D., a great fire spread through the city devastating many of her communities which preceded a swift decline in population and no reconstruction. By the time of the arrival of the Aztecs the city was little more than an ancient ruin, full of temples that her people had painted red so as to glow in the Mexican sun. The Aztecs viewed Teotihuacán as a holy place, where the sun, the moon, and the universe were

created, where the Gods met to plan creation. It was the Aztecs who named the city *Teotihuacán, the place where men become Gods*, and in some translations, *the place where the Gods touch earth*. The original name of the city, and the languages spoken there by the people who built the city are unknown. A recent glyph that represents the city has been translated as *the place of the precious sacrifice*, and the city was also referred to as *Tollan* ("place of cattails" or the "place where people are thick as reeds"), a name also used centuries later for the Toltec capitol of Tula. There is archeological evidence that the city was a multi-ethnic place with different quarters where lived the Zapotecs, the Mixtecs, the Maya, and the Nahua (Aztecs). The Totonacs, a Gulf Coast Mexican people, have always maintained that they built the city, a story later corroborated by the Aztecs.

The two truly dominant Mayan cultures at this time were centered at Tikal in Guatemala's Petén, which had aligned itself with Teotihuacán, and Calakmul located in the Campeche region of Mexico. These two cities dominated the region around the 500 A.D. and struggled with each other for trading rights which eventually led to open warfare. Calakmul finally made an alliance with the Maya at Caracol (in present day Belize) and defeated Tikal in 562 A.D. But Tikal was not through and in 695 A.D. they managed to defeat and overrun Calakmul and once that was done the Mayan culture under Tikal began to flourish as never before with new cities springing up all across Mayan territory, but within a century, by about 750 A.D., social and political changes were being felt as trade declined and more and more cities were abandoned.

The collapse of Teotihuacán in the 7th century sent shock waves through the peoples of Mesoamerica as cultural and scientific advancement became mired in what is known as the *Middle Classic Hiatus*. Although I am covering the *Classic Period* in its entirety, it is actually broken up into the *Early Classic Period* and the *Late Classic Periods* which are separated by the *Middle Classic Hiatus*, a period when there was a marked decline in the building and erection of dated monuments, particularly at Tikal. New kings and warlords strove to make their cities the dominant centers of the Mayan civilization after the loss of the Teotihuacán culture as the Mayan culture flourished despite broad-based internal conflicts and revolts. It was during this time that the Petén was changing from a grassland to the tropical rainforest it is today. The *Late Classic Period* was an era highlighted by the acceleration of the Mayan civilization.

By 850 A.D., militaristic outsiders had set up their own settlements along the *Usamacinta River* on what is today the border between Mexico and Guatemala. These were the years of the Mayan decline, the end of the *Classic Period*, and the emergence of the *Post Classic Period* which spanned the years from 900 A.D. until the time of the Spanish Conquest in the 1500s. At this time some of the Petén Maya fled into nearby Belize and the Yucatán, while most headed south into the Guatemalan highlands to the south. These areas were made up of many fragmented groups of Maya and strife and disorder was rampant in the numerous small, scattered Mayan settlements.

Other Mayan cities such as Cobá, Muyil, Tulum, Xel-Há and Tankah flourished during the *Classic Period* and became important trading centers with links to cities in the Yucatán, the Petén, and Campeche. These links were so strong that they even transformed the architectural style which is clearly influenced by that of the Petén.

During the *Late Classic Period*, from 600 A.D.-950 A.D., the Mayan civilization began to fall apart due to several factors, the most notable being an increase in conflict, which was most likely due to competition over natural resources. The years after 700 A.D. are often called the *Terminal Classic Period* and is marked by the rapid growth of the Mayan cities in the Yucatán, and after 900 A.D., the abandonment of the southern lowland cities. Tikal was deserted in the 9th century (nearby El Pilar never made into the *Post-Classic Period*), while the more residential areas followed shortly thereafter, yet it is during this period that Chichen Itzá flourishes in the Yucatán.

Post-Classic Period
900 A.D. – 1521 A.D.

The *Post-Classic Period* is the era of the decline of the Mayan civilization, the most decadent, degenerated, and militaristic period in the history of the Maya, and the period ends with the arrival of the Spanish. During this period the hub of Mayan cultural development moved north from the Maya lowlands in Guatemala and Belize to the Yucatán where the Maya first met the Spanish. In the Yucatán Peninsula, the Mayan cities there reached their peak during this period with commerce as their driving force. Mayan traders paddling canoes from Tabasco and Campeche rounded the Yucatán and headed south with goods for trade.

During the *Post Classic Period* Tulum and the inland port of Muyil prospered while Cobá developed into an important regional trading center in the Yucatán, but by the end of the 1200s, the once-great Mayan cities of Chichen Itzá and Uxmal, which were then inhabited by the Toltec-Maya, were abandoned. The Toltecs first appeared in Central Mexico in the 10th century A.D. when they built their capital city of Tula. The Toltecs are believed to have been refugees from the northern Teotihuacán culture, fleeing its fall in 700 A.D. Little is known of the Toltecs due to the destruction of their city by Aztecs seeking building materials so much of what we do know about them comes from legends handed down by other cultures. We do know that the Toltecs were highly militaristic and used that might to dominate their neighbors and sometime after 1200 A.D., the Guatemalan central highlands were invaded by a group of Toltec-Maya which radically altered life in the region.

The highlands had been populated by a peaceful, spiritual group of Maya and the militaristic Toltec-Maya soon set up a series of competing "empires" dominated by the K'iché Maya, who were located in the central highlands and still abound today (you'll sometimes see K'iche spelled Quiché, this is because the area they settled in is called Quiché-there are many Mayan dialects spoken amongst today's Maya in Guatemala, but *K'iché* is the most common, especially along the Río Dulce). The Toltecs controlled the more dominant tribes such as the K'iché, the Mam, the Kaqchikel, and the Tz'utujil establishing a new hierarchy and bringing with them new gods and a new language that blended with those of the Guatemalan Maya. Beginning around 1400 A.D., the K'iché, under the direction of the Toltec-Maya, began to exert their influence in the area and by the latter part of the 1400s controlled some one million people, completely dominating the once powerful Mam and Kaqchikel. In 1475, the great K'iché king Cuicab, the man who has been described as the mastermind of the K'iché expansion, passed away and with him went much of the K'iché authority. Soon various conquered tribes of Maya began to break away from K'iché control and for the next half-century the various Mayan tribes in Guatemala were locked in constant conflict with one another as their settlements reflected defensive positions as opposed to a setting better suited to an agrarian subsistence.

The coming of the Spaniards had been foretold in Mayan prophecies. It was written that a pale-skinned people from the east who worshipped one God would arrive and catastrophe would soon follow bringing the end of their world. The death knell for the Mayan empire sounded the day that Columbus, on his fifth voyage to the New World, 1503-1504, encountered some Mayan traders in a canoe southwest of Cuba. But the first Europeans to actually visit the Yucatán Peninsula were probably Juan Dias de Solis, and Martin Pinzon, former companions of Christopher Columbus, who were shipwrecked on the peninsula in 1511 and held captive by the Maya. What the Mayan oracles did not prophesize was the coming of one man, Gonzalo Guerrero. In 1511, a Spanish galleon foundered on Arrecife Alcaranes near Cabo Catoches, north/northeast of Isla Contoy, and twenty people washed ashore. After two years only two members of the party survived the rigors of life ashore, Guerrero and Friar Jerónimo de Aguilar. De Aguilar was rescued by Hernán Cortés in 1519, but Guerrero decided to stay with the Maya Because of his bravery and his skills as a warrior Guerrero won the trust of the chief of Chetumal who made him a nakóm, or captain. Guerrero married a Mayan noblewoman and adopted the Mayan dress and customs. Guerrero and his wife had three children, the first mixed race children, mestizos, in Mexico.

When Spanish soldiers first set foot on the Yucatán Peninsula they found a Mayan civilization, estimated at up to one million people, beset by hardships and at war with itself, but this did not deter the Maya from putting up a fierce resistance to the invaders. In 1517, a Spanish expedition led by Francisco Hernandez de Córdoba set sail from Cuba in search of slaves and new lands and landed on Isla Mujeres claiming the island for Spain. Heading for Cabo Catoche the Spaniards experienced the first Mayan resistance, Mayan warriors attacked them and Córdoba himself was killed. The surviving Spaniards retreated to their boats to return to Cuba where they claimed that the peninsula was rich in gold. The following years saw more and more expeditions targeting the Yucatán Peninsula starting in 1518 when Juan de Grijalva landed on Isla de Cozumel and viewed the cities of Tulum and Xel-Há from the sea.

In 1519, Hernán Cortés, with a fleet of 11 ships and a force of 550 men landed at Isla de Cozumel, a Mayan commercial and religious center, where he rescued Friar Jerónimo de Aguilar. In 1511, a Spanish galleon foundered on *Arrecife Alcaranes* near Cabo Catoche, north/northeast of Isla Contoy, and thirteen people washed ashore. After two years, only two members of the party survived the rigors

of life in the Yucatán amid the Maya, Guerrero and Friar Jerónimo de Aguilar, who were kept as slaves by the Maya. Aguilar was only given field work, but Guerrero, with his knowledge of European war tactics, earned the favor of the chief of the Chetumal Maya, Nacanchán, when he advised him on inter-Mayan conflicts. When de Aguilar was rescued by Cortés, Guerrero decided to stay with the Maya, he had already married Nacanchán's daughter, and had earned the rank of *nakóm*, the equivalent of a captain. Guerrero and his wife had three children, the first mixed race children, *mestizos*, in Mexico. Branded a traitor by Cortés, Guerrero is said to have been responsible for Mayan victories against the Spanish at Chetumal and several other battles in the Yucatán. Nobody really knows what happened to Guerrero but it believed that he died in Honduras fighting the Spanish around 1536.

In 1521, Cortés eventually north and then west on a journey that would lead him into the Gulf of Mexico to Veracruz and culminate in the conquest of Tenochtitlán, the capital of the Aztecs who were at the height of their thousand-year-old civilization at this time and who, within three years of the arrival of Cortés, were conquered by 500 Spanish Conquistadors and treacherous Indian allies such as La Malinche. La Malinche was the flip side of the Guerrero betrayal coin. An Aztec princess from Jalisco, La Malinche was captured in war and eventually given to Cortés. She had several children with Cortés and helped him defeat the Aztecs, explaining which tricks the Aztecs would use and how to counter them. Cortés rewarded her by abandoning her to return to Spain and marry a high-born Spanish noblewoman.

In 1523, Cortés dispatched Pedro de Alvarado to Guatemala to use "minimum force" and to "preach matters concerning our Holy Faith." De Alvarado and his army of over 600 soldiers and horsemen engaged a huge K'iché force estimated at 30,000 under the command of Tecún Umán near the deserted Mayan city of Xelajú. The well-armed warriors of de Alvarado were decimating the Mayan fighters when the battle suddenly ended as de Alvarado killed Tecún Umán in hand-to-hand combat. The K'iché were defeated but the Kaqchikel decided to form an alliance of sorts with the Spanish allowing the Spanish to establish their first base in Guatemala next to the Kaqchikel capital of Iximché In 1526, the Kaqchikel broke away from their Spanish allies and moved deeper into the mountains and began to wage a guerilla style war forcing the Spanish to move their base to present day Antigua where they established the first capital of Guatemala, Santiago de los Caballeros on St. Cecelia's Day, November 22, 1527.

De Alvarado's army continued to fight battle after battle with the highland Maya but the Spaniards never gained control over the more remote regions. In 1537, the Church stepped in and succeeded where de Alvarado failed. Missionaries under the guidance of Bartolemé de las Casas convinced the renegade Maya to accept both Christianity and Spanish sovereignty and by 1540 the last of the highland Maya were brought under Spanish control. Years later de Alvarado, who had controlled Guatemala like his personal fiefdom, enslaving and abusing the Maya and turning their lands into Spanish estates, was killed beneath a rolling horse during a battle in Mexico.

Unlike the Aztecs, the conquest of the Maya was not such an easy task, they had no centralized government whose fall would be the end of the conflict, in fact, so scattered were the communities that the Spaniards were sometimes able to turn one group of Indian against another. However, when it came to the Spanish, the Mayan warriors put up a fierce resistance, but despite their valiant struggle, the superior weaponry of the Spaniards, combined with their ability to attack on horseback, proved too much to overcome even though it took the Spaniards until 1546 to finally gain control over the peninsula. On December 8, 1526, Francisco de Montejo was put in charge of a military force set to conquer the Maya and colonize the Yucatán Peninsula. In October of 1527, Montejo and his men landed on the coast in an area where the Maya were friendly to the Spaniards, so friendly that the Maya even helped the invaders build thatched-roof huts. Montejo's settlement was called Salamanca de Xel-Há and was short-lived as the Spanish fell victim to tropical disease. Before long Montejo returned to the Yucatán Peninsula at Campeche where he headed inland to the north leaving his son, known as El Mozo, in charge of the garrison at Campeche. Another of Montejo's officers, Alonso Davila, headed for Quintana Roo in search of gold in 1531, and finding none arrived in Chetumal only to find the city in ruins. The Maya, upon learning of Davila's approach, torched the great city before fleeing into the jungle to return time and time again over the next 18 months in guerilla raids against Davila's men, finally forcing the Spaniards to retreat from Chetumal.

Several more years passed until the Spaniards again returned to Quintana Roo fully bent on conquest. Gaspar Pachero, and his son Melchor, landed on the peninsula in 1544 and found a Maya civilization debilitated by disease and drought and split into two rival groups making conquest by the Spaniards that much easier. Savagely fighting their way to Bacalar, the father and son founded Salamanca de Bacalar, but the poverty and desolation of the area forced many colonists to abandon Bacalar and return to Mérida.

The Spaniards, victorious at last, divided the Yucatán into landholdings called *encomiendas* that they seized as "spoils of war." The conquerors became the new masters as colonial plantations sprang up throughout the region and the Maya were forced to labor for the estates (haciendas) planting and harvesting cacao, cotton, and tropical hardwoods as well as gathering honey and beeswax, all for export. The Maya were enslaved and treated harshly, but their spirit was not broken, which led to several uprisings against their colonial masters. The first Mayan rebellion occurred in 1546 in Valladolid and Bacalar, and in later years more revolts occurred from 1639-1761 when an uprising with religious overtones at Jacinto Creek was the forerunner of the Caste War of 1847, which lasted for more than 50 years.

Inland, resident Franciscan friars had discovered the Maya and were shocked at what they thought to be the work of Satan, body mutilation and human sacrifice in the name of religion. The friars decided that it was their sacred duty to God to eliminate these blasphemies and bring the surviving Maya to Christianity. The friars, under the direction of Friar Diego de Landa, destroyed thousands of Mayan idols and de Landa personally manipulated the destruction of 27 codices filled with characters and symbols that he could not understand but took to be the words and drawings of Satan. The destruction nearly wiped out all traces of Mayan civilization, and today only three codices from that era remain intact, one in Madrid, one in Paris, and one in Dresden. De Landa did however write a manual for other priests concerning the Mayans, his scribe was the source of much of this information, especially the Mayan alphabet. The ancient Maya had an extensive written language that was both phonetic and ideographic. Words were written in hieroglyphs, each picture having its own meaning, and the Maya could arrange these pictures in a form to create words, sentences, and even tell a story. Unfortunately nobody could make the Mayan alphabet work and the work was ignored for over 4 centuries. A volume of Maya text was rescued from a library in Berlin when the Russians liberated the city in 1945. The Russian soldier who rescued the work, a student of languages and a mathematician, struggled for years and finally put the pieces together using the text and de Landa's alphabet. But the true key to Mayan languages was not discovered until the 1970s when a group of young linguists at Palenque discovered that the glyphs were actually an alphabet.

De Landa was recalled to Spain and spent a year in prison while awaiting word on his guilt or innocence of the charges of "despotic mismanagement." Although de Landa can be blamed for the loss of the history of the Maya, he did in fact pen a book in his own defense, *Relaciones del as Cosas de Yucatán*, which describes daily living in a Mayan village in great detail including the growing and preparation of food, the social structure, and the Mayan priesthood and the sciences including a formula that unlocked some of the secrets to Mayan mathematics and astronomy. Redemption for the loss of a culture? Hardly... but it was all that we were left with. De Landa was eventually cleared of all charges and returned to the Yucatán as a Bishop where he remained until his death in 1579.

But, not all Catholic missionaries were as hard line as de Linda, in fact de Linda's replacement while in prison, Bishop Toral, was far more compassionate to the Maya than his infamous predecessor. Toral was a humanitarian who was appalled by the treatment of the Indians and attempted to make changes to alleviate their suffering. The Franciscan hierarchy refused to see things Toral's way and no changes were made until shortly before Toral's death in 1571 when his changes were implemented in a *Royal Cedula* that prohibited the Franciscan Friars from shaving heads, flogging the Maya, and keeping prison cells in their monasteries as well as bringing about the release of Indian prisoners. Many of the Maya were baptized into the Catholic faith and the friars educated the people and did their best to protect them from hacienda owners in search of slaves.

On September 28, 1821, after three centuries as a Spanish colony, the independent republic of Mexico was born. But many wealthy hacienda owners in the Yucatán, dissatisfied with their new centralized government and the land reforms that it was imposing upon them, declared their independence from Mexico, and in 1847, with the Mexican government, preoccupied with the Mexican-American War and the hacienda owners still bickering about independence, the Maya became lost in the cracks. They Maya had suffered for years and nobody cared enough about them to do anything to alleviate their suffering. A fostering hatred for the ruling class, the blancos, exploded with a fury in 1847 in what has come to be known as the *Caste War*, a conflict that was to last for seven years and decimate the Mayan people and encourage a further half-century of guerilla encounters.

The *Caste War*, so called because of the complex racial levels or castes that the Spanish had developed to differentiate the mixed bloodline of the Mexican people, began as a rebellion in Tepich and quickly spread to Tihosuco, Ichmul, and Sacalaca on the Yucatán-Quintana Roo border. Showing no mercy to the white landholders, the Mayan goal was to remove them from the Yucatán so that the Mayan people could be free once more. So fierce were the Mayan warriors, and so successful, that by the Spring of 1848 they had the majority of the blancos trapped inside the cities of Mérida and Campeche. The blancos appealed for assistance from Spain, France, and the United States but no help came and the mayor of Mérida was within one day of evacuating the city when something quite unexpected occurred. Historians suggest that the Maya were within a week of driving their foes into the sea when the tide of battle turned almost overnight. To understand what happened, one must understand the religious significance of the land, and specifically of corn, maize, to the Mayan people. Within days of victory, the entire Mayan army to a man packed up their belongings and returned to their fields to plant their corn thanks to the appearance of a winged ant. In Mayan philosophy life and time are cycles, and the cycle at that time indicated it was time to plant their crops. The Maya knew that the rains would soon come and if their corn, the gift of sustenance from the gods, was not in the ground the gods would be insulted and angry. Just as the dawn of their victory approached the winged ant made its appearance. The winged ant, the harbinger of the rains, was a bit early but the Maya still returned to their fields to plant their corn. Not a very good move from a military standpoint, their return to the fields allowed the entrapped blancos to re-fortify their defenses and send for reinforcements offered by the Mexican government if the landowners would forget their independent views and support a unified Mexico. Troops from Mexico City and Cuba soon arrived along with 1,000 mercenaries and it wasn't long before the Maya found themselves under attack and the lands the blancos had lost were regained and the captured Maya sold as slaves to Cuban plantation owners. Thousands of the Maya hid in the jungle for decades or fled across the border into British Honduras, now Belize to escape the slavers. By 1855, the Caste War was officially over and although the government controlled the peninsula, the Mayan rebels fled to the jungles of central Quintana Roo where, with the help of gun-runners from British Honduras, they sustained regular guerilla attacks will into the early 1900s when disease, starvation, and repeating rifles finally put an end to the conflict.

After the debacle at Mérida and Campeche the Maya were defeated and demoralized, but certain Mayans resurrected a religious cult that allowed the Mayan to regain their spirit and reorganize, all it took was a "miracle" involving some carvings on a tree, a priest, and a ventriloquist. In 1850, a mestizo from Peto named José Maria Barrera carved three crosses into the bark of a tree in a community located near the border with present day Belize. The cult of the *Talking Cross* dated to a pre-Columbian oracle representing the gods of the four cardinal directions and the symbols of the three crosses supposedly transmitted a message from God that was given to the faithful on October 15, 1850 in a sermon by Juan de la Cruz. The priest employed a ventriloquist named Manuel Nahuat as the mouthpiece of the crosses to tell the Maya what God wanted them to do. The community came to be called Chan Santa Cruz, Little Holy Cross, and the inhabitants became known as *cruzobs*, followers of the cross. A temple was built to house the crosses that were kept in the inner sanctum called La Gloria. The community thrived selling timber and dealing in arms and the people that came to Chan Santa Cruz in large numbers rediscovered their self-esteem and began to organize. Taking advantage of period of poor relations between Campeche and Mérida which ended with Campeche seceding from the state of Yucatán in 1857, the Chan Santa Cruz Indians took the fort at Bacalar which gave them control of the coast from Cabo Catoche in the north to the border with British Honduras. At first the Indians killed their captives, but beginning around 1858 they began to keep white male prisoners as slaves working in the fields and forests and the women captives as domestic servants or concubines. The Chan Santa Cruz Indians were in complete control of Quintana Roo for over 40 years as a truce with the Mexican Government was sometimes in effect, sometimes

not. Quintana Roo was isolated, it was not connected by road to the rest of Mexico, which was unified and progressing as a nation and a people, so when President Porfrio Diaz came to power in 1877 he cast his eye on the Yucatán Peninsula.

In 1892, Mexico and British Honduras signed a peace treaty and arms sales to the Mayans were outlawed. This did little to put a halt to Mayan hostility and the peninsula remained a dangerous no-man's land of sorts and the military campaign against the Chan Santa Cruz Indians continued. In 1898, Payo Obispo, now known as Chetumal, was founded by Lt. Othón P. Blanco and designated capital of the territory. In 1901, the Mexican army, under the command of General Ignacio Bravo, attacked the Indians and set up a garrison in Quintana Roo that was regularly supplied by a railroad that the army constructed. Over the ensuing years the army continued to raid Mayan settlements and on November 15, 1902, President Porfrio Diaz made Quintana Roo a territory of the Mexican republic after years of being part of the state of Yucatán. Although the area was ripe for colonization, President Diaz used the region primarily as a penal colony for years (until this practice was ended after the Revolution) and the government of Mexico had little control over the region until around 1910 when the army began to make inroads in their control of the Mayan population. During these years the Mexican army continued to raid Mayan settlements until around 1915 when the army left the peninsula to the Maya who refused to submit to the Mexicans. That same year the region was again declared to be part of the state of Yucatán until 1931 when Quintana Roo was again separated from Yucatán.

From 1917-1920 hundreds of thousands of Indians died from influenza and smallpox, which had been introduced by the Spanish. As the older leaders passed away, new Mayan leaders emerged, once such man was General Francisco May, the headman of Yokdxonot-Guardia, the site of the *Talking Cross*. May led his troops in skirmishes against the Mexicans for years before seeing the inevitable and demanded, and received, a negotiated settlement with the government. In 1935 peace officially came to Quintana Roo when the Chan Santa Cruz Indians, under the leadership of General May, signed a formal peace treaty with the government of Mexico. The Maya were granted land parcels thanks to President Lazaro Cardenas who gave half the usable land in Quintana Roo to the poor.

The Mayan People

Mayan society was well defined; at the top of the Mayan social ladder was the ruler, the King, who was the earthy manifestation of the Gods. When a ruler died he was buried in a tomb deep inside a pyramid, an offering of jade, pottery and food arranged around his resting place. Below the King's station were the Priests followed closely by the Lords, nobles, warriors, artists, merchants, and on the bottom rung were the peasants, the farmers, who supplied the food and labor for building the temples and palaces of the upper classes.

The Mayans lived according to their place in society; their cities, which were primarily ceremonial centers, were home to the nobility and the priests (who would carry out daily religious duties, particularly sacrifices), but the great majority of the Maya were farmers who lived simple lives in thatched houses amid forest gardens well outside the city. The reason for this is wedded to the nature of agriculture in a tropical rainforest where plots of land, even when the farmers use slash and burn agriculture (*milpa*), would be unsuitable in 2-4 years due to a lack of nutrients (growth is rapid in a tropical rainforest and the nutrients supplied by animal feces and decaying flora is used up quickly), sometimes this length of time could extend to as much as 7 years if the land was weeded by hand instead of with tools. It is suggested that 70-acres of land were required to support a family of five, so simple math will show you that depending on the size of the community, most of which were small, the land would soon be depleted and a move to more fertile land was necessary.

The Maya had a great sense of physical beauty that differed from the other peoples in Mesoamerica. The Maya prized a long, backward sloping forehead, and in order to attain this look, infants would have their skulls bound with boards. The Lucayans in the Bahamas, and the Flathead Indians in Montana developed similar practices. Crossed-eyes were also an important item of physical beauty; infants would have objects dangled in front of their eyes in order to permanently cross their eyes (and this is still occasionally practiced today). Some Maya would have their teeth filed down to a point and place Jade in the holes.

The average Mayan's diet consisted of beans, tomatoes, peppers, and several other fruits and vegetables with corn being a staple, usually in the form of tortillas. Honey produced from bee keeping was not only found on the table, it was used in commerce. But the wealthy Maya were blessed with a richer diet consisting of fish, fowl, and other game meats, and the occasional chocolate drink made of cocoa and chilies. The Maya referred to chocolate as *The Drink of the Gods* and would make it in many forms from a frothy drink to a pulpy mush.

One of the most eye-catching aspects of the Mayan people is their colorful clothing in an exotic and seemingly infinite variety of colors. While most Maya wore simple cotton clothes, much as they still do today, the ruling class and merchants wore jewelry, feathered headband, and other decorations. Those in the know can tell which village a Mayan woman is from by the coloring of her *huipil* (pronounced *weep-peel*), the woman's colorful blouse whose designs date to pre-Columbian times. These designs, besides denoting the wearer's village or region, may display religious or mystical meanings. The *huipil* is a square or rectangular piece of material with a hole cut in the center and is usually embroidered around the neck in a cross-like shape. Then the *huipil* is folded in half and the sides sewn together allowing for arm holes. The *huipil* is tucked into the *corte*, a skirt that is wrapped around the body like a sarong, and it is held in place by a belt called a *faja*. In colder climes, in the highlands, some Mayan women wear a *tzute*, another rectangular cloth that is worn across the shoulders like a shawl or cape. The dress for today's Mayan man differs from the more traditional Mayan women's garb, exhibiting more of a Spanish influence. Single men normally wear brighter clothes than married men and both married and single men wear a *huipil*-like garment though with less decoration than the women's *huipil*. Both men and women wear colorful woven belts, while wide, leather or cloth belts called *mecapal* are used to carry heavy loads. Men might also be seen wearing a *tzute*-like garment as well as hats which are usually worn for ceremonial events. Mayan women will wear jewelry but Mayan men do not, however they may sometimes carry a bag called a *moral*.

The pre-Columbian Mayans were a spiritual people with a highly developed religion that the Spaniards either could not or would not acknowledge. Their religion was the center of life, very ritualistic, and to the Maya the natural and the supernatural planes were as one. Their gods, many of whom were reptilian, reigned supreme, and the Maya world was inhabited by good and evil spirits (consequently Mayan gods had a duality to their nature, each god having a benevolent and malevolent side). Their principal Gods were Itzamná and his wife, Ixchel (sometimes shown as Ix Chel), the mother and father of all the other gods. Ixchel was also the goddess of birth, fertility, and weaving. Ixchel taught women how to weave and Mayans came from all over their world to worship at her shrine on Cozumel.

Kinich Ahau, *Lord of the Solar Face*, was the Mayan's *Sun God* who appears in the huge masks at Kohunlich. Ah Mucen Cab, who appears in carvings at Tulum and Chichén Itzá, is the descending god who is also a *Sky Bearer* and *God of the Bees, He Who Watches Over The Honey*. The Mayan religion, due to its origins in agriculture, required accurate predictions of time with accommodations to the cycles of the rain forests. Cycle dependent, Mayan religion strove to allow Mayans to synchronize to these cycles. Mayan priests created a calendar with 18 months, each containing 20 days, plus 5 unlucky days, as well as a religious calendar that had 260 days. They believed each day was a God that carried the weight of the day on its back. The Mayan calendar begins on August 13, 3113 B.C. (by our modern calendar's dating, although some scholars claim it is August 11, and others August 6, which is the Chinese estimation of the midpoint between the summer solstice and the autumn equinox), and ends December 20, 2012 A.D. (a date that some Doom-sayers predict to be the end of Earth itself), a 5,125 year cycle.

The Mayans had their own beliefs concerning the history of the world and their own civilization which are outlined in more detail in the next section on the *Popol Vuh*. Their belief that the world had been created five times and destroyed four times was later adopted by the Toltecs. They believed in an afterlife, but heaven was reserved for only for those who had been sacrificed or who died in childbirth, everybody else went to *Xibalba*, a terrible place ruled over by the *Gods of Death*. The Maya believed that there were five different cardinal directions, four of which were associated with colors. North was white, the place of wisdom and purification, south was yellow, the place of life and expansion, east was red, the place of light and generation, west was black, the place of death and transformation, and the center was associated with a huge Ceiba tree, *wakah-kan*, that was the center of the universe. It has been suggested that the ceiba tree is actually the *Milky Way* as it appears in the night sky, and the three starts of Orion are said to be the hearthstones of Creation set down by the gods (one reason that three hearthstones are part of the cooking fire in most Mayan homes to this day).

The Maya worshipped 13 Gods in 13 heavens and 9 Gods of the *Xibalba*, the nine worlds of Hell. Between the heavens and *Xibalba*, was our earthly plane of existence which is often shown in Mayan art as a two-headed crocodile or a turtle in a great lake. In Mayan mythology, there were four *Tulans*, or *Tollans* as they are sometimes shown, one represented Heaven, one represented *Xibalba* (Hell), and the other two represented the path of the sun, east and west, with the Mayan people originating in the West.

Mayan cities had ball courts located at their ceremonial core and there is a lot of speculation about the game. Little is known of how the game is actually played, but what we do know is that the game involved two individuals or teams of 2-3 players, each of which was only able to hit the ball with their hips, shoulders, backs, elbows, or wrists. The object of the game appears to be to get the ball out of your opponent's section of the court without it touching the center channel (ball courts generally had a flat central channel and sloping parallel sides). In the latter years of the Mayan civilization, particularly in Central Mexico, the ball courts were larger with stone hoops on each side wall for scoring, these hoops can be seen at the greatest of all Mayan ball courts, the court at Chichen Itzá. The players wore helmets, belts, and padding to protect themselves as they flung themselves about. But this was not a casual contact sport, it was downright deadly in one sense. Carvings left behind indicate that members of one side or the other were sacrificed after the games. Some scholars claim it was the fate of the losing team, while other hold that the winners earned and honorable sacrifice. Even more say the game was just a way of settling disputes or for allowing prisoners a last chance at freedom. Whatever the reality of the game was, only the best athletes were selected to play and for them it was an honor to be sacrificed. Personally though, I cannot imagine people lining up to play this game, but I'm not an ancient Mayan either.

The Popol Vuh and Mayan Mythology
"Are utzijoxik wa'e k'ak atz'ininoq,
k'akachamamoq, katz'inonik, k'akasilanik,
k'akalolinik, katolona puch upa kaj."
"This is the account of how all was in suspense,
all calm, in silence, all motionless, still, and the
expanse of the sky was empty."

The above are the opening lines from the *Popol Vuh*, the *Council Book*, or the *Book of the Community*, the book of Mayan scriptures whose most complete copy is written in the language of the K'iche Maya.

When the Spanish, under the direction of Friar Diego de Landa, destroyed thousands of Mayan idols (and de Landa himself personally destroyed 27 codices fill with Mayan characters and symbols), some Mayan priests and scribes clandestinely made copies of some of their older hieroglyphic works using the Latin letters the Spanish had taught them. One of these books was discovered in Chichicastenango in 1702 by Father Francisco Ximénez, a Spanish missionary priest, who made a copy of it and translated it into Spanish. Somehow this copy made its way to a hidden corner of the library at the University of San Carlos in Guatemala City where it was discovered in 1854. Within a few years French and Spanish versions were printed and the *Popul Vuh* has been in print in one form or another ever since. Although the tome is indeed based on early Mayan hieroglyphic texts, as you read the *Popol Vuh* you will see and feel the Spanish influence upon the translated version, most notably the mention of the Spanish governors of Guatemala as being the successors of early Mayan rulers. One must wonder if the Spanish influence stopped there, the entire volume smacks of the *Book of Genesis* at times, the similarities in the two creation theories are amazing, but are they truly coincidental?

The *Popol Vuh* details the creation myth of the Mayan people in which the *Creators*, Tepeu and Gucumatz, who is also known as *Kukulkán* and called *Quetzalcoatl* by the Aztecs, were the first two beings to exist and were the wisest of sages. A third being, Huracan, known as the *Heart of Heaven*, also existed but is given less of a personification; he is known as the *God of Storms* (notice the similarity in his name and the name the pre-Columbian Arawaks gave the seasonal storms of the Caribbean?). Tepeu and Gucumatz decide that in order to preserve their legacy they need to create a race of beings who would worship them, so Huracan creates the race of man while Tepeu and Gucumatz advise and guide him. Earth is created first, followed by animals who did not worship their *Creators,* causing the animals to be banished to the forests for eternity. Next Huracan turns to the creation of man, first making him out of mud, but they just crumbled away or dissolved with water. Tepeu and Gucumatz summon other Gods to assist in the creation of man, and the next version is created of wood but wooden man has no soul or brain and they soon forgot the *Creators* who bring a black resinous rain down upon the heads of wooden man and in the rising flood waters wooden man takes to the trees where they become monkeys.

Finally man is made of corn and the Gods are at last successful. This is one reason corn is so important to the Maya, not only is it the base of their diet, it is the very essence of who they are. After the telling of the creation story, the *Popul Vuh* recounts the struggles of the hero twins Hunahpu and Xbalanqué, in defeating the lords of *Xibalba*, the underworld, or hell as we would likely call it. In the saga, an earlier set of ball-playing hero twins, Hun-Hunahpu and Vucub Hunah, play so loudly that they disturb the Lords of the Underworld, Vucub Caquix and Hun Came. The twins are summoned to *Xibalba* where the demon Lords defeat them in a ball game and kill them. The daughter of one of the Lords of the Underworld is impregnated by the decapitated head of Hun-Hunahphu and flees to live with the twin's mother where she gives birth to the hero twins, Hunahphu and Xbalanqué. The twin's grandmother hides all manner of ball playing equipment from the twins, but the twins succeed in getting a rat to show them the gear. Before long the twins are playing ball and disturbing the Lords of the Underworld who summon them for a ball game. The twins play the Lords for days and nights and are unbeatable so the Lords decide to burn them. Learning of this plan, the twins arrange for a seer to instruct the Lords to dispose of the twins in a certain way and the next day the twins jump into a flaming pit. The Lords grind their bones to dust and throw them into the river where the twins are resurrected with the faces of fish and return to *Xibalba* where, disguised as carnival dancers, they perform magical feats, even decapitating and resurrecting the other. The Lords see these amazing feats and want to be decapitated and revived. The twins gladly comply in decapitating them, but they do not resurrect them, defeating them forever. The twins then resurrect their uncles, Hun-Hunahpu and Vucub Hunah, who were buried beneath the ball court in *Xibalba*. This tale is often seen depicted in Mayan art.

The Maya Today

The greatest question concerning the Maya themselves, is what happened to them? Do not think of the Maya as a dead civilization, they are very much alive and still inhabit much of Central America from Mexico to Nicaragua, and their culture has remained amazingly intact despite the influences of the modern world and the bloodthirsty near-genocide perpetrated upon them over the last couple of centuries by the government of Guatemala.

Many of the people you meet in your travels in Central America may well be Mayan or at least have Mayan blood in them. In more traditional areas, such as Chichicastenango in Guatemala, you'll meet Mayans wearing the colorful Mayan style of clothing that harks back to an era long, long ago. Many Maya still choose to live in a time-honored manner and may limit their contact with outside influences. Corn still plays an important part of their diet, and even though some may speak Spanish, many of the Mayan dialects are still spoken, especially *K'iche* which you will find spoken along the *Río Dulce*.

Ancient Mayan Cities

There are SO MANY Mayan sites in Central America that I simply cannot list them all, so with that in mind I'll only cover here the best known and most visited sites, and one recent discovery.

El Mirador

El Mirador, *The Lookout*, is the largest and most elaborate of all Mayan cities and home to the largest pyramid the Maya ever built, a structure that rivals the ancient pyramids of Egypt. The site is extremely difficult to visit, if you plan to view the ruins of El Mirador you'll have to hire guides from the nearby village of Carmelita for around US$200-$300 for the five day trip through the jungle to the city and back on pack mules and horseback. It is also possible to visit El Mirador by helicopter but you can expect that luxury to be quite pricey. (Helicópteros de Guatemala; 502-2381-7777) There is talk of a road being built in the next year or two that will allow researchers and equipment into the site, but that is one of those things that may never get finished much less started

El Mirador, first discovered in 1926 in the Petén, was first photographed by air in 1930, but remained untouched by researchers until 1962 when Ian Graham spent 10 days there mapping the site. Graham, an explorer and a member of the *Corpus of Maya Hieroglyphics Project*, is also the discoverer of the 2,000 year old city of Cival (east/northeast of Tikal) in 1984. A detailed research project on El Mirador began in 1978 and archeologists quickly realized that much of the site was not a contemporary of Tikal (as first thought), but predated it by centuries, flourishing around 1000 B.C. and reaching its apex around 200-300 A.D. with a peak population of around 80,000-100,000. At this time El Mirador went into a period of decline it was abandoned and re-occupied several more times until around 800-900 A.D. Today, the El

Mirador basin is protected by the *Mirador Basin National Park*, officially established on April 18, 2002 as a *Special Archeological Zone* protecting some 600,000 acres and prohibiting roads throughout the area.

El Mirador covers some ten square miles with the center of its architecture covering a bit over one square mile in area. The most impressive site here is the pyramid named *La Danta*, some 230' high (the tallest structure the Maya ever built), followed closely by *El Tigre* at 180' high (which has 6 times the surface area of *Temple IV* at Tikal). *La Danta* and *El Tigre* are on opposite sides of the city and while *El Tigre* greets the morning sun, *La Danta* observes the coming of night. El Mirador is also home to the tomb of an ancient Mayan king, *Great Fiery Jaguar Claw*, one of a dynasty that goes back over 600 years before the birth of Christ. The site is also the center of a series of raised stone pedestrian causeways, one of which links El Mirador with the city of Nakbé some nine miles away.

If you wish to visit El Mirador or Nakbé you can look up Adonis Lopez in San Andrés, just across the lake from Flores. Adonis, who does not speak English, can be reached at 502-5619-8465 or at 502-5578-1832. Adonis charges US$300 each for two people for the six-day trip from San Andrés. If you have a larger group the price will go down accordingly. Viajes Tivoli speaks English and can arrange a six day trip for US$375 per person and can be reached at 502-5554-0433 (the price goes down for a five-day trip or for more people). The Carmelita Cooperativa (867-5629) is a co-op of over 100 guides and charges US$235 for two people to El Mirador (they also add on a 15% tip). The guide you get is dependent on who is next in the lineup. For up to four people the price goes up to US$261 per person (this is to pay for a cook), but when you get a group of ten together the price drops to US$221. The trek begins in the small village of Carmelita where the road from Flores ends near the Mexican border. You can reach the co-op at 502-7861 1809. *Tikal Connection* (502-5575-4335), formerly *Ecomaya*, also handles tours to El Mirador and they can be reached at 502-7926-4981, or by email at info@tikalcnx.com. They may not answer your emails, they didn't respond to several of mine. If you wish to fly into El Mirador contact *Helicópteros de Guatemala*, 502-2381-7777, or email them at Roventas@intelnet.net.gt. Prices start about US$600 per flight hour for four passengers, estimated round trip flight time from Guatemala City to El Mirador is almost 5 hours.

Tikal

Tikal is probably the most visited of all the ancient Mayan cities, primarily due to the convenience of access to the site. Located deep in the jungles of the Petén a few hours north of Río Dulce, the first settlers here arrived around 900 B.C. with first construction of which there is evidence of beginning around 200 B.C.-100 B.C. The ruins at Tikal are part of the *Tikal Biosphere Reserve*, a 222 square mile protected area that was declared a *UNESCO World Heritage Site* in 1979. Although easily visited as a day trip, the trek through the site can cover 27 miles of trails and it's best to stay overnight here to gain a full experience and view the dawn from atop one of the pyramids (if you're lucky you'll hear a jaguar in the night).

There are over 4,000 structures located at Tikal, the most interesting are the *Great Plaza* which is surrounded by stelae and sculpted altars with grand temples (I & II) at each end of the plaza. *Temple I*, the *Temple of the Great Jaguar*, was built around 700 A.D. by Ah Cacao whose tomb is inside the structure (Ah Cacao also constructed *Temple II*). *Temple III* is the *Temple of the Jaguar Priest* and was constructed around 810 A.D., while the tallest structure is *Temple IV*, The *Temple of the Double Headed Serpent*, which rises to 212' above the jungle floor and was built around 470 A.D. by Yaxkin Caan Chac. Temple V was built around 750 A.D. and rises to 190', while *Temple VI* contains the longest Mayan hieroglyph to found to date. Southwest of the *Great Plaza* is the *Plaza of the Great Pyramid*, which, along with structures to its west, forms an astronomical complex.

It is believed that Tikal was abandoned about 900 A.D. and was re-discovered in 1695 by a Spanish priest. Leaving the Tikal to the jungle, it wasn't until 1848 that a government expedition opened up the site to researchers. Finally, in 1951, access was allowed to the site for one and all after the construction of an airstrip, previously all entry was done by horseback. In 1956, excavation and restoration of the site was begun in earnest with most of the work completed by 1984. However, even today new projects are underway to restore more parts of Tikal and as little as ten years ago a workman, mowing the grass in the Great Plaza, stumbled upon a hitherto unknown *Stela*.

Quirigúa

Located just a few miles from Morales on CA9, the road to Guatemala City from Río Dulce, near Km marker 204, sits a small road that leads off to the south through a banana plantation to the ruins at Quirigúa. As you enter the parking lot, located in the middle of field of bananas, you'll park your vehicle under the hardwoods and visit the visitor center/museum to view ancient Mayan carvings before strolling about the grounds to view the remarkable stelae that stand here.

Here you'll find 500 year-old trees, ancient Mayan altars and temples, and a dozen of tallest stelae in the Mayan world, over 20'. The largest, Stela "E," measures 35' in height, is 5' wide, weights 65 tons, and was carved from a single block of stone quarried by the Maya. The temple here has three chambers and has a carved date that translates to 810 A.D. after which the history of this site ceases to be recorded. In 1979, Quirigúa was declared a *UNESCO Monument of the World's Heritage.*

Quirigúa was first settled sometime during the *Late Pre-Classic Period* by Mayan immigrants from the north, possibly from the Yucatán. Quirigúa, which appears to have been under the control of the rulers of Copán in Honduras, was valued for its location on the banks of the *Río Matagua*, and important Mayan trade route and source for jade. Around 737 A.D., Quirigúa won her independence for Copán when her leader, *Cauac Sky*, captured the leader of Copán, *18 Rabbit*. Quirigúa reached its peak around 790 A.D. but by 850 had faded from all but memory.

Copán

The Mayan ruins at Copán (sometimes called the "Art City") are located about 5 miles inside the border with Guatemala, and about ½ mile east of the town of Copán Ruinas on the road to San Pedro Sula. Copán was certainly not the largest Mayan city, at its peak around 550 A.D., it was home to only about 24,000 people during the Maya's *Classic Period*. Much of the Mayan artworks here are reproductions, the originals safely tucked away, protected from the elements and the wandering hands of thousands of tourists (the salts from your skin can corrode the stones). The principal attractions at Copán are the ball court, the *Acropolis*, the main park (*Las Sepulturas*), *Los Sapos*, the Hieroglyphic Stairway (this temple holds the longest known Mayan text, a lineage tree of Copán's rulers), and the new museum located in the visitor's center. The impressive *Copan Sculpture Museum* (http://asociacioncopan.org/sculpture-museum/) gives you a very good glimpse of how the Maya viewed and recorded their world through their art. Here is where you will find those protected artworks that I just mentioned, some 25,000 of them. Throughout the museum you'll find exhibits depicting aspects of Mayan religion, sacrifice, warfare, the nobility, the afterlife, and several other themes. If you don't like the museum you are welcome to stroll around the grounds or even enter the over 3.5 miles of archeological tunnels (a bit more expensive, an additional US$10, and probably best suited for those with a real interest in archeology). Only ten persons at a time are allowed inside the tunnels and they must have a guide. If you wish to view the ruins at Copán, make sure you find the right place, Copán Ruinas, not to be confused with La Entrada de Copán, a large industrial city that is almost 40 miles away, or the much larger town of Santa Rosa de Copán, the capital of the department (state) of Copán. Copán was declared a *World Heritage Site* by *UNESCO* in 1980.

Chichen Itzá

The ruins of Chichen Itzá (whose name means "in the mouth of the well of the Itzá") lie about 75 miles east of Mérida, roughly midway between Cancún and Mérida on Mexico's Yucatán Peninsula. During her prime, from around 800-1200 A.D., Chichen Itzá was the center of political, religious, and military might for all of the Yucatán, if not for most of Mesoamerica.

The architecture here is some of the most outstanding in all of the Mayan empire, though the structures are not as tall as those at El Mirador or Tikal, their mystery and uniqueness sets them far apart from the rest of the Mayan cities and they are separated into groups according to their age and builders, primarily the Toltecs.

The *Pyramid of Kukulkán* is one of the more unique structures in the Mayan world, and was structured to be just that. Only about 80' high, each side of the construction has 91 steps, with one step at the top that leads to the top platform, this makes a total of 365 steps. The pyramid was also constructed with the equinoxes in mind. On those dates, in the Spring and Fall, thousands of tourists converge on Chichen Itzá. When the shadow of the mid-afternoon sun is playing on northeastern angle of the pyramid it is reflected on the stairs creating alternating triangles of light and shade that give the illusion of a snake progressing down the steps in the direction of the *cenote*. The effect is most impressive as it touches the large sculpted head of Kukulcán at the bottom of the stairway, this effect could only have been obtained by very precise architectural and astronomical measurements.

The ball court, the largest of its kind in the Mayan empire, has a couple of interesting tribunals at either end of the patio. These tribunals were supposedly for the principal lords of the city and have very impressive acoustics. If you stand under the rings of one of the tribunals and clap your hands or shout, the sound is echoed seven times and you can have a conversation in a whisper with a partner in the other tribunal. The *Group of a Thousand Columns* is made up of a series of columns whose position is in the form of an irregular square and is believed may have once supported a thatched roof which may have housed a market place.

But one of the most interesting structures is *El Caracol*, not to be confused with the *El Caracol* found near the southern tip of Isla de Cozumel (which was primarily a lighthouse and an early warning system for approaching bad weather). *El Caracol*, also known as *The Observatory*, was used for astronomy as its windows were aligned with the four cardinal directions and the position of the setting sun at the equinoxes.

Chichen Itzá was first settled for agricultural reasons as the nearby *cenotes* (pronounced *say-no-tays*...sinkholes in the limestone bed that accessed an underground body of water were used as wells-hence the origin of the city's name) offered a source of fresh water for drinking and irrigation. Mayan settlements in the Yucatán were always constructed near a *cenote*, and Mayan cities were constructed near the largest *cenotes*. *Cenotes* can be as small as a well, or they can be of as grand a scale as the magnificent cenote at Dos Ojos, near Tulum, the longest underwater cave system in the world. One of the *cenotes* at Chichen Itzá later came to be used for what could be described as malevolent purposes. The *cenote* named *Xtoloc* provided the city with fresh water, while the other, the *Sacred Cenote*, the *Cenote of Sacrifice*, was the site where offerings of children and young women were made to appease the gods. In the *Sacred Cenote* have been found jewelry, pottery, figurines, and the bones of many humans, mostly children and many of these artifacts are on display at the *Peabody Museum* at *Harvard University*. There is some question as to the remains of children in the *cenotes*, it has been speculated that perhaps they fell in during play as opposed to being sacrificed.

Temple of the Great Jaguar, Tikal

The Grand Plaza at Tikal

Pyramid of Kukulkán, Chichen Itzá

Ruin at El Mirador

Hoop on ball court at Chichen Itzá

Palenque

Group of 1,000 Columns, Chichen Itzá

El Caracol

Palenque

Located about 9,000' above sea level in the Tumbalá mountains of Chiapas (a Mexican state named after the non-Mayan people who lived in the southern and western areas of the Yucatan), amid a thick forest of mahogany, cedar, and sapodilla trees, sits the ancient Mayan city of Palenque, once the capital of the Mayan state of *B'aakal*. The ruins sit on a ledge overlooking two worlds: to the north and east like fertile plains and swamps, while to the south and west lie lush green mountains. Palenque's location (which also gives it an average temperature of 79° and creates a morning blanket of fog giving the site a spectral quality) kept the ruins secret until a Spanish priest, Father Pedro Lorenzo de la Nada, discovered the site in 1567. The site sat dormant until 1787, when Captain Antonio del Rio was sent to survey Palenque. Del Rio claimed that the Maya could not have built the ruins here, and that ancient Greeks and Roman builders had made it this far. This claim was refuted by Juan Galindo, an Irish adventurer whose real name is unknown, who proposed that the Maya were indeed the architects and builders of Palenque. When Father de la Nada discovered Palenque it was known as *Otolum*, *Land with Strong Houses*, which de la Nada translated into Spanish to give the site the name *Palenque*, meaning *fortification*. This name also became connected with the nearby town, Santo Domingo del Palenque, which was built over some peripheral ruins in the valley below the main site. Palenque thrived from approximately 100 B.C. to its fall around 800 A.D., and was known as *Lakam Ha*, or *Big Water*, for the numerous springs and falls found at the site.

Palenque is notable for giving the world what may well be the best known Mayan King, *Hanab Pacal Votan*, more commonly referred to as *Pacal the Great* who ruled from 625-683 A.D. Inside the *Temple of Inscriptions*, which sits atop a pyramid, is a long hieroglyphic text that details the city's ruling dynasty as well as the achievements of *Pacal the Great*. A concealed stone slab on the floor of the temple reveals the entry to Pacal's tomb that sits at ground level deep inside the pyramid. Found inside Pacal's sarcophagus was the richest cache of jade ever found in a Mayan tomb, each piece hand carved and bound with gold wire. In 1994, researchers discovered another temple of three rooms deep inside the pyramid, and in the middle room they found the remains of a woman they dubbed the *Red Queen* because she was covered in cinnabar. There are no glyphs to identify this mystery woman so speculation abounds as to who she was and what was her place in Palenque society.

One of the greatest architectural achievements of Pacal's years was the *Palace* and the long vaulted tunnel underneath it through which a steady stream of water flowed, an aqueduct that also flowed underneath the city's main plaza. Located in the northern part of the city are the ruins of an un-excavated ball court and natural pool underneath a waterfall on the Río Otulum. The pool is called the *Queen's Bath* and today is still used by swimmers and bathers.

Iztapalapa

In April of 2006, archeologists announced the discovery of a massive 6th century pyramid buried underneath a hill where the people of Iztapalapa have been enacting the Crucifixion since 1833. Ceramic fragments and several ceremonial structures on the hill suggested the possibility of a site nearby but it wasn't until a team of researchers dug exploratory trenches in 2005 and 2006 that the possibility became a reality. The 500' by 500' by 60' tall temple, *The Hill of The Star*, is of Teotihuacán construction and was built around 500 A.D.; today it sits in a squalid barrio just outside Mexico City.

Using the Charts

For the soundings on the charts I use a computerized hydrographic system in my *Data Acquisition Vessel* (*DAV*), a 12' aluminum runabout gratefully supplied by *Quintrex* and *Boater's Exchange* of Rockledge, Florida. For my hydrographic system I use an off-the-shelf GPS and sonar combination that gives a GPS waypoint and depth every two seconds including the time of each observation (*WAAS* where applicable). The software used records and stores this information in an onboard computer. When I begin to chart an area, I first put the bow on a well-marked, prominent point of land and take GPS lat/long readings for a period of at least 5 minutes. I use the average of all these positions to check against the lat/long positions shown on the topos that I use to create the charts. I also use cross bearings to help set up control points for my own reference and to double check the GPS and WAAS readings. At this point I begin to take soundings.

My first objective is to chart the inshore reefs after which I'll plot all the visible hazards to navigation. These positions are recorded by hand on my field notes as well as being recorded electronically. I rely primarily on my on-site notes for the actual construction of the charts. The soundings taken by the system are later entered by hand, but it is the field notes that help me create the chart graphics. The computer will not tell me where a certain reef ends or begins as accurately as I can record it and show it on my field notes. Next I run the one-fathom line as well as the ten-fathom line (if applicable) and chart these. Here is where the system does most of the work though I still stop to take field notes. Finally, I will crisscross the entire area in a grid pattern and hopefully catch hazards that are at first glance unseen. It is not unusual to spend days sounding an area of only a couple of square miles. This takes a lot of fuel as well as a lot of time when transferring the data to the chart!

Due to the speed of the *DAV* each identical lat/long may have as many as ten or twenty separate soundings. Then, with the help of *NOAA* tide tables, the computer gives me accurate depths to one decimal place for each separate lat/long pair acquired on the data run. A macro purges all but the lowest depths for each lat/long position (to two decimal places). At this point the actual plotting is begun including one fathom and ten fathom lines. The charts themselves are still constructed from outline tracings of topographic maps and the lat/long lines are placed in accordance with these maps.

These charts are as accurate as I can make them and I believe them to be superior to any others. They are indeed more detailed than all others showing many areas that are not covered, or are incorrectly represented by other publications. However, it is not possible to plot every individual rock or coral head so piloting by eye is still essential. On many of the routes in my guides you must be able to pick out the blue, deeper water as it snakes between sandbanks, rocky bars, and coral heads. Learn to trust your eyes. Remember that on the banks, sandbars and channels can shift over time so that once what was a channel may now be a sandbar. Never approach a cut or sandbar with the sun in your eyes, it should be above and behind you. Sunglasses with a polarized lens can be a big help in combating the glare of the sun on the water. With good visibility the sandbars and heads stand out and are clearly defined. As you gain experience you may even learn to read the subtle differences in the water surface as it flows over underwater obstructions.

All courses shown are magnetic. All waypoints for entrances to cuts and for detouring around shoal areas are only to be used in a general sense. They are meant to get you into the general area, you must pilot your way through the cut or around the shoal yourself. You will have to keep a good lookout, GPS will not do that for you. The best aids to navigation when near these shoals and cuts are sharp eyesight and good light. The charts will show both deep draft vessel routes as well as some shallow draft vessel routes. Deep draft vessel routes will accommodate a draft of 6' minimum and often more with the assistance of the tide. Shallow draft vessel routes are for dinghies and small outboard powered boats with drafts of less than 3'. Shallow draft monohulls and multihulls very often use these same routes.

Not being a perfect world, I expect errors to occur. I would deeply appreciate any input and corrections that you may notice as you travel these waters. Please send your suggestions to Stephen J. Pavlidis, C/O Seaworthy Publications, 2023 N. Atlantic Ave. #226, Cocoa Beach, Florida, 32931, or email me at stevepavlidis@hotmail.com. If you see me anchored nearby, don't hesitate to stop and say hello and offer your input. Your suggestion may help improve the next edition of this guide.

A final note: If you are familiar with my past guides, you'll notice that I've strayed from my usual cartography in this publication. I feel the need to protect some skippers from themselves. The charts for the northern coasts of Guanaja and Roatán in the Bay Islands of Honduras do NOT have a lat/long grid on them, as do certain other reef entrances in the Northwestern Caribbean. Why you may ask? Simple I reply. I've noticed that some navigators have taken to watching the cursor on their chart plotters instead of the waters around them. In one particular instance that I know of a skipper who went hard aground and bent his 4" rudder shaft (no, he was not using one of my charts).

With this in mind I have decided that on the aforementioned charts I would omit the lat/long grid to avoid such a problem in the future. As a result you cannot plot your position on these charts, you cannot count on them being to scale, treat them as you would a sketch chart, in other words, you MUST use your eyes to get you through these passages. Why only on these charts you may ask? The areas covered on charts that I've drawn with no lat/long grids are protected by fringing reefs and the passes through the reefs are not marked and difficult to discern in all but the best of visibility, an error here could be very costly. I have included waypoints to place you just off the reef entrances, from there you will have to pilot your way in by eye. I know some of you may not appreciate this, but it is with good intentions I assure you. Call me old-fashioned, but I insist that you pilot by eye through these areas.

Legend

☐ water depth less than 1 fathom	☐ water depth over 10 fathoms
☐ water depth between 1 fathom and 10 fathoms	
— – — large vessel route-6' draft	♂ light
— · · — shallow vessel route	⚓ anchorage
+ rock or coral head	⊕ GPS waypoint
+ + + + reef	◉ tower
══════ road	Ⳑ wreck--above hw
m mooring	⟨+++⟩ wreck-submerged
dm dinghy mooring	☐ building

List of Charts

The prudent navigator will not rely solely on any
single aid to navigation, particularly on floating aids.

IMPORTANT!

If there is a discrepancy between this guide and any reef or shoal, believe the reef or shoal!

All charts are to be used in conjunction with the text. All soundings are in feet at Mean Low Water. All courses are magnetic. Projection is *Transverse Mercator*. **Datum** is WGS84. North is always "up" on these charts. The Index charts are designed strictly for orientation, they are NOT to be used for navigational purposes.

The author and publisher take no responsibility for errors, omissions, or the misuse of these charts. No warranties are either expressed or implied as to the usability of the information contained herein. Always keep a good lookout when piloting in these waters.

The charts of the northern shore of Jamaica, the Cayman Islands, the Bay Islands of Honduras, and the mainland of Honduras will be covered from east to west as most cruisers approach these areas from this direction. The charts of Roatán in the Bay Islands of Honduras cover the southern shore from east to west, and then the northern shore from west to east.

If you're familiar with my past guides, you'll notice that I've strayed from my usual cartography in this publication. It seems that I feel the need to protect some skippers from themselves. The charts for the northern coasts of Guanaja and Roatán in the Bay Islands of Honduras, and the charts for the cays lying southwest of Utila do NOT have a lat/long grid on them. Why you may ask? Simple I reply. I've noticed that some navigators have taken to watching the cursor on their chart plotters instead of the waters around them. In one particular instance that I know of a skipper when aground hard and bent his 4" rudder shaft trying to enter a harbor using only his chart plotter. With this in mind I have decided that on the aforementioned charts I would omit the lat/long grid to avoid such a problem in the future. As a result you cannot plot your position on these charts, you cannot count on them being to scale, treat them as you would a sketch chart, in other words, you MUST use only your eyes to get you through here these passages. Why only on these charts you may ask? Simple I again reply. The northern shores of Guanaja and Roatán are protected by fringing reefs and the passes through the reefs are not marked and difficult to discern in all but the best of visibility, an error here could be very costly. I have included waypoints to place you just off the reef entrances, from there you will have to pilot your way in by eye. I know some of you may not appreciate this, but it is with good intentions I assure you. Call me old-fashioned, but I insist that you pilot by eye through these areas.

Note: NOAA and DMA charts do not show some of the reefs and heads charted in this guide. Always keep a good lookout when piloting in these waters.

Chart #	Chart Description	Page #
	NORTH COAST OF JAMAICA	
Chart JAM-1	Port Antonio	75
Chart JAM-1A	Foster's Cove	80
Chart JAM-1B	Port Maria	81
Chart JAM-2	Oracabessa	83
Chart JAM-3	Ocho Rios	85
Chart JAM-4	St. Ann's Bay	87
Chart JAM-5	Discovery Bay	89

Index of Charts

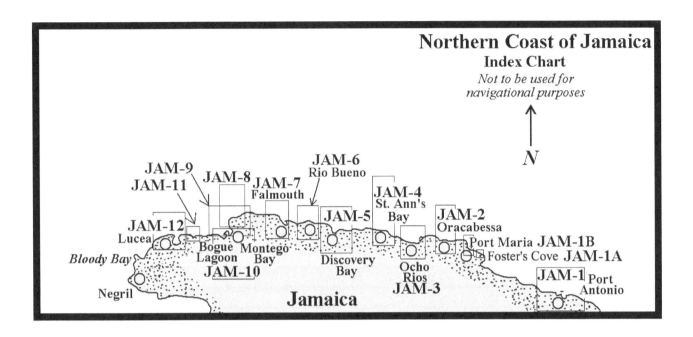

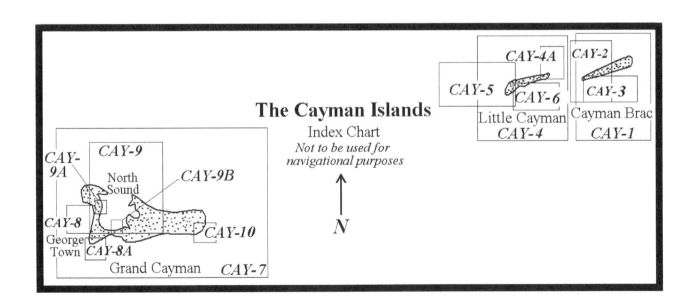

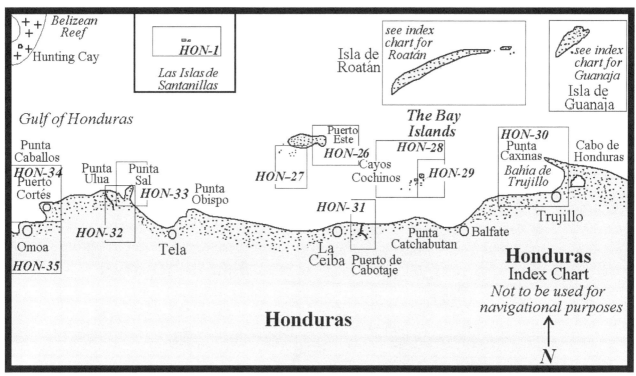

Belizean Reef

Hunting Cay

HON-1

Las Islas de Santanillas

Gulf of Honduras

Isla de Roatán

see index chart for Roatán

The Bay Islands

see index chart for Guanaja

Isla de Guanaja

Punta Caballos

HON-34

Puerto Cortés

Punta Ulua

Punta Sal

HON-33

Punta Obispo

HON-32

Omoa

HON-35

Tela

Puerto Este

HON-26

HON-27

Cayos Cochinos

HON-28

HON-29

HON-31

La Ceiba

Puerto de Cabotaje

Punta Catchabutan

Balfate

HON-30

Punta Caxinas

Bahía de Trujillo

Cabo de Honduras

Trujillo

Honduras
Index Chart
Not to be used for navigational purposes

N

Honduras

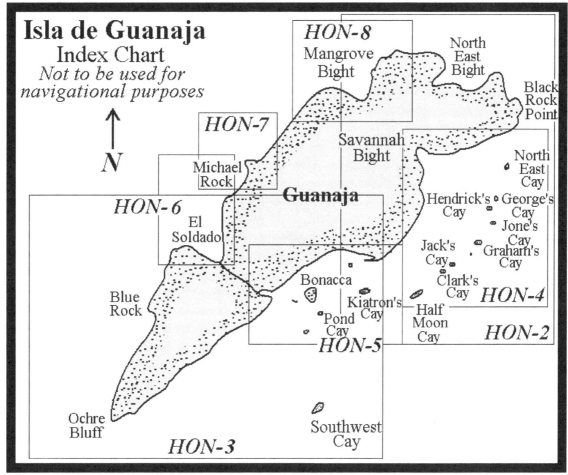

Isla de Guanaja
Index Chart
Not to be used for navigational purposes

N

HON-8

Mangrove Bight

North East Bight

Black Rock Point

HON-7

Savannah Bight

Michael Rock

Guanaja

North East Cay

Hendrick's Cay

George's Cay

Jone's Cay

HON-6

El Soldado

Jack's Cay

Graham's Cay

Clark's Cay

HON-4

Bonacca

Blue Rock

Kiatron's Cay

Half Moon Cay

HON-2

Pond Cay

HON-5

Ochre Bluff

Southwest Cay

HON-3

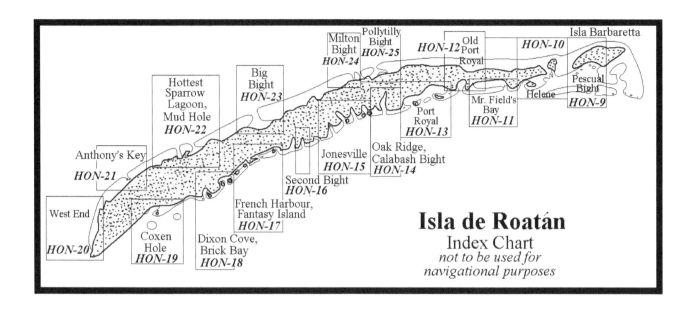

Milton Bight *HON-24*
Pollytilly Bight *HON-25*
HON-12 Old Port Royal
HON-10
Isla Barbaretta

Big Bight *HON-23*

Hottest Sparrow Lagoon, Mud Hole *HON-22*

Pescual Bight *HON-9*

Mr. Field's Bay *HON-11*

Helene

Port Royal *HON-13*

Anthony's Key *HON-21*

Jonesville *HON-15*

Oak Ridge, Calabash Bight *HON-14*

Second Bight *HON-16*

French Harbour, Fantasy Island *HON-17*

West End *HON-20*

Coxen Hole *HON-19*

Dixon Cove, Brick Bay *HON-18*

Isla de Roatán
Index Chart
not to be used for navigational purposes

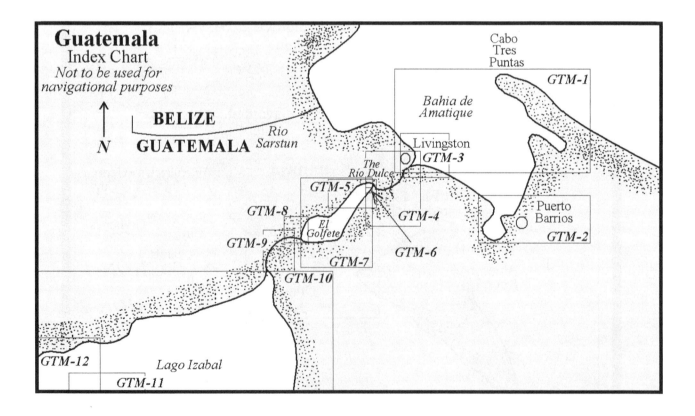

Guatemala
Index Chart
Not to be used for navigational purposes

N ↑

BELIZE

GUATEMALA *Rio Sarstun*

Cabo Tres Puntas

GTM-1

Bahia de Amatique

Livingston *GTM-3*

The Río Dulce

GTM-5

GTM-8

GTM-4

El Golfete

Puerto Barrios

GTM-2

GTM-9

GTM-6

GTM-7

GTM-10

GTM-12

Lago Izabal

GTM-11

Heading to the Río Dulce

In this section we will discuss routing information for those headed to the Northwest Caribbean, and in particular the *Río Dulce*. I've chosen the *Río Dulce* as the ending point for these routes as it is such a wonderful hurricane shelter and the ultimate destination of most cruisers who enter these waters.

For more information on currents pertaining to route planning, see the section *Tides and Currents* in the chapter, *The Basics*.

From Florida

Cruisers that are used to crossing the *Gulf Stream* from Florida to the Bahamas face a similar scenario when heading to the Yucatán from South Florida and the Keys. Here you will have to cross the *Gulf Stream* as well as the *Yucatán Current*, which flows through the *Yucatán Channel* to become the *Loop Current* in the *Gulf of Mexico* and eventually the *Gulf Stream*.

The *Yucatán Channel* lies between the mainland of Mexico and the Island of Cuba to the east. It is deep along its eastern edge and shallows as it approaches the Mexican coastline. There is a tremendous flow of water passing through the *Yucatán Channel* into the *Gulf of Mexico* and the set of the current can surpass 4 knots at its axis. The eastern edge of this current lies about 20 miles off Cabo San Antonio, Cuba, and about 35 miles west of Cabo San Antonio the current strength is about 1 knot. About 50 miles east of Cabo San Antonio the strength is double, about 2 knots, while approximately 60-70 miles east of Cabo San Antonio the current increases to about 3 knots. Around 75-80 miles east of Cabo San Antonio you'll usually find the axis where the velocity can exceed 4 knots. Oddly enough, 15 miles further west, about 25 miles from the Yucatán coast the current strength drops to about 1 knot. The current in the *Yucatán Channel* is stronger in summer and the width of its reach wider, while in the winter the velocity decreases as does the current's width. Bear in mind that this is not cast in concrete, cruisers have reported both lesser and greater strengths at varying times of the year.

There are numerous eddies and counter currents generated by the current. One such eddy runs westward close in along both the Florida Keys while another runs along the northwestern shore of Cuba and can be as strong as ½-1 knot. This counter current has been reported as far as 30 miles west of Cabo San Antonio, Cuba. Along the southern shore of Cuba, between Cabo San Antonio and Cabo Cruz (north of Jamaica), you'll find a westerly setting current of about 1 knot depending on wind strength and direction, and a counter current closer in that sets in a southeasterly direction. At any time you are likely to see a reverse of the primary current flows in the Northwestern Caribbean, especially north of Jamaica, between Jamaica and the Cuban coastline. You'll also find eddies, counter currents, at almost any point in the Northwestern Caribbean between Jamaica and the *Yucatán Channel* that will set you in any of several directions depending on which side of them you are. A great way to get a handle on these eddies is to subscribe to Chris Parker's *Caribbean Weather Center* and check in daily on the SSB. Chris can tell you where the eddies lie and where you need to go to get on their best side and have them work for you.

Sailing from the Florida Keys to Isla Mujeres there are two routes to choose from and which one you choose will depend on the strength of the *Yucatán Current* and the *Gulf Stream*. The first route (the choice for those seeking to have the currents work for you) brings you southward across the *Gulf Stream* and then westward along the northwestern shore of Cuba, about 12-15 miles off, where you can pick up the westerly setting counter current of ½-1 knot. Soon after you pass the western tip of Cuba you'll lose that boost as the current dissipates around Cabo San Antonio.

The second route depends on the strength of the *Yucatán Current*. If the *Gulf Stream* is in its normal position favoring the Cuban side of the *Straits of Florida* you can plot a southwesterly course staying north of the current as you head toward Isla Mujeres. This route becomes difficult when the *Yucatán Current* is running strong as it passes through the *Yucatán Channel* making your southwesterly course towards Isla Mujeres hard to maintain even with favorable winds. It's not unusual for sailors to sail a bit west of the northern tip of the Yucatán Peninsula to get out of the *Yucatán Current* and then turn back to the southeast for Isla Mujeres even though they had favorable winds when the current pushed them northward at 4 knots.

For information purposes, the distance from Key West to Isla Mujeres is approximately 325 nautical miles on a heading of 235°, while the distance from the Dry Tortugas to Isla Mujeres is approximately 295 nautical miles on a heading of 230°. From Havana to Isla Mujeres the distance is approximately 274 nautical miles, part of it paralleling the northern coast of Cuba.

From the Windward Passage

Leaving from Great Inagua in the Bahamas, the Turks and Caicos, or Luperón on the northern shore of the Dominican Republic, the run through the *Windward Passage* varies from a reach to a run depending on wind direction. Bear in mind that the trade winds will be at their strongest from December through March and can make for boisterous sailing conditions, albeit off the wind (Webb Chiles once said: "…better a gale from behind than 20 knots on the nose.").

Vessels approaching the Bay Islands of Honduras and/or the *Río Dulce* from the eastern coast of the United States will find a nice reach or run once they have worked their way through the Bahamas to Great Inagua and the *Windward Passage*. Skippers approaching from the Turks and Caicos Islands or the northern coast of Hispaniola will enjoy the same conditions. Although longer in mileage, for some this route is preferable as it offers a considerable amount of downwind sailing compared to the route from Key West to Isla Mujeres where you must fight the current the entire trip. In fact, it's somewhere in the neighborhood of a thousand miles of downwind sailing from Great Inagua. Cruisers heading south of Hispaniola will also appreciate the downhill nature of the winds and seas as they approach Jamaica or head for the Bay Islands. The current will range from on the nose as you pass southwest through the *Windward Passage*, abeam from the *Windward Passage* to Jamaica, on the stern as you sail from Jamaica to the Caymans, and again it will be on the beam as you sail from the Caymans to the Bay Islands or the *Río Dulce*. This is in ideal conditions mind you, at any time of year a reversal or an eddy can form and you'll fight the current.

And let me make one more comment about the *Windward Passage*. This can be a very rough body of water, after all, it's not called *Windward* for nothing. Although it's only shown on *Pilot Charts* and only briefly touched upon in the *Sailing Directions for the Caribbean Sea*, the *Windward Passage* usually has a southwest setting current of about ¾ knot. At times however you can find a northeast setting

current flowing through the *Windward Passage* at speeds that I have seen at times to be over two knots although generally it is between .75 and 2 knots. When you add this to a moderate northeast breeze, the *Windward Passage* can be reminiscent of the *Gulf Stream* when you have wind against current, and it will take you quite a while to get out of the flow, usually about ten hours or so depending on your speed as you head southwest through the passage. Don't even think about heading west to get out of the current, you might find that you're heading into an easterly flowing current that works its way along the southern shore of Cuba, while the currents close in to Haiti are reported to be in the range of ¾ knot setting in a northerly direction near Pearl Point. Use caution north of Cape Mole, Haiti, where this northward flowing current meets the current that sets west along Haiti's northern shore.

Cruisers headed to the *Windward Passage* need to be aware of the *IMO Traffic Separation Scheme* (http://www.imo.org/en/OurWork/Safety/Navigation/Pages/ShipsRouteing.aspx) that lies east of Cuba's Punta Maisi and makes good use of the northward flowing current found there (this current has been reported to reverse with northerly winds). The traffic separation scheme allows for a two mile wide corridor for northbound vessels and a two mile wide corridor for southbound vessels. These corridors lie within Cuba's 12-mile territorial limit so bear that in mind if you plan to go that route. If you're not comfortable with that, keep 12 miles east of Punta Maisi and you'll be out of the traffic separation scheme as well as Cuban territorial waters.

The following are some sample routes that I have employed. If you leave Matthew Town, Great Inagua you can head for a waypoint at 20° 00.00' N, 74° 00.00' W (approximately 206° at 60 nautical miles), which places you in the *Windward Passage*. From this position you can change your course to approximately 239° for Port Antonio, Jamaica, which lies at a distance of approximately 175 nautical miles, giving you a total of about 235 miles from Matthew Town. You can also head for Port Antonio from *Sapodilla Bay* in the Caicos Islands (Providenciales). From *Sapodilla Bay* head southwest in the *Freighter Channel*, the 12' deep channel leading from *South Dock* on Providenciales to the sea between *Southwest Reef* and *Molasses Reef*. A waypoint at 21° 35.75' N, 72° 23.25' W, will bring you to the southwest end of the channel and clear of the reefs. From this position you can take up your heading to a waypoint in the

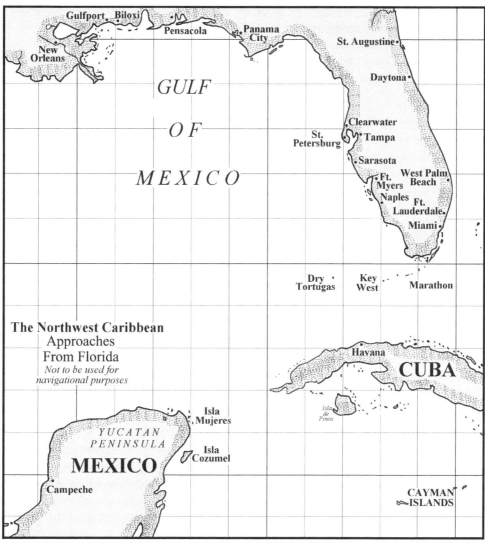

The Northwest Caribbean
Approaches
From Florida
*Not to be used for
navigational purposes*

GULF

OF

MEXICO

Gulfport   Biloxi
Pensacola
Panama City
New Orleans

St. Augustine

Daytona

Clearwater
St. Petersburg   Tampa
Sarasota
Ft. Myers   West Palm Beach
Naples   Ft. Lauderdale
Miami

Dry Tortugas   Key West   Marathon

Havana   CUBA

Isla de Pinos

Isla Mujeres
YUCATAN PENINSULA
MEXICO   Isla Cozumel

Campeche

CAYMAN ISLANDS

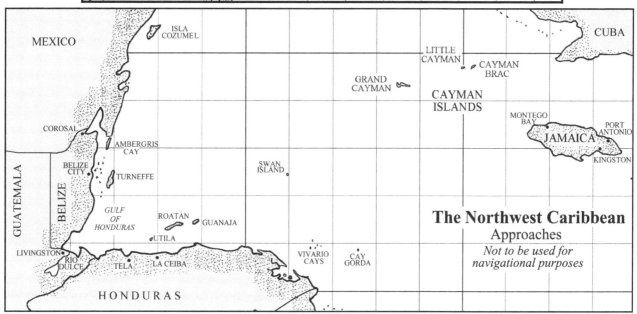

MEXICO

ISLA COZUMEL

CUBA

LITTLE CAYMAN
CAYMAN BRAC

GRAND CAYMAN

CAYMAN ISLANDS

MONTEGO BAY
JAMAICA   PORT ANTONIO
KINGSTON

COROSAL

GUATEMALA   BELIZE

AMBERGRIS CAY
BELIZE CITY
TURNEFFE

GULF OF HONDURAS
ROATÁN   GUANAJA
UTILA

LIVINGSTON
RIO DULCE   TELA   LA CEIBA

SWAN ISLAND

VIVARIO CAYS   CAY GORDA

The Northwest Caribbean
Approaches
*Not to be used for
navigational purposes*

HONDURAS

Windward Passage at 20° 00.00' N, 73° 46.00' W, where you'll take up an approximate course of 244° for 189 nautical miles to Port Antonio. If I'm leaving from Luperón in the Dominican Republic, I will head for a position north of the island of Tortuga at 20° 14.50' N, 72° 50.30' W (you can safely pass between the mainland of Haiti and the island of Tortuga, but if you leave Luperón at daybreak you'll pass Tortuga at night so it's safer to pass well north of the island), and then to a waypoint in the *Windward Passage* at 19° 57.60' N, 73° 40.00' W, and then to the waypoint at Port Antonio, Jamaica. Bear in mind that the *United States Coast Guard* maintains a very strong presence in the *Windward Passage* and that they often board and inspect yachts passing through these waters.

When you are ready to leave Jamaica, I suggest playing along the northern shore, stopping at any or all of the lovely anchorages there to arrive at the western end of the island (it's approximately 90 miles from Port Antonio to *Montego Bay*) to stage for your next leg. I prefer to clear out at *Montego Bay* and then anchor overnight at Lucea or *Bloody Bay* just south of North Negril Point (it's far easier to depart from *Bloody Bay*), leaving early the next morning from there. This knocks a few miles off your trip and your outward clearance is good for 24 hours anyway.

From the western end of Jamaica you have several choices, you can head to the Cayman Islands, the Swan Islands (*Las Islas Santanilla*), or you can head directly for Isla de Guanaja in the Bay Islands (*Las Islas Bahía*) off the northern coast of Honduras. From Montego Bay, Jamaica, the southwestern tip of Cayman Brac lies approximately 132 nautical miles distant on a heading of 307°, while the northeastern tip of Grand Cayman lies approximately 187 nautical miles from *Montego Bay* on a heading of 290°. Cruisers might be interested in knowing that the deepest part of the Caribbean lies between Jamaica and the Cayman Islands and is known as the *Cayman Trench*, sometimes called *Bartlett Deep* or the *Bartlett Trough*. The *Cayman Trench* is a submarine trench on the floor of the sea beginning at the southeastern tip of Cuba and lying east/northeast to west/southwest with a maximum depth of 25,216'.

Also from *Montego Bay*, Great Swan Island lies about 350 miles away on a heading of 260°, but don't take up this heading from *Montego Bay*, it's best to anchor off Negril in *Bloody Bay* and leave from there (see the chapter on the northern coast of Jamaica). From Grand Cayman, Great Swan Island

lies approximately 182 nautical miles distant on an approximate heading of 233°.

From Great Swan Island, Isla de Guanaja in the Bay Islands lies approximately 120 nautical miles distant on a heading of about 245° (this is a general heading, once you enter the waypoints into your GPS your heading will change a bit). If you are headed for the *Río Dulce*, you can work your way westward through the Bay Islands to Isla de Utila where Cabo Tres Puntas lies approximately 94 nautical miles away on a heading of 265°. A great stopover is Puerto Cortés on the Honduran mainland's western coast (see text in the chapter on Honduras).

Bear in mind that the northern edge of the northwest setting current that flows through this part of the Caribbean (see the section *Tides and Currents*) flows along the southern shore of Jamaica with a strength of about 1 knot, a bit more closer in, and a bit less farther offshore. Another branch of the same current sets west/southwest through the *Windward Passage* and thence along the northern shore of Jamaica to meet up with the current that flows along Jamaica's southern shore. Their combined flow passes south of the Cayman Islands and then northwest into the *Yucatán Channel*. At any time you are likely to see a reverse of this flow, especially north of Jamaica, between Jamaica and the Cuban coastline. You'll also find eddies, counter currents, at almost any point in the Northwestern Caribbean between Jamaica and the *Yucatán Channel* that will set you north or east depending on which side of them you're on. A great way to get a handle on these eddies is to subscribe to Chris Parker's *Caribbean Weather Center* and check in daily on the SSB. Chris can tell you where the eddies are and where you need to go to get on their best side and have them work for you.

A final note, if you don't like going to weather, do not try this passage in reverse, it's hard on the wind and the current.

From the Eastern Caribbean

Vessels heading to the Northwest Caribbean from the islands of the Eastern Caribbean will have a fantastic run/reach with following seas, but trying to return to the Eastern Caribbean will involve returning to the Bahamas through the *Straits of Florida* after your Northwestern Caribbean cruise to beat back to the DR, Puerto Rico, and the Virgins. You can of course attempt to regain the easting you gave up to arrive in the *Río Dulce* by retracing your route, but it will be against the wind and the current, an uncomfortable proposition at best and one that is very hard on boat and crew.

If you are heading west from the islands of the Eastern Caribbean I suggest that you favor the waters south of Puerto Rico and Hispaniola and making your way to Jamaica to follow the routes mentioned in the last section. This route is best for sailboats, as you are able to make the most of the trade winds. Passing north of the islands of Puerto Rico and Hispaniola often blocks the trades and makes sailors dependent on local coastwise wind patterns. I would try to avoid the banks located on the *Nicaragua Rise* lying between Jamaica and the northeastern tip of Honduras' *Mosquito Coast*. Don't get me wrong, its safe enough to pass between the *Rosalind Bank* and the *Pedro Bank* (south of Jamaica) in deep water, but in several places on the *Nicaraguan Rise* the waters may go from 1,500' to 12' in a very short distance (such as on the *Seranilla Bank* or from over 1,000' to 9' as on the *New Bank*; both of these banks are marked by lights). This makes for a piling up of the trade wind powered seas and it can be extremely rough for the average cruising boat. If these rough seas were not enough to convince you, bear in mind that you'll miss a lot of quality cruising along the coast of Jamaica, and Île à Vache off Haiti should not be missed either. There's a marina on Île à Vache that now carries fuel.

From Panama

Vessels entering the Caribbean from the *Panama Canal* generally tend to make a clockwise circuit of the Caribbean, heading east is hard on even the best boat and crew, but it can be done and often is. There is a lot of fishing activity along this route due to the number of shallow banks so you'll have to keep a very sharp lookout for fishing vessels as well as the shallow banks along this route. If you wish to anchor on these banks you must be certain to time your arrival so that you'll have optimum visibility to navigate your way through the reefs.

From Colón, you can head north and find shelter at Cayos de Albuquerque (Columbia), a little over 200 miles northwest of Colón. The Cayos de Albuquerque are a small reef-encircled area with two small islands along its eastern side. There is a Colombian military base located on the northernmost island and the *Commandante* will want to check your paperwork

when you arrive. The southernmost island is home to a fishing camp that is often busy and is a good place to pick up some local seafood. Just north of Cayos de Albuquerque is Cayos del Este Sudeste which also has a small Colombian military presence. The bases here are in touch with the base at Isla de San Andrés (further north) by HF radio on a daily basis and vessel movements are recorded for security reasons.

There is good shelter at Isla de San Andrés and a marked entrance channel (red-right-returning) that leads to a large anchorage on the northeastern tip of the island off *Nene's Marina*, well protected by a reef to windward You must use an agent (check on VHF ch. 16 to find one, there are several) to clear *Customs* here. You must have a *Zarpe* from your last port of call listing Isla de San Andrés as your next destination or you will need a letter, in Spanish, explaining your unscheduled stop. Fuel and water (at *Nene's Marina*-6' at MLW) is available as well as provisions and hardware items.

The next stop northward can be *Bahía Catalina* on mountainous Isla Providencia (Colombia), west of the *Roncador Bank*, and approximately 55 miles from Isla de San Andrés. Providencia is located at the southern edge of a reef-strewn bank with Low Cay at the northern end. The main harbor lies just off the main town of Santa Isabel and offers protection from all winds save westerlies. Here too you'll need a ship's agent to clear *Customs*, you can find one on VHF ch. 16. If you need fuel it can be delivered to the town dock by truck or you can jerry-jug it. Limited provisions can be found along with a few small restaurants. Heading north from Isla Providencia, you will pass west of the *Roncador Bank*, and head north to pass between the *Serrana Bank* and the *Quita Sueño Bank*. Both of these banks offer some shelter in the lee of reefs, but beware, both are known as ship graveyards as the many wrecks thereabouts will testify.

Continuing northward you'll come to the *Seranilla Bank,* an 18 by 24 mile coral and sand bank with four cays. A navigational light is located on Beacon Cay along with a Colombian marine outpost. Beacon Cay is the most hospitable of the cays on the *Seranilla Bank.*

From the *Seranilla Bank* it is advised to proceed in the deep-water channel west of the *Roncador Bank*. Jimmy Cornell, in his excellent work, *World Cruising Routes*, suggests a waypoint at 14° 30' N,

79° 30' W, west of the *Seranilla Bank*, as a turning point to the *Yucatán Channel* or the Cayman Islands. Mr. Cornell also suggests that if headed for the Bay Islands of Honduras to pass outside of Gorda Cay and north of Hobbies Cay as you approach the Honduran coastline.

Skippers headed to the Northwest Caribbean from the canal are advised to avoid the poorly charted reefs and shoals off Nicaragua and to exercise extreme caution off the *Mosquito Coast* of Honduras and Cabo Gracias à Dios. When rounding Cabo Gracias à Dios use caution as shoals and offshore reefs abound; although they are shown on charts, their actual locations should be viewed as suspect since their lat/longs may be off by miles.

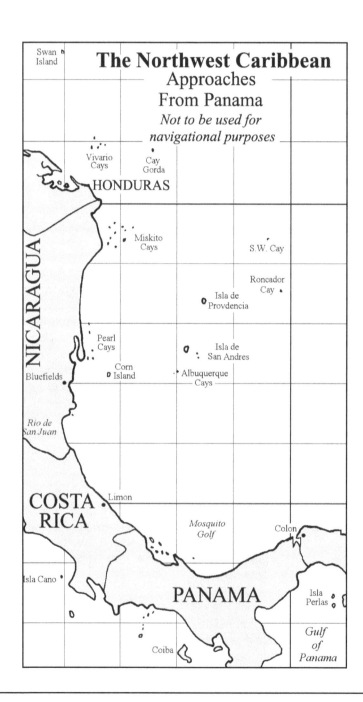

Jamaica's Northern Coast

Sounds of laughter everywhere
And the dancing girls swaying to and fro
I must declare that my heart is there
Though I've been from Maine to Mexico
Harry Belafonte
Jamaica Farewell

Port of Entry:
Kingston (Port Royal), Port
Antonio, Montego Bay, Ocho Rios, Discovery
Bay, Kaiser, Bowden, Port Esquivel
Fuel: Port Antonio, *Montego Bay*, Kingston
Haul-Out: Port Antonio
Diesel Repairs: Port Antonio, *Montego Bay*
Outboard Repairs: Port Antonio, *Montego Bay*
Propane: Port Antonio, *Montego Bay*, Kingston
Provisions: Port Antonio, Ocho Rios, Falmouth,
Montego Bay
Time Zone: Eastern (no Daylight Saving Time)
Electricity: 110 volt, 60 cycle

In a word…Jamaica. With the exception of perhaps Tahiti, few islands can conjure as many evocative images as Jamaica. Although Columbus named the island *St. Jago* (*Santiago*), the island's Indian name managed to survive Columbus' moniker. The name *Jamaica* has its origins in the Arawakan term for *Land of Wood and Water*, or *Land of Springs*, *Xaymaca*, early Spanish historians and cartographers replaced the "X" with a "J" and the name appeared for the first time in 1511 as *Jamaica*.

Today the name Jamaica brings to mind beautiful beaches, Reggae Music, Bob Marley, Blue Mountain coffee, rum, ganga, Rastafarians, all-inclusive resorts at Ocho Rios, Negril, and *Montego Bay*, and scores of tales of the old pirate days at Port Royal.

There is all this and more in Jamaica today. Yes, there are beautiful secluded beaches, excellent trade wind sailing, some fine, protected anchorages, and a cuisine that is quite unique to this charming island, add to this natural wonders such as *Reich Falls*, the *Río Grande*, the majestic *Blue Mountains*, and couple it with a friendly people and a *mañana-mañana attitude*, and you have the makings of a cruiser's paradise (if I may explain, most cruisers know what a *mañana attitude* is, it's that "it'll be done soon" thing that is so prevalent in paradise, well, *mañana-mañana* means that "…it will be done soon, but don't hold your breath, maybe tomorrow, or maybe the day after, we'll see").

No discussion of cruising the waters of Jamaica can be complete without a word to two about security. Before I ever came to Jamaica I asked various other cruisers about Jamaica and their thoughts on the island. The responses I got were extremely negative. Most told me not to go there, that there was too much violence on the island. Of course, none of these cruisers had ever been to Jamaica where, I will admit, there is a certain amount of crime and violence, the majority of which is between several bands of ne'er-do-wells, with little crime being committed upon visiting tourists. And these same cruisers were all heading to the waters of Venezuela where crime upon cruisers, including cold-blooded murder, is not uncommon. I couldn't understand their line of reasoning.

In more recent times, a German couple I met anchored overnight at *San San Beach* (just a few miles east of Port Antonio), a small bay that they were warned about (it's great for a daytime visit, but not for overnight). Around 2300, on their SECOND evening in the anchorage, two men swam out, boarded their boat, bound the couple and robbed them at gunpoint. When informed of the crime, the local police seemed almost indifferent. Just as you would not walk in certain areas of your own home town at night, the same holds true for parts of Jamaica, especially Kingston. Keep away from the banks south of Jamaica which I've been warned are often used by South American smugglers moving their products northward. Use caution! Use your common sense! Carry your money in traveler's checks. But don't miss out on so very much because of fear and doubt. Shakespeare once wrote: *Doubt is a thief that often makes us fear to tread where we might have won*. Like the commercials say: Come to Jamaica!

And if security wasn't enough to worry you, now I must mention the state of the roads on the island. If you plan to rent a car and drive around Jamaica I have to warn you that the roads are some of the worst that you'll encounter in the Caribbean. Although there are many good roads near Kingston, and some new 4-lane construction between Ocho Rios and *Montego Bay* on the northern coast, for the most part the roads are narrow with many switchbacks, rife with potholes, and at night many drivers run their high beams all the time. And if you blow out a tire on a pothole like I did and have to buy one on the road, don't forget to keep a receipt and the original tire, the car rental places are used to such damages and can sometimes return the tire for a refund, and they'll know if you changed the tire, they're hip to such things and they check (like I said, the roads are rife with potholes). Also, keep an eye out for speed traps and police checkpoints.

Customs and Immigration

To begin with, please note that cruising vessels will find it best to clear at Port Antonio, Ocho Rios, and *Montego Bay* along the northern coast. Although there are Ports of Entry at Port Kaiser, Port Esquivel, and *Discovery Bay*, these offices are used primarily for commercial vessels.

Also note that it is VERY important to fly your Quarantine flag until granted pratique! This is one formality that should not be ignored.

When you arrive in Jamaica and take a slip or anchor out, immediately notify authorities on shore, either a marina or the *Montego Bay Yacht Club* and they will arrange for the proper authorities to visit you and handle your clearance. Remember to report immediately, arriving on a Sunday and not reporting until Monday is not acceptable.

Officers will advise you when to remove your Quarantine flag and replace it with a Jamaican courtesy flag. Do not attempt to arrive in Jamaica without a courtesy flag, it is considered bad form.

One last note on clearing at Port Antonio. When clearing in, you can clear *Customs* at the marina but you will also have to walk about three blocks to the Police Station to clear with the local Police.

Clearing Quarantine
One of the first officers to visit your vessel will be the Quarantine office who will have several forms for you to fill out regarding the health of all aboard and whether or not any animals are on board. The office will also want to know about certain foodstuffs and their expiration dates, and whether or not your boat has a holding tank. Note that Port Antonio is a "no discharge zone" and if you do not have a holding tank you will be asked to use the facilities at the marina.

Clearing Customs
When entering Jamaica all visiting boats must have a clearance from their last port of call, all necessary boat documentation forms and identification for the crew, as well as a list of stores and a crew list.

Customs is the office in charge of vessel movements in Jamaica and they will give you clearance to your next port of call. If you clear out of

Port Antonio headed for *Montego Bay* you will need clearance for *Mobay* and when you arrive there you will need to check in with *Customs* there. You can also stop before *Mobay*, at perhaps Ocho Rios, and if anybody asks just say you were too tired to go any further that day. Not reporting to a Customs officer at a port in transit is a violation of Jamaican law.

Fees
Normally there are no fees to clear into Jamaica. Normal working hours for *Customs* and *Immigration* are from 0800 to 1700 (1600 in some ports), with an hour break at lunch. Clearance outside these hours may entail an overtime fee, while clearance on Saturdays, Sundays, and public holidays are charged at double-time. Jamaica *Port Authority* monitors VHF channels 11, 12, and 13. As of this writing, Jamaica levies a departure tax for those leaving by air of J$750.

Firearms
All firearms and ammunition must be turned over to *Customs* who will keep them in bond for you until you clear out (be sure to give *Customs* 24-hour notice of your departure so that they may retrieve your firearms and have them waiting for you).

Fishing
If you wish to fish you'll need to obtain a fishing license. If you bring a Jamaican with you on your fishing trip you won't need a license as Jamaicans are allowed to fish the waters of their country.

Pets
Jamaica does not have rabies and intends to keep it that way; therefore no animals may be imported. All dogs, cats, and birds must stay on the boat and are not allowed ashore under any circumstances, in fact, regulations state that you must keep your dog's poop and seal it in plastic bags to be dumped at least 3 miles offshore.

Importing Parts
If you need parts for your boat shipped into Jamaica, they can be sent duty-free if you check with *Customs* prior to shipping and fill out the right form, however there is a small processing fee for this service which is much less than the duty involved on most parts, US$10 as of this writing.

Clearing Immigration
Immigration may give you 90 days with one 90-day extension, longer stays require permission from *Immigration*. Citizens of Canada and the United

States do not need visas, only valid passports or expired passports less than one year old, or proof of citizenship such as a birth certificate or voter's registration card with a photo id. Having a pre-typed crew list will help expedite the officer's duties.

Commonwealth citizens and those from nations who have reciprocal agreements only need a valid passport (no visa) and can stay for up to six months. Citizens of Australia and New Zealand need a passport but no visa for stays of less than 60 days.

Clearing Out
When clearing out you have 24 hours to leave the country unless you have firearms to retrieve, in which case you must leave Jamaican waters immediately after receiving your weapons and clearance papers.

Ports of Entry:
Kingston (Port Royal), Port Antonio, Montego Bay, Ocho Rios, Discovery Bay, Kaiser, Bowden, Port Esquivel.

Tides

Tides in Jamaica are primarily diurnal, one high and one low each day, and are small, generally about 1 foot or less. There is a westward setting current off both the northern and southern coasts of Jamaica of about .7-1.0 knot with a reported current of up to 2-3 knots two miles off Morant Point. At times, the westward setting current has been reported to reverse its direction, especially during periods of westerly winds.

A Brief History

As with nearly all the islands of the Caribbean, Jamaica was first settled by Arawaks who arrived around 650 A.D.-900 A.D. from the Orinoco region of Venezuela and the Guianas. There is a huge variation in the numbers of Arawaks living on Jamaica at the end of the 15th century, estimates vary from 10,000 to 1,000,000 living on the island they called *Xaymaca*, the *Land of Wood and Water*, the *Land of Springs*. But one thing is fairly certain, the Arawaks on Jamaica were not under attack by the Caribs as their cousins in the Eastern Caribbean were.

Christopher Columbus, The *Great Discoverer*, stumbled across Jamaica quite by accident. Columbus had heard of *Xamayca* from the Indians on Cuba and while sailing along Cuba's southern coast on his second voyage to the New World was blown

off course and spotted Jamaica high on the horizon. Columbus arrived on Jamaica later that year and named the island *St. Jago (Santiago)*, but the island's Indian name survived Columbus' moniker. Early Spanish historians and cartographers replaced the "X" with a "J" and the name appears for the first time in 1511 as *Jamaica*.

Columbus arrived on the northern coast of Jamaica on May 5, 1494, and named the island *St. Jago*, or *Santiago*, after St. James. His fleet was greeted by 70 canoes full of hostile Arawakan warriors who had heard of the violent tendencies of Columbus' men from their Amerindian cousins on Hispaniola. Columbus continued on his route ignoring the Indians and he anchored on May 6 at *St. Ann's Bay* (which he named *Santa Gloria*) on the northern shore of Jamaica and had his interpreter reassure the Indians of his good intentions. Columbus' fleet was in dire need of repair and the Admiral sought to anchor his vessels at the mouth of the *Rio Bueno*. When his ship's launch approached the shore it was attacked with blow darts, but the Spaniards quickly repelled the attackers.

After this incident many curious natives arrived at the bay and Columbus ordered his men to fire upon them with crossbows. This did the trick. The next morning the Arawaks returned with food, heaping platters of fish and fruit, and the Indians begged Columbus and his men not to leave. But on May 9, the repairs completed, Columbus and his fleet sailed west where they discovered the *Golfo de Buen Tiemp*, now known as *Montego Bay*. Columbus arrived at Portland Bight during the second week of August, 1494, and named the bay *Bahía de la Vaca*, *Cow Bay*, because of the number of manatees, sea cows, that he saw there. Columbus sailed away only to return to Jamaica three years later when he became stranded at *St. Ann's Bay* for a year after the loss of two of his caravels.

Although Columbus claimed *St. Jago* for the Spanish sovereigns in 1494, the island was not occupied until 1509-1510, when Juan de Esquival arrived from Santo Domingo on Hispaniola with a group of settlers. The Spaniards settled in along the northern coast of Jamaica at St. Ann and built a town called *Sevilla Nueva*, *New Seville*, in 1510, and began a search for gold. Surrounded by swamps, fever hit the group hard and King Charles I finally permitted the survivors to move to the southern side of the island where they constructed the town of *St.*

Jago de la Vega, St. James of the Plain, which is now known as Spanish Town.

The island of Jamaica was eventually given to the family of Christopher Columbus in 1540 as their personal estate, but nothing ever came of the Columbus family's short dominion over the island, in fact, the Spanish colony on Jamaica never grew very large or flourished. The indigenous Amerindians died by the thousands of European diseases and those that survived that did not survive the Spanish. By the mid-1600s there were no Amerindians left on the island and it would take the arrival the British to change things for the better.

In 1596, a British force of 500 men under the command of Sir Anthony Shirley landed near Kingston and eventually sacked the poorly defended Spanish Town. In 1643, Spanish Town was again sacked by a much smaller force under the command of Captain William Jackson. Spain did nothing to help her colonists on Jamaica and continued that policy until her people were driven from Jamaica entirely, but not before becoming a thorn in the side of the British.

In May of 1655, nearly three centuries of British rule began when 38 English ships and almost 8,000 soldiers landed at *Passage Fort* in Kingston Harbour and marched toward Spanish Town, under orders from Oliver Cromwell who was seeking revenge for the deportation of English settlers from St. Kitts in 1629 and the subsequent numerous attacks on British shipping by the Spaniards. As part of a plan called the *Western Design*, Cromwell first sent his troops, under the command of Admiral William Penn and General Robert Venables, to take Santo Domingo on Hispaniola.

Failing miserably at that, Cromwell sent the survivors (the British lost over 4,000 men in that poorly executed attack) to Jamaica where on May 11, the entrenched Spanish colonists (only about 1,500, of which only about 500 could bear arms) decided to surrender after being promised that they would not be harmed and would be allowed to leave the island. The Spanish freed some 1,500 slaves and emptied the town of anything of value before the arrival of the British and fled into the hills and to the northern coast of Jamaica where many fled to Cuba while others held out against the British for almost five years.

When the British arrived in Spanish Town they found it empty and in anger destroyed most of the settlement. The freed slaves fled to the mountains and were organized into a fighting force by Don Cristóbal Amaldo de Ysassi, the Spanish Governor of Jamaica at the time. Ysassi's plan was for the freed slaves to harass the British troops until the Spanish could return and retake the island. These freed slaves, who would later become known as the *Maroons*, settled in St. Catherine Parish and along the *Río Juana*. The name *Maroon* is the British corruption of the Spanish *cimarrones*, meaning *wild* or *untamed*. The numbers of the *Maroons* grew as more and more runaway slaves flocked to their cause, and their continual raiding of the British plantations was a thorn in the side of the British colonists. The British offered land and full freedom to any *Maroon* who surrendered, but their offer fell on deaf ears. The *Maroons* continued to fight the British for the next 76 years costing the British many lives lost, hundreds of thousands of pounds, and some 44 acts of the *Assembly*. For more information on the *Maroons*, see the section entitled *The Maroons* in the chapter *The Local Cultures*.

By October of 1655, British General Sedgwick arrived from England and took charge of the fledgling colony and shortly after their arrival most of the settlers, Sedgwick included, succumbed to fever. Sedgwick's replacement General Brayne, feared a retaliatory attack by the Spanish from Cuba and fortified the defenses of the island. As expected, in 1657, de Ysassi, returned to Jamaica leading two contingents of guerilla forces from Cuba into the interior of Jamaica via the northern coast of Jamaica. General Brayne's replacement, General D'Oyley, attacked the Spaniards by sailing around the island from Kingston and defeated Ysassi near Ocho Rios in 1657 at the *Battle of Los Chomeros* and again at Río Nuevo in 1658 in the largest battle ever fought on Jamaica's shores. Even though he was defeated by a much stronger British force, Ysassi continued to hold out in the interior until 1660 when he and his men fled to Cuba in canoes. In 1661, D'Oyley was appointed Governor of Jamaica and established the first governing council on the island. During this time many of the officers who served under Penn and Venables in 1655 were presented with huge estates and who immediately began building defenses of their lands as well as Kingston and constructing no less than five forts at Port Royal.

In 1663, the British made the first real efforts at suppressing the *Maroons* who were rumored to have murdered every white man they came across. A former *Maroon*, Juan Lubolo, turned traitor and led a British contingent against his own people, but was defeated. This led to a very short and very uneasy peace between the *Maroons* and the British colonists. For more information on the Maroons, see the section *The Maroons* in the chapter *Local Cultures*.

By this time Port Royal was emerging as a pirate haven and in 1673, the famed pirate, Sir Henry Morgan became Lieutenant-Governor of Jamaica only to be replaced by Lord Vaughn in 1674, but later to reclaim the position in 1680. Morgan, who had successfully attacked and plundered Porto Bello and burned the old city of Panama less than three years earlier, and many other buccaneers moved their base of operations from the island of Tortuga, north of Hispaniola, to Port Royal, and the booty they brought to the docks to sell and trade enriched all involved. The British on Jamaica gained much by supporting the buccaneers and offering them safe haven. Not only did the buccaneers serve as protection for Jamaica from the Spanish, they also raided Spanish shipping and sold their goods at Port Royal with 10% of the take going to the Jamaican authorities. In 1688, Morgan died and was buried with honors at Port Royal.

Hot on the heels of this new income came the sugar industry, backed by then Governor Sir Thomas Modyford, who also pushed for cocoa production. This brought a huge influx of slaves to the island's new plantation economy by 1675. In 1690, a slave rebellion erupted at Chapelton in Clarendon but was eventually suppressed and the ringleaders executed. However, a large group of slaves, mostly *Coromantees*, an extremely brave and warlike people from Africa's *Gold Coast*, escaped into the interior of Jamaica and aligned themselves with the *Maroons* already living there.

Two years later an event occurred which would forever change the map of Jamaica, and roust the buccaneers from their nests. On June 7, 1692, at approximately 1140, everybody in the city of Port Royal was startled by what sounded like thunder from the north. Just as quickly the ground began to shake from the first of three shockwaves. Houses began to shake and fall, the second shockwave came and did little more damage, but the third tremor was the worst, it was felt all over the island of Jamaica. A great part of Port Royal was engulfed by the sea and thousands perished, their bodies floating for days in the harbor or rotting on land as minor quakes shook the area for several days. The survivors tried to rebuild the

city, but in 1704 a fire broke out and destroyed every building except the forts.

In 1694, one year after the destruction of Port Royal, the town of Kingston was laid out on land that was, at that time, private property. But it wasn't long before Kingston became a major settlement. At this time Jamaica was becoming known as a great sugar producing country with plantations also growing cocoa and sarsaparilla. At this time there were three classes of people in Jamaica, the white men who owned the property, the plantations, and ruled the land, were at the top of the pecking order. The second class was also made up of white men, but for the most part these men were little better than slaves (for an interesting take on this watch the movie *Captain Blood* starring Errol Flynn). It was the custom in those days for Great Britain to send criminals to her colonies for periods of 5-10 years. These men were purchased like slaves by the planters and were treated the same as any of their other slaves. After they had served their time these men, if they survived, were granted their freedom. The third class was the slaves brought over from West Africa who had little if any hope of ever being free unless they were fortunate enough to escape and hook up with the *Maroons*.

France and England happened to be at war in 1694 when a French fleet under Admiral du Casse attacked Jamaica. For an entire month his fleet landed troops on the northern and eastern shores of Jamaica and plundered every plantation they could find. On July 19, 1694, 1,500 experienced French troops landed at Carlisle Bay in Clarendon to find it defended by only a few hundred British colonists and some slaves. The colonists were soon backed up by several hundred more from nearby plantations and after several days of fierce fighting the British drove the French back to the sea, but not before the French troops had destroyed some 100 estates and plantations and stole 1,300 slaves.

In 1702, British Admiral Benbow sailed from Port Royal in search of du Casse and his fleet. Benbow found the French off the coast of Columbia and attacked them immediately. For five days Benbow and his fleet relentlessly fought the French before Benbow was wounded in the leg. In light of Benbow's condition, coupled with fierce French resistance, two of the Admiral's officers, Captains Kirby and Woods, persuaded the British fleet to return to Port Royal and safety. Kirby and Woods were tried for their conduct and shot, and Admiral Benbow died a few months later and was entombed in a Kingston church where his remains still lie today.

For the next three decades the British were kept quite busy on Jamaica with the Maroons in what is called the First Maroon War. The Maroons were very active during these years and made regular attacks on plantations and their owners. Agriculture was taking a downswing and it was reflected in the economy with some dismay about the future of Jamaica. In 1711, a great storm destroyed much of the parish of Westmoreland and took many lives and still the Maroons fought their guerilla war. In 1718, coffee was introduced into Jamaica by then Governor Sir Nicholas Lawes. Pirates were also becoming a thorn in the side of planters at this time and Lawes did much to repress piratical activity on his island. The First Maroon War was in full swing and in 1728 two regiments of British soldiers had to be brought in from Gibraltar to protect Jamaican planters and their estates. Finally, the British managed to wipe out a Maroon stronghold in the *Blue Mountains* called Nanny Town which was a great boost for the Brits against the Maroon warriors.

On January 6, 1738, Cudjoe, the great Maroon leader, and Colonel Guthrie of the British Army met and signed the peace treaty with an exchange of hats as a sign of friendship. Although historians claim that the treaty was signed under a huge tree called *Cudjoe's Tree* and today called the *Kinda One Family Tree*, Maroon historians claim different. They say the *Peace Cave* was the sight of the official signing, Colonel Guthrie and Cudjoe performing a blood brother ceremony instead of exchanging hats. The official document is even harder to discern, some day that it is in the care of a trusted Maroon elder and its location a secret of the highest priority. The treaty gave official recognition to the Maroons as a free people and deeded them 1,500 acres of land. It also allowed them to administer their own laws, gave them freedom from taxes, allowed the Maroons to hunt wild boar anywhere except within 3 miles of a town or plantation, and it bound the Maroons to fight with the British should any outside party attempt to invade Jamaica, such as the French from Haiti or the Spanish form Cuba. The Maroons were also bound to hand over any new runaway slaves and in later years some Maroons became slave hunters.

Although the next 50 years saw peace on the home front with the Maroons, England was at war with Spain and in 1741 some Jamaican troops took part in a disastrous attempt to capture Cartagena by Admiral Vernon and another failed attempt the following year when Governor Trelawney sought to capture the Isthmus of Panama. At home, several more slave rebellions broke out and Jamaica suffered from storms and earthquakes once again. In 1754, Kingston became the capital of Jamaica and the Assembly began to hold their meetings there.

A large slave rebellion in 1760 took place in St. Mary under the leadership of a slave called Tacky. The slaves seized the town of Port Maria on the northern coast and murdered all the white people they could find. British troops put down the violent rebellion killing some 400 slaves and deporting another 600 to British Honduras, now known as Belize. By 1775, there were almost a quarter of a million people living on Jamaica, of which over 192,000 were slaves. Jamaicans received a scare when in 1778, a French fleet sailed for the West Indies and martial law was declared on Jamaica fearing the flee was intent on taking Jamaica. All of the island's defenses were fortified and the legendary Horatio Nelson was made governor of Fort Charles in Port Royal in 1779, but the French fleet failed to arrive in Jamaican waters.

But a few years later another French fleet was intent on taking Jamaica when Admiral Rodney defeated the French Admiral de Grasse off Dominica on April 12, 1782, at the Battle of The Saintes. Rodney brought the captured French ships to Port Royal and the grateful residents of Jamaica erected a marble statue of their hero in Spanish Town Square.

After the American Revolution, many Loyalists fled to Jamaica while some went to the Cayman Islands, Canada, and the Bahamas, bringing their slaves with them, but it would not be long now until the slaves were free. In 1772, several British judges declared that should a slave set foot in England that he or she would become free. This was due to Granville Sharpe who took three slaves to England to secure their freedom. In 1793, a detachment of British troops and black soldiers from Jamaica went to Haiti to come to the aid of British planters who were irate over France freeing the slaves on the island. The troops took a few Haitian cities with many of their ranks dying from disease. The British were eventually routed by Toussaint l'Ouverture just as trouble once again arose with the Maroons in Jamaica.

The Second Maroon War broke out when 300 Trelawney Maroons revolted when two Maroons were flogged in *Montego Bay* instead of being handed back to their own people for punishment. The British employed 5,000 troops and quickly rounded up the Maroons using dogs to flush them from their hiding places in the mountains and forced them to sue for peace. A reward of 10 pounds was offered for every Maroon captured during this period.

After the signing of the peace treaty to end the *Second Maroon War*, the British decided that it was high time to get rid of the Maroon problem entirely. The government captured some 543 Maroons and exiled them to Halifax, Nova Scotia, on June 26, 1796. The Canadian government quickly found out that the Maroons were not the fine settlers they first thought them to be and decided that the best course of action was to remove the Maroons from Canadian soil. After much negotiation with the government of Sierra Leone in West Africa, the Maroons were shipped off to Freetown Harbour, Sierra Leone, on October 1, 1880, completing a circle begun almost two centuries before when the Maroon's ancestors were stolen from their homelands in West Africa.

The beginning of the 19th century brought a boost to the economy when the largest crop of sugar ever produced in Jamaica was exported in 1803. In the same year Kingston became a true city with a Mayor, 12 Aldermen, and 12 Counselors. In 1805, another French fleet threatened the island, but never actually attacked Jamaica, eventually being defeated by Lord Nelson at the *Battle of Trafalgar*. Jamaica's importance as a naval base declined after the Battle of Trafalgar and the goods previously smuggled into the island for sale and barter diminished as well. In 1807, the slave trade between Africa and Jamaica was abolished by an act of Parliament and after March 1, 1808, no more slaves were brought to Jamaica, although by this time over one million salves had been imported from Africa and by the time the trade was abolished there were almost 320,000 slaves on the island of Jamaica who suddenly found themselves worth much more to their owners since there was no new supply. As a result the way slaves were treated changed as they were no longer worked beyond the limits of their endurance. Many slaves were allowed to cultivate a small piece of land one day in every two weeks for their own sustenance. Those with an overage of product were allowed to sell their crop and many slaves suddenly found themselves with money; some slaves subsequently purchased their own freedom or freedom for their children.

Even with all the advances in the way the slaves were treated, to the consternation of the Jamaican planters the slaves still rebelled. In 1808, there was a mutiny by black recruits of the 2nd West India Regiment at *Fort Augusta*; the recruits were shot and killed by their superiors. In 1809, a conspiracy of rebellious slaves was discovered in Kingston. The ringleaders were put to death when it was discovered that they intended to burn the city and murder all the white inhabitants. In 1823, the British government drafted a set of instructions for making the lives of the slaves easier but the Jamaican planters objected to any interference on their island saying that their current code kept the slaves "...happy and comfortable, in every respect, as the labouring class in any part of the world."

The abolitionists in England stood up on one side of the issue while the Jamaican planters took up a reciprocal stand claiming injustice in the way that Britain was interfering in their lives. Some slaves heard of the debate and got the idea that the King had granted them freedom and that they were wrongly being kept in bondage by their owners. On December 28, 1831, a huge slave insurrection, the *Christmas Rebellion*, broke out in St. James Parish and rapidly spread to the parishes of Trelawney, Hanover, Westmoreland, St. Elizabeth, and Manchester and was hugely instrumental in bringing about the abolition of slavery on Jamaica. Led by a Sam Sharpe, the 20,000 slave strong rebellion lasted for over four months until May 23, 1832 when the slaves were tricked into laying down their arms. Some 400 of the rebellion's leaders were rounded up and hanged in *Charles Square* in *Montego Bay* (now known as *Sam Sharpe Square*), while hundreds of others were whipped. Sharpe's remains were buried in the sand along the edge of the bay but were later recovered and today lie beneath the pulpit at the *Burchell Baptist Church*.

In 1832, the Earl of Mulgrave became governor of Jamaica and urged new measures aimed at better treatment of the slaves, but the local politicians declined to act on the governor's suggestions and the British Parliament decided it was time to act decisively and passed The Abolition Act on August 28, 1833, which stated that all slave children under the age of six should be set free. The act also allowed for a 6 year period of apprenticeship from 1834-1840 after which every slave in the British Empire would be set free. The ruling also permitted some £20,000,000 to be paid to the slave holders as recompense with

£5,853,975 going to the Jamaican slaveholders. The apprenticeship system failed miserably and by August of 1838 was allowed to cease by an act of Parliament and Jamaica's slaves found themselves to be free at last with celebrations all over the island including a ritual burial of slave chains and shackles in Spanish Town.

Many of the newly freed slaves did not wish to work for their former owners complaining of the small wages offered and the planters in return began to order their former slaves off their lands, destroying their huts and felling the fruit trees they were cultivating. With no effective and economic workforce the plantations began to go out of cultivation, which was not helped by a drought between the years of 1839-1841. In 1841, planters imported new workers from Africa to work their lands but the immigrants failed as slave replacements and the practice quickly ended. Soon indentured servants from India began to arrive on Jamaica's shores as they did in many other Caribbean islands but still the sugar economy only got worse. Even with a free trade agreement Jamaica could not compete with Cuba on the world's sugar market and the economy remained in a downward spiral. A cholera epidemic in 1850 didn't help matters, wiping out over 32,000 people and which was soon followed by a smallpox epidemic that also took many lives. Many sugar plantations folded and England had to lend Jamaica vast amounts of money to pay off the debts that the tiny island had accumulated as the disputes between the dwindling number of planters and the laborers continued which had grown year by year as the planter's profits shrank.

Part of Jamaica's economical problems was due to the transition from a slave economy to a wage labor economy as most slaves refused to work for the starvation wagers offered by the sugar estates and chose to fend for themselves. But the planters were still in power as only property owners had the right to vote. The *Morant Bay Rebellion* of 1865 came about during the American Civil War years when the U.S. naval blockade of Jamaica cut off vital supplies and former slaves, desperate over conditions and injustice rebelled only to have the uprising quelled in short order. In retribution for the uprising some 600 were executed and almost as many flogged, while thousands of homes were burnt. The brutality of the government's response provoked an outcry in England which in turn marked the beginning of a more liberal era on the island during which time the Crown took over the local government and some great

strides were made. In 1869 a communications cable with Europe was established, the local rail line was extended, nickel coins were first used in Jamaica, and a college was established by 1876 and the first scholarship awarded in 1881.

By 1898, the economy of Jamaica was still in a bad way, there had been another drought and Jamaican sugar was selling at very low prices, and bananas had not yet become a major export. The government did something that we would consider extraordinary today, they cut their own costs with much internal opposition. By the beginning of the 1900s a line of steamers was inaugurated between Jamaica and England which helped open up the market for Jamaican bananas. On January 14, 1907 a massive earthquake destroyed Kingston at 3:30 PM. Over eight hundred persons were killed and the city nearly leveled by a series of three shocks that took place within 20 seconds. But within a few years Kingston was rebuilt including new public and government buildings. Over the next two decades the island's economy improved thanks in no small part to the burgeoning banana, coffee, and cocoa export business. The railway system was enlarged, a number of schools and hospitals were constructed, and more and more people were becoming landowners (and some women property owners achieved the right to vote). When World War I came about Jamaica answered the call sending some 10,000 men to the front, but suffered from a lack of shipping to take her products to market as happens to some countries during wartime. The Jamaican soldiers fought bravely, especially in Palestine against the Turks.

Soon banana growers banded together to obtain the best prices for their goods and to ensure timely shipments. By 1938 labor disputes would often erupt into violence and Jamaica's first labor union was established. World War II came and saw the United States enter into an agreement with Britain which allowed the U.S. to build a base at Portland Bight and another in Clarendon Parrish. In 1947, an important conference took place in *Montego Bay* in which representatives of all the British Caribbean peoples met to give consideration to uniting under a single government. What would have happened had they said yes to that idea is anybody's guess. Some say it would have been a mistake, others say it would have given the nations involved an economic boost and world status. But either way, it never truly came as some would have hoped about after years of reports and debates, it became more an economic federation that a true Caribbean nation as some had hoped.

In 1957, a final *Federation Conference* took place on Jamaica and the term *West Indies* was adopted for the federation and Trinidad was elected as the federation's capital. That same year Jamaica received full internal self-government from the Crown which meant a complete change of the political structure that had existed for nearly 300 years. One of the government's first acts was a vote by the people of Jamaica on whether or not to stay in the *West Indies Federation*, by a small majority Jamaica voted to withdraw from the newly formed federation and in turn she asked Britain for her independence in 1962.

On August 16, 1962, Jamaica became an independent state within the British Commonwealth and Alexander Bustamante was the first Prime Minister. Jamaica's post-independence politics were dominated for years by two cousins, Bustamants, who formed the first trade union in the Caribbean just prior to WWII and later formed the *Jamaican Labor Party* (*JLP*), and Norman Manley, whose *People's National Party* (*PNP*) was the first political party on the island when it was convened in 1938. Manley's son, Michael, led the *PNP* towards democratic socialism in the mid-1970s, causing a capital flight at a time when Jamaica could ill afford it. Inflation soared above 50%, unemployment skyrocketed and society became increasingly polarized, culminating in fully-fledged warfare during the campaigns preceding the 1976 election. Heavily armed groups of *JLP* and *PNP* supporters began killing each other in the partisan slums of Kingston and a state of emergency was declared. But the *PNP* won the election by a wide margin and Manley continued with his socialist agenda which did nothing to please the government of the United States.

Economic sanctions were established against Jamaica and soon businesses ceased their backing of Manley and the Jamaican economy, and tourism in particular, went into a sharp decline. During this time Jamaicans lived as if they were under siege and almost 700 people were killed in events leading up to the elections of 1980 which were won by the *JLP*'s Edward Seaga.

Edward Seaga turned around the Jamaican economy, severed ties with Cuba, and supported President Ronald Reagan and the government of the United States, in fact, when Reagan became President in 1980, Seaga was the first foreign ruler to visit the new leader in Washington D.C. So close did Jamaica's ties become with the United States that Jamaica even provided troops for the 1983 invasion of Grenada.

In 1989, a "reinvented" Michael Manley returned to power. Manley quietly re-established relations with Cuba, but gone from his administration were the anti-U.S. rhetoric that characterized his earlier administration. Due to failing health, Manly retired in 1992 and handed over the reins of government to Jamaica's first black Prime Minister, Percival James Patterson. A year later Patterson defeated Seaga in an election and Seaga never again gained the support he once had. Patterson won again in 1997, but in 1999, Jamaica erupted in nationwide riots after Patterson's government announced a 30% increase in the gasoline tax. Almost immediately sugarcane fields around Kingston and *Montego Bay* were burned and arson and looting was rampant. Within three days of this announcement the government rescinded the gasoline tax.

In July of 2001, a renewal of gang violence claimed 27 lives and just a few months later, in January of 2002, seven more lives were lost for the same reasons. In February of 2002, the police retaliated by killing five people who were leaving a crime scene and immediately people began complaining about police violence. But even with all the violence clouding the issues, Patterson won a fourth term in office and announced that he hoped that Jamaica would be a republic by the time he leaves office in 2007. We shall soon see...

Transiting the North Coast

In this guide I'll discuss only the northern coast of *Jam*aica from east to west, from Port Antonio to *Montego Bay*, since most cruisers headed to the Northwest Caribbean will likely take that route, especially those approaching from the *Windward Passage* and the Eastern Caribbean. But before we begin our exploration of Jamaica I'd like to take a moment and mention a few things you'll want to know as you travel along the island's northern coast.

To begin with, as you head west along Jamaica's northern shore, do not plug in a waypoint and head directly to it, there may be a headland or point blocking a direct route, you must keep a good watch along this shoreline, several shoals lie a mile or more offshore in places. And if that's not enough to watch out for, you're likely to find the floating markers for fish traps, and there will a LOT of these, anywhere inside the 100-fathom line. These markers may range from small buoys to empty water bottles that you won't see until almost upon them.

Usually there is a ¾-1 knot westerly setting current along Jamaica's northern and southern shores, but if you're too close in you might pick up a counter current, an eddy, at any time. Along Jamaica's northern coast these eddies are usually more noticeable between Galina Point and Port Antonio, but bear in mind that sets in any direction may occur at any time and can be as strong as a reported 2 knots (with 2-3 knots being common in the vicinity of Morant Point).

With this in mind you can travel close in along Jamaica's northern shore during the daytime, but if you plan to do it at night, stay well offshore, I'd suggest at least three miles, and preferably five miles off. At times, the westward setting current has been reported to reverse its direction, especially during periods of westerly winds.

If you need shelter from a strong front and/or northerly winds and swells, the best harbors for protection are at Port Antonio, *Montego Bay*, and especially in *Bogue Lagoon*. Ocho Rios, Oracabessa, and Falmouth can give some protection and will suffice if nothing else is available. If you need marine supplies you'll have to go to Kingston on the southeast coast by bus, taxi, or rental car. A few minor supplies like fuel filters can be found in *Montego Bay*, but the only true marine suppliers and repairmen are located in Kingston.

Port Antonio

*I've never met a woman
as beautiful as Port Antonio.*
Errol Flynn

Important Lights:
Folly Point Light, L Fl W 10s
Titchfield Light, Q G beacon
Galina Point, Fl W 12s
Waypoints:
Port Antonio - ½ nm N of entrance channel
18° 11.75' N, 76° 26.80' W

Galina Point - 1½ nm N of
18° 25.50' N, 76° 53.00' W

That much used quote of Errol Flynn's is as true today as it was half a century ago, without a doubt, this is one of the most picturesque areas of Jamaica. Errol Flynn had a lot to do with popularizing Port Antonio, he had a home on Navy Island and was responsible for bringing many friends and celebrities to Port Antonio in the 1940s and 1950s. A list of who's who in Port Antonio would include names like Rudyard Kipling, Randolph Hearst, poet Ella Willa Wilcox, Robin Moore (who came to the area to write *The French Connection*), and J. P. Morgan Jr. who was known to winter aboard his yacht *Corsair III* in the harbor. Flynn's yacht, *Zaca*, was also at home in the harbor at Port Antonio. But enough talk of celebrity visitors, the area itself is a celebrity in a manner, portions of the movies *Club Paradise* and *Cocktail* were filmed nearby.

I've visited nearly every island in the Caribbean and very few of those can compare with the stark beauty of Jamaica as you approach her coastline, specifically the Port Antonio area from offshore. To the east of Port Antonio you'll see the heights of the *John Crow Mountains* and the *Blue Mountains* looming like a huge, dark wall on the horizon, home to some of the best coffee in the world as well as the highest point in Jamaica at 7,402' (*Blue Mountain Peak*).

Porti, as Port Antonio is commonly called, is one of the wettest areas on the island of Jamaica, averaging nearly an inch of rain per day, 360" per year!

Cruisers heading west into the Northwestern Caribbean, and even most headed south to Panama, usually make Port Antonio their entryway to Jamaica, and for good reason. The harbor offers excellent protection, fuel, good dockage, and a new haul-out yard, and almost as important, Porti is untouched by the massive tourism meccas of some of Jamaica's more popular stops such as *Montego Bay*, Ocho Rios, or Negril.

Navigational Information
As shown on chart JAM-1, a waypoint at 18° 11.75' N, 76° 26.80' W, will place you approximately ½ nautical mile north of the entrance channel into *East Harbour*, but the best protection will be found in *West Harbour* which is gained by the deep channel between Titchfield Peninsula and Navy Island. An easy landmark on the entrance from seaward is the lighthouse on Folly Point, which has been in

Port Antonio with Navy Island in the background

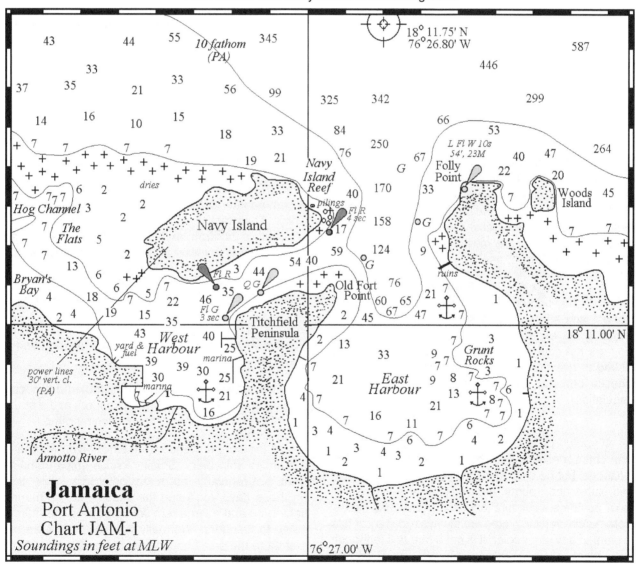

18° 11.75' N
76° 26.80' W

43   44   55   10 fathom   345   587
                (PA)
      33   446
37   35   21   33   56   99   325   342   299
  14   16   10   15   18   33   84   250   66   53
                                                L Fl W 10s
        7 7   7   7   7   19   21   Navy   76   54', 23M   40   47   264
  + + + + + + + + + +   Island   G   67   Folly   22
      + + dries   + +   Reef   250   170   33   Point   20
  7 7 7 7   6   2   2   + + +   pilings   40   7   Woods   45
Hog Channel 3   2   Navy Island   Fl R   158   G   Island
  7   The   2   4 sec   17   G   + +   7   7
  7   Flats   5   59   124   9   ruins
  7   2   Fl R 3   44   54   40   G   76   7
  13   Fl R   Q G   + + +   21   7
Bryan's   6   + + +   35   + + Old Fort   60   1
Bay   4   18   6   7   5   22   46   Point   65   67   47   7
  2   4   19   15   35   Fl G   Titchfield   45   + +
                  3 sec   Peninsula
        43   West   40   2   13   33   9   3
     yard &   Harbour   25   9 7   Grunt   1
     fuel   39   marina   7 7   Rocks
power lines   39   39   30   25   21   East   9   8
30' vert. cl.   30   7   Harbour   13   7 7 6
  (PA)   30   marina   21   21   8 7
      7   16   4   7   16   11   7   7 7   1
           1   3   4   7   6   7   6   2
Annotto River   1   3   4   3   2   4
              2   1

Jamaica
Port Antonio
Chart JAM-1
Soundings in feet at MLW

18° 11.00' N

76° 27.00' W

operation for over a century. Another landmark is the conspicuous small stand of palm trees atop a hill about 1 mile east of the entrance to *East Harbour*.

From the waypoint head mid-channel staying between the red and green buoys. You can anchor in *East Harbour* but most cruisers don't as it is susceptible to swell and no place to be in northerly winds and seas. The better anchorage lies in the southeastern end of *West Harbour*.

You can pick up a mooring here (call *Errol Flynn Marina* on VHF ch. 16 for availability-the new moorings have 18" diameter numbered balls) for just US$12 per day (for 2 persons or less-$2 for each additional person aboard) and this price includes full usage of the marina's shore side facilities such as the new dinghy dock, Wi-Fi, use of the marina pool and beach, showers, toilets, a laundry, and security. What a deal! The 25 moorings are new and are good for vessels up to 40' and are constructed of a huge, heavy duty, big ship chain Vessels over 40' in length will be directed to another part of the harbor and will be required to use their own anchoring gear. You can also hail the marina on VHF ch. 16/09 to arrange a slip.

There is a channel that leads through the reef and past the flats out into deep water well west of Navy Island. *Hog Channel*, see Chart JAM-1) with a controlling depth of 7' and one spot of just under 6'. Powerboats can use the channel but sailboats are restricted by the 35' vertical clearance of the power lines that lead from the mainland to Navy Island as shown on the chart.

What You Will Find Ashore
Both the harbor and marina are "no discharge zones" and all vessels at slips, at anchor, or on a mooring are expected to use their holding tanks. If you are not equipped with a holding tank you will be asked to use the shore side facilities (no one really checks but you are expected to comply with the regulation).

Getting Around
If you don't care to walk around Port Antonio you can catch a minibus for about $2 to one of the local beaches, but be sure to set the fare first. Taxis have red plates and "robots" are illegal taxis, vehicles that take customers for hire and don't have red plates; commercial vehicle plates are always red, if a car has a plate of any other color, it is not a true taxi (although they have to earn a living too). You won't find as

many taxis and buses here as you will at the more touristy areas such as Ocho Rios or *Montego Bay*, but that adds to the charm of undiscovered Porti. If you wish to take a taxi for a tour, be sure to set the price first, I cannot emphasize this enough, always set the price first. You'll find the buses a bit slow by U.S. standards, but then this is not the U.S. Most buses will be crowded, and they're not likely to be air-conditioned. Buses run from Port Antonio to the locations discussed in the following paragraphs.

Customs and *Immigration*
If you need to clear in, you'll be directed to tie up at the *Errol Flynn Marina* to await officers from *Quarantine*, *Customs*, and *Immigration*. The *Quarantine* officer will explain that no waste is to be pumped into the harbor at Port Antonio, if you don't have a holding tank you'll have to use the facilities at the marina. When they officers have completed their formalities you will be instructed to remove your "Q" flag and replace it with the Jamaican courtesy flag. After all of this you will be asked to walk three blocks to the Police Station to check in with the local Police.

Marine Facilities
Marinas
The modern, full-service, and friendly *Errol Flynn Marina* (http://errolflynnmarina.com/) is one of the finest in the Caribbean. The marina, which monitors VHF ch. 16 and 09, offers 32 fixed berths and can accommodate some of the largest yachts in the word. Their facing dock can handle vessels to 350' LOA with a 24' draft, and their "giga-yacht" dock can accommodate a vessel to 600' LOA with a 32' draft.

All slips include full electric (110/220/450 volt, 30 amp, 50 amp, and 100 amp, single and 3-phase electricity). fresh water, phone service, cable TV, Internet access, and a pump out. Other amenities include shower and laundry facilities, a pool, and a crew bar.

The marina also has a designated helicopter landing area with room for four choppers at the south end of *West Harbour* near the launching ramp.

At the northern end of the *Errol Flynn Marina* is the cruise ship pier. Smaller cruise ships come to Porti, not regularly, but every once in a while, and on those days you'll see the security at the marina tighten up and a large tent set up outside the marina gates for vendors. Normally you can walk from the marina to the small beach past the cruise ship dock, but when the ship's in you better pick up a pass at the marina office or you can expect to be questioned, but only when a cruise ship is in port.

Boatyards

On the west side of the harbor, across from the *Errol Flynn Marina*, is their boatyard with a 100-ton *Travelift* (24' wide) that can accommodate a vessel to 100' LOA, drafts to 12', and weights to 220,000 lbs. The yard can repair and store boats and is a designated "free zone" so all parts are duty-free.

The yard itself has water and power throughout, 24-hour security, and modern ground tackle to insure yachts are bunked and stored safely and securely. A crane is currently used to haul beamy vessels but a submersible lift is in the works to permit hauling of vessels with beams up to 36'.

All standard maintenance and repair services are offered including high pressure cleaning, scraping, barrier coating, gel coating, fiberglass repair and anti fouling application. The underwater services offered include zinc replacement, cutlass bearing removal and replacement, plus shaft straightening and propeller repair. Seacock servicing and folding propeller servicing is also included. Additional topside services can also be arranged, including mast stepping. Immediately adjacent to the *Travel Lift* slip is the 100-foot state of the art fueling jetty, which features both high speed and conventional dispensing pumps. Both gasoline and low sulphur diesel fuels are available.

Dockside sanitary pump-out services are available both at the marina and the shipyard if required. It is important to note that the shipyard and marina have been designated a duty and tax free zone by the Jamaican Government, which permits all, supplies and parts to be admitted at near stateside prices (plus shipping of course).

Marine Services

For good all-around service the answer is *Port Antonio Marine Services* (876-289-2890, admin@ port-antonio-marine-services.com). These folks can handle refrigeration and AC repairs, electrical and electronic problems, hull repairs and painting, and all manner of mechanical work!

Provisions

If you need groceries, visit *Sinclair's* or one of the several fresh fruit and vegetable stands on *West Street* and *Harbour Street* and at the *Musgrave Market* near the clock tower in the central square. Almost across the street from *Sinclair's* is a *Scotia Bank*, a good spot to change money.

Dining

Dining out in Porti is inexpensive and it begins at the *Errol Flynn Marina* where you can grab a bite at *Maybelle's Pub on the Pier* or *Norma's at the Marina* restaurants. To top off a meal here, visit *Scoops* ice cream parlor, located in the marina promenade.

THE place for cruisers is the *Rooftop Terrace*, a short walk away; you can see the two story bar from the cockpit of your boat if you're tied up at the new marina. Ladies need to be aware that the streets of Porti tend to be mostly male at night; it's a very lively place.

Most of the eateries in Porti lie on *West Street*, here you'll find two nice bakeries, the *Three Star Lion Bakery*, and *CC's Bakery*, home of the "holey bulla," a traditional Jamaican treat served in an unusual manner, it has a hole in it. Across the street is *Chenel's Pizza Pub* serving pizza, rotis, and Jamaican staples. Just a few doors up *West Street* is *Cartoons*, a good place for snacks, and *Devon House I Scream*, offering some of the finest frozen treats and fruit juices on the island. This Kingston-based ice cream parlor has locations all over the island of Jamaica.

If you crave Chinese food you can visit *Golden Happiness* at the corner of *West* and *Harbour Streets*, or *Shadows* at 40 *West Street*, where you can also get breakfast and Jamaican dishes. On *Allan Avenue* you have several choices for dining, *Troy's* (a little shack on the beach that serve up veggie patties, fresh seafood, and good fruit juices), *K-S Kozy Knook* (great seafood and a very popular watering hole for the locals just outside of town on the beach), and the popular *Anna Bananas*, one of the best places to dine in Porti if you're looking for good Jamaican dishes and a nice waterfront setting.

If you're in search of fine dining, you can visit *San San Tropez* or *Mille Fleurs* at the eco-friendly *Mocking Bird Hill Hotel* (east of the *Trident Castle*-see below; http://www.hotelmockingbirdhill.com/) where you will experience terrace dining with a spectacular view of the harbor, and if you haven't spent enough money on dinner, you will have a second chance in their boutique. The hotel's art gallery, *Gallery Carriacou*, offers regular exhibitions focusing on the work of local artists.

Navy Island

Just across the channel from the Titchfield Peninsula, and to your port side as you enter the channel leading into the harbors of Port Antonio, lies 64-acre Navy Island. Originally, the island was given to Governor Lynch of Jamaica for services to the Crown and named Lynch's Island. Later the island was used by the British Navy (hence the name) for barracks and storage in the early 1700s. The island was abandoned by the Royal Navy in 1773 and little remains of the fortifications from the years of their usage of the island.

The island was the destination for Captain Bligh who discharged a cargo of breadfruit here in February of 1793 and careened his vessel in the shallows some six years after being set adrift in the Pacific by mutineers on the *HMS Bounty*. In 1947, Errol Flynn came to Port Antonio and fell in love with Navy Island, purchasing the island to be used as his private retreat for his friends and loves. Here Flynn moored his beloved 118' gaff-rigged schooner *Zaca* and entertained the likes of celebrities such as Rita Hayworth, Tony Curtis, and Jackie Gleason aboard (contrary to rumors, Flynn did not have a house on the island, rather he had a thatch-roofed cabin built around a tree near his schooner).

One of the rumors concerning Flynn and Navy Island claims that Flynn lost the island in a poker game less than ten years after he acquired the island (other rumors claim that Flynn won the island the same way). Flynn was responsible for planting the distinctive low row of beautiful Royal Palms on the island.

In later years, the island's *Admiralty Club* and some associated villas flourished until 1992 when the island was abandoned following an employee rebellion against lessee Harry Eiler. Another rumor alleges that the island is today owned by actor Louis Gossett Jr., but if that's so, Mr. Gossett has yet to do much with it as the infrastructure still appears slowly to be decaying as of this writing.

Discovering Port Antonio

The busy little town of Port Antonio boasts several fine examples of Victorian architecture as you'll find when you stroll up *Gideon Avenue* and visit the Titchfield area. On the grounds of the *Titchfield High School* are the old cannons of *Fort George*, built by the British. A few steps from the marina is the old train station where you will find the *Portland Art Gallery* presenting the work of a number of Jamaican artists.

The *Port Antonio Crafts Market* on *West Street* is a great spot to pick up locally produced crafts and artwork, paintings, straw work, leather goods, and carvings, all sold by "hagglers," the local word for street vendors. As with most markets, bargaining is a way of life here and overly aggressive venders are not uncommon. *City Centre Plaza* on *Harbour Street* offers duty-free crystal, china, and jewelry while *St. George's Village* on *West Street* and *Harbour Street* has several nice eateries and gift shops. There's a post office on *West Street* across from the clock tower and the police dock.

On Folly Point Peninsula, on the eastern side of the entrance channel leading into *East Harbour*, you'll find an historic house that stands as a tribute to a lost love. *The Folly* was built in 1902 for Alfred Mitchell, an American banker, and was one of the grandest mansions in all of Jamaica. Mitchell built the mansion for his sweetheart who could not come to Jamaica and with nobody to inhabit the house, it quickly fell into disrepair. In 1935, the roof collapsed due to the use of saltwater in the concrete mix (the reason it was called *Folly*), and the once grand mansion was left to decay to nature's forces. Today little remains standing, a few pillars and portions of a staircase. But even the remains of this once ornate manor are an attraction, the ruins were featured in music videos by Shabba Banks and Lauryn Hill.

Also located here is the 130 year old *Folly Lighthouse*, one of the oldest working lighthouses in the Caribbean and visible as far as 28 miles out to sea. The light gives the *Errol Flynn Marina* the distinction of being the only marina in the Caribbean that has a marked and buoyed entrance channel and a lighthouse. The lighthouse is a great spot for photos, especially if the heavy seas are running. Lighthouse keeper Lincoln Ward (876-447-2703) will welcome you and be happy to be your guide.

A short distance east of Port Antonio is the *Trident Castle*, now the *Trident Hotel* (http://castleportantonio.com/). The castle was constructed in the 1970s as the home for German Baroness Zigi Fami who had huge land holdings in the area. Falling on hard times, the Baroness was forced to sell the structure and the new owners began to indulge their creative urges in elaborate additions. The huge hotel cannot be mistaken; it looks just like a castle with huge towers topped by pointed roofs.

To the east of Port Antonio you find the beaches of *Frenchman's Cove* (three miles east of Porti), *San San Beach*, *Dragon Bay*, *Winnifred*, and *Boston Beach*. *Frenchman's Cove* and its stunning beach is set amid a lush tropical garden, but the ruins of a 60-year old resort stand in tribute to a bygone era when this was the playground of the rich and famous. Today though, *Frenchman's Cove* is host to an annual all day-all-inclusive party that lures party monsters from all over the island every October.

If you enjoy golf, you'll be happy to know there is an 18-hole course just across the road from *Frenchman's Cove*. Two miles east of *Frenchman's Cove* is *San San Beach*. Here you can visit Monkey Island (sometimes shown as Pelew Island-a water taxi will take you to the island and supply you with lunch and rum punch for US$40 per person: 876-993-3209; local fishermen can often be hired to take you to Monkey Island for about US$10 per person). *Low Bridge Place Restaurant & Bar* is located near *San San Beach*. Owned by a Jamaica couple, this offers true Jamaican cuisine at its finest. Do not, I repeat, do not attempt to anchor overnight off *San San Beach*, it's a good day stop, but not for overnight.

The nearby *Blue Lagoon*, once called simply *Blue Hole*, was made famous by the 1980 movie of the same name although the movie was not filmed here, it was filmed entirely in Fiji. Enclosed by tall cliffs, the water of the *Blue Lagoon* looks (and is often touted as being...) bottomless due to its dark blue

Rafting on the *Río Grande*

hue, but it is really only about 180'-200' deep. Here you can snorkel the *Blue Lagoon Reef* or simply swim through the cold mineral water bubbles that flow to the surface amid the lush flora along the shore. If you visit the *Blue Lagoon Restaurant* you can view the photos of many celebrities who have dined there as you yourself sample their authentic Jamaican dishes (with live music on the weekends).

Nearby *Dragon Bay* is the site where parts of the movie *Cocktail* were filmed at the *Dragon Bay Hotel*. A mile to the east is *Winnifred's*, sometimes called *Fairy Hill*, which is home to one of the nicest public beaches on the island and the locale depicted in the movie *Club Paradise*. Still a bit further east is *Boston Bay*, a quaint site with fishing boats bobbing in the water, this spot is best known for its jerk pork and chicken, said to be the best on the entire island of Jamaica!

Just west of Port Antonio, *Crystal Springs* is a wildlife and bird sanctuary offering 158 acres of birds, some of which are so tame they'll light on your hand. If you hike down to the *Spanish River* you can visit a waterfall with a spring fed pool ideal for swimming. A bit under three miles southeast of Porti are the *Nonsuch Caves* where you can examine fossilized sea life and evidence of Pre-Columbian Jamaican Arawaks. *Athenry Gardens* is nearby with great views and lots and lots of tropical flora. About ten miles west of Porti at the *Daniels River Gorge*, you'll find the *Somerset Falls*, where you can climb a concrete stairway (slick!) that leads up the 400' falls. About 45 minutes east of Porti you'll find the famous *Reach Falls*, the site of a *Playboy* magazine shoot in the past.

One of the best days you could spend in the Port Antonio area would be to raft down the *Río Grande River*. Here you can take a 2½-hour trip down the river, passing banana tree after banana tree and entering the *Blue Mountains* through a narrow pass called *Lover's Lane*, or *Lover's Rock*. Errol Flynn actually got this business going when he noticed how Jamaicans would pole small, bamboo rafts loaded with bananas down to the coast for shipment. In the 1950s, this ladies man began floating down the river with young women and named the narrow section *Lover's Lane* for obvious reasons. Soon cooing tourists were rafting down the river and local raftsmen poled their rafts of bamboo like Caribbean gondoliers. There are other rivers in Jamaica that you can raft down, but the Río Grande started it all. Alongside

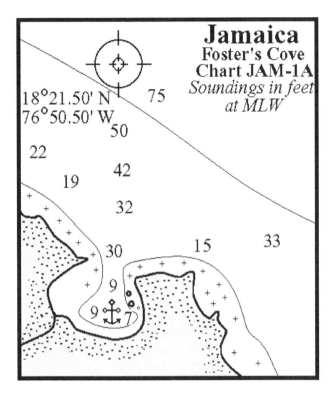

Jamaica
Foster's Cove
Chart JAM-1A
Soundings in feet at MLW

18°21.50' N
76°50.50' W

the river is the *Rafter's Restaurant* with a bar and souvenir shop.

The *Blue Mountains* should not be missed on your visit to Port Antonio. This 28 mile long range is among the longest in the Caribbean, and one of the highest at 7,402' at the highest point, *Blue Mountain Peak*. Here you'll find some of the finest hiking in the Caribbean, waterfalls galore, and of course the famous *Blue Mountain Coffee*. Both the *Blue Mountain Range* and the *John Crow Mountains* are national parks, being granted that status in 1993. As you approach Port Antonio from the east or north, your first view of Jamaica will be the *John Crow Mountains* as the *Blue Mountains* lie just west and south.

Foster's Cove

(Salt Bay)
Waypoints
Foster's Cove - ¼ nm N of entrance
18° 21.50' N, 76° 50.50' W

Situated approximately ten miles west of Port Antonio, *Foster's Cove*, often shown as *Salt Bay*, is a small, quiet, and sheltered cove that can be used in prevailing winds but is never to be considered when the wind or seas have any northerly component to them.

Navigational Information
As shown on Chart JAM-1A, a waypoint at 18° 21.50' N, 76° 50.50' W, will place you approximately ¼ nm N of the entrance to the cove. From the waypoint, head south and pass through the 300' wide gap between the conspicuous headlands. Watch out for the rocks on the northeastern shore of the bay. You are likely to see several small fishing boats anchored in the bay.

Once inside you can head as far south as your draft permits to drop your anchor. *Foster's Cove* is quite secluded, there is no town nearby and no amenities.

Port Maria

Waypoints
Port Maria- ¼ nm NE of Cabarita Island
18° 22.50' N, 76° 53.00' W

Just a few miles west of *Salt Bay* is Port Maria where you can anchor in *Port Maria Bay* in settled weather in the lee of Cabarita Island.

Navigational Information
As shown on Chart JAM-1B, a waypoint at 18° 22.50' N, 76° 53.00' W, will place you approximately ¼ nm NE of Cabarita Island. From the waypoint head SW until you can round up and anchor south and east of Cabarita Island. Although you can anchor in *Little Bay*, the entrance is narrow and the bay is deep.

What You Will Find Ashore
Lying between the *Othram* and *Pagee Rivers*, Port Maria is the capital of the parish of Saint Mary and was originally named Puerto Santa Maria, the second town established by the Spanish in Jamaica. Once a busy port, today the town is home to some 7,500 people and occasionally suffers from flooding of the *Othram River*.

On a headland between *Little Bay* and *Port Maria Bay* sits *Fort Haldane*, built in 1759 and named after General George Haldane, then Governor of Jamaica. The fort was constructed to protect Port Maria from Spanish raids and used as a garrison to keep the slaves of Port Maria under control.

Fort Haldane had a role in the famous Tacky's Rebellion On Easter Sunday, 1760. On this date, a runaway slave named Tacky (a Maroon of Ashanti descent), along with a group of slaves from nearby plantations, murdered their masters and killed the guards at Fort Haldane and taking arms and ammunition. In 1780, a hurricane destroyed most

Cabarita Island, Port Maria

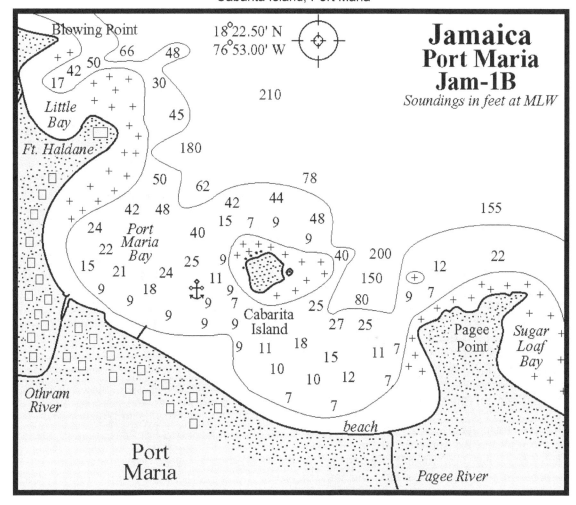

of the fort and the decision to abandon the fort was made and the garrison moved to Ocho Rios. Parts of the garrison building and the unique rotating cannons are all that are left today.

Nearby is Sir Noel Coward's 7-acre estate, *Firefly*, which once served as the home of Sir Henry Morgan. Other buildings worth visiting in Port Maria include the St. Mary's Parish Church, built in 1861 (the church won an award in 1987, Heritage in Architecture), and the St. Mary courthouse, built in 1820 and which now houses the Port Maria Civic Centre.

Oracabessa Bay

Waypoints
Oracabessa Bay - ½ nm N of point E of bay
18° 25.50' N, 76° 56.40' W

Oracabessa Bay - ¼ nm NW of ent. old marina
18° 24.85' N, 76° 56.78' W

Oracabessa Bay - .1 nm NW of anchorage ent.
18° 24.50' N, 76° 57.05' W

Navigational Information
Heading west from Port Antonio you will need to keep a sharp eye out, you'll find numerous fish traps close to shore in less than 100 fathoms of water. Before taking up a course for the entrance to *Oracabessa Bay* you must first clear three points of land, the first being Sim Head (sometimes shown as Ship Head or Ship Rock), the headland just a couple of miles west of Navy Island. Once clear of Sim Head you can head to a waypoint at 18° 25.50' N, 76° 53.00' W, which will place you 1½ miles north of Galina Point, the next point of land you must clear (you can clear Galina Point ¼ mile off and clear all dangers).

Once clear of Galina Point you should head west to clear the point north/northeast of *Oracabessa Bay*. A waypoint at 18° 25.50' N, 76° 56.40' W, will place you approximately ½ mile north of the point in deep water. Once clear of the point you can follow the shoreline southwest to head for a waypoint at 18° 24.50' N, 76° 57.05' W, which places you .1 nm northwest of the entrance channel to the anchorage in *Oracabessa Bay* on Chart JAM-2.

From this waypoint you may head generally southwest, paralleling the shoreline at least ¼ mile off, to enter the small but protected anchorage by keeping between the reef to port and the jetty to

starboard. Some charts show a lit range on the entrance (93° 15'), but when I surveyed the harbor in 2006 it was not in operation nor could I find someone who knew when it worked last or when it will again be operating. Once inside the small basin anchor wherever your draft permits and if northerly swells are forecast you'll be better off in the northernmost part of the small anchorage area.

In days past there was a marina in Oracabessa, *Oracabessa Marina*, just south of Santa Maria Island. The marina is just a memory now but the narrow entrance channel leads to a tiny protected harbor that is blocked by a small bridge and today only permits dinghy exploration. As shown on Chart JAM-2, a waypoint at 18° 24.85' N, 76° 56.78' W, will place you approximately ¼ nautical mile northwest of the deeper water that leads to the entrance channel. From the waypoint parallel the shoreline of the small peninsula to your south as you head south/southeast to the mouth of the narrow creek that lead to Santa Maria Island. There may or may not be a small white buoy to mark the opening. Remember, this is for dinghies only.

What You'll Find Ashore
Oracabessa Bay, from the Spanish *Orocabeza* (Golden Head), is best known as the location of *Goldeneye*, the home of author Ian Fleming, the creator of the James Bond novels. Fleming first came to Jamaica in 1943 when he was serving in the British *Naval Intelligence Division* in the *Blue Mountains*. In 1947, he paid £2,000 for a piece of land on the northern coast of Jamaica near *Oracabessa Bay* that was a racetrack at one time. Fleming constructed a simple yet elegant beach house to be used as his winter home and named it *Goldeneye* after a botched anti-Nazi *NID* operation which Fleming himself had been involved. Fleming and author Noel Coward immediately found themselves in a competition of sorts as Coward stressed that his Fleming's *Goldeneye* was inferior to Coward's own *Firefly* overlooking Port Maria. *Firefly* sits on a hill about two miles west of Port Maria and was Noel Coward's home from its construction in 1956, until Coward's death in 1973, (he died in his bedroom and is buried on the property. *Firefly* was built upon the site of an ancient Arawak settlement where many artifacts were found and which later was used as a lookout by the pirate Sir Henry Morgan (it is said that you can see Cuba on a clear day from this vantage point).

Over the years *Goldeneye* played host to numerous celebrities from Truman Capote to

Oracabessa Bay

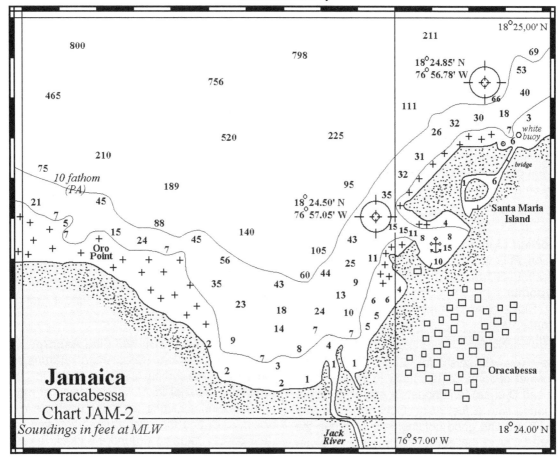

Jamaica
Oracabessa
Chart JAM-2
Soundings in feet at MLW

Evelyn Waugh while Fleming and his wife, Blanche Blackwell, mother of Jamaican music entrepreneur Chris Blackwell, enjoyed being the heart of a glamorous jet-set crowd. Finally, in 1952, Fleming, who now had a new wife, Lady Anne Rothermere, began his series of James Bond novels with *Casino Royale*. It is said that Fleming took the name of his hero, James Bond, from the author of *Birds of the West Indies*. Sadly, Ian Fleming died on August 12, 1964, just before the release of what some consider the greatest James Bond movie ever, *Goldfinger*. Today, both *Goldeneye* and *Blue Harbour* are exquisite resorts with *Goldeneye* probably taking the crown as Jamaica's most exclusive, and one of the biggest attractions in Oracabessa is *James Bond Beach* where you can rent a PWC, take a helicopter tour of the area (http://jamaicahelicopterservices.com/), enjoy a horseback ride, or simply relax at a beach bar/grill.

A short walk east of the anchorage area brings you to the heart of downtown Oracabessa where you'll find a roundabout in town that serves as a market and central location for taxis.

Dining
For fine dining try the *Sea Palm* restaurant in the *Golden Seas Hotel* were you'll be served heaping portions of excellent Jamaican dishes, pastas, kebabs, and seafood. Just cross the street is *Big Mamma's Jerk Centre* specializing in...what else? Jerk pork and chicken! But for my liking, I prefer *Total Delight* located at the downtown market for the finest, authentic Jamaican dishes. On a hill outside of town is *Dor's Sea Cliff Fish Pot* with the best seafood in the area. If you desire ice cream, there's a *Devon House I Scream* shop located in Oracabessa.

Ocho Rios

Important Lights
Beacon, Fl G 5s
Beacon, Fl G 1.5s
Waypoints
Ocho Rios - ¾ nm N of marked entrance Channel
18° 25.50' N, 77° 07.00' W

Ocho Rios (Spanish for *Eight Rivers*), the garden center of Jamaica, is usually just called Ochi (pronounced O-chee), and boasts a nice little harbor and a marina with a fuel dock; Ochi is also a Port of Entry. You'll find good holding here although the waters are busy in the daytime with jet skis, water skiers, and touristy charter catamarans going to and fro. Ochi and St. Ann Parish make up the spiritual center of Jamaica, home to the likes of Bob Marley, Marcus Garvey, and Winston Rodney, as well as a tourist center that is fast becoming one of Jamaica's finest and most popular, in fact, the first exclusive tourist hotel on the island, the great house of the *Shaw Park* sugar plantation, was constructed here in 1923.

Navigational Information
From *Oracabessa Bay* you can parallel the shoreline westward staying at least 1 mile offshore, or head to a waypoint at 18° 26.30' N, 77° 02.40' W, which places you 1 mile north of Frankfort Point. From this position you can again follow the shoreline west or head to a waypoint at 18° 25.50' N, 77° 07.00' W, which will place you approximately ¾ mile north of the marked entrance channel as shown on Chart JAM-3. From this waypoint you can head south until you are able to pick up the marker buoys for the channel entrance and follow them in a southeast direction until you can round the cruise ship dock and enter *Ocho Rios Bay*. Sometimes, if the cruise ship docks are full, you'll have to swing wide to the east to round the stern or bow of one of the cruise ships, you'll have good water to do this. Conversely, if the cruise ship docks are empty, you can pass between the dock and the mooring bollards in deep water. Occasionally, when the cruise ship docks are full, you'll see a cruise ship tied up at the more commercial *Reynold's Pier*. The holding, sand and mud, is good in *Ocho Rios Bay*. If you need to get out of northerly swells it's best to anchor as far north in the bay as possible in the lee of the jetty. When northerly swells are running the jetty and the offshore reefs protect the bay for the most part though some swells do find their way in from the northwest and the bay can be very uncomfortable; at these times you're better off at *Oracabessa Bay*.

There is a small, protected marina inside a cove at the southwestern end of *Ocho Rios Bay* as shown on the chart. *Ocho Rios Marina* offers bow or stern-to dockage with electricity, water, and a fuel dock with diesel and gasoline.

What You Will Find Ashore
Jamaica's *North Coast Highway* runs along the shore here becoming *DeCosta Drive* in Ocho Rios and runs parallel to *Main Street* where most of the shops, vendor's stalls, and the market are located. In town you'll find the main bus station and numerous taxi drivers hanging around the clock tower and car

park to take you here and there. You'll find many hotels in the area, several of which are all-inclusive. The town is tourist oriented, so don't expect a lot of boater's amenities save for the one small marina.

The top attraction in the Ocho Rios area is, without a doubt, *Dunn's River Falls*, located just west of town. *Dunn's River Falls* is a series of waterfalls that cascade down from the hills to the sea, in fact, when you leave Ocho Rios heading west by sea, you will pass by the final falls as it empties into the sea. You can climb the falls, there is an entrance fee, and a sure-footed guide will lead you and carry all your cameras just in case you should slip as you climb the falls in groups, working your way upwards hand-in-hand.

Dining

There are several small mini-markets in town, and even a *Devon House I Scream* ice cream parlor as well as a *Burger King* and a *KFC*. For locally flavored dining, fresh seafood, visit the outdoors cookers on *Fisherman's Beach* (see Chart JAM-3) just west of town. In town are dozens and dozens of fine eateries, everything from Chinese and Pizza to Indian, Thai, and Vegan cuisine. To the right of the cruise ship docks is the huge craft market while *Main Street* is home to 11 shopping malls.

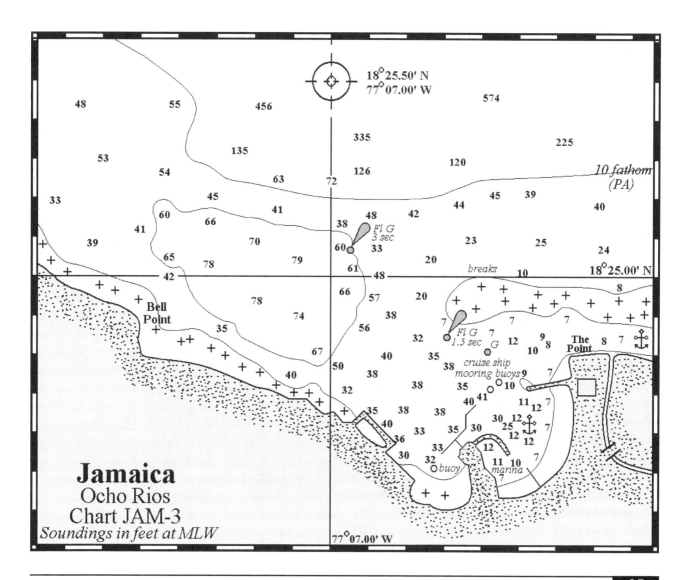

Jamaica
Ocho Rios
Chart JAM-3
Soundings in feet at MLW

Ocho Rios

The marina at Ocho Rios

St. Ann's Bay

Important Lights
Channel entrance W, Fl R 3s
Channel entrance E, Fl G 3s
Waypoints
St. Ann's Point - 1 nm N of
18° 27.50' N, 77° 10.25' W

St. Ann's Bay - ½ nm NNE of entrance channel
18° 27.40' N, 77° 11.75' W

The harbor at St. Ann's is not one of the best anchorages along the northern shore of Jamaica, but it does offer a bit of refuge in settled weather, or in periods of light east-southeast winds and seas. When Columbus landed here in 1494 he named the bay *Santa Gloria* and in 1510 the Spanish built their first settlement in Jamaica just outside of St. Ann's and named it *Sevilla Nueva*, now known simply as Seville.

Navigational Information
Heading west from Ocho Rios you must clear a small headland before you can take up your course for *St. Ann's Bay*. I call this un-named point St. Ann's Point for lack of a better name, and a waypoint at 18° 27.50' N, 77° 10.25' W, will place you approximately one mile north of this point. Be certain that you keep a sharp eye out for reefs and fish traps through here and never try to enter St. Ann's at night.

From the waypoint off St. Ann's Point, you can head for a waypoint at 18° 27.40' N, 77° 11.75' W, which will place you approximately ½ mile north/northeast of the marked entrance channel leading into *St. Ann's Bay* as shown on Chart JAM-4. From this position head generally south/southwest to split the red and green markers where you should be able to pick up the range (lit-193°; never try to enter this

harbor at night) to enter the bay, keeping an eye out for the conspicuous reef to starboard. Keep an eye out for there are shoals to port and starboard upon entry that may be difficult to discern in even good conditions, but when you are between the two outer markers (if they are still there) you can take up a course of 193° and you should be fine, but keep a sharp eye out, both for the shoals and on your depth sounder. You can anchor in the middle of the harbor or just to the east where you'll be in the lee of a reef in prevailing winds.

Another option is to head west once inside the harbor, following the channel of deep water past Reader's Point to anchor in the lee of another shoal area that offers a bit of protection from the west and southwest. There is a small anchorage area to the east of the harbor in the lee of a small cove and reef (holding is fair to good in sand, mud, and rocks), which is reached by threading your way through two small reef systems, and with poor visibility this would be a dangerous passage to say the least, plus, if the wind shifted at night you'd never find your way out. There is a small patch of deeper water to the west of *Lee Reef*. This area should not be considered for an anchorage as it offers no real shelter in prevailing conditions and entry is restricted to a bar with 4' over it a MLW. Never attempt to stay in *St. Ann's Bay* if northerly swells are forecast.

What You Will Find Ashore
The small but lovely town of St. Ann's will delight you with its old-fashioned charm and the Friday and Saturday open-air market on *Main Street* will do its best to separate you from your dollars. The sloping streets of the town house many small shops and eateries that you'll enjoy investigating (that is if you enjoy investigating small shops and "off the beaten

path" diners). In town, the courthouse dominates *Main Street* as it has since its construction in 1860. The *Peter Martyr Church* is the first stone church built in Jamaica, it was constructed by the Spanish in 1524. The public library boasts a large statue of Marcus Garvey (see the chapter *Local Cultures-Rastafarians*) who was born in St. Ann's.

Dining

The two main thoroughfares in St. Ann's are *Main Street* and *Bravo Street*, and located on *Bravo Street* is a nice locally flavored diner called *Square One* serving all kinds of tasty meals and snacks. *The Mug*, one of the best seafood restaurants on the island, is located on the coast highway, and features Wednesday night *Mug Nights* when barbecued chicken and fish is added to the normal menu and the owners keep the place open until 0100. West of town, towards Priory, where you can find all sorts of

snack and jerk vendors on the highway is the *Seafood Specialists*, serving what their name implies.

Discovery Bay

Important Lights
Entrance channel outer W, Fl R 7.5s
Entrance channel outer E, Fl G 7.5s
Entrance channel inner W, Fl R 5s
Entrance channel inner E, Fl G 5s

Waypoints
Discovery Bay - 1½ nm N of entrance channel
18° 28.90' N, 77° 24.28' W

Discovery Bay is home to an immense *Kaiser* bauxite plant which ships the better part of two million tons of bauxite to the U.S. every year. The town of *Discovery Bay* is home to many plant workers, as well as a string of shops, hotels, and eateries along the main road. In all honesty, *Kaiser* does a lot for the local community, they fund all manner of community

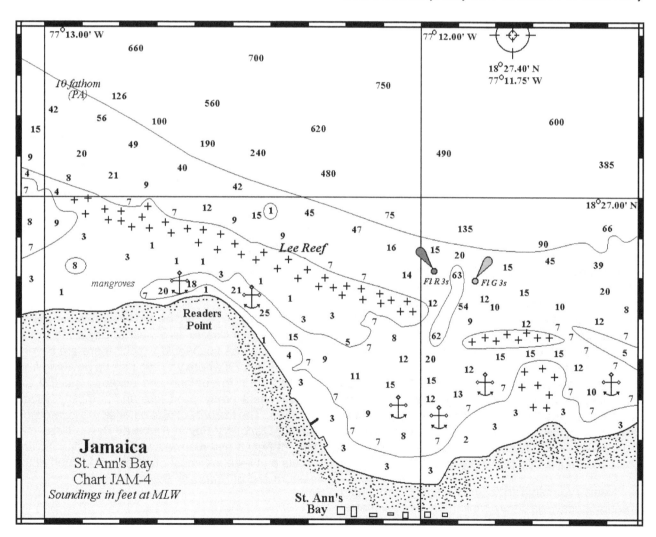

Jamaica
St. Ann's Bay
Chart JAM-4
Soundings in feet at MLW

projects including the annual push cart derby held every August, in fact, most of the push cart scenes in the movie *Cool Runnings* were filmed here.

Navigational Information

Heading west from *St. Ann's Bay* you must first clear Flat Point before making your way to the waypoint that places you outside of the channel leading into *Discovery Bay*. Staying at least one mile offshore, head for a waypoint at 18° 30.00' N, 77° 18.50' W, which will place you approximately 1¾ miles north of Flat Point. From this position you can take up your course to the waypoint at the entrance to *Discovery Bay*. A waypoint at 18° 28.90' N, 77° 24.28' W, will place you approximately 1¾ miles north of the marked entrance channel leading into *Discovery Bay* as shown on Chart JAM-5. From this waypoint steer approximately 193° to pick up the first two outer markers. There is a working lighted range here as this bay gets a considerable amount of commercial traffic exporting bauxite from the docks on the southern shore of the bay. A very good landmark here is the huge orange-stained dome that sits just west of the orange-stained commercial docks (the docks here were cast as the base for Dr. Julius No in the James Bond movie entitled *Dr. No*).

In prevailing winds the best spot to anchor is along the eastern shore of the bay and just north of *Puerto Seco Beach*. There is a *Customs* office just west of the commercial docks, but the officers there are not used to dealing with cruisers and may suggest you clear at *Montego Bay* or Ocho Rios instead.

What You Will Find Ashore

Just across the road from *Puerto Seco Beach* is a small shopping center, easy to access by landing your dinghy on the beach which is usually crowded on the weekends. Here you'll find several shops, a bakery, and a Chinese food takeout. Nearby is the *West Indies Marine Research Laboratory* (http://www.mona.uwi.edu/cms/dbml.htm) where the only decompression chamber in Jamaica is located. On the western shore of the bay is the open-air museum known as *Columbus Park* which focuses on Columbus' landing here as well as craft sales. The very straight road leading away from the park was used by ganga smugglers in the 1970s as an airstrip. Government installed concrete bollards on the sides of the road put a stop to this practice.

Nearby you can visit the *Green Grotto Caves* (http://greengrottocavesja.com/) which lie approximately two miles from the spot where Columbus is said to have landed in 1494. These limestone caves have a lot of history in them, first serving as shelter and religious site for pre-Columbian Arawaks, the caves were later used as a hideout by the Spanish fleeing the British in 1655, and by runaway slaves in the 18th century. During World War I and World War II the caves were used by smugglers running guns to Cuba. Here you will descend over a hundred feet into the earth through passageways and caverns where you'll come to the *Green Grotto* itself, a wonderful, deep underground lake of clear, green water.

If you take highway *B3* inland from *Discovery Bay* and take a left in the small town of Alexandria, you'll come to the *Bob Marley Centre and Mausoleum* in Marley's hometown of Nine Mile. Bob Marley's resting place is the number one tourist destination in the parish of St. Ann. On site is a vegetarian restaurant as well as a gift shop selling Bob Marley memorabilia. After you pay your entrance fee and sign in you will be escorted by a Rasta guide through the compound to visit Bob's house, single bed, BBQ pit, and "meditation stone." If you wish to stay overnight there's a small hotel just across from the compound where you can get a room for about US$40 per night. If you have a tent you may camp free inside the compound. If you're there on Feb. 6, Bob Marley's birthday, you can help celebrate the occasion with other festive souls.

Provisions

Vegetarians will want to visit *Afiya*, a health food store that also serves delicious vegan dishes. There are several supermarkets located in the *Runaway Bay* area, the best of which is *A&B Value Mart*, the largest one on the strip and it also has a pharmacy on site (located by the gas station).

Dining

The best places to dine are located in the hotels, some are all-inclusive so expect to pay a fee to use their facility. As you would expect, there are several roadside stands where you can pick up anything from roasted meat to seafood and ackee. The *CD Bar & Grill* offers pretty good fare and is mostly a local hangout. The majority of nice eateries are located just east of *Discovery Bay* at *Runaway Bay*, a three-mile strip of beach and highway where you'll find several hotels and eateries, most of which are located at the eastern end of *Runaway Bay* at Salem.

Discovery Bay

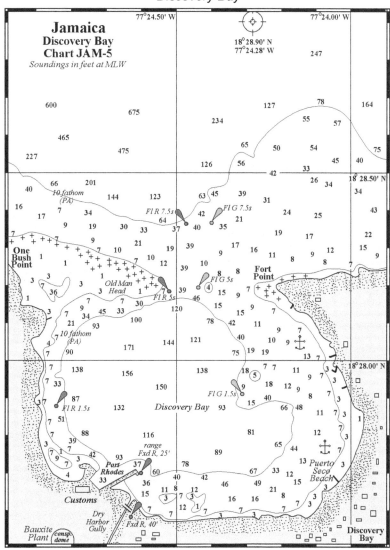

Jamaica
Discovery Bay
Chart JAM-5
Soundings in feet at MLW

Rio Bueno

Waypoints

Rio Bueno - ¾ nm N of harbor entrance
18° 29.00' N, 77° 27.35' W

Less than three miles to the west of *Discovery Bay* lies a small but deep bay at the mouth of the Río Bueno where you'll find the town of the same name. Río Bueno, the site of some scenes in the Anthony Quinn movie, *A High Wind in Jamaica*, may best be described as being over its former glory. The buildings in town, many of which date to the 1700s, are decaying and the biggest thing the town has going for it is a huge animal feed factory.

When Christopher Columbus discovered Jamaica in 1494, it is believed he anchored overnight in this small harbor as it fits so well the description of the horseshoe-shaped bay that the Admiral of All Oceans describes in his log. For the cruiser however, the harbor offers little protection except in winds from east through south to west and is no place to be if northerly swells are forecast, it can be a deathtrap for small vessels in the winter months.

Navigational Information

When approaching from *Discovery Bay* you may follow the shoreline westward staying a minimum of one mile off to avoid reefs to make your way to the waypoint that will lead you into *Rio Bueno*. You can also work your way to a waypoint at 18° 29.00' N, 77° 26.35' W, which will place you approximately 1.5 miles north of the point, from this position you may then take up a course to the *Río Bueno* waypoint at 18° 29.00' N, 77° 27.35' W. From this waypoint you can head south to enter the harbor at the mouth of the *Río Bueno* as shown on Chart JAM-6. As you approach the mouth of the bay, keep an eye out for

the shoal on the western side of the harbor, it only has 5' of water over it. In prevailing winds the best anchorage is along the eastern shore of the bay, and don't forget, this harbor is a deathtrap in strong northerly swells.

What You Will Find Ashore

There is a bit of history in *Río Bueno*, just east of town you'll find a bridge over the *Río Bueno* that was originally built by the Spanish and now is the border between Trelawney Parish and St. Ann Parish. Closer to town are the remains of a British-built fort (1778) named after then British Secretary of War, Henry Dundas. On the western side of town is the biggest, and some may say only draw to *Río Bueno*, the *Gallery Joe James*. Set in a 17th century warehouse, the building houses an art gallery, hotel, restaurant (*The Lobster Pot*-great Sunday brunch), and studio for Joe James, a well-known Jamaican artist who's usually around to guide you through his gallery and sell you his works. Also west of town is

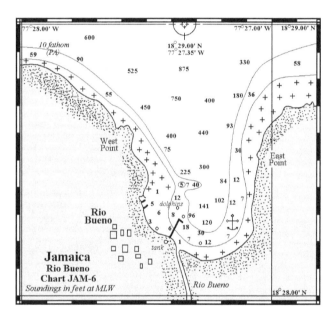

Port Rhodes, *Discovery Bay*

Cruise ship dock at Falmouth

the *Arawak Sunset Bar* where the owner will take you on a tour of the small cave located there.

Two miles outside of town is the *Grand Lido Bravo* (http://www.grandlidoresorts.com/), a silly all-inclusive resort that was constructed to resemble a "real" Jamaican town including a town square. Here you'll find first rate accommodations, gyms, pools, spas, a 9-hole golf course, several bars and restaurants, and even a special adult only nudist section. Just a bit west, between the small towns of Braco and Duncans is a rather unique spot, *The Plane Stop*, an open-air jerk center set amid the wrecked fuselage of an old drug smuggling plane.

Falmouth Harbour

Important Lights
Falmouth Harbour Light, Fxd R
Rose Hall Lighthouse, Fl (5) W 30s
Waypoints
Falmouth Harbour - ½ nm NE of
18° 30.35' N, 77° 38.15' W

The town of Falmouth is architecturally pleasing with an interesting collection of Georgian buildings while the bay offers good protection from northerly winds and seas and boasts two marinas (provided you don't draw too much), *Glistening Waters* and *Fisherman's Inn*, sometimes called *Rose's by the Sea*.

Since the last edition of this guide, Falmouth has become a major cruise ship port along Jamaica's northern coast. There is now a deep and well-marked entrance channel leading to a huge new wharf (see chart and photo).

Falmouth is the capital of Trelawney Parish (since 1790) and is named after Sir William Trelawney, the parish governor during the plantation era when 88 sugar plantations bought and sold slaves on the same Falmouth docks from which they exported their sugar. Where today's market is located there once stood a cage used as a jail for drunken sailors of two centuries ago.

The advent of steam powered ships signaled the end of prosperity for Falmouth as its harbor was too shallow for these larger ships. Before long sugar was diverted to other ports and by the end of the 19th century Falmouth was little more than a ghost town. Falmouth made a bit of an economic comeback as the marketplace for Trelawney Parish when the *Albert*

George Market was constructed in 1896 and is still a hive of activity on Wednesdays, the traditional market day in Falmouth. Scenes from the movie *The Wide Sargasso Sea* were filmed in and around Falmouth.

What You Will Find Ashore
Glistening Waters Marina (http://www.glisteningwaters.com/) has a very good restaurant/bar (good seafood-some say the best on the island of Jamaica) and sits right on the edge of the main road between Ocho Rios and *Montego Bay* so catching a bus isn't too difficult. The restaurant is one of the best seafood restaurants on the northern coast and the marina offers several small charter boats suitable for night cruising in the phosphorescent waters of the *Luminous Lagoon* (officially called the *Oyster Bay Phosphorous Lagoon*) where fish leave luminescent trails when they swim around your boat as tiny organisms light up when the water is agitated, a swim here will be an unforgettable experience. Next door, *Fisherman's Inn* has rooms to rent, a nice restaurant, and offers night tours to the *Luminous Lagoon* (half-price if you dine at their restaurant). If you'd like to slowly ride a bamboo raft down a river, the nearby *Martha Brae River* is the place for you. Nearby, *Time N Place* is a good little beach grill.

In town you'll find a hardware store, *The Leaf of Life*, a good grocery store, *Super S Plus*, and if you're looking for a place to dine, you have many to choose from. *Juicie Patties* (http://fenntechltd.com/juicipatties/) is part of a chain and has a franchise in Falmouth, and if they don't serve up a pattie to your specs, try *Nice and Spicy* on the square in town.

Montego Bay

Important Lights
Montego Bay Light #1, Fl R
Montego Bay Light #2, Fl R 5s
Montego Bay Light #3, Fl R 3s
Montego Bay Light #4, Fl R 5s
Montego Bay Light #5, Fl R 3s
Montego Bay Light #6, Fxd G
Waypoints:
Montego Bay Point - 1 nm N of
18° 32.00' N, 77° 53.70' W

Montego Bay - ¼ nm N of entrance channel
18° 28.30' N, 77° 56.20' W

Montego Bay, or as it's better known, *Mobay*, is the second biggest city on the island of Jamaica, the largest city on the north coast, and the undisputed heart of the island's tourism industry. Lying on the shores of *Montego Bay*, the area was originally called *Bahía de Manteca*, *Bay of Lard*, by the Spanish due to the lard manufacturing that went on centuries ago when wild boar roamed the brush and hillsides around *Montego Bay*. *Montego Bay* prospered for a while as a sugar and banana exporting port, but those days are long gone, the bananas now being shipped out of Kingston and Port Antonio.

The area grew as a resort based on *Doctor's Cave Beach* when celebrities and socialites from all over the world flocked to frolic in the mineral-spring fed waters that fed the bay. Today numerous hotels overflow with tourists on a daily basis who come here to enjoy *Doctor's Cave Beach*, *Walter Fletcher Beach*, *Cornwall Beach*, *Tropical Beach*, and *Rose Hall Beach*. *Walter Fletcher Beach* is home to the *Aquasol Theme Park* and is a very popular destination in its own right, and *Rose Hall* is home to the *Rose Hall Great House*, once the home of Annie Palmer, a well known witch who murdered three husbands and numerous slave lovers.

Cruisers must bear in mind that the waters of *Montego Bay*, from the airport to the *Great River* west of town (includes *Bogue Lagoon*) are now part of the *Montego Bay Marine Park* and spearfishing

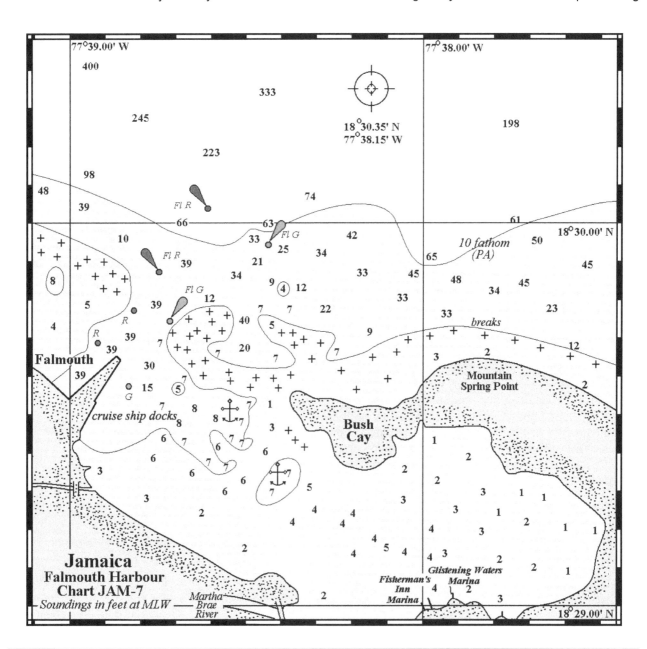

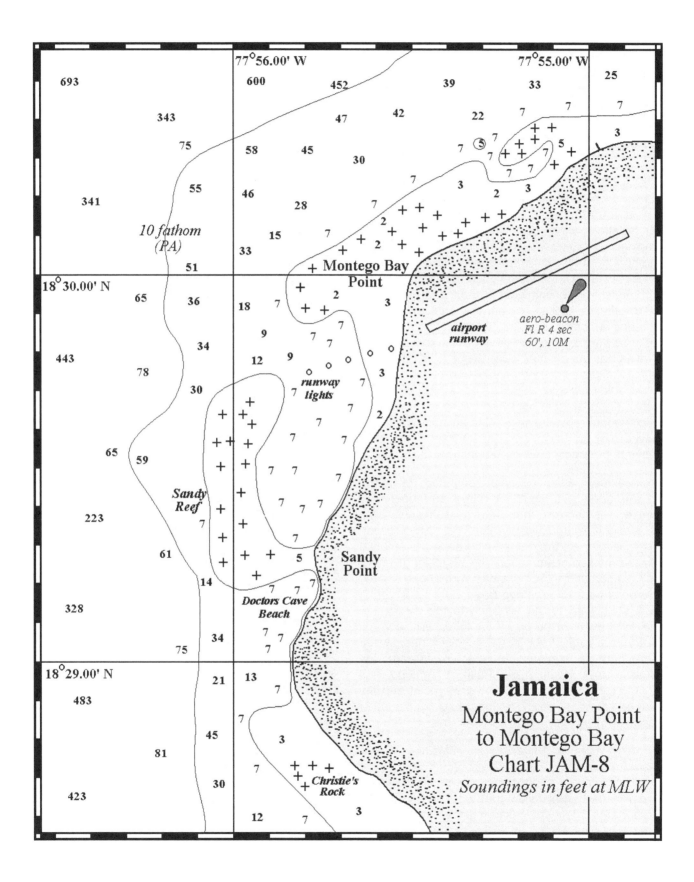

77°56.00' W   77°55.00' W

693   600   452   39   33   25

343   47   42   22   7   7   7

75   58   45   30   7   5   7   3

55   46   28   7   3   2   3

341   15   7   2   7

10 fathom
(PA)   33   7   2

51   Montego Bay Point

18°30.00' N   65   36   18   7   2   3

34   9   7

443   78   12   9   7   2   airport
runway   aero-beacon
Fl R 4 sec
60', 10M

30   runway
lights   7   3

65   59   7   2

Sandy
Reef   7   7

223   7   7   7

61   7   7

14   5   Sandy
Point

328   Doctors Cave
Beach   7   7

34   7   7
75   7

18°29.00' N   21   13

483   7

45   7

81   3

30   7   Christie's
Rock

423   12   7   3

Jamaica
Montego Bay Point
to Montego Bay
Chart JAM-8
Soundings in feet at MLW

is illegal. For more information you can phone 876-952-5619 or visit their office at *Pier One Marina* (http://pieronejamaica.com/marina/, 876-952-2452). However, the *Jamaican Coast Guard* has informed me that you may fish in the anchorage basin off the yacht club.

Navigational Information

There are two good anchorages in the *Montego Bay* area, one is located by the *Pier One Marina*, and one is just off the *Montego Bay Yacht Club* dock. These anchorages are fine in normal conditions, but I urge you to move to *Bogue Lagoon* for protection during strong winter storms or when a hurricane or tropical storm threatens. During the winter, when strong winds and seas from the west through the north affect the island, the anchorages mentioned can be anywhere from uncomfortable to untenable. There is no offshore reef to prevent the large rollers from entering *Montego Bay* and these anchorages can become very agitated and even untenable at times. Waves can break right over the jetty at *Pier One Marina*, and a *seiche* action develops at the *Montego Bay Yacht Club* when incoming waves bounce off the concrete cruise ship docks and echo into the small basin where most cruising boats anchor. If you are aware that contrary seas are forecast you should move to the safety of *Bogue Lagoon* for the duration.

Montego Bay, although bounded by reefs to the north and south, is large and open. If you're approaching from the west the entrance is straightforward passing north of the Freeport Peninsula where the cruise ships dock and entering via the marked channel from the waypoint given. If you're approaching from the east, you'll need to clear the point north of *Montego Bay* before turning your bow southward to the entrance to the harbor. A waypoint at 18° 32.00' N, 77° 53.70' W, will place you over a mile north of *Montego Bay* Point in deep water. From here you may head more southwestward (see Chart JAM-8, *Montego Bay* Point to *Montego Bay*) until you can head south for the waypoint and the harbor entrance, easily distinguished by the outer green buoy as shown on Chart JAM-9.

A waypoint at 18° 28.30' N, 77° 56.20' W, will place you approximately ¼ mile northwest of the marked entrance channel as shown on the chart. From the waypoint follow the large buoys into the harbor area where you can turn to the east to anchor near *Pier One Marina* or to the south to head into the basin by the *Montego Bay Yacht Club*. In the northeastern corner of the harbor at *Montego Bay* is a small jetty enclosed anchorage that is often crowded with local boats, and which is also home to *Pier One Marina*. The anchorage offers good holding and easy access to a grocery store and fast food restaurants just across the main road.

On the southwestern side of the harbor at *Montego Bay* is the *Freeport Peninsula*, sometimes called *Montego Freeport*, which has been developed from what were once mangrove islands. Here you'll find the cruise ship docks, the *Montego Bay Yacht Club*, and the *Montego Bay Free Zone*, where a great many products such as T-shirts are produced for export. As you head south/southwest past the cruise ship docks to the basin by the *MBYC*, you'll pass several lighted buoys, one just off the yacht club which has a series of orange floating markers trailing it. When American cruise ships are in port you must pass west of these orange markers, thanks to 9-11. Don't worry, there's plenty of water there.

You can anchor in the small basin just off the yacht club docks in 6'-20' of water with fair to good holding in a thick sand/mud bottom. Don't try to anchor here in a strong blow, you're much better off in *Bogue Lagoon* as evidenced by a few boats on the beach at the southern end of the basin. Boats at the yacht club are moored bow or stern to and must use their own anchors (use caution if you're told to anchor on the eastern side of the dock, it can get pretty rough there during the daytime if the easterly trade winds are up. If you haven't cleared in the yacht club office will alert *Customs* and *Immigration* for you.

What You Will Find Ashore

The land area that we call *Montego Bay* is divided into three distinct parts; the crowded streets of the city of *Montego Bay* itself, the "hip-strip," that 1½ mile stretch of road from town northward past *Doctor's Cave Beach* and on out to the *Dead End Bar*, and the outlying areas where you'll find homes, hotels, and villas along the beaches and perched on the hillsides.

If you follow *Howard Cooke Boulevard* into town you'll pass the *Crafts Market* on *Harbour Street*, and come to *Highway A-1*, also called *Barnett Street* (two other craft markets exist in *Mobay*, one in the hotel area, next to the *Fantasy Hotel*, and the other on *Fort Street*, the site of an old 17th century fort). As *Barnett Street* reaches the downtown area it becomes *St.*

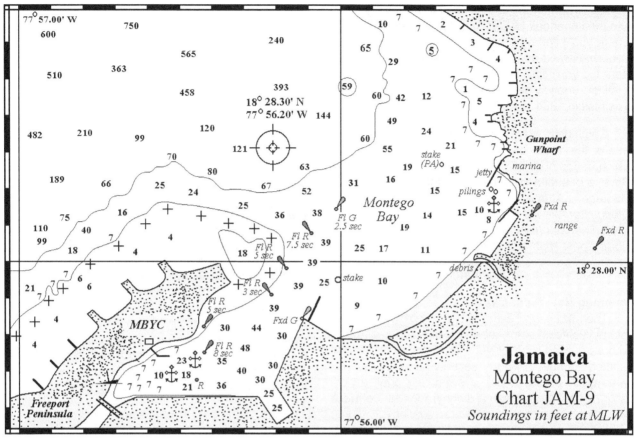

77° 57.00' W   750
600   240
           565
        363
510   393
      458   18° 28.30' N
              77° 56.20' W   144
          120
482   210   99
       70
189   66   25   80
         25   24
       16   25
75   40   +   +   +
110   7   4
99   18   4   4
    7 +
21 7 6   6
  7 4
    +   4
      MBYC
    +   4
Freeport
Peninsula

10
65   7   2
   29   3
60 42   4
   49   7 7
60 55 24   7 5
      21   4
  stake 19 15   7
  (PA)   7
31 16   15   Gunpoint
Montego   jetty Wharf
Bay   14 15 10 marina
    19   8 pilings
25 17 11   7
      debris   Fxd R
         range Fxd R
39
25 stake 10
9
7 7
7

36 38
Fl G
2.5 sec
Fl R
7.5 sec 39
Fl R
5 sec 39
Fl R
3 sec 39 25
Fl R
5 sec 39
30 44 Fxd G
Fl R 48 30
8 sec 35 40 30
10 18 30
23 21 R 36 25
7 7 7   25

Jamaica
Montego Bay
Chart JAM-9
Soundings in feet at MLW

18° 28.00' N

77° 56.00' W

The view from the pool at the *Montego Bay Yacht Club*

James Street (check out the *St. James Bakery* here) and then changes to *Fort Street* in the center of town where you'll find a hub of activity called *Sam Sharpe Square*, named after the leaded of a slave rebellion. Here too you'll find *The Cage*, which at one time was a jail for runaway slaves, and *The Courthouse*, which was built in 1804, and destroyed by fire in 1824.

Continuing north you'll come to a roundabout where the road divides into *Gloucester Avenue*, which heads north to the hip strip area, and *Queen's Drive*, a beautiful road that leads into the hills to Fort Montego. After the passing through the hip strip *Gloucester Avenue* eventually passes the roundabout at the *Sangster International Airport* and becomes the *North Coast Highway*.

Marinas

Montego Bay Yacht Club

The *Montego Bay Yacht Club* (http://www. mobayyachtclub.com/) has a very nice restaurant with very good food at very good prices, a TV and reading lounge, 24-hour security, Internet access (also Wi-Fi on the dock), a swimming pool, a pool table, a laundry service, a dinghy dock, a fuel dock with diesel, gasoline, and water available. If you need anything for your boat, ask the dockmaster or the yacht club office for their advice, they'll be glad to assist you, they can even arrange for you to clear in or out of Jamaica.

The folks here at the *MBYC* are not at all stuffy, they're quite friendly and can be a big help in filling in any information gaps you may have about Jamaica and her waters. There is a laundry service available at the yacht club, the charges is US$5 per load to wash and the same to dry, plus a 15% government tax (it's a nice idea to tip the lady that actually does your laundry J$100). You can buy time at the marina's bar for their computer to access the Internet, as little as ½ hour or as much as 50 hours. Cruisers who wish to dinghy in from the anchorage must register with the yacht club and pay a fee of US$6 per day per person for full use of the facilities.

Pier One Marina

Pier One Marina is home to several tourist charter boats and may be full, it might be better to phone ahead for a slip if you need one (876-954-3229). Most slips are bow or stern to but I have seen a boat tied up along the inside of their western dock. The marina's

restaurant offers a good food with a very nice view of *Montego Bay* and reasonable pricing. There is a small fishing tackle store on site, *Sea Supply*, that also carries some minor boating supplies.

Getting Around *Montego Bay*

There are a couple of ways to get around town besides renting a car. You can get a regular taxi, which will cost you anywhere from US$5-US$8 just to go to the grocery store from the *MBYC*, or you can catch what's known as a *route taxi*, taxis that run specific routes and only charge J$50 per ride. You can pick up a route taxi right outside the entrance to the *MBYC*, and you can also make them an offer to take you wherever you need to go even if it's off their route, most of these drivers are flexible.

Paradise Express Ferry intends to initiate the first high speed marine excursion service operating between the Jamaican North Coast tourism towns of Montego Bay, Negril and Ocho Rios, serving the 3.3 million annual international tourists that visit the North Coast resort areas. The service will utilize modern high-speed passenger catamaran ferries, providing safe, environmentally friendly operations.

Provisions

The *MBYC* is very convenient to the Mega mart where a five-minute taxi ride will take you to this "buyer's club" type of supermarket that is stocked with almost everything you could want.

As you take the road leading into *Montego Bay* from the Freeport Peninsula and the *MBYC* you'll come to a traffic signal at the north/south coast highway, also called *Howard Cooke Boulevard*. Go straight here and at the next intersection, at the corner of *Alice Eldemire Drive* and *Southern Cross Blvd.* in Bogue, you'll find a *Scotia Bank ATM* kiosk next to a *Texaco* station, a *KFC*, a *Fontana Pharmacy*, a *Shop Smart Appliance & Bedding Centre*, and a large *Super S Plus* grocery store with an ATM just inside the front door on the left. If you are in search of duty-free liquors you're in luck! Just across from the cruise ship dock is a small shopping center catering primarily to the cruise ship passengers. Here you'll find a duty-free liquor store and a small medical/surgical clinic.

Dining

So now that you're settled in at *Montego Bay*, if you're a normal cruiser you're probably thinking about dining out, so let's take a look around town and see what's available besides *KFC*, *Burger King*, *McDonalds*, and *Pizza Hut*.

Across the street from the *MBYC* is an all-inclusive beach resort, *Sunset Beach*, that charges US$45 per day for all you can eat and drink and access to their facilities, a good deal if you ask me even though they only allow you on site from 1000-1800 (if you tell them you're from the *MBYC* the price is only US$30, they offer special deals to those in the neighborhood). There is also a small *Scotia Bank ATM* by the gate to the resort.

Using *Pier One Marina* as a starting point on *Gloucester Avenue*, and heading north along the shoreline you'll enter what's known as the hip strip, the center of *Mobay*'s tourist haunts. Just as begin to enter the area you'll come across the *Pelican Restaurant* (http://www.pelicangrillja.com/) on the east side of *Gloucester Avenue*. This is a very popular restaurant with local folks that has been in operation for over 30 years. Their food is good, reasonably priced, not cheap mind you but not pricey either, but their biggest attraction has to be their fantastic ice cream dishes, reason enough to drop in on a hot day.

Almost across the street is the multi-colored *Margaritaville* and its neighbor, *Marguerite's* (www.margueritesjamaica.com/). These two restaurants are as different as night and day. *Margaritaville* (http://www.margaritavillecaribbean.com/locations/montego-bay/) attracts a young clientele, party animals, and people that want to watch giant screen TV or take a ride on the waterslide that runs from the upstairs bar directly into the bay. *Marguerite's* on the other hand is elegant and reserved, with special flambéed dishes to delight even the most discriminating cruiser's palate (reservations are suggested, oh, and it can be pricey). Almost across the street from *Margaritaville* is the *Coral Cliff Entertainment Centre*. Primarily a casino, the *Centre* has opened a unique game room called *Chillin*, a winter wonderland complete with falling snow and an ice bar where everything is made of ice. *Coral Cliff* even supplies coats and gloves for those of you who forgot to bring winter clothing.

The *North Coast Highway* offers many fine places to dine. You can begin your search for gastronomic delights at *Half Moon Village* (http://halfmoon.rockresorts.com/) where you'll find the elegant *Sakura Japanese Restaurant*, as good as any Japanese restaurant anywhere. *Sakura's* offers free transportation from local hotels and the *Montego Bay Yacht Club*; you can phone the restaurant at 876-953-9686 for more info. Also at *Half Moon Village* is

the *Royal Stocks English Pub and Steakhouse*, fine eatery featuring steaks and seafood along with a large selection of traditional ales. *Royal Stocks* also offers free transportation; phone them at 876-953-9770.

Around town you'll find the *Richmond Hill Inn* on *Union Street* with its panoramic view of *Montego Bay* and its classy ambiance. The *Town House* on *Church Street* was built in 1765 and features local artwork on its walls. The *Town House* is open Monday through Saturday for lunch and dinner and offers free transportation from local hotels and the *MBYC*. The *Vineyard* at the *Coyaba Beach Resort* (http://www.coyabaresortjamaica.com/) offers dining in a trellised garden and reservations are suggested. But if you want true Jamaican food, not the touristy fare, and if you want it in a down-to-earth setting, you can't do better than the *Kit Kat Restaurant* at *Verney's Tropical Resort* (http://www.verneyresort.com/) on *Leader Avenue*. With a hilltop view of the city this open-air eatery features the best of Jamaican cooking, this is the spot for REAL Jamaican cuisine.

The *Seagrape Terrace*, at the *Half Moon Hotel*, is an open air dining experience right on the beach with both buffet and *a la carte* offerings (dinner is *a la carte* only). *Seagrape Terrace* offers nightly floor shows and dancing to the sounds of a steel pan band. At the *Sandals Royal Jamaican Resort* (http://www.sandals.com/main/montego/mo-home/) on the *North Coast Highway* you'll find *a good restaurant* ocated on a small island just off the resort's beach.

Also at *Sandals* is fine Italian restaurant, *Cucina Romana*, serving excellent Italian dishes with a great antipasti buffet, and *Tokyo Joe's*, another fine Japanese restaurant (dinner only and closed on Fridays). *Sandals* is an all-inclusive resort and arrangements must be made with management for visitors. Further north and east along the coast you'll come to *Rose Hall* where you can dine at *Ambrosia* located at the golf course across the street from *Wyndham Rose Hall*. *Ambrosia*, which is closed on Wednesdays, serves Mediterranean cuisine in a lovely garden setting and is pricey to say the least, at least by my humble standards.

One of the best eateries in *Montego Bay* lies just up the road at *The Pork Pit* on *Gloucester Avenue* across from the *Walter Fletcher Beach*. Popular with the locals, this no-frills establishment serves up some of the best jerk pork on the western side of Jamaica. Nearby is *The Native* with their impressive Friday and

Sunday lunch buffet. *The Native* is quite different from most places you'll find on the hip strip; walking into *The Native* is like walking into a colonial British restaurant complete with bamboo chairs and tables and a lovely verandah just high enough off the street to be out of the hustle and bustle.

In town, just past the *Fairfield Theater*, is *Day O Plantation* (http://www.dayoplantation.com/), a wonderful little restaurant owned by Paul Hurlock, who is also the inventor of an electric car called the *Electrogen* that is on display in his restaurant. Paul is also an accomplished musician with several recordings to his credit and you can hear him play every night at his restaurant with the *Cabot Paul Steel Band*. The *Jamaican Bobsled Café* offers gourmet pizza, but if you just want to roam and find the perfect spot for your meal, simply take a stroll up or down *Gloucester Avenue* and choose your own dining experience from the dozens that lie on this boulevard.

To the west of *Montego Bay* you'll find several excellent restaurants, though pricey by some cruiser's standards. The *Lethe Estate* is about 20 minutes west of town and offers gourmet dining in an elegant atmosphere, you'll have to dress nice for this one, no shorts and t-shirts. In Reading try *Norma's* at the *Wharf House*. Norma Shirley's restaurant is known for its nouvelle Jamaican cuisine and is kin to the restaurant of the same name in Kingston and has been featured in several well-known culinary magazines.

Round Hill is another elegant restaurant where you'll dine by candlelight under the stars. Although it is one of Jamaica's dressier restaurants there is a casual Monday beach barbecue complete with bonfire. *Round Hill* offers a live jazz band performing after dinner on Tuesday and Thursday nights and on Friday nights you'll view a Jamaican folkloric floor show.

Just across the bay you'll find *Dervy's Lobster Trapp* (http://lobstertrapp.com/) where the owner, Derby, will prepare your lobster on his brick and charcoal grill. In Bogue Hill is *Julia's*, one of Jamaica's most praised culinary hotspots and a favorite of visiting celebrities, the place to go to see and be seen. The menu is primarily Italian and your meal is accompanied by the singing of the owner. Reservations are required and dress is just short of formal. In nearby Granville, you can dine on the 3,000 acre *Barnett Estate* (http://www.bellefieldgreathouse. com/) at *Bellefield Great House & Gardens,*, operated by *Elegant Resorts International*, which should give you an idea of the ambiance of this place. Guide tours of the *Great House* are available and the grounds are open to visitors.

Rose Hall Estate

Along the northern shore of Jamaica, about six miles east of *MoBay*, is *Rose Hall*, home of the *Rose Hall Great House* (https://rosehall.com/tours/) which is easily seen from offshore. The huge white stone mansion is unmistakable; it sits back off the highway (A-1) surrounded by manicured grounds and tended gardens. The Great House is the center of numerous tales of voodoo, murder, and Annie Palmer, the *White Witch of Rose Hall*. *Rose Hall Plantation* was built in the 1770s by owner and mayor, then known as the *Parish Custos*, John Palmer.

There are two stories to the *Rose Hall* lore. In one, Annie Palmer was born Annie Marie Patterson in either England or Ireland and moved to Haiti as a very young girl. Here she learned the arts of voodoo before her arrival in Kingston, Jamaica, at the age of seventeen. Eager to find a husband, young Annie Patterson, due mostly to her good looks and the fact she was white, soon fell in with Kingston society where she met John Palmer, grandson of the builder of *Rose Hall*. Annie and John Palmer married in 1820 and the happy couple settled at the *Rose Hall* estate. The marriage was not a happy one and feeling the seven-year itch, Annie took a young slave as her lover. When John Palmer discovered the affair he severely beat Annie, but his young wife would have her revenge. Annie placed poison in her husband's wine and as he lay dying in his bed she finished the job by smothering him with a pillow.

The new mistress of *Rose Hall* took two more husbands over the years and is said to have murdered them also, stabbing and strangling them both. She then killed a succession of white bookkeepers and slaves with whom she had been sleeping. She was a cruel mistress, even to those she did not have as lovers, doling out severe punishments for minor infractions. Annie Palmer was murdered in her bed in 1831, strangled, and her killer was never discovered. It is said that she was murdered by an old crone, the grandmother of a young woman who was Annie's rival for the attention of a young Englishman, who magically set a "vampire" onto her.

But there is another tale of Annie Palmer, the one who is buried in a crypt next to the great house. This Annie Palmer was the exact opposite of the *White Witch of Rose Hall*, being virtuous and peaceful. She may have been confused with Rosa Palmer, the original mistress of *Rose Hall* who had four husbands and was known for her less than virtuous ways. Somewhere between the two ladies a legend arose and now a favorite tourist site sports photos of the *White Witch of Rose Hall* staring at the camera from the safety of a mirror in the *Rose Hall Great House*.

Legendary Country star Johnny Cash had an estate located nearby and reported ghostly encounters in the Great House. He even wrote a song about Rose Hall and the White Witch entitled "The Ballad of Annie Palmer."

Bogue Lagoon

Waypoints
Bogue Lagoon - ¼ nm NW of entrance channel
18° 27.28' N, 77° 57.70' W

Bogue Lagoon - inner waypoint at entrance ch.
18° 27.205' N, 77° 57.548' W

Bogue Lagoon - start of channel exiting lagoon
18° 27.05' N, 77° 57.04' W

Bogue Lagoon has, without a doubt, the best shelter on the northern coast of Jamaica, and it can even be used as a hurricane hole (which is exactly what local boaters do as would I if I were here and a hurricane threatened). Vessels with drafts to 6½' can enter the bay with little problem, but a draft of 7'-8' will need to play the tide. Use extreme caution in entering during periods of poor visibility and never attempt this entrance at night! Take it slow and easy through here and keep one eye on your depth sounder. The bay is a marine part fish sanctuary and the denizens of the waters (snook and tarpon here) are protected.

Navigational Information
As shown on Chart JAM-10, a waypoint at 18° 27.28' N, 77° 57.70' W, will place you approximately ¼ mile northwest of the unmarked entrance channel through the reefs as shown on the chart. If you are approaching from the north, from *Montego Bay*, give the reefs west of the Freeport Peninsula a wide berth. From the waypoint you'll easily see the reef on the southern side of the entrance channel, it dries in places at low water and is quite visible even at high water.

From the waypoint you can head in on an approximate heading of 113° magnetic, but this heading should only be used as a reference, the idea being you must keep the highly visible southern reef at least one boat length to starboard and steer toward the center of the opening of the mangrove island and the point of land that just northward from the southern shore of *Bogue Lagoon*. There is a small cone-shaped hill in the distance when sighting between the island and point and you can use that as a reference as well. There is a minimum depth of 7' through here. As a reference I can also give you an inner waypoint for the entrance, but don't try to steer toward this waypoint, use your eyes and pilot accordingly, I cannot stress that enough! The inner waypoint is 18° 27.205' N, 77° 57.548' W, and once through the channel and inside the reef you can turn to port to begin your passage through the markers and into the deeper water of *Bogue Lagoon*.

As you'll notice on the chart, there are several markers leading northeast and then southeast into the bay. These markers, although they're steel posts set in concrete, have not been maintained and you can't tell which are red and green anymore, but you should be able to discern the channel by counting the markers, provided they're all still there. You can also head straight across the shallow bar lying southeast of the entrance channel but there is a shallow spot of 3' along this route, it's far safer and easier on the blood pressure if you follow the markers.

As shown on the chart, as you turn to the east/northeast, the first marker you'll keep to starboard and the second to port. Then you'll enter a channel between four sets of markers, these are fairly obvious. When you pass the last of the four sets of markers turn to the southeast and you'll take one more marker to starboard and ahead of you you'll see another pair of markers very far apart, split these and you'll soon find yourself in 20' of water. Anchor wherever your heart desires, there is good holding here and good protection to be found from any wind direction. If you have been here before, you'll notice that the old *Jamaica Rose Marina* is no longer in operation though their dock still stands.

What You Will Find Ashore
Along the shoreline are many private residences while along the northern shore is a wonderful little spot to dine, the *Houseboat Grill* (http://thehouseboatgrill.com/). You can anchor off anywhere you like and dinghy in and secure to their railing, climb aboard,

and have a great meal with a nice view of your boat at anchor in the vivid green waters of *Bogue Lagoon*. The two-story restaurant is closed on Mondays, but during the week they are quite busy, they're a very popular spot and they serve superb cuisine with a menu that changes every couple of weeks, they even have a lobster pen where you can choose your own lobster; and ladies, no heels please.

The folks that run the *Houseboat Grill* also offer tours (very informative tours complete with breakfast and lunch) into Cockpit Country to their old family home, the *Hilton Estate*, at St. Leonards. Ask about it at the restaurant, pick up a flyer at the *Montego Bay Yacht Club*, or email them at hiltonhiday@n5.com.jm

When leaving *Bogue Lagoon*, you can eyeball your way out along the same route you took to come in. If you need a waypoint, and so many cruisers do these days, a position at 18° 27.05' N, 77° 57.04' W, will place you just south of the two innermost markers. From here follow the channel out the same way you entered keeping the very visible southern reef well to port as you exit.

Mosquito Cove

Waypoints
Mosquito Cove- ¼ nm N of entrance
18° 28.00 N, 78° 06.50' W

Mosquito Cove offers good protection when the wind and seas do not have any northerly component to them. Quite a few local small boat owners favor *Mosquito Cove* as a hurricane hole.

Navigational Information
The main danger is the easily seen *Bruckner Reef* as shown on Chart JAM-11. As shown on the chart, a waypoint at 18° 28.00 N, 78° 06.50' W, will place you approximately ¼ north of the entrance. Then entrance channel carries about 20' of water and is about 250' wide with rocks on both sides so exercise caution when entering. You can anchor in about 10'-15' of water in the SE corner of the bay just off the small town.

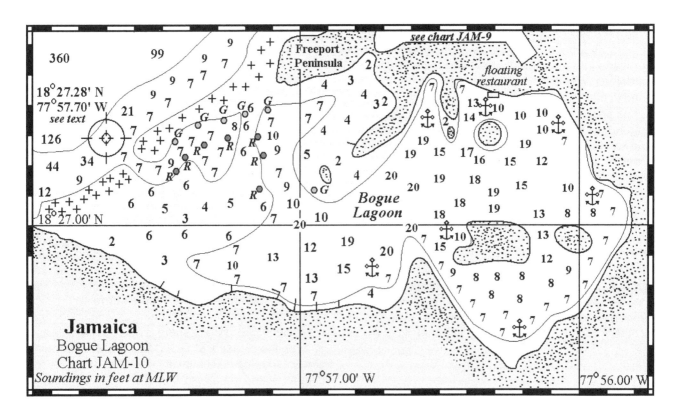

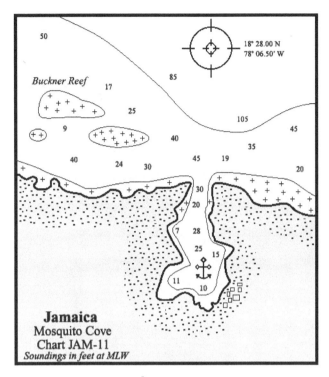

18° 28.00 N
78° 06.50' W

Buckner Reef

Jamaica
Mosquito Cove
Chart JAM-11
Soundings in feet at MLW

Lucea

Important Lights
Flagstaff Reef Light, Fl R 4s
Waypoints
Lucea; outer waypoint - 1¼ nm NNW of entrance
18° 28.40' N, 78° 09.80' W

Lucea; inner waypoint - 1¼ nm NNW of entrance
18° 27.65' N, 78° 09.75' W

Lucea, pronounced Lucy, is the bustling capital of Hanover Parish and the location where Sir Henry Morgan kept ships moored when he was the Lt. Governor of Jamaica. During the sugar years the town flourished as planters exported their product here, but today, only a bit of molasses is exported, that and the gem of the Lucean economy, their tasty Lucea yam.

The topography around Lucea is quite different from that along the rest of the northern coast of Jamaica. Gone are the mountains, in their place stand gentle rolling hills as the Jamaica begins to flatten out along her western shore.

Navigational Information
Heading west from *Montego Bay* keep at least one mile (or more) offshore to avoid inshore dangers. A waypoint at 18° 28.40' N, 78° 09.80' W, will place

you 1¼ miles north/northwest of the entrance into the harbor at Lucea. From this waypoint you may head to an inner waypoint at 18° 27.65' N, 78° 09.75' W, which places you approximately ½ mile north/northwest of the entrance into the harbor as shown on Chart JAM-12. From this waypoint head continue on into the harbor on an approximate heading of 175° keeping between the red buoy marking *Flagstaff Reef* to port and the green marker lying north of the western end of the *Lucea Marine Terminal* to starboard along the eastern shore of the bay at Cane Point.

The harbor offers protection in prevailing winds from NE to SE, and in those conditions your best anchorage will be in the lee of the eastern shore; another option is to anchor in the southeastern part of the harbor just off Barbary Hall. Winds from SE to NW are blocked by the land surrounding this harbor, but never try to stay here during periods of northerly winds or seas.

What You Will Find Ashore
Although the marine terminal for Lucea is on the northeastern side of the harbor, the town of Lucea is located on the western side of the bay. The town of Lucea itself is just a reminder of its past glory. The general state of disrepair of Lucea's buildings has prompted many supporters to push for Heritage status for their town though little progress has been made in that direction.

The focus in downtown Lucea is her central park complete with bus drivers competing for passengers, and a covered central market on the east side of the town square, the *Cleveland Stanhope Market*, which on Saturdays and Sundays spills out into the street as the throngs of vendors push their wares onto the throngs of buyers. The 19th century courthouse is topped with a huge clock tower, seemingly out of shape and place here. In fact, the clock tower, which has been keeping perfect time for over 170 years, was originally ordered by St. Lucia but shipped to Lucea instead (Lucea's Spanish name is Santa Lucea-they must not have had *UPS* or *FedEx* back then). The top of the tower resembles the top of an old style German army helmet, said to be due to a local planter of Germanic heritage who bankrolled the tower with the assurance that he had a hand in the design. The local folk so liked the clock tower that they took up a collection to pay for it and kept it.

The *Hanover Parish Church*, which dates to 1725, boasts several monuments as well as a small

Lucea

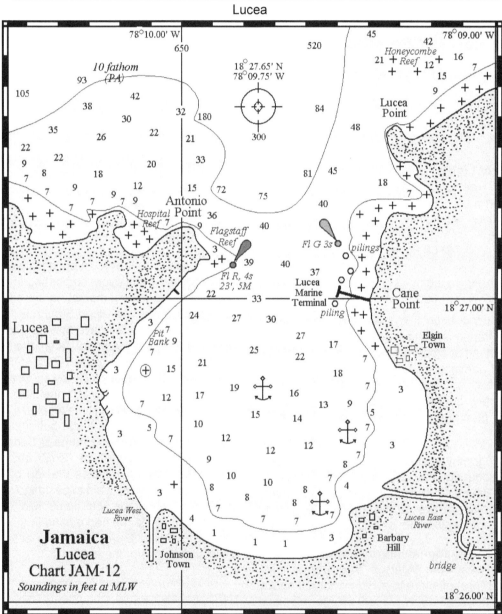

Jamaica
Lucea
Chart JAM-12
Soundings in feet at MLW

Jewish cemetery inside its grounds. Between the church and the sea is the *Rusea School*, founded in 1777 from contributions from Martin Rusea. A French religious refugee, Rusea washed ashore at Lucea and was so touched by the generosity of the local population that he left his entire estate to Lucea upon his death in 1764. There is a small road that begins about 200 yards west of the church and leads to the *Hanover Museum* (http://museums-ioj.org.jm/?p=573) located in the old police barracks. The museum boasts exhibits including prisoner's stocks, miscellaneous pots, lead weights, measures, an old wooden bathtub, and a gift shop with a snack bar and restrooms.

Nearby, and partially hidden from view, are the remains of *Fort Charlotte* on the edge of the harbor. The fort, which was rebuilt in 1761 and whose original construction date is unknown, is still home to three rotary mounted cannons which never fired a shot in defense. The fort was named after King George III's Queen.

The town of Lucea boasts several nice hotels and even more eateries. *Vital Ital* is a favorite of Rastas and vegans, while *D&S Restaurant* offers good pasta and burgers in an informal setting. For true Jamaican fare, try visiting any of the vendor's stalls at the market or visit the *Hard Rock Café* (not connected with the U.S. chain of the same name).

Bloody Bay

Important Lights
Negril Point, Fl W R 2s

Bloody Bay lies just to the north of Negril and is a great final stop in Jamaica. You might enjoy clearing out in *Mobay* at the *MBYC*, and then taking a leisurely sail down the coast to anchor at Bloody Bay for the night before heading to the Cayman Islands or Honduras. It shortens that trip by a few miles and the bay itself is lovely, a long white sand beach with very few folks around, most of the action being centered on the beaches of Negril just around the next point to the south, you'll probably be the only boat there. From Lucea keep a mile offshore and follow the shoreline southwest to *Bloody Bay*. Round North Negril Point and anchor just off the beach as far north as possible to avoid the jet-skis and other annoyances.

Bloody Bay is the spot where the pirate Calico Jack Rackham was captured along with lady pirates Anne Bonney and Mary Reade. *Bloody Bay* earned its name from the whalers who used to dump tons of whale parts into the bay turning the waters blood red.

Just south of *Bloody Bay* is *Red Bay* and Negril. Two points of land south is located the *Negril Lighthouse* at the southern end of *Red Bay* (just west of the town of Negril). Sitting high atop a cliff, this majestic lighthouse was originally powered by oil lamps and then gas, but today is solar powered.

The Cayman Islands

Port of Entry:
Cayman Brac, Grand Cayman,
Little Cayman (see text - *Customs and Immigration*)
Fuel: Cayman Brac, Grand Cayman
Haul-Out: Grand Cayman
Diesel Repairs: Grand Cayman
Outboard Repairs: Grand Cayman
Propane: Grand Cayman
Provisions: Grand Cayman
Time Zone: Eastern (no Daylight Savings)
Electricity: 110 volt, 60 cycle
Important Lights: See Appendix A

The Cayman Islands, that well known offshore banking haven, lie roughly 180 mile northwest of Jamaica and approximately 340 miles northeast of Roatán in the Bay Islands of Honduras. Three islands make up the Cayman Islands: Grand Cayman, the largest and the capital of the island chain, and the Lesser Caymans, sometimes called the *Sister Islands* on Grand Cayman, Little Cayman, and Cayman Brac, which lie approximately 75 miles east/northeast of Grand Cayman.

The Cayman Islands are formed of coral reefs that grew atop mountains peaks, kin to the peaks in Cuba's *Sierra Maestra* range and part of the submarine *Cayman Ridge* that extends northward from Honduras to Cuba. The abundance of marine life makes these islands an extremely popular diving attraction and Grand Cayman's *Seven Mile Beach* is rated one of the world's finest. George Town is one of the world's offshore banking centers with over 500 banks located here and was featured in the book and movie *The Firm*. Grand Cayman attracts many ex-pat millionaires who appreciate the island's lenient tax and banking regulations. All around the harbor you will see colorful gingerbread buildings that define Cayman architecture.

Cayman Brac is riddled with caves and wrecks and is said to have provided some inspiration for Robert Louis Stevenson's *Treasure Island*. Little Cayman, only about 5 miles west of Cayman Brac, is known for its abundant wildlife, spectacular bonefishing, and *Bloody Bay*, a breathtaking dive and snorkel experience. Oh, and one more thing, if you wish to pronounce the name of these islands correctly, as one who lives here would, you must put the accent on the second syllable, as in Cay-MAHN, not CAY-man.

The depth of the waters around the Caymans vary from 23,500' in the *Cayman Trench*, approximately 100 miles east/southeast of Grand Cayman, to 80'-120' on the steep-to coral sand ridge known as the *Cayman Bank*, about 9 miles west/southwest of the Northwestern tip of Grand Cayman. You will never notice when you're over the *Cayman Trench*, but you can tell when you're on the *Cayman Bank* where the water is a bit discolored and the surface usually has some strong ripples about. If you need a lat/long, try 19° 20' N, 81° 35' W. If you plan to dive here You will have plenty of company, it's a popular spot with charter dive boats and tourist carrying submarines, so exercise caution.

If you plan to be in the Cayman Islands for October, you will have a chance to enjoy and partake in their annual *Pirate's Week*, a national festival chock full of music, street dances, costumes, games, a kid's day, sporting events, *Heritage Days*, and lots of food and drink. The highlight is a mock "pirate invasion" from the sea when two old-time sailing vessels full of bloodthirsty pirates make a "surprise" invasion at George Town, Grand Cayman where thousands of people line the streets to take part or just watch. The week is finalized with a "trial and sentencing" of the assembled pirates.

Customs and Immigration

If you are approaching from Jamaica, you may clear in at either Cayman Brac or at Grand Cayman. Little Cayman is not equipped to handle vessels arriving from international waters (there is no *Mosquito Control* officer on the island) although you are able to clear out from Little Cayman. If you clear in at Cayman Brac and wish to go to Grand Cayman, you must clear out before departing whether it be from Cayman Brac or Little Cayman. When arriving in Grand Cayman you can ask *Port Authority* via VHF if you can clear at one of the marinas in *North Sound*.

Cayman Islands' *Customs* requests that you fly a Q-flag <u>AND</u> a Cayman Islands courtesy flag when entering their waters. Vessels entering the waters of the Cayman Islands are required to contact *Port Authority* as soon as possible.

Clearing Immigration
Immigration allows an initial stay of 30 days. When you receive your *Immigration* slip keep it with your passport, it is the equivalent of a *Tourist Identification Card*. Extensions (CI$50 for first extension, CI$100 for every other extension up to six months) to the stay

granted by *Immigration* are available and proof of financial resources are required.

Fees

When you arrive in either Cayman Brac or Grand Cayman you can expect to be boarded by a *Mosquito Control* officer who will spray your vessel and charge you US$31.25. If you clear in at Cayman Brac this procedure will not have to be done again at Grand Cayman if you retain your receipt and make no other landfall between the Lesser Caymans and Grand Cayman (such as a detour to Cuba). If you need to clear in at Cayman Brac call *Port Authority* or *Brac Customs* on VHF ch. 16 and await instructions. If you need to clear at Grand Cayman head for the commercial docks and call *George Town Port Security* on VHF ch. 16 for instructions.

If you are flying into the Cayman Islands an onward or return ticket is required. There is a US$25.00 departure tax if departing by air from the Cayman Islands. When entering by boat there are no fees when clearing in except for the mosquito spraying charge, and there are no clearing out fees when departing Little Cayman for Grand Cayman, but when clearing out for another country, whether from Grand Cayman, Little Cayman, or Cayman Brac, there is a fee of CI$3.00, or US$3.80.

Immigration extensions are CI$50 for the first month and CI$100 for each month thereafter up to six months. Overtime is US$70. Arriving on a bank holiday incurs a fee of CI$72. Forms for clearing in or out cost CI$3.

Visas

Citizens of Andorra, Argentina, Austria, Bahrain, Belgium, Brazil, Chile, Costa Rica, Denmark, Ecuador, El Salvador, Finland, France, Germany, Greece, Guatemala, Iceland, Irish Republic, Israel, Italy, Japan, Kuwait, Liechtenstein, Luxembourg, Mexico, Monaco, Netherlands, Norway, Oman, Panama, Peru, Portugal, San Merino, Saudi Arabia, Spain, Sweden, Switzerland, and Venezuela need a visa for entry into the Cayman Islands.

Mosquito Control

A visit by *Mosquito Control* is required for entrance into the Caymans. They will ask you to close all of your hatches and ports and require you and your fellow crew members to stay on deck while they spray the inside of your boat. The service costs US$31.25.

Firearms and Spear Guns

Note that spear guns, live plants or plant cuttings, fruits, and vegetables are prohibited items. All spear guns, pole spears, Hawaiian slings, flare guns, and firearms are required by regulations to be confiscated for the duration of your stay in the Cayman Islands. Although the *Customs* officers throughout the Cayman Islands are bound by the same regulations, it seems that it is up the individual officer's discretion as to what items to retain during your stay. I've had *Customs* in Cayman Brac leave my pole spears aboard and retain my flare gun, while just a week later in Grand Cayman I've had *Customs* retain my pole spears and not my flare gun. If you clear in at Cayman Brac, and wish to clear out at Little Cayman heading west to Grand Cayman, it is possible for you to pick up your firearms at Cayman Brac *Customs* and transport them to Little Cayman where you will turn them over to Little Cayman *Customs* for the duration of your stay then you can pick them up as you clear out for Grand Cayman.

Picking up or Dropping off Crew

If you are dropping off crew on Grand Cayman you must show *Immigration* a copy of the airline ticket and the crew member so they can be removed from the crew list. If you are picking up crew on Grand Cayman and they are flying in on a one way ticket, you must produce a letter from the skipper inviting them aboard the boat, a copy of the vessel's clearance papers, the documentation for the vessel, and if possible a letter from the marina where you are staying.

Pets

All dogs and cats entering the Cayman Islands must be accompanied by an import permit issued by the *Cayman Islands Department of Agriculture*. You can request an application form by writing to: *Veterinary Services, Department of Agriculture*, P.O. Box 459, G.T., Grand Cayman, Cayman Islands, B.W.I. (phone: 345-947-3090; fax: 345-947-2634; http://www.gov.ky/portal/pls/portal/docs/1/1079588. PDF). All pets must be permanently identified by a microchip implant or a tattoo. Dogs and cats must have received a rabies vaccination not less than 30 days nor more than one-year prior to entry in the Cayman Islands. After vaccination a blood test must be taken to check for protective antibodies against rabies. Your pet may then enter the Cayman Islands six months after the date of the blood test.

For information concerning waiving the 6-month period contact the *Department of Agriculture*. Also, within 14 days of your departure for the Cayman Islands your pet must be examined and issued an official *Veterinary Health Certificate* issued by a licensed veterinarian and stamped by a government vet (such as a *USDA* vet in the United States, a *Canadian Food Inspection Agency* agent, or *DEFRA* in the United Kingdom). A single entry fee of CI$51 will be charged or a multiple entry fee of CI$150 will be assessed by the *CIDA*. All this can be handled by fax. Parrots are required to have a CITES certificate from their country of origin.

All animals and documents are subject to examination at the port of entry by an approved inspector. Should the animal fail to meet entry requirements, the *Chief Agricultural and Veterinary Officer* may at his discretion and at the expense of the importer, order that the animal be refused entry and returned immediately or be destroyed. Detention or quarantine is NOT an option in the Cayman Islands. All dogs staying in the Cayman Islands for longer than 30 days must be licensed with the *Department of Agriculture*.

Dogs and cats are prohibited entry if they are imported from any country in Asia, Africa, or Central and South America, as well as Cuba, Mexico, Puerto Rico, Haiti, and the Dominican Republic. The following dogs are not permitted in the Cayman Islands: these breeds include but are not limited to Mastiffs, Staffordshire Terriers, Rottweilers, Shar Pei, Japanese Tosa, Bull Mastiff, Malinois, Argentino Dogo, Neapolitan Mastiff, Japanese Akita, Fila Brasileiro, Fogue de Bordeaux, Vatahoula Leopard Dog, Pit Bull Terrier, and the American Bulldog.

Ports of Entry:
George Town, Grand Cayman,
The Creek on Cayman Brac. Blossom Village
(*Owen's Sound)* on Little Cayman

Getting Around

If you plan to rent a car here you will need to have a valid driver's license and you will need to purchase a visitor's permit for US$7.50 from your rental agent. The only form of public transportation is found on Grand Cayman where you will have access to minibuses that serve 8 routes. The buses look like minivans with a circled number on the front; for example: *Route 1*, yellow, and *Route 2*, green, cover George Town to *West Bay*, while *Route 5*, red, goes to *Gun Bay* on the east side of the island. There are bus stops in downtown George Town and all

along *Seven Mile Beach* and around the perimeter of the island. Daily bus service is from 0600-2300, Sunday through Thursday, and even later during the weekend. Fares cost anywhere from CI$1.50-$3.50, or US$1.88-$4.38.

Some taxi routes are a set rate as per government regulations, while other taxis are metered, usually the newer taxis have meters. If you don't wish to take a bus or a taxi, there are car, bike, and scooter rentals available. Driving is on the left.

Medical Facilities

Medical facilities in the Caymans are very good. There is a well-equipped hospital on Grand Cayman, the *Chrissie Tomlinson Memorial Hospital* (http://chrissietomlinson.com/), and a smaller facility on Cayman Brac) which can cope with most routine medical and dental problems. Also in George Town is the *Cayman Islands Health Services Authority* (https://www.hsa.ky/). *Health City Cayman Islands* is located on *Sea View Road* (http://www.healthcitycaymanislands.com/)

Serious cases are transferred to Miami (make sure you have adequate insurance in case you need an air ambulance). For medical or police emergencies dial 911 or 555. The area code for the Cayman Islands is 345.

Moorings

There are numerous public moorings in the Cayman Islands, these are 18"-30" white buoys with a blue strip and they usually have a yellow poly-painter. These moorings are free and the smaller buoys are designed to hold a vessel of 60' while the larger buoys are reserved for vessels from 60'-100'. The Cayman Islands would prefer if you used a mooring instead of anchoring in their waters as it is a serious offense to anchor so as to damage coral (the waters off George Town, Grand Cayman, are patrolled on a regular basis). Please respect the dive boat operators who must use these same moorings, particularly the ones over the M/V *Tibbets* at Cayman Brac. You can pick up one of these moorings in the afternoon and stay the night, but it's a show of courtesy to vacate the mooring in the morning so the dive boats can access the site.

The only place where you might be questioned about using a mooring is in *Dick Sesinger's Bay* on the southern shore of Cayman Brac. Here you will find several moorings off the resorts that are used primarily by the resort's dive boats. Although you are allowed by law to use these moorings, always ask first. One time I entered the bay and the *Customs* boat directed me to one of the *Dive Tiara* moorings for an overnight stay. The resort later hailed me on the radio and asked if I had engine trouble and told me that it was no problem to stay on the mooring, they would notify their incoming dive boat and direct him to stay at the dock overnight, and yes, I did have engine trouble.

Tides

The tides in the Cayman Islands are primarily diurnal with one high and one low each day, though on some days the tides will be semi-diurnal with two highs and lows per day, and are generally in the range of 1'. The currents in and around the Cayman Islands generally set to the west, though a northward flowing current can be found south of Grand Cayman at times, and a southward and/or eastward flowing current can be found between Cuba and the Cayman Islands at times.

Weather

One last note on the weather that affects the Cayman Islands. When sailing these waters you might hear of a *biami*. A *biami* is a fierce storm that originates in Cuba and moves, generally, southward. *Biami* is the that name I've heard *Brackers* (residents of Cayman Brac) use to describe the storm which is usually preceded by lightning, always packs a lot of wind, and may last for over 24 hours. If you see lightning to the north, this might be a *biami*, and it might be time to think about reefing those sails. You will also see the term *biami* used in the section on the *Río Dulce* in Guatemala where it also describes a particularly fierce storm

A Brief History

He hath founded it upon the seas
Psalm 24, Verse 2
The Cayman Islands Motto

The Cayman Islands were discovered by the *Admiral of All Oceans*, Christopher Columbus, on May 10, 1503, during his fourth and last visit to the New World. Columbus was actually on his way from Panama to Hispaniola when his fleet was driven off course by strong winds and he sighted the Lesser Caymans, Cayman Brac and Little Cayman. It is said that Columbus found the islands so full of turtles that they looked like rocks from offshore and he named the islands *Las Tortugas*, *The Turtles*.

Over the next century and a half the islands went through several name changes and played host to many ships as sailors used the islands to replenish their fresh water supplies as well as filling their larders with turtle meat and various fowls. For a while they were called *Lagartos*, meaning *alligator* or *large lizard*, and finally, around 1540, the *Caymans*, a derivative of the Carib word for the crocodile, *caymanas*, which, according to seafarers such as Sir Francis Drake and William Dampier, were found on the islands along with certain "...large lizards." Drake, who visited the islands between 1585-1586, reported sighting large "edible serpents," some up to 10' in length as described by one of Drake's men.

A few years later a French cartographer showed the island of Cayman Brac with crocodiles in its waters and text that described the creatures. According to the *Cayman Islands National Archives*, there are written accounts dating back to the 1830s of men shooting the crocodiles for Sunday sport. Nobody on the islands today can remember seeing a crocodile, but a 1993 archeological dig on Grand Cayman, and a 1996 dig on Cayman Brac, proved the existence of the crocs.

In 1655, the Cayman Islands came under British control when the nearby island of Jamaica was taken from the Spanish by Oliver Cromwell's army, but the islands did not officially became a British territory until the signing of the *Treaty of Madrid* in 1670. A group of British deserters fled Jamaica with escaped slaves and settled on Grand Cayman in 1658. Their surnames were Watler and Bodden, and today some of these island's oldest families are the Watlers and the Boddens, descendants of these same colonists. A report in the *National Archives* names Isaac Bodden as one of the original 21 settlers at Bodden Town and reports that there were some 39 families of around 200 white people and about the same number of slaves living on.

The first recorded settlements were actually recorded on Cayman Brac and Little Cayman during the years of 1661-1671. The settlers were Jamaicans who were removed back to Jamaica after 1671; the Spanish later destroyed the settlements.

The first Royal land grant in Grand Cayman was recorded in 1734 and covered some 3,000 acres between Prospect and *North Sound*, the beginning of permanent colonization. Other land grants soon followed until 1742 and the settlements developed and even prospered thanks to slave labor.

Sir Henry Morgan is also rumored to have stopped in the Caymans occasionally as did other pirates and privateers who sought Spanish gold. Tall tales tell us that there is quite a bit of pirate booty buried in the Cayman Islands, treasure caches were supposed to have been left behind by Sir Henry Morgan, Blackbeard, George Lowther, Thomas Antis, and Neal Walker, whose booty is still to be found on Little Cayman.

When the *Treaty of Utrecht* officially ended privateering in 1714, France and Spain ceased hostilities toward other European countries and the Cayman Islands became a refuge for out of work buccaneers. In 1724, Sir Walter Scott wrote in *The Pirates*, that Grand Cayman was "...a place requiring caution." But as the golden age of piracy faded into the past, the settlements on the Cayman Islands prospered and by 1741 several permanent land grants were awarded to families whose descendants still live on the islands.

The Cayman Islands are tax free, and that is said to be due to a series of events linked to the *Wreck of the Ten Sails*. In November of 1794, the British naval vessel the *HMS Convert*, the flagship and protector of a 58-ship merchant convoy from Jamaica to England, ran aground on the reef at East End, Grand Cayman. The stricken ship set off a signal to warn the other vessels in the convoy, but it was received in error and nine other ships wound up on the reef attempting to close with the flagship. Although 8 lives were lost, the people of East End were responsible for saving the lives of the rest of the crew and passengers, including a member of the Royal family (though some claim there were no Royals aboard), and it is reported that King George III bestowed a tax free status upon the people of the Cayman Islands as a reward (though records do not support this tale). During the court martial Captain Lawford, the master of the *Concord*, testified that a northbound current set them 20 miles off course and onto the reef.

By the beginning of the 19th century, the Cayman Islands boasted a population of 933, 545 of whom were slaves. At this time Cayman built sailing vessels were catching turtles and venturing to Jamaica for trade. Soon schooners were ferrying cargo such as cotton, mahogany, and sarsaparilla to Jamaica, and local shipbuilding, fishing, and turtling were to support many Cayman islanders for the next 150 years.

The Cayman Islands first true representative form of government was born on December 5, 1831, when residents met at the *Pedro St. James* great house in George Town and decided that representatives for the five different districts of Grand Cayman should be appointed for the purpose of forming local laws for better government. Elections were held on December 10 and on December 31 the first *Legislative Assembly* met in George Town, Grand Cayman. In 1833, Britain passed a law freeing the slaves after a 5-7 year apprenticeship program and by 1835 full emancipation was in effect except for those slaves registered in the apprenticeship program, however, no Cayman Island slaves were registered as the registry office was in Jamaica.

Most of the freed slaves turned to fishing and turtling, and the sea provided a good livelihood for most. Shipbuilding became a major industry on Grand Cayman at this time as well. For the next 100 years the Cayman Islands remained relatively isolated, only merchant seaman came and went, sustaining the economy for a while and Caymanians became famous for their resourcefulness and independent spirit. It wasn't long before the reputation of Cayman Islanders as outstanding sailors and turtle fishermen grew as many men joined the merchant marine and earned reputations as some of the finest ship's captains and seamen in the world. But despite the best efforts of the Cayman Islanders, nature would have a word to say about the economy of the islands. Hurricanes and a depletion of the green turtle population forced many residents to leave the islands for a better income in Cuba, Honduras, and Nicaragua.

The Cayman Islands were formally annexed to Jamaica in 1863 and soon ships were regularly plying the waters between the Caymans and Jamaica carrying freight, mail, and passengers. Jamaica appointed a *Commissioner* in the Cayman Islands to oversee the day to day operation of the government as it was becoming too difficult to handle Cayman affairs from Jamaica. Under the new Commissioners the Cayman Islands began to prosper as schools, a bank (just one), a hospital, and a roadway system were constructed.

One of the most memorable events in recent Cayman Island history was the Hurricane of 1932, which hit on Tuesday night, November 7th with winds estimated at 150mph and a storm surge of 30'. A day later the hurricane hit Cayman Brac with winds of 200mph and a storm surge of 32'. The Caymans were completely devastated with Cayman Brac being hit the hardest with a total of 69 lives lost. Many were washed out to sea while many survived by climbing trees to escape the surge. The Caymans took many years to recover from that tragedy and you will still find some old timers that remember the hurricane vividly.

A commissioner by the name of Sir Allen Cardinall is often described as being the man responsible for bringing the Cayman Islands into the 20th century. Cardinall served from 1934-1940 and brought the first wireless station to Grand Cayman in 1935, created a network of roads on Grand Cayman, and was the first to recognize the tourism potential of the islands claiming that the beach in *West Bay*, Grand Cayman was the "...most perfect beach for bathing in the West Indies." The first cruise ship, the *Atlantis*, arrived in Grand Cayman in 1937, the same year that the first tourism booklet about the islands was published.

In the 1950s, several major hotels opened on Grand Cayman along with a hospital, and *Barclay's Bank*, which heralded the beginning of the islands as a financial center. In 1953, the *Owens Roberts Airport,* was built on Grand Cayman and a year later an airstrip was built on Cayman Brac. By 1957 tourism began taking hold on *Seven Mile Beach* boosted by Bob Soto who began the island's first recreational diving business, introducing world to the underwater delights that the Cayman Islands had to offer.

In 1959, the Cayman Islands ratified their first constitution which provided a Legislative Assembly of 12 elected members and an Executive Council comprised of 2 elected members. The Commissioner was replaced by an Administrator who presided over the Legislative and Executive Councils and who was bound to consult with the Executive Council before exercising his powers of office. The island's first *Tourist Board* was formed in 1966 launching a serious effort at tourism promotion overseas, and which we see today was very successful over the years.

When Jamaica became independent in 1962, the Cayman Islands elected to remain under British rule as a Crown Colony and the power that was once held by the Governor of Jamaica was transferred to the

local Administrator whose title changed to Governor in 1971. A new constitution was drafted in 1972 which also brought minor changes to the makeup of the Legislative Assembly and the Executive Council.

Today we know the Cayman Islands as an offshore banking haven (begun back in 1966 when the first banking and trust laws were passed) and as a world class diving destination. The *Tourist Board* became the *Department of Tourism* in 1974 and in 1991, increased population and development meant more representatives were needed in the Assembly. In 1993-1994, the Assembly was expanded to 15 elected members and the members of the Executive Council became known as Ministers.

On September 11 and 12, 2004, *Hurricane Ivan* hit Grand Cayman, HARD, with sustained winds of 165 mph and gusts to 208 mph, and estimated 30' seas which blanketed parts of the island with water 8' deep in places (the locals were happy that Ivan hit at low tide). Grand Cayman will take a long time to recover from *Ivan*, the devastation is awesome, the entire reef along the southern shore was changed, parts of the reef wound up on the south shore road. Some old timers say *Ivan* was worse than the Hurricane of 1932, although *Ivan* did no damage to either Little Cayman or Cayman Brac. Two people died on Grand Cayman, one perished in a shelter in Bodden Town, another was found in his boat in the mangroves at *North Sound*. All over the island you will see the evidence of destruction, a desert of sand where trees once stood, a lake which once was a woodland, and sand everywhere, at times the southern shore east of Bodden Town looks like it is covered in a layer of snow, except it's sand that washed up from *Ivan*.

Cayman Brac

Waypoints
Cayman Brac -1 nm NE of northeast tip
19° 46.00' N, 79° 43.00' W

Scott's Anchorage - ¼ mile north of jetty
19° 41.82' N, 79° 52.75' W

Cayman Brac - 1 nm SW of West End Point
19° 40.00' N, 79° 54.00' W

Cayman Brac was given the suffix *Brac*, which is Gaelic for *bluff*, by Scottish fishermen who settled on the island in the 1600s. The island is usually just called *Brac* by the folks that live there, who are known as *Brackers* and for the most part live on the northern

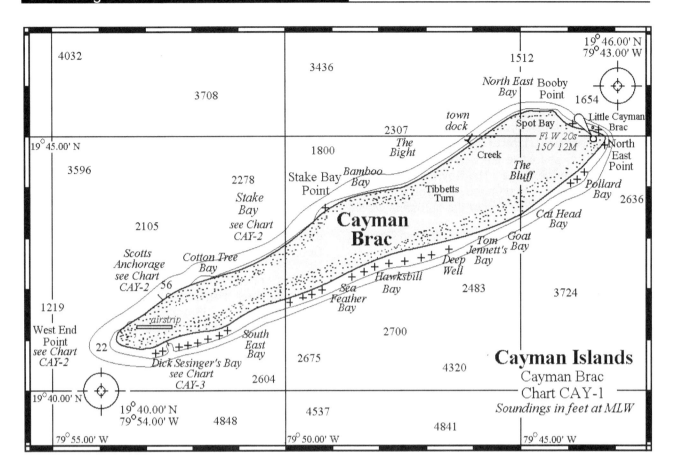

The bluff at the northern tip of Cayman Brac

side of the island. There are approximately 1,500 people living on this wonderful little island where crime and unemployment is practically non-existent and Brackers enjoy a high standard of living with the added benefit of no income taxes! I've mentioned in previous guides about how friendly some local folks are, but here on Cayman Brac, it's not just those who are involved with the tourist industry that are friendly, it's a natural part of every *Brackers* makeup, these folks are genuinely friendly, warm, hospitable, and very proud of the island and their heritage, and are anxious to share this with you. Today the government is pushing tourism on the island and with its backing the tourism industry is slowly growing here bringing a greater prosperity to the local economy. If you'd like to learn more about Cayman Brac and her people I suggest that you visit the *Cayman Brac Museum* at *Stake Bay* with its fascinating collection of Brac antiques, some of which are relics of past shipwrecks that date back to the 1700s, while others are donated from the homes of locals.

The bluff for which the island is named is actually a towering limestone plateau rising to 140' above sea level and dominating the eastern half of 12-mile long by 1½ mile wide Cayman Brac. This prominent landmark allowed Columbus to sight the island on his fourth voyage to the New World. The bluff is literally riddled with caves (over 170 documented) and a delight for spelunkers. Most of the caves lie at the foot of the bluff while others can only be reached by a short, but sometimes rugged climb. The largest of the caves is called *Great Cave* and offers a number of chambers for your exploration (watch out for the harmless fruit bats). Some of the caves are said to contain lost treasures of pirate gold, but what you will most likely find is *Caymanite*, a stone only found in the Cayman Islands, usually in the crevices in the limestone bluff. Newly popular on Cayman Brac is the sport of rock climbing, a natural when you consider the bluff is a great platform for vertical cliff climbing. Cayman Brac is also a haven for avian life and is a stopping point for several species in their migratory paths. Here and there you will find nature parks and parrot trails providing you with a good opportunity to explore and view the local flora and fauna.

The Creek, Stake Bay
Waypoints
The Creek - 200 yards NNW of town dock
19° 44.81' N, 79° 46.12' W

Cayman Brac, *Stake Bay* - ¼ nm offshore
19° 43.80' N, 79° 51.00' W

Navigational Information
If you're approaching from Jamaica, a waypoint at 19° 46.00' N, 79° 43.00' W, will place you approximately 1 mile northeast of the northeastern tip of Cayman Brac as shown on Chart CAY-1. If you wish to approach Cayman Brac via its southwestern tip, a waypoint at 19° 40.00' N, 79° 54.00' W, will place you approximately one mile southwest of West End Point, also shown on Chart CAY-1. Bear in mind that as you approach Cayman Brac from Jamaica, you might see a flashing red light from 10-20 miles off, this is not a point of land, it is the antenna tower at *Stake Bay*.

From the waypoint off the northeastern tip of Cayman Brac you can pass close inshore, at least ¼-½ mile off as you head southwest along the northern shore of the island to the main settlement of The Creek where you will clear in.

A waypoint at 19° 44.81' N, 79° 46.12' W, will place you approximately 200 yards north/northwest of the main dock (see photo). As shown on Chart CAY-2, a waypoint at 19° 43.80' N, 79° 51.00' W, will place you in *Stake Bay*, about ¼ mile offshore. You can also pick up a mooring at *Scott's Anchorage* and dinghy in from there. A waypoint at 19° 41.82' N, 79° 52.75' W, will place you approximately ¼ mile north of the rock jetty where you will see several moorings available. You can also drop your anchor anywhere along the rocky shoreline in sand, never in coral! In most conditions these are good anchorages, but the north shore is no place to be with any northerly seas running. Even on calm nights the north shore can be a bit rolly when the wind dies and there is any sea at all from the east or southeast. Although it doesn't look like it on paper, *Stake Bay* actually offers a small bit of protection from the southwest, however southwesterly seas can work their way around the point to give you a bit of roll.

What You Will Find Ashore
Customs and Immigration
To begin the clearing in process, which won't take long, call either *Port Authority* or *Brac Customs*

The town dock at The Creek, Cayman Brac, you can clear in here

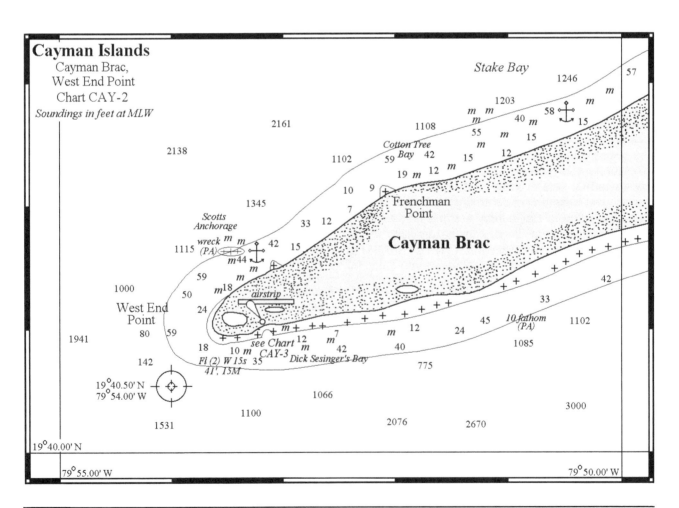

Cayman Islands
Cayman Brac,
West End Point
Chart CAY-2
Soundings in feet at MLW

on VHF ch. 16. You will likely be directed to the large concrete town dock, conspicuous by the warehouse and cranes behind it (*Port Authority* will also direct you to close all the hatches on your boat until the *Mosquito Control* officer sprays your boat and releases you).

The dock is a bit high for most cruising boats (but it has good water depth, anywhere from 11-20 feet) and it can be a rough place if any seas are running. If you're uncomfortable with tying up there you will find a mooring in front of the small boat harbor and ramp just to the west of the town dock. Make sure that *Port Authority* and *Customs* are aware you will be tying up there instead and ferrying out the *Customs, Immigration,* and *Mosquito Control* officers in your dinghy. Another option is to pick up a mooring in *Stake Bay* and dinghy the officers aboard from there; the *Customs* office is located by the antenna tower on shore at *Stake Bay*.

Diving the M/V Captain Keith Tibbetts

Great diving abounds in the Cayman Islands and Cayman Brac is no exception to that rule with dozens of wrecks in her surrounding waters. One of the biggest attractions for *SCUBA* divers here is the wreck of the M/V *Captain Keith Tibbetts*, also known as the *Russian Destroyer*, a 330' long frigate lying in 50'-110' of water near *Scott's Anchorage*. The *Tibbetts* was sunk in September of 1996 and is complete with guns fore and aft and a great variety of sea life (the hatches have been barred to ensure the safety of divers). The ship lies within 15' of the surface so even snorkelers can get a good view of it, in fact, on calm days you can see it quite nicely from the deck of your boat as you putter about over the top of it. The dive site lies west of the small rock jetty in *Scott's Anchorage* and can be found by locating a trio of mooring balls about 10 yards apart. One mooring is attached to the ship's stern, another to her bow, and the third is attached to her anchor. Wall diving is very good here on Cayman Brac and usually starts around 70'-100', while shallow reef dives such as *Greenhouse Reef* or *Radar Reef* offer spectacular corals rising close to the surface.

Dick Sesinger's Bay

Waypoints
Dick Sesinger's Bay - ¼ nm S of entrance
19° 40.81' N, 79° 53.15' W

Along the southeastern shore of Cayman Brac is a small break in the reef which leads to a very calm and protected stretch of water with depths of 6'-8' at MLW in *Dick Sesinger's Bay* as shown on some maps of Cayman Brac.

Navigational Information
As shown on Chart CAY-2, and in greater detail on CAY-3, a waypoint at 19° 40.81' N, 79° 53.15' W, will place you approximately ¼ mile south of the entrance channel into the bay. From the waypoint you will notice the pilings that mark the channel through the reef, a green one on the western side of the channel, and two on the eastern side of the channel. Never attempt to enter the channel in moderate to strong southerly winds, you will find seas breaking all the way across the entrance that can fling your vessel unto the bottom if you are not extremely careful. Never enter the channel and turn to the east early in the morning when the sun is in your eyes, you will never see the shoals, for the same reason never head west in the channel late in the day when the sun is low. There is a range for the entrance, you will see the markers ashore.

From the waypoint you will notice a range on shore, follow it in favoring the eastern side of the channel. Keep your eyes open and proceed cautiously. Once inside past the inner marker you must make a sharp, almost 90°, turn to starboard to follow the channel past the resort. Pay no mind to the dock off your port bow on shore, it's the *Brac Reef Resort* dock and you cannot tie to it. As the channel leads to the east you will notice that it has a few red and green markers that lie at the outermost edges of the channel, by no means hug one of these, keep as much as you can to where you estimate the middle of the channel lies and avoid the dark, grassy shoals. As you approach a small dock you will notice some dive boat moorings just off the dock, pass between the moorings and the dock even though your inclination says to go south of the moorings, the deeper water is between the moorings and the dock.

If a mooring is not available proceed eastward and anchor east of their moorings in 6'-7' of water. About 150' east of the easternmost *Dive Tiara* mooring you can find a pair of engine blocks on the bottom in mid-channel; you can tie to these or set an anchor in the sandy bottom, the holding ranges from fair to good here depending on how and where you set your anchor.

Author's boat anchored in *Dick Sesinger's Bay*

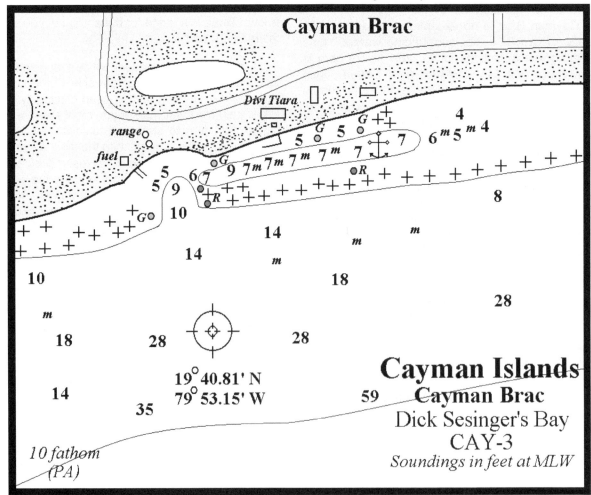

This anchorage is very well protected and you can ride out the fiercest frontal passages safely once inside, provided you don't swing out of the narrow channel into shallow water. The fringing reef that protects this small bay dries at low water and does a wonderful job of breaking almost all incoming seas. There is a fairly strong westerly setting current through this anchorage and in most cases you will lie to the current instead of the wind.

What You Will Find Ashore

Ashore on Cayman Brac there's no public transportation, but there are several companies that rent cars and scooters and there's even a taxi, but the driver will have to be called as she has another job, there's just not that much need for a full-time taxi on Cayman Brac. There are several nice hotels on the island and a very busy airstrip, *Sir Captain Charles Kirkconnell International Airport*. There are two main roads on the island, the most heavily traveled, *A6*, follows the northern coast from West End past places like Knob Hill, Banksville, Half Way Ground, Molucca Heights, Tibbetts Turn, and *Spot Bay*, some of which are not shown on any maps. On the southern shore of Cayman Brac you will find *A7* that leads from West End past *Brac Reef Beach Resort* (http://www.caymanbracbeachresort.com/) and several nice caves before ending up at *Pollard Bay*.

If you need to pick up some fuel there are three gas stations on the island, but you will have to dinghy your fuel out to your boat via your jerry jugs. There are several grocery stores on the island, the largest is *Kirkconnell's*, located in *Stake Bay* just around the corner from the *Customs* office, and *Billy's Supermarket* is located on the road near *Stake Bay*. If you need to do some laundry you can go to the small shopping center called *Foster's Corner* on the road to the airport where you will find *Brac Suds*.

If you just want to find a good place to eat on shore you can try *Aunt Sha's*, *The Captain's Table* (with their pirate Captain statue just outside), *Edd's Place* (local and Chinese dishes as well as Jerk Chicken), the *G&M Diner*, *La Esperanza*, and *Sonia's Restaurant,*. Two of my favorite eateries are *Angie's*, a very popular spot with locals and tourists, and *Seaview*, usually just called "*Blackie's*" with what they claim is a drive up, but it's more like drive up, order, and wait, but their ice cream is worth the wait. If you need medical help there is a small hospital on the island, *Faith Hospital*, and you can phone them at 345-948-224.

Little Cayman

Waypoints
Little Cayman- 1 nm NE of East Point
19° 43.50' N, 79° 56.50' W

Little Cayman, Main Channel- ¼ nm NE of
19° 42.73' N, 79° 57.65' W

Little Cayman- ½ nm SW of West End Point
19° 39.20' N, 80° 07.00' W

The island of Little Cayman, only about 10 miles long and 2 miles wide, lies approximately five miles west of Cayman Brac and is quite low compared to her easternmost sister. Little Cayman is not as heavily populated as Cayman Brac, with around 150 folks permanently residing on the island, the locals are vastly outnumbered by the local iguana population, something on the order of 10:1. So numerous are the iguana on Little Cayman that you will often see signs (painted by local artists Janet Walker and John Mulak) announcing "Iguana Crossing" and "Iguana Right of Way" posted throughout the islands to protect these reptiles that reach lengths of over 5'.

This island seems made for those who want to get away from it all; it was once home to several die-hard fishermen (you will find world class bonefishing on the flats here) and divers who lived here with few if any creature comforts. A well-known resident was the famous actor Burgess Meredith, who sadly, is well remembered for his role of *The Penguin* on the old *Batman* TV show. Meredith had a home on the northwestern tip of the island and like everybody else on the island in those days, got his electricity from a generator, the island's first true electrical service didn't come online until 1991. Today the island's entire economy is based on the divers that flock to the dive resorts (*Reef Divers* (http://www.reefdiverscaymanbrac.com/) and the *Little Cayman Reef Resort*) (http://www.littlecayman.com/) in *Owen's Sound* on the southern shore of Little Cayman.

Navigational Information
If you are approaching Little Cayman from Cayman Brac I hardly need to give you any waypoints, only 4 miles separate the two islands. If you wish to pass along the northern shore of Little Cayman and head towards Bloody Bay you can head for a waypoint at 19° 43.50' N, 79° 56.50' W, which will place you approximately one mile northeast of East Point at the northeastern tip of Little Cayman as shown on Chart CAY-4. From this position you may proceed along

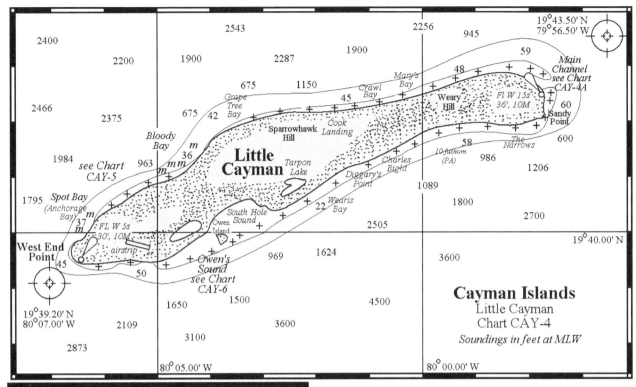

Cayman Islands
Little Cayman
Chart CAY-4
Soundings in feet at MLW

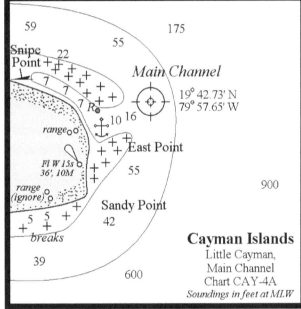

Cayman Islands
Little Cayman,
Main Channel
Chart CAY-4A
Soundings in feet at MLW

the northern coast of Little Cayman toward *Bloody Bay* keeping clear of the reefs of the northeastern tip of the island. If you wish to approach Little Cayman's north coast via West End Point, a waypoint at 19° 39.20' N, 80° 07.00' W, will place you approximately ½ mile southwest of West End Point as shown on Chart CAY-4 and in greater detail on Chart CAY-5.

From this position you can pass west of the point to turn northeast towards *Bloody Bay*.

At the northeastern tip of Little Cayman, as shown on Chart CAY-4, and in greater detail on Chart CAY-4A, it is possible to find shelter from westerly winds, more specifically, winds from the south/southwest through the west/southwest. Just north of Sandy Point and East Point, just past the light, you will find a range consisting of a large white triangle as the front mark, and a large white square that acts as the rear mark. The pair mark a wide and deep entrance channel through the reef called *Main Channel*. Don't confuse this range with a smaller range that lies southwest of Sandy Point that is used primarily by dive boats, the waters inside are shallow, 4'-6' in most places.

As shown on Chart CAY-4A a waypoint at 19° 42.73' N, 79° 57.65' W, will place you on the range just outside the break in the reef. Enter on the range and you will find the deeper water passing between the reef and the northeastern tip of the island by the conspicuous barge near Snipe Point. The bottom is rock and sand and the holding ranges from fair to good depending on where and how you set your hook. If you're seeking shelter from the westerly winds in the prelude to a frontal passage this is a good spot for that, but once the wind and seas move into the northwest it will be time to head to *Owen's Sound* to anchor. If your draft allows, you will be much better off in *Owen's Sound* for any sort of a blow (but not a hurricane, never consider staying at Little Cayman or Cayman Brac in the event of a named storm).

An even better spot to ride out a frontal passage, and the best anchorage on the island as far as I'm concerned, is in *Owen's Sound* on the southern shore of Little Cayman as shown on Chart CAY-4, and in greater detail on Chart CAY-6. The only problem with this anchorage is the depth of the water, or to be more specific, the lack of depth. A draft of 6' can enter and find shelter here, but vessels with deeper drafts, although they can enter, will be hard pressed to find room to anchor outside of the entrance channel.

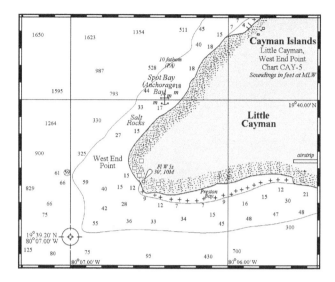

Owen's Sound

Waypoints
Owen's Sound - ¼ S of entrance
19° 39.25' N, 80° 04.45' W

As shown on Chart CAY-6, a waypoint at 19° 39.25' N, 80° 04.45' W, will place you ¼ mile south of the well-marked entrance channel. When approaching this waypoint do not allow your vessel to get too close to the reef that lies east of the channel, the reef itself stretches almost 100 yards to seaward, to the south, from the red light on the eastern side of the entrance channel. The channel is marked by two privately maintained lights, red and green, both flashing once every 5 seconds, and a range ashore consisting of a white triangle as the front mark and a white square as the rear mark. The front mark is light with a quick flashing green light at night while the rear mark is lit with a quick flashing red light. These lights are to assist the dive boats entering after a night dive on *Bloody Bay Wall*, they are not meant to lead you into a shallow harbor that you've never been into before. Don't try to enter *Owen's Sound* at night if you've never been here before. If you have any questions about the depths here you can try to hail *Reef Divers* on VHF ch. 16 for more information.

From the waypoint, enter the wide channel (it's wider than the channel at the *Divi Tiara Resort* on Cayman Brac!) and once inside and just past the reef on the eastern side of the channel turn to starboard and head towards Owen's Island. Avoid the dark shoals that you see closer in towards shore in the entrance channel, they only have about 4' of water over them. As you make your turn to the east you will see a small mooring about ¼ mile east of the channel.

If it's not taken go ahead and pick it up, but be warned that there's only 6' of water there at MLW. You can anchor in 6'-8' of water just east of the channel, about halfway between the channel and the mooring. The bottom is sand and the holding is good. Shallow draft vessels can work their way in closer to Owen's Island to anchor in the lee between Owen's Island and the mainland of Little Cayman in 4'-6' of water. Watch out for shallow spots as you work your way through here, you will definitely be steering around some sandy shoals and shallow grassy patches. *Owen's Sound* affords very good protection from northerly swells and winds. During the prelude to a frontal passage, when the wind veers from southeast to southwest and builds, *Owen's Sound* gets quite choppy, but the long fringing reef breaks all the big seas, leaving only a small chop and a lot of surge to throw you around, nothing dangerous, only uncomfortable. At the northeastern end of the anchorage is tiny, uninhabited Owen's Island. The island only lies about 100-200 yards offshore and offers a nice little beach and lots of mangroves to explore. The bay to the northeast of Owen's Island, *South Hole Sound*, is very shallow, 3' in most places, and is only suitable for dinghy exploration or shallow draft vessels.

What You Will Find Ashore
The main settlement on Little Cayman is called Blossom Village (and is sometimes shown as South Town) and it's located just inland at the southwestern end of *Owen's Sound*. Here you will find Larry, the *Customs* officer. Larry is who you will need to find when you're ready to clear out before departing for Grand Cayman, and he's not too difficult to locate. He's either at his home/office in Blossom Village

Owen's Sound, Little Cayman

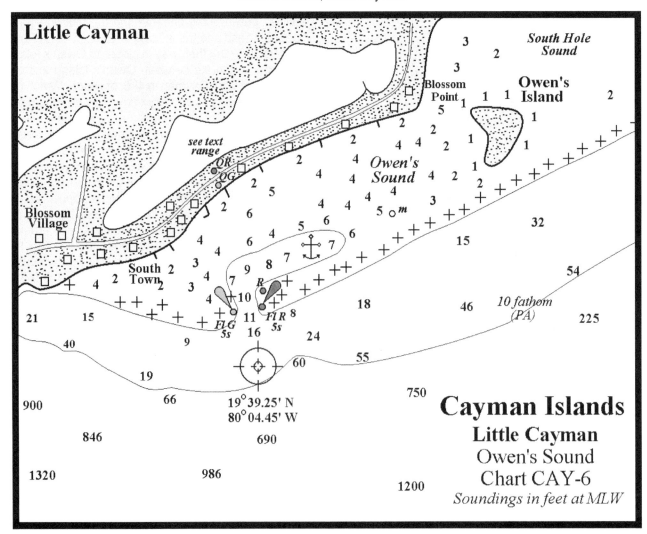

along with his dog, Casper, or at the airport clearing a flight. If you can't get in touch with Larry on VHF ch. 16 (give a hail to *Little Cayman Customs*), then dinghy in to the main dock, it's the westernmost one in the center of *Owen's Sound*, and take a short stroll to the west along the shoreline until you come to a small boathouse and ramp, but no dock (it was destroyed in a hurricane in 2004 along with Larry's boat). Larry's house is about a hundred yards inland of this boathouse in the main settlement of Blossom Village.

In Blossom Village you will find the airstrip, several hotels, a car rental company, a gas station, a resident nurse, and a very nice restaurant that I highly recommend, *The Hungry Iguana*. In town, at the *Village Square* complex you will find the *Village Square Grocery and General Store*, a bank (only open on Mondays and Thursdays from 0900-1430), a boutique, and a realty office.

Along the shores of *Owen's Sound* you will find a couple of nice dive resorts, *Reef Divers*, the *Little Cayman Reef Resort*, and the *Southern Cross Dive Resort* (http://www.southerncrossclub.com/), all of the dive resorts have restaurants and bars on site. A nice stop is the *Little Cayman Museum* (http://www.littlecaymanmuseum.org/), or the *Cayman Islands National Trust* (http://www.nationaltrust.org.ky/) office where you can garner a wealth of information about Little Cayman and visit their gift shop which showcases local artwork and offers several nice gifts for sale. The museum contains artifacts that date back over 150 years and offer a view of island life before tourists began arriving

On the north side of Little Cayman you will find moorings at *Bloody Bay*, as shown on Chart CAY-4, which will enable you to dive the *Bloody Bay Wall*, one of the most spectacular dive sites in the world. Jacques Cousteau hailed the waters of Little Cayman as one of the three best dive sites in the world, and a former *National Geographic* Magazine reporter named the *Bloody Bay Wall* as the number 7 dive site on the planet. The wall begins around 20' and plunges nearly vertical to over 1,200'. Southwest of *Bloody Bay* is deep *Spot Bay*, sometimes called *Anchorage Bay*, where you can pick up a mooring or drop the hook in good holding sand.

The main road on Little Cayman is officially *A8* (and just as officially it's called *Guy Banks Road* on the southern part of Little Cayman) and runs the entire circumference of the island. It's just off this road that you will find a brackish mangrove pond that is the *Booby Pond Nature Reserve* (sometimes called the *Governor Gore Bird Sanctuary*, http://www.nationaltrust.org.ky/#!governor-michael-gore-bird-sanctuary/clrv), a protected wetland under the *Wetlands Convention* signed in Ramshir, Iran, in 1971. Besides the frigate birds overhead, you will find a colony of 5,000 pairs of red-footed boobies that nest here, the largest red-footed booby colony in the Caribbean. The reserve is the largest bird sanctuary in the Caribbean and is also home to colonies of snowy egrets, terns, herons, and black frigate birds. Not that you're likely to find one at the bird reserve, but Little Cayman is home to one of the oldest reptile species in the New World, the tree climbing *anolis maynardi*, which has no other name. The females are green and the males brown, and they blend in perfectly with the surroundin, g foliage. Somebody needs to name these lizards!

Continuing north you will pass *South Hole Sound*, the body of water that lies east and north of Owen's Island. Here you will find the *Crossover Road*, or is it's more formally called, *Spot Bay Road*, which takes you over to the northern shore of Little Cayman just west of *Jackson's Pond*. If you don't take the crossover road you can continue northeastward towards Sandy Point. You will pass by brackish *Tarpon Lake*, a favorite stop for anglers in search of the 3-15 pound tarpon that can be caught in the lake. At Sandy Point you will find a stop sign where you can pull off the road to access the pink sand beach to be found here. The road continues around Little Cayman and begins to head southwest along the northern shore of the island where you will come back to the *Crossover Road* at *Bloody Bay* and *Jackson Pond*.

Grand Cayman

Waypoints
NW tip - 2 nm N of Boatswain Point
19° 25.00' N, 81° 25.00' W

Grand Cayman, SE tip - 2nm S of eastern reefs
19° 15.00' N, 81° 05.00' W

Grand Cayman, SW tip - 1 nm S of Sand Cay
19° 14.00'\ N, 81° 24.00' W

Grand Cayman is 22 miles long and varies from 4-8 miles in width with the highest point being only 60' above sea level at East End, so you're not likely to see the island until you're very close to it except

Marked channel with range
that leads into *Dick Sesinger's Bay,* Cayman Brac

Iguana crossing on Little Cayman

Author's boat at *Owen's Sound*, Little Cayman

Iguana on Little Cayman

Friendly sign on Owen's Island, Little Cayman

Larry, the *Custom's* Officer on Little Cayman,
and his dog Casper

at night when you can see the lights from Grand Cayman 10-15 miles out to sea when approaching from Little Cayman. For the most part, Grand Cayman is surrounded by a barrier reef system with the exception of the western shore, the location of the lovely *Seven Mile Beach* (which is really more like 4 miles long). The eastern end of the island at Gorling Bluff, is marked by a light, and the barrier reef has several small breaks that allow small craft access to the shore.

The currents off the eastern tip of Grand Cayman are strong and irregular and tidal rips often form between Gorling Bluff and Collier's Point. If you are approaching Grand Cayman from the north, from Cuba, do not be distracted by any onshore lights, you may be viewing lights that are several miles inside the reef at *North Sound*. Stay at least 1 mile off the northern shore to avoid the inshore reefs, especially near *North Sound*. If you're approaching the eastern side of Grand Cayman, stay at least 1½ miles offshore to avoid the reefs that stretch out almost a mile offshore at the southeastern tip of the island at *Gun Bay*. Along the southern shore you can come close in places, but to avoid any problems I suggest staying at least 1½ miles off to avoid the reefs at *Frank Sound* and *South Sound*.

Navigational Information

If you wish to approach Grand Cayman from the east, and want to transit the southern coast of the island, you can head for a waypoint at 19° 15.00' N, 81° 05.00' W, which will place you approximately 2 miles south of the reefs off the southeastern tip of Grand Cayman as shown on Chart CAY-7. From this waypoint you can head just south of west for a waypoint at 19° 14.00' N, 81° 24.00' W, which will place you approximately one mile south/southwest of *Sand Cay Light*. From this waypoint you can round the southwest tip of Grand Cayman and head to *Hog Sty Bay*.

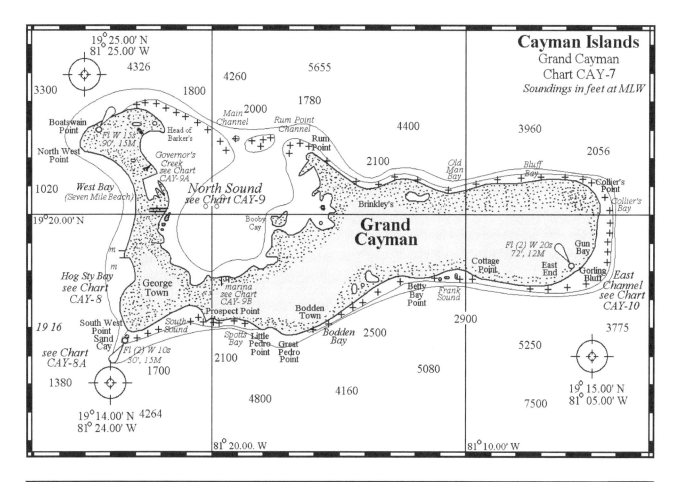

Welcome to Hell, Grand Cayman

Hell, Grand Cayman

If you are approaching Grand Cayman from the east and wish to pass north of the island to gain access to *Hog Sty Bay*, a waypoint at 19° 25.00' N, 81° 25.00' W, will place you approximately 2 miles north of Boatswain Point. From this position you can round the northwestern tip of Grand Cayman and proceed to *Hog Sty Bay* as shown on Chart CAY-7.

George Town

George Town is the capital of the Cayman Islands as well as a MAJOR cruise ship destination and offshore banking center. So popular is George Town with the tourists that some 1.3 million per year visit here via cruise ships and airlines. Over half of the Cayman's 30,000 residents reside in George Town, but don't look for a bustling Caribbean metropolis, this is still very much an island community, once you get out of the tourist traps along the waterfront and *Seven Mile Beach*. George Town was once known as *The Hogstyes*, a far cry from today's modern financial center that rivals Zurich and Tokyo. And if you'd like to watch TV while you're on Grand Cayman, there are two local stations, channel 22 and channel 27.

Navigational Information

When you're within 10 miles of Grand Cayman you should call *George Town Port Security* on VHF ch. 16 to notify them of your impending arrival. The anchorage for small vessels lies northwest of George Town's concrete pier in 15'-40' of water as shown on Chart CAY-8, and Chart CAY-8A. The holding is fair to good in sand and light mud. You can pick up a free mooring if you'd like, they're orange with a blue

stripe, the moorings that are white with a blue stripe are dive boat moorings and can be utilized if needed, but expect to hear about it from an irate divemaster.

You can tie up your dinghy at the dock that is used for cruise ship launches, just be sure to leave room for the launches to land. You can also anchor north of town along *Seven Mile Beach* (which is really only about four miles long). When a frontal passage threatens small craft must move to the wonderful protection offered by *North Sound*, but do it early, heavy northerly swells can cause entry problems in the channels. For more information on *North Sound*, see the next section. Shelter from northerly swells and winds can also be found along the southern shore of Grand Cayman at *South Sound*, see Chart CAY-8A.

Although the anchorage in *Coconut Walk Bay* is good in fair weather, I believe that you will appreciate the anchorages in *North Sound* much better (does it sound like I'm trying to sell you on *North Sound*?). Heading south from *Hog Sty Bay* parallel the shore and enter *Coconut Walk Bay* between Sand Cay and the mainland of Grand Cayman. From here work your way around the point to anchor wherever your draft allows. Keep a sharp lookout for scattered heads and small patch reefs. Never try this route at night.

What You Will Find Ashore
Customs and *Immigration*

Cruisers are required to hail George Town Port Security when within VHF range on ch. 16. When you arrive at the docks on the west side of Grand Cayman

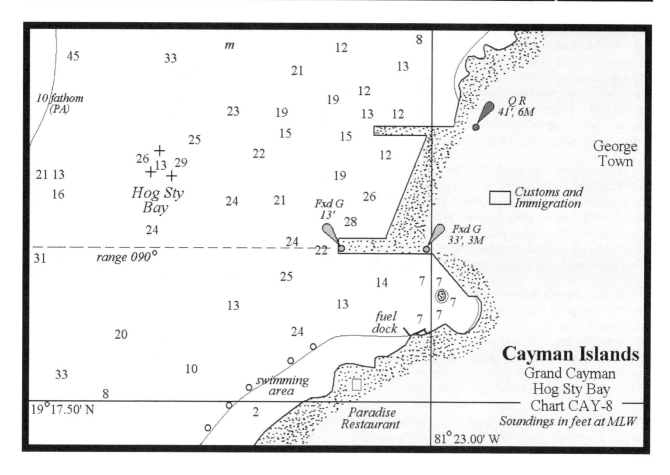

45   33   *m*   12   8
            21   13
10 fathom   12
(PA)   13
      23   19   19   12
            15   15
      25   22   12
26 +   13
   +13 29   19
21 13 +   26
16   *Hog Sty*   24   21   *Fxd G*   28
      Bay   *13'*
      24   — 24
                          —22
31   range 090°   *Fxd G*
                             33', 3M
      25   14   7 7
            13   13   7
20   24   7
            10   *fuel*   7
33   *dock*
      8   swimming
           area
19°17.50' N   2   *Paradise*
                    Restaurant
                    81° 23.00' W

Q R
41', 6M

George
Town

Customs and
Immigration

Cayman Islands
Grand Cayman
Hog Sty Bay
Chart CAY-8
Soundings in feet at MLW

George Town, Grand Cayman, with cruise ships at anchor

hail them again and they will direct you where to tie up. To avoid any congestion with cruise ships plan to arrive on a Sunday but plan on paying an overtime charge (approximately US$100 including *Mosquito Control*). While awaiting room at the docks, or if you do not feel you can safely come alongside the docks, you are permitted to use one of the orange mooring balls. If necessary, the officials will come out to you.

If you advise *Port Authority* that you wish to enter *North Sound* and head to a marina there, they will assist in having the officials come to your dock to clear you. In truly bad weather from the NW, you can go to *Spotts Bay* on the south side of Grand Cayman (see Chart CAY-7) and ask to clear from there, but bear in mind that the cruise ships will also go to *Spotts Bay*.

If you haven't already cleared with *Immigration* and the *Mosquito Control* officer in Cayman Brac, you will need to handle these matters in George Town. To begin the process you must call *Port Security* on VHF ch. 16 and they will direct you to the dock. As shown on Chart CAY-8, you will probably be directed to the north side of the northern most dock especially if the cruise ships are in port. If the dock is too rough, if there's too much surge, you can anchor out and dinghy the officers out to your boat. If the western shore of Grand Cayman is untenable, you will be directed to an anchorage on the south shore in *South Sound*.

If you're going to tie up to the concrete dock in *Hog Sty Bay* be sure to use plenty of fenders and long, stout dock lines. There are several bollards available but they're far apart, setting up spring lines would be a good idea as well. If the cruise ships are in port they'll probably be offloading passengers on this north dock so when you tie up do so as far to the east on the dock as you can. If you don't want to deal with the cruise ship hassles, clear in on a Sunday or Monday, there are usually no cruise ships in port on those days, but there is a US$70 overtime charge for clearance on Sundays.

The government offices are located just southeast of the dock in a two-story yellow building, *Customs* is on the first floor and *Immigration* is on the second floor, but you will only need this information when you clear out, when you clear in remain on your boat and the officers will come to you. Once you've cleared *Customs* you can anchor off the town or a bit northward, off *Seven Mile Beach*, or do what I do,

head to the safety and security of *North Sound* (more on that area in a moment).

Medical

For medical needs, there are numerous doctor's offices and clinics around George Town, and a large hospital just south of the commercial docks.

Veterinarians

If you need a vet try the *Cayman Animal Hospital* (http://www.caymananimalhospital.ky/) at 946-VETS, or *Island Veterinarian Services* at 949-0787 (http://www.islandvetservices.ky/).

Marine Facilities
Marine Supplies

A mile or so east of *Hurley's* is *Melody Marine*, a marine supply and fishing tackle store.

Marine Repairs

Compass Marine is a small marine service operation offering fabrication and expert rigging, electronics, mechanical, and fiberglass repair. *Compass Marine* is a dealer for *Hall* spars, *Mack Sails*, *Quantum Sails*, and *Blue Water Marine Paints*. Owner Mike Farrington is a qualified boat builder and avid sailor and can handle repairs on anything from a dinghy to a 105' schooner. *Compass Marine* is located at 147A *Dorcy Drive* in George Town and can be reached by phone at 345-949 0660, or you can email Bill at bill@compassmarine.ky (web site: www.compassmarine.ky).

Sail Repair

Near *Hurley's* is *Windward Sailing and Canvas*,(http://www.caymanwindsurf.ky/), the only place in the Caymans for your sail, canvas, or boat cushion repairs; call Monika at 916-3055

Fuel

Just south of the commercial dock, and south of the conspicuous rock shown on Chart CAY-8, is a *Texaco* fuel dock. Here you can get gasoline, diesel, and potable water, but use plenty of fenders as the dock is notorious for surge, especially when the cruise ships are in port and their lighters are ferrying passengers ashore in this busy little cove. I prefer to get fuel at the *Kaibo Yacht Club* or *Harbour House Marina* (http://www.harbourhousemarina.com/), both in *North Sound*. Just south of the *Texaco* dock is the *Paradise Seaside Grilol* (http://paradiserestaurant.ky/) right on the waterfront.

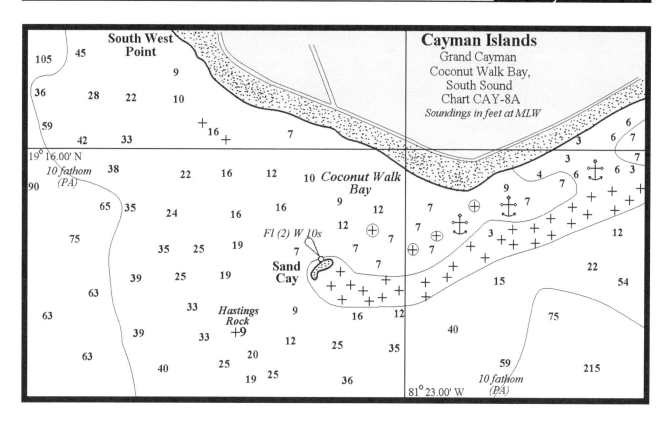

Cayman Islands
Grand Cayman
Coconut Walk Bay,
South Sound
Chart CAY-8A
Soundings in feet at MLW

South West Point

Coconut Walk Bay

Fl (2) W 10s

Sand Cay

Hastings Rock

19° 16.00' N

10 fathom (PA)

81° 23.00' W

10 fathom (PA)

South Sound, Grand Cayman, cruise ships in background

Internet

North of the dock is a *Texaco* station, where, if you go east for less than half a block you will come to the *Marquee Center* where you will find *Café Del Sol*, the place to go for Internet access.

Provisions

If you need to do some major provisioning here, you will find almost anything you could want, but it will be expensive, up to 30% more than U.S. prices. *Kirk's* on *Harbour Drive* is a good choice, so is *Foster's Food Fair* (http://fosters-iga.com/fff/) at *Seven Mile Beach* (2 locations) and the airport, but my favorite is *Hurley's* (http://hurleys.ky/home.php) at the roundabout south of the airport on *Bodden Town Road*. But like anywhere else, one store will likely have something you want that the other doesn't. In the same complex as *Hurley's* is a *Blockbuster Video*, a good toy store, and a book/hobbies store, *Books by the Bay*.

Dining

If you head north from the commercial docks, you will find *the Cayman Cabana* (http://www.caymancabanarestaurant.com/), THE place to be for the younger set, though all will feel right at home here. Located on the waterfront, Nelson Dilbert has been brewing *Old Dutch* beer here for over 15 years, one of only two breweries in the Cayman Islands. The barstools were constructed by craftsmen in Bodden Town, while the sign above the entrance was crafted by inmates at Northwest Prison, it seems everybody has something to do with this wonderful piece of *Caymanicana* (yes, I know that's not a word, but it could be, couldn't it?).

Sometimes you will find local fishermen selling fresh fish from the rocks below and south of *Cayman Cabana*; they'll have a small scale set up and you can walk or dinghy up to purchase your next meal. The *Greenhouse Cafe* (http://www.greenhousecayman.com/) now serves Lionfish with only a few minutes from "diver to diner."

Just past *Cayman Cabana* is *Rackam's Pub* (http://rackams.com/), a *Burger King*, the *Lobster Pot Restaurant* (http://www.lobsterpot.ky/), and the *Wharf Restaurant*, a VERY fine dining establishment complete with live music nightly (http://www.wharf.ky/).

Cox Lumber (http://www.tibbettslumber.com/), and *Uncle Bill's Home Improvement Center* (http://

www.unclebills.ky/), a *KFC*, a *TCBY*, the *Captain's Bakery and Grill*, the *Thai Orchid Restaurant* (http://www.thaiorchid.ky/), *Papa John's Pizza* (http://www.papajohns.ky/), the *Billy Bone's Beach Bar*, and the very popular *Coconut Joe's* (http://www.coconutjoecayman.com/), quite a selection of fine eateries from which to choose.

Laundry

Across the street from the docks and a bit to the east is a *One-Hour Martinizing* laundry service that's VERY expensive; two loads, washed, dried and folded cost US$30.

Discovering George Town

The main north/south road that runs along the western shore of Grand Cayman is called *Harbour Drive*, at least that is what it's called in town. North of George Town it's called *North Church Street* and south of town it's called *South Church Street*, and all along its length you will find all manner of duty-free shops, boutiques, grocery stores, restaurants, hotels, condos, and banks, and banks, and banks.

In the heart of town, just across the street from the commercial docks, there are hundreds of little boutiques and gift shops catering to tourist's interests from rare gems and fine watches to t-shirts and resort-wear. Here too you will find the air-conditioned *Cayman Islands National Museum* (http://www.museum.ky/) in the old courthouse on *Harbour Drive*, a *Harley Davidson Grand Cayman* (http://www.harleydavidsoncayman.com/) store, and the local *Hard Rock Café*. The museum is a wonderful place to spend a few hours and learn something about the history and culture of these islands. The main bus depot sits about a block east of the cruise ship docks.

Right on the waterfront at *Fort Street*, are the remains of *Fort George*, built in 1790 to protect the island's residents from the French and Spanish. In town look for the impressive, white clock tower; the clock is steam powered and was built in 1937 as a monument to King George V, for whom George Town was named. If you need to handle some mail while here you can visit *Elizabethan Square*, just north of the commercial docks. Here you will find a post office and a *FedEx* office. If you have an *American Express* card you can have your mail sent to you at: Your name, Your Boat's name, C/O *Cayman Travel Services*, *American Express*, PO Box 1759-GT, Elizabethan Square, George Town, Grand Cayman, Cayman Islands, BWI. It's best to check first with *Cayman Travel Services* (http://www.caymantravel.ky/) to see if this service is operating when you arrive, their phone number is 345-949-5400.

There are several art galleries on Grand Cayman that might pique your interest. In George Town, *The National Gallery of the Cayman Islands* (https://www.nationalgallery.org.ky/) hosts a variety of touring art exhibitions featuring local artists and collections. The *Esteban Gallery* is locally owned and managed and features what has been described as a "new interpretation of art. Located on the corner of *Fort Street* and *North Church Street* in George Town, the gallery features the work of Horacio Esteban and other local artists.

The *Kennedy Gallery* presents fine Caymanian art, prints and originals, as well as bronze sculptures. The gallery (http://kennedygallerycayman.com/) is located at the *West Shore Center* (http://shop7mile.com/discover-our-malls/west-shore-center/), close to the *Marquee Center* and the *Butterfly Farm*. At the *Sunset House Hotel* (http://www.sunsethouse.com/) on *South Church Street*, one mile south of George Town, you can visit Cathy Church's *Underwater Photo Centre and Gallery* (http://www.cathychurch.com/). Cathy's vibrant prints bring the marine world to life in color and black and white. The gallery has a small retail shop where Cathy's work is available to one and all. Here too you may rent underwater photography equipment and take lessons so you too can bring back some stunning underwater photos of your own.

North of George Town lies the famous *Seven Mile Beach* on *West Bay* (see Chart CAY-7). Although in reality it's only 5.5 miles long, *Seven Mile Beach* is dotted with hotels, condos, restaurants, and private homes along the beautiful green and blue waters of *West Bay* (home to several marine parks designed to protect and preserve the environment for ages to come). The waters are teeming with marine life, corals, snorkelers, glass-bottom and submersible tourist conveyors, para-sailors, and jet-skis, or as they're more commonly called these days, *PWC*, personal watercraft. The area called *West Bay* lies just north of the beach and is more akin to the "real" Grand Cayman complete with homes and families, not condos and tourists.

At the northeastern bend in *West Bay* is a public beach, boat ramp, and small dock that you can tie your dinghy to while you explore. About ½ mile south along the harbor road is a large *Foster's Food Fair* (http://fosters-iga.com/fff/), a very well-stocked grocery store. This dock is also where you will want to tie up to go to Hell.

Just a bit inland and north of the dock is the community of Hell (a walk of a little over a mile), located appropriately on *Hell Road*, a very popular spot for tourists who wish to send a letter with the postmark "Hell." But a catchy moniker is not the only draw for this community. Here you will find a peculiar rock formation that has evolved from the skeletons of shells and corals that have solidified over the millennia by salt and lime deposits. Researchers have found petrified forms of sea life here that are said to be 20 million years old.

At the north end of *West Bay*, along the shoreline from Northwest Point to Conch Point, you will find the *Cayman Turtle Farm* (https://www.turtle.ky/), the only green turtle farm in the world. At one time the Cayman Islands were full of turtles, the reason Columbus named the islands *Las Tortugas*, but today their numbers have been badly depleted and the green sea turtle is now an endangered species. The turtle farm exists to provide the local market with fresh turtle meat preventing the hunting of the animal in the wild, and to replenish the waters with hatchlings and yearlings. There are over 100 circular tanks in which some 16,000 turtles are raised in every stage of development. Since its inception in 1980, the Turtle Farm has released over 30,000 turtles into the sea. At the snack bar and restaurant you can sample turtle dishes as well as next door at the well-known *Cracked Conch of the Sea Restaurant* (http://www.crackedconch.com.ky/).

North Sound

Waypoints

North Sound - turning point to channels from W
19° 24.00' N, 81° 21.00' W

North Sound, Stingray Channel - ¼ nm N of
19° 23.10' N, 81° 20.43' W

North Sound, Main Channel - ¼ nm N of
19° 22.90' N, 81° 19.72' W

North Sound, Rum Point Channel - ¼ nm N of
19° 22.80' N, 81° 17.50' W

North Sound, Governor's Creek - ¼ nm ENE of
19° 21.55' N, 81° 21.90' W

North Sound, Kaibo Yacht Club - ½ nm SW of
19° 21.00' N, 81° 17.00' W

Harbour House Marina - ¼ nm N of channel
19° 18.10' N, 81° 19.50' W

As far as I'm concerned, huge *North Sound* should be the focus for any voyage to Grand Cayman. Here you will find two marinas, a haul-out yard, a fuel dock, several unique dive and swimming sites, and numerous places to anchor to find protection from any wind direction. The canals that lie off the sound are lined with some very nice houses and you can find good shelter in the *Governor's Creek* area, although it may seem like you've anchored in somebody's backyard.

Navigational Information

There are three entrances to *North Sound* as shown on Chart CAY-9, from the west they are *Stingray Channel*, *Main Channel*, and *Rum Point Channel*, and with the exception of *Stingray Channel*, they are well-marked. I do not advise entering *North Sound* at night unless you have become thoroughly familiar with the waters and entrance channels. When approaching the entrance channels to *North Sound* from the west, from *West Bay* and George Town, you must clear Northwest Point and Boatswain Point (see Chart CAY-7), both of which can be passed ¼ mile off, and then work your way eastward keeping clear of the reef that begins on the western side of Conch Point as shown on Chart CAY-9. This reef breaks in most conditions and is fairly easy to see (a lot of it is above water). To avoid the reef I suggest staying

north of 19° 24.00' N as you work your way eastward. If you have good visibility and are not daunted by the reef on your starboard side, you can work your way eastward by paralleling the reef, keeping to the 5-fathom line a couple of hundred yards north of the reef. Either way you choose, exercise caution.

From the west you can head to a waypoint at 19° 24.00' N, 81° 21.00' W, which will be your turning waypoint. From this position you can head to the waypoints I am about to give you at the beginning of each entrance channel, *Stingray Channel*, *Main Channel,* and *Rum Point Channel*.

We'll now discuss entering *North Sound* from the three channels, but before I continue I want to suggest that first-time visitors to *North Sound* use *Main Channel* as opposed to the other two. *Main*

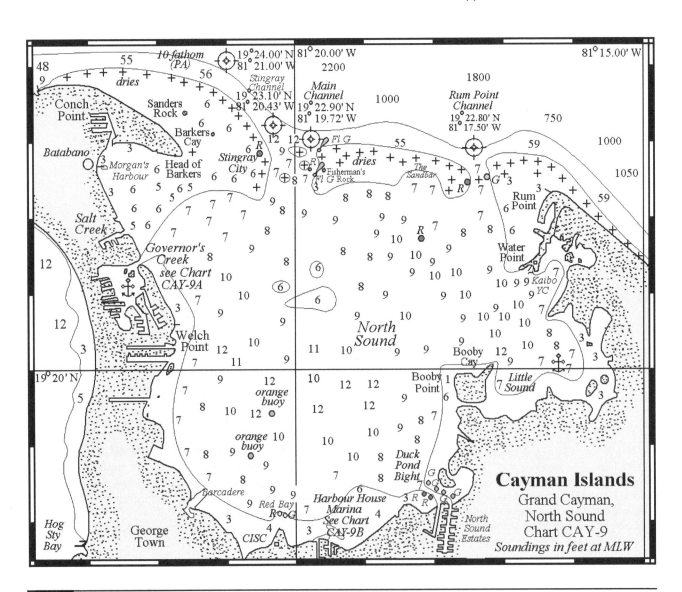

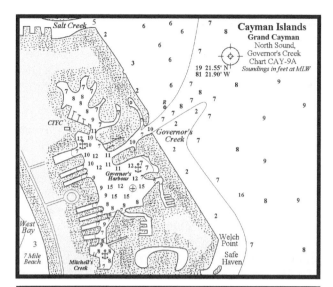

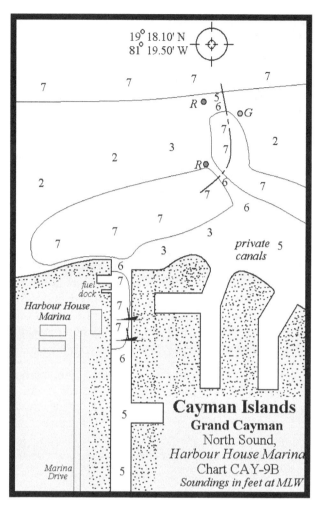

Kaibo Yacht Club, North Sound, Grand Cayman

Governor's Harbour with *Cayman Islands Yacht Club* upper center

Channel is well-marked and it's wide and easy to see in most conditions. With that in mind, now let's enter via *Stingray Channel*.

From the above mentioned turning waypoint, you can head generally south/southeast to a waypoint at 19° 23.10' N, 81° 20.43' W, which puts you past the end of the reef on your starboard side and at the mouth of *Stingray Channel* (*Stingray Channel* once was as well-marked as her two sister channels, but *Hurricane Ivan* in 2004 changed all that and the marks may not be replaced).

From this position you can see a shoal well to port; head southward and then southeastward once past this shoal, paralleling the lie of the reef on your starboard side, and you are in *North Sound*. Once inside the reef you can turn to starboard to anchor behind the reef in the vicinity of the red buoy, this is the area known as *Stingray City*, a popular tourist attraction where divers and snorkelers hand-feed the stingrays that congregate here.

From the turning waypoint the outer green marker for *Main Channel* is easily seen. You can head to a waypoint at 19° 22.90' N, 81° 19.72' W, which will place you at the northern end of the entrance channel. From this position you can look southward and see the inner markers, pass between those and you are in *North Sound*.

To access *Rum Point Channel*, leave the turning waypoint and head to a waypoint at 19° 22.80' N, 81° 17.50' W, which will put you north of the marked entrance channel (I don't advise using *Rum Point Channel*, it's shallow, only about 7' at MLW, and it has a large head in the middle of the channel just south of the markers; you will have a much easier entry if you use *Main Channel*). As you approach the waypoint you must do so from the north to avoid the reefs on either rise of the channel as the markers are a bit south in the channel as you can see on the chart. Favor the western side of the channel and keep and eye out for the large coral head in the center of the channel just inside the markers.

On the west side of *North Sound* you will find the entrance to *Governor's Creek* and the *Cayman Islands Yacht Club* as shown on Chart CAY-9 and in greater detail on Chart CAY-9A. A waypoint at 19° 21.55' N, 81° 21.90' W, will place approximately ¼ mile east/northeast of the entrance into the *Governor's Creek* canals. From the waypoint head into the canal keeping the red buoy to starboard and keeping off the

visible shoal to port. Once inside keep favoring the port side of the channel and wind your way back until you enter *Governor's Harbour*. A turn to starboard here will bring you to the *Cayman Islands Yacht Club* and the anchorage just south of their seawall.

You can head further south from the *CIYC* and work your way through the canals to enter protected *Mitchell's Creek* where you can anchor in 7'-12' of water and a grassy bottom. The advantage of anchoring here is that you can tie your dingy to the seawall and a short walk will put you on *Harbour Drive* to the west. You will have to thread your way through a couple of shallow areas, 6' at MLW, but keeping to mid-channel and going slow will get you through unless your draft is simply too deep.

The *Kaibo Yacht Club* is one of my favorite marinas on Grand Cayman although it is quite a distance from downtown George Town. Located on the eastern side of the sound on the Kai Peninsula just south of Rum Point and east of Water Point. You can't see the marina when you enter *North Sound*, but once inside the reef you can head generally east/southeast to a waypoint at 19° 21.00' N, 81° 17.00' W, which will place you approximately ½ mile southwest of the marina. From the waypoint head northeast into the little cove where you can't miss the marina, it has the biggest metal roof in the cove and you will find 7'-8' of water right up to the docks with an occasional 6' spot to either side.

At the southern end of *North Sound* you will find the entrance channel to *Harbour House Marina* (http://www.harbourhousemarina.com/). As shown on Chart CAY-9B, a waypoint at 19° 18.10' N, 81°19.50' W, will place you just off the entrance channel leading to the boatyard. From the waypoint you will see several markers that define the channel which has a controlling depth of 5' at MLW in one spot right at the mouth of the channel. Remember that all markers inside *North Sound* are privately maintained so their configuration might change by the time this guide is published.

From the waypoint head southward passing between the two red markers and one green marker. Once past the inner red marker, turn to port and head for the marina staying between the very visible shoal (visible only if there's good light) and the shoreline. When you are north of the canal off the western shore where the marina is located, turn to port and enter the canal, you will find a 6' at MLW but for the most part you will find 7'. The fuel dock is about 100 yard down the canal to starboard, just past the haul-out basin. If you need assistance *Harbour House Marina* monitors VHF ch. 16. Around the next point to the west of *Harbour House Marina* is a narrow, marked channel that has a controlling depth of 4' at MLW, and leads to the docks and clubhouse of the *Cayman Islands Sailing Club* (http://www.sailing.ky/).

To the east of *Harbour House Marina*, at *Duck Pond Bight*, you will find the marked entrance channel to *North Sound Estates*. The channel and the canal will take 7' most of the way in; compared to a lot of the canals off *North Sound* this is a lot of water. With the exception of *Governor's Creek*, most canals only have about 4' 6" of water and so are used primarily by shallow draft powerboats.

What You Will Find Ashore

One of the most popular tourist destinations in *North Sound*, and one that you will probably want to visit, is *Stingray City* (http://www.stingraycitycaymanislands. com/). There are actually two *Stingray City* sites, one just to the west of *Stingray Channel* in about 12' of water, and the other to the east of *Main Channel*, usually called *The Sandbar*, in about 3'-10' of water, both locations are easy to find, simply look for all the local boats ferrying out crowds of tourists. *Stingray City* was inadvertently created at the beginning of the 20th century when fishermen, returning to port, would stop just outside the channel to clean their catch and dump the entrails overboard. It didn't take long for the local stingray population to discover the free buffet and today they are quite used to visitors feeding them squid, so much that I believe they expect to be fed.

Marine Facilities

Marinas

Cayman Islands Yacht Club

At the time of this writing the *Cayman Islands Yacht Club* (http://www.ciyachtclub.ky/#), the *CIYC*, boasts a fuel dock with diesel and gas, and dockage for vessels to 150' and drafts to 7'. If you would like to telephone the yacht club before you arrive on Grand Cayman to check on the availability of dockage, contact the club at 345-747-2492.

If you're approaching the marina by land, turn to the east on *Yacht Drive*, just off the harbor road at *Seven Mile Beach*. You can anchor just off the yacht club but the holding is iffy, the grassy bottom makes for poor holding, it would be best to dive on your anchor or perhaps set two if a blow is forecast.

The one good thing about a blow is that it will keep the no-see-ums away, and they can be thick here on windless nights.

It is possible to arrange for *Customs* and *Immigration* clearance at the marina with advance approval. Pilot service is available from *Main Channel* for $100. The marina tends to be used by tourist and dive boats and other commercial operators so it is fairly busy during the day but there are still a number of live-aboard boats here too.

Barcadere and the George Town Yacht Club

The *Barcadere* (http://www.barcadere.com/) is the newest marina facility on Grand Cayman, in fact, parts of the marina are still under construction. The 20-acre mixed use development is centered around the marina located on the southwestern shore of *North Sound*.

The marina's 83 concrete and hardwood docks can accommodate vessels up to 150' in length with a maximum draft of 8' (local pilots are available and recommended for deep draft vessels). Slips are complete with 30 amp, 50 amp, 100 amp, and 200 amp single phase electric and 100 amp and 200 amp 3-phase electric, 60hz. All slips have potable water, dockside *ValvTect Marine Fuel* (duty-free for transient vessels), free pump out service, free Wi-Fi, showers, 24-hour security, *and Customs* and *Immigration* clearance (with 48-hour advance notice), Future developments include a hotel and condos, a retail village with a convenience store, liquor store, clothing boutique, laundromat, a multi-level storage rack that can accommodate boats up to 40' LOA, and a tackle shop. The marina monitors VHF ch. 16 and can be reached by phone at 345-949-3743.

On site is a boatyard with a huge 100-ton *Travelift*, and *Scott's Marine* (http://scottsmarinecayman.com/) with a boat showroom, chandlery, and boat repair services. *Scott's Marine* can handle all manner of repair from hulls to electronics and mechanicals.

A new development, and one that is set to open as this edition is published, is the opening of the *George Town Yacht Club* (http://gtyachtclub.com/) on the waterfront at *Barcadere*.

Accessible by land or sea, and with parking for cars and boats, the *George Town Yacht Club* (*GTYC*) includes a club house with a restaurant and bar, changing rooms with showers and lockers, and a recreational fountain/pool for kids and the young at heart.

The second floor club house features a member's lounge with large screen TVs for sports, artwork by Guy Harvey and a private bar area with a huge balcony overlooking *North Sound.*

Harbour House Marina

Harbour House Marina is a boatyard and chandlery with a diesel dock; they're really not a marina in the proper sense of the word although they do have slips for rent complete with 30 amp and 50 amp electric, water, duty-free fuel, and dockside shower facilities.

Harbour House Marina has a 75-ton lift that can haul a boat with a 24' beam and a crane that can haul boats with beams up to 33'. Here you will find a huge, two-story, 8,000 square-foot chandlery with everything you could need including some rigging supplies. What they don't have they can usually *FedEx* in for you in a couple of days. Also located on site is a diesel repair shop, *Marine Power* (http://www. marinepower.ky/). *Harbour House* can haul and paint your boat, as well as handle all your welding, rigging, fiberglass, and mechanical needs, and if that wasn't enough, they can fix your prop too. Other guides have stated that *Harbour House Marina* handles sail repairs, this is because *Windward Sailing and Canvas* used to be located on site, now they've moved about a mile west on the south shore road (http://www. caymanwindsurf.ky/kit/repair/).

If you're arriving at *Harbour House Marina* by road, take the southern road, *Shamrock Road*, and turn north onto *Marina Drive* at *McRuss' Grocery Store*. Go to the end of *Marina Drive* and the road will end at the entrance to the yard. If you're arriving by sea, give the marina a hail on VHF ch. 16 before entering the channel or phone them at 345-947-1307 (email: jonathon@harbourhousemarina.com or mark@harbourhousemarina.com). *Harbour House Marina* is closed on Sundays.

Kaibo Yacht Club

The *Kaibo Yacht Club* (http://kaibo.ky/) offers floating docks that will accommodate a vessel to 80' and a 7' draft, 50-amp electric, RO water, a pay phone, a fuel dock offering diesel and gasoline, and a friendly restaurant.

Although by road it's a fair distance from the hustle and bustle of George Town, this is an oasis for the cruising sailor who just wants to get away from all of the commotion of the cruise ship tourists. Since most car rental agencies in George Town won't come out this far to pick you up (it's a 45-minute ride from George Town) I simply call *Cico Avis* (345-949-2468), they'll come out to pick you up at the *Kaibo Yacht Club* and that will save you a CI$40 cab ride into town. The *Kaibo Yacht Club* also has a small store on site, *The Chandler's Shop*, which offers the usual t-shirts and gifts along with cold beverages, ice cream, snack foods, and various sundry items.

Let's discuss what's around the *Kaibo Yacht Club*. Heading out of the driveway of the *KYC*, you will soon come to the beginning of the *North Shore Road* at Rum Point where you will find the *Rum Point Club* (http://www.rumpointclub.com/). Here you'll find a long dock used primarily by commercial boats (there's only about 3' of water at the outer end). Rum Point received its name from an incident in which several barrels of rum washed ashore here after a shipwreck. The *Rum Point Club* sits at the tip of Rum Point and is a great spot to while away some time. The club offers watersports rentals, a small dock suitable for dinghies and small boats, volleyball, hammocks, beachside lounging, the *Treasure Chest Gift Shop*, *Red Sails Sports* (http://www.redsailcayman.com/), and the *Rum Point Restaurant*. Sundays are popular with local boaters and the place fills up with powerboats.

Morgan's Harbour Marina

Just east of Hell and north of *Governor's Creek* you will find Batabano located on the northeastern side of *North Sound*. Here you can visit the *Calypso Grill* at *Morgan's Harbour Marina* (http://morganscayman. com/), which is not really a marina, just a dock where a couple of local fishing boats tie. The docks here were destroyed by *Hurricane Ivan*, but are not back up and running. The waters leading to the dock barely carry 5' and there is 7' around the docks, three small finger piers with a fuel dock.

In the restaurant, husband and wife team Richard and Jane Schweiger insist on using only locally caught fish to easily satisfy any seafood craving you might have and possibly create some new addictions, like the Fresh Fish Ceviche. The reputation of the Morgans Harbour Sunday barbecue means that locals and visitors often make the trip to this restaurant to enjoy lazy Sunday afternoons overlooking the water. And if their restaurant doesn't do the trick for you, there are two others to choose from.

East End, East Channel

Waypoints
East Channel - ½ nm E of channel entrance
19° 18.80' N, 81° 04.00' W

The eastern end of Grand Cayman, simply called East End, is one of the most untouched areas in the Cayman Islands. The offshore reefs are home to several wrecks.

The treacherous reef off the eastern shore of Grand Cayman parallels the shoreline, but at the southeastern end of the island it is farther offshore than at the northern end. Here you will find *East Channel*, a passage through the reef that leads to good water inside, 7'-12' deep in some places. The entrance is tricky and it has a dogleg to the south to avoid some coral as shown on Chart CAY-10, but the tricky part doesn't end there, inside there are numerous scattered shoals and heads, much of which has been changed since *Hurricane Ivan*, so if you've been in here before, expect things to be a little different.

The mouth of *East Channel*, marked by a piling on the northern side, can break in moderate to heavy seas and appear quite daunting, and it should NEVER be attempted at night, in periods of poor visibility, or when you are experiencing heavy following seas. I've tried to enter with 20-25 knots of northeast wind and the seas were breaking all the way across the channel, not all the time though, in the lulls I could discern the channel entrance, but I prudently went around the south side of Grand Cayman instead of taking a chance on entering that day.

Navigational Information
As shown on Chart CAY-10, a waypoint at 19° 18.80' N, 81°04.00' W, will place you approximately ½ mile east of the entrance to *East Channel*. From the waypoint head west entering the channel by keeping the piling on the northern side of the channel to starboard. You will have to pilot your way in here by eye, once inside you will need to turn to port to avoid some shoals directly in front of you.

What You Will Find Ashore
At *Gun Bay* you find a pair of cannons from the *Wreck of the Ten Sails* as well as a monument to that tragedy as well as some other notable wrecks that occurred on the east reef. If you'd like to dive the wrecks, see the folks at the *East End Dive Lodge* at the southeastern tip of Grand Cayman, south of *Gun Bay*. *Gun Bay* has one very nice little restaurant,

Vivine's Kitchen, a good spot to try "all your native dishes" as the sign reads.

Driving Around

First let's discuss what we'll find if we head south from the commercial docks in George Town and then east along the southern shore. By the way, the phrases "going country" or "going to the tropical side" refer to taking a trip to the east end of Grand Cayman. If you head south on *Harbour Drive* from the docks you will enter a residential section south of *Paradise Restaurant* with many nice homes along the waterfront as well as inland. A mile or so south of George Town is the *Grand Old House* (http://www.grandoldhouse.com/), sometimes called *Chef's Tell*, an old plantation era house that sits on the edge of the sea and offers an above average dining experience. Further along, at *South Sound*, you will find the *Bikini House*, a small beachfront bar tucked in along the waterfront.

The road that parallels the southern shore of Grand Cayman has several names, at some point or another it might be called *Jackson Road, Poinciana Road, Bodden Town Road, Shamrock Drive, Church Street*, the *Eastern Highway, A2, A3, A4*, but it doesn't matter, just head east, you won't get lost. As I mentioned earlier, at the roundabout southeast of the airport on *Bodden Town Road* you will find a nice mall with a larger *Hurley's* supermarket (http://hurleys.ky/home.php), my favorite, along with a *Blockbuster Video*, a good toy store, and a book/hobbies store, *Books by the Bay*. A mile or so east of *Hurley's* is *Melody Marine*, a marine supply and fishing tackle store, and *Windward Sailing and Canvas*, the only place in the Caymans for your sail, canvas, or boat cushion repairs; call Donna at 947-2649. Just a bit further east of *Melody Marine* is *Marina Drive* at the intersection where you will see *McRuss' Grocery*.

At the southern end of Grand Cayman, south of Savannah and west of Bodden Town, you will find the *Pedro St. James National Historic Site*, a restored great house atop a limestone bluff with a stunning view. The *Pedro St. James Castle*, often just called *The Castle* (http://pedrostjames.ky/), was built by Englishman William Eden with slave labor in 1780 when only 400 people lived on Grand Cayman. At one time it was a plantation great house, a courthouse, a jail, the *Government Assembly* building, and a restaurant. It is the birthplace of democracy for the Cayman Islands when Caymanians met here to form the first assembly on December 5, 1831. It is one of the largest homes on the island and certainly the oldest still standing. The house survived numerous hurricanes until 1970 when it was destroyed by a fire. Now it has been rebuilt and is the centerpiece of a historic park with a visitor center and an audiovisual theater complete with a laser light show.

Continuing eastward on the south shore road you will come to Bodden Town, once the largest settlement on Grand Cayman and the first capital of the Cayman Islands. Here you will find *Gun Square* where two cannon, once used to guard the channel through the reef, are now stuck muzzle-first into the ground. A few hundred yards east of *Gun Square* you can visit the *Pirate Caves* (http://www.piratescaves. ky/caves.html) where it's said that pirates of old left their treasure which has now been buried under centuries of hurricane damage. You will find a lot of

Ship's lead keel from wreck near *East Channel*

Ship's prop from wreck at *East Channel*

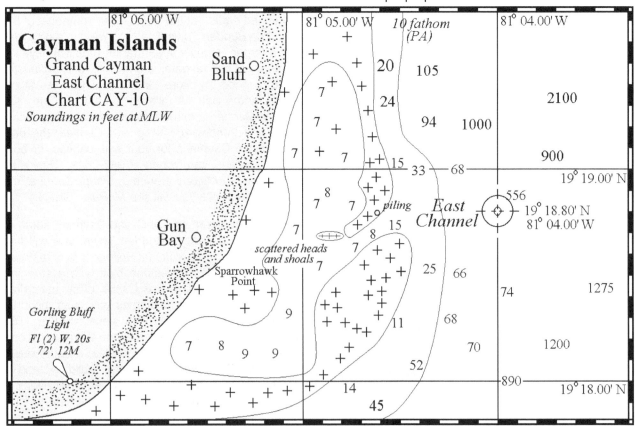

pirate artifacts on display here and a mini-zoo where the kids can feed freshwater stingrays. There is a 4 mile long stone wall at Bodden Town that's known as Grand Cayman's "Great Wall of China," which was built to protect the local residents from pirate attacks, unfortunately most of it was destroyed by *Hurricane Ivan*. Just east of Bodden Town is a small roadside stand called *Wood's Jerk Center*, a good spot to pick up some jerk chicken or pork. If you need something to drink you can stop in at the *Pitstop Bar* for a cold one, they're almost next door.

Heading east again you will come to Breakers and Blowholes where you will find the *East Side Fish Fry* right on the beach, *Vernon and Cora's Convenience Store*, a *Texaco* station with some limited grocery items, and the *Pirate's Cove Restaurant and Bar*. Blowholes is named after the shoreline where incoming waves erupt into geysers of saltwater shooting straight up through cracks and holes in the ironshore. Heading east from Breakers you will come to *Frank Sound Road*, which heads north to the north shore road and is covered in the next section on *North Sound*. If you head east from the intersection at *Frank Sound Road* you will soon come to East End, and that is covered in the section *East End*.

Beginning on the northern shore of Grand Cayman, a couple of miles east of Rum Point is the *Driftwood Beach Bar* with a Sunday barbeque from 1300-1900. A mile east at the corner of *Hutland Road* and the main road is *Chisson's Store*; here you can catch a bus into George Town at the covered bus-stop on the corner. Just a mile or so east of *Chisson's Store*, just before you enter the community of *Old Man Bay*, is the *Over The Edge Café* (http://www.overtheedgecayman.com/) right on the waterfront. In *Old Man Bay* you will find a small store, the *Old Man Bay Grocery*, and if you continue east you can follow the curve in the road as the *North Shore Road* turns into *Frank Sound Road* and heads south across the island, or you can take a left at the curve and continue east along the northern coast towards the east end of the island. Check out the snorkeling only a hundred yards or so offshore at *Old Man Bay*.

Frank Sound Road leads southward from *Old Man Bay* to the main highway that runs along the southern shore of Grand Cayman from East End to George Town. About 2 miles south of *Old Man Bay* is the turnoff for the 200-year old *Mastic Trail*, a footpath through the very heart of Grand Cayman that showcases a mangrove swamp,

woodland areas, and an agricultural area. If you're heading north on *Frank Sound Road* from the south shore road, which is called *Bodden Town Road* in this part of the island, the park lies approximately 2.5 miles north.

If you intend to head eastward along the north shore road instead of turning south on *Frank Sound Road*, you will eventually come to the northeastern tip of Grand Cayman where you will find the *Reef Resort*, and a nice little Internet spot, the *Thirsty Surfer Liquor Store and Internet Café*, with lots of snacks, goodies, and a few grocery items. Here too is *Castro's Hideaway Beach Bar and Grill* located behind the resort on the beach.

Continuing along the north shore road you will begin heading south on the eastern shore of Grand Cayman which is covered in more detail in the previous section *East Channel*.

Honduras

Ports of Entry:
Puerto Castillo (Trujilllo), La Ceiba (*La Ceiba Shipyard*), Puerto Cortés on the mainland, Coxen Hole (Roatán), Bonacca (Guanaja), and Puerto Este (Utila) in the Bay Islands (Islas de la Bahía).
Fuel: La Ceiba, Roatán, Guanaja, Utila
Haul-Out: La Ceiba, French Harbour
Diesel Repairs: La Ceiba, Roatán
Outboard Repairs: Roatán, La Ceiba, Utila
Propane: Roatán, La Ceiba
Provisions: Roatán, Utila, Guanaja, La Ceiba
Time Zone: Central Time Zone
Electricity: 110 volt, 60 cycle
Important Lights: See Appendix A

Honduras is located at the widest part of the isthmus of Central America and is the second largest republic in Central America. Just offshore are the enchanting Bay Islands, Las Islas de la Bahía, one of 18 departments into which Honduras is divided. A recent war against crime has dropped the crime rate in Honduras by 56%, good news indeed for the visiting yachtsman.

If that is not enough to entice you to these waters, couple that news with the fact that the Honduran government is very open to cruisers, promoting cruising in her waters by allowing a *Zona Libre*, a *Marine Free Zone* (no duty on imported marine supplies) at *Puerto de Cabotaje*, slashing cruising permit fees, and in general fostering an environment that will attract voyaging visitors to her shores.

Honduras has three distinct topographical regions, the interior highlands which constitutes approximately 80% of the total land area, and the Caribbean and Pacific lowlands. The interior highlands, whose terrain has been difficult to traverse and even more difficult to cultivate (the land lacks the rich volcanic ash found in other Central American countries), has not been highly developed although it is home to the majority of the population of Honduras. The western border of Honduras, which borders Guatemala, is primarily wooded and mountainous, while on the eastern border the lower mountains there merge with those of Nicaragua.

Between the mountainous eastern and western borders is a depression that runs from the *Caribbean Sea* to the *Golfo de Fonseca* and the Pacific coast. Tucked into one of these sheltered valleys

of the interior highlands is the capital of Honduras, Tegucigalpa, located over 3,000' above sea level. As mountainous as Honduras is, it is an oddity perhaps that the country has no active volcanoes inside its borders.

The coastal plain along the northern coast of Honduras is the most exploited. East of La Ceiba the coastal plain, the Caribbean lowlands, is only a few miles wide, while east and west of this area the plains extend inland along broad river valleys. The largest of these river valleys, along the *Río Ulúa* near the Guatemalan border, is Honduras' most developed area with San Pedro Sula, the country's industrial capital, located here.

At the northeastern end of Honduras, along the Nicaraguan border the Caribbean lowlands broaden again to an extensive area known as *Mosquitia*, the *Mosquito Coast*, Honduras' least developed area and one that consists primarily of swamps and mangroves near the coast. The entire Caribbean lowlands tend to have a wet climate with consistently higher temperatures and humidity.

The Pacific lowlands area is the smallest topographical area of Honduras. Averaging only 12-14 miles wide along the northern shore of the *Golfo de Fonseca*, the land is flat, swampy, and composed mostly of alluvial soils that have washed down from the mountainous areas. The *Golfo de Fonseca* is generally shallow and the water rich in marine life. Several islands in the *Golfo* are eroded volcanoes part of a chain of volcanoes that extends along the Pacific coast of Central America. The Pacific lowlands have a tropical wet/dry climate with a distinct wet and dry season.

About 90% of the population of Honduras is *mestizo*, but you'll also find small groups of European, African, Asian, Arab, Garifuna, and Mayan descent. Spanish is the principal language, although some English is spoken along the northern coast and on the Bay Islands while you'll also hear some Mayan and Garifuna dialects as you travel here and there in Honduras.

One last note, and this concerns provisioning. If you ask the packers to double bag your goods at the checkout, be very specific, otherwise they're apt to put double bags on the items, yet put double the amount in each bag as well!

Customs and Immigration

Before we begin our discussion of Honduran regulations concerning clearing in and out, let me touch upon the "CA-4 Agreement." The "CA-4 Agreement," developed between the nations of Guatemala, Honduras, El Salvador, and Nicaragua, was implemented in the summer of 2006 and allows free travel of CA-4 citizens amongst all four countries. However, Americans and all other foreign nationals will now be granted one 90-day stay in the CA-4 countries, with only one 90-day extension permitted by visiting the *Immigration* office of any CA-4 country, and will no longer be granted a new 90-day stay as tourists crossing any border between the CA-4 countries. At the end of your initial 90-day stay, youi must leave for a non-CA-4 country for 72 hours or get an extension.

A tourist visa card must be purchased on entry. This new CA-4 visa applies to the following countries:- Guatemala, El Salvador, Honduras, and Nicaragua. The length of stay (normally 90 days) applies to the whole group and only one extension will usually be granted. To remain in the region longer, a 3-day visit to a country outside the CA-4 area must be made and a new visa will be issued on re-entry.

Coxen Hole (Isla de Roatán) is the principal Port of Entry for the Bay Islands and clearance in the Bay Islands is generally simpler than at the mainland ports, the officials in the Bay Islands are used to dealing with cruisers. Puerto Este on Utila is not an official Port of Entry, but the Port Captain will issue a cruising permit and give permission for a few day's stay so you can relax before heading to Coxen Hole for clearance. If clearing in at Guanaja (Bonacca) do not move your vessel until the formalities are complete. Several boats that have gone to El Bight prematurely have been fined.

When arriving all vessels must fly the Q-flag. Captain and all crew must visit *Immigration* and the Port Captain with the vessel's clearance from the last port of call.

Cruising Permit

A cruising permit is required in Honduran waters although checking in and out of every port is not necessary, you'll only have to check in on arrival and check out on departure from Honduran waters. Cruising permits are issued for 30 days.

Immigration

A tourist card must be purchased upon entry. For those that do not require a visa, *Immigration* usually issues stays of 30 days which can be extended and cruising permits are issued for 30 days.

To enter Honduras, citizens from the following countries will need a valid passport (but no visa): Argentina, Australia, Canada, Chile, Columbia, Costa Rica, Denmark, El Salvador, Finland, France, Germany, Greece, Guatemala, Iceland, Ireland, Italy, Japan, Netherlands, New Zealand, Norway, Panama, Peru, Poland, Portugal, Spain, Sweden, Switzerland, United Kingdom, United States, and Uruguay. Visitors from other nationalities must have a valid visa or tourist card. Visas are usually issued for 90 days.

Fees

Immigration extensions cost US$22 per 30 days. There is a US$3 entrance fee, a US$3 departure fee, and a US$30 departure tax if you or your crew flies out of Honduras. The Port Captain will charge you US$20 to clear in and US$30 to clear out. Overtime charges apply and seem to be at the discretion of the officer. If you use an agent to clear there will be an agent fee to deal with.

Honduras is known for the inconsistency of her fees. Some *Immigration* officers charge US$5 instead of US$3, while vessels on the Pacific coast have reported paying only US$2 for an exit zarpe. There is a report of an officer in La Ceiba charging US$100 for a "Port Handling Fee."

Firearms

All firearms must be declared upon arrival.

Fishing

Spear fishing is not permitted by anyone, including Honduran nationals, anywhere in Roatán (the sole exception is for taking lionfish and for that you must take a class and get a license). Foreign nationals are not permitted to take lobster or conch at any time anywhere in Roatán while Hondurans can only take them outside the park boundaries during the open season. Fishing is only permitted by hook and line except for Lionfish spearing ($20 permit fee).

Pets

All animals aboard must be declared upon entrance.

Protected Areas

In the Bay Islands, all of Utila is a sanctuary except for the settlements. Guanaja and her reefs are also protected as are the *National Marine Park* of Barbareta and West End, both on Roatán, and the Cayos Cochinos. Boats are not permitted to anchor in protected areas and will have to use a mooring (free).

Clearing Out

Upon departure from Honduran waters a clearance is issued by the Port Captain and *Immigration* must be visited for an exit stamp on your passport.

Ports of Entry:

Puerto Castillo (Trujilllo), La Ceiba
(*La Ceiba Shipyard*), and Puerto Cortés
on the mainland, and Coxen Hole (Roatán),
Bonacca (Guanaja), and Puerto Este (Utila) in
the Bay Islands (Islas de la Bahía).

A Brief History

The history of Honduras begins long, long ago with the first settlers, hunter gatherers who came to Honduras either by the *Bering Strait* land bridge or across the Pacific Ocean on rafts. Either way, Anthropologists theorize that these early Hondurans arrived about 10,000 B.C. and stayed only a short while before moving on to South America. Honduras became a crossroads of sorts for South American and Mesoamerican peoples and between 3,000-1,000 B.C., three distinct groups migrated into the area. From South America came the ancestors of today's *Pech* and *Tawahka-Sumu Indians* who settled in northeastern Honduras and Nicaragua, while north central Honduras saw an influx of *Jicaque* from North America who may be related to the early Sioux.

By the time of Christ, other groups from Mexico and Guatemala migrated to Honduras to be followed shortly by a group that moved into western Honduras around Copán that would build one of the greatest civilizations ever known in the Americas, these people were to become known as the *Maya* (for more detailed information on the *Maya* see the section *The Maya* in the chapter *Local Cultures*).

By the fifth century the magnificent Mayan city of Copán was constructed as evidenced by the first glyph that was positively dated to 426 A.D. The glyph relates the accession to the throne of Yax J'uk'Mo' to the throne of Copán and the beginning of the dynasty that was to reign for four centuries ending sometime around 822 A.D. Around 900 A.D., the independent city-states of the Maya abruptly collapsed for reasons that are still not understood though researchers theorize that the population grew too big for the surrounding land to sustain.

After the disintegration of the Mayan civilization Honduras was populated by numerous tribes and sub-tribes such as the *Lenca* in western and south-central Honduras, and the *Chortí Maya* who dominated far western Honduras and who number over 4,000 in that region today. Most of central and north central Honduras was occupied by the *Tolupan*, while farther east, in what is today known as Olancho and Mosquitia, were the *Pech* (numbering about 2,500 today) and the *Sumu*, and scattered throughout western, southern, and northern Honduras the *Aztecs* maintained several trading posts. These tribes shared commercial ventures, and a few even went to war with each other, but there was no dominant tribe, no central group, which made conquest far easier for the Spanish invaders that were soon to come.

As was so often the case in the Caribbean, the first European to visit Honduras was Christopher Columbus whose first stop was at Guanaja in the Bay Islands. Columbus' first stop on the mainland of Honduras was at Punta Caxinas, near present day Trujillo, where a Spanish priest said the first Mass in the mainland Americas (the spot is now marked by a concrete cross). Columbus, who named the land *Honduras* meaning *depths* for the deep water he found off the coast, then headed east and his fleet was battered by severe weather until they rounded a cape and entered the calmer waters off Nicaragua. The Admiral was so pleased with the improved weather that he named that cape Cabo Gracias a Dios.

For almost two decades after Columbus' visit only a couple of Spanish explorers visited Honduras until 1522 when an expedition led by Gil González Dávila entered the Golfo de Fonseca (on the Pacific coast of Honduras) overland from Panama. Over the next two years, six more Spanish expeditions converged on Honduras, their only true goals being the acquisition of wealth and power for the explorers involved. In 1524, Dávila again returned to Central America, landing near the mouth of the Río Dulce in present day Guatemala and establishing a small community there before marching through the center of Honduras and on into Nicaragua. The Spaniards settled on the northern coast at Trujillo in 1525 and soon began exploring the much cooler central highlands where

Comayagua was established as a mining center and the capital in 1537 and it remained the political center of the nation until 1880 when Tegucigalpa became the capital of Honduras.

The local Indian tribes continued to fight the Spanish into the latter 1530s and almost managed to drive the Spaniards from their lands (one has to wonder had all the indigenous people in Central America banded together under one great leader what the outcome would have been).

One leader in particular, Lempira, whose name means "gentleman of the mountain," was unusually successful against the European invaders. Believed to have been born in 1499, Lempira, is now one of the Honduras' national heroes. Chief of the *Lenca* tribe, Lempira organized some 30,000 fighters into a resistance force to be reckoned with, a force the Spanish could not defeat in battle. Lempira successfully resisted the Spanish forces aligned against him by captain Alonso de Cáceres, the governor of Coyocutena, an area that today is known as the *Department of Lempira*. When de Cáceres could not defeat Lempira on the battlefield he resorted to treachery and deception. Under the white flag of truce, de Cáceres sent two representatives to Lempira to negotiate a peace treaty in 1839. During the meeting with Lempira, de Cáceres' men shot and killed the great warrior chief in effect killing the resistance movement entirely; within a year the indigenous peoples were defeated by the Spaniards. Today Lempira's name is synonymous with the indigenous people's heritage and so honored is this great leader that Honduras' currency is named after him. By 1841, the numbers of indigenous Indians were hovering around 8,000, approximately 1% of what their numbers were when the Spanish arrived in Honduras.

In 1570, gold and silver were discovered near Tegucigalpa and the Spanish began shipping their new-found treasures back to the mother country. These Spanish treasure ships drew a great number of pirates to this part of the Caribbean feeding off captured Spanish vessels. Primarily British, Dutch, and French, these pirates led countless raids on towns and ships along what is known as the *Spanish Main* as Spain's treasure fleets sailed from Venezuela to Honduras and onward, out into the Atlantic and back to Spain often using Roatán in the Bay Islands as a base for their forays.

Although Spain was holding fast in the interior of Honduras, the British came to the Bay Islands and the Caribbean Coast of Honduras attracted by great stands of mahogany. After an appeal by chiefs of the *Miskito* region, a British protectorate was declared over Honduras' coastal waters which lasted until 1859 when they were was relinquished to Honduran control.

On September 15, 1821, representatives of Honduras, Guatemala, El Salvador, Costa Rica, and Nicaragua, declared their Independence from Spain in a formal *Act of Independence* signed by Brigadier Don Gabino Gainza, the last of Spain's Captain Generals in the New World. Two groups in Honduras vacillated between independence and joining the Republic of Mexico and by early 1822, Honduras declared her loyalty to the Emperor of Mexico, Augustín de Iturbide, just as her four neighbors had done, some by force. Within a year Iturbide was deposed and the five Central American nations formed the *United Provinces of Central America*. In 1838, after a long period of social and economic differences with her neighbors, and strife amongst Central American leaders (conservatives versus liberals) brought about the collapse of the *Federation* in 1838 even though Honduran General Francisco Morazán tried unsuccessfully to maintain the *Federation*, and as a result, on November 15, 1838, Honduras became a separate republic.

Born in 1792, Francisco Morazán, often described as the George Washington of Central America, was the last Honduran President of the *United Provinces of Central America* and ruled from 1830-1842. Born to an upper-class family, Morazán was self-educated in Tegucigalpa and spoke fluent French. Morazán was a champion of Central American federalism and fought valiantly but lost in his bid to prevent Mexico from annexing Honduras after 1821. In 1829, Morazán led the liberal army in a civil war to defeat the conservative government and a year later became President of the *United Provinces of Central America*. During his tenure Morazán suggested numerous reforms, some of which specifically targeted restricting the power of the Catholic Church in Honduras. After the *Federation* fell apart in 1838, Morazán was exiled in 1840 by a Guatemalan leader named Rafael Carrera. But two years later, in 1842, Morazán returned to Honduras and attempted to restore the *Federation* by staging a coup in Costa Rica. Defeated by a conservative army, Morazán was executed on September 15, 1842, the anniversary of Central American Independence. It is said that Morazán was given command of his own execution and that he ordered his firing squad to fire upon him, and when he said "I'm still alive" ("Estoy vivo"), they fired once more, ending this visionary's life.

Since she gained her Independence, Honduras has endured countless coups, rebellions, rigged elections, and underhanded dealings in her government, but one of the most famous incursions into the country came about in 1860, at the hands of an American mercenary named William Walker who had seized control of Nicaragua and sought to do the same in Honduras, was caught and executed in Trujillo and today his tomb is a tourist attraction.

William Walker was an American filibuster famed for his military exploits in Central America in the mid-1800s. At this time in history, adventurers known as filibusters participated in military action designed to take control of parts of Central America with the intent of annexing the captured territory to the United States, an exaggerated expression of the concept of *Manifest Destiny*.

Walker was born in Nashville, Tennessee, in 1824, and graduated from the University of Nashville at 14. By the age of 19, Walker had a medical degree and at 25 was a physician in Pennsylvania. Walker later studied law in New Orleans, and a few years later became a journalist in California where he co-owned a newspaper, *The Crescent*, where a young writer named Walt Whitman worked on staff. And even with all these early successes, before his life was over Walker was to become better known as the President of Lower California and the Emperor of Nicaragua.

Between 1853-1860, William Walker hired soldiers of fortune and made several attempts to wrest control of territories in Mexico and Central America, and even invaded lower California, conquered the city of La Paz, and declared it an independent republic. Walker then annexed the nearby Mexican state of Sonora and renamed it the Republic of Sonora and established himself as "President." A result of Walker's actions in Sonora was the *Gadsden Purchase* whereby Mexico sold part of Sonora to the United States.

Walker was driven out of Sonora by the Mexican military in 1854 and then surrendered to U.S. Forces and was charged with violating neutrality laws but was later acquitted. Walker then turned his attention to Central America where chaos reigned as Democrats

and Legitimists fought each other for control. The Democrats invited Walker to join the fight and in 1855, with an army of 58 men called *The Immortals*, Walker arrived in Nicaragua.

Within a year his *Immortals*, and a local Democrat force, the *Leonese*, a liberal militia from the town of Leon, captured Grenada and Walker installed himself as President of Nicaragua. Walker immediately confiscated all foreign investments and re-instituted slavery as the United States became one of the first countries to recognize his authority. With the slogan "Five or None," Walker gave other Central American countries much to consider, mainly where would he invade next? Costa Rica bravely took steps to stop Walker by invading Nicaragua with some 9,000 men, however Walker's forces repelled the invaders. But when Walker tried to follow the Costa Ricans into their country his invasion failed just as miserably as disease wiped out soldiers on both sides.

During the fighting a young Costa Rican drummer boy, Juan Santamaria, became a national hero when he torched a fort where Walker's army was encamped. Walker was driven out of Costa Rica in mid-1857 by a Central American alliance that defeated him at Santa Rosa (now a Costa Rican national monument) and Walker surrendered to a United States Naval officer and was returned to the United States where he once again faced neutrality violations. Walker landed in New Orleans where he was greeted as a hero, visiting President Buchanan before heading to New York to begin trying to once again rebuild an army.

By the end of 1857, Walker had succeeded in forming another army and attempted to invade Nicaragua again but was thwarted by the British Navy who barred his forces from landing in Nicaragua. Walker returned to the States and, seeking to form yet one more army to try to invade Central America, wrote a book entitled *The War In Nicaragua* to propagate his cause and raise funds. In 1960, Walker had again sailed south with a new army but was unable to land in Nicaragua, held off by the British Navy, so he and his army landed in Honduras planning to move overland into Nicaragua. In short order the British turned Walker over to Honduran authorities, who, within six days, stood the 36 year-old William Walker in front of a firing squad in Trujillo and executed him. Today his tomb can be found in the municipal cemetery in Trujillo, this man who might have changed the history of our hemisphere if not checked. His epitaph reads: William Walker, Fusilado, September 12, 1860."

Just before the turn of the century a lack of funds resulted in a small town becoming an industrial giant in Honduras. In 1888, a projected railroad line from the Caribbean coast to the capital ran out of money when it reached the town of San Pedro Sula and as a result San Pedro Sula grew into Honduras' main industrial center and second largest city.

As Honduras entered the 20th century, three United State's fruit companies, *United Fruit*, the Vaccaro brothers (who would later be known as *Standard Fruit*), and *Cuyamel Fruit*, owned 70%-75% of all Honduran banana plantations, all the products of which were intended for U.S. markets. During these years many of the smaller banana farms were either bought out or forced out of business. In 1913, banana exports accounted for well over 60% of Honduras' total exports as the nation earned the moniker "banana republic." So embedded was the banana industry that for over a century the movers and shakers of the banana trade shaped the politics of Honduras. Where William Walker failed in his bid to control Honduras, the U.S. fruit companies succeeded.

The early 1900s were marked by political unrest which resulted in an occupation by United States Marines in 1932. This led to General Tiburcio Carias Andino establishing his strong military dictatorship that same year, which led to several decades of military rule. In October of 1955, young military reformists staged a coup and installed a provincial junta which paved the way for assembly elections in 1957. The new assembly installed Dr. Ramon Villeda Morales as President and then transformed itself into a national legislature with a six-year term. During this liberal assembly's term, 1957-1963, the military began a transformation, separating itself from politics and any one political party as their new military academy graduated their first class in 1960. Villeda was removed from office in a bloody coup in October of 1963 as a group of military officers exiled certain Liberal Party members and took control of the national police. Once again the military came into control, led by General Lopez Arellano, who ruled Honduras until 1970.

In 1969, El Salvador invaded Honduras in what was to become known as the *Football War*. The two nations had been disagreeing about their borders for almost two centuries and it finally came to a head during a *World Cup* qualifying match between the two countries. The conflict was sparked by the deportation and alleged mistreatment of some 20,000 El Salvadoran immigrants in Honduras, victims of Honduran vigilantes. On July 14, a month after two heated soccer matches, and a cancelled third game (many Honduran fans were beaten in El Salvador at the second game and a rag was hoisted on a flagpole when the band played the Honduran National Anthem), El Salvador bombed several sites inside Honduras and even invaded the country by land making their way deep into Honduran territory. The Honduran air force bombed the Salvadoran fuel depot the invaders found they could advance no further.

The *Organization of American States*, the *OAS*, succeeded in convincing El Salvador to withdraw after threatening the country with economic sanctions and military intervention, and although the war only lasted 100 hours, over 5,000 people were killed. The International Court in the Hague eventually settled the dispute awarding each country some of the disputed lands.

A civilian president, Ramon Cruz, came into power briefly in 1970, but the discontent of the people after the 1969 *Football War* came to a head and in 1972, General Arellano staged another coup and took office again, only to be deposed in the mid-1970s by internal scandals. But General Arellano's successors, General Melgar Castro who ruled from 1975-1978, and General Paz Garcia who ruled from 1978-1983, continued to build and modernize the military, the physical infrastructure, and the telecommunication systems of Honduras. The economy began to grow during this period as a greater international demand for Honduran products merged with the availability of foreign investments.

When Somoza was overthrown in Nicaragua in 1979, the Honduran military began to rethink plans of turning over the reins of government to civilians. A new assembly was elected in 1980 and general elections were held in November of 1981. A new constitution was approved in 1982 as the Liberal Party government of President Roberto Suazo Cordoba came into power.

In the years between 1979 and 1985, U.S. military and economic aid to Honduras increased from $32 million to over $282 million. A grateful Honduras responded by agreeing to base an estimated 15,000 Nicaraguan Contras who were to join the U.S. military in joint maneuvers.

Conversely, U.S. aid for development assistance dropped during those years from 8% to 6% as some 70% of Honduras' children were malnourished. During these years the U.S. used Nicaraguan refugee camps inside Honduras as bases for operations designed to destabilize the Sandinista government of Nicaragua. The U.S. was also training Salvadoran military at Salvadoran refugee camps that were also located inside Honduras. Public knowledge of some 12,000 Cubans operating in Honduras and the exposing of the Iran/Contra scandal resulted in huge anti-American demonstrations in Tegucigalpa. The Honduran government changed its stance towards assisting the U.S. military, refusing to sign a new agreement with the U.S. and taking steps to remove the Contras from the country.

But President Suazo Cordoba still needed U.S. aid to battle a recession and an growing threat posed by the Sandinista government in Nicaragua and a civil war in El Salvador. Following a very strange election in November of 1985, Jose Azcona Hoyo assumed the Presidency.

The Liberal Party actually had several candidates on the ballot and claimed victory as their candidates received more votes than the National Party Candidate, Rafael Leonardo Callejas, who received a total of 42% of the popular vote. Of the Liberal Party Candidates, Hoyo received only 27% of the total popular vote, yet became President due to the fact he received more votes than any other Liberal Party candidate. Hoyo's election marked the first peaceful transfer of power between civilian presidents in over 30 years of Honduran military rule. However, four years later Callejas returned and won the presidential election, taking office in January of 1990. Callejas immediately began to place the military under civilian control and created an Attorney General's office.

When the Contra War ended in 1990 and the Contras finally left Honduras, the nation's primary woes have been economic. An ebbing of exports along with a shrinking GNP, coupled with very little aid from the U.S., forced Honduras to increase its European market. In 1996, the civilian government of President Reina made a huge step forward in removing the military from all levels of government by naming his own defense minister instead of accepting the nominee of the military. Reina brought about a certain amount of fiscal health by reducing inflation, increasing economic growth, and reducing public debt.

In October of 1998, Hurricane Mitch devastated parts of the Bay Islands and hit hardest the mainland of Honduras. Mitch spawned three days of torrential rains causing landslides and floods that buried entire towns and destroyed over 100 bridges throughout the country. The Río Choluteca flooded and left the capital city of Tegucigalpa in an ocean of mud and across the nation some 13,000 people died and another two million were left homeless. It took over two years to clean up the country but Honduras will feel the effects of Mitch for a long time to come.

In 1999, a maritime border conflict arose with Nicaragua. Honduras claimed her maritime border at 15° north latitude, while Nicaragua claimed the border at 17° north latitude, which would cover all of Honduras' Caribbean coastline as well as Guatemala's, and even parts of the shoreline of Belize. Verbal assaults flew on all fronts and Nicaragua imposed a 35% tariff on all imported Honduran goods until the matter finally went to the *International Court* in the Hague.

In 2002, newly elected President Ricard Maduro made great progress in the areas of tourism and the war against crime. Although some say his reforms are too heavy handed, expanding police powers to enter private homes, Maduro established a tourist police and even learned of crime reduction from former New York Mayor Rudy Giuliani. Although the public was behind his anti-crime efforts, the criminals were not, a prison riot in April of 2003 left 86 prisoners dead. Maduro also advocated new border procedures and was part of a Central American delegation that met with U.S. President Bush to push for reduced tariffs and the adoption of a *Central American Free Trade Agreement*.

Las Islas Santanilla

(The Swan Islands)
Waypoints:
Las Islas Santanilla- 1 nm N of Isla Grande
17° 26.00' N, 83° 56.00' W

Las Islas Santanilla, James Bay- ¼ nm NW of
17° 25.00' N, 83° 56.40' W

Approximately 120 miles northeast of Isla Guanaja in the Bay Islands of Honduras, and approximately 15 miles south of the rhumb line from George Town, Grand Cayman to Guanaja, lie *Las Isla Santanilla*, the Swan Islands (sometimes shown on charts as Las Islas del Cisne), a perfect stopover for vessels bound for the Bay Islands of Honduras from the Cayman Islands, Jamaica, or the *Windward Passage*. The Swan Islands are made up of Isla Grande (*Great Swan*), Isla Pequena (*Little Swan*), and Booby Cay, a tiny island off the southwestern tip of Great Swan Island. The waters between Booby Cay and Great Swan Island are so shallow that one can walk between the two at low tide. The islands have developed fringing reefs lying just off their shores, particularly along their northern shore. Isla Grande is approximately 2 miles long while Isla Pequena is only about 1½ miles in length but is home to the highest spot in the islands at a whopping 78' above sea level. Isla Pequena is the smaller of the pair of islands, but is higher in elevation.

A Brief History

The Swan Islands were discovered by Christopher Columbus on *St. Anne's Day* in 1502 and were therefore named *Las Islas Santa Ana*. The islands offered little in the way of colonization, but they did serve as a pirate haunt from the 16th-18th centuries. The islands are said to be named after a Captain Swan, the master of the *Cygnet*, a ship sent to the Caribbean by London merchants in 1680 on a commercial voyage. The *Cygnet* was attacked by pirates and Swan was forced to join them and it is believed that Captain Swan may have become one of the buccaneers that dominated these waters.

Almost a century later, in 1775, the islands first appeared on a chart as the Swan Islands. Later still, in 1860, the notorious William Walker occupied the islands during one of his attempts to conquer South America. After Walker was executed Honduras claimed the islands but to no avail as the islands were put under United States sovereignty in 1863 by the *Guano Islands Act*. It would be over 100 years before Honduras would officially gain control of the Swan Islands.

At the beginning of the 20th century, the *Swan Island Trading Company* (sometimes shown as the *Swan Islands Commercial Company*) took title of the Swan Islands from a Captain Alonzo Adams, the self-proclaimed "King of the Swan Islands," who staked a claim to the islands claiming them as abandoned property. In the early part of the 1900s, the *Swan Islands Trading Company* leased part of Great Swan to the *United Fruit Company* who planted over 15,000

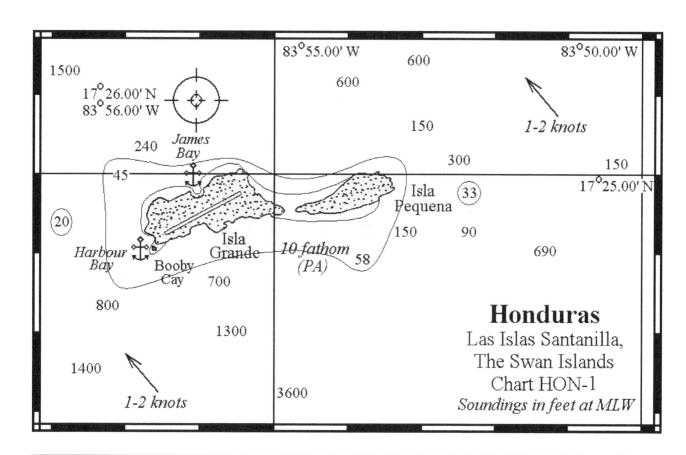

coconut palms on the island. The company pulled out after several years, but provided valuable hurricane weather data from 1928-1932. In 1938, the *United States Weather Bureau* established a weather station on the island that was only occupied during hurricane season. A few years later, in 1940, the weather station was manned full time.

In the late 1940s, the *United States Agriculture Department* used Great Swan as a quarantine station for Latin-American cattle bound for the states; the quarantine station was abandoned in 1949, only a few years after its inception. In 1946, an aircraft navigational beacon was installed on the island by the FAA and remained in use until 1971. In 1960, a 50,000 watt radio station, *Radio Swan*, was constructed on Great Swan Island. The station as intended to broadcast propaganda to Cuba shortly after Castro's rise to power and was owned by a New York company called the *Gibraltar Steamship Company*, which did not own any steamships. In 1961, the station's name was changed to *Radio America* and its headquarters moved to Miami, Florida.

I've heard rumors that Great Swan was home to a transmitting station during the *Bay of Pigs* invasion (allegedly sending coded messages to operatives inside Cuba), and in later years, the island was used as a re-supply base for planes assisting the Contras in Central America. Of course these are just rumors.

While all this was going on, Honduras laid claim to the islands in 1920, but did not press the issue until the 1960s. Honduras claimed that when Columbus landed here in 1502 to pick up wood, this made the islands part of the Spanish colonial empire, and of course Honduras was the rightful heir to the islands. The United States countered claiming that in 1863, *Secretary of State* William Seward laid claim to the islands on the behalf of the United States of America just a few years after George White landed on the islands, claiming them for the United States in 1857. After much wrangling back and forth, on November 22, 1971, the United States and Honduras signed a treaty that put the islands under Honduran sovereignty as of September 1, 1972. The U.S. continued to operate a weather station on Great Swan until 1980 when it was transferred to the government of Honduras.

There is talk about a huge development that is planned for the Swan Islands. Current plans call for the Swan Islands to become one of the world's most beautiful and exciting destinations, a tax haven where people can retire or just vacation. There are to be no property or income taxes, but there is a planned 12% sales tax and 12% duty on items not for resale on the island. I've seen the architect's drawings (*Swan Island Development, LLC*, in partnership with *Fantasy International Resorts* and *Caribbean Investment Associates*) of the completed project that shows a huge marina and cruise ship dock on the northern shore of Great Swan along with condos and a huge new airstrip. The planned capital city, to be called Cygnet, will be home to 5,000 people (quite crowded for so small an island in my humble opinion) with four resorts, casinos, and numerous clubs, restaurants, grocery stores, banks, boutiques, and theaters. Cygnet is slated to be the world's first city designed exclusively for electric vehicles, no automobiles will be allowed on the islands should this plan ever come into being.

We'll just have to wait and see what the future will bring, the location of the Swan Islands in the center of the Northwestern Caribbean, which is quite prone to hurricanes, may be the biggest obstacle to this imposing project.

Navigational Information

If approaching the Swan Islands from the Cayman Islands or the Bay Islands of Honduras, head for a waypoint at 17° 26.00' N, 83° 56.00' W, which will place you approximately one mile north of Isla Grande as shown on Chart HON-1. From here you can head around the western tip of Isla Grande to the recommended anchorage at *Harbor Bay*, or head south to the alternative anchorage at *James Bay*. Nearby hazards to navigation includes the *Rosario Bank* which lies approximately 62 miles north of Isla Santanilla and has depths ranging from a reported 24' to over 200', and the *Misteriosa Bank* approximately 87 miles north of Isla Santanilla, which is 24 miles long and 2-7 miles in width with depths ranging from 42'-161' over a coral bottom. Use caution here as seas can pile up in these shallow areas.

The only anchorages to speak of are both located at Isla Grande. The "requested" anchorage lies at the southwestern tip of Isla Grande at *Harbor Bay*, but it's no place to be in moderate or stronger southeast winds as the bay becomes untenable. Visiting vessels are "requested" to stop at *Harbor Bay* so the military can check your documents, they cannot grant pratique or issue a cruising permit for Honduras, nor should you surrender your outward clearance from your last port, keep that until you officially clear in at your next port of call. There is a small dock in *Harbor Bay that* can be used by vessels to allow access by the marines unless there's any surge at all in the anchorage. *Harbor Bay* is located at the extreme southwestern tip of Isla Grande in the lee of Booby Cay as shown on Chart HON-1 and the entrance is straightforward from the west.

If *Harbor Bay* is untenable, you can anchor on the northwestern side of Isla Grande at *James Bay*. A waypoint at 17° 25.00 N, 83° 56.40' W, will place you approximately ¼ mile northwest of the 50-yard wide entrance channel to *James Bay*. You'll have to dodge a few coral heads but once inside you can anchor in 7'-12' of water over a sand bottom, but there's only room for one or two boats. Neither of the anchorages mentioned offer any protection from northerly winds and seas.

What You Will Find Ashore

Today, the only people that inhabit Isla Grande are a few Honduran marines, a couple of farmers, and a small, ever-changing group of fishermen. There is no fresh water on the island, all of the island's drinking water is either rainwater collected in cisterns or bottled water brought in by the military. There are no stores, there are no Internet cafés, and there is no fuel to be had here.

Islas de la Bahía

(The Bay Islands)

Las Islas de la Bahía, the Bay Islands of Honduras, lie approximately 20-30 miles offshore and parallel the northern shore of the Honduran mainland for about 75 miles in a southwest/northeast alignment. The principal islands in the group are, from southwest to northeast, Isla Utila, Isla de Roatán, and Isla Guanaja. Along with three smaller islands, Isla Barbareta, Morat, and Isla Helene, there are some 65 smaller cays scattered about. South of Roatán, about 1/3 of the distance from the mainland to Roatán, lie the Cayos Cochinos (the Hog Islands), which are also included in this section.

The equatorial current in the vicinity of the Bay Islands runs in a westerly direction north of the islands while the counter current usually sets in the opposite direction south of the islands. When northerly winds are blowing the strength of the equatorial current is lessened and sometimes not even felt at all. The tidal rise and fall is greater at Roatán than anywhere else in the island group and the set is west and north on a rising tide and south and east on the ebb. You may often notice a counterclockwise eddy just north of Isla de Utila

The Bay Islands of Honduras offer a very different world from that of mainland Honduras. The history of the Bay Islands includes many disputes between the Spaniards and the British during colonial times, with the British actually controlling the islands during most of that period bestowing upon the islands a unique heritage. English is widely spoken in the Bay Islands with Spanish being almost a second language in a country, Honduras, where Spanish is the principal tongue. There is a huge ex-pat community here which has added to the infrastructure that we can all enjoy.

Roatán, the largest of the group, has the greatest tourism industry, much of it geared for divers, though more and more resorts are being constructed that offer satisfaction for the tourist in other vistas. Because of this tourist base prices are higher for food and fuel here while they're cheaper in nearby Guanaja. Utila is known for its excellent diving (the tourist focus of this island is without a doubt DIVING) and its party atmosphere (well, diving may actually be a secondary focus at times), while Guanaja, which was devastated by *Hurricane Mitch* in 1998, is enjoying a revitalization and is a unique destination in itself with no roads and a capital, Bonacca, which sits on a small cay just offshore, most of it on stilts. What I'm trying to say here is that all the islands in this group are different yet alike, and yet quite apart from each other in flavor as you will soon see

When transiting the waters of the Bay Islands you'll find that the depths will come up on you quite suddenly, going from 150' to 10' in depth in a boat length it seems, while at other times the shoals lie farther to seaward from the breaking reefs that you would imagine. A lot of the reefs however are easily discernible as they dry at low water or have gotten to the point that they are continually above water now even though they're not shown as such on any charts.

One last word, if you rent a car in the Bay Islands, or in Honduras, driving is done on the right.

Isla de Guanaja

Waypoints:
NE tip, 1 nm SE of light at Black Rock Point
16° 29.30' N, 85° 48.15' W

Isla de Guanaja is the most easterly of the Bay Islands, lying about 15 miles east/northeast of Roatán and sometimes shown as *Bonacca* on older charts, will probably be your first landfall in the Bay Islands when approaching from the *Windward Passage*, Jamaica, the Cayman Islands, the Swan Islands, or from the islands of the Eastern Caribbean.

Isla Guanaja was discovered by Christopher Columbus on July 30, 1502, on the fourth and last voyage to the New World by the *Admiral of All Oceans*. Columbus was met by giant canoes holding 25 Paya Indians in each one, and when they went ashore, Columbus's men found excellent quality drinking water with which they could re-supply their casks. Columbus noted that he had "...never tasted water of better quality." Guanaja was so covered with thick Caribbean pine that Columbus named Guanaja *Pine Island*, sadly, most of the trees that covered Guanaja were destroyed by *Hurricane Mitch*, but the island has rebounded very well indeed and is as beautiful a place as you could want to find. As you sail around Guanaja you'll see evidence of Mitch nearly everywhere in the trunks of trees still standing minus their bark, leaves, and limbs. Guanaja is very lightly touched by tourism, it's quite a unique getaway as it's often overlooked as most visitor's interests are focused on Roatán and Utila.

There are approximately 10,000 people living on Guanaja, 8,000 of which live in tiny and cramped Bonacca (sometimes shown as *Guanaja Settlement* on some charts and as *Sheen Cay* on others) which is usually just referred to as The Cay. A few folks live at *Mangrove Bight* on the northern shore of Guanaja, and more still live at *Savannah Bight*, Guanaja's second largest settlement.

The island is home to several small waterfalls that are within easy hiking distance and offer clear water and pristine settings. On the northwestern side of Guanaja, just inland from the *End of the World Resort* (located on *Michael Rock Beach*) and the *Island House Resort*, is one of the island's loveliest waterfalls, only a short 30 minute hike away. You can take your dingy to the resorts or take a water taxi from Bonacca to the resorts (the water taxis also offer waterfall tours, how convenient).

Another option if you wish to see the island and don't wish to take your boat, is to hang out at the water taxi dock in Bonacca and check out who's going where and what it will cost you to ride along. Boats headed to the north side take the short canal into *Bahía Pine Ridge* and then head up the northern shore past Michael Rock to *Mangrove Bight* in the relative comfort and safety offered by the fringing reef. Generally a boat headed to *Mangrove Bight* will take you as a passenger for about US$5, but that price can change, and don't forget, then you'll need to make arrangements for accommodations or a return trip. Usually the boats arrive at the water taxi dock in the morning to sell their wares or drop off passengers, then leave at midday, and some return again in the afternoon. Some of the more pricey "express" boats going to the north side can charge you as much as US$30 per trip.

Guanaja is home to some marvelous reef systems, especially on the northern side of the island, as is Roatán. The reefs are home to some 90% of all species of corals and sponges found in the world and there are over 30 breathtaking snorkeling spots where the corals and marine life come to within a few feet of the surface. Today the *Posada del Sol Resort* is working in conjunction with *Texas A&M University* on several reef studies in Guanaja's waters.

For the best in local knowledge visit the *Airport Hilton Hotel*, have a drink at the *Last Stop Bar*, and you'll find a wealth of information in the owner, Andy, whose dad, Capt. Al, built the bar. If you wish to rent a small motor boat, this is the place to ask about it, or you can call them at 453-4469.

A final note about navigating your vessel in Guanaja. The waters of Guanaja contain a number of old houses built on stilts over the water, groups of old pilings, and shoals that are hard to see until you're almost on top of them. I don't recommend plying these waters at night, during periods of poor visibility, or heading into the sun when the glare blinds you as to the dangers that may lie on your vessel's course. I tried to find and chart every shoal, but being an imperfect world, some may have been missed, so use caution when navigating inside the reef at Guanaja from *Savannah Bight* southward, and especially on the northern shore of the island.

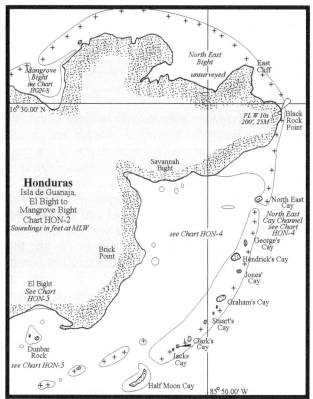

Savannah Bight

Waypoints

Savannah Bight, NE Cay Channel- ¼ nm ESE of
16° 28.65' N, 85° 48.80' W

Navigational Information

When approaching Guanaja from the east, from
Jamaica, Swan Island, or Grand Cayman, you can
head for a waypoint at 16° 29.30' N, 85° 48.15' W,
which will place you approximately 1 mile southeast
of the light at Black Rock Point. From here you can
choose to pass through the reef into the sheltered
waters of *Savannah Bight* or head further south to
pass through the reef closer to Bonacca (which we
will discuss in the next section, for now let's talk
about entering *Savannah Bight*). From the waypoint
southeast of Black Rock Point you can head to a
waypoint at 16° 28.65' N, 85° 48.80' W, which will
place you approximately ¼ mile east/southeast of the
entrance channel that lies south of North East Cay as
shown on Chart HON-2 and in greater detail on Chart
HON-4.

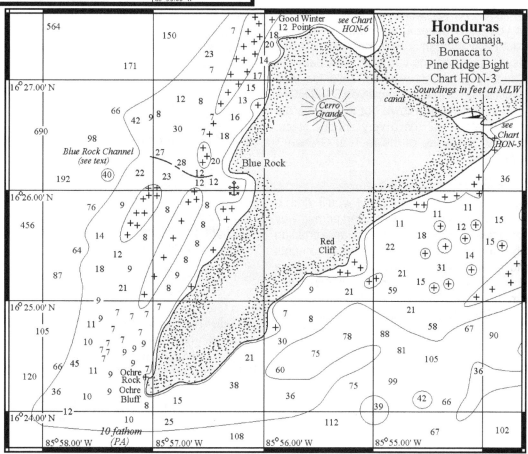

From the waypoint you can easily pass through *North East Cay Channel* and once inside you can round to starboard to anchor in the lee of North East Cay, turn more to the west to head for the town of *Savannah Bight*, turn to port to pass inside the reef to anchor in the lee of the reef or to pick up a mooring at Graham's Cay, or you can make your way southwestward to Bonacca or *El Bight*. Bear in mind that Honduran officials want you to clear in at Bonacca before dropping the hook at any of these anchorages. Never attempt to enter via *North East Cay Channel* with heavy following seas, the channel will break all the way across.

Once inside the reef the waters of the bight will vary from 70' to 20' with a few isolated shoals here and there that you must wind your way around. Most of these shoals are shown on the chart, but there may be one or two that I missed so keep your eyes open and don't try to work your way through the sound with the sun low and in your eyes or at night. Soon after leaving the channel at North East Cay you will spot a large shoal to port as you head for the settlement of *Savannah Bight*, it's marked by a rock that sits above water at low tide and the shoal is easily passed on its northern side. As you work your way toward the settlement you'll find several more shoals that you must pick your way through, it's not that difficult really, they're easy to see, and you can then pass between the town and some shoals with old buildings atop them lying just south of town as shown on Chart HON-4. You can anchor west of town but in a moderate southeast breeze this can be a very choppy place, you're better off in the lee of the reef, at Graham's Cay, or at *El Bight*.

What You Will Find Ashore
In the town of *Savannah Bight* you'll find a shipyard at its western end that is utilized primarily by the shrimping fleet. The yard can haul a large cruising boat easily but you'll have to make arrangements beforehand, they may be too busy. In town are a few small shops selling basic grocery items, but if you need real provisioning you're better off going to Bonacca, that's where everybody in *Savannah Bight* goes for their groceries. In the center of town is the *Pirate's Landing Disco* with a dock for their customers. This is a loud and busy place on the weekends and quite often during the week too.

If you wish to visit the settlement of *Savannah Bight* from Bonacca, you can take the regularly scheduled boat, the *Sava*, from the taxi dock in

Bonacca. From Savannah you can walk along the only road on Guanaja which leads from *Savannah Bight* to *Mangrove Bight* on the northern side of the island past the old, unused airstrip. The walk is not difficult and only takes about an hour and a half, but be forewarned, bring mosquito repellent.

About halfway between *Savannah Bight* and *Mangrove Bight* you'll come to *Marble Hill*, a tree covered, rocky outcrop on the west side of the road. Just on the other side of the hill is Plan Grande, a pre-Columbian ceremonial site that was mapped in the 1930s just before it was pillaged and destroyed. Today little remains of the site but you can still walk around and look if you'd like, and some locals will be happy to act as your guide for a fee. I'm told that a group of researchers from the *Instituto Hondureño de Antropologia e Historia*, the *IHAH*, is planning an excavation of the site in the near future (http://www.ihah.hn/).

Graham's Cay

If *Savannah Bight* isn't for you, I'm sure Graham's Cay will be. Graham's Cay, once called Josh's Cay, is named after a new owner who operates a small resort on the island and offers a half-dozen free moorings for those who are interested (though in the lee of the reef, it can get a bit choppy when the wind is above 20 knots from the northeast through the southeast).

Navigational Information
Once inside the reef via the channel at North East Cay, you can turn to port and head southwest paralleling the lie of the reef until you can pick up a free mooring or drop your hook in the sand in the lee of Graham's Cay as shown on Chart HON-3.

From Graham's Cay it's an easy sail or motor to *El Bight* or Bonacca with few obstructions as shown on Chart HON-2 and in greater detail on Chart HON-5.

What You Will Find Ashore
Graham's cay is one of my favorite stops, besides the free moorings, good diving, cool breezes, and easy access to the facilities ashore, Graham, who monitors VHF ch. 06 (hail *Graham's Cay*), is VERY accommodating to cruisers. Besides the free moorings Graham offers free ice, water, and a laundry wash (you'll have to dry on board your boat), and he asks nothing in return, but good manners dictates that you at least frequent his bar and restaurant and

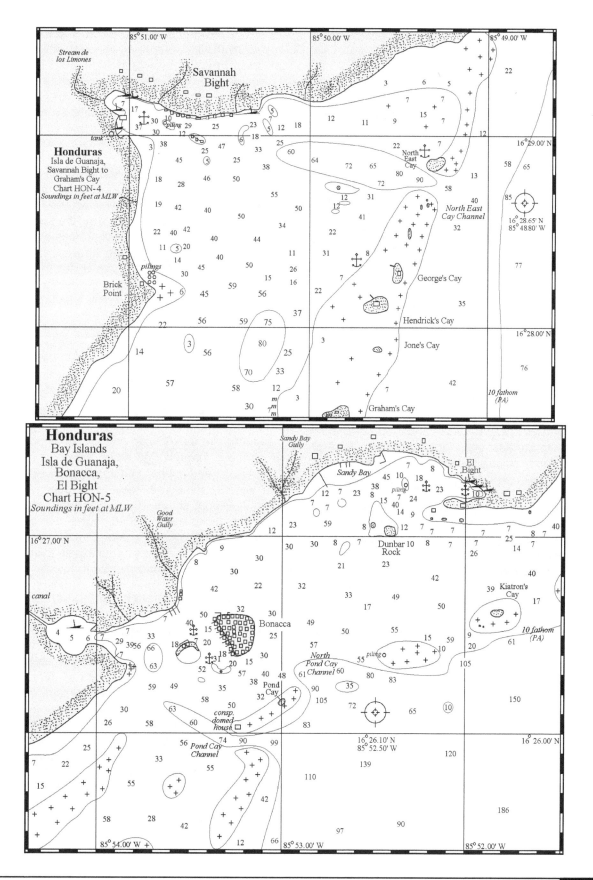

put some *lempira* in his till. Graham also offers *Wi-Fi* but availability is limited to guests of the key.

El Bight

El Bight is a very protected anchorage, not what I would call a "hurricane hole" by any means, but it does offer shelter and good holding from anything short of a full blown hurricane. Before I go any further, let me remind you that you will need to clear in at Bonacca before anchoring at *El Bight*. I've heard third hand tales of folks who have been fined for dropping the hook in *El Bight* before clearing in. I checked with the *Capitan de el Puerto de Bonacca* on this and he would only say yes, you must clear before anchoring at *El Bight*.

Navigational Information

Located northeast of Bonacca as shown on Chart HON-5, the entrance is easy, passing between Dunbar Rock and the point of land that is the southern shore of *El Bight* if you're approaching from *Savannah Bight*, or, if you are approaching from Bonacca, by passing west of Dunbar Rock and being careful to avoid a couple of shallow spots as shown on the chart, you can then pass north of the shoal lying north of Dunbar Rock to enter *El Bight*. Use caution when rounding the point to the east of *El Bight*, the waters here are 7'-8' in depth several hundred yards off the point.

If you'd like to get the most effect from the wind at *El Bight* you'll need to anchor at the extreme western end of the cove, just north of the ruins of an old house and pilings, but if you want the best shelter head in as far as you can past the wrecks and you'll be as snug as the proverbial bug-in-a-rug, but you'll have to deal with mosquitoes and no-see-ums as they love any windless spot like this.

What You Will Find Ashore

There is a very nice little bar, *The Crazy Parrot*, on the southern shore of *El Bight* with an equally nice dinghy dock. Nearby is a German restaurant, *Manati Bar and Restaurant Instituto Hond*, serving excellent German cuisine at a very reasonable price.

Bonacca

Waypoints:
Pond Cay Channel- ¼ nm SE of
16° 26.10' N, 85° 52.50' W

Bonacca is the capital of Guanaja, the largest settlement (even though it only encompasses some 100 acres), and the hub of all activity that's Guanaja related. The waters off the western shore of Bonacca are teeming with water taxis, vendors, and all manner of small craft go back and forth from Guanaja to Bonacca, and most either don't know or don't care about the *Rules of the Road*, be careful as some of these skippers will pull out right in front of you, fearlessly cross your bow, and come so close you'll think they're going to ram you.

Bonacca, often shown on other charts as *Guanaja Settlement*, or Sheen Cay, is one of the most unique communities in the Caribbean. Actually built upon two cays, Hog Cay and Sheen Cay, the town consists of less than 100 acres that is home to more than 8,000 people. Nearly all the houses are two and three stories tall and many are built on stilts. The "streets" are little more than 5' wide cement walkways while in some places you'll cross wooden walkways over small waterways.

I'd like to paint a picture of Bonacca as a *Venice of the Caribbean*, but I truly can't. True, there are some narrow water passageways that bisect the town, but they are usually filled with debris, garbage, and raw sewage that is allowed to flow into the waters in town creating an unholy stink on some days, and these passages are barely wide enough for a local *cayuco* to squeeze through. All along the shore you'll see businesses and houses constructed on pilings above the waters, some with their living quarters directly over their boat sheds. In 1998, *Hurricane Mitch* hit Bonacca hard, many houses were destroyed and most of those that were spared that demise lost their roofs. But the islanders rebuilt their town in short order and it is all the stronger for it.

Navigational Information

When approaching Bonacca from outside the off-lying cays, make sure you clear Half Moon Cay (see Chart HON-2) before making your way to the entrance at *North Pond Cay Channel* as shown on Chart HON-5. Here, a waypoint at 16° 26.10' N, 85° 52.50' W, will place you ¼ mile southeast of the channel. From the waypoint pass between the reef to starboard which is marked by a piling at its western end at the time of this writing, and the reef that lies east of Pond Cay. This entire Pond Cay reef system is conspicuous by the domed house that sits on stilts at the southwestern tip of the shoal. Once inside *North Pond Cay Channel* you can turn to port a bit to pass to the west of Bonacca avoiding the shoals that sit just west of the town as shown on the chart. Anchor

Guanaja off the starboard bow

House on Guanaja

Dunbar Rock, Guanaja

Bonacca, Guanaja

Street scene, Bonacca, Guanaja

Zapata's store, Bonacca

Savannah Bight, Guanaja

wherever your draft allows if you need to clear, and make sure that your anchor is set well.

What You Will Find Ashore
Customs and Immigration
The *Port Captain's* office is at the head of the water taxi dock, the southernmost large dock on the west side of the settlement and noticeable by its two story gazebo. You'll have to anchor off the island and dinghy in so try to secure your dink well on the inside as far as possible, the dock is a VERY busy place, the hub of activity on the Bonacca waterfront with small boats constantly coming and going. The dock is really meant for water taxis although the occasional fruit vendor will tie up there long enough to sell his or her wares. Don't block the dock with your dinghy; the painted admonition *Solo Taxis* means *Taxis Only* in English. It's not too difficult to find a place to tie up your dinghy while you scramble up the dock or seawall and head into town; just make sure that it's okay with the landowners for you to leave your dink there for a short period.

Vessels may not move from Bonacca until pratique has been granted, I've heard third hand of boats that were fined for anchoring in *El Bight* before clearing. When you come ashore it's a good idea to have some *Lempira* in your pocket to pay the cost of clearance. First you'll have to visit *Immigración*, then the Port Captain's office, *El Capitan de el Puerto*, all near the water taxi dock. You can get change at *Zapata's* store or at *Bancahsa* across from the taxi dock and at *Banco Atlantida*.

Garbage
If you need to drop off some garbage, on the north side of Bonacca, just east of the fuel dock, is a small dock where the garbage boat is secured. You are permitted to leave your bagged garbage on the boat Mondays through Saturdays from 0600-1000 and from 1300-1600, but please don't leave your garbage on the dock, place it on the boat itself.

Fuel and Propane, Marine Supplies
At the northwestern tip of the island are a couple of fuel docks, *Texaco* and the *Extra Gas* dock, both of which have good fuel but *Texaco* also offers fresh water. Here too is located *Extra Shine Boat Repairs*. If you need hardware, propane, fuel, or diesel and *Yamaha* outboard repairs go across the waterway to *Wilmont Bay Service* on the tiny island (commonly referred to as Alcatraz) just west of the *Texaco* fuel dock. *WBS* also carries *Sherwin Williams Paint*, ice,

and purified water. *WBS* is open Monday through Saturday from 0730-1700 and on Sundays from 0730-1500.

Medical
If you have a medical emergency phone 504-9758-8289, if yours is not an emergency phone 504-453-4471. If you require the services of a Dentist call Jill Haylock at 504-453-4188. Her clinic is above her mother's store, a yellow two-story tienda. Jill is only on the island two weeks a month so be sure to call first.

Internet
The *Baytech Cyber Cafe* and *Internet Now* both have Internet access but space is limited.

Provisions
The best place in town to provision is *Zapata's Store* on the western side of the island. You'll see the store, and the dock has over 15' alongside which makes it very convenient for all vessels. Besides *Zapata's* you can also get groceries at *Novedades Ega*, *Novedades Susy*, and *Casa Sicaffy* which is one of the best stocked stores in Bonnacca.

On most Friday mornings, a boat from the mainland arrives with fresh produce destined for the various tiendas and produce stands. If you happen to be waiting in *Zapata's* you can sample some of their Friday morning cinnamon buns.

Dining
For dining try *The Pirate's Den* located in the center of Bonacca features fresh locally caught seafood and the usual beef and chicken dishes. *The Pirate's Den* opens at noon with daily lunch specials and Fridays is BBQ day with draft beer all day. *Mexi-Treats* is a delightful air-conditioned Mexican restaurant located in front of *Banco Atlantida*. The *Best Stop Restaurant and Bakery* is one of my favorites. Terry Zapata is the chef and cooks up great burgers, wings, and dogs as well as all kinds of breads, pastries, and pies every morning and serves them up in his family style restaurant.

The Canal to Pine Ridge Bight

From Bonacca it is possible to take your dinghy up a canal to *Pine Ridge Bight* and the northern shore of Guanaja. Although the canal was dredged to 9' in the late 1980s, it is now far too shallow for most cruising boats, the controlling depth is just a bit under 4' near the northern end. When entering the first bay from Bonacca stay to the north side of the channel and then stay south of the pair of wrecks in the inner bay.

The Northern Shore

The northern shore of Guanaja offers several nice anchorages that are best enjoyed when the wind is light and southeasterly. Never attempt the channels on the northern shore in poor visibility (you'll never see the reefs), heavy winds or following seas, and never attempt to stay here when northerly seas are forecast, you may be trapped inside until the seas subside. If you are approaching the northern shore of Guanaja from the east, or from *Savannah Bight* or Bonacca, stay at least two miles off the northeastern shore of the island to avoid the off-lying reefs. As you begin to parallel the northern shore as you head southwestward, stay about ½ mile outside the visible reef line, any closer in and you may find yourself in 2-5 fathoms of water with a lot of shallow heads scattered about as the reef is ill-defined in some places. On the bright side, you can enter inside the reef at the southwestern tip of Guanaja and parallel the shoreline all the way north to *Michael Rock Channel* where you'll have to go outside to access *Mangrove Bight*, unless you draw less than 3' in which case you can continue northward paralleling the shoreline and dodging heads and patch reefs, but it's easier to go outside at *Michael Rock Channel*.

If you're familiar with my past guides, you'll notice that I've strayed from my usual cartography in this publication. It seems that I feel the need to protect some skippers from themselves. The charts for the northern coasts of Guanaja and Roatán in the *Bay Islands* of Honduras do NOT have a lat/long grid on them. Why you may ask? Simple I reply. I've noticed that some navigators have taken to watching the cursor on their chart plotters instead of the waters around them. In one particular instance that I know of a skipper when aground hard and bent his 4" rudder shaft. With this in mind I have decided that on the aforementioned charts I would omit the lat/long grid to avoid such a problem in the future. As a result you cannot plot your position on these charts, you cannot count on them being to scale, treat them as you would a sketch chart, in other words, you MUST use only your eyes to get you through these passages.

Why only on these charts you may ask? Simple I again reply. The northern shores of Guanaja and Roatán are protected by fringing reefs and the

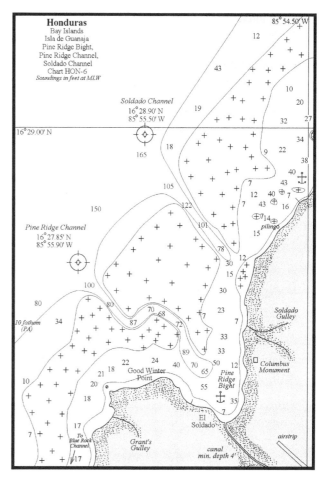

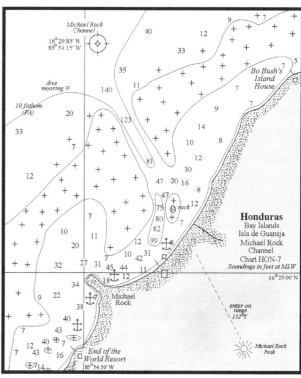

passes through the reefs are not marked and difficult to discern in all but the best of visibility, an error here could be very costly. I have included waypoints to place you just off the reef entrances, from there you will have to pilot your way in by eye. I know some of you may not appreciate this, but it is with good intentions I assure you. Call me old-fashioned, but I insist that you pilot by eye through these areas.

The settlements and resorts on the northern shore of Guanaja offer little for the cruiser except calm anchorages (except during periods of heavy northerly swells), some of the most beautiful beaches on the island, and absolutely superb reef diving, it's hard to imagine why anybody would want to come here.

Pine Ridge Bight

Waypoints:
Soldado Channel- ¼ nm NW of
16° 28.90' N, 85° 55.50' W

Pine Ridge Channel- ¼ nm NW of entrance ch.
16° 28.85' N, 85° 55.90' W

Pine Ridge Channel- ¼ nm NW of
16° 27.85' N, 85° 55.90' W

Blue Rock Channel- NW waypoint
16° 26.22' N, 85° 57.13' W

Blue Rock Channel- intermediate waypoint
16° 26.10' N, 85° 56.75' W

Blue Rock Channel- ¼ nm SW of Blue Rock
16° 26.03' N, 85° 56.46' W

El Soldado and *Pine Ridge Bight*, sit at the end of the canal that leads northwest from the south side of Guanaja as shown on Chart HON-6. The anchorage has little to offer save a stopover to view the *Columbus Monument* on the eastern shore of the bight. The monument marks what is believed to be the spot where Columbus landed in 1502, but is unfinished, it seems that Spain donated some money for the monument and a museum, but not all of it went to that cause and nobody seems to know where exactly the monies are.

Navigational Information
There are several ways to enter *Pine Ridge Bight* and the waterway that runs along the northern shore of Guanaja all the way to Michael Rock. Chart HON-6 shows the tricky *Pine Ridge Channel*, and the not so tricky *Soldado Channel*, but if I'm approaching from the southwest tip of Guanaja, I prefer to parallel the coastline northward as shown on Chart HON-3, it is far easier than attempting *Pine Ridge Channel*, it's also inside the reef for most of its length, making for calmer waters if any seas are running on the northern side of the island side of the island. As shown on Chart HON-3, you can stay approximately ¼ mile off the western shore of Guanaja and be in 2 fathoms of water nearly all the way from Ochre Bluff to Good Winter Point (also shown on Chart HON-6).

If you intend to enter via *Pine Ridge Channel* from offshore, a waypoint at 16° 27.85' N, 85° 55.90' W, will place you ¼ nautical mile northwest of the entrance to the channel. From the waypoint enter the channel and follow it as it doglegs between the reefs. Never try this channel in poor visibility. If you intend to enter via *Soldado Channel* a waypoint at 16° 28.90' N, 85° 55.50' W, will place you approximately ¼ nautical mile northwest of the entrance to the channel. From the waypoint enter this rather straightforward channel between the reefs until you come to the deeper water inside and can turn to port or starboard to head to your destination.

If you intend to exit *Pine Ridge Bight* and head to Roatán, you can either leave via *Pine Ridge Channel* or *Soldado Channel* as shown on Chart HON-6, or you can leave via *Blue Rock Channel* that starts just south of Blue Rock as shown on Chart HON-3 (you can also anchor just south of Blue Rock in prevailing conditions). Even though it's shallower, I much prefer *Blue Rock Channel* to *Pine Ridge Channel*; on days with poor visibility I can easily exit from *Pine Ridge Bight* via *Blue Rock Channel* when I can't even see where the inside entrance of *Pine Ridge Channel* lies.

To find *Blue Rock Channel* head south from *Pine Ridge Bight*, rounding Good Winter Point and working your way southward toward Blue Rock as shown on Chart HON-6 and Chart HON-3. Just south of Blue Rock you will come to your easternmost waypoint for *Blue Rock Channel* at 16° 26.03' N, 85° 56.46' W, which places you approximately ½ mile southwest of Blue Rock (you can also anchor in the small cove south of Blue Rock in settled weather, never if northerly swells are running). REMEMBER, use the *Blue Rock Channel* waypoints ONLY as a guideline, pilot your way through these reefs by eye, ignore that the waypoint is telling you if something does not look right, trust your eyes and your depth sounder.

From the waypoint you'll be heading just a bit north of west to an intermediate waypoint at 16° 26.10' N, 85° 56.75' W, and then to the western waypoint at 16° 26.22' N, 85° 57.13' W, at which time you can head to the waypoint south of the shoals lying southeast of Barbaretta. As you can see on Chart HON-3, *Blue Rock* Channel winds its way through two reefs and allows you to pass north of a third, and the distance between the reefs is far wider than *Pine Ridge Channel* though not nearly as deep, but plenty deep enough for a 9' draft. Never attempt this passage when heavy westerly or northerly seas are running, at night, or in periods of poor visibility. You can also enter *Pine Ridge Bight* via *Blue Rock Channel*, simply follow the above directions in reverse.

Michael Rock

Waypoints:

Michael Rock Channel- ¼ nm NNW of entrance
16° 29.85' N, 85° 54.15' W

Navigational Information

Michael Rock Channel is one of the easiest channels to enter along the northern shore of Guanaja, due in no small part to the natural range of *Michael Rock Peak*, the highest point on Guanaja (and in fact, the highest point in all of the Bay Islands). As shown on Chart HON-7, a waypoint at 16° 29.85' N, 85° 54.15' W, will place you approximately one-quarter mile north/northwest of the entrance to *Michael Rock Channel*. From the waypoint line up on *Michael Rock Peak*, 150° T, and enter the channel, but don't just follow the range in without keeping one eye on the reefs and one eye on the depth sounder (it seems that you will need three eyes for this passage). Very soon you'll need to turn to starboard to avoid the shoal with the rock in its center as you head towards the house with the dock. You'll have deep water all the way in, almost until you reach the area of the house and dock. You can anchor here or head around Michael Rock to anchor off the *End of the World Resort* (http://www.endoftheworldresort.com/). Keep between the reef and the shoreline, easy to do in good light, and you'll have 25'-40' of water all the way to the resort except for the three shoals just off the club. Cruisers heading south from Michael Rock or north from *Soldado Channel* are advised to pass to the west of the shoals off the resort's dock, you'll have 30'-40' of water there, and between the two shoals that lie southwest of the dock as shown on Chart HON-6 and Chart HON-7.

You can also anchor on either side of Michael Rock as shown on the chart, but the holding on the south side is a bit grassy so make sure your anchor is dug in well.

What You Will Find Ashore

The *End of the World Resort*, a favorite place for local folks as well as tourists, offers a bar and restaurant on the beach (with Saturday and Sunday barbecues featuring local seafood) along with all manner of water-sports, Internet access, and several hiking trails including a 2-hour hike to a waterfall. The resort also offers cozy cabins located on the hills above the water, you'll see them as you sail along the shoreline. Nearby is *Caseta 2000*, a nice little island bar complete with sand floor, a great view of the Caribbean, and cold beer.

Hikers among you can follow a trail past the beaches northeast of Michael Rock and inland a bit to arrive at *Mangrove Bight*. Along this walk you'll find *Bo Bush's Island House* dive hotel (http://www.bosislandhouse.com/), a great spot to get away from it all on an island where people go to get away from it all. Owner Bo is bilingual and a very experienced diver with a thorough knowledge of these waters.

Mangrove Bight

Waypoints:

Mangrove Bight- ¼ nm NNW of entrance
16° 30.75' N, 85° 52.65' W

Well, the good news is that *Mangrove Bight* has been rebuilt. Devastated by *Hurricane Mitch* in the morning hours of October 26, 1998, local residents watched in horror as thirty-foot seas entered the bight and destroyed their docks and homes in short order. Within two years the town had been rebuilt though it still sits right on the waterfront.

Navigational Information

If you are approaching *Mangrove Bight* from *Savannah Bight*, from the eastern side of Guanaja, give the reefs along the northern shore of Guanaja, as shown on Chart HON-2, a wide berth!

As shown on Chart HON-8, a waypoint at 16° 30.75' N, 85° 52.65' W, will place you approximately ¼ mile north/northwest of the channel leading into *Mangrove Bight*. From the waypoint enter the channel, in good light it's easy to see, and keep the piling on the reef to starboard as shown on the chart and bear in mind that the piling is set well south of the

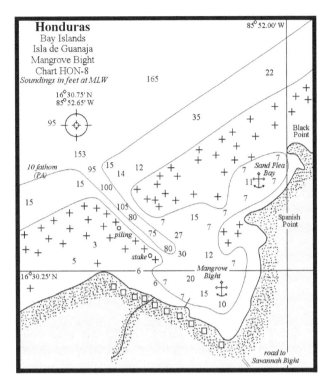

northern edge of the reef and so does not mark the northwestern tip of the reef. Further in is a smaller stake that marks the southern end of the same reef, keep it well to starboard also. Your passage through this channel will be a gently curving course to port as shown on the chart. The channel is deep and you can stay in over 10 fathoms all the way in. If you find yourself suddenly in less than 5 fathoms you've strayed to one side or the other. Once past the stake and shoal to starboard, you can turn in towards the town (not too soon though or you'll go aground) or anchor at the head of the bight. You can also work your way up into *Sand Flea Bay*, but I must warn you, there's a reason it's named that!

What You Will Find Ashore

Ashore you'll find several small stores where you can pick up a few basic supplies and some fresh fish or produce as well as a couple of *comedores* where you can get a burger or a fish dinner. From *Mangrove Bight* you can follow the small road southward to *Savannah Bight* as I mentioned in the section *Savannah Bight*. However there is another small trail you can follow from the western end of *Mangrove Bight* that leads up and over a small hill and down into *Sandy Bay* on the southern shore of Guanaja by *El Bight*. The hill rises to 412' and its flat peak is a popular camping spot. This is a long hike, it will probably take you at least a day.

Roatán

Roatán is the largest of the Bay Islands, approximately 29 miles wide by about 2 miles wide at its widest point, and the three small islands at its northeastern tip, Helene, Morat, and Barbaretta are generally considered to be part of Roatán, though the residents of Helene will tell you differently. There is a mountainous ridge that runs along the center of the island making for superb hiking through woodlands and rainforest with stunning ocean vistas for your enjoyment. Roatán's shoreline is indented with deep water inlets (most of which are called bights), that have offered a safe haven to mariners for centuries. Along the shoreline you'll find ironshore to mangroves, to lovely white, sandy beaches backed by swaying palm trees and small houses built on stilts at the water's edge, while the offshore reefs offer some of the most spectacular diving in the world.

The people of Roatán are amazing, most speak English, in fact some entire communities, such as Helene, speak only English. In fact, you often don't know which language you'll use when you approach an islander until they speak.

It has come to my attention that some of the places on Roatán are misnamed. The locals refer to places by their land names, the cruisers refer to places by the water names, and the real estate agents use another system entirely. This is why *Second Bight* is often called *Parrot Tree Plantation*, while French Harbour can be either a town, or the bay to the west of Old French Harbour. At West End, there was no West Bay until the 1990s because there was no tourism until that decade. So bear all of this in mind as you travel along these shores and I'll try not to confuse you too much in this chapter.

Ferries

Galaxy Wave Ferry operates between Roatán and La Ceiba with 0700 and 1400 departures from Coxen Hole and 0930 and 1630 departures from La Ceiba. For more information call 504-445-1795 or email for more information, info@Roatánferry.com. The ferry also visits Utila and will bring you to La Ceiba in about two-hours of air-conditioned comfort complete with refreshments and videos.

Getting Around on Roatán

The principal means of transportation here are the many taxis that seem to be everywhere. These white sedans are quite affordable and easy to get. If you need a taxi just stand by the road and flag one down as it passes by. Rates range from US$1-2 in town, while it may cost as much as US$5-10 to go to French Harbour or West End from Coxen Hole. The taxis all tend to look alike, they all appear to be small, white *Toyota Corollas* with yellow squares on the side with their number on it; a few may have a "Taxi" sign on the roof. Make sure you say "Collectivo" as an "express" will cost more.

There is also regular bus service between the major communities on Roatán with buses running, on the average, about every half hour. There are buses that run from Coxen Hole to West End that cost about US$.50.

Rental cars are readily available and prices are reasonable and vary from under US$50-100 per day depending on the vehicle you choose (there is a 16% government tax on every rental). Roatán has a paved road that connects the most important communities on the island from West End through Coxen Hole to Punta Gorda to the east. Here the paved road turns to dirt and continues east to the areas of *Paya Bay*, *Camp Bay*, Port Royal, and several other smaller communities.

A word about driving on Roatán, there are a lot of potholes, perhaps not quite as bad as the roads along the northern shore of Jamaica, but still a lot of potholes. You really don't need a map on Roatán, there's only one main road and the turnoffs are well marked.

Medical Assistance

There are several clinics and one hospital (in Coxen Hole and not recommended) on the island, and a dive compression chamber for divers. Larger medical centers are available on the mainland in San Pedro Sula and La Ceiba. Emergencies can be handled by air ambulance, and a number of resort owners and individuals have their private planes at the airport on Roatán.

Located in Coxen Hole is the *Woods Medical Centre* (504-2445-1080; http://www.mmex.org/missionrecords/wood-medical-center) open 24/7

and located almost directly across from *Immigration*. *Woods* is the best place on the island for quality medical care. Anthony's Key has a top-notch clinic, *Clinica Esperanza*, 504-2445-3234; http://clinicaesperanza.org/) on site with a dive compression chamber and a laboratory, they're located just west of Anthony's Key on the south side of the road. *Clinicas MediCentro* is located in the *Megaplaza Mall* at French Harbour. Call to set up an appointment, 504-9496-1928. Dr. Leslie has a small clinic in Oak Ridge at the taxi stand plaza, call 504-435-2219 or 504-435-2373 for more information.

There is an optometrist located on Roatán at *Optipon* (504-9982-7376 or 504-9702-0097) which is located in either *French Harbour* or Coconut Place near the airport, depending on the day.

If you need a dentist call the *Roatán Dental Centre* in the *Megaplaza* at *French Harbour*, Dr. Hayman Grant, at 504-2480-5275, or 504-9778-9678 (email: drhrghond@yahoo.com). Dr. Grant had a practice in the US for 15 years and speaks fluent English.

Also in *French Harbour,* next to *Gio's Restaurant,* are the dental offices of Dra. Miriam Espinoza (office: 504-408-3549, cell: 504-9985-2243). Nearby is the office of Dr. Jorge Lanza Valldares (French Harbour office: 504-408-3549, La Ceiba office: 504-440-0269) who is open on Thursdays and Fridays and specializes in Orthodontics and Cosmetic Dentistry. Other Dentists are Drs. Jorge and Ligia Lanza, 504-9995-3751. In Oak Ridge, you can visit Eunice for teeth cleaning and a dental checkup. Eunice can be reached at 504-445-0430 and her house is located about 5 minutes from the taxi stand, the first house on the right on the right.

In case of a medical emergency you can dial 911. For Police call 199, for Fire assistance call 198, for an ambulance call 195, and to reach the hospital in Coxen Hole phone 504-445-1227.

If you need a veterinarian, *Animal Kingdom* is located in *Sandy Bay* and you can call Dr. Santiago Soto at 504-9909-0595. Dr. Calderone of the *Clinica Veterinaria Centaurus* (504-9995-2260), visits *French Harbour* on Wednesdays from his office on the mainland. On Utila, Dr. Loretta Potts runs the *Utila Animal Rescue and Pet Care* (http://www.utilaanimalrescure.org/), and in La Ceiba, Dr. Bueno is a vet that can be reached at 440-2539.

The Southern Shore

The southern shore of Roatán is where most of the larger settlements and the nearly all of the marine services are located. The southern shore has several very protected anchorages, a couple of possible hurricane holes, and the better nightlife, while the northern shore offers solitude and some of the best diving on the fringing reef that stretches for almost the entire length of the island. If you've got the time to explore Roatán, you should do both shorelines. We'll cover both shorelines in this chapter beginning with the southern shore from east to west as if you were approaching from Guanaja, and the northern shore from west to east as if you were doing a circumnavigation of the island.

Isla de Barbareta

Waypoints:
Pigeon Cay- ¼ nm SSE of entrance
16° 24.60' N, 86° 07.35' W

W of Pigeon Cays- ¼ nm S of
16° 24.45' N, 86° 08.60' W

Shoals SE of Isla Barbaretta-1 nm S of SE tip
16° 23.50' N, 86° 05.90' W

Isla de Barbareta, along with her sister islands Isla Helene and Morat, make up a trio of cays that lie off Roatán's northeastern tip and are considered a part of Roatán itself, though there are some folks in Helene that will beg to differ. Isla de Barbareta is private and permission must be granted before coming ashore. The caretaker is Pepper and can usually be found on the island.

Navigational Information

If you are approaching from Guanaja, make for a waypoint at 16° 23.50' N, 86° 05.90' W, which lies about 1 mile south of the southeastern tip of the shoals lying southeast of Isla Barbareta. From the waypoint you can parallel the shoals heading west keeping in deep water well clear of the visible reefs.

A waypoint at 16° 24.45' N, 86° 08.60' W, will place you ¼ mile south of the entrance channel that lies south/southeast of Pelican Point (sometimes shown as Pelikan Point) as shown on Chart HON-9. From this waypoint, head north-northwest between the two highly visible reefs as you work your way northward to anchor in *Pascual Bight*. There is a large shoal area that is shown on the chart, the least depths are 6'-7'

with many spots of 10'-12' and several shallow coral heads. You can work your way through this area but it's far easier on your nerves if you bypass it to the east.

For the more daring among you, there is a channel leading in from the east, from the Pigeon Cays, but I find the waypoint and entrance channel shown on Chart HON-9 to be far easier to use, and safer. However, for those of you used to eyeball navigation, a waypoint at 16° 24.60' N, 86° 07.35' W, will place you approximately ¼ mile south/southeast of *Pigeon Cay Channel*. From the waypoint you'll notice the Pigeon Cays to the northeast of you and several small patches of reef that dry at MLW. You'll pass between the westernmost of these small dry patches and the visible reef to port, you'll see the channel between the two, follow it in a generally northwest direction as it doglegs between shoals and comes out into the deeper water south of Pelican Point on Isla Barbareta.

Helene and Morat

Waypoints:
Helene Harbour- ¼ nm S of entrance channel
16° 24.45' N, 86° 12.70' W

Morat- ¼ nm SSE of entrance channel
16° 25.20' N, 86° 10.90' W

Morat is a small island west of Isla de Barbaretta, and Helene is the first community you'll come to as you head west along Roatán's southern shore.

Navigational Information

Morat has a small little harbor that offers protection from all winds save those from a southerly direction as shown on Chart HON-10. A waypoint at 16° 25.34' N, 86° 10.96' W, places you approximately ¼ mile south/southeast of the tricky entrance channel, use caution when entering here and never attempt this route at night or during periods of poor visibility. From the waypoint head up the slightly curving channel keeping *Hog Reef* to starboard and the unnamed reef to port to anchor in the lee of Morat wherever your draft allows.

To enter the harbor at Helene, proceed westward, south of Isla Morada, sometimes shown as Rose Island, to a waypoint at 16° 24.45' N, 86° 12.50' W, which places you approximately ¼ mile south of the entrance channel. From the waypoint head into the harbor passing between the huge reef system west of

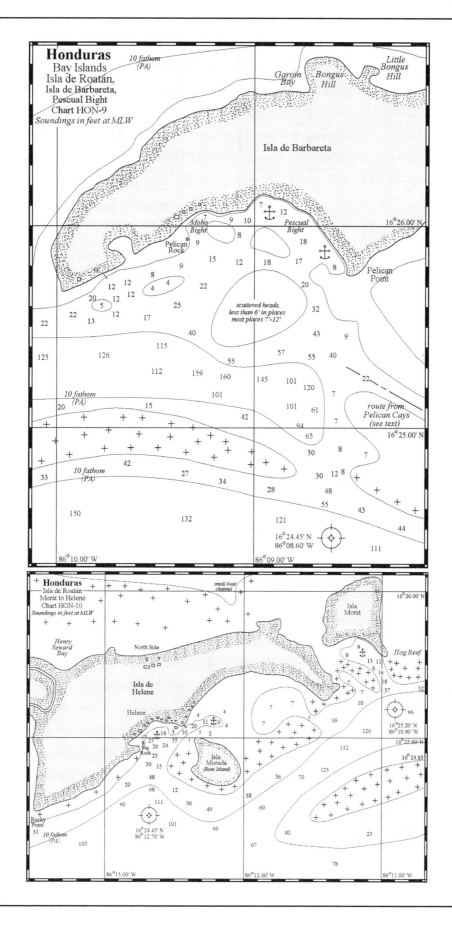

Honduras
Bay Islands
Isla de Roatán,
Isla de Barbareta,
Pescual Bight
Chart HON-9
Soundings in feet at MLW

10 fathom (PA)

Garoin Bay

Bongus Hill

Little Bongus Hill

Isla de Barbareta

7 12

Moho Bight

9 10

Pescual Bight

8

Pelican Rock

9

18

15 12 18 17

8 12 4

4 22

20

8

Pelican Point

12 12

4

20

20 12

5 12

25

scattered heads, less than 6' in places most places 7'-12'

32

22 22 13 12 17

40

43 9

125 126

115

57 55 40

55

112 159 160

145 101 120

7

10 fathom (PA)

101

101 61

route from Pelican Cays (see text)

22

20

15

42

94

7

16°26.00' N

16°25.00' N

65

42

30

8

7

33

10 fathom (PA)

27

34

30 12 8

28

48

150

132

121

55 43

44

16°24.45' N
86°08.60' W

111

86°10.00' W

86°09.00' W

Honduras
Isla de Roatán
Morat to Helene
Chart HON-10
Soundings in feet at MLW

small boat channel

16°26.00' N

Isla Morat

Henry Seward Bay

North Side

Hog Reef

8

8 13 11

8

16

Isla de Helene

7 18 37 32

Helene

7 7

10

96

4 11 9 4

7 7 16

16°25.20' N
86°10.90' W

16 3 35

120

16°25.00' N

1 2

Big Rock

25 20 24

35

16°24.83'

25

30 15

Isla Morada (Rose Island)

112

48

56 70

125

20

68

12

38

60

90

111

30 49

60

40

23

Rocky Point

31

10 fathom (PA)

16°24.45' N
86°12.70' W

101

60

67

78

105

86°13.00' W

86°12.00' W

86°11.00' W

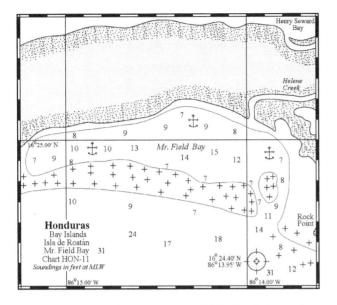

Isla Morada and the area around Big Rock to anchor either just off the town, which has more surge, or anchor well past the cut between Isla Morada and Helene as shown on the chart.

What You Will Find Ashore

Helene is a small fishing community where many of the folks, population of 60 or so, speak English and are all related in some way or another. If you like a guide ask for Larry, and if you would like to go ashore and eat, the pink building is home to the *First Stop Restaurant* serving up locally caught seafood. There's also a dive operation here, located on the point, and there are caves nearby to explore, just ask Larry.

Mr. Field Bay

Waypoints:
Mr. Field Bay- ¼ nm SSW of entrance channel
16° 24.40' N, 86° 13.95' W

Just west of Helene is a large reef protected cove called *Mr. Field Bay* that offers good protection from all directions, the reefs break the seas from the south while the low stretch of Roatán to the north offers excellent shelter from the fiercest northerly winds.

Navigational Information
As shown on Chart HON-11, a waypoint at 16° 24.40' N, 86° 13.95' W, will place you approximately ¼ mile south/southwest of the entrance channel into *Mr. Field Bay*. From the waypoint pass between the reef lying west of Rock Point and the visible reef to port. This can be a tricky passage, never attempt it at night or during periods of poor visibility. As you enter

the channel you'll come to a large reef in the middle of the channel at the northern end of the channel, the deeper water is to the eastern side of this reef, once past the reef anchor where your draft allows.

Old Port Royal

Waypoints:
Old Port Royal Harbor- ¼ nm SSE of entrance
16° 24.40' N, 86° 15.93' W

Old Port Royal is the next stop as we travel along the southern shore of Roatán westward. Old Port Royal was once the site of an ill-fated settlement by a group known as the *Providence Company* who tried to colonize this area between 1630-1640. In 1978, the hills above the harbor were designated the *Port Royal Park and Wildlife Refuge* in order to protect several indigenous species and to preserve the watershed for the people of eastern Roatán.

Navigational Information
As shown on Chart HON-12, a waypoint at 16° 24.40' N, 86° 15.93' W, will place you approximately ¼ mile south/southeast of the channel. From the

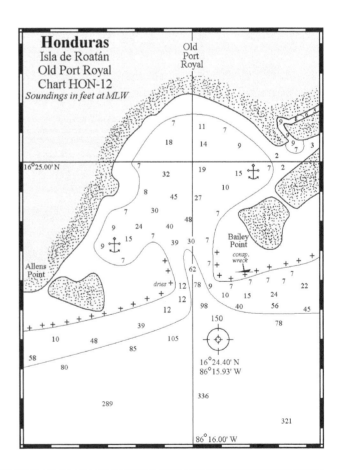

waypoint head a bit west of north into the deep channel between the unnamed cay off Allens Point and Bailey Point as shown on the chart. Once inside the harbor you can anchor wherever your draft allows.

Port Royal

Waypoints:

Port Royal Harbor- ¼ nm SSE of Fort Cay Ch. 16° 23.90' N, 86° 17.45' W

Port Royal Harbor- ¼ nm SSE of Lime Cay Ch. 16° 23.50' N, 86° 18.45' W

Port Royal was once the site of English pirate camps who named the bay after their favorite haunt in Jamaica. In 1740, the British occupied the bay building two forts to protect it. *Fort Frederick* was constructed on the mainland with one rampart and six cannon. *Fort George* was of course built on what is now called Fort Cay or George's Cay and had one rampart and seventeen cannon. The forts saw little use until their destruction in 1782 by the Spanish. Today you can still view the remains of *Fort George*, but the remains of *Fort Frederick* are now part of the base of a private home.

Navigational Information

There are actually two bays that make up what I have placed together as Port Royal as shown on Chart HON-13. Port Royal is actually the easternmost bay while *Lime Cay Bight* lies to the west. You can easily pass between the two bodies of water on the inside of the reef or use a channel through the reef to access the deeper water outside.

If you wish to enter Port Royal, a waypoint at 16° 23.90' N, 86° 17.45' W, will place you approximately ¼ mile south/southeast of the *Port Royal Channel* that lies just west of Fort Cay as shown on Chart HON-13. From the waypoint you can head straight up the deep, wide channel and anchor wherever your heart desires and your draft allows, but most head to the southeastern part of the bay to anchor in the lee of Careening Cay (Comfort Cay). There are several areas where you'll be anchoring in depths of 40' but you can still find places with less water to drop your hook. Expect the harbor to be buggy on a windless night.

You can head west to *Lime Cay Bight* by passing Cow and Calf on either the north or south side. I prefer to take Cow and Calf to port, passing between the cay and the mainland in order to avoid the reef system lying south of the cay.

If you wish to enter *Lime Cay Bight* from seaward you can head for a waypoint at 16° 23.50' N, 86° 18.45' W, which places you approximately ¼ mile south/southeast of the marked *Lime Cay Channel* between Lime Cay and the reef system lying east of the Conch Cays. At the time of this writing the channel had one red marker that lies just west of Lime Cay, keep it to starboard, and one green marker further inside, keep it to port and you're there.

What You Will Find Ashore

It's possible that over the next few years a marina may be built here, either in Port Royal or *Lime Cay Bight*, so keep an eye open for that, at the time of this writing rumors were floating around hot and heavy hinting to this possibility. In Port Royal you'll find a lovely house and dock with a huge "Welcome Cruisers" sign on it. If the folks haven't moved and the new owners taken down the sign, you need to give them a shout on Ch. 68 or Ch. 72, their hail is *Chili Chili*, and they want to welcome you to Port Royal.

If you need a welder or fabricator, visit Peter Schmitt on his square-rigger, *Crazy Horse*, located on the northern side of Port Royal by Cow and Calf, he has a complete machine shop and does exceptional work. Peter monitors VHF Ch. 68 and Ch. 72.

In *Lime Cay Bight* you'll find the *Mango Creek Resort* (http://www.mangocreeklodge.com/; monitors VHF Ch. 72-you'll notice the huge wind generators in the hills behind the resort), which has several moorings for rent as well as several colorful cabanas on stilts along the waterfront that can be yours for the asking (and the paying). The resort also serves up breakfast, lunch, and dinner with some notice. Their breakfasts are absolutely worth the trip in to shore, eggs your way and stacks of pancakes and platters of potatoes.

On the northern side of the bay, almost at the end of the road to the east, you'll find *La Sirena* and its owner Jimmy. Here you can grab a drink or enjoy a meal in a palapa sitting over the water amid the loveliest surroundings. If you phone ahead, 3320-6004, your food will be hot upon your arrival.

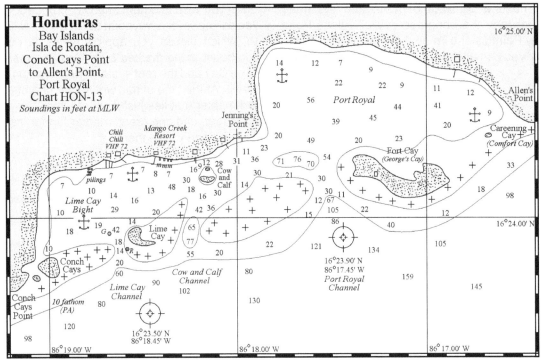

Honduras
Bay Islands
Isla de Roatán,
Conch Cays Point
to Allen's Point,
Port Royal
Chart HON-13
Soundings in feet at MLW

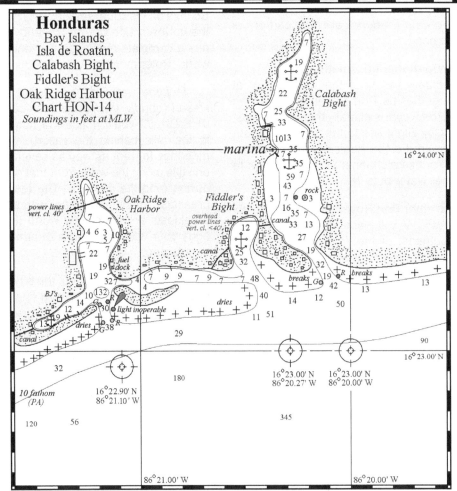

Honduras
Bay Islands
Isla de Roatán,
Calabash Bight,
Fiddler's Bight
Oak Ridge Harbour
Chart HON-14
Soundings in feet at MLW

Calabash Bight

Waypoints:
Calabash Bight- ¼ nm S of entrance channel
16° 23.00' N, 86° 20.00' W

Calabash Bight offers good protection for the cruising vessel and could even be used in the event of a hurricane if you tucked yourself well up into the northern extremity of the bay. Bear in mind that if you plan to stay in *Calabash Bight* for a hurricane that you'll be sharing this spot with a lot of local boats, many of them large, unattended, steel, shrimpers! Most folks here monitor VHF ch. 72 or 22.

Navigational Information

A waypoint at 16° 23.00' N, 86° 20.00' W, will place you approximately ¼ mile south/southeast of the entrance channel as shown on Chart HON-14. Line up and pass mid-channel between the reefs and the red and green buoys that mark the channel's edge. Once inside pass about ½ boat length to the west of the white buoy, this is a narrow channel between two shoals and caution must be exercised.

What You Will Find Ashore

Nearby is the *Tropical Beach Resort* offering offshore fishing as well as diving packages, but as of this writing their ownership has changed and they may no longer accept outside guests. There is some good news though…as of this writing a new Internet café opened at the entrance to the canal joining *Calabash Bight* with *Fiddler's Bight.*

Marine Facilities

Marina

Located on the west side of *Calabash Bight* is the new mini-marina, *Turtlegrass Marina* (http://www.turtlegrass.net/) and their *Turtle Shack Restaurant.* The marina has 400' of dockage (they can handle boats up to 48' LOA with a draft of 9') one 30' wide catamaran slip, and two free moorings. Hail the marina on VHF ch. 72 for more information. The restaurant is open on Tuesdays and Thursdays but owner Mark will make fresh bread with a day's notice (his bread is hot, fresh, and sometimes delivered to your boat). The marina is proude of their endless happy hour and their endless cooler of beer.

The marina offers 30 amp electric, RO water, Wi-Fi, and can have clean diesel delivered to the dock at a competitive price. The marina also offers bottom cleaning along with consulting and sometimes installation of solar, diesel, and wind generator combos. The marina also offers computer Networking and Repair services.

Laundry

For your laundry needs seek out Miss Curly who is located at the southern end of the eastern shore of *Calabash Bight,* her's is the low dock off the blue house.

Fiddler's Bight

Waypoints:
Fiddler's Bight- ¼ nm SSE of entrance channel
16° 23.00' N, 86° 20.27' W

Fiddler's Bight is small and is used more by local boats and shrimpers, in truth *Calabash Bight* is the better anchorage.

Navigational Information

A waypoint at 16° 23.00' N, 86° 20.27' W, will place you approximately ¼ mile south/southeast of the entrance to *Fiddler's Bight* as shown on Chart HON-14. From the waypoint you can enter between the two visible reefs, beware that the entrance is more of a dogleg than shown, to anchor wherever your draft allows, but don't go too far north, that's where you'll find some low hanging power lines, vertical clearance less than 40'.

Oak Ridge

Waypoints:
Oak Ridge Harbor- ¼ nm SSE of entrance ch.
16° 22.90' N, 86° 21.10' W

In days past the harbor at Oak Ridge was a refuge for pirates fleeing from the Spaniards, then later it was a boat building center, but today it is a shrimper's port, make no mistake about that, and many of the citizens here are of British descent. Oak Ridge is a small, picturesque community built upon the shrimp trade and it has managed to retain much of its charm even though it now is connected to the rest of Roatán by road. Today you'll find a fuel dock here, a couple of nice restaurants, a few grocery stores, hardware stores, and even a place where you can surf the Internet.

Navigational Information

A waypoint at 16° 22.90' N, 86° 21.10' W, will place you approximately ¼ mile south/southeast of the entrance channel as shown on Chart HON-14. From the waypoint pass between the visible reefs keeping the non-working light to starboard upon entering and passing between the two sets of red and green buoys. The light itself is a concrete structure about 20' tall with cement platform on top. The light stands on the reef itself so don't try to take it close upon your starboard side when entering.

Once inside you can turn to port to anchor in the small arm of the bay that stretches westward, do not anchor north of the shoal by the low hanging power lines, vertical clearance 40', this is a favorite spot for local thieves to find their next victim. If fact, *Calabash Bight* is a much better anchorage as is *Jonesville Bight* to the west. If you must stay here I'd recommend *Oak Ridge Marina*, also known as *Sandy's Marina,* directly across from *BJ's*. At the western end of the small arm of the bay in front of *BJ's* is a canal leading west. You can utilize this canal to dinghy as far west as Carib Point inside the reef.

What You Will Find Ashore
The *Reef House Resort* (http://www. reefhouseresort.com/) sits on the small cay across from the main dock in Oak Ridge and offers good rooms and even better food. *BGA Bank* also has an office here and buses stop here daily, *BGA* is located by the huge shrimp plant on the western shore of the harbor.

Marine Facilities
Marina
In the western bight of *Oak Ridge Bay,* across from BJ's, is *Sandy's Marina.* The marina offers 4 slips and one slip for a catamaran, all with finger piers. Sandy's also provides water, a washing machine, and good local information.

Fuel
The fuel dock at *Sandy's Marina* is for jerry-jugging only and they usually don't carry diesel, but there is another dock in the harbor you can try. On the western side of the bay, next to the taxi stands and market, there is a finger pier (*Roy Mart*) and cement dock that is often blocked by ships involved in loading and offloading. There is 12' at the dock and you can jerry jug your fuel unless their new hose is installed. At the time of this writing there is a 50 gallon minimum.

Sail and Canvas Repairs
If you need some sail or canvas repairs done while you're at Oak Ridge, phone Judy at 504-435-1501. She does great work, uses *SailRite* gear, and is accessible by dinghy or water taxi.

Medical
Dr. Leslie has a small clinic at the taxi stand plaza, call 504-435-2219 or 504-435-2373 for more information. In Oak Ridge, you can visit Eunice for teeth cleaning and a dental checkup. Eunice can be reached at 504-445-0430 and her house is located about 5 minutes from the taxi stand, the first house on the right.

Provisions
Oak Ridge is a good spot to pick up a few things you might need, a few groceries, a hardware item you require, but not a place to do any sort of major provisioning, do that at *Eldon's* in *French Harbour.*

Across the street from *BJ's* is the *J&D Store*, a good spot to pick up a few needed basic groceries. You can also pick up some groceries at *Commercial Hessie,* the *Bodden Supermarket,* and the *C&A Save Center. Miss Claire's* has a good selection of staples and basics and good frozen meats (not to mention 12 volt deep cycle batteries, *Clint's* also carries batteries). *J&D's* is a bit larger and also carries a good selection of basics.

Just up the road from *BJ's,* in Barrio Lempira, is a small produce stand with reasonable prices. At the intersection of the road with the main highway is another produce stand that restocks on Mondays.

Every Saturday morning there is a market at the taxi and bus stop in Oak Ridge. This is the perfect time to acquire some quality beef or pork, cut on the spot, by Dave, the butcher from Diamond Rock. Shrimp is also available from local shrimpers at the market.

Dining
For dining out, or just to surf the net, visit *BJ's Restaurant* and visit the owner, BJ. *BJ's*, who have their own dinghy dock, is the place to be on Saturday when most cruisers in the area dinghy over for a jam session which goes on until later in the afternoon.

Hog Pen Bight

Waypoints:
Hog Pen Bight- ¼ nm SSE of entrance channel
16° 23.05' N, 86° 21.75' W

Hog Pen Bight offers little to the cruiser save good protection from all weather.

Navigational Information

As shown on Chart HON-15, a waypoint at 16° 23.05' N, 86° 21.75' W, places you approximately ¼ mile south/southeast of the well-marked entrance channel. From the waypoint head just a bit west of north until you can pick out the red and green markers as shown on the chart, the green marked is backed by a white maker further inside. Split the markers and head up into the bay avoiding the shoal in the center, and although you can pass it on both sides (if you draw less than 7'), the deeper water is to the east of the shoal. You can anchor wherever your draft allows but the best protection is offered at the extreme northern end.

Jonesville Bight, Bodden Bight

Waypoints:
Jonesville Bight- ¼ nm S of entrance channel
16° 22.80' N, 86° 22.35' W

Jonesville Bight is home to one of the most popular cruising destinations on Roatán, *Bodden Bight*, home of the *Hole in the Wall Bar*, the reason so many cruisers opt for this anchorage.

Navigational Information

As shown on Chart HON-15, a waypoint at16° 22.80' N, 86° 22.35' W, will place you ¼ mile south of the entrance channel into *Jonesville Bight*. From the waypoint had northward through the red and green markers as shown on the chart, past Jonesville Cay and into the harbor itself. Once inside you can anchor on the eastern side of the harbor or head northwest to anchor in *Bodden Bight*.

Those wishing to anchor in *Bodden Bight* will at first wonder how in the world did those sailboats already anchored there got under those power lines? The power lines will appear daunting at first but there is a way under them. To the east of *Bodden Bight*, across much of the bay, the clearance under the power lines is around 30'-40', but on the western side of the harbor the clearance increases to almost 80' along the western shoreline.

As you approach the northern part of *Jonesville Bight* you'll see a small red buoy in front of you as shown on the chart. Keep the red buoy to starboard and avoid the shoal to port as you pass the green buoy on your port side. You're heading for the peach colored house on the shore. Stay close inshore as you parallel the shoreline into *Bodden Bight* and you'll be fine.

If you wish to head east inside the reefs by dinghy, it's possible to do so from Jonesville keeping to the channels along the shoreline all the way to *Calabash Bight*.

What You'll Find Ashore

Marinas

There is a small marina to port as you enter Jonesville Bight, it's called Jonesville Point Marina (504-9967-3803) and has 4 side-tie slips available. The docks are low and fixed and I cannot recommend riding out a hurricane here.

Dining

Jonesville is another one of Roatán's picturesque fishing communities and was established in 1852. One of the town's best eateries is *Art's Restaurant* on the waterfront and open for breakfast, lunch, and dinner with a wide variety of seafood, beef, and chicken dishes in a family atmosphere and a setting of objects that have been recovered from the sea. The *Reef House* and *Henry's Cove Hotel* also offer good dining. *Puky's* offers a very nice Sunday BBQ.

Without a doubt, the biggest attraction for cruisers here is the *Hole in the Wall Bar* in *Bodden Bight*. Accessible only by water, the world famous (or should be) owner Rhonda (Bob Lee passed away in January 2013) offers a great Sunday BBQ (starting at 1300) and a full-service bar.

Propane

If you need propane call *Venta de Gas Butano* at 435-2435.

Provisions

For groceries try *Super Tienda de Juventud* behind the shrimp boat docks, 2435-1514.

Laundry

If you're in Jonesville or *Bodden Bight* and need to have some laundry done, get on your VHF and call *Yvonne* on ch. 72, she will put you in contact with Gladys who provides laundry services on Mondays, Wednesdays, and Fridays.

Carib Point Bight

Waypoints:

Carib Point Bight- ¼ nm SE of entrance channel
16° 22.45' N, 86° 22.90' W

Carib Point Bight offers little except for good protection in all conditions except strong southerly or southeasterly blows when the harbor gets a bit surgy.

Navigational Information

As shown on Chart HON-15, a waypoint at 16° 22.45' N, 86° 22.90' W, places you approximately ¼ mile southeast of the entrance channel. From the waypoint head in a northwesterly direction until you can make out the center of the channel lying west of the reefs lying off Bennett Cay and east of the shoal off Carib Point. Once inside proceed north on either side of the bay to anchor on the eastern or western part of the shoal that splits the harbor as shown on the chart.

Neverstain Bight

Waypoints:

Neverstain Bight, ¼ nm S of entrance channel
16° 21.90' N, 86° 23.74' W

Neverstain Bight, although it seems to have nothing to offer, has excellent snorkeling outside of the harbor itself.

Navigational Information

As shown on Chart HON-15, a waypoint at 16° 21.90' N, 86° 23.74' W, places you approximately ¼ mile south of the entrance to the harbor. From the waypoint head northward into the bay and work your way around to port to anchor where your draft allows, the bay gets very shallow the further west you steer.

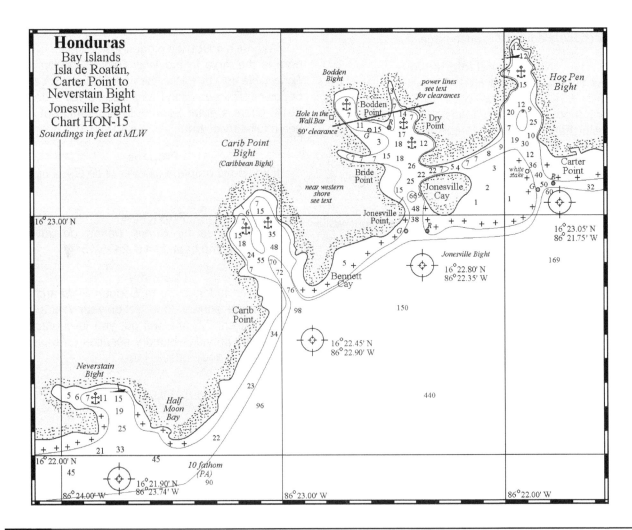

Parrot Tree Marina, Second Bight

Second Bight

Waypoints:
Second Bight- ¼ S of entrance channel
16° 21.80' N, 86° 24.50' W

Second Bight is home to the largest marina on Roatán, the *Parrot Tree Plantation Marina*, part of the exclusive *Parrot Tree Plantation* complex.

Navigational Information
A waypoint at 16° 21.80' N, 86° 24.50' W will place you ¼ mile south/southeast of the marked entrance channel as shown on Chart HON-16. The channel is narrow, only 100' wide, but it carries 22' of depth. From the waypoint, heard towards the opening, you'll see a red marker, keep it to starboard. Past the red marker you'll see two steel rails to starboard and one to port, pass between the two and the very visible shoals and you're inside *Second Bight*. The marina docks are directly in front of you. The marina suggest a heading of 328° as you enter the channel, keep your eyes on the shoals as the channel is only 100' wide.

What You'll Find Ashore

Marina
Here you'll find *Parrot Tree Plantation*, a 168-acre gated community that is home to *Parrot Tree Plantation Marina,* an upscale, full-service marina that can accommodate boats up to 150' in length and drafts to 13'. The marina offers 20 slips, some of which can accommodate a vessel of 75' (and several hundred feet of side-tie dockage, enough to accommodate a vessel of 170'), with 30 and 50 amp, 120 and 240 volt single-phase electric, water, phone service available, fuel, excellent security, garbage disposal, and bathrooms on site. The marina monitors VHF ch. 63 and reservations can be made by email, dockmaster@parrottree.com

Fuel
The *Ebanks Agency* will deliver fuel to *Parrot Tree Plantation Marina* (or any marina), minimum 100 gallons. You can phone the agency at 504-9945-3811.

Dining
The meeting place for folks here is the *Parrot Tree Coffee House*, open from 0700-1500 daily and on Sundays from 0900-1500. *The Coffee House* features an assortment of coffees and other beverages along with delicious fresh bagels, breakfast, lunch, and snacks of all sorts. *The Coffee House* also caters. You can dine on their lovely terrace overlooking the marina or inside where you can enjoy the air-conditioning on those hot days.

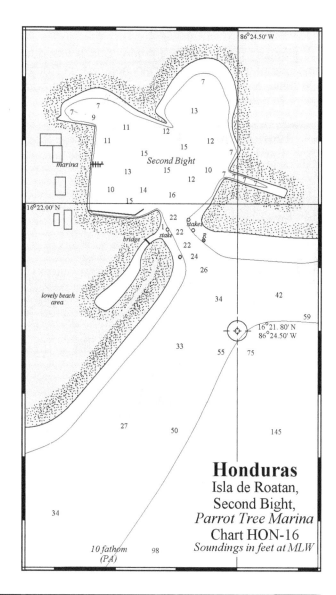

Honduras
Isla de Roatan,
Second Bight,
Parrot Tree Marina
Chart HON-16
Soundings in feet at MLW

The *Santé Wellness is* now open offering full spa service and massages. They can be reached at 504-9944-2695. For more information on the marina and condo development you can telephone the *Parrot Tree Plantation Marina* at 504-9706-9240 or you can email them at reservations@parrottree.com.

Old French Harbour

Waypoints:
Big Cay Channel- ¼ nm SSE of entrance channel
16° 21.30' N, 86° 25.80' W

Old French Harbour- ¼ nm SSW of entrance
16° 20.85' N, 86° 27.00' W

Now we are coming to the heart of Roatán cruising, the area between Fantasy Island and *Old French Harbour*.

Fantasy Island offers a marina and a fuel dock and one of the most popular anchorages on Roatán lies between Fantasy Island and *Old French Harbour*, which in itself is home to a nice marina.

Navigational Information

As shown on Chart HON-17, a waypoint at 16° 21.30' N, 86° 25.80' W, will place you ¼ mile south/southeast of *Big Cay Channel*. *Big Cay Channel* won't allow you to access the fuel dock at Fantasy Island, but it will allow you, if your draft is shallow enough (less than 5'), to access *CoCo View Marina* at the *CoCo View Resort* just east of Fantasy Island.

From this waypoint head in between the markers until you can round the point to work your way into *CoCo View Marina* as shown on the chart. If you need to access the fuel dock at Fantasy Island pass by *Big Cay Channel* and make your way to the next waypoint at the entrance to Old French Harbour.

Heading westward from *Big Cay Channel* the next waypoint at 16° 20.85' N, 86° 27.00' W, is the gateway to *Old French Harbour,* the anchorage at *French Cay Harbour*, and Fantasy Island as well. From the waypoint you can head northward in the wide channel between Big French Cay and the unnamed point to port. If you wish to enter *Old French Harbour*, keep heading north until you can follow the channel

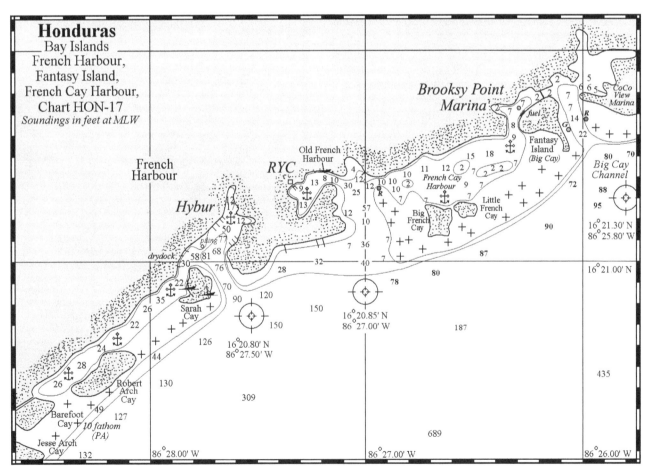

as it curves to port into *Old French Harbour*. On the northern shore is the newly refurbished *Roatán Yacht Club*, formerly the *French Harbour Yacht Club*.

If you wish to venture to Fantasy Island or to anchor in *French Cay Harbour*, head north from the waypoint until you can take the red marker to starboard and turn towards the east. You will pass between the mainland of Roatán and Big French Cay as you work your way north of east to Fantasy Island keeping a close lookout for the shoals scattered about in *French Cay Harbour*.

At Fantasy Island you'll want to work your way around to the northern shore if the island where the fuel dock is located, always call the resort before approaching either their marina or fuel dock for instructions and availability. There are currently 12 moorings available in *French Cay Harbour*, most of them courtesy of the *Marine Park Service*.

What You Will Find Ashore
The amenities to be found ashore are easy to get to from both *Old French Harbour* and *French Harbour* (see next section). I will list the marinas in this section and all the marine and shopping options in the next section on *French Harbour*.

Dinghy Dock
Located in *Old French Harbour*, just east of the *Roatán Yacht Club*, is the "shrimp dock," the dock most cruisers use to access the shore here. This is a private dock that the owner, Mr. Bobby, used to graciously allow cruisers to use for free, but I am informed that Mr. Bobby now charges US$10 per day for tying up your dinghy here. Please note that you

CoCo View Resort and Marina

may only use the dock until 1700 daily, do not access this dock after that as Mr. Bobby let's his guard dogs out at that time. You can also tie up at the *Roatán Yacht Club* (for a small daily fee which is waived with a purchase at the restaurant/bar) or at *Frenchy 44s*.

Marinas

Brooksy Point Marina
Brooksy Point Marina (http://brooksypointyachtclub.com/), located in a snug cove just west of Fantasy Island, is the newest marina on this part of Roatán. Owners Mike and Lilo offer 14 slips, a bar, shower, Wi-Fi, water, electric, garbage disposal facilities, laundry facilities and hot showers. Guests at the dock have access to these amenities as do cruisers anchored or moored in the harbor for a weekly fee of US$15.

Brooksy Point Marina

Fantasy Island, French Cay Harbour in background

Brooksy Point Marina is more than just a place to dock your boat. Mike and Lilo will happily make a diesel, gas, or propane run for you if necessary. Mike has also set out red and green markers to lead you into the marina. If you still have trouble finding your way in contact the marina on VHF ch. 72.

CoCo View Marina

The *CoCo View Marina and Resort* (http://www.cocoviewresort.com/) is one of the oldest on Roatán and the diving offered here is excellent, starting just off the beach here and at Fantasy Island. Both the *CoCo View Resort* and the *Fantasy Island Resort* offer dive packages and can take you wherever your heart desires for the best diving on the island.

It is unfortunate that the *CoCo View Resort* has had some bad experiences with cruisers so that now the cruising community is not welcome at the resort. Apparently cruisers took advantage of the free Wi-Fi and the resort's guests could not access the Internet because of the bandwidth being used by the cruisers. If that was not bad enough, some cruisers walked out on their bar bills and took advantage of free meals to which they were not entitled. At this point, only the resort's dive facilities are open to cruisers.

Fantasy Island

Fantasy Island Resort and Marina is under new management and their prices are very competitive. The marina has a fuel dock and requests that cruisers give advance notice and schedule their visit to the dock (they open at 0900 on Tuesdays and Fridays).

The marina has side-tie berths for up to 20 vessels, 110/220V AC, water, and cable TV. There are an additional 20+ docks without power or cable TV. Water is available for free but it is not potable. The resort allows you to land your dinghy here as well. Guests are given full use of the resort's facilities such as Wi-Fi, Internet in the lobby, shops and restaurants, pool tables, hot showers and restrooms, tennis courts, a volleyball court, kayaks, two private beaches, and beach towels. Marina guests also receive a 20% discount at the bar, gift shop, and on dive trips.

Other services include boat cleaning and maintenance, bottom cleaning and zinc replacement, propane, bottled water, same day laundry service, dive tanks filled, potable water delivered to your boat, massage, shuttle to the airport, and the best buffet on the island!

For more information you can contact Pete Doodson (dockmaster), on VHF ch. 71, by phone at 504-3171-4239, or by email at fdockmaster@fantasyislandresort.com.

Roatán Yacht Club

The *Roatán Yacht Club* (504-9490-0042) has recently been refurbished and is becoming one of the favorite stops for cruisers on the southern shore of Roatán.

The marina has 19 deep water slips with 110/220 volt AC electric. The marina also offers free water to guests (within reason), is a short walk from *Eldon's Supermarket* (504-2455-7517) on the main road, and boasts a great restaurant and bar, *Jack's Harbour View Restaurant* which does indeed have a harbour view and offers live music from time to time.

The marina has a guest house with rooms for rent, free Wi-Fi in the "cruisers area," a gift shop, cable TV on the docks, a laundry service, and access to nice walking trails. This is the spot to rent a car and tour the island, and if you're interested, If you do rent a car, be sure and pick up a remote control from the marina that will allow you to access the gate at any hour so you can leave and enter the marina at your whim.

French Harbour

Waypoints:
French Harbour- ¼ nm SE of entrance channel
16° 20.80' N, 86° 27.50' W

Just west of *Old French Harbour* lies the entrance to *French Harbour*, home to one of the largest shrimping fleets in the Western Caribbean and the economic hub of Roatán.

The entire area of *French Harbour* is a marine reserve and thus under the protection of the *Roatán Marine Park Service, RMPS*. The taking of any marine life here is prohibited. The *RMPS* installs and maintains mooring buoys that are, as of this writing, free. For more information you can phone the *RMPS* at 504-2445-4206 (http://www.roatanmarinepark.com/).

French Harbour has a daily VHF radio net on ch. 74 at 0900 daily. VHF ch. 72 is the hailing channel for *French Harbour*.

Navigational Information

As shown on Chart HON-17, a waypoint at 16° 20.80' N, 86° 27.50' W, will place you approximately ¼ mile southeast of the entrance channel into *French Harbour*. From the waypoint head generally northwest into the deep wide channel until you can turn to starboard to anchor off town (not recommended as it's TOO BUSY with the shrimping boats), or until you can turn to port to pass between the mainland of Roatán and Sarah Cay (watch out for the shoal on the northern shore, it's marked by a piling) and anchor in the narrow waterway between Roatán and the offlying cays. Here you can venture well to the southwest to anchor and avoid most of the traffic that moves about in *French Harbour*.

What You Will Find Ashore

East of *French Harbour*, about a mile, you'll soon come to *Arch's Iguana Farm*, a must-see on the outskirts of French Cay where you'll find over 2,800 iguanas of four different species living on the property. Go slow as you approach as there are iguanas are all over the place, orange ones, green ones, big ones with huge spikes running down their backs (I saw one that was 6' from nose to tail), and small ones that will run across the road in front of you on their two hind legs. There's also a huge aviary with all sorts of parrots and macaws, a couple of spider monkeys, and pens where Arch raises tarpon, lobster, and turtles. The entrance fee is quite reasonable, only US$5 per person.

Marine Services

Haul Out

There are a couple of places to haul out in the *French Harbour* area. Bear in mind that these yards are set up for the commercial fleet, they can assist in an emergency. *Hybur* has a haul out, call Nadine at 504-455-7590, and there is also the *French Harbour Marine Railway*, their contact number is 504-3362-2172.

Fuel

My first choice for fuel would be to head to *Brooksy Point Marina* and ask Mike to jerry jug some fuel for me. But if I needed a large amount of diesel I would head for Fantasy Island's fuel dock, or *Hybur Shipping* in *French Harbour*. There's really not a fuel dock here, more like a steel structure you can tie to while you refuel with a large nozzle that some small sailboats may not be able to accept. The fuel dock itself, southern-most dock that is surrounded by fence, is usually filled with large ships with their spring lines blocking access. It's best to check out the dock first by dinghy. For more information about fueling at *Hybur* call Nadeen Thompson at 504-2455-7512 or email Nadeen at nadeen_thompson@hotmail.com

Marine Supply

Hybur Shipping has a chandlery located on their property. Most items are geared for the commercial fleet, but there are lots of goodies here that will interest cruisers. *Cool Wind Supply*, located in the *McNab Plaza*, is a *West Marine* distributor and they're open Monday through Friday from 0800-1700. You can contact *CWS* by phone at 504-2455-7771, or by email at coolwind@globalnet.hn.

Located next to *Sun Super Mart* is the *Parker Store* stocking some marine necessities such as hoses, batteries, filters, and impellers. They are open Monday-Friday from 0800-1700, and on Saturdays from 0800-1200. You can reach them by phone at 504-2455-5156, 504-2455-5157, or by email at esantos@cendema.com.

On the road heading west towards Coxen Hole, about ½ mile from the *Shell* station, is *Wood's Building Supply and Hardware* (504-2455-7508), and next door is *Hybur Supplies*, a marine supply outfit that's geared towards the shrimping fleet.

Refrigeration and AC

For refrigeration parts and repairs try *Friopartes*, open Monday through Friday from 0800-1700 and on Saturdays from 0800-1200 (504-2480 5263, email: geren_Roatán@friopartes-hn.com). If you just need a good tech to handle your repair, try Anastacio Marin at 504-9656-5230 or Gerald Bodden at 504-3315-5132.

Cool Wind Supply, located in the *McNab Plaza*, can also handle your AC repairs (504-2455-7771, email: coolwind@globalnet.hn). *CWS* is also a *West Marine* distributor and they're open Monday through Friday from 0800-1700.

Sail Repair

If you need sail or canvas repair, visit *Valdina's* (504-2455-5605 or 504-9781-0880), open Monday through Friday from 0800-1700 and on Saturdays from 0800-1200.

Banks

If you need to restock your wallet, you'll find several banks in French Harbour. *BGA*, *Futuro*, *Banpais* (ATM), *Sogerin*, *Banco Bamer* (ATM), *Banco Continental* (ATM), and *Banco Atlantida* all have

Roatan Y C. - 3000   Family First View   516 42. 20
Fantasy Isld

offices here. *BGA* and *Banco Atlantida* offer cash advances on your *Visa* card. *Eldon's Supermarket* has an ATM inside their store.

Laundry

If you require a laundry service while in the *French Harbour* area, hail Stephen on VHF ch. 72 or phone him at 504-9850-1711. Stephen, usually just called "the laundry guy," will pick up from your dock around 0900 and return your laundry the same day. Stephen will also act as a personal shopper if you need something from town.

Pharmacy

Open daily from 1000-2200, *Farmacia Internacional* is located at *French Harbour*. You can phone them at 504-2455-5831.

Propane

Located across from *Ace Hardware* is *SolGas* (504-2455-7507). You can bring your tank to them for a refill or they'll come to you (ashore, not at a dock) for refills of four or more tanks. Across from *Hybur* is *Tropi Gas*, where you can get your propane bottles filled, even the aluminum ones. Mike at *Brooksy Point Marina* will make a propane run for guests at the marina.

Provisions

If you take a right leaving the marina quickly you'll come to *Eldon's Supermarket*, the best place for groceries on Roatán. The *Eldon* chain is now called *Sun Super Mart* and this particular location has an ATM inside. Hours are Monday through Saturday from 504-2425-3190 and on Sundays from 0700-2100. *Eldon's* is within walking distance of the *Roatán Yacht Club*.

There are numerous little stores in and around *French Harbour*, you'll enjoy walking through here searching for fresh produce or whatever. The *Mini Super La Perla 2* is next to a small vendor area where you can find everything from fresh veggies to gifts and t-shirts. On the road leading west to Coxen Hole you'll find the *Bahía Seafood Market*, and *Plaza Jackson*, a shopping mall where you'll find the *House of Meats* meat market. Located at the new *Roatán Mall* is a *Mega-Plex Grocery Store*, a nice, new, large supermarket.

Located in the *Hybur* area is the *Mariscos Hybur Seafood Market*, open Monday through Friday from 0800-1700 (504-2455-7588). Nearby is the aptly named *Bulk Gourmet* offering a large selection of imported meats (USDA Black Angus Beef), wines, spirits, the best local seafood along with organic and gluten-free products. Open Monday through Friday from 0900-1700, and on Saturdays from 0900-1300, the store also offers a free pick-up and drop-off service for groups of three or more (504-9937-6762, 504-9510-7361, email: thebulkgourmet@yahoo.com, info@thebulkgourmet.com).

There is a shrimp packing plant across from the *RYC* that sells five pound boxes of fresh, frozen shrimp. Nearby is *Rex Seafood* where you can pick up frozen seafood, beef, pork, and chicken (504-9961-5253).

Dining

Just across the street and up the hill from the marina to the left is a *Police Station*. Past the station is the *Golden Fish Restaurant*. Further down the road still is *Gio's Restaurant* (famous for their King Crab), located in the same building as a medical clinic and a *Credomatic* bank branch. One of the best restaurants on the island is *Romeo's* located at the *Casa Romeo Hotel* and offering some of the finest gourmet cuisine to be found on Roatán.

On the harbor road, across from the shrimp boat docks is *Cappuccino's Ice Cream Shoppe*, one of my personal favorites. Nearby by is *Restaurante Lakiba* and the *Cool Runnings Restaurant*, both good spots for locally flavored food and atmosphere. Located at the new *Roatán Mall* is an *Applebee's*, a *Wendy's*, and a *Sarita Ice Cream Shop*.

On the water at *Old French Harbor*, next to *Arch's Iguana and Marine Park* (http://www.archsiguanaandmarinepark.com/), is *Frenchy's 44*, a fairly new restaurant and a very popular one (http://www.littlefrenchkey.com/). Although the prices tend to be on the upper end, the varied menu as well as the service are first rate. Wednesday is Karaoke night. Just across from the iguana farm is a new bar called *Gecko*, owned by the folks from *Frenchy's*.

Brick Bay

Waypoints:
Brick Bay Channel- ¼ nm SSE of entrance
16° 19.65' N, 86° 28.65' W

Brick Bay, once called *Brig Bay*, is the center for diving on this part of the island. The bay is home to two marinas, *Brick Bay Marina* and the upscale *Barefoot Cay Marina*.

Navigational Information

As shown on Chart HON-18, a waypoint at 16° 19.65' N, 86° 28.65' W, will place you approximately ¼ mile south/southeast of the marked entrance channel into *Brick Bay*. From the waypoint pass between the outer markers as shown on the chart and work your way around to port to enter the small cove where *Brick Bay Marina* is located, or, if you prefer, you can turn to starboard once clear of the reef lying west of Jesse Arch Cay to head into *Barefoot Cay Marina* for a slip or to pick up a mooring just off the marina.

What You Will Find Ashore

Marine Facilities

Marinas

Barefoot Cay Marina

Barefoot Cay Marina is a very nice resort geared toward the upper end clientele and is separated from the mainland by a small canal only 100 yards wide.

Barefoot Cay Marina

Brick Bay Marina

Brick Bay Marina is the site of the old *CSY* operation from years past and boasts a nice restaurant, the *Subway Dive Shop*, a swimming pool, rooms for rent, 595' of dock space that can accommodate a yacht up to 150' LOA with a 9' draft. The marina also has two moorings for rent. The marina boasts 30 amp and 50 amp electric, water, cable TV, showers, and Wi-Fi.

There is another small dock next to *Brick Bay Marina*, it has six dock spaces and is really not a

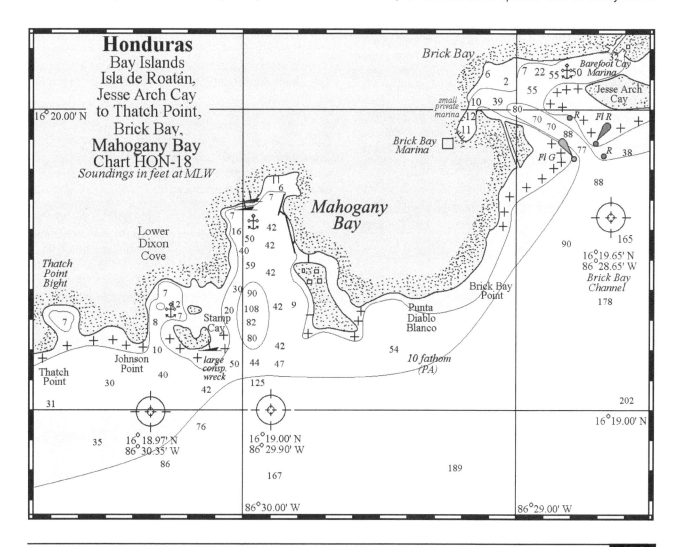

Brick Bay Marina

marina per se, it is more of a private site that rents dock space.

Fuel
If you need fuel, *Bay Island Petroleum*, *BIP*, has a station located on the green dock at *Barefoot Cay Marina*. You can hail them on VHF ch. 11, phone them at 504-2455-6465, or reach them on the Internet at www.bipRoatan.com (biproatan@gmail.com).

The *Ebanks Agency* will deliver fuel to *Brick Bay, Marina* with a minimum of 100 gallons. You can reach the agency by phone at 504-9945-3811, they will deliver to any marina on Roatán.

Marine Supplies
Just off the main road near *Brick Bay* is *Blue Seas Seafood* where you can pick up *Racor* and *Cummins* filters (504-2445-1509).

Mahogany Bay

Sail and Canvas Repair
Located in *Brick Bay* is *Roatán Awning & Canvas* to assist in your canvas and sail repairs. For more information call Dave Marshall at 504-3385-7457, or email him at daveRoatán@yahoo.com.

Mahogany Bay

Waypoints:
Dixon Cove- ¼ nm S of entrance
16° 19.00' N, 86° 29.90' W

Lower Dixon Cove- ¼ nm S of entrance
16° 18.97' N, 86° 30.35' W

Mahogany Bay (formerly *Dixon Cove*) and *Lower Dixon Cove* are two small bays just west of *Brick Bay* and while they offer little ashore, they offer a peaceful anchorage for the tired mariner, with the exception of *Mahogany Bay*, now a major *Carnival Cruise Line* destination.

Navigational Information
As shown on Chart HON-18, a waypoint at 16° 19.00' N, 86° 29.90' W, will place you approximately ¼ mile south of the entrance channel into *Mahogany Bay* and southeast of the conspicuous wreck on Stamp Cay.

From the waypoint head north favoring the left hand side of the channel, closer to the wreck than the *Carnival Cruise Line* complex. Enter the bay and wherever your draft allows keeping well clear of the cruise ships and their docks

A waypoint at 16° 18.97' N, 86° 30.35' W, will place you approximately ¼ mile south of the entrance into *Lower Dixon Cove*. From the waypoint head northwards keeping between the point to port and the large reef system that lies west of Stamp Cay. Once inside watch out for the shoal directly in front of you and turn to port to anchor in the lee of Stamp Cay and the small rock north of it.

What You Will Find Ashore
On the southeastern shore of *Dixon Cove* is Everett Cay which is connected to the mainland by a small bridge. Everett Cay is now home to the *Carnival Cruise Line* complex and offers two cruise ship berths with accommodations for up to 8,000 passengers including shopping, inland excursions, and a unique chair lift that takes guests from the welcome center to the beach.

At the northern end of *Mahogany Bay* is Roger Quiqq's *Jolly Roger Snorkeling Cruises* dock (http://jollyrogerroatan.com/). Roger hopes to dredge the area soon, install a larger dock, and open his docks up to transient boats.

Coxen Hole

Waypoints:

Coxen Hole- 4 nm N of *Seal Bank*
16° 18.70' N, 86° 32.80' W

Coxen Hole- ¼ nm E of *Seal Bank*
16° 18.30' N, 86° 32.10' W

Coxen Hole- ¼ nm W of *Seal Bank*
16° 18.20' N, 86° 33.20' W

Coxen Hole, the largest town on Roatán and the capital of the Bay Islands, is a very, very busy place. In town you'll find narrow streets full of small stores and vendors displaying their colorful wares (everybody seems to be selling electric fans, they're

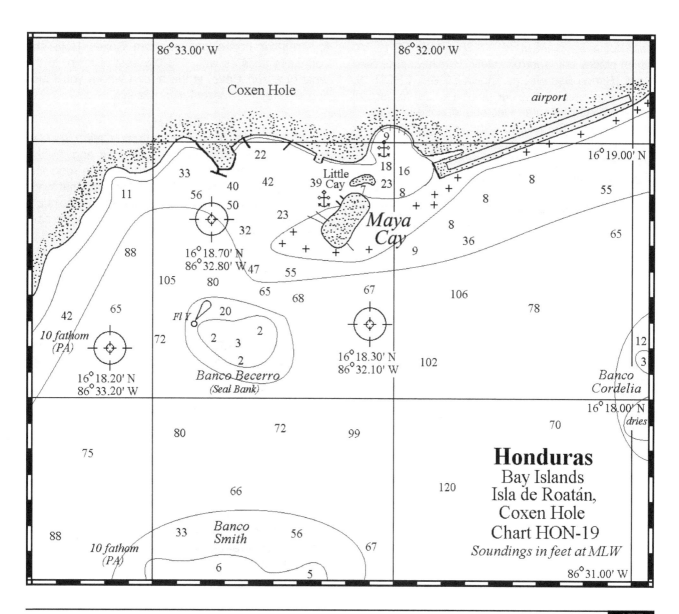

a hot item here), with people strolling or riding their bicycles everywhere, especially on the weekends. Although there aren't any tourist attractions here to speak of, the town is the hub for Bay Island politics and banking with all the major government offices and several banks located here. The city is also the gateway to Utila and the mainland of Honduras as ferries from both places stop here daily.

Coxen Hole is said to have been named after John Coxen, a pirate who lived on Roatán between the years of 1687-1697. Researchers have found a different spelling of the name, John Coxon, but it seems that the two may be one and the same man even though there is a conflict with the dates pertaining to their years on Roatán.

Navigational Information

If you're approaching from the east, you can head for a waypoint at 16° 18.30' N, 86° 32.10' W, which places you approximately ¼ mile east of *Seal Bank (Banco Becerro)* as shown on Chart HON-19. When approaching this waypoint it's best to parallel the shoreline of Roatán westbound close in to avoid shallow *Banco Cordelia* as shown on the chart. From this waypoint pass between the visible shoal south and west of Maya Cay (formerly known as Osgood Cay or Big Cay) and *Seal Bank* to round up northward into the harbor and anchor where your draft allows. Bear in mind that this is a busy, dirty harbor that often has a lot of surge. If you have to clear *Customs* (the *Port Captain, El Capitan de el Puerto*) and *Immigration* I'd suggest Utila, Guanaja, or La Ceiba on the mainland instead, I for one don't care much for the anchorage at Coxen Hole, but some folks don't mind it at all.

If you are approaching from the west, parallel the shoreline avoiding *Banco Smith* as you work your way to a waypoint at 16° 18.20' N, 86° 33.20' W, which places you ¼ mile west of *Seal Bank*. From this waypoint pass between the shoreline and the yellow flashing buoy that marks the western tip of *Seal Bank* and make your way to the anchorages in the harbor.

What You Will Find Ashore

Customs and Immigration

Both the *Port Captain* (504-445-1262) and the *Immigration* (504-445-1326) offices are located across from *Banco Atlantico* behind a small park, I do not recommend clearing out at Coxen Hole, instead I would suggest that if you are leaving Roatán visit Lilu at *Brooksy Point Marina* and she can get you cleared with a minimum of effort, it's worth the small fee she

charges. Either that or wait to clear out from your next Honduran port of call.

Banks

Banco BGA also has offices in Coxen Hole with services that include cash advances on your Visa card, and if you are headed west, bear in mind that there is no bank in West End. *Banco BGA* is open from 0800-1130 and from 1300-1600 Monday through Friday and is open on Saturday mornings. *Banco BAC-Credomatic* also has an office in Coxen Hole and an *ATM* machine. If you need medical assistance the *Wood Medical Center* (502-445-1080) is now open in Coxen Hole, they've moved into a large, new building and are open 24 hours, and they've got the best care on Roatán.

Getting Around

If you need transportation on Roatán itself, you'll find regular buses running from Coxen Hole and countless taxis as well. To the east of town, to the west of *Dixon Cove*, is the airport where you'll also find several fine car rental companies.

Internet

For Internet access I suggest *Café Que Tal*, located at the corner of the main road and *Thicket Mouth*, this is the intersection of the main road that runs the length of Roatán and the side road that leads into Coxen Hole, next to the *Casi Todo Bookstore* (a great spot for tourist info). *Que Tal* is open daily except Sunday from 0800-1600 serving breakfast and lunch along with deli sandwiches, fresh fruit frescos and home-baked cookies. Just past *Que Tal* is *Paradise Computers,* an Internet access site with a great snack bar for hungry net surfers.

Provisions

The place to go for groceries in Coxen Hole is the old *H. B. Warren Grocery* which has now been taken over by *Eldon's* and is now a *Sun Super Mart*. Here you'll find all manner of provisions, clothes, toys, and housewares. The store is located near the dock by the *Port Captain's* office and *Immigration*, next to the Parque.

Other grocery stores include the *Bay Island Grocery Store, Bodega Julysa, Commercial Herrera, Deposito Ricardos, Mini Super Diana, Mini Super Patsy, Petrosun Mart,* Pulperia *El Iriangulo, Purtidora Zapota,* and *Vicassy Grocery Store*. On the main highway, several blocks from the downtown area of Coxen Hole, is *Plaza Mar*, a supermarket with a great selection in a large location that also supplies some restaurants.

Dining

Everywhere you look in Coxen Hole there are dozens and dozens of tiny shops and stores and along the waterfront you'll find a magic shop, a video store, and a medical clinic within a stone's throw of each other. The streets are packed with vendors and their colorful wares and are quite lively, even more so on the weekends. Just east of the main area is *Mary Ann Sea Man's Restaurant and Bar* and a bit further is an ice cream shop while a bit west is the *Hondutel Cyber Café*. You can also access the Internet at the phone company's headquarters in Coxen Hole, *Honddusoft*, upstairs in the *Bonillla Building* next to *Paradise Travel*. If you need a pharmacy, *Pharmacy Roatán* is on the road leading out of town to the main road.

I can also recommend *El Paso*, in the hotel of the same name next to the *Cayview Hotel*. They may look worn at the edges but the seafood is excellent and the prices reflect that. *Sol Caraibe* also has Internet access and a fine Honduran buffet on the second floor of the *King Solomon Building* just across from the *HB Warren Grocery Store*. On the road into Coxen Hole from the airport is a very nice Chinese restaurant, *Halu Kiliki*, as well as a *Bojangle's Fried Chicken* and a *Pizza Inn*. For fine gifts and crafts, as well as some of the best Honduran cigars, visit *Yaba Ding Ding*, the local nickname for pre-Columbian artifacts which sits east of town on the harbor road.

Maya Cay

Located in the center of the harbor at Coxen Hole, Maya Cay, formerly Osgood Cay, is Roatán's newest attraction. This little island features two secluded beaches, excellent snorkeling, a 70,000 gallon swimming pool, a 5,000 square foot lounging deck, lush garden paths through colorful and aromatic local flora, an animal rescue center, an artisan plaza, and one of Roatán's cultural centers where you can visit a reconstruction of the Mayan ruins in Copan on the mainland (*The Bay Island's Interpretation Center and Ethnic Honduran Art Exhibit Center*).

When it's time to eat you can visit the *Ironshore Bar and Restaurant* to try a local beer or one of their many cocktails such as the *Monkey Lala*.

West End

Waypoints:
West End- ¼ m W of channel entrance
16° 17.72' N, 86° 36.34' W

West End is one of the finest places to stay while cruising Roatán; it's a diver's haven and the anchorage offers wonderful beaches with good protection (except for winds and seas of any strength from any westerly direction-you won't want to be here when strong winds are blowing and equally heavy seas are rolling in from south through west to north). If you're interested in such things, the *Luna Beach Resort* (http://www.lunabeachresort.com/) near the southern end of the bay was the setting for the TV show *Temptation Island* which aired a few years ago.

Please note that the waters of West End are a "No Anchor," "No Fishing," and "No Discharge" zone. If you visit the park's office you'll see the seized spear guns mounted on the wall, testimony to the rigorous enforcement of the no fishing regulations here. If you intend to dive the waters of the park you'll have to leave a $10 donation at the office.

West End has many problems when it comes to dealing with the cruising population. A few years ago the officials of the *West End Marine Park* (http://www.roatanmarinepark.com/) came up with a workable plan to put a halt to anchoring in the bay at West End and installed moorings to accommodate transient vessels. The *West End Marine Park* installed 30 nice moorings in the waters of the bay; some moorings are screw types, others are concrete blocks.

Recently, the mayor of West End ordered the moorings removed and an end to anchoring in the bay. As of this writing the moorings are still there, as are their painters, lying on the bottom. If you want a mooring you'll have to dive and pick up a line to secure your vessel. Cruisers are currently doing this and they are not asked to leave. However, the solution to this problem lies in the future and there's no telling how it will turn out.

Navigational Information

As you round Punta Oeste at the western end of Roatán, and begin heading north along the island's western shore, you'll soon come to West Bay, whose entrance channel is marked by a red and green float. Although the bay and channel carry enough water to enter and anchor, you'll want to avoid it like the plague unless you enjoy jet skis roaring by your boat all day long, this is an exclusive tourist development

Punta Oeste, Roatán, *West Bay* in background

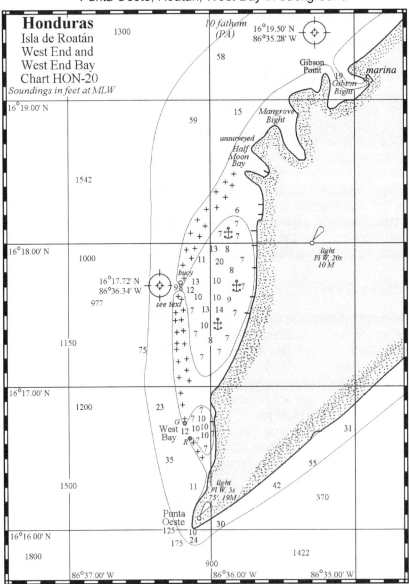

Honduras
Isla de Roatán
West End and
West End Bay
Chart HON-20
Soundings in feet at MLW

and a watersports playground, not a calm, peaceful anchorage. Instead, head north just a bit further to anchor off West End.

Although other publications will tell you there are two entrances through the reef at West End, I'm going to show you what is known as the southernmost one, it is marked, hard to miss, and it's a bit easier to enter than its more northern counterpart. As shown on Chart HON-20, a waypoint at 16° 17.72' N, 86° 36.34' W, will place you approximately ¼ mile west of the entrance channel. From the waypoint you will see a pair of small buoys that mark the northern edge of the channel. These buoys replace an old piece of dredge pipe that was stuck vertically in the reef and which stood there until a barge pushed it over in April of 2006.

The entrance through the reef will appear daunting to say the least, it's narrow, not too deep, and there are a couple of coral heads you'll have to work your way around, they do not look as deep as they really are. From the waypoint head eastward keeping the buoy close on your port side, not so close as to be able to reach out and touch it, but close. You'll see the heads in the channel even though you'll have 8' of water in most of this narrow channel.

Some folks like to line up the dock at the *Luna Beach Resort* on their bow and head in on it keeping the piling to port. I don't favor that idea, I'd rather keep an eye on the reefs around me in this particular instance. As a guideline you can keep the buoys to port and steer 090°T. Never attempt this channel at night or in periods of bad visibility or heavy following seas. Once you're about 75-100 yards past the piling you can turn to either port or starboard and anchor wherever your draft allows. Pick a nice sandy spot as there's a fair amount of sea grass here, you might want to dive on your anchor to make sure it is set well.

What You Will Find Ashore

On shore, casual, laid back West End is simple to navigate, there's only one sandy, shady road and everything is located on or off that road including numerous beach bars, boutiques, and almost 20 dive shops, next to Utila this is the cheapest place to get *PADI* certified. If you're visiting West End by land you can take one of Roatán's public buses departing from the front of the *H.B. Warren* in Coxen Hole. The trip usually takes about 20 minutes and the buses run from 0600-1830, Monday through Saturday with limited service on Sundays. There are no banks at West End so bring all the cash you'll need with

you. If you enjoy rainforest canopy tours there's a nice one on the main road just outside West Bay at *Gumbalimba Park* (http://www.gumbalimbapark.com/index.html).

The VHF hailing channel is the same as *French Cay Harbour*, ch. 72.

Fuel
If you need fuel while you're here you'll have to jerry-jug it; *Woody's Groceries* sells diesel in one-gallon milk jugs, there is no fuel dock.

Laundry
If you need to have your laundry done while at West End, the *Bamboo Hut* offers a wash and dry service for all. Another option is to call Larry on his cell at 504-3347-6604. Larry has a low per pound rate and is open every day except Sundays.

Dining
If you're looking for something to eat you won't have to go far in West End to find a good eatery. One of the best is *Diane's Garden of Eat'n* with great food AND service. You'll just have to walk up and down the road and choose where you'll want to dine that particular day, choosing from *Bite on the Beach* (one of the most popular hangouts; http://www.biteonthebeach.net/index.html), *Rick's* (quite the famous spot on Roatán and located above *West End Divers*, where you'll also find the *West End Coffee Shop*), *Les Boucaniers*, *Denny's Diner*, the *Cannibal Café* (not a great name for a diner if you ask me but their Tex-Mex is fantastic, if you can eat three of their burritos they're free; http://www.seabreezeroatan.com/cafe.html), *Brick Oven Pizza*, *Sundowners*, the *Twisted Toucan*, *Chili's*, *Mango Verdi*, the *Blue Channel Pub* (with a movie every night and Internet access), the *Eagle Ray Bar and Grill* (on stilts on the water), Foster's Barking Monkey (also on stilts above the water; http://fostersbarkingmonkey.com/), the *Lobster Pot*, *Black Pearl*, *Pura Vida Italian Restaurant and Pizzeria*, and *Pinocchio's*, also Italian.

Along with dive shops and diners you can find several nice gift shops and boutiques and even a couple of places to rent scooters and bikes, *Capt. Van's* (at *Half Moon Bay*; http://www.captainvans.com/), and *Roatán Rentals* (http://roatansalesandrentals.com/).

A Catholic Mass is held at *Bamboo Hut* every Saturday evening and if you're into working out you'll find a gym located at the *Beach House*, open Monday through Saturday with separate schedules for men and women.

The Northern Shore of Roatán

If you're familiar with my past guides, you'll notice that I've strayed from my usual cartography in this publication. It seems that I feel the need to protect some skippers from themselves. The charts for the northern coasts of Guanaja and Roatán in the Bay Islands of Honduras do NOT have a lat/long grid on them. Why you may ask? Simple I reply. I've noticed that some navigators have taken to watching the cursor on their chart plotters instead of the waters around them. In one particular instance that I know of a skipper when aground hard and bent his 4" rudder shaft.

With this in mind I have decided that on the aforementioned charts I would omit the lat/long grid to avoid such a problem in the future. As a result you cannot plot your position on these charts, you cannot count on them being to scale, treat them as you would a sketch chart, in other words, you MUST use only your eyes to get you through these passages. Why only on these charts you may ask? Simple I again reply. The northern shores of Guanaja and Roatán are protected by fringing reefs and the passes through the reefs are not marked and difficult to discern in all but the best of visibility, an error here could be very costly. I have included waypoints to place you just off the reef entrances, from there you will have to pilot your way in by eye. I know some of you may not appreciate this, but it is with good intentions I assure you. Call me old-fashioned, but I insist that you pilot by eye through these areas.

Gibson Bight

Waypoints:
Roatán, Gibson Bight- ¼ nm NNW of entrance
16° 19.50' N, 86° 35.28' W

Just north of West End is *Gibson Bight*, home to *Gibson Bight Marina*.

Navigational Information
As shown on Chart HON-20, a waypoint at16° 19.50' N, 86° 35.28' W, will place you approximately ¼ nm NNW of the entrance into *Gibson Bight*. The entrance is narrow, between two reefs (never try to enter here at night or in heavy following seas), but easily seen in good visibility. Once inside the bay you'll find good water, 12'-17'. A turn to port will bring you into the basin of the marina which has 8' at MLW.

What You'll Find Ashore
Gibson Bight Marina (http://www. gibsonbightmarina.com/) offers 8' of water in the basin, a boat ramp, 24-hour security, electrical and water hook ups at each slip, a fuel dock, and a concrete sea wall. Future amenities include an office, store, and dry boat storage.

Sandy Bay, Anthony's Key

Waypoints:
Anthony's Key Channel- ¼ nm NNW of entrance
16° 19.80' N, 86° 34.50' W

Sandy Bay is often called the cultural center of the island of Roatán, and as home to the *Roatán Museum*, *The Institute for Marine Sciences* (http://www.roatanims.org/), and the *Carambola Botanical Reserve* (http://www.carambolagardens.com/), it's no wonder Sandy Bay is known in this regard.

The biggest draw for the mariner is without a doubt *Anthony's Key Resort*. *Sandy Bay* is larger than West End, but it certainly doesn't feel like it. Both *Anthony's Key Resort* and the *Bay Island Beach Resort* have dive shops on site to help you enjoy the reef.

Navigational Information
As shown on Chart HON-21 a waypoint at 16° 19.80' N, 86° 34.50' W, places you approximately ¼

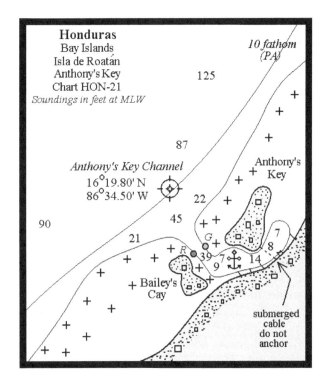

Anthony's Key Resort

mile north/northwest of the entrance to the anchorage off the resort. From the waypoint head generally south/southeast between the red and green markers and anchor off the resort. Don't anchor too far east to avoid the submerged power lines.

What You Will Find Ashore

Anthony's Key Resort (http://www.anthonyskey. com/) is the focus for watersports and diving here and the nearby *Oceanside Inn*, *Roatán Sunrise Resort*, *Tri R Resort*, and the *Bay Islands Resort* offer accommodations for the weary cruiser. *The Roatán Museum* is open from Thursday to Tuesday and an entrance fee of US$4 is charged to all except guests of *Anthony's Cay Resort*. *The Institute for Marine Sciences* at *Anthony's Key Resort* offers a dolphin encounter (US$75 for 30 minutes) at 1000 and 1500 daily, except Wednesday, during the week with three shows each day during the weekend at 1000, 1300, and 1600. Here again, there is a US$4 entrance fee but guests of *Anthony's Key Resort* are admitted free. *The Dolphin Café* is located adjacent to both the dolphin encounter and the museum on Anthony's Key. The *Blue Parrot*, located in the *Sundancer Villas*, offers up great food and is convenient to Coxen Hole as well. The *Bay Islands Resort* offers Internet service as well as a nice little store stocked full of munchies, toiletries, gifts, and clothes. On the beach at *Sandy Bay* is the *Sunset Bar and Grill* and the *Sandy Bay Internet Café,* while a mile past the *Sunset Bar* on the main road is the entrance to the *Roatán Butterfly Garden*.

The nearby *Tropical Treasures Bird Park* boasts over 80 different tropical birds on display including several varieties of macaws, parrots, and toucans, most of which are indigenous to Honduras. At the time of this writing this bird park was open, but it may close soon so bear that in mind.

Located just off the highway across from the entrance road to *Anthony's Key Resort* is the *Carambola Botanical Reserve* where you can walk trails well inland to places such as the *Iguana Wall*, a sheer rock cliff that is a home and breeding ground to iguanas and parrots.

If you need medical assistance here, *Anthony's Key Resort* is home to the *Cornerstone Medical Center* (monitors VHF ch. 26) which has the only hyperbaric chamber on Roatán. There is a wonderful clinic here too, *Clinica Esperanza* (http://clinicaesperanza.org/) run by the amazing Nurse Peggy.

Mud Hole

Waypoints:
Man O' War Channel- ¼ nm NNW of entrance
16° 21.80' N, 86° 31.45' W

Hottest Sparrow Channel- ¼ nm N of entrance
16° 22.20' N, 86° 30.65' W

Navigational Information
Two good bays for anchoring and exploring the reefs are found at Mud Hole and in *Hottest Sparrow Lagoon*, but neither one should be considered when strong northerly seas are running although some shelter can be found when the wind shifted northeast it would be uncomfortable at best. As shown on Chart HON-22, a waypoint at 16° 21.80' N, 86° 31.45' W, will place you ¼ mile north/northwest of *Man O' War Channel*. From the waypoint find the channel by eye and follow it as it curves softly to the east and anchor in Mud Hole or behind Little Cay as your draft allows.

A bit further east is *Hottest Sparrow Channel* leading into *Hottest Sparrow Lagoon*, sometimes shown as *Turtling Bay*. As shown on Chart HON-22, a waypoint at 16° 22.20' N, 86° 30.65' W, will place you approximately ¼ mile north of the very deep channel. Head southwards down the center of the channel and anchor in *Hottest Sparrow Lagoon* or south of the unnamed cay as shown on the chart.

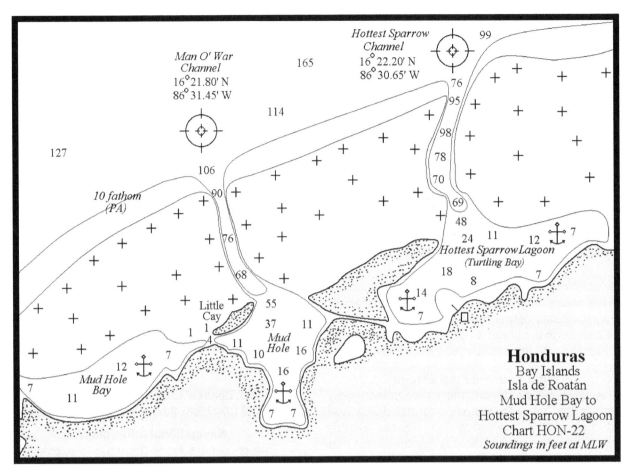

Man O' War
Channel
16°21.80' N
86°31.45' W

Hottest Sparrow
Channel
16°22.20' N
86°30.65' W

10 fathom
(PA)

Little
Cay

Mud
Hole

Hottest Sparrow Lagoon
(Turtling Bay)

Mud Hole
Bay

Honduras
Bay Islands
Isla de Roatán
Mud Hole Bay to
Hottest Sparrow Lagoon
Chart HON-22
Soundings in feet at MLW

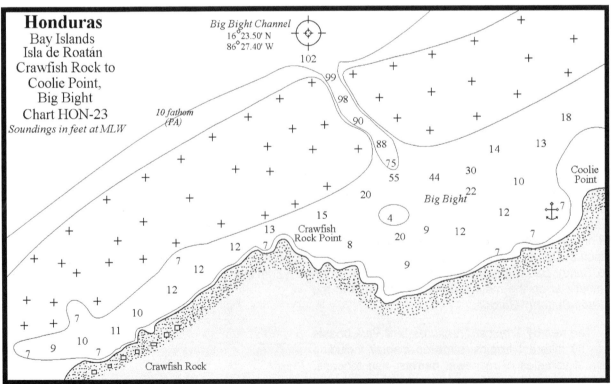

Honduras
Bay Islands
Isla de Roatán
Crawfish Rock to
Coolie Point,
Big Bight
Chart HON-23
Soundings in feet at MLW

Big Bight Channel
16°23.50' N
86°27.40' W

10 fathom
(PA)

Coolie
Point

Big Bight

Crawfish
Rock Point

Crawfish Rock

Big Bight

Waypoints:
Big Bight Channel- ¼ nm NNW of entrance
16° 23.50' N, 86° 27.40' W

The next anchorage along the northern shore is at *Big Bight*, and it's possible that we will see some big changes here over the next few years. At the time of this writing a local entrepreneur was not far from obtaining a permit for a huge marina here, so keep an eye open in the future for docks and a marked entrance channel.

Navigational Information

As shown on Chart HON-23, a waypoint at 16° 23.50' N, 86° 27.40' W, will place you approximately ¼ mile northwest of the entrance to *Big Bight Channel*. From the waypoint head generally southeast until you can pick up the reefs on either side of the channel and then head straight down the center of the deep channel. You can anchor wherever you prefer, either to the east behind Coolie Point or anywhere inside the bay. You can also anchor east of Coolie Point as shown on Chart HON-24. If your draft is shallow you can work your way along the northern shore inside the reef, but I wouldn't suggest this unless you draw 3' or less and have the tide with you. You can also anchor to the west off the small community of Crawfish Rock.

Johnson Bight, Milton Bight

Waypoints:
Milton Bight Channel- ¼ nm NNW of entrance
16° 24.50' N, 86° 24.80' W

Johnson Bight Channel- ¼ nm NNW of entrance
16° 24.20' N, 86° 25.50' W

Navigational Information

As shown on Chart HON-24, a waypoint at 16° 24.20' N, 86° 25.50' W, will place you approximately ¼ mile north/northwest of *Johnson Bight Channel*. From the waypoint you can head down the channel to anchor in Johnson Bight, but I must warn you, this is an extremely narrow channel and there may not be room for you to turn around if you make a mistake. It might be prudent to access the anchorages here by using the *Milton Bight Channel*.

As shown on Chart HON-24, a waypoint at 16° 24.50' N, 86° 24.80' W, will place you approximately ¼ mile north/northwest of the entrance to *Milton Bight Channel*. From the waypoint head down the channel avoiding the false channel that appears to head off to the east about midway. Once through the reefs you can anchor in *Johnson Bight* or *Milton Bight* as you prefer.

Pollytilly Bight

Waypoints:
Pollytilly Bight Channel- ¼ nm NNW of entrance
16° 24.70' N, 86° 23.90' W

Navigational Information

As shown on Chart HON-25, a waypoint at 16° 24.70' N, 86° 23.90' W, will place you approximately ¼ mile north/northwest of the entrance channel

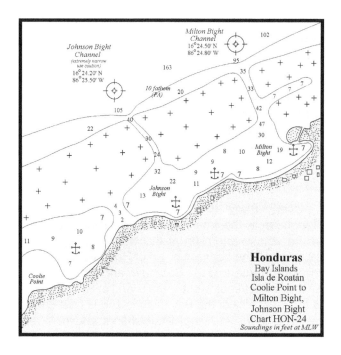

Honduras
Bay Islands
Isla de Roatán
Coolie Point to
Milton Bight,
Johnson Bight
Chart HON-24
Soundings in feet at MLW

Milton Bight

Pollytilly Bight

leading into *Pollytilly Bight*. The entrance is fairly straightforward like any of the reef entrances along this northern shore. Ashore is a small community of the same name. You can head east to anchor in the lee of the reef at Cañabraval and you can almost work your way to Punta Gorda.

What You Will Find Ashore

If you catch a ride or walk up to the main road you will find that you're close to Punta Gorda, a huge Garifuna community and home to an emergency medical clinic, the *Doc Polo Galindo Clinic* on the main road. In Punta Gorda you'll find one small hotel, a pool hall, and several small eateries and stores.

O'Henry and Roatán

Over a century ago, a young fugitive from the United States arrived in Honduras aboard a rusty freighter during the "Banana Boom" years. Just

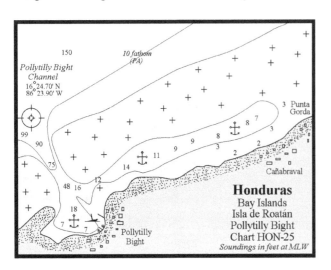

another gringo drifter with a past, William Sydney Porter was wanted by United States authorities for bank fraud. Porter had been an employee of an Austin, Texas, bank when an audit discovered a shortage of thousands of dollars and the evidence pointed directly at William Sydney Porter who was now spending his time between Trujillo and Roatán instead of enduring a trial and a certain guilty verdict.

When Porter's wife fell ill the fugitive decided to return to the United States to be with her during her final days. He was apprehended and sentenced to three years in a federal prison where Porter discovered he had a natural flair for writing, producing many short stories for magazines during his incarceration. To conceal the fact that he was an inmate Porter used the pen name "O'Henry" and by the time his 3-year stretch was up O'Henry was appearing in all of the best periodicals of the day with collections of his tales being translated into dozens of languages.

Although little is known of O'Henry's specific activities during his stay in Honduras and Roatán, it is believed his time here is reflected in some of his stories. For instance, in his *Cabbages and Kings* many of the tales take place in the town of *Coralio* in the imaginary Central America republic of *Anchuria*. It has been suggested that *Coralio* could be Coxen Hole, Roatán, or Trujillo on the mainland, and that the word *hondo* (Honduras) means depth while *ancho* (Anchuria) means width. Of course all of this is speculation concerning the writer's imagination where local characters retire to a hammock drunk every day, and where others try to sell shoes to *Coralians* where bare feet is the norm.

O'Henry passed away in 1910 but remains one of America's most beloved authors. His dramatic and humorous surprise endings are part of the charm of his tales where the fates of his characters are often reversed; where rogues and drifters become gentlemen, perhaps this was born of his own real life experience.

Utila

Utila, Party Central for the Northwestern Caribbean, is the smallest of the Bay Islands and lies at the southwestern tip of the chain, approximately 19 miles off the northern coast of Honduras, about 21 miles from Puerto de la Cabotaje, and approximately 16 miles west/southwest of the island of Roatán. Utila is the least hilly of the Bay Islands and is best known for its inexpensive diving, whale sharks, and the divers that come here, who, along with the backpackers, make for a real party atmosphere. As of 2006, Utila now has a port captain and an *Immigration* officer as well, now you can clear in and out where as before you could only clear out.

A note about the charts on Utila. I have removed the lat/long grid for the charts of the cays lying southwest of Utila. This is an area where you MUST pilot your way by eye through the shoals, you've no business trying to pilot here using a chart plotter. Keep one eye on the depth sounder, one eye on the waters around you. If you are heading west to the Río Dulce, instead of heading well south to clear the reefs lying southwest of Utila you can pass around the north side of the island and then west, the reefs do not extend to the north of Utila.

Puerto Este

(East Harbour)

Waypoints:
Puerto Este- .1 SW of entrance channel
16° 05.15' N, 86° 54.10' W

Navigational Information

There are three entrances into the harbor at *Puerto Este*; there's an entrance along the shore on the west side of the harbor which entails making a dogleg between two shoal areas, one at the eastern side of the bay just west of the conspicuous light which is the entrance favored by the dive boats and ferries but for me is a bit narrow with shallow reefs on both sides, and a third entrance, which is fairly well marked and deep. Never attempt any of these entrances during periods of poor visibility or at night.

As shown on Chart HON-26, a waypoint at 16° 05.15' N, 86° 54.10' W, will place you approximately .1 mile southwest of the marked (as of this writing) entrance channel leading into *Puerto Este*, also known as *East Harbour*, or *East Harbor*. From the waypoint you'll be passing between two shoal areas, the shoal on the western side of the channel is marked by a white stake as of this writing. You'll be entering the harbor in a northeasterly direction and once inside you can continue northeastward to anchor off town wherever your draft allows and your fancy agrees, and if you don't like loud music anchor farther out. For the most part the holding is not very good in the bay, the bottom in most places is sea grass over thin sand over coral, make sure your anchor is set well here. Don't forget that if you choose to anchor near

the town dock or anywhere between the town dock and the easternmost entrance to the bay that you will have to endure the worst of the ferry wakes as they come and go from Utila.

What You Will Find Ashore

If you need to clear in or out, you'll find the office of the Port Captain, *El Capitan de el Puerto*, and *Immigration* are near the commercial dock in *Puerto Este* near the *BGA* (just across from the town dock; there is also a branch of *Banco Atlantido* about ½ block away-both banks will exchange dollars for *Lempira*, but only *BGA* will cash traveler's checks and advance cash on your *VISA* card). Just past *Bush's* grocery at the eastern end of the harbor is a small video store where you can get a cash advance on your *VISA* card but be aware that they will charge a 7% fee for this service). There is a VERY nice gift shop just across the street from the video store that is definitely worth a visit, it's not your usual tourist trap.

If you're going to be walking around Utila don't fret, you can't get lost, there's only one road and it follows the shoreline along the harbor. Although it's basically a pedestrian thoroughfare, you'll have to watch out for the few cars on the island as well as the occasional motorcyclist and all the bicycles, both privately owned and rentals. If you would like to visit the mainland of Honduras from Utila, there is daily ferry service from *Puerto Este* to *Puerto de Cabotaje* (La Ceiba), via the *Utila Princess* (two trips per day; http://www.utilaprincess.com/. If you need fuel there is a dock at the northeastern end of the harbor where you can pick up some diesel.

Puerto Este, often just referred to as Utila, is located between two small bays, or lagoons, *Big Bight Lagoon* (*Upper Lagoon*) and *Blue Bayou* (*Lower Lagoon*) as shown on Chart HON-26. The entrance to the *Big Bight Lagoon* is between the old airstrip (and is spanned by a LOW bridge) and town and is home to a few of the local businesses such as *Sharkey's*. *Blue Bayou* is found at the end of the main road through town at Blue Bayou where you'll find a small beach (there is an entry fee). Between the lagoon and the sea is the exclusive *Laguna Beach Resort* (http://www.lagunabeachresort.info/) with great diving just off the beach. *Billares Marina* is located in *Blue Bayou*, but it is primarily a private marina, check with *Billares* if there is a slip available. The route to the marina has a controlling depth of about 3'. For more information you can reach the marina by telephone at 504-425-3294.

Puerto Este, Utila

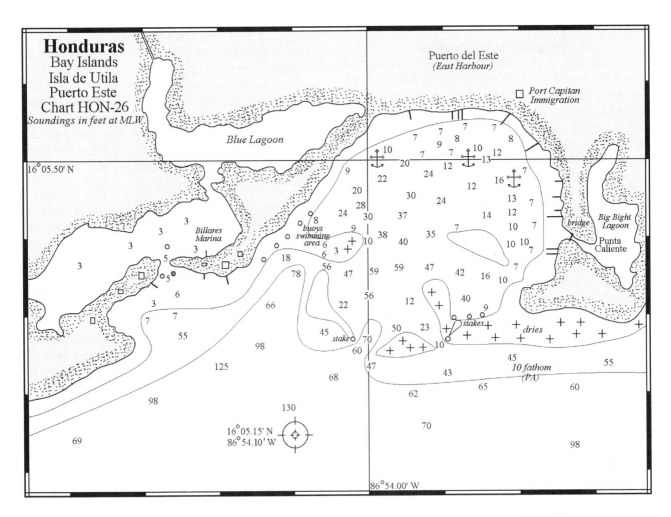

Honduras
Bay Islands
Isla de Utila
Puerto Este
Chart HON-26
Soundings in feet at MLW

Puerto del Este
(East Harbour)

Port Capitan
Immigration

Blue Lagoon

16°05.50' N

Billares
Marina

buoys
swimming
area

Big Bight
Lagoon

bridge

Punta
Caliente

stakes

dries

stake

10 fathom
(PA)

16°05.15' N
86°54.10' W

86°54.00' W

Provisions

The best places for groceries on Utila is *Bush's Supermarket* which recently expanded and is now double in size. You can also try *Henderson's*, the *Meat Mart* (across from *Tranquilo*-great freshly butchered meats), *Supermarket Rose* (west of *Tranquilo's*), and *Samantha's 7-11*. There is also a bakery in town, *Thomson's Bakery*, offering a different special every day and one of the best places for breakfast. But if you are of a different mind, and if your heart is set on ice cream, visit *Munchie's Ice Cream and Food Emporium* located at *Island House*, Utila's oldest house. *Munchie's* offers more than just ice cream, they also have snack such as baked potatoes and nachos.

The *Utila Food Company* (http://utilas.wix.com/foodcompany) offers the best spices, spice packages, fresh foods, deli meats, and everything in between. Their goodies are available at *Ronie Ramon's Veggie Stand* and *Wardy's*, both in Sandy Bay, and *Bobby's Supermarcado* at Puerbo in front of *Paradise Divers* (http://www.paradisediversutila.com/).

Internet

There is a dentist in town as well as a couple of places to access the internet, *Howell's*, across from *Bush's Supermarket*, *Mermaid's Corner*, and the *Mango Tree House* at *Mango's Hotel*. For scooter and ATV rentals see *Bodden Rentals*. There are now two Spanish schools in town if you wish to try to learn the language before you head west to spend the hurricane season on the Río Dulce.

Dining

There are dozens of nice places to eat on the island and several friendly places to just hangout, drink, and party with whoever happens to be on the island at the time. *Tranquilo* is probably the most popular hangout for the cruising crowd, they have a place to tie up your dink and they're located right on the water. Behind *Tranquilo's* is *The Grill* (good food), which features some of the best and most economical food on the island, and they will also serve you at *Tranquilo's*. Nearby, *Skid Row*, a laid back local hangout, offers daily lunch specials. For fried chicken visit *Mermaid's Corner* where you can surf the net while eating the best fried chicken since my mother's fried chicken in Atlanta half-a-century ago.

Next to *Tranquilo's* is *Coco Loco* right on the water. While this is a nice bar, it has gained a bad reputation amongst cruisers and I will leave my description of the bar at that. The *Bundu Café* is under new management and is a very popular place for those who delight in the best coffee to be found in the Bay Islands. *The Mango Inn Bar & Grill* (http://www.mangoinnbarandgrill.com/) features great wood-fired pizza served with delicious pepper oil. The restaurant is unique in that you'll find a lot of hummingbirds flittering about the well-placed feeders during the day, and at night, when the mosquitoes are out, bats will come, drawn by the feeders, and chase away all the mosquitoes.

Try *Mango's Inn* on Sunday for a good BBQ, and if you are vegan, Mango's offers a vegetarian menu during the week and upstairs you'll find a nice wine shoppe. *Capt. Jack's* also has a great BBQ on the weekend.

The *Looney Lagoon Bar and Restaurant* is located at *Crosscreek* and offers good music as well as good food and even breakfast. The *Bar in the Bush*, located on the road to Pumpkin Hill, is a very popular place with the younger crowd. Opening at 2300 and closing at dawn, the *Bar in the Bush* features techno/dance/rave music and is the all-night party place.

One of the most popular places on the island is *The Jade Seahorse* (http://jadeseahorse.org/), just up from the town dock and one of the most unique restaurants in all of Honduras. Owner Neil is an artist and he has created a unique tree-house bar connected to platforms and sitting areas by bridges and walkways and tunnels. The bathroom is a must see! Another popular cruiser hangout is the *Colibri Hill Resort* (http://build.colibri-resort.com/) with their huge pool and pool bar, nice rooms, and massage services.

There is only one "mountain" on Utila, unlike her neighbors Roatán and Guanaja, Utila is not as rugged topographically. There is a trail that leads up *Pumpkin Hill* and the caves there are rumored to contain pirate loot from days of yore.

Gunter's Driftwood Gallery is where you'll find a variety of carved wooden items as well as coral jewelry and some paintings. Owner Gunter, Austrian by heritage, opened up a dive shop here many years ago, it's now known as *Eco Marine*.

The southern tip of Utila and offlying cays as seen from the northwest

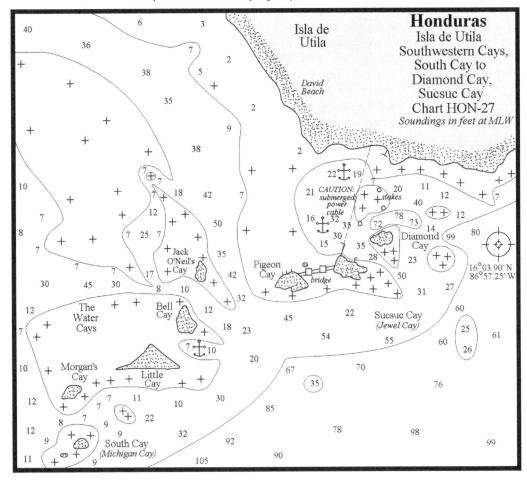

The Cays Southwest of Utila

Waypoints:
Diamond Cay- ½ nm E of
16° 03.90' N, 86° 57.25' W

Southwest of Utila are a group of small off-lying cays and a couple of nice anchorages and tons of reef diving and snorkeling opportunities. Some of the cays, such as Bells Cay, South West Cay, Sandy Cay, and Morgan Cay are privately owned, some of which are for rent.

Navigational Information

As shown on Chart HON-27, a waypoint at 16° 03.90' N, 86° 57.25' W, will place you approximately ½ mile east of Diamond Cay. From the waypoint pass to the north of Diamond Cay, between Diamond Cay and the mainland, avoiding the visible shoal that is shown on the chart. Once past the shoal angle towards Sucsuc Cay avoiding the reef area to starboard which is marked by three stakes as of this writing.

As you pass Sucsuc Cay anchor wherever you feel comfortable but the best spot is in close to the shore of Utila in about 10' of water, but watch out for the submerged power-line that stretches from Utila to Sucsuc Cay (see Chart HON-27). This power-line is buoyed by small floats and in some places is only 6' under water, use caution here and keep your eyes open. There is also a deep but very narrow channel between Sucsuc Cay and Diamond Cay, but don't attempt it if any seas are running, the coral lies close aboard on both sides of the channel. You can also anchor in the Water Cays in settled weather as shown on the chart.

West of these cays are some narrow channels that wind their way between shoals west of Utila. There are only one or two places to safely anchor for any periods and they lie between Ragged Cay and the mainland of Utila and are no place to be in winds or sees out of the west or north.

What You Will Find Ashore

The Water Cays are some of the prettiest of the cays southwest of Utila, and a very popular place for camping amongst the backpacker set. They are also home to the annual *Utila Sunjam*, a techno-music party held the first week of August (http://sunjamutila.com/). The other huge Utilan event is the *Utila Carnival* held during the third week of July in *Puerto Este*.

Sucsuc Cay is the most populous of the offshore cays and here you'll find several places with rooms for rent, a dive shop, a couple of small stores (it's cheaper to buy provisions in *Puerto Este*), and a few small but nice restaurants such as *Susan's* or *Maggie's*

Cayos Cochinos

Waypoints:
Cochino Grande- ½ nm W of NW tip of
15° 59.00' N, 86° 29.50' W

Cochino Grande- ¾ nm E of
15° 58.10' N, 86° 27.90' W

Lower Monitor Cay- ½ nm S of entrance channel
15° 56.50' N, 86° 29.05' W

Shoal on rhumb line to La Ceiba
15° 54.68' N, 86° 32.15' W

Cayos Cochinos, the Hog Islands, once called the *Masaqueras* by early colonists, lie about 20 miles south of Roatán and about the same distance northeast of La Ceiba on the mainland of Honduras. The islands of the Cayos Cochinos can be seen from La Ceiba on a clear day, but they usually appear as one mid-sized mountainous island instead of 13 different islands.

The two major islands in the group are Cochino Grande and Cochino Pequeño as shown on Chart HON-28, but only Cochino Grande is inhabited, if you don't count the small group of rangers and scientists stationed on Cochino Pequeño (sometimes shown as Cayo Menor).

The Cayos Cochinos were designated a *Marine Protected Area* in 1993 by the government of Honduras and a decade later, in 2003, was declared a *Marine Natural Monument*. The entire archipelago within a 5-mile radius has been declared a biological preserve by the Honduran government and is now set aside as a national marine park, home to the *Coral Reef Foundation Research Institute*. You are welcome to visit the institute but you must make an appointment first, just call them on VHF ch. 83 (*Coral Reef Foundation*). The park is protected and anchoring on the reefs is absolutely prohibited (but there are moorings available). Fishing in the waters of the Cayos Cochinos is also prohibited and is enforced by a contingent of park rangers on Cochino Pequeño. The venerable *Smithsonian Institution* has entered into a 100-year commitment with the government of Honduras to help manage the park and conduct reef studies to determine the impact of population on this pristine nature reserve.

The park has recently instituted a per-person and a per-boat fee structure for foreign flag vessels (Honduran vessels pay a little less) and all visitors. The boat fees are charged by the day, month, or year, but you must keep your receipt to show the Honduran marines that will board your boat to see if your fee is paid or to collect any monies due. Foreign flag vessels under 30' must pay US$5 per day, US$10 per month, or US$20 per year; foreign flag vessels from 30'-55' must pay US$10 per day, US$20 per month, or US$48 per year; foreign flag vessels from 55'-90' are charged US$20 per day, US$40 per month, and US$80 per year; foreign flag vessels over 90' are charged US$50 per day, US$100 per month, and US$200 per year. Foreign visitors are charged US$10 per day, US$20 per month, and US$40 per year. I'm also told that licensed Captains do not need to pay, however that rule may change.

Lower Monitor Cay, Cayos Cochinos

Local sailor, Cayos Cochinos

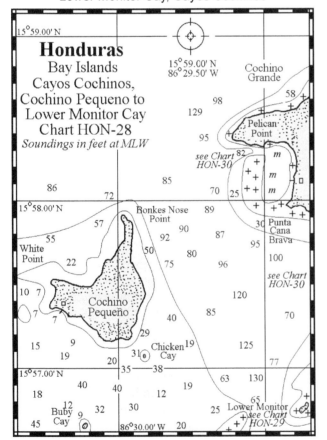

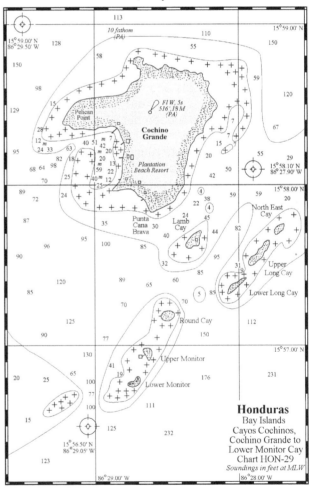

Getting to the Cayos Cochinos

The only way to get to the Cayos Cochinos is by boat, either your boat or somebody else's. *Garifuna Tours* (http://garifunatours.com/), one of the largest eco-tour companies in Honduras, offers daily trips to Cayos Cochinos at 0700 from their offices in La Ceiba. You can hire a boat in Nueva Armenia on the mainland for the trip to the Cayos Cochinos or you can take the weekly *Plantation Beach Resort* boat from La Ceiba. The *Plantation Beach Resort*, located on Cochino Grande, has a fast jet-boat that leaves the *Puerto Cabotaje de la Ceiba* (see the section on *La Ceiba*) which lies just east of La Ceiba, on Saturday afternoons at 1700. The boat returns to La Ceiba the following Saturday morning and costs US$30 one way.

Also available on the weekends are trips from *Puerto de Cabotaje* to the Cayos Cochinos aboard the *Utila Princess*, US$65 (includes a light lunch), and you can book this trip at *Mango Tango* in the *Zona Viva* in La Ceiba. You can hire your own boat in Nueva Armenia. From La Ceiba take the road to Trujillo and go to Jutiapa, about 23 miles from La Ceiba, here you will pick up a dirt road that will take you five miles to the town of Nueva Armenia that lies near Punta Catchabutan, nearly south of the Cayos Cochinos. There's also a bus that leaves La Ceiba at 1130 daily for Nueva Armenia. Once in Nueva Armenia see Rene Arzu to arrange passage, it's a small community and everybody knows Rene. All trips to the Cayos Cochinos depart in the early morning hours so you'll have to stay overnight in Nuevo Armenia, but don't worry, Rene's sister has a small hotel with rooms for rent and she'll even arrange for your dinner and breakfast. Another alternative is to stop by the *Caribbean Sands Resort* (504-443-0035) about 12½ miles east of La Ceiba in the town of Roma. The resort offers organized one-day tours to the Cayos Cochinos.

A final note on the Cayos Cochinos. One of the jobs of the military patrols on the islands is the protection of the resident pink boa constrictor. These rare snakes are coveted by collectors and a pregnant female can be worth up to US $30,000 on the black market.

Navigational Information

If you're approaching the Cayos Cochinos in your own boat, here's what to do. Vessels heading for the Cayos Cochinos from the north, from Utila, Roatán, or Guanaja can make for a waypoint at 15° 59.00' N, 86° 29.50' W, which will place you in deep water about ½ mile west of the northwestern tip of Cochino Grande. From this waypoint head south past Pelican Point to round to port and enter the mooring field in the cove on the western shore of Cochino Grande as shown on Chart HON-29. If you're approaching at night there is a new light on Cochino Grande that flashes white every five seconds.

Vessels approaching from Trujillo can head for a waypoint at 15° 58.10' N, 86° 27.90' W, which will place you approximately ¾ miles west of Cochino Grande and in a position to pass between North East Cay and Lamb Cay to round the southern tip of Cochino Grande as shown on Chart HON-29.

Vessels heading to the Cayos Cochinos from La Ceiba or Trujillo, can make for a waypoint at 15° 56.50' N, 86° 29.05' W, which will place you approximately ¼ mile south of the deep entrance channel lying between Lower Monitor Cay and the shoal that lies to the west/southwest of Lower Monitor Cay as shown on Chart HON-29. From this waypoint head generally north, staying in the deeper water that lies about mid-channel, and head northwards to the mooring field at Cochino Grande

When entering the mooring field in the bay off the western side of Cochino Grande and off the *Plantation Beach Resort* don't stray too close to shore as shown on the chart, there's a rocky shoal there just waiting for your keel. Anchoring is not permitted in the Cayos Cochinos so you must pick up a mooring. At this time there are eight moorings available with plans to add four more. The moorings at Cochino Grande are not uniform in appearance, one might be an orange ball while the next may be a plastic soft drink bottle, but they are connected to good moorings, the park rangers have assured me of that. For more information on the moorings available, and how large a vessel each one will support you can hail the *Plantation Beach Resort* on VHF, they monitor channel 12 and answer to the hail *Trinity*. You'll find that when the wind is up gusts will blow down the hillside to turn your boat on her mooring to face almost every direction at times. Soon after you've secured your vessel to a mooring you'll be visited by a boat with a park ranger aboard and a couple of Honduran Marines to collect the park fees. If you need assistance at any time during your stay in the Cayos Cochinos, you can call the Honduran Marine base, *Cayo Menor*, on VHF ch. 71.

Vessels heading southwest to La Ceiba, and in particular *Puerto de Cabotaje*, can exit the Cayos Cochinos via the deep channel that lies west of Lower Monitor Cay as shown on Chart HON-29. From the mooring field at Cochino Grande, head out into the deeper water between Cochino Grande and Cochino Pequeño and head southward to pass between Lower Monitor Cay and the shoal that lies to its west/southwest. Once past the above mentioned waypoint you can take up your course for the waypoint off the jetties at *Puerto de Cabotaje*, but bear in mind that in the vicinity of 15° 54.68' N, 86° 32.15' W you'll pass over a shoal area with a least depth of 25', if this makes you nervous simply head more to the south, that's where the deeper water lies.

What You Will Find Ashore

On Cochino Grande you'll find the *Plantation Beach Resort* where you can dine and surf the Internet if you need to catch up your emails. For those interested in hiking the island, several trails originate at the resort with one trail leading to the very peak of the island at the lighthouse where you'll enjoy a 360° panorama with a 20 mile radius on a clear day.

In the mooring field of Cayo Cochino you'll see a large white house on the side of the hill, this is the home of ex-pats Hoss and Lori Pollard who are very helpful to cruises and who answer to the call sign *Eagle's Nest* on VHF ch. 12.

At the southeastern end of the bay is the *Plantation Beach Resort*, primarily for divers, this is where you'll find the only phone in the park (504-442-0974). The staff speaks English and offers Internet access, water, laundry service, video rentals, and will send and receive mail for you (*Plantation Beach Resort*, APTO #114, La Ceiba, Honduras), not only do they offer all that, they will accept bagged garbage, but just don't drop it off on their dock or grounds. All dives in the park must now be done with a certified divemaster as per park regulations. On the northwestern shore of Cochino Grande is Jan Jones' clinic, but unfortunately Jan is only here two months out of the year since she's retired. However her clinic is still in operation and desperately need supplies so if you can bring anything or offer any items from your own medical kit, please do so. Jan needs everything from band-aids and peroxide to vitamins, out of date prescription medicines, and even bars of soap.

The cays to the southeast of Cochino Grande offer fine snorkeling and lovely beaches, but of course you can't anchor here, but there is one mooring available (it's best just to dinghy over in fair weather from Cochino Grande). Lower Monitor Cay is home to a lovely fishing village complete with cayucos on the beach and thatch-roof houses, a wonderful photo opportunity at worst. The Garifuna community here is called Chachauate and while there is no running water or electricity, you can find food and even overnight accommodations.

The Northern Coast of Mainland Honduras

The Northern coast of mainland Honduras offers several lee-side anchorages such as Trujillo, Puerto Cortés, and Omoa, and two anchorages at Punta Sal, Puerto Escondido and Laguna el Diamante, that offer good all-around protection. Not to be outdone, if you head upriver at *Puerto de Cabotaje* near La Ceiba you can tie up at *La Ceiba Shipyard* offering the best in protection and amenities.

Trujillo

Waypoints:
Trujillo- 1½ nm NW of Punta Caxinas
16° 03.00' N, 86° 02.00' W

Bahía de Trujillo is the easternmost harbor covered in this guide along the mainland coast of Honduras. To the east of Trujillo is the area known as *La Moskitia*, or the *Mosquito Coast*. This area is sparsely populated, inaccessible by land, and home to the largest tract of virgin rainforest in Central America. Inhabited by several indigenous groups, the name does not come from the area's abundance of mosquitoes, it originates with the Miskito Indians who live there. There is a regular boat that services the area and you can check on its schedule and rates at the muelle in *Puerto de Cabotaje* near La Ceiba.

Trujillo lies at the foot of two mountains, *Mt. Capira* and *Mt. Calentura*, atop a small bluff overlooking the bay of the same name, *Bahía de Trujillo*. The modern port town of Puerto Castillo, which lies at the northern end of the *Bahía de Trujillo*, is a *Port of Entry* for Honduras so you can clear in or out there.

The beach at Trujillo lies below the ruins of an old Spanish fort and here you'll find many *champas* where you can eat and drink while listening to music. To the east of the bay is *Laguna de Guaimoreto*, a protected area and national park.

Christopher Columbus landed near Trujillo on August 14, 1502 (the first time he actually set foot on the North American continent), during his fourth voyage to the New World. Columbus noticed the water color in the local waters and named the area *Golfo de Honduras, The Gulf of the Depths.*

A few years later, in 1508, Vicente Yañez and Juan Diaz de Solis arrived at Puerto Castilla and not knowing that Columbus had already christened the site, named it *Cabo de Honduras,* or *Cape of the Deep Waters.*

During Colonial times Trujillo, because of its location and the fact that it was home to a large, deep bay, became an important port for homeward bound Spanish ships from the New World. The settlement of Trujillo was founded shortly after the conquest of Mexico by Juan de Medina on May 18, 1525, but was not declared a city until the Conqueror of Mexico, Hernan Cortés visited a short time later.

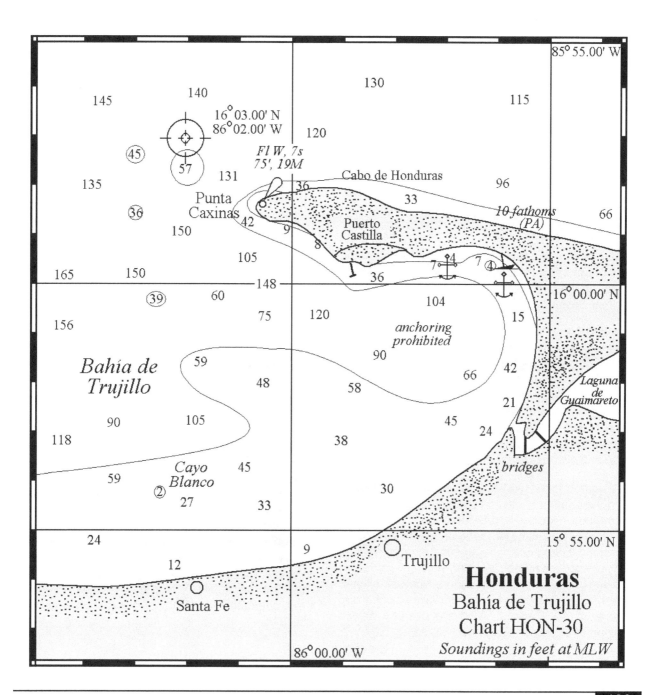

Honduras
Bahía de Trujillo
Chart HON-30
Soundings in feet at MLW

One of the first bishoprys in Honduras was established in Trujillo by Cortes but even this could not insure sustained growth for the city due to the climate (hot and humid) and British pirates who took their toll on the city. Although the city was abandoned several times its strategic location convinced Spain to redouble her efforts in keeping Trujillo inhabited including building a monastery there. In order to defend Trujillo against the pirates a fortress, *Fortaleza de Santa Bárbara* (*El Castillo*), was built sometime around 1550 (though some research indicates it may have been as late as 1590), but the attacks continued well into the 18th century. As a result of the seemingly never-ending pirate attacks, Trujillo was burned and destroyed several times and totally abandoned on a few other occasions.

In 1860, an American mercenary named William Walker, who had seized control of Nicaragua and sought to do the same in Honduras, was caught and executed in Trujillo and today his tomb is a tourist attraction.

William Walker was an American filibuster famed for his military exploits in Central America in the mid-1800s. At this time in history, adventurers known as filibusters participated in military action designed to take control of parts of Central America with the intent of annexing the captured territory to the United States, an exaggerated expression of the concept of *Manifest Destiny*.

Walker was born in Tennessee and graduated from the University of Nashville at 14 and by 19 had a medical degree. He started out at 25 as a physician in Pennsylvania, then studied law in New Orleans, and later became a journalist in California where he co-owned a newspaper, *The Crescent*, where a young writer named Walt Whitman worked on staff. Before he died Walker also proclaimed himself the President of Lower California and the Emperor of Nicaragua.

Between 1853-1860, William Walker hired soldiers of fortune and made several attempts to wrest control of territories in Mexico and Central America, and even invaded lower California, conquered the city of La Paz, and declared it an independent republic. Walker then annexed the nearby Mexican state of Sonora and renamed it the Republic of Sonora and established himself as "President." A result of Walker's actions in Sonora was the Gadsden Purchase whereby Mexico sold part of Sonora to the United States.

Walker was driven out of Sonora by the Mexican military in 1854 and then surrendered to U.S. Forces and was charged with violating neutrality laws but was later acquitted. Walker then turned his attention to Central America where chaos reigned as Democrats and Legitimists fought each other for control. The Democrats invited Walker to join the fight and in 1855, with an army of 58 men called *The Immortals*, Walker arrived in Nicaragua. Within a year his *Immortals*, and a local Democratic force, captured Grenada and Walker installed himself as President of Nicaragua causing other Central American countries to wonder where Walker would invade next. Costa Rica bravely took steps to stop Walker by invading Nicaragua, however Walker's forces repelled the invaders. But when Walker tried to follow the Costa Ricans into their country his invasion failed just as miserably as disease wiped out soldiers on both sides. During the fighting a young Costa Rican drummer boy, Juan Santamaria, became a national hero when he torched a fort where Walker's army was encamped. Walker was driven out of Costa Rica in mid-1857 by a Central American alliance that defeated him at Santa Rosa (now a Costa Rican national monument) and Walker surrendered to a United States Naval officer and was returned to the United States where he once again faced neutrality violations. Walker landed in New Orleans where he was greeted as a hero, visiting President Buchanan before heading to New York to begin trying to once again rebuild an army.

By the end of 1857, Walker had succeeded in forming another army and attempted to invade Nicaragua again but was thwarted by the British Navy who barred his forces from landing in Nicaragua. Walker returned to the States and, seeking to form yet one more army to try to invade Central America, wrote a book entitled *The War In Nicaragua* to propagate his cause and raise funds. Walker took up a strong pro-slavery stance, and in 1960 had again sailed south with a new army but was unable to land in Nicaragua, held off by the British Navy, so he and his army landed in Honduras planning to move overland into Nicaragua. In short order the British captured Walker and turned him over to Honduran authorities, who, within six days, stood the 36 year-old Walker in front of a firing squad in Trujillo and executed him. Today his tomb can be found in the municipal cemetery in Trujillo, this man who might have changed the history of our hemisphere if not checked.

Navigational Information

The *Bahía de Trujillo* is a huge harbor and there's plenty of area to anchor on the eastern and southeastern side of the bay. Although the bay offers protection for northerly and northeasterly swells, it is not the place to be when the winds and seas have any westerly component to them.

As shown on Chart HON-30, a waypoint at 16° 03.00' N, 86° 02.00' W, will place you approximately 1½ miles northwest of Punta Caxinas. From the waypoint head south past Cabo Honduras to turn to the east and head towards the eastern shore of *Bahía de Trujillo* clearing well to the south of Puerto Castillo, the commercial port in the bay and the spot for clearing *Customs* and taking on fuel and water. Anchor on the northern shore of the bay, anchoring south is prohibited. Anchor between the port and the conspicuous wreck to the east.

If you're proceeding west from Trujillo, beware of the reef shown as *Cayo Blanco* on Chart HON-30.

What You Will Find Ashore

The dining and drinking establishments in Trujillo are concentrated downtown and along the beach by town and by the airport and those that are not within walking distance are easy to reach by taxi. And, just to be on the safe side, don't walk the beaches of Trujillo at night alone, do it in a group.

If you need to change your dollars into *Lempiras* you can to that at *BGA* (just off the square in town), *Banco Atlantida*, *Banchasa*, and *Banco de Occidente* which is also the local *Western Union* office. *Banco Atlantida* and *Banco Occidente* both will give you cash advances on your *Visa* or *MasterCard*. If you need to have your laundry done visit *Lavandería Colón*, across from the *Hotel Mar de Plata*. The *Immigration* office is located in the Garifuna barrio of Cristales. Between Puerto Castilla and Trujillo is *Casa Kiwi*, a backpacker's hangout with laundry service, hammocks, dorms, and a no-dogs and no-chickens policy.

If you plan to dine at only one place in Trujillo, it must be the *Rogue's Gallery*, or *Jerry's* as it's often called. Owned by expat Jerry, the bar is located right on the beach and is open from 0700-2200 daily and serves up the best gringo food around, you can't beat their breakfasts although seafood is the specialty of the house. For fine dining visit the *Lempira Restaurant* located in the *Villas Brinkley Hotel*. Offering some of the finest views of Trujillo, the cuisine here is prepared by European chefs and their soup and salad bar is usually enough for most patrons.

The *Bucanero Restaurant* is located in the *Colonial Hotel* on the main square in town and offers an international menu and a full bar, while the *Pantry*, just a block and a half from the park, offers breakfast, lunch, and dinner buffets in a family setting. Their pizza is some of the best in town and they also feature an international *à la carte* menu. One of the oldest restaurants in town is *Restaurante Granada* and they feature fine meats and seafood. Near the airport beach you'll find *Restaurant Isabella* at the exquisite *Christopher Columbus Beach Resort* and a new place, the *Gringo Bar* right on the beach next to *Bahía Bar*.

In the Garifuna barrio of Cristales you'll find a bit of Garifuna culture at the *Copacabana*, a lively bar with loud Garifuna music. And if you're in search of Garifuna crafts then you'll want to visit *Gari Arte*.

There is quite a lot to do in and around Trujillo and if you wish to explore the surrounding areas, *Turtle Tours* (http://www.turtletours.de/turtle-tours/) is an excellent local tour operator that offers a variety of tours of Trujillo and all of Honduras. *Turtle Tours* is located at the *Villas Brinkley Hotel*. *Turtle Tours* can also assist you in visiting the Moskito region if you're so inclined. Regular air and ship traffic offer good opportunities for you to visit this rather isolated area.

One of the most popular stops near Trujillo is the *Cuyamel Caves* just south of town. The caves, which date back to pre-Columbian times, are notoriously difficult to find as only a few people actually know where they are. Approximately four miles from Trujillo, on the road to Tocoa, you'll find the *Aguas Calientes Resort*, a natural hot spring with a spa on site, the *Salud y Vida* spa. You can take a bus from Trujillo but the resort is not a normal stop so make sure the driver is aware that you want to get off the bus there. In the mountains south of Trujillo you can visit the *Capira y Calentura National Park* where hiking trails will take you through the rainforest to a waterfall on the *Río Negro*. If you can make it to the top of Mt. Calentura you will be rewarded with an excellent panorama of the Bay Islands. *Fucagua* is a non-profit organization that is actively participating in the conservation of the park and for more information about the park you can visit *Fucagua's* office on the second floor of the *Kiosk* located at the central park in Trujillo.

If you take the dirt road from Trujillo west you'll pass several new housing developments as you come to the *Campamento Hotel and Restaurant*, a full-service resort that even permits you to pitch a tent on their property for US$5 per night which includes use of their facilities such as the bathrooms and showers. Their restaurant will sit you amidst the palm trees and serve you up such exotic meals as iguana or tepesquintle. About six miles west of Trujillo is the Garifuna community of Santa Fe, where the real draw is *Pete's Place*, sometimes called *Comedor Caballero*, or *El Caballero*, arguably the best place for seafood on this stretch of coast. Continuing west you'll soon come to another Garifuna community, Guadeloupe, where you'll find some unique Garifuna artisans who have set up shop here. Nearby is *Hacienda Tumbador,* and old Honduran cattle ranch that now preserves the local crocodiles.

La Ceiba and Puerto de Cabotaje

Waypoints:
Puerto de Cabotaje- ¼ nm NNW of entrance
15° 48.18' N, 86° 45.67' W

Tegucigalpa piensa,
San Pedro Sula trabaja,
Y La Ceiba divierta!

Tegucigalpa thinks,
San Pedro Sula works,
And La Ceiba parties!

La Ceiba, the largest city on the northern coast and the third largest city in Honduras is home to over 100,000 people many of whom refer to their home as *Honduras' Girlfriend*. La Ceiba is an old port city with a lot of charm, but the heart of today's La Ceiba is the open-all-night party district, a rowdy place by anyone's standards where you'll see Hondurans, Cubans, and Norte Americanos all partying side by side till the sun comes up in the *Zona Viva*. By far, the biggest party takes place every May, *la Feria de San Isidro*, when some 200,000 revelers from across Honduras and the Caribbean descend on La Ceiba for a weeklong whirlwind of parties, dances, live music, and floats with scantily clad women aboard culminating in a grand Saturday night blowout. The Sunday following *Carnival* finds the streets empty and quiet save for the occasional barking dog or chirping bird, most folks don't even bother to wake up until the soccer matches come on TV.

La Ceiba was first settled by a small group of Garifuna from Trujillo in 1810, and later by immigrants from the Olancho region in the 1820s. One of these *olanchanos*, Manuel Hernandez, built his house near a large *ceiba* tree which soon became the town's gathering spot as workers and passersby enjoyed the shade, the area became known as La Ceiba after the tree. Sadly, the ceiba tree was cut down in 1917 when construction began on a *Customs* office, but the name of the town remained. Once the main port for fruit exports, La Ceiba has now ceded that role to Puerto Castilla (the port on the northern shore of *Bahía de Trujillo*), but remains the administrative hub for the *Standard Fruit Company*, now *Dole*.

The town of La Ceiba has a large pier at the center of its waterfront, but there is no truly sheltered place to anchor off the town except in the most settled of conditions when you can anchor west of the dock (which does nothing to break any easterly swells). I've seen other cruising guides that claim that there are no good harbors along the Honduran mainland from Trujillo to Punta Sal. Those guides are not entirely wrong, they're simply outdated, that certainly was the case at one time, but no more. In November of 1993, La Ceiba proudly opened the *Puerto Muelle de Cabotaje* about two miles to the east of the city of La Ceiba at what is shown on older charts as *Barro Boca Vieja*. The facility was designed to accommodate the shrimping fleet and commercial vessels from the Bay Islands, but it is also a great boon to cruising boats who now stop here to stay at *Lagoon Marina* or *La Ceiba Shipyard*, or to haul out and enjoy the duty-free zone for marine parts and supplies. The marina and shipyard facilities are located up a narrow river well inside the very protective breakwater behind which you can anchor if there's no room available at the marina or yard. Here too you can catch one of the daily ferries to Utila or Roatán.

Navigational Information
Due to the good facilities located inside *Puerto de Cabotaje*, I will not show a chart of the anchorage off the town of La Ceiba itself. It is more of an open roadstead and the large pier offers little if any lee.

As shown on Chart HON-31, a waypoint at 15° 48.18' N, 86° 45.67' W, will place you approximately ¼ mile north/northwest of the entrance through the breakwaters. From this waypoint enter staying mid-channel between the jetties or a bit to the east of mid-channel, do not stray to the west of mid-channel, favor the eastern side of the channel. The water will shallow from 25'-30' to 9' in places, but don't worry, there's plenty of water in the channel (as long as you draw less than 9' and the tide is high). Once

Puerto de Cabotaje, mainland Honduras

La Ceiba Shipyard, Puerto de Cabotaje

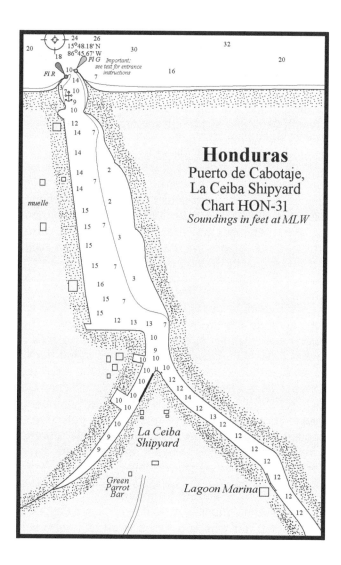

Honduras
Puerto de Cabotaje,
La Ceiba Shipyard
Chart HON-31
Soundings in feet at MLW

Waterfall in the mountains near La Ceiba

Expats Bar, La Ceiba

inside the jetties you can anchor to starboard behind the western jetty or continue up river past the *muelle* (the town dock or wharf) to starboard, favoring the west side of the small harbor to avoid a shoal on the east side of the bay. Once past the *muelle* turn to port and then to starboard to go upriver to the marine facilities. A quarter mile or so upriver you'll come to a spot where two small rivers meet, and directly in front of you you'll see the haul-out basin for the *La Ceiba Shipyard* (VHF ch. 69) which has side-tie docks on both small rivers (the dock to the west currently has power).

If you continue a few hundred yards up the eastern river you'll come to the currently closed *Lagoon Marina* (it is listed for sale so its future is uncertain). You'll have roughly 9'-15' of water in either river, but go slow, the rivers are narrow and you might find yourself sharing the waterway with an outgoing vessel. If you need to clear in or out from here *La Ceiba Shipyard* offers free rides into La Ceiba where you'll find the *Port Captain* and *Immigration* offices. If the weather is settled you can also anchor off the large dock located west of *Puerto de Cabotaje* and walk into town to clear, but the weather will have to cooperate as this is a very uncomfortable anchorage in all but the most settled of weather.

What You Will Find Ashore

Marine Facilities

Boatyards

La Ceiba Shipyard may be the finest boatyard in the Northwest Caribbean with a complete group of *marine services available* the yard is professionally managed and very welcoming to transient vessels. Although the yard is not a marina in the proper sense of the word, they do have side-tie dockage available and are more than happy to have transient vessels stay for a while as long as the docks are not needed for their yard customers (every time I've been here I've always found dockage available, and by the way, the yard monitors VHF ch. 69, their phone number is 504-441-9426, and their email address is laceibashipyard@gmail.com).

The yard has a 120-ton *Travelift* (they can haul vessels to 100' LOA or a multihull with a beam of up to 25' 4") and offers storage on the hard for cruisers who wish to leave their boat in a safe place for a season or two. The yard can carry out all phases of marine repairs including sandblasting, hull repair (wood, glass, and metal), hull and deck painting,

diesel and outboard repairs (the yard is now a *Yanmar* dealer), rigging and sail repair, electronics service, carpentry, hydraulics and refrigeration, prop and shaft repairs, life raft certification, and they also allow do-it-yourselfers or paid crew to work on their own vessels.

If you plan to leave your boat on the hard here you will need a document from the shipyard stating that you will be leaving the country by private yacht to avoid buying a return trip ticket when flying back into Honduras.

There is 24-hour security on site, usually there are three armed guards patrolling the 14-acre site day and night, you'll feel very, very safe here. The shipyard also can arrange to have your laundry done and your propane tanks filled. If this is not enough for you let me tell you what they offer you for FREE. Free Internet, free phone calls to the U.S. or Canada (three per day with a five minute maximum for each call; phone and Internet access is only available during office hours, Monday through Thursday from 0700-1700, and on Fridays from 0700-1600, the office is closed on the weekends), and free transportation to town at 0900 and at 1400 (also only during the week, not on the weekends), I know of no other marina or boatyard anywhere that is as accommodating to the cruiser.

La Ceiba Shipyard does not accept international personal checks or traveler's checks for the payment of yard services, however they do accept *Visa*, *MasterCard*, and *American Express* along with approved checks drawn on a Honduran

Marinas

La Ceiba Shipyard has a few slips available as long as they are not required for yard usage, The slips have full electric, water (the marina also sells 5 gallon jugs of purified water, the water at the docks is potable but it has a high iron content and may leave a residue on your boat), and you'll find showers ashore; there is no fuel dock but the yard can bring fuel to your boat, just tell them how many gallons you require. *Lagoon Marina*, which sat just a few hundred yards upstream of the shipyard, is now closed, listed for sale, and its future is uncertain.

Marine Supplies

For marine supplies, your first choice is *La Ceiba Shipyard*. The boatyard has a large and very well stocked chandlery on site so they might have what you need on hand. If you need to order an item they can quote current *West Marine* prices and have the items shipped in from the U.S., orders in by Wednesday are usually at the yard by the following Friday.

La Ceiba Shipyard has been designated as a *Marine Duty Free Zone* and all parts imported via the yard, either by customer's orders or from the yard's *West Marine* catalog are received free of all duties and taxes (you will need to provide *La Ceiba Shipyard* with a copy of your documentation or allow them to make a copy of it). However, you will have to pay all shipping charges and the yard will tack on a handling charge which can be as high as 25%. If you intend to have something shipped in for your vessel, check with the office first and let them walk you through the paperwork, if the paperwork is not completed correctly, and if the items shipped are not addressed in the proper manner, you might find yourself paying a hefty duty and tax.

You can also visit *Motores Kawas*, 504-2443-2161, they're actually an auto parts outlet but they do carry marine supplies. For hydraulic hoses, bearings, o-rings and associated products visit *Central de Mangueras*, their number is (504) 440-0750. The local *Yamaha* dealer is *UltraMotor* (http://www. ultramotorhn.com/) at *Barrio el Centro, 13 Calle*, and *Avenida 14 de Julio*, and can be reached by phone at 506-2427-8510.

Getting Around in La Ceiba

Getting around town is best accomplished by taking a taxi from *Puerto de Cabotaje*. The taxi drivers hang out on VHF ch. 11, and a few hang out on VHF ch. 08. When you find a driver you like, you should call him or her either by phone or by radio, they appreciate repeat business and some go out of their way to help you, although some will try to get more *lemps* than their ride is worth. Sometimes you can cut a deal at night if you have more than two people in the taxi, and often you can hire a car and driver by the hour with some crafty negotiations.

Taxis in and around downtown La Ceiba usually charge around 15-25 *lemps* for downtown stops, but the marinas located at *Puerto de Cabotaje* are a bit farther away so the fares are higher. One drive in particular, Miguelito, hangs around the *La Ceiba Shipyard* quite a bit and can be trusted, you can hail him on VHF ch. 08. If you plan to rent a car, hitchhike, or explore by bicycle, it's easy enough to find your way around. There are two main avenues (*Avenidas*) that run perpendicular to the coast, *Avenida San Isidro*

and *Avenida 14 de Julio*. The streets (*Calles*) that run parallel to the coast are numbered consecutively with *Calle 1* running adjacent to the shoreline.

Money Changing

In town it's not too difficult to change your dollars into *Lempiras* or get a cash advance on your credit or debit card. The huge *Mega Mall* (both *La Ceiba Shipyard* and *Lagoon Marina* can drop you off here) has several *ATM*'s on site and banks can be found all over the downtown area. On *Avenida San Isidro*, across from the *Hotel Iberia*, is *Credomatic* where you can get an advance on your credit card, *VISA* or *American Express*; also on the same street is *Master Cambia*, while next to *Farmacia Aurora* is *Honducard*. You can also get the same rates as the banks give at *Supermercado Los Almendros* located at the *Hotel Principe*.

Internet

For Internet access in downtown La Ceiba, of course *Expats* has Internet access, or you can visit the *Internet Café* located at *the Centro Comercial Panoyotti* in downtown La Ceiba. Open Monday-Saturday from 0800-2200, they offer Internet access as well as long distance phone service. You can reach them by phone at 504-443-4152 or email them at: laceiba@hondusoft.com. After you've surfed the net you might want to grab a bite to eat at *Mixers Comida Buffet*, a great little cafeteria style restaurant in the came center. Also located downtown is *Café@Café* (Monday-Saturday, 0700-2000), a gourmet cafeteria/Internet café located next to the *Plaza del Sol* shopping center on *Avenida San Isidro* across the street from *Motores Kawas*. *Café@Café* offers gourmet coffees and teas to sip while you're munching on their exotic pastries, gourmet sandwiches, or simply surfing the net. *Avenida San Isidro* is also home to many banks and is close to the main square.

Medical

If you need emergency medical assistance call 504-443-0969 or 504-443-970. The *MediCentro Clinic* is a modern and well-run clinic located in downtown La Ceiba. Dr. Omar Zuniga is a dermatologist at *MediCentro* who speaks English and can be reached by phone at 504-24401259. Mammograms are available at *MediCentro* with no appointment necessary.

Dr. Wilfredo Sandoval speaks English and is a very competent doctor. His office is on the second floor of *Banco Seguarador Hondureno, Edificio*

Commercial, on *Ave la Republica* near the *Hotel Paris.* If you need the services of an eye doctor, Dra. Alicia Ponce speaks English and shares an office, *Hospital Oftamalogico Ponce,* with her husband, Dr. Luis Danilo D. Ponce (504-9982-7376) on *Blvd. 15 de Septiembre.*

Dra. Florencia Portillo is a good dentist and endodontist also on *Blvd. 15 de Septiembre* (504-2443-2817) next to *Banco Continental* and Dr. Ponce's office.

Provisions
Provisioning is easy and relatively inexpensive in La Ceiba. *Super Ceibano* has four stores around town, with their *Super Ceibano #1,* across from the park downtown, has the best selection, with *Super Ceibano #2* just a few blocks away. I've been told that *Super Ceibano* has been purchased by *Walmart* so some changes may be in the works, including a name change.

For overall choice and value, I prefer the *Supermercado Mega* at the *MegaPlaza Mall,* a large two story air-conditioned mall on the road from Puerto de la Cabotaje into town. The mall is also home to several *ATMs* and a cinema that usually shows English speaking movies with Spanish subtitles.

You can also pick up some groceries at *Supermercado Los Almendros* located by the *Hotel Principe. D'todo,* located on *Avenida 14 de Julio,* and *Fiesta Imports* both bring in U.S. products from *Sam's Club* and *Cosco* for resale in Honduras and they like *Super Ceibano* and *Supermercado Mega,* take credit cards. *Casa Colorado,* a good place for bottled beverages and spirits, also takes your credit card, but you'll have to pay a premium to use it there.

For baked goods try one of the two locations of *Laura's Bakery,* one in the yellow building at *La Merced 13 Calle,* and a second location on the second floor at the *Mega Mall.* The *Mega Mall* also boasts an *Applebee's,* a *Pizza Hut* sits across the street, and a financial section where several banks are located. *Super Paiz* is located at *Ave de la Republica* and *Calle 7* and is owned by *Walmart.*

Dining
By far, the most popular bar in town, and one of the best places in La Ceiba to get a meal, is *Expatriates (Expatriados),* or *Expats* as it's more commonly called, and you'll feel right at home among all the ex-pats and locals that frequent the second floor establishment with its large open verandah located in the *Naranjal* section of La Ceiba. The bar has a great menu, a couple of TVs, an assortment of fine Honduran cigars including the bar's own brand, *Expatriados.* There's also free Internet access, a dartboard, and a bulletin board to keep you up on the latest goings on in La Ceiba.

Expatriates also has a second location in the mountains and offers free van service to and from the downtown bar starting at 1100 daily. *Expats* says that they'll even pick you up or drop you off at *La Ceiba Shipyard* when you're ready to return from the mountains or from *Expats* in La Ceiba, I've been dropped off there from the mountain location, but when I'm at *Expats* in La Ceiba the driver always seems to be somewhere else and it will take him an hour to get back so it might be easier to call a taxi (taxis monitor VHF ch. 11 in La Ceiba and a trip to or from the shipyard to downtown should not cost over *L*50 during daytime hours, a bit more at night or if there are several people going-occasionally you'll find a roguish taxi driver who'll try to charge you *L*100 for one person, they think just because you're at the shipyard you're a rich gringo, ignore them and find another taxi; taxis in La Ceiba itself are usually about *L*15 for in-town stops). At the mountain location you can go horseback riding, relax in the fresh water pool, or take a dip in the nearby *Río Cangrejal.* As of this writing rumors are flying around that *Expats* is closing their location in the mountains and planning to open one in Trujillo, so keep your eyes open for changes here.

One of the best restaurants in Honduras, *Ricardo's,* located in La Ceiba on *Avenida 14 de Julio,* offers a full bar, great steaks, seafood, and diet sensitive entrees. You can dine inside or outside and sample their extensive salad and pasta bars. One of the newest restaurants in town is *El Patio* located on *Avenida 15 de Septiembre* near La Ceiba's bus terminal (*Termino de Autobus*). *El Patio* is a branch of the famous restaurant located in Tegucigalpa and serves up some of the best Honduran food you'll find in La Ceiba. The new Bay *Islands Restaurant* is located in Barrio Potreritos across the street from the *Bueno Veterinary Hospital.* Specializing in island style food the focus is on meats and seafood. One of my favorites is *Le Rustique,* a small and very informal French restaurant located on a rooftop on the third floor of the *Moran Building* on *Avenida San Isidro. Le Rustique* also caters and reservations are suggested (504-963-8653).

Another one of La Ceiba's best restaurants is located, like so many other fine restaurants, on the beach. *Meson del Puerto* has an old-world colonial décor with an open beach deck for outside dining. Just across the street is *Caribeños*, a new restaurant that features typical Honduran cuisine for breakfast, lunch, and dinner amid the cool breezes and great views of the La Ceiba shoreline. Most of these beach-side restaurants can be found in *Zona Viva* on *Calle 1*. *Restaurante Miramar* is located at *the Turicentro Barra Vieja,* at the end of *Calle 1*. Here you'll dine while viewing visiting birds and turtles in a tropical garden setting. *Paseo Universitario*, a branch of the same restaurant from Tegucigalpa, offers excellent local dishes and they're located at *Calle 1* and *Avenida 14 de Julio*. Nearby is *Las Brisas de Naturaleza* right on the beach. Here you can dine on some of the best seafood in La Ceiba and when you do you must try their *topado*.

In La Ceiba, as in most cities, many of the best restaurants are found in and near the better hotels in *Zona Viva*. *El Portal* is located at the *Hotel El Colonial* and features Thai cuisine in air-conditioned comfort. *Los Olivos* is located next to the *Barcelo La Aurora Hotel* on the road heading east to Tela. Here, in an informal garden setting you can dine on fine BBQ dishes and Arabian cuisine. On the same road you'll find the *Golden Palace Restaurant*, one of the most exclusive restaurants in all of La Ceiba featuring a delicious International menu and featuring steaks and Chinese cuisine. Also on the road to Tela you'll find *Autopollos Al Carbon* in the *Toronjal* district. This is one of the few 24-hour restaurants in La Ceiba and they serve excellent chicken and cold beer.

At the *Partenon Beach Hotel* (http://www.hotelpartenonbeach.com/) you'll find *Touché*, open for breakfast, lunch, and dinner, emphasizing a French theme. *Café Giarre* is a delightful European flavored sidewalk café located at the corner of *Avenida San Isidro* and *13 Calle*, just below the *Posada de Don Giuseppe Hotel*. The *Dutch Corner*, located next to the *2001 Amsterdam Hotel* on the beach, is open for breakfast, lunch, and dinner and features an inexpensive menu featuring baleadas, chicken, ribs, and delicious banana fritters. Across the street is a wonderful little spot called *Mango Tango* where you can dine on Honduran cuisine while singing karaoke… actually you should never try to sing while dining, didn't your mother ever tell you not to sing with your mouth full? Nearby is *My Friend (Mi Amigo)*, located right on the beach at the end of the road by the hotel.

The Honduran equivalent of *Starbucks* has got to be *Expresso Americano* with three locations, one at the *Hotel Paris* on *Parque Centro*, one at the *Mega Mall*, and one at the *Goloson Airport*. *Cafeteria Cobel*, located across the street from the *Hotel Principe*, is a dining tradition in La Ceiba and is open for breakfast, lunch, and dinner.

Driving Around La Ceiba

For general shopping pleasure, La Ceiba is the home of Honduras' largest department store, *Tiendas Carrion*. Not to be outdone, the newcomer is *Super Tiendas Palmira* carrying everything from clothes to sporting goods. If you're looking for quality Honduran cigars, try *Ex-Pats*, they have a good selection. For local arts and crafts visit *Mayart* on *Avenida San Isidro*, or *Artesanias Valle de Ángeles*, also on *Avenida San Isidro*. To find true local art you can visit Virginia Castillo, an accomplished local artist, at her home in the *Toronjal* district, she no longer has her gallery but still sells her works out of her home.

On the road heading east to Trujillo you'll find a lot to do and several nice places to dine. Just east of town is the *Río Cangrejal* where you can raft downstream and experience Class II, III, and IV rapids, all within a short drive from La Ceiba.

A few miles east of La Ceiba is the *Villa Rhina Club and Resort* featuring the *Villa Rhina* restaurant alongside pleasant natural pools and a river. This is a great spot to spend a day immersed in nature hiking in the mountains or dining at the beach. The resort also offers transportation to and from La Ceiba, you can call them at 504-443-1222.

In the Garifuna village of Sambo Creek 12 miles east of La Ceiba you'll find three nice restaurants, *La Champa, Sambo Creek, El Mirador*, and *Helen's*. *La Champa* offers typical Honduran seafood dishes, a complete bar, and spectacular views of Cayos Cochinos. *Sambo Creek*, owned by an American ex-pat, serves up great food at even better prices right on the beach and shares the same spectacular views of Cayos Cochinos. This is also the only restaurant in Sambo Creek where you can buy ice cream. Every evening except Tuesdays they serve up live Garifuna music and have four cabins available as well as a boat you can charter to take you to the Cayos Cochinos.

El Mirador, located at the *Hotel Canadian*, is owned by a French Canadian couple who serve up international food with indoor and terrace seating where you can enjoy a great view of, what else, the Cayos Cochinos. Nearby and right on the beach is *Helen's*, where you can enjoy their swimming pool for a nominal fee. In the nearby Garifuna village of Corozal you'll find *Brisas del Mar*, a quaint seafood restaurant set on a beautiful beach. A few yards past the road to Sambo Creek you'll find *Glenda's Paradise Hot Springs* where the natural hot water is about 105° F, 40° C. There is also a cold water pool on site as well as a snack bar. There are several daily buses that run to and from the main bus terminal in La Ceiba that make stops in the *Sambo Creek*/Corozal area.

Just past Km marker #209 you'll come to a small river at Los Chorros. When you pass the bridge walk up past the fence along the trail for about 100 yards where you'll find a small snack bar. Only a few yards away you'll find the first of a series of small swimming pools, there will be more the further upstream you go. It's best to come here during the week as it's very crowded on the weekends and holidays.

About 13 miles east of La Ceiba, in the community of Roma, you'll find the *Palma Real Beach Resort & Villas;* with its great view of the Cayos Cochinos (it seems that every establishment along this stretch has great views of those lovely islands) is probably the best beach hotel in all of Honduras. Adjacent to the resort is the *Water Jungle Aqua Park*, an extensive jungle theme park that is the largest of its kind in Honduras. The park offers a large food court, swimming pools, games for the kids, huge water slides, and a wave pool.

About 15 miles east of La Ceiba you'll find the *Fig Tree Medical Center* operated by Dr. Sebi, a rehabilitation and rejuvenation center specializing in the treatment of cancer and diabetes by making use of special natural diets combined with the natural hot springs in the area.

About 16 miles east of La Ceiba is a small ocean-side bay called *Laguna de Cacao*. The bay is surrounded my mangroves full of birds and monkeys. The people of the small village here make there living producing cacao, a prime ingredient in the manufacturing of chocolate. Here you can see the cacao bushes, a sugar plantation, and an ox-driven sugar mill. If you'd like you can walk through the village to a small canal where a dugout canoe will take you on a trip through the mangroves and allow you to sneak up the local wildlife.

If you head west from La Ceiba, you'll come to the huge *Pico Bonito Cloud Forest National Park*, a few miles outside of town. *Pico Bonito* is one of the most diverse parks in Central America covering land from the beach to the mountains, some of which rise to over 7,500', and it's THE landmark when making landfall at La Ceiba.

The park is named after *Pico Bonito*, the large mountain lying just south of La Ceiba, an important landmark especially when arriving from the sea. Park access is limited but you can visit the lower areas of the park. The entrance to the park is on the road to Tela and San Pedro Sula just past El Piño. Once past the *Quebrada Seca Bridge* take the second left, and follow the road towards the mountains for approximately one mile where you'll find the start of the *Río Zacate* trail. The trail leads you up into the forest for about 1.5 miles along the course of the *Río Zacate* to a pleasant waterfall with several nice swimming holes. The river got its name from the *zacate* grass, a forked, clinging sawgrass that grows everywhere up and down the length of the river.

In La Ceiba there are many tour operators such as *La Moskitia Ecoaventuras* (http://www.lamoskitia.hn/), *Omega Tours* (http://www.omegatours.info/), *Tourist Options* (http://www.hondurastouristoptions.com/en/), *Jungle River Lodge* (http://www.jungleriverlodge.com/), *Rios Honduras*, and *Garifuna Tours* (http://garifunatours.com/), who can arrange a tour of the park for you and most include lunch with the journey. *The Coco & Bamboo Bar & Restaurant* at the *Jungle River Lodge* serves a regular menu as well as vegan entrees. The lodge is located within a working coffee and cacao plantation and is home to the *Tropical Butterfly Farm and Gardens* (http://hondurasbutterflyfar.tripod.com/), open to the public from Wednesday through Sunday from 0800-1630.

The butterfly farm is home to over 12,000 butterflies and other insects from 68 countries with over 9,000 from Honduras alone. As you tour the farm you'll visit each step in the life cycle of a butterfly and can observe them in great detail before entering the *Butterfly House* where thousands of butterflies flutter about feeding on nectar and mating, what a life. Also on site is a serpentarium, housing over 20 different kinds of snakes and reptiles. If you are adventurous you can enjoy a canopy tour from the folks at *Highline Zipline Canopy Tours* (http://www.jungleriverlodge.com/canopy.html), the first canopy tour on Honduras' northern coast. The tour starts at the *Jungle River*

Lodge and takes you across the river and into the forest of the park.

Tela

I will not show a chart for Tela, it's basically an open roadstead anchorage, much like La Ceiba, and I see no reason why one would want to anchor there. However, it is a wonderful destination and easy to get to from Puerto Cortes so I will give you some basic information about the town and what you'll find there.

Tela is basically your sleepy little banana-republic seaside town, but that will soon change as the future brings new investors here to take advantage of Tela's main attraction, her beaches. Her location also helps, Tela is only 50 miles from a major airport at San Pedro Sula and 60 miles west of La Ceiba and her airport, and improved highways, along with regular bus service from La Ceiba, are bringing more and more people to enjoy Tela. And when those visitors arrive in Tela they are discovering that there is more to her charm than just beaches.

Founded by the conquistador Cristobal de Olin on May 3, 1524, Tela was built along the banks of a small river next to an Indian community called *Tehuacan* which had all the amenities for a healthy settlement, good water, good soil, and food for the taking. The city received her name, *Triunfo de la Cruz*, for her founding date was the *Day of the Holy Cross* in the Catholic faith. A rather long name you must admit, which is why it as eventually shortened to T'dela and by 1829 was simply, Tela. The original name is now the name of a small hill along the shoreline next to the city.

As Spanish ships loaded with the treasures of the New World made their return trips to Europe buccaneers prowling the waters of the Trujillo/Puerto Cortés/Havana route found easy prey off the Honduran coast. As the pirates made themselves at home in Tela several places were renamed by them. Today's *Bahía Tornabe* was then called *Turn Bay* and *Punta Izopo* was then *Punta Bishop*.

In 1797, the ancestors of today's Garifuna were taken from their homes on St. Vincent and marooned on the island of Roatán and were later moved to Trujillo where they dispersed along the northern shore of Honduras. By 1808, the Garifuna had established themselves in Tela and for the most part remained until around 1889 when they set up small communities just to the east of the hill known as El Triunfo and another to the west at San Juan.

From 1860-1900, the economy of Tela was based on bananas, promoted by the city, and traded on a small scale. But after the turn of the century the city fathers offered small concessions to investors to help improve the economy of Tela and during these years the city of Tela itself took form with territorial boundaries established, schools constructed, and public lighting installed downtown. After the turn of the century and lasting for a dozen years the government of Tela issued small concessions to investors to nurture the city's economy.

The city prospered and territorial boundaries were established, schools constructed, and public lighting installed. In 1912 a huge concession was granted to the *Tela Railroad Company*, the company that monopolized the banana plantations and produced the famed *Chiquita* banana. This period of up and down fortune lasted until 1976 when the company moved their base of operations to La Lima (just outside of San Pedro Sula) and a steady growth of tourism began while cattle ranching and agriculture also made great strides. Tela still retains the air of a small banana town and when strolling around downtown in the Tela Nueva district you can visit the *Villas Telemar Hotel*, once the living quarters for many of the *Tela Railroad Company's* executives.

For your dining pleasure one of the best restaurants in town is *Cesar Mariscos* just across from the beach and specializing in seafood. Located on the beach by the hotel of the same name is *Sherwood* serving great breakfasts and an even better *tapado*. *Luces Del Norte* serves breakfast, lunch, and dinner and offers books for sale as well as a book exchange. *Mango* offers Internet access, music, and movies on the river by the *Garifuna Museum*. For an early breakfast (0600), try *Cafeteria Tuty's* in the heart of Tela across from Garifuna Tours.

The largest hotel in Tela, *Villas Telamar*, offers a couple of good dining options from a beach restaurant with a limited menu in a tropical setting, to an indoor restaurant in an elegant setting that features buffet lunches on the weekends as well as live music. For pizza visit *Pizzeria El Bambino* on the main boulevard in town, they also serve up good pasta dishes and have a playground for kids. In the Garifuna village of San Juan is *El Tucan*, located at the *Honduras Shores Plantation*. This restaurant features seafood and a large pool with a swim-up bar. Nearby is *El Pescador*, a waterside restaurant with moderately priced seafood dishes.

Punta Sal and Laguna el Diamante

Waypoints:
Punta Sal- 3 nm WNW of
15° 56.00' N, 87° 39.00' W

Puerto Escondido- ½ nm NW of entrance
15° 54.85' N, 87° 38.50' W

Laguna el Diamante- ½ nm NW of entrance
15° 54.00' N, 87° 39.40' W

I'll begin this section with a warning. A couple of years ago a cruising boat was boarded here and the skipper died. Since then the number of cruisers here have dropped off considerably. I would not anchor here alone, but with other boats and an all night shared anchor watch.

The peninsula of Punta Sal is a long, narrow ridge a couple of hundred feet high and the surrounding 782 square kilometers are a Honduran national park, *Parque Nacional Jeanette Kawas*. The park includes Puerto Escondido and *Laguna el Diamante*, the two popular anchorages here, but it also protects the *Los*

Micos, *Tinashí*, and *Río Tinto* lagoons, the Martínez and Chambers canals, and the *Río Ulúa* and *Río Chamelecón*.

The park, previously known as the *Punta Sal National Park*, is named after Jeanette Kawas, a leader in the fight to protect Punta Sal much to the chagrin of some very powerful folks, in particular the *National Campesino Union*, an African palm cooperative, and a Honduran Colonel, Mario "El Tigre" Amaya, both of whom claimed ownership of the lands of the peninsula. Kawas was successful and Punta Sal was named a national park in 1994 but she paid the ultimate price, she was gunned down the following year and her murder is still unsolved.

Navigational Information

As shown on Chart HON-32, a waypoint at 15° 56.00' N, 87° 39.00' W, will place you approximately three miles west/northwest of Punta Sal. From this waypoint you can head southeast to a waypoint at 15° 54.85' N, 87° 38.50' W, which will place you approximately ½ mile northwest of the entrance to Puerto Escondido, or you can head a bit west of

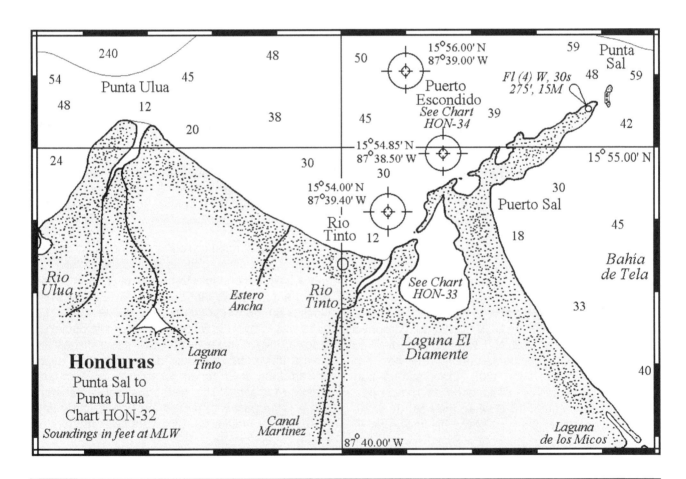

south to a waypoint at 15° 54.00' N, 87° 39.40' W, which will place you ½ mile northwest of the entrance to Laguna el Diamante. These last two waypoints and the entrances to Puerto Escondido and Laguna el Diamante are shown in greater detail on Chart HON-33.

If you are entering *Puerto Escondido*, beware of the submerged rocks on both sides of the channel as shown on Chart HON-33, you might not see them until you are upon them. Stay mid-channel and enter on 162° T. Inside the best holding is in the northeast corner of the bay in about 10'-15' of water. Puerto Escondido is no place to be in strong westerly winds and seas.

The entrance to *Laguna el Diamante* can be a bit tricky if you've never been there before. The problem is that if you are approaching the entrance from a position too far to the east you'll see the channel between the rock that sits on the northern side of the channel and the mainland and you could easily mistake it for the entrance channel. IT IS NOT THE ENTRANCE CHANNEL. It is shoal and rocky and no place you would care to be. Make sure you keep that offlying rock to port upon entering the bay! The entrance channel *to Laguna el Diamante* carries 10'-15' of water and inside you'll find depths of 7'-9' throughout except for the southern part where the water shoals. The best anchorage is in the northern part of the bay, well protected in all wind conditions. However, if you go too far north in the bay the bottom is soupy and you might have trouble getting your anchor to set.

This area is a park and don't be surprised if park officials come by to collect a US$3 fee for park usage.

What You Will Find Ashore
What will you find ashore here? Several trails to explore and more than one might imagine from what seems an isolated outpost. The anchorages here are beautiful, *Puerto Escondido* has steep hills covered with palm trees and a white sand beach on its southern shore.

Laguna el Diamante is surrounded by a hilly jungle growth with a rough trail (you might want to bring a machete as it's not well maintained) at the northern end of the bay that will take you the hundred yards to the lovely beach in *Puerto Escondido*. This trail is said to have been planted with fruit trees by pirates of old and along the way you can pick up bananas, oranges, and even avocados. All around

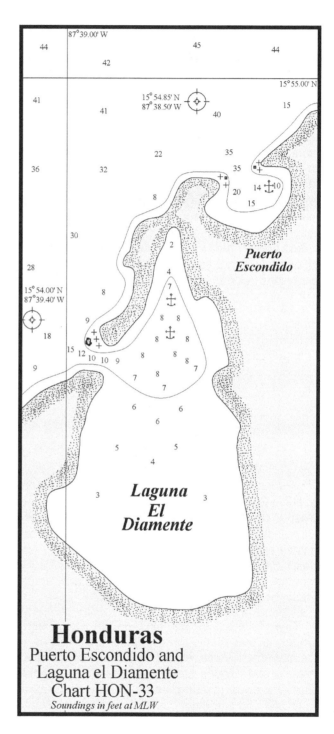

Honduras
Puerto Escondido and
Laguna el Diamante
Chart HON-33
Soundings in feet at MLW

you the jungle is full of howler monkeys, parrots, frigate birds, and all manner of seagulls and finches.

If you need provisions here you'll be amazed that with a bit of determination and luck you'll be able to find a few. You'll often see fishermen from the local village fishing in the lagoon and they're quite open to selling or trading you part of their catch, usually robalo (snook), or snapper. But if you're looking for more, real provisions so to speak, the village of *Río Tinto* is less than a mile away from the entrance to *Laguna el Diamante*. It's about an hour's hike away, through the jungle, over some hills, and across a river, but don't let that scare you away, it's all part of the adventure, and if you'd like you can pick a lot of fresh fruits on the way. Of course, if you'd like you can take the dinghy outside to reach the village, just head south. The village has a few small stores (beer, basic canned goods, toilet paper, rice, freshly baked bread), a couple of dozen homes, and lots of niños that will act as a guide for you and carry your provisions back for you.

As an interesting side note, and if you're into music, in *Laguna el Diamante* you can pick up a local radio station at 94.9 FM that plays English speaking pop tunes from the 1960s, 1970s, and 1980s with few commercials.

Puerto Cortés

Waypoints:
Puerto Cortés- ¾ nm WNW of Punta Caballos
15° 51.20' N, 87° 58.60' W

Puerto Cortés is an excellent stopover if you are heading to or from the *Río Dulce*. If you are heading west, it can be a great overnight stopover between Utila and Cabo Tres Puntas. If you are heading east, it is an excellent place to clear into Honduras as you head to the Bay Islands or La Ceiba. If the wind is forecast to be westerly, this is not a good anchorage, you're better off at *Laguna el Diamante*.

One of the busiest ports in the Caribbean, Puerto Cortés is one of the most important port cities in Central America with most of the goods that Honduras imports and exports coming across her docks, only Puerto Barrios (actually Santo Tomás de Castilla) in Guatemala can even come close to giving Puerto Cortés any competition.

Puerto Cortés was originally founded in 1524 as Puerto Caballos, *Port of Horses*, after Spanish Conquistador Gil Gonzáles Dávila was caught in a terrible storm and was forced to throw several horses overboard. Ravaged by pirates and epidemics, the Spanish moved their operations from Puerto Cortés to the safer harbor of Omoa towards the end of the 1600s. The latter 1800s saw the Honduran Caribbean coast, and Puerto Cortés in particular, become home to all manner of rogues and shady individuals, as the nation's golden Banana Republic years were ticking away. Honduras had no extradition laws until 1912. In 1890, the Louisiana Lottery, outlawed in its home state, moved to Puerto Cortés and became one of the largest lotteries in the world for a short period. Even today the port area can best be described as "seedy," but luckily there is so much more to Puerto Cortés.

Navigational Information
As shown on Chart HON-34, a waypoint at 15° 51.20' N, 87° 58.60' W, will place you approximately ¾ mile west/northwest of Punta Caballos. Do not head straight for this waypoint if approaching from the east, you must first pass north of Punta Caballos. At this waypoint you will see a red buoy to port, that marks the western edge of the shipping channel, and unless you draw as much as a freighter you're okay passing west of it. From the waypoint you can head southeast passing between a pair of red and green lighted buoys to continue generally southeast towards the conspicuous water tower by the Honduran Navy base at the southeastern end of the bay.

Do not anchor off *Coca Cola Beach* (south of the Navy base and named after a *Coca Cola* warehouse located nearby), it's much safer to anchor off the mouth of the river outflow north of the Navy base in 10' of water. There is an armed guard on the point at the Navy base, and on the other side of the river is a bonded warehouse also with an armed guard...good news for cruisers.

What You Will Find Ashore
Customs and Immigration
Clearing in and out at Puerto Cortés could not be easier. To come into town take your dinghy under the bridge and tie up at the dock of the restaurant on your left. Enter the restaurant and talk to the owner, he's Italian but speaks good English. He will hail a taxi for you to take you to *Immigration* and the Port Captain's office.

The *Customs* office sits across the street from the *Post Office* on the main road by the docks. The *Immigración* office is located at 5th *Avenida* between

3rd and 4th *Calle*, 504-665-0582, and the *Port Captain's* office is located two doors down.

First you must visit *Immigration* and then the Port Captain and you are done. No fees. No hassles. The Port Captain issues 90-day visas and sometimes he charges and sometimes he doesn't. Other times he might charge an anchoring fee. It is speculated that it all depends on the attitude of the cruisers who are clearing.

Getting Around

Puerto Cortés is conveniently located near Honduras' industrial center at San Pedro Sula, and the traffic between the two, one a major port and one an inland industrial capital, can be quite heavy at times as you might expect. The two cities are connected by a modern 4-lane highway so you can drive the approximately 35 miles in about 45 minutes or take a one-hour bus ride (buses run every 15 minutes). There is also railroad service between Puerto Cortés and Tela operating on Fridays and Sundays. The train leaves the Puerto Cortés railroad depot at 0700 and arrives in Tela at 1100, then leaves Tela at 1300 and arrives in Puerto Cortés at 1800

Marine Facilities

Boatyard

Puerto Cortés has a lot more to offer than just a bustling waterfront, one of the best things about Puerto Cortés is the Honduran Navy base where you can haul your boat very economically. The yard boasts a 100-ton *Travelift* and allows you to work on your own boat but if you plan to do that bring EVERYTHING

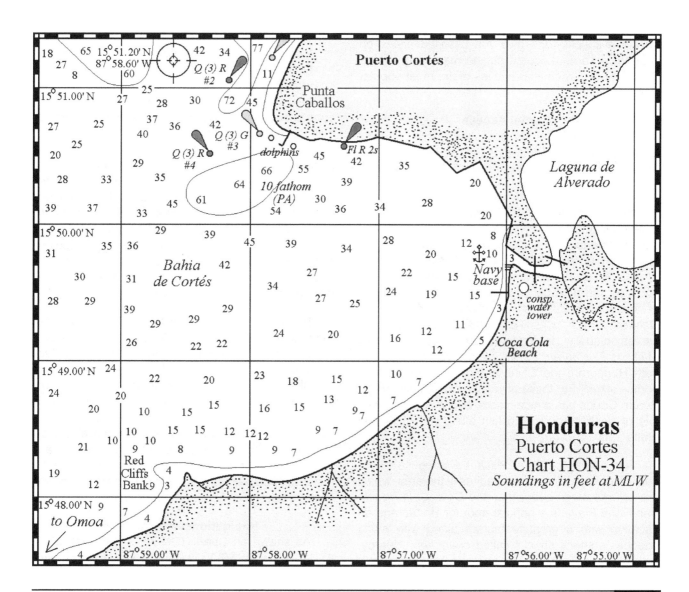

Honduras
Puerto Cortes
Chart HON-34
Soundings in feet at MLW

you need with you, nothing is available in Puerto Cortes except for basic hardware supplies, and don't forget at least one 100' extension cord with 15-amp ends (typical household ends in the United States).

If you wish to avail yourself of the boatyard, do not tie up at the Navy pier or enter the haul out area with your boat, they are guarded and you could, technically, be in violation of the law. It is best to dinghy in (and not to the Navy base) and walk up to the front gate of the base to make arrangements to haul your boat. English is not spoken here so please have an interpreter with you unless you have a good grasp of the Spanish language. Please note that the showers in the boatyard do not have hot water and that there is no pressure washer available in the yard.

Changing Money
In town you'll find *BGA* and *Banco Atlantido*, both of whom will exchange dollars for lempira, cash traveler's checks, and give you cash advances on your *VISA* card. Located on the main road by the docks are several mini-branches of the most popular Honduran banks.

Internet Access
If you need Internet access *Cheisser Internet* is one block east of *Wendy's*, while *Rudon's Cyber Mundo* is four blocks west.

Dining
Downtown there are numerous inexpensive eateries including a *Wendy's* and a *Pizza Hut* if you desire American fare. Without a doubt, the best restaurant in town is Matt's (2nd *Avenida* between 6th and 7th *Calle*) where the owners speak English and you can dine on large portions of fine seafood at moderate prices. A block away is *Restaurant Candiles*, which looks like an ordinary *champas*, but serves up quality Honduran cuisine. Just across from *Matt's* is *Restaurant Peking*, where you can dine on both Honduran and Chinese fare in three different portion sizes. For those of you who love such things, Puerto Cortés has a nice market every Saturday with lots of fresh produce and fish along with gifts and crafts.

Just past *Coca Cola Beach* is Cieneguita where you'll find some of the best beaches in the area, which are still not much better than the *Coca Cola Beach*. The *Hotel Playa* is a popular spot for Hondurans on vacation with a great restaurant along with many beachside snack shacks called *champas*. Nearby, the *Palmeras Beach Hotel* also has a good restaurant

with a variety of seafood dishes and a really good breakfast menu. If you'd like to take a tour of the area by mountain bike, see Roberto Alvarez Jr. at the *Hotel Playa* and he can arrange for you to visit his Honduras on first class bicycles. At the far end of the beach is the *Ancla Bar and Restaurant* serving good seafood dishes at moderate prices. Heading east from Puerto Cortés you will arrive at the Garifuna communities of Travesía and Bajamar, two of the most important Garifuna communities in Honduras. Bajamar has an annual Garifuna dance festival that is popular for locals and tourists alike. In Travesía, *Restaurante Fronteras del Caribe* sits under the palm trees on a lovely stretch of beach.

Omoa

Waypoints:
Omoa- ½ nm NW of Punta de Omoa
15°47.30' N, 88° 03.50' W

Omoa, only a few miles from the Honduran border at Tegucigalpita, is one of the oldest towns in Honduras and was once the site of a massive Spanish fortress, *El Castillo de San Fernando de Omoa*, the largest colonial-era fort that the Spanish built in Central America (constructed between 1752-1773). Originally constructed to protect the shipments of silver bound from the mines of Tegucigalpa to Spain, the fort was captured by a joint force (over 1,000 men) of British soldiers and Miskito Indians in 1779. In later years the fort was to fall into the hands of Spanish Loyalists, a force of Francisco Morazán's soldiers, and even a group of Guatemalan soldiers. After independence in 1821 the fortress was used as a jail (1853) and later abandoned. Today the fortress is a national monument and is open to the public.

Even with all her history, Omoa is often remembered today in an odd way, it is the locale where the S/V *Fantome* used to moor to take on passengers for cruises in the northwestern Caribbean. If you don't already know, the *Fantome* sank south of Guanaja during *Hurricane Mitch* in 1999. Today Omoa is a pretty laid back place with a few nice hotels and restaurants, nothing really fancy, just funky, and it's a favorite with backpackers and the site of an annual fishing tournament. If the wind is forecast to be westerly, this is not a good anchorage, you're better off at *Laguna el Diamante*.

Navigational Information
As shown on Chart HON-35, a waypoint at 15° 47.30' N, 88° 03.50' W, will place you approximately

½ mile west/northwest of Punta de Omoa. From this waypoint pass south of the point and angle in towards shore to anchor off the eastern shore of the bay as your draft allows but keeping a channel open to the town dock.

What You Will Find Ashore

Internet

Roli's has Internet access, nice rooms, laundry service, bikes for the use of the guests, and is a great place for information; speak to the Swiss owner, Rolan Gassman.

Dining

If you're looking for a place to eat, the beach area is wall-to-wall *champas*, eateries, and restaurants. One of the best of the "snack shacks" is located next to the *Flamingo Hotel*, the *Pulpería y Comida Rápida*. *Aquí Champa* and *Champa Johnson* are also worth mentioning and worthy of your business. But the best place in town to dine, in my humble opinion, is *Il Punto*, or *Punto Italian* as it's sometimes shown. Here you can feast on fine pastas and deli meats and sample the best of the owner's wine cellar. *Il Punto* is located near the beach just off the main road.

Vying for the title of best restaurant in Omoa is *Río Coto*, a branch of the restaurant of the same name located in nearby Río Coto, lying between Omoa and the Guatemalan border. *Donde Pancha* is a good local restaurant where the owner, Pancha, will personally cook your meal. Swiss owned, *El Botin Suizo* is also located on the beach and offers good food with a full bar. The big gringo hangout in Omoa is *El Paraíso de Stanley* and is open every day until the last customer leaves.

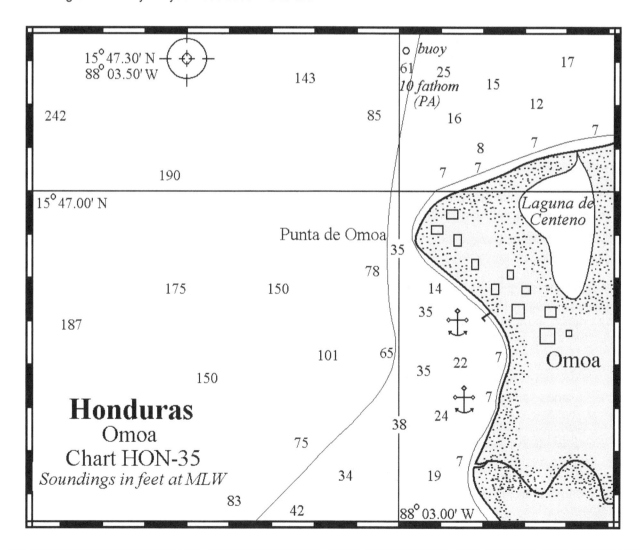

Honduras
Omoa
Chart HON-35
Soundings in feet at MLW

Republica de Guatemala

The Land of Eternal Spring

Port of Entry:
Livingston, Puerto Barrios
Fuel: Livingston, Río Dulce
Haul-Out: Río Dulce
Diesel Repairs: Río Dulce
Outboard Repairs: Río Dulce, Puerto Barrios
Propane: Río Dulce, Puerto Barrios
Provisions: Río Dulce, Livingston, Puerto Barrios
Time Zone: Central Time Zone
Electricity: 110 volt, 60 cycle
Important Lights: See Appendix A

Guatemala, or more precisely, the Republica de Guatemala, is often called *El Pais de la Eterna Primavera*, the *Land of Eternal Spring*, thanks entirely to its good weather that is enjoyed all year round. Almost every cruise to the Northwestern Caribbean focuses on Guatemala and the hurricane protection offered by the *Río Dulce* area from Livingston to Lago Izabal on Guatemala's Caribbean coast.

Guatemala's topography is volatile to say the least and offers several different landscapes along with volcanic activity and the occasional earthquake. The muggy Pacific coast of Guatemala is home to many black-sand beaches while just a little distance inland the Pacific coastal plain rises to a mountainous heartland where most of Guatemala's people reside. Here you'll find volcanoes and breathtaking mountain scenery.

The western highlands are home to more than 35 volcanoes that reach heights of over 12,400', some casting a red glow into the sky at night. The mountainous areas of Guatemala can be freezing at night during the winter even though Pacific coast temperatures may be in the 90s.

As the central mountains become hills once again to the east, they blend into a coastal plain on the Caribbean coast where you'll find mangrove swamps, banana plantations, and tropical growth such as palm trees nearly everywhere. To the north and northeast of the mountainous interior lies the huge, flat, virgin rainforest known as the Petén, the center of Mayan culture for centuries and the site of some episodes of the TV show *Survivor* that aired in September of 2005. The show was filmed at Yaxha,

between Flores and Melchor de Mencos. Three "lost cities" were found in the Petén over the last few years, one of which, Wakná, was only recently discovered by satellite imagery. The Petén is one of the best preserved rainforests in Latin America and is home to a variety of wildlife including jaguars, ocelots, tapirs, and a variety of monkeys and avian life including parrots and storks. Further south, near Cobán, you can attempt to get a glimpse of the very elusive and rare *Quetzal,* the national bird of Guatemala. The Petén has only two seasons, hot and dry or hot and humid, many will say that is true of all of Guatemala, but it's not. The highlands are usually very cool, even in the hottest part of summer, and rarely does one need air-conditioning there. In reality though, the dry season is from November through May and the rains can be counted on from June through November.

The highest point in Guatemala is at the top of *Volcan Tajumulco* at 4,211 meters. The peak is one of an estimated 38 volcanoes of which 3 are active, *Fuego*, *Pacaya*, and *Santiaguito* (although one volcano near Antigua just became active in 2003). *Volcan de Agua* is easily seen from Guatemala City and is located very close to Antigua, and from *Lago Atitlán* you can easily see three volcanoes, *Atitlán*, *San Pedro*, and *Tolimán*, all inactive. The Guatemalan volcanoes are the highest and most active in Central America and the accompanying earthquakes can be the most devastating although it's unlikely that you'll ever notice one if you're on the *Río Dulce*.

Guatemala is divided up into 22 departments (*departmentos*), roughly the equivalent of a state. The *Río Dulce* is located in the department known as Izabal, sometimes referred to as the *Jade Coast*. Guatemala's people, nearly 14,000,000 of them, are primarily a blending of two cultures, most noticeably the Maya, the most ancient and distinctive culture in Central America, and the Ladinos, equal in numbers to the Maya yet more urban and commercial. Besides the Maya and the Ladinos you'll likely meet Garifunas (along the Caribbean coast) along with a smattering of Chinese and non-Maya Xincas as well as a hefty group of ex-pat Americans and Europeans.

An estimated 80% of Guatemala's people live in the southern part of the country while the more northern and eastern areas are more thinly populated. In the central highlands you will find that the Maya dominate the mountainous areas as well as northwestern Guatemala and to an extent the Petén region as well. And you really won't get an idea of the nature of the people of Guatemala by judging those you meet in the capitol, Guatemala City, or even those you'll meet in *Río Dulce*. To find the true nature of Guatemala's people visit the smaller communities and places like Panajachel or Antigua where the people are warm, affectionate, and you'll even see lovers walking hand in hand down the city's streets.

After you arrive in Guatemala and settle in on the *Río Dulce*, you'll want to take several land trips to visit the true heart and soul of this wonderful country. You'll want to visit the Mayan ruins at Tikal, Quirigúa, and Copán in Honduras, the breathtaking colors of the Sunday morning market at Chichicastenango, *Lago Atitlán*, *Semana Santo* (*Holy Week*) in Antigua, Las Verapaces for nature herself (including whitewater rafting and views of the elusive *Quetzal*, the national bird of Guatemala), the beaches, fishing, and surfing of the Pacific coast, and the tarp covered market in Morales where you can get lost in the maze of sheltered alleys, all this and so much more.

On a final note, medical care is very good in Guatemala, and if you don't have medical insurance the hospitals will usually accept you with payment up front and the bill will be a fraction (about US$750 for an appendectomy) of what it would be in the United States (where it can be difficult to even get a doctor to see you if you're a new patient).

Customs and Immigration

Before we begin our discussion of Guatemala's regulations concerning clearing in and out, let me touch upon the "CA-4 Agreement." The agreement, developed between the nations of Guatemala, Honduras, El Salvador, and Nicaragua, was implemented in the summer of 2006 and allows free travel of CA-4 citizens amongst all four countries. However, Americans and all other foreign nationals will now be granted one 90-day stay in the CA-4 countries, with only one 90-day extension permitted by visiting the *Immigration* office of any CA-4 country, and will no longer be granted a new 90-day stay as tourists crossing any border between the CA-4 countries. You must leave a CA-4 country for 72 hours to be permitted to return and gain a new Visa.

A tourist visa card must be purchased on entry. This new CA-4 visa applies to the following countries:- Guatemala, El Salvador, Honduras, and Nicaragua. The length of stay (normally 90 days) applies to the whole group and only one extension will usually be

granted. To remain in the region longer, a visit to a country outside the CA-4 area (at least three days out of a CA-4 country) must be made and a new visa will be issued on re-entry.

Although the CA-4 agreement was agreed to by the participating countries it is often not enforced for U.S. passport holders. A weekend trip to Copan to view the ruins will get you another 90 days as you return to Guatemala. A trip to Belize or Honduras for lunch will to the same when you return to Guatemala.

A final note, look for a Port Captain's office to be constructed in *Río Dulce* in the near future.

Clearing In at Livingston

Most cruisers clear at Livingston but you can no longer clear in or out of Livingston on Sundays as the officials take that day off. A word of warning, you'll need to change some dollars into Quetzales before you visit *Immigration*. The bank in Livingston has moved further up the street on the right and the ATM is usually out of service, so if you need Q's and the ATM isn't working then you have to visit the bank with your passport and credit card and they will give you enough money to handle your clearance, but that is all. If you still don't have enough then speak with Raul (if he is doing your paperwork-see next paragraph) and you can usually work something out.

For those of you who have been to Livingston before, Raul Morales Veliz is no longer the *Customs* officer in Livingston, he is now the proud owner of *Naviera Servimar,* also in Livingston. Raul's office is on the second floor of the yellow building behind and to the left of *La Buga Mama*, a short walk from the main dock (no, you won't have to walk all the way up the hill). Internet service and cold drinks are available while you wait for Raul to handle all the legwork of clearing in or out as well as passport extensions. For more information you can phone Raul at 7947-0888 or 5510-9104, or email him at navieraservimar@ gmail.com.

If there are a number of boats waiting to check in at Livingston, six or more, those vessels that use Raul for an agent will be serviced first while all other boats will have to wait until after lunch. This is important if you wish to get upriver before nightfall. Once a month (this is announced on the daily VHF net) Raul comes to *RAM Marine* and handles boat extensions and passport renewals.

The phone number for *Aduana* (*Customs*) in Livingston is 502-7947-0073. The phone number for the *Port Captain* in Livingston is 502-7947-0029.

Customs

When you arrive at Livingston to clear in you must first call *El Capitan de el Puerto de Livingston* on VHF ch. 16. He'll give you instructions on how to come in and clear, actually he and his entourage will come to your boat first. Cruising yachts will be issued 3 months stay on arrival with a special permit consisting of a sticker that must be displayed prominently on the boat. The sticker will be attached by the *Customs* officer in the first port of entry. Extensions for boat navigational permits cost US$150 for an additional 9 months. After the initial 12 months, you may obtain a permit for an additional 12 months for US$150 for an indefinite number of years. Vessels are required to be located in an *INGUATE* registered marina.

Immigration

Guatemala changed their visa regulations in 1996 and today citizens of most countries no longer need a visa. Depending on your country of origin *Immigration* will grant stays of 30-90 days that can be extended by application at least one month prior to expiration. You will be expected to bring a clearance from your last port of call. You'll also need to request a cruising permit showing where you intend to visit.

Current *Immigration* documents now come in 90 day and 12 month versions (*Immigration* no longer issues the 9 month document). Passports should always be carried if travelling inland. Prior visas are not required by nationals of the European Union, Argentina, Australia, Belize, Canada, Costa Rica, Ecuador, El Salvador, Honduras, Israel, Japan, New Zealand, Nicaragua, Norway, Switzerland, and the USA.

Firearms

Cruisers will need to declare all firearms upon entry to Guatemala. Firearms will be held by police or the port captain during the stay in port.

Fees

The clearance fees are as follows:
Check In
US$50.00 Cruising Permit
Q 60.00 Customs
Q 225.00 Immigration
Q 175.00 Port Captain
Q 100.00 Doctor
Check Out.

Q 160.00 Immigration 2 persons
Q 25.00 Customs
Q 165.00 Port Captain
The fees shown apply only to Monday-Friday clearance; on Saturdays a Q100 overtime fee will be applied. There is a daily fine for overstaying one's permitted time.

Pets

Animals must be declared and have up-to-date health certificates. They are not permitted to land.

Clearing Out

The law states that your boat MUST leave Guatemala after its one-year extension is expired, but if it cannot for some reason, you must meet with the *Port Captain* in Livingston and have a legitimate reason why it cannot leave. You can have someone with your power of attorney handle the extensions for you. Only approved marinas such as *Bruno's* can do this at this time; *Tortugal* and *Tijax* can handle the matter as well but they have to go through an approved agent. Although the law states that you must be in a marina for your one year extension, some cruisers at anchor use the agent as well.

When you are planning to leave the *Río Dulce* you should once again contact Raul and let him do the legwork for you. If you are staying at the *Amatique Bay Marina & Resort* in Puerto Barrios and wish to clear out, you can call Raul (he lives in Puerto Barrios, 7947-0888 or 5510-9104, or email him at navieraservimar@gmail.com.), and he will come to the marina to pick up your paperwork and bring it back to you that night or the next day.

Visiting the Sapodilla Cays

Vessels that have cleared into Guatemala can now leave the *Río Dulce* if they are only visiting the Sapodilla Cays and return to the *Río Dulce* without having to check into another country. Vessels must go through normal check out procedures and when they arrive in the Sapodilla Cays must have a ranger sign their *Zarpe* so they can return to Livingston and check back in. This procedure saves the expense and time involved with clearing into and out of Belize.

Ports of Entry:
(Caribbean Coast)

Livingston (closed on Sundays), Puerto Barrios, Santo Tomás de Castilla (the officials here usually direct yachts to Livingston or Puerto Barrios

Security

A cruising guide to Guatemala would be incomplete without a section on security precautions to take while in the country. Not that Guatemala is inherently any more dangerous than any other place such as New York or Los Angeles, but crime is not unknown here though most of it is carried out by Guatemalans on Guatemalans.

The place where crime is most rampant is in Guatemala City. The city is divided into zones, zonas, and several zones such as *Zona 5* and *Zona 8* are not to be ventured into by gringos in the daytime much less the nighttime. *Zona 10*, the hotel zone, is probably the safest zone of all and I frequently will stroll there at night with no worries.

If you come across a political gathering or demonstration it's best to avoid it, you, as a foreigner, will stick out as if you were painted pink from head to toe, and who knows, the demonstration may be against what you might stand for, so for safety's sake try to avoid such gatherings.

Semana Santo, *Holy Week*, is the biggest religious holiday of the year in Antigua, and you can be sure the pickpockets will be out in force.

One last word, so as not to incite the locals, it's not a good idea to take photos of children without asking their parent's permission. Unfortunately there are rumors floating around about foreigners abducting children in the more remote areas.

Those bound for the *Río Dulce* usually clear at Livingston. I suggest that if possible you should anchor at Tres Puntas and head to Livingston at first light to clear as early in the morning as you can spending the rest of the day working your way up the *Río Dulce* to El Golfete, perhaps *Texan Bay*. Do not anchor overnight in Livingston! If you do spend the night in Livingston be sure that anything left on deck is locked because the chances are good it won't be there in the morning if it's not chained and locked. This included dinghies in davits and motors mounted on the pulpit railing.

A Brief History

The history of Guatemala is thick with conflict, racism, strife, revolution, coups, counter-coups, civilian massacres, and even a U.S./CIA backed invasion. Guatemala has only recently, within the last decade, made progress towards peace, and the tale begins long, long ago.

The earliest settlers of *Mesoamerica*, that part of the North American continent known as Central America stretching from north central Mexico to Panama, were the descendants of the first arrivals in North America, Stone Age hunter-gatherers who came to this continent via the Bering land bridge between Siberia and Alaska some 25,000 years ago.

The first settlers of which there is any physical proof were the *Clovis* named after the location of a find of stone spear tips at Clovis, New Mexico, who settled in the central highlands of Guatemala somewhere between 11,000-9,000 B.C. The physical proof, a collection of stone tools and spear tips, is dated to 10,000 B.C.-9,000 B.C., but it is speculated the *Clovis* had actually been residing in Guatemala for some 1,000-2,000 years prior to that.

A recognizable pattern of settlements has been traced to as early as 8,000 B.C., just as mankind was making the shift from hunting to a more agrarian way of life as the ice age was retreating and larger game was rapidly becoming scarce with the warming climate. This period, known as the *Archaic*, was to last until about 1,800 B.C. and saw the development and domestication of plants such as corn, peppers, beans, and squash. At this time, the Petén, now a rainforest, was an area of savannahs and woodlands, a perfect land for the burgeoning Mayan culture's *Pre-Classic period* (2,000 B.C. to 1500 B.C.). For a more detailed history of the Maya, see the section *The Maya* in the chapter *The Local Cultures*.

By 2,000 B.C., fishing and farming villages were prevalent on Guatemala's Pacific coast and were the forerunners of the great Mayan civilization which dominated Central America for centuries. By 1,000 B.C., the *Olmecs*, Mesoamerica's "mother culture," began constructing ceremonial pyramid-like structures in Central America and their work has been found along Guatemala's Pacific coast as well as at Copán in Honduras and even as far south as El Salvador.

During the Maya's *Middle Pre-Classic Period*, from around 1,000-300 B.C., the Mayan population was growing, particularly in the Petén, and what may have been the first Mayan city was built at Nakbé, which dominated the Mayan civilization until about 100 B.C. when the focus shifted to El Mirador in the northern part of the Petén. The only rival El Mirador had was Kaminaljuyú, a city built on the site where modern day Guatemala City is located.

The greatest question concerning the Maya themselves, is what happened to them? Towards the end of the *Late Pre-Classic Period* (200-300 A.D.), El Mirador, the greatest city in the Mayan world was abandoned sometime around 250 A.D. and conjecture as to why is all we have. Was it disease, famine, warfare? Nobody knows for certain but evidence points to a long, dry climatic period. To the south the *Ilopango* volcano in El Salvador erupted and covered much of that region in ash forcing the abandonment of Kaminaljuyú around the same time as El Mirador. The Pacific trade routes were disrupted and normal trade now focused more to the north bringing more of a Mexican influence to the cities of the Petén.

At this time *Mesoamerica* enters the Mayan *Classic Period*, their greatest period of achievement which is introduced by the creation of a calendar and a system of writing. Northward, in Mexico, sat Teotihuacán, a city of some 250,000 people with a dominant, and sometimes violent nature. Teotihuacán spread her influence from Mexico southwards into Honduras and even rebuilt Kaminaljuyú in Teotihuacán style.

But even for all that, the two truly dominant Mayan cultures at that time were centered at Tikal in Guatemala's Petén, which had aligned itself with Teotihuacán, and Calakmul located in the Campeche region of Mexico. These two cities dominated the region around the 500 A.D. and struggled with each other for trading rights which eventually led to open warfare. Calakmul finally made an alliance with the Maya at Caracol (in present day Belize) and defeated Tikal in 562 A.D. But Tikal was not through and in 695 A.D. they managed to defeat and overrun Calakmul and once that was done the Mayan culture under Tikal began to flourish as never before with new cities springing up all across Mayan territory, but within a century, by about 750 A.D., social and political changes were being felt as trade declined and more and more cities were abandoned.

The collapse of Teotihuacán in the 7th century sent shock waves through the peoples of *Mesoamerica* as cultural and scientific advancement became mired in what is known as the *Middle Classic Hiatus*. New kings and warlords strove to make their cities the dominant centers of the Mayan civilization after the loss of the Teotihuacán culture as the Mayan culture flourished despite broad-based internal conflicts and revolts.

By 850 A.D., militaristic outsiders had set up their own settlements along the *Río Usamacinta* on what is today the border between Mexico and Guatemala. These were the years of the Mayan decline, the end of the *Classic Period*, and the emergence of the *Post-Classic Period* which spanned the years from 900 A.D. until the time of the Spanish Conquest in the 1500s. At this time some of the Petén Maya fled into nearby Belize and the Yucatán, while most headed south into the Guatemalan highlands to the south. These areas were made up of many fragmented groups of Maya and strife and disorder was rampant in the numerous small, scattered Mayan settlements.

By the end of the 1200s, the once-great Mayan cities of Chichen Itza and Uxmal in the Yucatán, which were inhabited by the Toltec-Maya, were abandoned. Shortly thereafter the Guatemalan central highlands were invaded by a group of Toltec-Maya which radically altered life in the region. The highlands had been populated by a peaceful, spiritual group of Maya and the militaristic Toltec-Maya soon set up a series of competing "empires" dominated by the K'iché Maya, who were located in the central highlands and still abound today (you'll sometimes see K'iche spelled Quiché, this is because the area they settled in is called Quiché-there are many Mayan dialects spoken amongst today's Maya in Guatemala, but *K'iché* is the most common, especially along the *Río Dulce*). The Toltecs controlled the more dominant tribes such as the K'iché, the Mam, the Kaqchikel, and the Tz'utujil establishing a new hierarchy and bringing with them new gods and a new language that blended with those of the Guatemalan Maya.

Beginning around 1400 A.D., the K'iché, under the direction of the Toltec-Maya, began to exert their influence in the area and by the latter part of the 1400s controlled some one million people, completely dominating the once powerful Mam and Kaqchikel. In 1475, the great K'iché king Cuicab, the man who has been described as the mastermind of the K'iché expansion, passed away and with him went much of the K'iché authority. Soon various conquered tribes of Maya began to break away from K'iché control and for the next half-century the various Mayan tribes in Guatemala were locked in constant conflict with one another as their settlements reflected defensive positions as opposed to a setting better suited to an agrarian subsistence.

In 1521, Spanish invaders under the leadership of Hernán Cortés took the Aztec capital of Tenochtitlán in Mexico and in 1523, Cortés dispatched Pedro de Alvarado to Guatemala to use "minimum force" and to "preach matters concerning our Holy Faith." De Alvarado and his army of over 600 soldiers and horsemen engaged a huge K'iché force estimated at 30,000 under the command of Tecún Umán near the deserted Mayan city of Xelajú. The well-armed warriors of de Alvarado were decimating the Mayan fighters when the battle suddenly ended as de Alvarado killed Tecún Umán in hand-to-hand combat. The K'iché were defeated but the Kaqchikel decided to form an alliance of sorts with the Spanish allowing the Spanish to establish their first base in Guatemala next to the Kaqchikel capital of Iximché In 1526, the Kaqchikel broke away from their Spanish allies and moved deeper into the mountains and began to wage a guerilla style war forcing the Spanish to move their base to present day Antigua where they established the first capital of Guatemala, Santiago de los Caballeros on *St. Cecelia's Day*, November 22, 1527.

De Alvarado's army continued to fight battle after battle with the highland Maya but the Spaniards never gained control over the more remote regions. In 1537, the Church stepped in and succeeded where de Alvarado failed. Missionaries under the guidance of Bartolemé de las Casas convinced the renegade Maya to accept both Christianity and Spanish sovereignty and by 1540 the last of the highland Maya were brought under Spanish control. Years later de Alvarado, who had controlled Guatemala like his personal fiefdom, enslaving and abusing the Maya and turning their lands into Spanish estates, was killed beneath a rolling horse during a battle in Mexico.

As Guatemala entered her period of Spanish Colonial rule, the capital city of Santiago de los Caballeros entered a prolonged period of mourning initiated by de Alvarado's widow, Beatriz de la Cueva (de Alvarado's first wife's sister), who had herself appointed the new governor and then painted the entire palace black, inside and out. On September 10, 1541, a huge mudslide flowed down the sides of the Aqua volcano and buried the city. The survivors moved the city a short distance away and the new Santiago de los Caballeros became the administrative center for six provinces, Costa Rica, Honduras, Nicaragua, El Salvador, Guatemala, and Chiapas, now part of Mexico (Santiago de los Caballeros was to rule Guatemala until 1773 when it was destroyed by

a series of earthquakes and the capital again moved, this time to what is now known as Guatemala City).

Along with the Spanish, the most powerful force in Guatemala was the Catholic Church whose Franciscan friars first arrived here with de Alvarado in 1523. By 1532, the Franciscans had company, the Jesuits, the Dominicans, and Mercedarians. Guatemala's first Bishop, Francisco Marroquín, awarded these early missionaries huge tracts of land and indigenous peoples as slaves to farm those lands and earn huge tax-exempt incomes for their owners. This was just the beginning of the exploitation of the Maya which has endured even until this century. In the highlands, scattered Mayan villages were relocated and between 1543 and 1600, some 700 new settlements were constructed, each centered around a Catholic church. Local farmers were pressed for tithes and the new Mayan converts to Catholicism found that their labor was exploited and would remain so for centuries.

The office of the *Inquisition* was set up in Santiago de los Caballeros, and between 1570-1582, religious persecution was at its height, but little is known of the exact nature of the *Inquisition* in Guatemala as no records were kept. By the latter part of the 1700s, the Spanish Crown grew tired of the Church's uncontrolled abuse of power and wealth in her lands and began to limit the Church's power and impose taxes on her religious orders and the conflict reached a climax in 1767, when Carlos III ordered the Jesuits banned from all Spanish colonies

Finding little silver and no gold in Guatemala, the colonial economy here was agrarian based with the largest crops being tobacco, cacao, chicle, cotton, and the most valuable of all, indigo, while on coastal ranches a few cattle were raised. The labor force for the Spanish ruling class came by way of a system of *repartamientos* whereby indigenous Maya were transported to the plantations of the Pacific coast as slave labor. In the central highlands, the Maya were going through many cultural changes dictated by their Spanish lords even as diseases brought to Guatemala by the Spaniards ravaged the Mayan population, in some places taking 50%-90% of the people. All in all, the two centuries of Spanish colonial rule transformed Guatemala and her people, creating a new economy, new cities, a new religion, and an extremely racist hierarchy, but in all fairness to the Maya, their culture persevered, they refused to be wiped out, they absorbed what the Spanish dealt to them and came out as strong as ever.

During the Spanish colonial period, Guatemala's wealth and power was concentrated in the hands of those who were actually born in Spain, the *chapetones*, while those born of Spanish blood who were born in Guatemala, the *Creoles*, and those of mixed blood, the *Mestizos*, were left wanting, and the indigenous Maya were so far removed from wealth and power as to be non-existent. But change was in the air.

In the chaos that followed Napoleon's invasion of Spain an air of reform swept through the Spanish colonies, but the *chapetones* and the Church resisted change, they wanted to maintain the status they so enjoyed. On September 15, 1821, Brigadier Don Gabino Gainza, the last of Spain's Captain Generals in the New World, signed a formal *Act of Independence* which maintained the status quo under new leadership and even recognized the power of the Catholic Church (the first of many *Declarations of Independence* that Guatemala was to endure). Hearing of this, the Emperor of Mexico, Augustín de Iturbide, sent troops into Guatemala to annex the new nation, but this union lasted less than one year.

In 1823, a second *Act of Independence* (which sought to abolish slavery and create new, liberal reforms) joined together several Central American states into a rather loose federation modeled after the United States of America. The first president was a Salvadoran General named Manuel José Acre, who, after a bitter feud with his own party, broke away to try to form his own government which inspired others to do the same as a group of liberals from El Salvador, Honduras, and Guatemala united under the leadership of Honduran General Francisco Morazán. Under Morazán's leadership, Mariano Gálvez became the leader of Guatemala and many reforms took place during his watch; religious orders were abolished, the death penalty was dropped, and Gálvez instituted trial by jury, a school system, and a new law code.

While all this was going on rebellion was brewing in the mountains. While Guatemala was struggling for independence and those of Spanish blood were finding new prosperity, the Maya in the highlands were struggling for their very survival. Besides having to bear the burden of two centuries of harsh Spanish colonial rule, a cholera epidemic in 1823 killed thousands and only added to the Maya's misery. A young leader emerged, the illiterate but charismatic Rafael Carrera, who led the Maya on a march on Guatemala City. Now in command, Carrera recognized only one authority, the Church, and his reforms cast aside the more liberal reforms of Gálvez as religious orders were restored and the more traditional Spanish titles were reinstated. The conservatives sided with Carrera for they knew he would support their unpopular positions. Under Carrera, Guatemala fought a long and costly war with Morazán and his federation eventually proclaiming Guatemalan independence in 1847. For a short period in 1867, Carrera had to deal with an internal uprising as the western state of Los Altos declared their independence in defiance of the new Guatemalan leader; the revolt ended in a short while and Los Altos returned to the republic.

Following Cerrera's death in 1865, several liberal uprisings took place under the leadership of men such as Serpio Cruz (who was captured and executed in 1870), Francisco Cruz, and the very successful Justo Rufino Barrios who was active in suppressing the Los Altos revolt of 1867. Barrios left Mexico and entered Guatemala in early 1871, with an army of 45 men which grew day by day until Barrios took Guatemala City on June 30 of that year. Miguel García Granados became the new leader of the republic and Barrios the Commander in Chief. Granados was soon overthrown by a revolt and Barrios returned to Guatemala City in 1872 and installed his troops in the local barracks and set up elections which Barrios himself won.

A bit of a tyrant and egotist, Barrios set out to revitalize the school system and clamped down on the Church and her activities prompting his excommunication and Barrios' subsequent expulsion of the Archbishop from Guatemala. The military and police thrived under Barrios as the railroad and telegraph were introduced to Guatemala, but his greatest reform was the restructuring of Guatemala's agricultural economy and the emergence of coffee as a principal export (which brought a huge boom to the economy and in turn helped to reshape the country).

Most of the new coffee plantations were owned and operated by Germans and most of the coffee was exported to Germany. The new German society was welcomed with open arms while the Maya were still considered little more than a labor force. Although most of the Germans were forced to leave Guatemala during World War II, their impact can still be felt today in the Verapaz highlands.

As a result of the coffee boom, many Mayans lost their lands, and some their freedom, as the government began to confiscate unused or communally owned lands in 1873, to sell to the highest bidder. If that were not bad enough, in 1876, Barrios ordered community leaders to supply a work force for the plantations, up to ¼ of the local male population were sent to the plantations as little more than slave labor. Soon, highland villagers rose up in revolts that lasted into the early years of the 20th century, and many Maya had their villages burned to the ground while their leaders were executed, and isolated incidents like this were to re-occur periodically even until more recent years.

Barrios sought U.S, assistance in solving the border dispute with Mexico, a dispute that some of Barrios' detractors claimed was centered more on Barrio's personal holdings than Guatemalan territorial rights. Even as Mexican troops entered Guatemala to seize the disputed lands of Chiapas and Soconusco, Barrios was leading his army into El Salvador where he was killed at Chalchuapa on April 2, 1885 while attempting to realign El Salvador with his views of a unified Central America.

Barrios tenure was followed by several shorter terms while the next major player on the Guatemalan power scene was Manuel José Estrada Cabrera, who was elected in 1898 and overthrown in 1920 after a financial crisis and several assassination attempts. However, during the years under Cabrera, Guatemala made advances in public health, construction, agriculture, and education (although teachers were forbidden to criticize Cabrera's administration), but by the time of his downfall Cabrera was on the verge of insanity and was forced to leave the country.

The most important event to occur during the Cabrera years was the emergence of the United Fruit Company in Guatemala. The United Fruit Company had its origins in Costa Rica years before when Minor Keith was contracted to build a railroad from San José to the Pacific coast. Short on funds Keith sought to raise capital by growing bananas on land granted to him for the railroad. So profitable was his newfound business venture that he soon merged his Tropical Trading and Transport Company with rival Boston Fruit Company and thus was born the United Fruit Company. In 1901, United Fruit bought a small

tract of land in Guatemala and in 1904 was awarded a contract to complete a railroad from Guatemala City to Puerto Barrios with provisos granting the company 100' on either side of the railroad tracks, no taxes for 99 years, a promise that the government would not interfere with United Fruit Company activities, and company acquisition of the Pacific railway in 1912 (although United Fruit did help build some schools in Guatemala, the company was opposed to building highways because they would compete with their railroad monopoly). In this manner United Fruit gained a monopoly over transport in Guatemala as they already controlled the port at Puerto Barrios.

Suddenly banana cultivation boomed and by 1934 United Fruit controlled massive amounts of land in Guatemala (UFC controlled over 40% of the country's best lands) and was exporting 3.5 million bunches of bananas annually while employing some 25,000 Guatemalans. But United Fruit was not just a banana exporter, their reach extended into many layers of Guatemala's economy and political circles as well as neighboring Honduras and was soon the largest coffee exporter as well. So long were United Fruit's arms that they were known as el pulpo, the octopus. United Fruit was exempt from almost all taxes and completely controlled the roads in Guatemala along with the country's only Caribbean port. So successful was United Fruit from an economic standpoint that in the years from 1900-1930, their profits doubled 14 times.

Cabrera's successor, Carlos Herrera, sought to terminate United Fruit Company contracts which as you may suspect did not go over well. Herrera's tenure lasted little more than a year before he was replaced by General José María Orellano in December of 1921. Orellano had an ambitious young man as his Minister of War, Jorge Ubico, who had some 290 political opponents killed in 1926, the same year Orellano died of a heart attack. Following Orellano's death a fierce power struggle ensued between Ubico and Lazaro Chacón which the radical Chacón won handily. Chacón was soon caught in a bitter fight between Guatemala's farmers and the United Fruit Company and eventually died of a stroke in 1930 setting the stage for the re-emergence of the charismatic Jorge Ubico, the godson of Rufino Barrios.

Ubico's first crisis was Guatemala's economy which was hit hard by the depression and he opened tariff-free trade agreements with the United States who pressured him to expel Guatemala's German population in the years leading up to World War II. Ubico initiated sweeping internal reforms including a massive road building program as well as crackdown on corruption and as he was known to be a friend to big business, he also assisted the *United Fruit Company* in their times of need by replacing the debt peonage system with a new vagrancy law the required landless peasants to work 150 days a year. Further laws that benefited the land owning elite included the right to shoot vandals and poachers on their properties which helped lead to more working class uprisings in the 1930s and 1940s.

It is suggested that Ubico had some mental problems, that he was paranoid and claimed he was the reincarnation of Napoleon Bonaparte. Ubico set up an intricate network of spies and informers who were especially active in the prelude to an election year. When an assassination plot was discovered in 1934, Ubico had some 300 people killed in just two days. Unable to stem the rising tide of discontent, Ubico was forced to resign in 1944 after a series of violent uprisings by the *October Revolutionaries*, a group of young, dissident military officers, students, and liberal professionals. Ubico was succeeded by Juan Frederico Ponce Viades who he was hardly any better than his predecessor and within a year faced a violent revolt and fled the country along with Ubico as Guatemalans demanded democracy and freedom. A joint military/civilian junta took over power in what was called "the handover" and in March, 1945, a new constitution was introduced which included suffrage for all adults while prohibiting all future Presidents from a second term. This began what was known as the *Ten Years of Spring*, a period of free speech and political activity, land reform, and forward progress for the republic.

A civilian president, Juan José Arévalo, was elected in 1945 and held the presidency until 1951 (surviving some 25 coup attempts) establishing a social security system in Guatemala as well as health reforms. There were two rivals for power following the Arévalo years, Colonel Francisco Arana and Colonel Jacobo Arbenz Guzmán, both of whom were members of the military junta that took power after Ubico's years. Arana was assassinated and of course suspicion fell upon Guzmán, but no charges were brought against him. Guzmán won the election with 65% of the vote and soon set in place his own socialist reforms, not the least of which was a new roadway to compete with the *United Fruit* railroad,

and the design of a new port next to Puerto Barrios (to also compete with *United Fruit* who owned the Puerto Barrios). Guzmán also initiated a series of lawsuits against foreign firms in Guatemala for unpaid taxes, irritating the Unites States and the major corporations that had a huge stake in Guatemala. Guzmán further antagonized foreign interests with his *Law of Agrarian Reform* in 1952, which allocated unused lands owned to be distributed to the landless peasants causing the *United Fruit Company* to lose some 15% of their land holdings in Guatemala, the first time since the arrival of the Spanish that a Guatemalan ruler offered something back to the masses. But the final nail in Guzmán's coffin came about when he granted the communist *Guatemalan Labor Party* legal status (in all fairness, Arbenz' government was not Communist, but it was certainly anti-American). This greatly upset the U.S. government who denounced the communist tendencies of the Guatemalan government and decided that the Guzmán government had to be overthrown.

In 1953, President Eisenhower okayed plans to overthrow the Guzmán government and the *CIA* hastily put together a small army of mercenaries in Honduras (*Operation PBSUCCESS*) with plans to invade Guatemala (as if it were a coincidence, the new *CIA* director, Allen Dulles, was also a member of the board of the *United Fruit Company*, who helped in their own way to engineer the coup). Many Guatemalan civilian and military leaders backed the U.S. stance and recognized Guzmán as a menace and the Guatemalan Army refused to defend the Guzmán government when the U.S. backed coup led by Col. Carlos Castillo Armas succeeded in taking control of the government from Guzmán. Guzmán knew the Guatemalan Army would not come to his aid so he purchased a huge supply of Czech arms that he was going to use to arm the people who supported him, but the arms shipment was intercepted at sea before it could arrive at Puerto Barrios. On June 27, 1953, Guzmán relinquished the presidency to Colonel Carlos Enrique Díaz the Guatemalan Army Chief of Staff, just as the *CIA* backed forces approached Guatemala City.

The military took control of the Guatemalan government after the overthrow (and immediately began receiving U.S. aid) and was to retain control for some thirty years as the economy dwindled and violence grew. In 1954, the U.S.-backed Castillo Armas was elected President and the gains the Mayans made were wiped away as Ladinos returned to the power structure. Armas revoked the constitution of 1945 and replaced it with a more restrictive version that outlawed left-wing parties, which in turn brought about the execution of large numbers of unionists and reformers. Armas surrounded himself with old-style Ubico supporters and all the lands that had been taken from *United Fruit* and given to the Maya were returned. Periodic rumors of coups plagued Armas' term until finally he was shot by his own bodyguard in 1957.

After a few months of turmoil General Ydígoras Fuentes took power and his extremely autocratic rule led to a failed coup by junior military officers in 1960. The officers, led by Marco Yon Sosa and Turcios Lima, escaped and went into hiding in the eastern highlands, establishing close ties with Cuba and forming the nucleus of the armed revolts that were to plague the Guatemalan government for the next 36 years. Ydígoras Fuentes was overthrown in 1963 and the U.S. (with the approval of JFK), fearful of another socialist government taking control, backed another military coup in which the Army again took over control under the leadership of Peralta Azurdia.

Azurdia was to rule for only three years, but during that time the Army came under nearly constant attack from guerilla fighters led by Sosa and Lima who had been trained in counterinsurgency by the U.S. when they were still in the fold. The *PGT*, the *Guatemalan Labor Party* aligned itself with a new party, the *FAR*, *Rebel Armed Forces*, Sosa and Lima's guerilla army representatives who advocated a return to the rule of Juan José Arévalo.

The elections of 1966 were won by Julio César Méndez Montenegro who was forced to sign a pact with the Army agreeing to stay out of their affairs, follow Army instructions, and allow the military a free hand in all matters of national security. Montenegro's first act as President was to offer a general amnesty for all guerillas which was immediately rejected by Sosa and Lima and new anti-Army campaigns begun. Failing to quell rebel activity in that manner, the Guatemalan Army developed a unit that terrorized the local peoples who were suspected of aiding the rebels. That, combined with the death of Lima in a car crash was the killing blow to the rebels in the eastern highlands and their focus shifted to the area around Guatemala City where the U.S. Ambassador, John Gordon Mein, was assassinated by *FAR* rebels in 1968. Although the government of Montenegro was aligned with the more socialist views of Arévalo

and Arbenz, the Army had true control and when the military joined with the right-wing *MLN*, political assassinations became commonplace as death squads such as the *Mano Blanco* and the *Ojo por Ojo* had free reign to kill peasants, students, unionists, and academics as Guatemala entered another two decades of political strife, electoral fraud, and violence.

During the years from the late 1960s to the early 1990s Guatemala's economy prospered but little wealth trickled down to the poorer classes. There was no fine line between the ruling elite and the poor who had no access to health care or education but were still being pressed into labor in the plantations. In 1970, right-winger Colonel Arana Osorio was elected President by a vote estimated to be only 4% of the entire voting-age population. Osorio's first act as President was to go on an anti-guerilla campaign stating "...if it is necessary to run the country into a cemetery in order to pacify it, I will not hesitate to do so." Before long the death squads reached new heights of violence in retaliation for rebel attacks on government installations and even members of the government.

A new group surfaced at this time, the *URNG*, *Guatemalan National Revolutionary Unity*, which was countered by a group of right-wing vigilantes called the *ESA*, the *Secret Anti-Communist Army*, which was responsible, along with the *Blanco Mano*, for the torture and murder of thousands of students, professionals, and peasants suspected of leftist activities, an estimated 15,000 during Osorio's first three years as President. Election fraud was rampant in the 1974 elections when the right-winger Kjell Laugerud was declared the winner while the *FNO*, the *National Opposition Front* claimed their candidate, General Efraín Ríos Montt was the true winner. Montt was finally persuaded to withdraw his claim in favor of an Ambassador post in Spain despite the backing of several members of the Army.

Laugerud's term in office was not as severe as his predecessors and he offered limited reforms and plans to colonize the Petén. His tenure was marked by a catastrophic earthquake on Feb. 4, 1976, which killed over 23,000 people and almost completely destroyed Puerto Barrios, cutting off the port from the rest of the country for months. A new group, the *EGP*, *Ejército Guerillero de los Pobres*, the *Guatemalan Army of the Poor*, surfaced in the Ixil area and soon new armed conflicts erupted prompting U.S. President

Jimmy Carter to cut off all aid to Guatemala due to "...the country's appalling human rights record." The *EGP* was formed around 1972 by some experienced guerilla fighters from the 1960s who crossed the border into Mexico and began to build a network of supports as there was little if any military presence in Ixil at the time. The *EGP*'s first armed assault was the execution of Luis Arenas, the owner of *Finca la Perla*, just north of Chajul. Arena, notorious for keeping hundreds of his employees deep in a system of debt/bondage, was shot in front of his laborers as he was counting out the payroll. That day the slogan of the *EGP* was born: "Long live the poor, death to the rich." This act brought an immediate and very bloodthirsty retribution from the military who began slaying and torturing suspected guerillas and sympathizers.

The 1978 elections were doctored by the Army and their candidate, the newly elected President, Brigadier General Fernando Lucas García which only served to bring about a new wave of violence across the country as the economy went downhill rapidly and guerilla bases in the mountains were being strengthened. Some of the worst massacres in Guatemalan history followed over the next decade. In that same year a group of villagers in Panzós arrived for a town meeting to solve land disputes only to find a group of soldiers waiting on them. The soldiers opened fire and within a few minutes over a hundred men, women, and children lay dead. What was not known to the villagers was that the Army had arrived in Panzós the day before the atrocity and with bulldozers had created two mass graves just outside town. Another fact that was not known to the villagers was that President García owned over 78,000 acres of disputed land outside Panzós. Panzós was the end of the Caribbean railway and a loading point for produce and goods to pass down the Río Polochic into and across Lago Izabal, making Panzós an important transshipment point where profits could be made.

In 1979, the *EGP* executed Enrique Brol, owner of *Finca San Francisco* located near Cotzal and that same day took the town of Nebaj and held a huge meeting in the town square. The *EGP* forced locals and tourists alike to attend and listen to their speeches denouncing the government of Guatemala and its policies. This soon brought a new wave of military attacks to the area and a fortification of Nabaj.

Political conditions in the capital city deteriorated so badly that political groups went underground as two opposition leaders were murdered and as well as more than a hundred members of the *Christian Democrats*. In January of 1980, a small group of Mayans joined with student activists and occupied the Spanish embassy in Guatemala City just as a meeting was taking place between the Spanish Ambassador and a group of prominent Guatemalan citizens. Government forces surrounded the embassy and a fire broke out inside the compound killing everyone but the Ambassador who managed to escape but was badly injured. In all, thirty-nine people died and some reports of that event suggested that the activists deliberately started the fire.

Stuck in a never-ending war against the rebels, the Army was suffering losses to the tune of 250 per month while the rebels were estimated to have 6,000 armed members and over 250,000 unarmed collaborators. As the guerillas widened their campaign across the country the Army set up civilian vigilante groups, *Patrullas de Autodefensa Civil*, *Civilian Self-Defense Patrols* (PACs) to assist in keeping "subversives" in check. Until the *Peace Accords* are signed in 1996, an estimated 600,000-1,000,000 Mayan were forced into the patrols. In the *PACs*, participation was considered voluntary but many Guatemalans, especially those in the northwest, had no choice but to join either the *PACs* or the guerillas. The Army also established *Iximché*, a special military unit that carried out various mass murders from 1981-1982, this was one of the first named "death squads" to wreak havoc on the population of Guatemala. Conflicts continued as the death squads took their tolls on the Guatemalan people and it is estimated that over 25,000 people lost their lives during the four years García ruled the country.

On May 24, 1981, 15 residents of the K'iché village of Los Cimientos, a small mountain community, went to the market in Finca San Francisco to sell their produce. Fourteen of them lost their lives as the Army surrounded the market and slaughtered nearly all of the men, women, and children who were there. The only Los Cimientos survivor was a nine year old child who had hidden under the bodies. After the attack the Army invaded Los Cimientos and accused the people there of being leftist sympathizers. The Army found two of the village elders, Mayan priests well into their 70s, lighting candles and praying in the local cemetery. The soldiers brutally killed the priests in front of the town folk. The rest of the population of Los Cimientos were warned to leave before the Army commenced bombing the village. The people of Los

Cimientos fled immediately, leaving all their worldly possessions behind and their last view of their village was of flames destroying their homes as some of their friends and neighbors were being tortured. The people of Los Cimientos began 13 years of living as refugees while being exploited as a labor force in the nearby plantations. In August, 1994, receiving no help from the Government, the people of Los Cimientos returned to their old homesteads, two-thirds of which had been occupied in the intervening years. The K'iché petitioned the government time and again to restore their lands as their quarrel with the Ixil, who had inhabited Los Cimientos in the absence of the K'iché, escalated. The Ixil destroyed K'iché crops, killed their horses, and installed a water system whereby they could shut off water flow to the K'iché. On June 15, 2001, the K'iché families in Los Cimientos were awoken at dawn by a group of men armed with baseball bats, machetes, sharpened sticks, and guns, and were told that they had two hours to leave Los Cimientos or they would be killed. To prove their deadly intent some of the armed men raped two K'iché women in front of their young children. Once again the K'iché fled their homes in Los Cimientos for the lands of Xeputul near Cotzal and six months later moved to Batzula Churrancho where they felt safer. To date, nobody has been arrested for the events of June, 2001, nor has anyone offered to help the K'iché return to their land even though Ixil leaders admitted that their people were responsible for the crimes and that the K'iché are the true owners of the land, but some Ixil vowed further violence if the K'iché returned.

In 2002, the Los Cimientos Maya gave up their hope of returning to their homes in Los Cimientos and were relocated to San Vicente. They lost 6,000 acres in Los Cimientos, with 5 pure water rivers, and 3-4 harvests a year of organically grown crops, for 2,000 acres in San Vicente, with one polluted river, and the chance of 2-3 harvests per year with the use of agricultural chemicals. The government of then President Alfonzo Portillo proclaimed this to be a great victory, second only in importance to the 1996 peace accords. The government promised the K'iche (in signed agreements) food support until their crops were established, new infrastructure and houses for those destroyed by the Ixil, as well as on-site health care. The Portillo government never fulfilled their obligations to the Los Cimientos K'iche causing the loss of several children to malnutrition and lack of medical care.

The 1982 presidential election was won by Aníbal Guevara, but on March 23, 1982, was overthrown in a coup staged by a group of junior military officers. The coup leaders asked retired General Efraín Rios Montt, who had lost the fraudulent election in 1974, to take command of the country. Huehuetenango born Montt, who had the backing of the Reagan administration (President Reagan said that Montt is "...a man of great personal integrity...," and even as Reagan spoke these words Montt's troops marched on La Dos Erres where, by the time the army left the village, five young women were raped, children were bludgeoned to death, and 160 people were dumped into the village well while still alive), formed a three-member junta to rule Guatemala, but within two months had dismissed his junta colleagues and assumed the Presidency. Montt offered the rebels an amnesty in June, but when the month passed and there were no takers, he vowed to rid Guatemala of the rebels by Christmas. Montt told an audience of poor Guatemalans that "If you are with us, we will feed you; if not, we'll kill you." The report of this appeared in the New York Times on July 18, 1982, the same day as the massacre at Plan de Sanchez.

On July 18, 1982, Guatemalan soldiers aided by PACs entered the community of Plan de Sanchez, about 95 miles north of Guatemala City, in search of leftist guerillas. The soldiers used machine guns and machetes to kill the villagers, some of whom they had forced into their homes only to set their houses on fire or toss in a hand grenade. When it was all over 226 people had been murdered. On July 18, 2005, current Guatemalan Vice-President Eduardo Stein visited Plan de Sanchez to formally accept government responsibility for the massacre. Stein's trip was prompted by a historic ruling by the Inter-American Human Rights Court who had decreed that Guatemala pay the survivors and relatives $7.9 million in damages.

In all fairness, one has to mention that the massacre at Plan de Sanchez came only weeks after two deadly guerilla attacks. On June 6, 1982, guerillas stopped a bus near Cotzal and executed 13 PAC leaders and their wives, and on June 17, 1982, guerillas entered the village of Chacalté (a community where the PAC had been very active) and killed over 100 people and wounded another 35. As if in further retaliation, on the evening of Oct. 13, 1982, Guatemalan soldiers entered the town of Santa Anita las Canoas and gathered up 14 suspected guerillas. The soldiers tied the men to fence posts and tortured them all night, their screams still haunt their family members in the village to this day. Finally, at dawn, the soldiers fired upon the men, killing them all.

Montt was successful in going after the rebels; the Army and the *PACs* recaptured nearly all guerilla held territory and under Montt's *Victoria 82* (*Victory 82*) "scorched earth" policy, guerilla activity lessened, but at a huge cost in civilian deaths as the campaign, which was designed to destroy the support base for the rebels made no distinction between guerilla combatants and the innocent Mayan population in targeted areas. Montt ordered the Army's *Archivos* intelligence unit to "...apprehend, hold, interrogate, and dispose of suspected guerillas as they see fit." Montt's brief presidency has been described as the most violent period of Guatemala's 36-year civil war which took some 200,000 lives, mostly unarmed indigenous civilians, Mayans, some 70,000 alone during Montt's 14 months in office. To be perfectly honest, both sides engaged in executions and torture, but vast majority of human rights violations were carried out by the Guatemalan Army and the *PACs*. In 1999, a report entitled *Memory of Silence*, revealed that the Army and the *PACs* were responsible for 93% of the reported human rights abuses.

During these years the Army abused the citizens of Guatemala in schools as well as on the killing fields. Members of the Army would often go to select schools where teen-aged young men were in attendance and wait for the students to head for home and "induct" the older, male students immediately into the Army, the students simply did not come home from school and the family knew what had happened. I'm told by men who were students then that they often had to hide from the soldiers, waiting inside school until the Army left before the students could depart for home.

On August 8, 1983, Montt was ousted by his Minister of Defense, General Óscar Humberto Mejía Víctores, who claimed that "religious fanatics" were abusing their government positions (it has been suggested that this coup was backed by the U.S. government who wanted Guatemala back on the road to democracy). Although seven people were killed in the coup Montt survived to found his own political party, the *Guatemalan Republic Front*, and to later be elected President of Congress in 1995 and again in 2000.

Víctores allowed a gradual return to democracy starting with a 1984 election for an Assembly to draft a democratic constitution. The first free elections in Guatemala in three decades were held on May 30, 1985, when Cinicio Cerezo, a Christian Democrat won with almost 70% of the vote. Cerezo's top priorities were an end to the violent civil war as well as legal and human rights reforms (although the government was criticized for failing to act on human rights violators). Cerezo was successful in moving the military away from the political zone (although Cerezo admitted that the Army still had 75% of the power in the country) and into the more traditional role of providing internal security, specifically by fighting the rebels that still plagued the countryside.

Although Cerezo's first two years were characterized by a stable economy and a marked decrease in political violence, dissatisfied military members made two coup attempts in May of 1988 and again in May of 1989, but Army leadership supported the government. But Cerezo was a bit of a fence sitter, accused of being both Communist and right-wing at various times, "non-confrontational" has been used to describe his term and people gradually became disappointed in his administration. During the latter years of Cerezo's term it became increasingly clear that the Army still ran the show, that the wealth was still controlled by the elite (at this time 65% of Guatemala's people lived below the poverty line), and that political violence was again on the upswing with 85 politically motivated murders in February of 1989 alone. Even the leaders of *GAM*, Guatemala's human rights support group, became victims of Cerezo's death squads.

On November 11, 1990, elections were held which were mired in controversy and an eventual runoff ballot gave the Presidency to Jorge Antonio Serrano (a former minister in Montt's administration), and Guatemala enjoyed the first transfer of a democratic civilian government to a democratic civilian government. Serrano's record was mixed, he had some success in consolidating civilian control over the Army, replacing a number of senior officers and persuading the military to engage in peace talks with the *URNG*, although it has been suggested many times that Serrano was just a front man that allowed the Army to take care of their real business of running the country. Serrano took a politically unpopular step when he recognized the sovereignty of Belize however he made up for that by stopping the fiscal slide that Guatemala was mired in and reducing inflation while creating real economic growth. In May of 1993, Serrano created his own coup claiming he must lead the country due to corruption in his own administration. Serrano illegally dissolved both Congress and the Supreme Court and tried to restrict civil freedoms in the name of fighting corruption. Suspected of being influenced by Columbian drug cartels and facing a coup of his own, Serrano fled the country and on June 5, 1993, Congress chose Ramiro de León Carpio to complete Serrano's term.

De León was not a member of any political party but he did have strong popular support. Disregarding calls for revenge against the military, De León overhauled the senior military commanders declaring that stability was his long term goal. Under De León the U.N. brokered peace talks progressed and his 1995 *Indigenous Rights Act* granted the Maya greater personal freedoms and even allowed state education in Mayan languages.

In 1996, new President Álvaro Arzú moved quickly towards peace and on December 26, 1996, after three decades of civil war with 150,000 dead, 50,000 missing, and over 1 million refugees, the *Peace Accords* were signed and peace came at last to Guatemala. Human rights abuses were investigated and within two days of publishing a paper on the abuses, Bishop Juan Geradi was bludgeoned to death in his garage. Although the people of Guatemala had been used to death squads and murder, for some reason Geradi's killing was a shock, this wasn't supposed to happen anymore, and in the days and weeks following the murder things only got weirder. A few days after the murder, hundreds of thousands of people gathered in Guatemala City for a silent protest while judges and prosecutors received death threats and fled the country. At one point a priest's dog was implicated in the assassination! If things were not strange enough, Geradi was succeeded by Bishop Mario Rios Mont, the former President's brother. As Arzú left office, Geradi's murderer or murderers were still at large and although politically motivated killings dropped off the crime rate soared in comparison. Guatemala suddenly found itself with the fourth highest incidence of kidnapping in the world with over 1,000 people abducted in 1997 causing law and order to be a major issue in the 1999 elections.

In the background, former dictator Rios Montt returns to politics as the elected head of the *FRG* winning his third term in 1998. Guatemala's first peacetime election in forty years was won by Alfonso Portillo in 1999. Portillo, a member of the *FRG*, a friend and ally of Montt, and an admitted murderer

(he killed two men in a brawl in Mexico and fled the country feeling he had no chance of a fair trial), claimed that if he could kill to defend himself, he could defend his people. Montt is elected the President of Parliament and in that role says, "I make the laws of Congress, I approve the budget of Congress, so I already am (national) President." Guatemalan politics takes on a "family" air as Montt's daughter is elected Deputy President of the Parliament, while Montt's son becomes head of finances for the Army.

In 1999, Nobel Peace Prize laureate Rigoberta Menchú Tum, in concert with Guatemalan human rights organizations, presented charges against Rios Montt and four retired Guatemalan Army Generals, two of whom were once President of Guatemala. Menchú Tum (whose father had been killed inside the Spanish Embassy in Guatemala City when government troops laid siege to the building killing 35 people, including four Spanish priests), petitioned the Spanish National Court and charged the men with torture, genocide, illegal detention, and state-sponsored terrorism. The five were indicted along with three other highly placed government officials who held their offices between 1978-1982. This would prove to be a long, drawn-out case, one in which Rios Montt has still not been held accountable for his actions (which include an estimated 300+ massacres during his 14 months in office). The Spanish court decides not to proceed, arguing that while there was strong evidence against the accused there is no reason why the case could not be heard in Guatemalan courts. However, members of the Guatemalan Parliament, such as Montt, are immune from prosecution by Guatemalan law. Later that same year U.S. President Bill Clinton publicly apologized for his country's support of Guatemala's past regimes, specifically that of Montt.

Portillo vowed to clean up the judicial system, get tough on crime, tax the rich, respect human rights, and bring to justice Geradi's killers. Finally, in June of 2001, an Army officer, Byron Lima Estrada, former head of the notorious *G-2* intelligence unit and a former member of the controversial *Presidential Security Unit*, the *EMP*, two other Army officers, and a priest who acted as an accomplice, were tried for the murder of Bishop Geradi. The military officers received 30 years each and the priest received a 20-year sentence. This was the first time the Army was actually helpless to defend their own, although a bomb did explode outside the home of one of the judges on the first day of the trial, and random shots were later fired at the courthouse, and there were several instances of intimidation of prosecutors and witnesses reported. Despite serving justice in the Geradi case, Portillo's years were plagued by scandal, a sagging economy, and an increasing crime rate, and after several kidnapping threats Portillo moved his family to Canada.

On June 17, 2002, some 8,000 former members of the *PACs* staged a demonstration in northern Guatemala demanding that the government pay them US $2,500 each for "services rendered to the fatherland" during the Guatemalan civil war. In 2003, Montt's *FRG* party pushes a bill through Parliament granting the former militia members US$660 each. At this same time reports began showing up that the former militia members were reactivating their intelligence-gathering network and that they were remaining loyal to Montt. Even some 7 years after the peace treaty was signed, an atmosphere of fear and intimidation lingered in Guatemala. A Bishop and several members of the Catholic Church received death threats just prior to a visit by Pope John Paul II while certain human rights organizers were subjected to similar intimidation.

On July 24, 2003, demonstrations rocked Guatemala City as the Supreme Court granted an injunction temporarily barring Montt from running for the presidency in the upcoming November elections. Some 3,000 demonstrators were given meals by the *FRG* in return for their protesting and the riots forced the closing of the US Embassy as Montt's supporters called for his return to power (Guatemala has a "no-second-term" rule for their presidents). The November 9, 2003, presidential election was won by the ex-mayor of Guatemala City, Óscar Berger in a runoff (Montt was a distant third with 11% of the vote; he was finally permitted to run for the office).

In May of 2004, Montt, the former 1980s dictator, was ordered held under house arrest on a charge of causing the death of radio reporter Hector Ramírez. Ramírez, a reporter for Guatemala's *Channel 7* television news and *Radio Sonora*, died as a result of a heart attack suffered while fleeing from *FRG* attackers who were beating him with sticks while he was covering the aforementioned protests in Guatemala City (the lack of police control and their lackadaisical attitude towards the protestors resulted in the dismissal of the head of the National Police). Similar reports came in from all over the city as *FRG* members and supporters attacked numerous other journalists. Montt was also accused of manslaughter

for instigating a fatal riot in 2003, and is named in lawsuits of directing the wholesale slaughter of tens of thousands of Mayans during his short, one year rule.

Charges are currently pending in both Spain and Guatemala as Gustavo Meoño, director of the Rigoberta Menchú Foundation, traveled to Spain to reactivate criminal proceedings against Montt. President Óscar Berger, remarked in an interview, "We're not going to allow anyone to be exempt from punishment. If someone committed acts outside the law, we will ask that justice be done." Montt's house arrest does not forbid him from traveling around Guatemala, and on November 20, 2004, he attended the wedding of his daughter Zury Mayté Sosa, a member of the Guatemalan Congress, to U.S. Representative Jerry Weller, a Republican from Illinois.

In September of 2005, the Spanish Constitutional Court ruled that Spanish courts could indeed try those accused of crimes against humanity even if the victims were not of Spanish origin. In June of 2006, a Spanish judge, Santiago Pedraz, traveled to Guatemala and interviewed Rios Montt and others charged with him. Some 15 defense appeals later Pedraz was prevented from interviewing Montt and his compatriots. On July 7, 2006, Pedraz issued an arrest warrant against Montt and former Presidents Óscar Humberto Mejiá Victores and Romeo Lucas García (who had, unknown to Pedraz, died in Venezuela in May of 2006). Also named were two retired generals, two ex-chiefs of police, and a former Minster of the Interior. In a July, 2006, press conference, 80-year old Rios Montt admitted that there were "excesses" that were committed by the army during his tenure in office, but he steadfastly denied his guilt. On May 10, 2013, Montt was convicted of genocide and crimes against humanity and was sentenced to 80 years in prison.

Bahía de Amatique

(Bay of Honduras)

The *Bahía de Amatique*, the *Bay of Honduras*, is the gateway to the *Río Dulce* as well as the commercial ports of Puerto Barrios and Puerto Santo Tomás de Castilla. The bay is silty from the run-off of several rivers and there is usually a lot of boat traffic, including a number of large freighters heading in and out of Santo Tomás de Castilla daily, as well as smaller craft ferrying people and goods between Livingston and Puerto Barrios.

The Río Sarstún

The *Río Sarstún*, pronounced *sar-stoon*, flows into the *Bahía de Amatique* and forms the border between Belize and Guatemala. *Sarstún* is a Mayan word meaning *healing stone*, and describes the stones used by Mayan healers to communicate with spirits. These stones are not found by their owners, rather the stones seek out their own particular owner, often just appearing to them as if supernaturally.

The *Río Sarstún* is best explored by dinghy or shallow draft vessel. The bar barely carries 4' at MLW but once inside the depths open up to 9' and more for a short distance inland, be prepared for bugs at sunset.

Los Siete Altares

Lying between the *Río Sarstún* and Livingston are the *Seven Altars*, *Los Siete Altares*, a series of beautiful waterfalls that lie just inland approximately 3

miles northwest of Livingston. Each of the waterfalls has a natural pool at its base and the jungle scenery is worthy of as much film as you care to shoot. Although you can anchor offshore and dinghy in for the short hike to the falls, I'd suggest renting a *lancha* and guide in Livingston. For a few *Quetzales* you can ride in a fast boat there and back, and not have to worry about anchoring your vessel on a lee shore. For obvious reasons the trip to the waterfalls will be much more enjoyable and scenic during the rainy season. Due to several incidents of criminal activity in years past, there is a bit of a police presence here to protect the many tourists that come here. To find the falls if you are anchored offshore, the path to the falls lies north of the small river, near the end of the beach.

Cabo Tres Puntas

Waypoints
Cabo Tres Puntas – 1 nm WNW of
15° 58.50' N, 88° 38.50' W

Cabo Tres Puntas is a good stopover point for vessels heading to or from the *Río Dulce* and the peninsula it is located on, a nature preserve, has

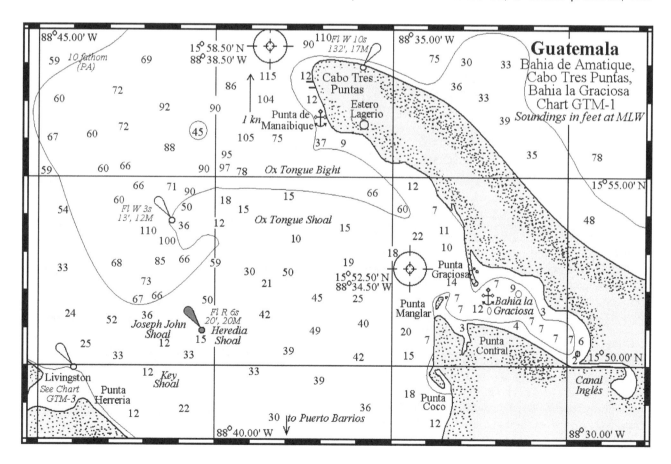

some of the best beaches on the Caribbean coast of Guatemala. For those heading to the *Río Dulce*, Cabo Tres Puntas offers a good overnight anchorage before leaving at first light to make the crossing of the Bahía de Amatique to Livingston to clear with the Port Captain and *Immigration*.

For those leaving the river, Cabo Tres Puntas makes a convenient overnight stop before heading west to Punta Sal, Puerto Cortes, or even Utila. On Chart GTM-1 you'll notice Punta de Manabique on the southwestern tip of Cabo Tres Puntas, on some locally drawn maps, the entire point is shown as Punta de Manabique instead of Cabo Tres Puntas, so be advised that the locals may call it by a different name.

Navigational Information

As shown on Chart GTM-1, a waypoint at 15° 58.50' N, 88° 38.50' W, will place you approximately 1 mile west/northwest of the northwestern tip of Cabo Tres Puntas. From here you can head south/southeast to anchor in the lee of the point wherever your draft allows, the further south you go the less roll you'll have to endure. Bear in mind that the bottom does come up quickly here so make sure your anchor is set well and don't forget that there is often a northward flowing current off western shore of the point that can be as strong as 1 knot.

For those of you heading to Livingston from Cabo Tres Puntas, you can take up an approximate course of 214° magnetic from the tip of Cabo Tres Puntas to the buoy off the bar at Livingston.

Bahía la Graciosa

Waypoints
Bahía de Graciosa – ½ nm WNW of entrance
15° 52.50' N, 88° 34.50' W

Bahía de Graciosa lies on the eastern side of *Bahía de Amatique*, north of Puerto Barrios, and makes for a shallow, but well protected anchorage, not quite what I would call a hurricane hole but it would do in a pinch.

Navigational Information
The entrance and interior of *Bahía la Graciosa* are home to several difficult to see shoals so use caution when entering. As shown on Chart GTM-1, a waypoint at 15° 52.50' N, 88° 34.50' W, will place you approximately ½ mile west/northwest of the small cays that lie north of Punta Manglar and the unmarked

entrance to the bay. From the waypoint head just a bit south of west to avoid the shoals on either side of you and enter the bay where you'll find depths of 7'-15' throughout most of it, anchor wherever your draft allows and be prepared for bugs and sundown. Keep an eye out for the sandbar that extends south of the entrance for about 200 yards.

What You Will Find Ashore
At the far eastern end of *Bahía la Graciosa* is *Canal Inglés*, named after the British loggers who built the canal between *Bahía la Graciosa* and the *Río Piteros*. The canal offers excellent bird-watching opportunities that are not to be missed.

Puerto Barrios

Waypoints
Puerto Barrios- 1½ nm north of entrance to bay
15° 46.00' N, 88° 36.90' W
Amatique Bay Marina- ¼ nm NW of entrance
15° 45.00' N, 88° 35.00' W

Most people think that Puerto Barrios is Guatemala's premier Caribbean seaport, at one time that was true, but today the bulk of the shipping is handled on the southern side of the bay at Santo Tomás de Castilla. Puerto Barrios was founded in the 1880s by President Rufino Barrios but it wasn't long before the *United Fruit Company* gained control of the port as well as the railway from Puerto Barrios to Guatemala City. Before long the *United Fruit Company* had a monopoly on all goods entering Guatemala from the Caribbean, charging heavy duties while the company itself was exempt.

The port of Santo Tomás de Castilla, just south of Puerto Barrios, is the actual importing and exporting center for Guatemala today as well as the headquarters for the Guatemalan Navy. Santo Tomás de Castilla is not a port of entry and authorities there will direct yachts to Livingston or across the bay to Puerto Barrios. Santo Tomás de Castilla was originally built by the Spanish in 1604 and was once inhabited solely by Black Caribs from St. Vincent. Pirates eventually ransacked the city and in 1843 the settlement was revived when a group of colonists from Belgium arrived here. Today there is little here save the docks and buses to Puerto Barrios.

Puerto Barrios is a mixture of cultures. The Spanish were here first, but the Garifuna came on the scene in 1797 and were soon followed by Belgian immigrants at Santo Tomás de Castilla in 1843. By the end of the 1800s indigenous K'ichi Maya who had lost their lands in Alta Verapaz arrived on the scene along with some Ch'orti Maya who were forced to relocate after being robbed of their lands in the east. At this point the focus for the community shifted to the eastern side of the Bay nearer the dock area of Puerto Barrios as new immigrants from Zacapa, Chiquimula, Baja Verapaz, and Honduras flocked to the area for work.

Navigational Information

If you are approaching from Livingston, the bearing for the light at *Bajo Villedo* from the Livingston sea buoy is approximately 125° magnetic and the distance is approximately ten miles. As shown on Chart GTM-2, a waypoint at 15° 46.00' N, 88° 36.90' W, will place you approximately 1½ miles north of the *Bahía de Santo Tomás de Castillo*, shown on some

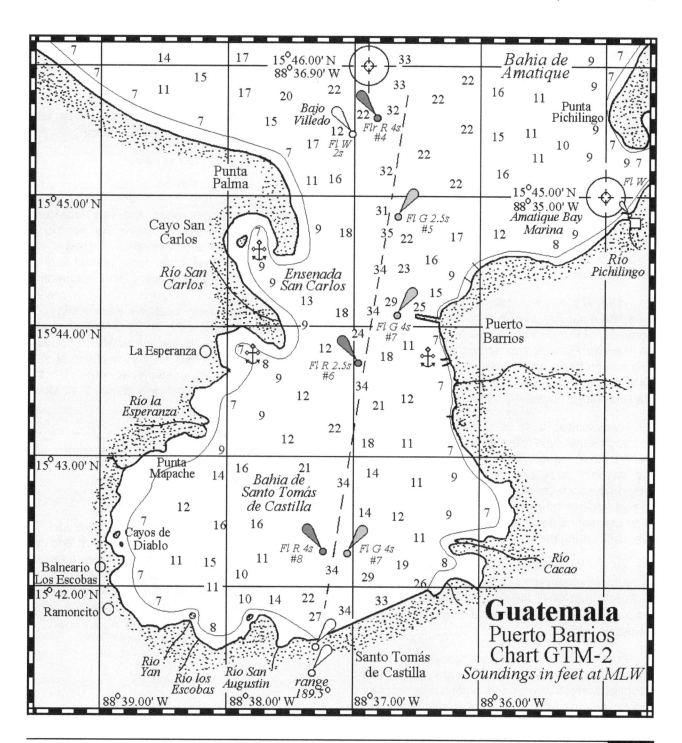

Guatemala
Puerto Barrios
Chart GTM-2
Soundings in feet at MLW

charts as *Bahía de Gálvez*, and approximately ½ mile north/northeast of the light that marks *Bajo Villedo* (8'-12' depths).

From the waypoint head south into the bay splitting the red and green lighted markers (lighted range on the southern shore of the harbor-189.5°) to anchor south of the pier at Puerto Barrios, anchoring north of the pier is prohibited due to traffic. You'll find a bit of current here, usually setting northwest at .25-1.5 knots, the strength of the current changing with the wind and sea conditions. The current also reverses setting southeast at about .25-.5 knots. The tidal range here, as in most of the Northwestern Caribbean averages about 1'.

I don't recommend anchoring off the town unless you absolutely need to clear *Customs* and *Immigration*, but if that's the case I'd suggest doing it in Livingston where it's safer and easier, and then if you like you can head south to explore Puerto Barrios. Anchorages can also be found on the western side of the bay off the small community of La Esperanza and in the protected Enseñada San Carlos directly across from and west of the commercial dock at Puerto Barrios.

There is a very nice marina in the Puerto Barrios area, the *Amatique Bay Resort and Marina*. Located northeast of Puerto Barrios in a resort complex built on the *Río Pichilingo* as shown on Chart GTM-2. The marina has a newly dredged channel (7') and is becoming a popular place for cruisers. The depths at the dock range from 8'-10' consistently.

A waypoint at 15° 45.00' N, 88° 35.00' W, will place you approximately ¼ mile northeast of the entrance to the marina at the mouth of the *Río Pichilingo*. From the waypoint you'll see the resort's lighthouse and jetty on the northern side of the entrance, keep them to port and enter the narrow river and wind your way in to the marina basin where you'll also find a *Shell* fuel dock selling diesel and gasoline.

What You Will Find Ashore
Almost whatever you need to find can be located in Puerto Barrios or shipped in. There are several banks in town, most just north of the main market center downtown.

Puerto Barrios is an exceptionally busy town with a huge market area and there are limited marine supplies here as well as auto parts stores, hardware stores, AC and refrigeration repair shops, alternator and starter repair shops, a musician's supply store, a computer shop, a VERY good machine shop, outboard motor dealers, a *DHL* office (the only server that has an office locally), several great restaurants, a *Domino's* pizza with two-for-one days on Tuesdays and Thursdays, and a movie theater with two screens at the *Pradera Mall* (http://praderaconcepcion.com/web/).

Customs and Immigration
If you need to clear in or out you must first visit the port captain, *El Capitan de el Puerto*, who will arrange for the necessary officials to visit your boat at anchor or at the marina, all of the offices are within a short walking distance, but since nearly all cruisers clear at Livingston, this might be a moot point. You can also clear in at *Amatique Bay Marina* (see below).

Marine Facilities
Marina
The *Amatique Bay Resort and Marina* offers 25 slips (nice concrete piers and very protected) and has plans in the works to raise that number to 180 with dry storage for boats up to 30' (power, not sail). The marina offers a fuel dock, Internet access, fax services, storage, showers and bathrooms, workshop, drydock, 2 heliports, hiking, a private beach, and tours to many locations, a swimming pool, two restaurants, boat care and maintenance, and assistance with *Customs* and *Immigration*. You can contact the marina on VHF ch. 68, by phone at 502-7931-0000 (http://www.amatiquebay.net/). By the way, their entrance channel now carries 7' at MLW, soon to be 8'.

Marine Services
For alternator, generator, and starter repairs and parts visit *Tecnielectrica Industrial* on the main road in Puerto Barrios.

Ferries
There is a public ferry leaving the town dock for Livingston at 1000 and again at 1700 daily, and any number of *lanchas* that leave whenever they are full. Two ferries leave every day for Punta Gorda in Belize, at 1000 and at 1400, and you must clear out with *Immigration* before you can purchase a ticket. The *Immigration* office is located at 9 *Calle*, two blocks north of the town dock (*muelle*).

Provisions

The best place to shop in Puerto Barrios is the *Mega-Mall Maxi Bodega*, probably the best-stocked supermarket east of Guatemala City.

Dining

There are several good restaurants in town, my favorite is *Safari* right on the water at *1st Avenida*. Here you'll find some of the best *tapado* along with strolling musicians and the occasional vendor hawking CDs. For Cuban food try *La Habana Vieja*, *Delfine's*, *Hibiscus Gardens* (for international fare; http://hibiscus-gardens.com/), *Restaurant El Castillo* (steak and seafood), *Campero's* (fried chicken-located at the *Mega-Mall*), and *Antojitos Doña Maria* for a large selection of good Guatemalan food. If you like pizza there is a *Domino's* (https://www.dominos.com.gt/) located in Puerto Barrios offering two for one pizzas on Tuesdays and Thursdays. The marina boasts two fine restaurants, *Puerto Chico* and *Mangos*.

Driving Around Puerto Barrios

If you are driving to Puerto Barrios from *Río Dulce*, around Km marker 259 start looking for the opening to a cave on the left hand side of the road. You'll see it somewhere between Km 260. There won't be a sign, keep your eyes peeled, the entrance is only a few feet off the road.

Morales, and her sister community, Bananera, have no access to the sea, lying off the main highway (*CA-9*) between Puerto Barrios and Guatemala City, just before the junction (*Ruidosa*) of the highway that heads west to *Río Dulce* and eventually Flores and Tikal (before *Ruidosa* if you are coming from Guatemala City). The town can be reached by bus from Puerto Barrios, *Río Dulce*, and Guatemala City.

Morales is a very busy town for being so small. There are several nice hardware/tool stores here, a *Post Office*, several auto parts stores, a very good *dispencia* (a grocery store called *Dispencia Familiar*-a sister store to the one in *Río Dulce*), a *GUATEL* office, several banks, a good meat market, and one of the most interesting open markets to be found. As you approach the main part of the community, Morales is the first town that you come to, and I can find little distinction between where Morales ends and Bananera begins, even folks who live there have confusing information to offer.

As you enter town from *CA-9*, you'll keep the railroad tracks to your left and after the road becomes one way, well, it's supposed to be one way but most folks don't honor the one way, you can continue on and you'll soon come to a turn off on the right that will bring you to the market streets. Here vendors and snack shacks line the sides of the streets but the best part of the market can't be seen from the road, you'll have to park your car or get off the bus and explore to find it. In the center of all of this there is a huge tarp covered area full of dimly-lit, narrow little alleys and passageways and wall-to-wall stalls. I think you could spend a day lost in here and probably not see it all. Now I'm told that this market is in Morales, I've also been told it is in Bananera, and the one I believe most is that it's in between the two.

Bananera was once the home of the *United Fruit Company* until the company's dominance waned in the 1960s. At one time this tiny hamlet was home to the most powerful group of men in the country next to Guatemala City, the men who influenced politicians and the wealthy upper class and virtually ruled Guatemala. Today *Bandegua*, a subsidiary of *Del Monte*, owns the old *United Fruit Company* holdings and you'll see their trucks in Puerto Barrios every day. *Bandegua* operates out of the same compound that once housed the *United Fruit Company*, complete with company store, private airstrip, and a private one-hole golf course. As you enter Morales and head for the open market, just across the railroad tracks to the east you'll see a long, high concrete wall, this is the old *United Fruit* compound, today the *Bandegua* compound. For the most part *Bandegua* has stayed away from the political arena in Guatemala, being quite content to export some two million bananas a year.

But in 1999, *Bandegua* laid off over 900 employees in the immediate area citing a slumping worldwide banana economy, sluggish Guatemalan production, and the damages to their plantations caused by *Hurricane Mitch*. Immediately the labor unions took up the cause of the workers and strikes were initiated as well as a roadblock of the Atlantic highway, *CA-9*, that runs between Puerto Barrios and Guatemala City, effectively cutting off the transshipment of all bananas. After much violence and charges of corruption, the union leaders who had called for the strikes resigned, and it seemed to one and all that *Bandegua* was flexing its banana-fed muscles. However, when all the dust settled in April of 2000, all the workers who had been laid off were re-hired.

One of my favorite restaurants is to be found here in Morales. On a side street that runs parallel to the main road, just a few hundred yards east of the *Bethesda Hospital Centro Medico* (http://hcmbethesda2009.galeon.com/), you'll find *Hotel Sol*, with a jewel of a restaurant, *Restaurante Sol*. The restaurant features Chinese food that is the best in the area; the portions are huge and the restaurant serves a very tasty pepper oil with every meal including to-go orders (and trust me, if you've been without Chinese food for a while, you'll want to take a meal home with you for later or the next day-definitely try their mixed fried rice, *mixto*, and their egg-rolls, which appear on the menu as *taco-chinos*).

The Río Dulce

The River that Swallows Gringos

In a few moments we entered the Río Dulce. On each side, rising perpendicularly from three to four hundred feet, was a wall of living green. Trees grew from the water's edge, with dense unbroken foliage, to the top; not a spot of barrenness was to be seen; and on both sides, from the tops of the highest trees, long tendrils descended to the water, as if to drink and carry life to the trunks that bore them. It was, as its name imports, a Río Dulce, a fairy scene of Titan land, combining exquisite beauty with colossal grandeur. As we advanced the passage turned, and in a few minutes we lost sight of the sea, and were enclosed on all sides by a forest wall; but the river, although showing us no passage, still invited us onward.

John Lloyd Stephens
1841

The *Río Dulce*, *Sweet River*, begins at the *Bahía de Amatique*, *Honduras Bay*, at the Garifuna community of Livingston, and is a favorite "hurricane hole" of many, many cruisers. In fact, the *Río Dulce* is probably the finest hole in the entire Caribbean offering excellent protection, economical prices, and an eclectic group of gregarious cruisers. During hurricane season you'll find hundreds of cruisers tied up to the docks at one of the local marinas and a few riding at anchor (many opt for the cheap marina rates so they can run their air-conditioners, I know I certainly do). With so many cruisers in one spot you're bound to have countless pot-lucks, swap meets, barbecues, dinghy races, and happy hours. But the river is not just a cruiser's Mecca, here too you'll meet many Guatemalans that live here year round as well as those who come here just to vacation and enjoy the water.

The *Río Dulce* is a protected area, from Livingston to *Lago Izabal*, however, at this point in time regulations are vague if not non-existent, and those that are in place affect only riverside construction. However, there is talk of one day requiring holding tanks of all vessels on the river. Only time will tell what regulations will be created and enforced on the river.

The *Río Dulce* is an aquatic community, if you want to move about on the river it must be by boat as there are no roads or paths outside of the towns of Río Dulce (Fronteras) and El Relleno except for the roads to San Felipe and El Estor and a path leading to the old *Mario's Marina* and *Mango's Marina* from the small village of Esmeralda. Fortunately all the houses and business on the river have a boat dock to make access easy. If you don't have a dinghy (or simply don't want to use it) you can get around by hiring a *lancha*, an inexpensive water taxi of sorts that is pronounced "launch-a." There's usually a group of *lanchas* at the docks in *Río Dulce* waiting to take you anywhere your heart desires, and they vary in size and style, call *Puerto Fronteras* on VHF ch. 68 to hail a *lancha*. Please notice that I'm using the name *Río Dulce* for the town that is often shown as Fronteras. All the road signs and maps show it as *Río Dulce*, not Fronteras, and all the Guatemalans know it by the same name. In fact, if you ask a taxi driver in Guatemala City, or even in Puerto Barrios, to take you to Fronteras, he'll likely take you to the border with Honduras (*frontera*), don't laugh, this has really happened.

Just about everybody monitors the local hailing frequency, channel 68, on marine VHF radio. Once contact is made please shift your traffic to a working channel. The national police monitor ch. 16 so if you have an emergency give them a hail on ch. 16 and also hail your fellow cruisers on ch. 68. Please note that the police only speak Spanish. There is daily VHF net at 0730 on ch. 69 that doesn't last too long, it only takes about 15-20 minutes to wrap things up. There are the usual calls for emergency and priority traffic followed by a mail call, weather, a services offered/needed portion, a buy-sell-trade portion, and then there are a few commercial announcements before the net ends.

One last word about spending time on the *Río Dulce*, beware of blisters on your hull. The folks at *La Ceiba Shipyard* tell me that nearly all boats that come out of the *Río Dulce* develop minor blistering problems after being in warm fresh water so bear that in mind and check your bottom before you venture far from the river.

Medical Care

Medical care is easy to access in the *Río Dulce*, there are five medical clinics in the area, two in *Río Dulce*, one in La Esmeralda that is open to everybody, and one at Ak' Tenamit on the river downstream of *El Golfete*. The clinic at Ak' Tenamit is staffed 24-hours a day with a nurse on duty (monitors VHF ch. 88). For more serious medical problems you can visit the *Clínica Médica San Jose* in Morales (5947-8015), a 24-hour emergency clinic with x-ray equipment, a lab and pharmacy, and a staff of doctors, not just nurses (not that there's anything wrong with nurses, it's just that sometimes you want to speak to a doctor). There is now a new hospital in Morales, *Bethesda*, modern and up to date, as well as a well-equipped eye clinic. But for the best care anywhere, you should see Dr. Karyn de Santa Cruz in Guatemala City. Dr. Karyn can be reached at her clinic at 2362-8681, or by cell at 5414-8686. Another highly recommended English speaking doctor is Dr. Leonel A. Ramirez who can be reached at his office in Morales, 7823-2060 or on his cell at 5412-0504.

The town of *Río Dulce* also has two dental clinics, the *Clínica Dental Armando Mejiá* on the road to San Felipe (no x-ray equipment) and *Clínica Dental Abel Aquire* located on the highway to the Petén, just north of *Río Dulce* (also no x-ray equipment, 7948-7743). But for the best dental care anywhere near the *Río* you must go to Morales and visit Dr. Sonia Olavarrueth, she can be reached at 4040-3333.

Let me throw in a few good words for a special couple that are doing so much for the people of the *Río Dulce* area, Mike and Karen Rhea. Mike and Karen first arrived on the river about 10-15 years ago on their trimaran after doing some missionary work in Florida. They were cruising Central American waters from Mexico to Panama, a voyage that originally began on the Sacramento River near their home town in California. Mike and Karen saw a crucial need for

health care in La Esmeralda, the 700-person village behind the old *Mario's Marina*. Within a year Mike and Karen received government approval to build, staff, and stock a clinic in the village, and using their combined skills, Mike is a skilled craftsman and Karen a nurse, they began construction on the clinic. Even during the construction phase Karen was seeing patients and providing medical care free to all, and today, cruisers far and wide have heard of the work in La Esmeralda and many who come here donate of their time, money, or medical supplies to give to the people of La Esmeralda which has dramatically improved the health of the people of the surrounding area.

Today Mike and Karen have embarked on an even more ambitious project, an orphanage and home for un-wed mothers and widows located just north of *Río Dulce* on the main road to Tikal. The orphanage and clinic are in dire need of many items and if you're coming to the Río it would be much appreciated if you could bring any of the following for donation: 4" gauze, vitamins, Tylenol, children's Tylenol, Ibuprofen, hydrogen peroxide, clean clothes, new or used eyeglasses, any type of skin cleanser, lice medicine, condoms, pregnancy test kits, and any medical supplies you can think of to bring, but please, do not offer out-of-date medicines (the clinic is licensed by the government and they can be shut down if they pass out expired medications). Also, if you just want to help, the clinic can use your assistance if you can spare the time. If you can't volunteer at the clinic, you might wish to spend a day with the kids at the orphanage, a good fix for grandparent cruisers who miss their grandchildren. For more information visit Mike and Karen's website at http://rayodeesperanza.org.

Now in their 6th year, *Guatemala Medical Travel* (a medical travel agency) works with 40-50 of the most highly skilled medical specialists, bringing them together with patients in need of affordable medical treatment. If this is what you might need, I heartily suggest that you check out their site at www.GuatemalaMedicalTravel.com and contact Lori Shea for more information at 502-4701-4520 or 502-5737-3023 (Guatemalan phone numbers; Lori@GuatemalaMedicalTravel.com).

If you need a vet, Dr. Angel Velasquez has his practice just on the edge of town and there are two vets who come to Río Dulce from Guatemala City two or three times a month, Dr. Wer and Dr. Andrade.

Transiting

Your passage up the *Río Dulce* will be absolutely unforgettable, but there are a few things we must discuss concerning the river. The *Río Dulce* is a large river, from ¼-1 mile wide for most of its length with the narrowest spot at the point at La Vaxca where the river narrows to about 100 yards wide at a bottleneck in the canyon. The waters of the *Río Dulce* are, for the most part, free of debris, but there are occasional hazards such as floating or submerged logs called "deadheads" and tree branches, but these hazards tend to be more common in the calmer spots away from the main flow of the river and in the smaller tributary rivers that flow into the *Río Dulce* although you're likely to spot a "deadhead" anywhere. A deadhead may appear as just the end of a log at or near the surface and its length may lie vertical in the water, use caution. The flotsam and jetsam is more noticeable after periods of heavy rain that wash all manner of debris down from the hills, you should always keep a sharp lookout when underway on the river.

The current in the river usually runs about ½-1 knot and slightly higher in the rainy season, depending of course on how much rain the area has had. During the early summer of 2006 the river was some 4'-5' above its normal level and the river ran stronger in the canyon between *El Golfete* and Livingston. Also note that the currents under the bridge in *Río Dulce* (Fronteras) are very strong at all times of the year. Normal currents in the river between *El Golfete* and Livingston run from ½–1½ knots most of the year, but can be higher during the rainy season, sometimes as strong as 3 knots.

A hazard unique to these waters are the huge floating masses of hyacinths which can completely cover an area when the wind is from the wrong direction. They may even appear as an island where there was none the day before. Usually interlaced with logs, these floating masses are often home to snakes, some of which may be poisonous, and all of them are looking for a way off their floating prison, be careful if you come alongside one of these floating islands in your dinghy or in the big boat.

Many of the smaller tributaries that join the *Río Dulce* and can be followed upstream for miles although the smaller rivers often are home to unseen submerged hazards such as logs, branches, and rocks. The depth of the waters here can also vary from shallow with rocks to deep within a boat length or two. It is fortunate that the waters are fairly clear and these hazards can often be easily seen by crew on the bow although it's best to explore some of these rivers by dinghy or in a *cayuco*. *Cayucos* are wooden canoes that the locals use for fishing, hauling goods, or just transportation, and if you are running the river at night you will need to be extra cautious as most of these *cayucos* don't have running lights. In many places along the river local fisherman will string nets at night, usually on either side of the point at El Castillo, about 1 mile upstream from the bridge at *Río Dulce* where the *Río Dulce* narrows just before it widens into *Lago Izabal*, in the waters south of *Mango's Marina*, and all along the shores of *Lago Izabal*. One of the worst places to encounter these nets is in *El Golfete* where the nets can even be found in the middle of the channel between Cayo Grande and Cayo Largo. I do not advise that you move about in *El Golfete* at night.

Weekends and holidays bring their own hazards as the river is very busy with scores of Guatemalans playing on the river in their powerboats and jet skis (just like South Florida, right?), so if you drop the hook on the river always use an anchor light, preferably at deck level as a light at that height is far easier to see than a masthead light which could be mistaken for a bright star or not even noticed at all.

Weather is a concern for all on the *Río Dulce*. There are two primary seasons here, the rainy season, May through October, and the dry season, November through April. I usually say that it's either hot and rainy or hot and not so rainy, but that's not completely true. During the dry season rain can occur at any time, but it is usually confined to just a shower during the afternoon or from 0000-0600, thunderstorms are rare during this part of the year. However, during the rainy season, thunderstorms are common and rain can occur at any time of the day or night, sometimes raining steadily for several days at a time without little if any break. When the daily storms come out of the east and southeast you can expect them to be short lived and not very fierce, however, if you have encounter a storm out of the southwest, locally called a *biami*, you can expect a bit of a blow, usually under gale force, for a short while.

While the river is fairly safe during storms with strong winds, *Lago Izabal* and *El Golfete* are another story. Short, steep seas with a short interval can build very quickly and can easily swamp a small boat or dinghy. These storms and seas usually occur in the afternoon so it's best to do your traveling in the morning and be in a marina or protected anchorage by about 1300 or before. Also, be advised that during the rainy season the level of the *Río Dulce* may rise by as much as 1'-2'. A final word on *El Golfete*. It's best to head east in this area early in the morning for by afternoon the wind will have picked up considerably and make heading downriver a real chore.

If you have a boating emergency on the river you should put out a distress call on VHF ch. 68 and 16, in that order, and you should not have a problem finding somebody to come to your assistance. There are no official search and rescue vessels on the river and few people monitor ch. 68 at night except perhaps those with insomnia.

Fuel on the river is not hard to find, besides the *Texaco* fuel dock in Livingston at the mouth of the river, there are two fuel docks near the bridge over the *Río Dulce*, *Esso* southeast of the bridge, and *Shell* (VHF ch. 73) located in *Shell Bay*, both offering gasoline and diesel. In Mariscos, on *Lago Izabal*, there are lots of niños that are willing to jerry jug your fuel cans from the dock to the nearby gas station for a few *Quetzales*.

One final note on the charts of the *Río Dulce* included in this book. From Livingston to *El Golfete* I do not show any waypoints or a lat/long grid on the charts, you really don't need them and you won't miss them at all, the distance is short so they really aren't necessary, of course I'm sure there are some of you that will disagree with me.

Livingston

Waypoints
Livingston - ¼ nm NE of sea buoy
15° 50.34' N, 88° 43.64' W

Livingston, the gateway to the *Río Dulce*, was once called *La Buga*, a corruption of the Spanish *La Boca*, which means mouth, since the community is at the mouth of the river, is the gateway to the *Río Dulce* and the place you'll need to stop to clear in and out of Guatemala. Livingston sits on the northern side of the mouth of the *Río Dulce* and was founded around 1795 by Black Caribs, now known as the Garifuna. There is no overland access to Livingston, although you may see cars and trucks in Livingston, none of them came overland, all arrived by sea.

CAUTION: If you are bound up the *Río Dulce*, I suggest that if possible you should anchor at Tres Puntas and head to Livingston at first light to clear as early in the morning as you can, spending the rest of the day working your way up the *Río Dulce* to *El Golfete*, perhaps *Bahía de Tejano* or *Bahía Buenavista*. Do not anchor overnight in Livingston! If you do spend the night in Livingston be sure that anything left on deck is locked because the chances are good it won't be there in the morning if it's not chained and locked. This included dinghies in davits and motors mounted on the pulpit railing.

Navigational Information
As shown on Chart GTM-3, a waypoint at 15° 50.34' N, 88° 43.64' W, will place you approximately ¼ mile northeast of the sea buoy and the entrance across the bar at Livingston. Now you will undoubtedly meet all sorts of cruisers who will give you waypoints for crossing the bar, inside waypoints, outside waypoints, waypoints where they ran aground, things like that. The waypoint I have given is to be used as a guideline, it is to be utilized to get you to the sea buoy, you'll have to pilot your way in from there. I don't recommend using waypoints to cross the bar, instead use your eyes and your depth sounder. Bear in mind that from time to time the position of the buoy may change due to storms and allowances must be made for that.

One important note: you will likely see some small buoys or flags paralleling your course and usually lying on the northern side of it (to starboard upon entering from the sea). Don't be fooled into thinking that these are channel markers, they are fishing markers, that is all, and if you get too close, well, to be truthful, you'll probably run aground before getting too close. I've seen boats of 7.5' draft enter

Sketch courtesy of Bob Smith

View from atop the hill in Livingston

Livingston waterfront, fuel dock in background

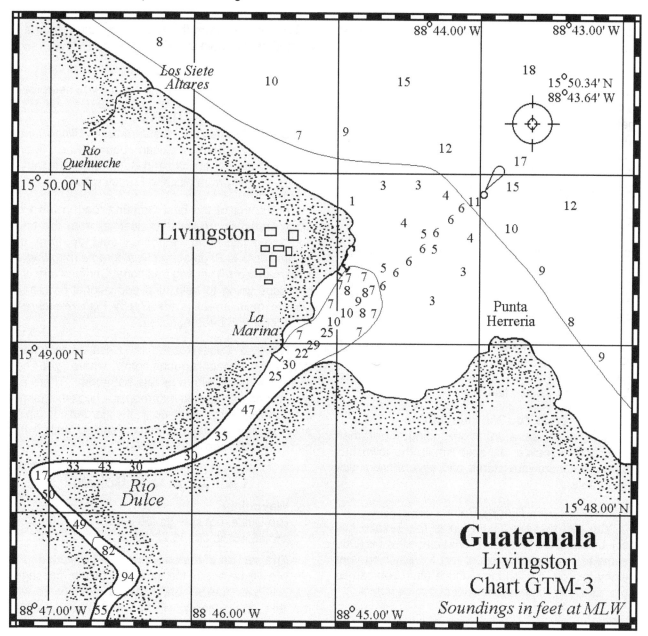

88°44.00' W

88°43.00' W

8

Los Siete
Altares

10

15

18

15°50.34' N
88°43.64' W

7

9

12

17

Río
Quehueche

15°50.00' N

3   3

1

4   11   15

4

6

12

Livingston

4

6

10

5 6

4

6 5

5 6

5 6 6

3

9

7 7 7

8 9 8 7

7 6

3

La
Marina

7
8
10 8 7

10 8 7

Punta
Herreria

15°49.00' N

7 25

10

7

22 29

30

25

3

8

9

47

35

30

30

33   43   30

17

50

Río
Dulce

15°48.00' N

49

82

Guatemala
Livingston
Chart GTM-3
Soundings in feet at MLW

94

88°47.00' W   55

88 46.00' W

88°45.00' W

the river with a good tide, and boats with up to 8' have been helped across the bar (there are several boats in Livingston that can haul you across the bar, but don't try this with an unprotected rudder or bolt-on keel, damage can result from the hard bottom-if you need a tow call the port captain). If you draw 6' or more, you should wait until the tide is rising, almost high, before entering.

For more information on the tide you can try to hail the port captain, *El Capitan de el Puerto de Livingston*, on VHF ch. 16 for the time of high water. You can also hail Raul Morales Veliz at *Naviera Servimar*, on VHF ch. 16, by phone at 502-7947-0888. Raul can arrange to have a power boat heel your vessel using a halyard from the top of the mast the help you get over the bar.

If you talk to ten people that have crossed the bar, you'll likely get ten different suggestions as to how to cross the bar. There is a tried and true method, used by commercial mariners for years and years, and it's quite simple. With the sea buoy on your stern, put your bow on the middle of the mouth of the *Río Dulce* and steer for that on a heading of 225° magnetic. If you look along the northern shore, you'll see a large commercial dock jutting out near the mouth of the river. For years pilots have been coming in on this heading and leaving on it as well. Head in on 225° and keep the end of the commercial dock just off your starboard bow. From the end of the dock the commercial boats will steer 45° to exit the bar, the reciprocal of the entrance heading, it works, and it carries you over the deepest part of the bar.

Once across the bar most folks who run aground make the mistake of turning to starboard too soon. Don't turn towards town to anchor until you're at least abreast of the *Texaco* fuel dock.

What You Will Find Ashore
Livingston has a lot more going for it than many people realize, although small, the town has some great hardware stores and several very nice restaurants.

Dinghy Dock
You can tie your dinghy up at the *Texaco* fuel dock but the local "boat boys" will want a few Qs (Q60 seems to be what they shoot for) for watching your dinghy for you, a good idea. Quite often you can tie up at *La Casa Rosada* just west of the town dock.

Customs **and** *Immigration*
When you arrive at Livingston to clear in you must first call *El Capitan de el Puerto de Livingston* on VHF ch. 16. He'll give you instructions on how to come in and clear, actually he and his entourage will come to your boat first. Cruising yachts will be issued three months stay on arrival with a special permit consisting of a sticker that must be displayed prominently on the boat. The sticker will be attached by the *Customs* officer in the first port of entry. For more information see the section *Customs and Immigration* at the beginning of this chapter.

Banks
Banco de Commercio is located on the left as you walk up the hill from the town dock, and *Bancafé* is located on the main street in town.

Fuel
There is a *Texaco* dock in town if you need fuel.

Dining
One of my favorite restaurants is *Tilingo Lingo Restaurant*, where Mexican born owner Maria Ouevedo serves Mexican and Garifuna cuisine, along with everything from pizza to French toast.

For some of the best Garifuna food in town try *Margot's*, while *El Malecón*, just up from the town dock, specializes in seafood. Just up from the *Texaco* dock is *Buga Mama Restaurante* (http://www.bugamama.org/) serving traditional Garifuna fare with proceeds going to help rural educational programs. On the main street is the *Happy Fish Restaurant*, good food with Internet access.

Near *La Casa Rosada* is *Casa de la Iguana* (http://www.casadelaiguana.com), where you can rent a bungalow with a private bathroom. There are also dorms with shared bathrooms, a book exchange, cold drinks, outdoor tables in the garden for dining and hanging out with breakfast served daily. For more info call Inga at 7947-0064.

Livingston to El Golfete

Waypoints
Río Dulce, hot springs- 50' S of
15° 46.46' N, 88° 48.72' W

The section of the passage from Livingston to *El Golfete* will be one of the most spectacular passages you will ever make. Short, and a motor even with the tide, the scenery will be worth every drop of diesel your vessel requires for this leg, and more!

Heading upriver from Livingston you'll soon enter the *Río Dulce* canyon where green, tree-shrouded cliffs interspersed with white, steep rock walls rise 300' on either side of you. I've seen it written that the first Tarzan movie was filmed here and when you see this area you'll agree that it would make quite the backdrop for such a cinematic undertaking. Vines hang to the water's edge and here and there you'll spy a tiny *cayuco* paddling close to the shoreline. Small houses dot the shoreline here and there as you approach the *Río Tatin*, *Río Lampara*, and *El Golfete*.

As shown on Chart GTM-3, as you head upriver from Livingston you will see a large dock to starboard, this is where in older days larger vessels would moor to off load their goods. Just past the dock are some power lines with an overhead clearance of about 85'. As you proceed upriver you can stay mid-channel and you'll have plenty of water, the only shoals to be found will be on the sharp curves as shown on Chart GTM-4.

A few miles upriver from Livingston is the mouth of the *Río Tatin* on the north side of the *Río Dulce*. If you turn up the *Río Tatin* you'll quickly find water that's less than 6' deep, so unless you're a very shallow draft vessel, it'll be a dinghy trip up this tributary, but it will be worth it. If you anchor inside the mouth of the river and head upstream in your dink, all the while watching for shallow rocks, you will soon come to a fork where the *Río Tatin* flows in from your right, and if you continue upriver you'll find a small waterfall and a spring fed swimming hole. To continue upriver you'll need to portage your dinghy in several places around fallen trees and across rocky patches. The local folks tell me that if you continue upriver far enough you will find yourself within walking distance of Livingston.

A short distance west of the *Río Tatin* is Ak Tenamit, a unique social center that was founded in 1992 and whose goal is to assist some 9,000 K'iché Mayans who have settled along the *Río Dulce* as a result of land reforms and the civil war. Operating programs for education, job training, and medical care, the center is staffed by volunteers who maintain the grounds, run the health clinic, manage the women's co-op, and teach in the school. If you can spend a few hours here volunteering it will be greatly appreciated and you just might walk away with a better understanding of the Maya.

Approximately ½ mile upriver of Ak Tenamit is a hot spring located a few feet inland on the northern shore of the *Río Dulce*. The hot sulfurous spring, called *Agua Caliente*, is not too difficult to find, there is a low wall and four orange markers that show its location, and if the river is not running too strong, like after a period of heavy rains, you can put your hand over the side of your dinghy and feel the warm water when you get close to the springs. Usually there are several folks enjoying the springs during the day, but they usually leave before sunset and you can have the whole place to yourself then. If you're carrying a handheld GPS in your dinghy, a waypoint at 15° 46.46' N, 88° 48.72' W, will place you about 50' south of the wall. Recently, a Mayan collective, *Communidad Barrios del Río Lampara*, has improved the rock wall at the springs, installed a small dock, and built a restaurant. There is a donation box for the springs in the palapa. On site you'll find that you can take a guided tour through the cave up the hill from the springs for about 15Q per person and tips for the guide. You can also hike about 150 yards up a steep but well maintained trail to the entrance to the cave.

A little more upriver from the *Río Tatin* is the mouth of the *Río Lampara* behind a small island on the south side of the river. The entrance is tricky for a big boat, but doable if not after a period of heavy rain which will bring down a lot of debris to confuse and block the entrance. The entrance channel in most conditions will take a draft of 6'. To enter the river, put your stern on Ak Tenamit and point your bow at the center of the mouth of the *Río Lampara*, and bear in mind that the river will be trying to push you downstream at ½- 1½ knots or more. With your stern on Ak Tenamit and your bow facing the center of the river, the island will be to port and the remains of a large tree that is imbedded in the shoal on the south side of the river will be to starboard. Head towards the center of the river on an approximate heading of 185°, this heading is to be used as a guideline. The deepest water may move slightly due to the flow of the rivers so you might have to feel your way in. Once you come alongside the south side of the small island you'll find the water depths 12'-20' which will continue for a short distance upriver before the river shallows and the bottom gets rocky.

Just to the east of the *Río Lampara*, on the southern shore of the *Río Dulce* (caution; the depth here is less than 3') is a small restaurant, *El Viajero*. Here you can eat upstairs in the breeze with a good view of the river and dine on some of the best garlic shrimp and fried *robalo* (snook) on the river. Next door is *Tienda Angelita* where you can buy gasoline and exchange your propane bottles (if they have Guatemalan valves on them).

As you head upriver on the *Río Lampara*, you'll pass a couple of small *tiendas*, one on each shore, and you'll soon come to a smaller river that enters from the east, just past this intersection is the *lancha* building business of Ingmar, who builds the best *lanchas* to be found on the *Río Dulce*. West of the mouth of the *Río Lampara* is the *Río Tameja*, another good dinghy exploration opportunity.

El Golfete

El Golfete, *Little Gulf* in English, is a widening of the *Río Dulce* that lies about 6 miles from Livingston, and is more reminiscent of a lake than a river. Ten miles long and three miles wide at its widest, *El Golfete* offers few hazards on the courseline from one end to the other, although there are some shoal areas close in to shore in places. If you see a pleasant anchorage for the night before proceeding upriver to the marina area of the *Río Dulce, El Golfete* and her bays are the perfect spot. But bear in mind, there has been some crime in the areas I'm about to mention and, with the possible exception of *Bahía de Tejano* and *Bahía Buenavista*, it's best to anchor with a buddy boat.

Cayo Grande

Waypoints
El Golfete, N- 1.4 nm SW of Cayo Grande
15° 46.60' N, 88° 50.10' W

As you enter *El Golfete* from the lower leg of the *Río Dulce*, immediately to your right you'll see Cayo Grande where you can find a pleasant restaurant and an equally pleasant anchorage. Cayo Grande is a protected area, and is uninhabited as of this writing.

Navigational Information
As shown on Chart GTM-4 and Chart GTM-5, as you enter the northeastern end of *El Golfete*, Cayo Grande will lie on your starboard side. You'll have deep water almost everywhere except right along the shoreline. As you enter *El Golfete* from the *Río Dulce*, there is a piling shown on Chart GTM-4 on the southern side of *El Golfete*, southeast of Cayo Grande, that was knocked down as this book was going to print, it probably won't be replaced so give that point a fair berth as the piling is just under the surface about 50'-75' offshore. Other cruisers report there are more than one submerged piling here.

You can pass between Cayo Grande and the mainland and anchor wherever you choose between Cayo Grande and the mainland, but the shallowest water will be at the northern end just past the northwestern tip of Cayo Grande, here you'll find depths of less than 20' without having to tuck in next to shore. This is a very comfortable anchorage when the afternoon winds pipe up in *El Golfete*, and believe me they will. Sometime after noon, almost every day, you can expect the winds to increase to 15 knots and often more creating a nice little chop on *El Golfete* making outbound progress slow and uncomfortable.

If you are heading southwest across *El Golfete* to Cayo Largo and the *Río Dulce* again, you can steer 230° T, and as you approach Cayo Largo, pass between the island and the conspicuous pilings that lie a mile to the west of it. Keep an eye out for two small buoys that lie east and northeast of Cayo Largo. Or, if you prefer to navigate by GPS, a waypoint at 15° 42.25' N, 88° 55.27' W, will place you approximately ½ mile northeast of Cayo Largo, between Cayo Largo and the piling as shown on Chart GTM-7. From this position pass between the piling and Cayo Largo and enter the *Río Dulce* as shown on the chart.

If you are approaching the northeastern end of *El Golfete* from the southwestern end by Cayo Largo as shown on Chart GTM-5, a waypoint at 15° 46.60' N, 88° 50.10' W, will place you approximately 1.4 miles southwest of Cayo Grande, from the waypoint it's a simple matter to pass south and east of Cayo Grande and re-enter the narrow confines of the *Río Dulce* heading towards Livingston.

What You'll Find Ashore
There are no trails on Cayo Grande, it is almost completely natural and supports all manner of wildlife from insects to frogs to snakes and toucans, the island is alive. There is a small restaurant just to the east of Cayo Grande. *Los Palafitos*, on the shore of the mainland. But the biggest draw here is *El Biotopo Chocon Machacas*, the manatee preserve located on the mainland to the west/northwest of the northern tip of Cayo Grande (Chart GTM-5).

In 1976, Thor Janson began a detailed study of the manatees in the *Río Dulce* area and discovered that *El Golfete* was a prime location to observe manatees. Thanks to the efforts of Thor Jason in impressing the government of Guatemala of the need to protect this shy, gentle creature that the government created the reserve as part of their *Río Dulce* protection plan.

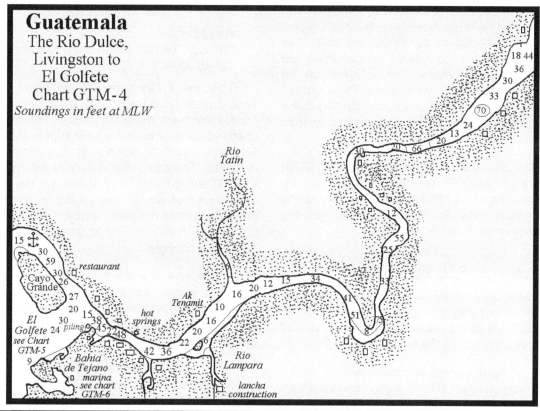

Guatemala
The Rio Dulce,
Livingston to
El Golfete
Chart GTM-4
Soundings in feet at MLW

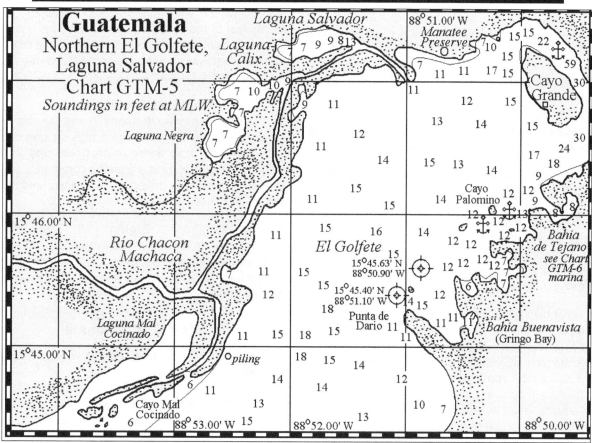

Guatemala
Northern El Golfete,
Laguna Salvador
Chart GTM-5
Soundings in feet at MLW

The reserve has a small dock and several hiking trails and camping is permitted here, but don't expect the reserve to be full of manatees...the manatees don't know that there is a reserve here and they are likely to be found anywhere in *El Golfete* or on the *Río Dulce*. Consider yourself fortunate if you happen to spy one of these elusive creatures, the *Río Dulce* manatees are not as open to human contact as their Florida cousins.

Located on the southern shores of the *Río Dulce* just before you enter *El Golfete*, you'll find a couple of small *tiendas* and a furniture shop where you can purchase handmade pieces for the home you are going to buy or build on the river.

Lagunas Salvador and Calix

Just west of the manatee reserve is a small river that leads to two very protected land-locked coves that would be excellent places to hide in the event of a hurricane approaching the area.

Navigational Information
As shown on Chart GTM-5, if you head west from Cayo Grande you'll come to the mouth of a small river that will lead you into *Laguna Salvador* and *Laguna Calix*. With 11' at the mouth of the river, you'll find 7'-10' all the way into *Laguna Salvador*. Just before you enter *Laguna Salvador* another small river branches off to the south and this leads into *Laguna Calix*. You'll find no less than 7' on this route as well. Both *lagunas* offer good holding in sandy mud, lots of mangroves, even more wildlife, and some very nasty bugs if there's no wind at dusk.

There is a narrow river that leads away to the south just before you enter *Laguna Calix*, this is only for dinghy exploration and even then you won't be able to make it through to the southern end of the river where it joins the *Río Chacon Machaca*, there are simply too many fallen trees blocking your passage, but there are one or two places where you can take the dingy outside, to the east, into *El Golfete*.

As shown on Chart GTM-5, it is possible to enter the mouth of the *Río Chacon Machaca* with a draft of 4' or less, but you'll have a maze of shallows, fallen trees, and small islands to work your way through, but if successful you'll be rewarded by several miles of pristine jungle river where you'll have to work your way around fallen trees and other debris that line the shores of this narrow river in places.

Bahía de Tejano

Waypoints
Bahía de Tejano- ¼ nm NW of entrance
15° 46.30' N, 88° 50.10' W

This lovely bay received the name *Bahía de Tejano* when Mike Payne opened up the *Texas Bay Marina* here several years ago. The marina has changed ownership and is now known as *Burnt Key Marina* however the name of the bay seems to be up in the air. The small village located nearby is named Cayo Quemado and I'm told that the bay itself was once shown on an old map as *Bahía Durate*. Since the situation has not been resolved, I will continue to call the bay *Bahía de Tejano*, at least until the name is officially changed.

The waters in and around *Bahía de Tejano* are alive with wildlife, you'll find plenty of fish and birds hereabouts, in fact some of the local *lancha* operators take their clients into the lagoons behind the marina for bird-watching trips.

Navigational Information
As shown on Chart GTM-5, and in greater detail on Chart GTM-6, a waypoint at 15° 46.30' N, 88° 50.10' W, will place you approximately ¼ mile northwest of the entrance into *Texan Bay*. From the waypoint head into the bay as shown on the chart and anchor wherever you choose or call *Burnt Key Marina* on VHF ch. 68 for a slip.

What You Will Find Ashore
Burnt Key Marina, formerly *Texan Bay Marina*, is now up and running in full force offering side tie slips with electricity and water at each slip and 24-hour security. The marina is a growing community of sorts as some folks have rented or purchased land nearby on which to live.

Dining
The marina has a great little restaurant on site, but the newest dining experience has been constructed by the founder and former owner of *Burnt Key Marina* back when it was *Texas Bay Marina*,

Bahía Buenavista
(Gringo Bay)
Waypoints
Bahía Buenavista inbound vessel- ¼ nm NW of
15° 45.63' N, 88° 50.90' W
Bahía Buenavista outbound vessel- ¼ nm NW of
15° 45.40' N, 88° 51.10' W

Bahía Buenavista, more commonly known as *Gringo Bay* and shown on Chart GTM-5, offers good holding all over the bay so please don't anchor near the moorings to give the boats there plenty of swinging room. The entrance is straightforward and deep.

Navigational Information

There are actually two entrances to *Bahía Buenavista*, one for outbound cruisers and one for inbound cruisers, and the waypoints given are on either side of the small cay that lies off the entrance into the bay as shown on Chart GTM-5. If you are inbound from Livingston (heading upriver), a waypoint at 15° 45.63' N, 88° 50.90' W, will place you approximately ¼ mile northwest of the cut between the offlying island and the mainland; from the waypoint head generally southeast into *Bahía Buenavista* keeping the small island to starboard.

If you are outbound (heading downriver) from the town of *Río Dulce*, a waypoint at 15° 45.40' N, 88° 51.10' W, will place you approximately ¼ mile west of the entrance into the bay; from the waypoint head generally south/southeast into the bay keeping the small island to port. Both of these routes have plenty of water and offer no obstacles or hazards.

What You Will Find Ashore

Here you'll find one of the *Río Dulce's* most lovable characters, Jennifer, a local painter who has a house in *Bahía Buenavista*. If you'd like to visit her studio or garden give Jennifer a hail on VHF ch.68 and she'll be happy to greet you if she's around. Jennifer is a good source of local information, courtesy flags, and smoked *robalo* (snook), and if you want the latest poop on the local security cautions by all means, contact Jennifer.

El Golfete to Río Dulce

Waypoints
El Golfete, Cayo Largo- ½ nm NE of
15° 42.25' N, 88° 55.27' W

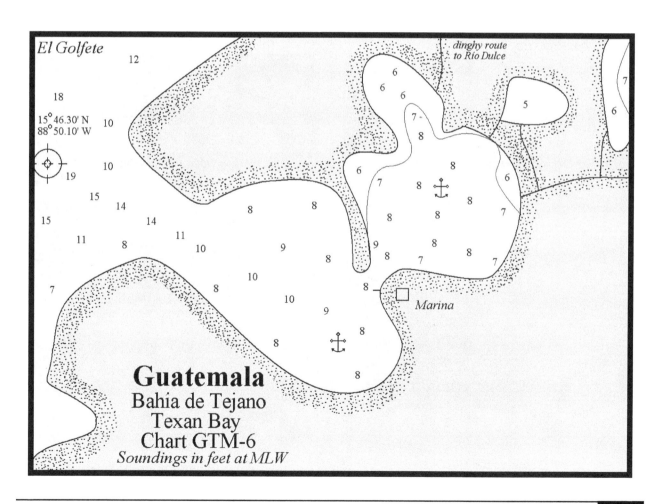

Río Dulce Photographs
all photos on this page courtesy of Bob Meredith, *S/V Barnacle*

Agua Caliente

Ak Tenamit

Amatique Bay Marina, Puerto Barrios

The *Shell* and *Puma* fuel docks, *Río Dulce*

Livingston waterfront

Waterfall at *Finca Paraiso, Lago Izabal*

Gorge on the *Río Dulce*

Statue near Livingston

The area from *El Golfete* to the bridge in the community of *Río Dulce* is the heart of this cruiser's mecca, and we'll cover this section with two charts, Chart GTM-8, which covers *El Golfete* to *Mango's Marina*, and Chart GTM-9, which will take us from *Mango's Marina* past the bridge.

Navigational Information

Heading southwest in *El Golfete* from Cayo Grande, you can steer for a waypoint at 15° 42.25' N, 88° 55.27' W, which will place you approximately ½ mile northeast of Cayo Largo, between Cayo Largo and the piling well to its east as shown on Chart GTM-7. This is an approximate course of 230° T. Keep an eye out for a white buoy just off this courseline as shown on Chart GTM-7. From this waypoint it's simple to pilot into the *Río Dulce* heading for the marina area as shown on the chart. Keep Cayo Largo to starboard and the river will open up before you as shown on the chart.

Outward bound vessels can keep Cayo Largo to port as they enter *El Golfete* from the *Río Dulce* and head generally northeastward to a waypoint at 15° 46.60' N, 88° 50.10' W, which will place you approximately 1.4 miles southwest of Cayo Grande

as shown on Chart GTM-5. From this waypoint pass Cayo Grande to port and enter the *Río Dulce* headed downstream for Livingston.

As you leave *El Golfete* and enter the *Río Dulce* again, as shown on Chart GTM-7 and Chart GTM-8, keep in mid-channel and avoid the shoals on the eastern shore of the river. As you start bearing more to starboard when you are north of *Laguna Escondida* you'll want to start to keep more to port of mid-channel to avoid the shoal area that ends at the mouth of the *Río Ciénaga* as shown on the chart. You can pass north of the shoal, passing between the end of the shoal and the mangroves on the point of land, but unless you have a draft of less than 5' you won't be able to cross back over the shoal near the mouth of the *Río Ciénaga*.

As shown on Chart GTM-8, *Río Seja* joins the *Río Dulce* just downstream from *Mango's Marina* on the northern shore. You'll notice that two rivers empty into the *Río Dulce* from the north, the mouths converging at the same point of land. The river to the west is wide and straight, and ¼ mile upriver are some low-hanging power lines, vertical clearance

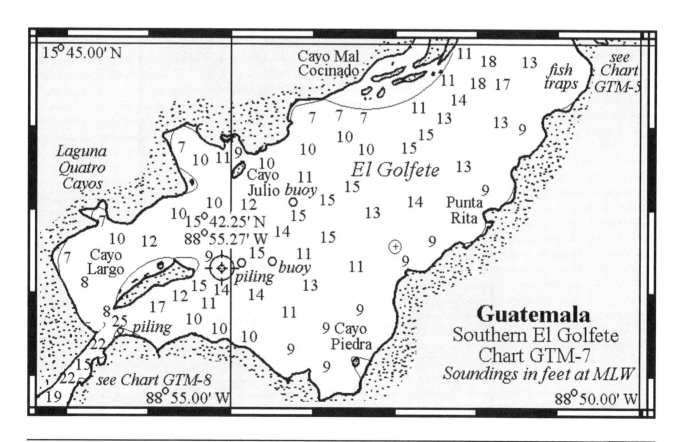

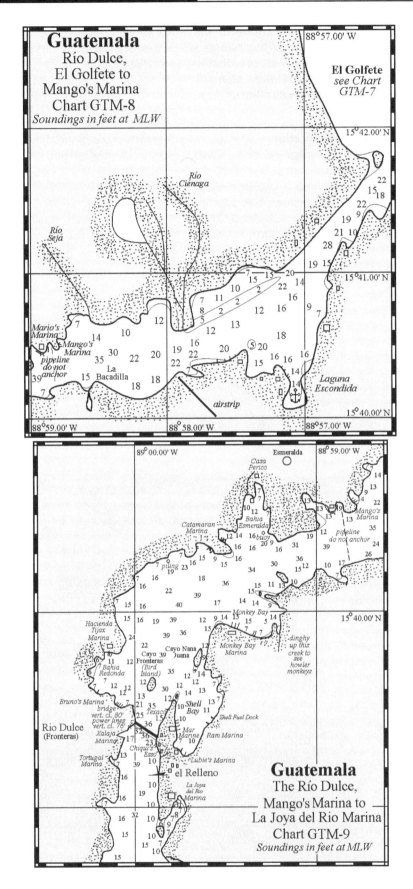

Guatemala
Río Dulce,
El Golfete to
Mango's Marina
Chart GTM-8
Soundings in feet at MLW

El Golfete
*see Chart
GTM-7*

Guatemala
The Río Dulce,
Mango's Marina to
La Joya del Rio Marina
Chart GTM-9
Soundings in feet at MLW

appears to be less than 30', but nobody can seem to tell me the exact height so this is an estimate. Past the power lines the river leads into a lovely lagoon that is definitely worth an exploratory dinghy expedition. The river to the east is the *Río Ciénaga* and boats can navigate this river for several miles as depths of 6'-8' are good for quite a way upstream, but you'll have to keep a sharp eye out for submerged logs.

You can anchor pretty much anywhere on the river that suits you, but if you wish to anchor near the old *Mario's Marina,* do not anchor just east of the marina's easternmost docks, there is a submerged pipeline here and anchoring is prohibited (see Chart GTM-9). Just to the southwest of the marina, less than a hundred yards off the dock as shown on Chart GTM-9 is a shoal that used to be called *Barry's Reef* for a previous owner.

You can anchor in *Monkey Bay* but beware; it has a reputation for poor holding, being called at times both *Mosquito Bay* and *Drag Anchor Bay.* As you approach the bridge you can anchor in either *Shell Bay* or in front of town in *Bahía Redonda.* If you have a tall mast you need to know that the bridge has a vertical clearance of 80', but the power lines beyond the bridge do not have such height. Nobody can give me an exact height on the power lines, but the consensus seems to be about 75', with a bit more on the eastern shore by *Chiqui's.* Beware of the strong currents under the bridge!

What You Will Find Ashore

Security
Cruisers will be happy to note that the Guatemalan Navy has resumed their 24/7 river patrols in February, 2013. The patrols are fully funded by the navy without funds donated by local businesses or marinas. The navy has 6 patrolmen on duty and added a second *Tibueron* patrol craft with a 74 hp *Yamaha* engine. For Semana Santo (Easter Week), and other high-season events, the navy will reinforce the security patrols. Here are the phone numbers for the navy patrol; Officer in charge, 502-5245-2569; patrol boat, 502-4482-7001

Internet
For Internet access in town, you can visit *Río Bravo Pizza.* Most of the larger marinas have Wi-Fi and some even have a computer you can rent to access the Internet. The local bowling alley, *Hoodie's Boliche,* also has Internet access.

A lot of folks have taken to using a "dongle," a small unit that looks like a flash drive and plugs into your USB port and connects your computer to the Internet by means of a nearby *TIGO* cell phone tower. It costs $30-$50 per month depending on the gigabytes you use.

Fuel
Ram Marine is the only marina on the river that has a fuel dock, but there are two places in town where you can get diesel and/or gasoline. The *Shell* fuel dock in *Shell Bay,* and the *Esso* fuel dock south of the bridge and also on the east side of the river, just past *Tienda Reed's* (*Chiqui's*).

Marine Facilities

Marinas
To begin with, let's discuss the 14 "tourist marinas" that you'll find here in the heart of the *Río Dulce.* The reader must know that businesses quickly come and go in places like *Río Dulce,* and if they're not coming and going they're changing, so allow for that when you arrive as one or two of these marinas may not be open, or they may be under new management and have changed names, but as of this writing this is what is available on the *Río Dulce.*

Another thing I'd like to mention is the power situation on the *Río Dulce.* The power grid in the area is not adequate for the electrical demands placed upon it at times and you will find that there are periods when you will have voltage drops, I've seen it drop below 100 volts before, and you will also experience frequent power outages (especially during and after a bad squall), but don't panic, you'll get used to it. Some marinas have backup generators for such times. And bear in mind that when you face your monthly power bill from your marina, that power in Guatemala is VERY expensive. With the exception of *Ram Marine* and *Mar Marine,* which both monitor VHF ch. 73, all of the marinas on the river monitor VHF ch. 68.

Mangos Marina
As shown on Chart GTM-9, as you head upriver, the first marina you will come to is *Mango's* (http://www.riodulcemangomarina.com/), a small marina that is usually full. The marina does have good electric and a pool but that's it as far as amenities. Mango's offers high speed *Wi-Fi,* a pool, common kitchen, potable water, a resturant, boat cleaning services, a laundry, dinghy and outboard storage, metered electric, launch service, shop space, and engine and sail repairs.

Catamaran Marina

A bit further west is *Catamaran Marina and Resort* (www.catamaranisland.com) on *Bahía de Esmeralda*. *Catamaran* offers 50 side tie slips (at good prices), 110/220 volt 50 amp electric, a swimming pool, a tennis court, a very nice restaurant and full-service bar, Internet access at your boat, small cabanas for rent, hotel usage for all guests, a good backup generator in case of power outages, however the marina does not permit either children or pets. Daily happy hours run from 1600-1900 at the pool bar.

Monkey Bay Marina

On the other side of the river and a bit closer to town is *Monkey Bay Marina* (http://www.monkeybaymarina.com/) where you'll get some of the best breeze on the river. *Monkey Bay Marina* is managed by cruisers and offers 22 deep-water side-tie slips for catamarans and monohulls with 110/220 volt, 30 amp and 50 amp electric (with generator backup), purified water, laundry, showers, wireless Internet, kayaks and day sailers for guest use, a workshop complete with a drill press, grinder, table saw, and planer, and a large *palapa* with a stove, BBQ, a refrigerator/freezer, food preparation and dining areas, and enough kitchen gear for all the folks who stay there and cook dinner out every evening. The marina is family oriented and children are highly welcome.

Hacienda Tijax

Just across the river and a bit more upstream is *Hacienda Tijax*, part of a much larger complex. *Hacienda Tijax* (http://tijax.com/) offers side-tie slips with water, electricity, showers, a swimming pool, a workshop for do-it-yourselfers, a hotel, restaurant and bar, laundry, *lancha* service, and Internet access.

As you head upriver past these marinas that I have mentioned, you'll soon come to the heart of the area, the bridge, where you'll find the two communities that are the center of activity and business on this part of the river. On the north side of the bridge is the town of *Río Dulce*, often referred to as Fronteras, and on the south side of the bridge is El Relleno, though both are usually referred to as *Río Dulce*, few people make a distinction between the two.

Bruno's Marina

On the northwest side of the bridge in downtown *Río Dulce*, southwest of Cayo Fronteras, usually just called Bird Island, is *Bruno's Marina* (http://

brunoshotel.com/). *Bruno's* has been serving cruisers for over 20 years and is internationally known. The marina has side tie slips with water, electricity (110 and 220 volt service), cable TV, 24-hour security, rooms for rent, a great restaurant, a shaded swimming pool, laundry service, and is centrally located near everything in town.

RAM Marina

Across the river from town is *Enseñada Nana Juana*, often called *Shell Bay*, and here you'll find several marinas and a haul-out yard, *Ram Marina and Yacht Club*,

RAM Marina boasts nautical and fishing supplies, a restaurant, covered storage and lockers, a convenience store, laundry facilities, gated parking, floating docks that can accommodate vessels to 75' in length with full power, water, cable TV, and Wi-Fi.

RAM has a *PUMA* gas dock right next door to the *Shell* gas dock. *RAM Marina* also offers hot dip galvanizing of your anchors, chain, and other gear, a soda blaster, and full service maintenance and repair.

Nana Juana Marina

Nana Juana Marina (http://hotelmarinananajuana.com/) is located next door to *Ram Marina* and offers cruisers a pool, bar, and restaurant. The marina offers free Wi-Fi, special yard rates for marina guests, nice bathrooms, community BBQs (five with Woks), a community room with chairs and tables. 110 volt and 220 volt electric, 24-hour security, a laundry, a propane refill service, a small DIY workspace, a dinghy dock, dinghy storage, and an oil cump facility.

Calypso Marina

Calypso Marina (http://www.calypsomarina.com/), is an authorized marina and although small, the marina can accommodate 20 boats in a very secure and boater friendly environment with 24-hour security, potable water, secure power connections, road access and other amenities.

La Joya Del Río Marina

La Joya Del Río Marina is probably the most protected marina on the *Río Dulce* located in *Laguna La Joya* (the site of the old *Suzanna's Laguna Marina*) between the bridge and Lago Izabal. The marina offers full electric, water, a laundry service, and has great rates.

Mar Marine

Mar Marine (http://marmarine.com/) is where you'll also find side-tie slips and an excellent diesel mechanic on staff, Rudy.

Capt. John's Marina

Capt. John's Marina (http://www.riodulcemarina.com/) offers services that no other marina can, notably, fuel polishing.

Tortugal Marina

A bit further upstream on the same side of the river is Tortugal Marina (http://tortugal.com/), a nice marina with a good staff and facilities. Thirty slips are available with full electric and water, a restaurant and bar, library, laundry, Internet, fax/photocopy/telephone service in the office, yacht maintenance, and long term storage.

Mansion del Río

On the other side of the river is Mansion del Río, and although they have a good restaurant and pool, they are geared primarily towards small, shoal draft powerboats.

Marine Facilities

Boatyards

If you need to haul out you have three choices, the new RAM Marina and Yacht Club yard in Shell Bay, and Astillero Magdelena, better known as Don Abel's (Don Abel Ramirez's boatyard). RAM Marine has a new 85-ton Travelift and an 8,000 lb. forklift for small powerboats. Don Abel's has two 150-ton marine railways (this means they can haul out large catamarans and trimarans-over 30' in width and boats up to 80 tons), a 75- ton marine railway, and an 85-ton Travelift, all with full marine repairs as well as a new prop shop! Cruisers can stay at their apartments and indulge in the ice cream shop and grocery store while hooking up to their Wi-Fi. Nana Juana Marina can haul catamarans to 50' LOA.

Marine Services

For refrigeration try SeaKist (http://www.seakistservices.com/, 502-5057-2093). If you need an electrician call Richard at 502-5687-0291. If you are in need of sail or rigging repair contact Cayo Quemado Sails at 502-5776-5856 (http://www.quemadosails.com/). Marine supplies can be found at Equipos del Río across from BanRural, 502-7930-5615. Windward Marine Electronics can help with your electrical or electronic needs, call them at 502-

5732-2802, or hail them on VHF ch. 68. For solar system parts and accessories try Sistemas Solares (http://www.solar.gt/i/) across from BanRural, 502-7930-5249. If you need a carpenter contact Manuel at 502-5758-5954.

Provisions

Some of the marinas on the river will have a small store, a tienda, on site. The tienda at Mario's Marina is one of the best and it makes it easy for cruisers staying there to top off their larder whenever necessary. Mario's offers gourmet meat selections from a choice butcher in Guatemala City and cannot be beat for taste or price. Everything from steaks to filet mignons to smoked pork chops and sausage. They also carry a wide variety of beverages, breads, snacks, and various canned goods as well as ice cream. If you're staying at another marina you can always dinghy over to Mario's or hire a lancha to drop you off and pick you up after you've completed your shopping.

There are numerous tiendas in the town of Río Dulce, where you can buy all the basics at low prices, and in the center of town, along the main road are numerous small tiendas and snack shacks where you can pick up anything from fresh fish, produce, meat, pots and pans, shoes, and even kerosene. You'll find a lot of competition here for your business, prices are negotiable so keep that in mind. On the weekends an even larger market is set up on the north bank of the Río Dulce under the bridge.

For shopping I prefer Miriam's Tienda (she also sells spirits) near Río Bravo Pizza, and Ingrid's just up from Bruno's, and of course Tienda Reeds, just past the bridge on the left, usually just called Chiqui's after owner Chiqui Lupitou. Chiqui's also offers fenced and guarded parking in the large lot behind the store if you wish to keep a car here for any length of time. Chiqui's has some good meats, telephone cards, and even marine supplies, batteries, and hardware items. Just up from Miriam's Tienda on the left at the main road is a great spot to find fresh produce vendors, If you walk up to the main road and take a right, about a block down on the right is Dispencia Familiar where you'll usually find the best prices in town but not the best meats. For fine meats try Pana Meats.

Dining on the Río Dulce

Now let's discuss where to dine while on the river. Without a doubt you can have a great time at the Cayuco Club at Mario's Marina as I've mentioned earlier. Just around the corner from *Mango's Marina*, up the small creek in *Bahía de Esmeralda*, as shown on Chart GTM-9, you'll find *Casa Perico*. *Casa Perico* will be happy to pick you up at your marina for their Saturday night *BBQ Buffet* or their Wednesday night *Pizza Buffet*.

As you approach the bridge both *Catamaran Marina* and *Hacienda Tijax* have very good restaurants. In *Shell Bay* you'll find *Mary's Restaurant* and across the street and under the bridge is a tiny *comedor* that sells some of the best fried chicken in town. On the other side of the bridge, *Bruno's* is an excellent place to dine as is *Río Bravo Pizza* (who also feature seafood besides pizza). On the main highway are dozens of small places to eat as well as folks selling food from carts and in small stalls alongside the road so it's a real adventure searching for something to eat at times; decisions…decisions…decisions. South of the bridge you can dine at *Tortugal Marina*, or at *Vista Río*. The *Hotel Kangaroo Bar and Restaurant* (http://www.hotelkangaroo.com/) offers both an Aussie and Mexican menu. And of course, the *Sundog Cafe* is up and running strong.

The Castillo

As you leave the *Río Dulce* and venture upstream into huge *Lago Izabal*, you'll pass the *Castillo de San Felipe de Lara* on your starboard side as you enter the lake. Locally known as *El Castillo*, or *The Castillo*, the fort stands on the western shore of the *Río Dulce* about ½ mile south of the bridge. In the early 1500s, Spain opened trade with Guatemala in the area that was then known as *Golfo Dulce* and warehouses were set up on the shores of Lago Izabal. The fort was built by the Spanish to protect their interests on *Lago Izabal* from the English pirates that were attracted by these rich warehouses. In 1595, King Phillip II of Spain ordered a tower, known as the *Sande* tower, built on the present site with 12 artillery pieces and manned by an equal number of soldiers. Although in an excellent location and with a very good field of fire, the *Castillo de San Felipe de Lara* was not entirely successful as a defensive measure, even though at one point the Spaniards went so far as to string a chain across the river to thwart pirates headed upstream. Over the next two hundred years the fort was destroyed several times, but the Spanish were resilient, rebuilding time and time again. The fort was first destroyed in 1604, and when it was rebuilt it was renamed the *Bustamante* tower after the Spanish captain that rebuilt it. In no time at all the

tower was again destroyed and in 1651 was rebuilt as the *Castillo de San Felipe de Lara* in honor of the King of Spain and the man who rebuilt the tower, a judge named Lara Mogrovejo.

Over the following years the fort was attacked several times and went into a period of decline even though several attempts at rebuilding it were poorly handled. Burned to the ground in 1684, the fort was rebuilt four years later, stronger and better than ever. Soon the attacks stopped and the fort fell into disuse, eventually becoming a prison like so many old forts seemed destined to do. Today *El Castillo de San Felipe de Lara* is a park and the waters surrounding the fort are buoyed for swimmers and no anchoring is permitted in front of the *Castillo*.

Lago Izabal

Lago Izabal, at 590 square kilometers, is the largest lake in Guatemala. Although in places the lake is 50' deep, the winds here can create a vicious short, steep chop in little time. The lake is fed my numerous small rivers, some of which are navigable by the average cruising boat, sail or power and which also contribute the water hyacinths that plague boaters on the lake and the river. The lake is surrounded by mountains, the *Santa Cruz Mountains* to the north where you'll find peaks rising to over 4,000', and the *Sierra de las Minas* to the south where those peaks top out at over 7,000'.

When navigating near the shoreline, within a mile and a half, you must always keep an eye out for fishing nets. Here men on shore will assist men in *cayucos* who will string a net out for over a mile from shore in a huge "U" shape. The only sign will be a *cayuco* offshore and men in the shallows

Sketch courtesy of Bob Smith

close in. You'll need to pass outside these *cayucos* to avoid getting entangled in the small diameter polypropylene line that is used for hauling the net and which of course floats a few inches below the surface. Do not attempt to move about on the lake at night, especially near the shoreline. All the anchorages west of a line from *Denny's Beach* to *Finca Paraíso* should be considered as questionable from a security standpoint, you should only travel here with a buddy boat, and when leaving your boat make sure it is locked, or better yet, leave someone aboard.

We'll begin our circumnavigation of *Lago Izabal* in a clockwise manner beginning at *El Castillo de San Felipe de Lara*.

Denny's Beach

Waypoints
Denny's Beach- ¼ nm NW of
15° 28.75' N, 89° 01.41' W

When headed south the first stop you'll likely make, and it's a good one, is *Denny's Beach*, *Playa Denny*, a popular destination for both cruisers and local boaters.

Navigational Information
After entering *Lago Izabal* at *El Castillo de San Felipe de Lara*, make sure that when heading southwest into the lake you don't pass east of a line between the Castillo and Punta de Dario, the waters here shoal quickly. A waypoint at 15° 28.75' N, 89° 01.41' W, will place you approximately ¼ mile northwest of *Denny's Beach*. From the waypoint you can anchor where your draft permits or if you wish to access a slip give *Denny's Beach* a hail on VHF ch. 63. The waters inside the *muelle* shallow to less than 6' so make sure you call ahead for instructions. *Denny's Beach* has potable water available on the *muelle*.

What You Will Find Ashore
Denny's Beach (http://dennysbeach.com/) is a great place to spend a couple of days and nights to get away from the "hustle and bustle" of *Río Dulce*. There's a nice little beach to swim off, a platform to dive off, a pleasant anchorage that's very safe except when the winds pick up and a 3' chop builds quickly.

The bar and restaurant are quite comfortable and *Denny's* full moon parties are not to be missed. *Denny's Beach* is a small lakeside resort with a wide range of accommodations for rent such as dorms,

cabanas, beach house rooms, to beachfront cabanas and luxurious villas. *Denny's Beach* also offers laundry services, Internet access, horseback riding, and tours to the ruins at Quiriguá and several other local attractions.

Mariscos

Waypoints
Mariscos- ¼ nm NW of town
15° 25.69' N, 89° 05.97' W

Mariscos, originally called *Bodegas*, is THE major town on the southern shore of *Lago Izabal*. A ferry used to run between Mariscos and El Estor but as of this writing sits idle. Here you can catch buses to *Río Dulce*, Puerto Barrios, and Guatemala City.

Navigational Information
As shown on Chart GTM-10, a waypoint at 15° 25.69' N, 89° 05.97' W, will place you approximately ¼ nm NW of Mariscos. Just anchor wherever you like and dinghy into town. If you stay ¼ mile offshore from *Denny's Beach* you should encounter no hazards save the occasional fishing net.

What You Will Find Ashore
Today Mariscos is rarely visited. When the road from El Estor to the main Flores-Puerto Barrios highway was built, the need to take goods and people across the lake by ferry to Mariscos dropped off dramatically and now the ferry is all but a memory. There's little here for cruisers save a small *farmacia*, a nice *tienda*, and bus service to Guatemala City.

Puerto Refugio, Río Oscuro

Waypoints
Lago Izabal, Puerto Refugio- ½ nm N of west tip
15° 24.65' N, 89° 16.30' W

One of the most protected anchorages on *Lago Izabal* can be found in *Puerto Refugio*, also known as *Enseñada de Balandras*, located at the southwestern end of the lake. It is alleged that pirates used this cove as a hideaway while waiting to waylay errant Spanish Ships heading downriver. The anchorage is protected from all but heavy southwesterly and westerly winds.

Navigational Information
As shown on Chart GTM-10, and in greater detail on Chart GTM-11, a waypoint at 15° 24.65' N, 89° 16.30' W, will place you approximately ½ mile north of the western tip of Punta Chapin. From the waypoint

round the shallows that lie west of the point and enter Puerto Refugio to anchor where your draft allows. As you round the tip of Punta Chapin to enter the bay, you'll notice a buoy to port; it explains in Spanish that this is a "Manatee Area."

What You Will Find Ashore

As shown on Chart GTM-10, just southwest of *Puerto Refugio* is the *Río Oscuro*, a pristine jungle river full of exotic wildlife, you might even see a crocodile or two here or in Puerto Refugio. There is a bar at the mouth of the river that limits drafts to under 6' depending on the amount of recent rainfall. The stunning, colorful *Río Zarquito* branches off the *Río Oscuro* not far from the mouth of the river and meanders off into the jungle and is certainly worth exploring by dinghy. Depending on the amount of rainfall the *Río Oscuro* is navigable for between 3-7 miles from its mouth.

Bocas de Bujajal, Río Polochic

Waypoints
Bocas de Bujajal- ½ N of Río Polochic
15° 28.90' N, 89° 21.50' W

The *Bocas de Bujajal* are the mouths of the *Río Polochic*, a very busy river in times gone by, and still not dead yet. There are several coves here that offer good protection to the cruising boat, but you must watch out for fishermen hauling out their nets

The *Castillo de San Felipe de Lara*

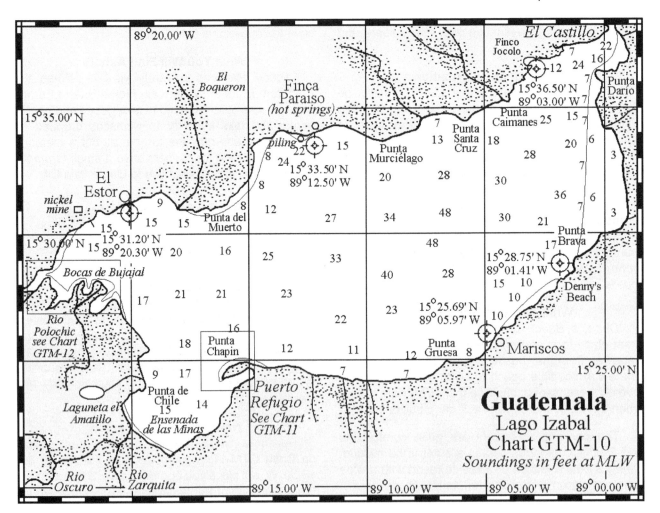

from shore. The *Río Polochic* was once used for hauling goods downstream to El Estor and then by ferry to Mariscos. Although you can work your way some thirty miles upriver, there are good times and bad times to enter the river, never try to enter during the rainy season, one good rain will wash down all manner of debris to foul and possibly damage your vessel, and don't enter during the peak of the dry season either, you might get upriver and find that the water has dropped significantly overnight and you might not be able to get back out for days or weeks.

Navigational Information

As shown on Chart GTM-12, a waypoint at 15° 28.90' N, 89° 21.50' W, will place you approximately ½ mile north of the mouth of the *Río Polochic*. From this waypoint you can head south to anchor in the unnamed bay between *Enseñada el Padre* and *Enseñada Boca Ancha*. Don't try to anchor in *Enseñada el Padre*, it shoals quickly and even the deeper areas will be laced with large sandy mounds covered with grass and lying only a foot or two under the surface. Use caution when entering this bay. The bay itself is used mostly by local fishermen and even though there is an entry into the *Río Polochic* system it can only be used by dinghies or *cayucos*.

Vessels may also anchor in *Enseñada Los Lagartos*, sometimes shown as *Enseñada Laguna*, which lies northwest of *Enseñada Boca Ancha* and west/northwest of the waypoint. The entrance has shoaled and drafts are limited to less than 6'.

If you wish to enter the *Río Polochic*, the entrance can vary from easy to extremely tricky, and sometimes it is downright impassable. The problem lies with heavy rains and the flotsam and jetsam that they bring down the river. I've been to the *Río Polochic* when a muddy bar extended over ½ mile out and was laced with logs and all manner of debris, and the entrance depth was only a few feet. At other times, usually during the dry season, the river is much more clear and easier to enter. Another problem you'll need to be aware of is that the bottom is extremely silty and if you're churning up the bottom by dragging your keel across the bar that you stand a good chance of clogging your raw-water intake and overheating your engine.

You will notice that the river appears to have two mouths, one on either side of the unnamed bay. The entrance between the unnamed bay and *Enseñada el Padre* is not passable, the only entrance is the mouth

to the west of the unnamed bay, between the bay and *Enseñada Boca Ancha* as shown on the chart. Once over the bar the river deepens to 10'-30' in places and narrows to less than a hundred feet not far upriver. The trip upriver is spectacular, first the banks are low and flat but as you wind your way upstream you'll be surrounded by mountains that rise over 2,400'.

El Estor

Waypoints
El Estor- ½ nm S of town
15° 31.20' N, 89° 20.30' W

El Estor received its name from the days when the pirates who sailed the waters of *Lago Izabal* came to the town to buy or steal the supplies they needed from "the store," hence the name, El Estor. Today El Estor has the opportunity for a new growth as the large, and very conspicuous nickel mine that sits on the shores of Lago Izabal just west of the town is re-opening under new Canadian management. When the mine began operations in the 1960s, an agreement between the mine's operators and the town called for the mine to make certain improvements to El Estor including streets, an electric grid, and a telephone system. Nearby is the small town of Panzós where over one hundred villagers were gunned down by the Guatemalan Army in 1978 during the height of the civil war.

In 1978, the elections in Guatemala were doctored by the Army and their candidate, the newly elected President, Brigadier General Fernando Lucas García. The elections only served to bring about a wave of violence across Guatemala as the economy went downhill rapidly and guerilla bases in the mountains were being strengthened.

Some of the worst massacres in Guatemalan history followed over the next decade. That same year a group of villagers in Panzós arrived for a town meeting only to find a group of soldiers waiting on them. The soldiers opened fire and within a few minutes over a hundred men, women, and children lay dead. What was not known to the villagers was that the Army had arrived in Panzós the day before the atrocity and with bulldozers had created two mass graves just outside town. Another fact that was not known to the villagers was that President García owned over 78,000 acres of disputed land outside Panzós. Panzós was the end of the Caribbean railway and a loading point for produce and goods to pass down the *Río Polochic* into and across *Lago*

Izabal, making Panzós an important transshipment point where profits could be made.

Navigational Information

As shown on Chart GTM-10, a waypoint at 15° 31.20' N, 89° 20.30' W, will place you approximately ½ mile south of the town of El Estor. Anchor wherever your draft allows but I suggest that you buddy boat with another cruiser to visit here and not anchor here overnight by yourself!

What You Will Find Ashore

El Estor is not just your sleepy little lakeside village, the folks are friendly and there are several places to dine and pick up some groceries. For dining visit *Hugo's Restaurante*, *Café Santa Clove*, or *Restaurante Chaabil* located lakeside (no alcohol).

You can catch a bus in *Río Dulce* that will bring you to El Estor. Buses leave about every 90 minutes from the north end of the bridge. Once in El Estor you can catch a bus to Cobán at the central park at the unfriendly times of 0100 and 0400. The route is

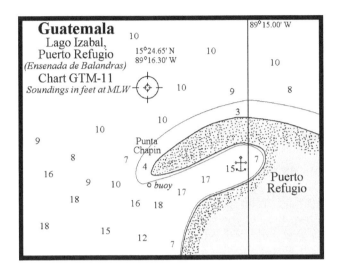

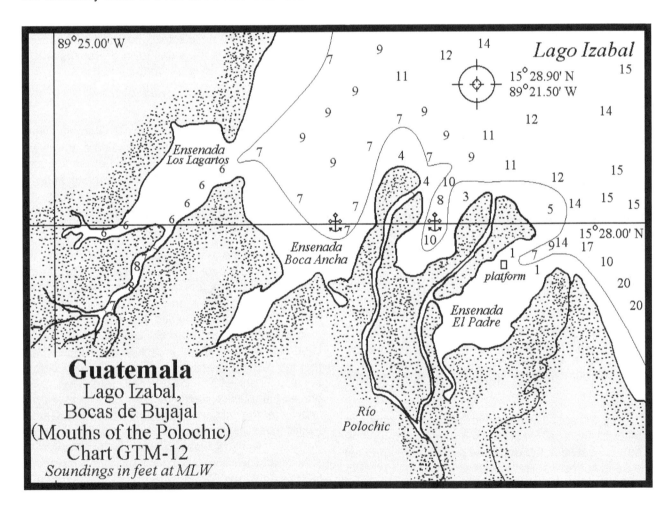

Guatemala
Lago Izabal,
Bocas de Bujajal
(Mouths of the Polochic)
Chart GTM-12
Soundings in feet at MLW

via a bumpy, unpaved road that runs up the beautiful *Polochíc Valley.* This area is infamous for being a hotbed of armed holdups of travelers. For the latest news on this situation check with the folks at *Hugo's Restaurante.*

Approximately 3 miles east of El Estor is the *Río Sauce* where you will find the stunning *Boqueron Canyon,* which is easier to drive to than visit by dinghy as there is one spot upriver where you must portage your dink for several hundred yards. Here, nearly vertical cliffs rise to over 750' above the *Río Sauce* while the river below roars through a jungle canyon and over and around huge boulders. For a few dollars locals will take you up the *Río Sauce* in a wooden canoe to explore the canyon. There is a small beach in the canyon, not far from the beginning of the trip, and they can drop you off there and return at a designated time to allow you some privacy.

Finca Paraíso

Waypoints
Finca Paraíso- ¼ nm SE of
15° 33.50' N, 89° 12.50' W

One of the most popular spots to visit on Lago Izabal is *Finca Paraíso,* Spanish for *Paradise Farm,* a communal farm that supports several families. You can also visit here by bus or taxi from the town of *Río Dulce* if you don't wish to bring your boat here.

Navigational Information
As shown on Chart GTM-10, a waypoint at 15° 33.50' N, 89° 12.50' W, will place you approximately ¼ mile offshore at *Finca Paraíso.* Watch out for the shoal and piling west of *Finca Paraíso* as shown on the chart. Anchor wherever you'd like and dinghy ashore.

What You Will Find Ashore
At *Finca Paraíso* you'll find a few rental cabins (with private bathroom facilities), a small restaurant (all at Don Julio's *Brisas del Lago*) and a wonderful hot springs that is worth the effort to visit. A 12-meter high hot spring waterfalls above the *Río Aguas Caliente* is the draw here and is easy to find. From the water it's about a 30-45 minute walk, but if you drive to *Finca Paríso,* the walk is only about 10 minutes from the parking lot just off the road. Though there is hot water at the falls that spring from a cave in the side of a mountain, the ponds beneath can be quite cool and absolutely picture postcard perfect. It's possible to explore the caves above the falls but you'll need to

bring a flashlight and you might wish to consider a guide as well unless you're the adventurous sort, and if you're a cruiser, chances are you're the adventurous sort.

Finca Jocolo

Waypoints
Finca Jocolo- ¼ nm SE of
15° 36.50' N, 89° 03.00' W

Navigational Information
On the northern shore if *Lago Izabal,* a bit over three miles west of *El Castillo de San Felipe,* is a small cove known as *Finca Jocolo.* As shown on Chart GTM-10, a waypoint at 15° 36.50' N, 89° 03.00' W, places you approximately ¼ mile southeast of the entrance. You can't miss the entrance, look for the large Ceiba tree on shore. Inside the anchorage you'll find good holding in hard sand once you make sure your anchor is set well. This is a great spot in northerly winds and also when the afternoon winds kick up a real chop on the lake.

The Rest of Guatemala

This cruising guide is not meant to be a complete travel guide to Guatemala, if you are looking for one of those there are plenty of good ones to be found. But in this section I will briefly touch upon some of the more popular places to visit while you're spending hurricane season on the *Río Dulce.* And no, I won't discuss each and every restaurant and Internet café here, but I'll just touch upon some of the highlights you should look for to enhance your stay in Guatemala.

Guatemala City

Guatemala City is the capital of Guatemala and if you plan to spend much time at all on the *Río Dulce,* you'll wind up here at least once. The city is divided into 15 zonas (zones), and each has its own grid system of roads, *avenidas* run north and south, and *calles* run east and west. Each *zona* is different and some are not recommended for a visit. The main zonas you'll be concerned with are *Zona 1,* where most of the cheaper hotels and bus terminals are located and you'll see perfect examples of Guatemala City's Spanish architecture (most of the older buildings in the city are located here), and *Zona 10,* where the finer hotels are located near the airport.

In *Zona 1* you'll find *Plaza Mayor,* Guatemala City's ceremonial center and its adjacent retail district. Sunday is the day to be in *Zona 1* along with thousands of Guatemalans who come here to stroll the streets, eat ice cream, listen to loud music, and spend money with any of the hundreds of street vendors you'll pass at the busy *Mercado Central* which replaced the original market building that was destroyed by an earthquake in 1976. On the square you can't miss the twin-towered *Catedral Metropolitana* and if you need a bit of a respite from the madness in the market head north a bit to *Parque Minerva* for some peace and quiet.

Zona 10 is usually called the hotel zone and for good reason, this is where you'll find the best hotels in the city and numerous restaurants and bars to go along with them. The best by far is the *Westin Camino Real* (http://caminoreal.com.gt/), it even has a casino downstairs and a room where you can hook up to the Internet. Just behind the *Westin* is the equally nice, but far less expensive (and my favorite), *Biltmore Express* (http://hotelbiltmore.com.gt/). The *Biltmore* offers full access to the goodies at her sister hotel, the *Westin*, and both offer secure underground parking. The *Biltmore* also offers a great daily breakfast from 0530 till 1000 consisting of sandwich meats, cereals, coffee, juice, all manner of breads, rolls, muffins, and fresh fruits. Just behind the Biltmore is one of my favorite restaurants, the *Inka Grill*. Down the road a bit is the *Howard Johnson*, nearly as nice but not as pricey as the *Biltmore* (US$66 versus US$85 per night), and they offer a breakfast as well which includes eggs cooked to order and pancakes. A few blocks away from the *Biltmore* is the *San Carlos* where you can get a room for about US$25 per night, but no air-conditioning (which is not really needed as Guatemala City is very cool at night due to its location in the highlands) and no dogs, *Otelito* takes small dogs, and they're located on 12 *Calle* 4-51. If you're going to bring your pet it's best to call ahead for permission. *Zona 10* is also home to several nice museums including *Museo Popol* with its outstanding Mayan and Spanish art collections, and the *Museo Ixchel* which offers exhibits of traditional arts and dress of Guatemala's central highland communities. In *Zona 13* you can visit the *Museo Nacional de Arqueología y Etnología* (http://munae.gob.gt/pages/museo.php?lang=ES) to view their impressive collection of Mayan artifacts. *Zona 4*, known as *4 Grados Norte* and situated near *Zona 10*, is a pedestrian zone and here you'll find numerous art galleries, bistros, several truly fine restaurants, a word of warning, *Zona 4* is not a good place to be wandering around at night.

The best shopping in Guatemala can be found in Guatemala City, though her open-air street market differs little from those you'll find in towns across the country. In Guatemala City you can find just about anything you need from mechanical parts to real American style grocery stores such as *Hiper Paiz* (much like a *Super Walmart*), and even a *Price Smart* (https://shop.pricesmart.com/ar/en/), one of the best places to shop in town. A *Walmart* (http://www.walmart.com.gt/) has being built in Guatemala City over the past few years. If you need hardware items you'll find *Ace Hardware* stores are located inside *Cemaco* (http://cemaco.com/) stores, while *Novex* (https://www.novex.com.gt/) is much like a *Home Depot* but on a smaller scale.

Antigua

La Antigua, one of the oldest and most beautiful cities in Central America, was the capital of Guatemala from 1543 until 1776 when the capital was moved 28 miles to the east to the present site of Guatemala City following a devastating earthquake. The city sits between three volcanoes, *Agua, Fuego,* and *Acatenango,* and its colorful buildings have survived 16 earthquakes and numerous floods and fires.

In 1523, Cortés dispatched Pedro de Alvarado to Guatemala to use "minimum force" and to "preach matters concerning our Holy Faith." In 1526, the Kaqchikel broke away from their Spanish allies and moved deeper into the mountains and began to wage a guerilla style war forcing the Spanish to move their base to present day Antigua where they established the first capital of Guatemala, Santiago de los Caballeros on *St. Cecelia's Day*, November 22, 1527. De Alvarado, who had controlled Guatemala like his personal fiefdom, enslaving and abusing the Maya and turning their lands into Spanish estates, was killed beneath a rolling horse during a battle in Mexico on July 4, 1541.

As Guatemala entered her period of Spanish Colonial rule, the capital city of Santiago de los Caballeros entered a prolonged period of mourning initiated by de Alvarado's widow after the death of her husband on July 4, 1541. Beatriz de la Cueva (de Alvarado's first wife's sister), who had herself appointed the new governor and then painted the entire palace black, inside and out. On September 10, 1541, a huge mudslide flowed down the sides of the Aqua volcano and buried the city. The survivors moved the city a short distance away and the new

Santiago de los Caballeros became the administrative center for six provinces, Costa Rica, Honduras, Nicaragua, El Salvador, Guatemala, and Chiapas, now part of Mexico (Santiago de los Caballeros was to rule Guatemala until 1773 when it was destroyed by a series of earthquakes and the capital again moved, this time to what is now known as Guatemala City).

Antigua today is known for many things, her aggressive street vendors, a problem with thieves breaking into cars that are not in protected parking lots, and her many Spanish language schools. *Las Capuchinas*, once a church, is now a museum and *Casa K'ojom* (http://www.kojom.org/) is a fascinating collection of Mayan related music, artifacts, and culture. On Sundays one should check out the bustling market in the *Parque Central*. But Antigua's biggest draw comes once a year, during *Semana Santo*.

Semana Santo in Antigua

If you can only visit Antigua once, I suggest you go during *Semana Santo*, *Holy Week*, the week before Easter, this is when Antigua truly is alive and the time you spend there will be one of those unforgettable memories that you will carry forever. Although the weeklong festivities center on the death of Jesus, all around you is a celebration of life in a carnival-like atmosphere with vendors selling their wares and all kinds of food items guaranteed to pique your interest.

The focus of *Semana Santo* is the processions with each of the five churches in Antigua having at least one procession as well as churches from surrounding communities, sometimes there are as many as five processions in one single day. So busy and crowded is Antigua during *Semana Santo* that some hotels are booked a year in advance for the three busiest days, Wednesday, Thursday, and Friday.

The processions, which originated with the Spanish (most say with Pedro de Alvarado) in the 1500s, actually begin several weeks before *Semana Santo* on Sundays and Wednesdays until Palm Sunday when the festivities of Holy Week actually begin. The processions march to the sound of slow drums, similar to a wedding march, as the *cucuruchos*, the robed men who carry the huge wooden platforms called *andas* on their shoulders, slowly sway from side to side. Other *cucuruchos* walk alongside them, ready to spell their comrades who will take time out to rest and later spell someone else. There may be as

many as 200 *cucuruchos* walking in two lines before each *anda* waiting for their turn to carry the *anda* for two or three blocks. There is even a man dressed as Jesus who goes through the *Stations of the Cross* along with Roman Soldiers on horseback as the processions wind through the streets of Antigua. The *cucuruchos* who carry the main platforms wear richly embroidered velvet robes of red, black, midnight blue, and purple, although on Good Friday they all wear black. Those that carry the platforms of the lesser saints or Mary Magdalene or John have simpler robes. The men carry the platform with Jesus while women, called *carcadoras*, carry the platform with the Virgin Mary while dressed in white with white lace mantillas on their heads except on Good Friday when they too wear black.

It's easy to tell when a procession is coming, it's usually preceded by firecrackers and the bands that accompany each platform can be heard blocks away. The bands can consist of 30 or more members with some trumpeters dressed as Roman Centurions in white, gold, and red with authentic looking period helmets and accompanied by chariots and magnificent horses lent by the owner of one of Guatemala's most exclusive stables. Besides the noise you'll see the cloud of frankincense from a distance as some of the larger processions being led by 40-50 men swinging incense burners. So intense is the cloud of smoke at times that people, even the incense swingers, wear masks over their faces to breathe. As the burners leave a cloud of smoke behind you'll soon seen the *anda* emerge eerily from the smoky haze.

Besides the processions, a prime ingredient in this mix is the creation of the *alfrombras*. An *alfrombra* is an extremely colorful work of art created on the streets of Antigua and made of colored sawdust, flowers, vegetables, baked items in the shapes of lambs and fish, and even colored bits of glass to make these portraits shine in the sun. Some alfrombras may show the Stations of the Cross, or they may simply be beautiful, intricate and colorful mandalas, or they may spell out something like *God is Love, Dios es Amor*. All of those who live on the street where the procession passes are expected to create an *alfrombra*. Although the creation of an *alfrombra* is primarily a family affair, some *alfrombras* are made by organizations such as the group of car mechanics or tire changers. When finished, the designs are guarded until the procession the next day. Sometimes the streets are blocked off by ladders, chairs, or cars to protect the *alfrombras*, while in some instances people hustle outside to create one as soon as the drums can be heard in the distance. If you care to assist in the making of an *alfrombra,* simply walk up and ask if you can help, you'll usually be welcomed warmly. If you just want to view the *alfrombras,* I'd suggest getting out on the streets at 0400 on Good Friday morning and view the creations that the people constructed overnight and awaiting the first procession at 0600. And by the way, although the processions may be blocks long, only the men and women carrying the *andas* are permitted to walk on an *alfrombra.*

The Saturday processions commemorate the sadness of Mary, the mother of Christ. Her image, and only her image, is carried through the streets by women dressed in black and preceded by the statues of angels clad in ornate, rich velvets. These processions wander the streets of Antigua for some ten hours before returning to the churches as everyone prepares for Easter Sunday.

The last processions on Easter Sunday are a bit different. Here, men and women carry the anda in street clothes and everybody is welcome to join them. Unlike the sadness of Good Friday's processions, the Easter Sunday procession is one of joy in Christ's resurrection. As the procession ends and the *anda* reenters the church, the church bells ring out and rose colored confetti is thrown down upon the crowd.

Panajachel and Lago Atitlán

One of the strangest nicknames for any place in Guatemala is the moniker sometimes given to the lovely town of Panajachel, *Gringotenango,* roughly translated it means *the place of gringos.* This is probably due to the number of old "hippies" that have flocked here over the years and the newer influx of young backpackers. But the real draw here, *Lago Atitlán,* Aldous Huxley described as the most beautiful lake in the world: "It is really too much of a good thing." *Lago Atitlán* is indeed one of the most stunning of all the sights you will see in Guatemala, it is the #1 tourist attraction in Guatemala and some will even go so far as to describe it as one of the *Seven Wonders of the World.*

Lago Atitlán is a caldera lake created when a collapsed volcanic cone filled with water. Some 100,000 years ago three volcanoes, *Santa Cruz, Zakilac,* and *Pakisis,* were formed. They were outlets for the same magma deposit, a *batholith.* Then, about 85,000 years ago, a huge eruption destroyed

the volcanoes and the ground over the magma deposit collapsed and the caldera that was to become *Lago Atitlán* was formed. Today *Lago Atitlán* is still surrounded by three volcanoes, *San Pedro, Atitlán,* and *Tolimán,* all of which are inactive. The lake itself is over 900' deep in many places and drains to the Pacific coast via an underground outlet. In 1955, the *Lago Atitlán* basin was declared a national park but you can hardly tell it today, so popular is it with the tourist crowd, not to mention the wealthy Guatemalan's who have moved to its shores after "discovering" the lake in the 1990s.

For those wishing to travel across the lake there is *lancha* service available, but for some locations it is cheaper and faster to take a bus. The *lancha* operators are notorious for overcharging tourists, gringos, so beware and check around before deciding on a *lancha* and a price.

There are some 13 communities surrounding the lake, and even more in the surrounding hills, some of which are very traditional Mayan villages where you'll hear the Kaqchikel Mayan dialect and the rare Tz'utujil dialect spoken by the descendants of people who once inhabited the slopes of the *San Pedro* volcano. The largest community, Panajachel, is almost a cosmopolitan resort compared to some of the smaller and more traditional villages, and during the 1960s and 1970s was Central America's favorite destination of "hippies" traveling through the region, many believing that Panajachel was a vortex energy field similar to the Pyramids in Egypt and Machu Picchu in Peru. Some of these same travelers have stayed in Panajachel and now operate cafés, boutiques, and other like-minded capitalistic ventures.

The most popular spots are of course Panajachel, but even more pleasant, and not quite so touristy are places like laid-back San Pedro la Laguna, a favorite of the hippie/backpacker crowds and a good place to enroll in one of the town's Spanish language schools, Sololá, sitting some 1800' above the lake with its centuries-old Friday market that was described by Aldous Huxley as "...a walking museum of fancy dress," and Santiago Atitlán where you'll find the drinking and cigar smoking deity *Maximón.*

An interesting afternoon phenomenon on *Lago Atitlán* is a strong afternoon easterly wind called *Xocomil,* the *Fury of the Demons,* the "wind that carries away sin." Legend has it that the *Spirit of the Lake* fell in love with a beautiful maiden from a village on the shores of the lake. When the maiden's parents realized this they took her away and she died of a broken heart. Since then the *Spirit of the Lake* desperately comes looking for her every day and it is said that he will not rest until he finds her. A north wind is said to mean that the *Spirit of the Lake* is discarding a drowned body after claiming its soul.

Chichicastenango

Chichicastenango, sometimes just called Chichi, is another must-see destination that I've seen described as Guatemala's tourism Mecca. Located nearly 7,000' up in the heart of the central highlands, the way to get there is from the south, from Sololá near *Lago Atitlán*. Chichicastenango is an important market town and no visit to Guatemala would be complete without a visit to the colorful Thursday or Sunday morning markets in this isolated community where these markets have been held for centuries (the Sunday market is the busiest and THE market that is not to be missed). And if you're in Guatemala in December, you should make every effort to visit Chichicastenango during the *Fiesta de Santo Tomás* with its parades, processions, dances, and the *Palo Volador*, where men dangle from ropes from a 60' pole.

In the square below the church you'll find the market, which has been going on for hundreds of years and is a blend of tourist oriented vendors and traditional Mayan weavers and artisans from the nearby communities. The best time to attend the markets is before 1000 when the tourist buses arrive. Here you'll find true Mayan workmanship alongside stalls selling imitation goods and the uninitiated will have trouble telling the difference. Bargaining is part of the process so bear that in mind, and be forewarned that some of the vendors there apply a very "hard sell" approach and some will even follow you around until you have to tell them to leave you alone.

A short distance outside of town, about ½ mile from the market, is the shrine of *Pascual Abaj*, where ancient Mayan ceremonies are still performed by a *brujo* with incense, alcohol, and chanting, while worshipers make offerings of anything from flowers to chickens. These ceremonies are very important to the Mayan people so do not disrespect any of those in attendance and do not take any photographs without permission. This goes for all of Chichicastenango as well, especially if you wish to take photographs of

children, always ask first and in many cases expect to pay something for the opportunity.

Quetzeltenango (Xela)

Quetzeltenango, usually just called Xela (pronounced Shay-lah), was once known as Xelajú, the K'iché word for "under the ten," possibly a reference to the fact that this highland capital sits amid numerous mountain peaks. Xela, Guatemala's second largest city (though nowhere near the size of Guatemala City), prospered for many years as a coffee-brokering and storage center until an earthquake and a volcanic eruption ended that financial boom. Today however it is THE higher learning center for Guatemala and home to 8 universities, over 100 private colleges, and over 70 language schools. In the center of town you'll find the *Parque Minerva*, built during the presidency of Manuel Estrada Cabrera (1898-1920) to honor the classical goddess of education as a way of inspiring Guatemalan youth. Just to the north of Xela is Olintepeque, a Mayan community whose primary output is the colorful textiles you'll see in so many markets. Towards the Pacific coast from Xela lies Zunil, THE garment center for Guatemala, and in the hills above town are the fabulous hot springs, *Fuentes Georginas*, where you can spend the night or just visit for the day and relax in the soothing hot springs.

South of Xela, Volcán Santa María rises to over 12,000' and if you'd like you can visit one of the tour operators (*Casa Iximulew* or *Adrenalina Tours*) in Xela to arrange for a climb. From atop the volcano you can see Mexico as well as the volcanoes surrounding Antigua and *Lago Atitlán*, as well as the still active Volcán Santiaguito, not as high as Volcán Santa María, but quite active and an awesome sight to peer down from the heights into the mouth of an active volcano. You are not permitted to climb Volcán Santiaguito due to its level of activity.

El Petén and Flores

Comprising some 1/3 of Guatemala's land area, the tropical rainforest of El Petén is sparsely populated, although in the last few decades it has increased from 15,000 to over 300,000, mostly refugees from the civil war that ended in 1996. This number is far down from the more than one million people that archeologists estimate lived here 1,200 years ago when the center of the Mayan civilization was located here in cities such as Tikal, Nakbé, and El Mirador. The main road leading into the Petén from Guatemala City goes right through *Río Dulce*, Flores, and Tikal, all of which are only a few hours north of the marine centers on the river.

Flores, the capital of the jungle covered northwestern department of El Petén, sits on the island of San Andres in *Lago de Petén Itzá* and is connected to the mainland towns of Santa Elena and San Benito (along with Flores, all three of these towns are often referred to as Flores) by a 1640' long man-made causeway. Founded by the Itzá Mayans as their capital, Tayasal, it was the last functioning Mayan ceremonial center in Guatemala at the time of the conquest. In 1697, the Spanish finally conquered the Itzá and the town of Flores was built atop the ruins of Tayasal and was originally used as a penal colony. The Spanish constructed a fort in Flores in the early 1700s, *El Castillo de Arismendi*, which served mainly as a prison until the 1980s.

The center of town is the main plaza which sits atop a hill in the center of the island and this is where the government offices will be found. Flores has excellent bus service to Guatemala City as well as Belize and in town are several nice hotels, some even have protected parking. The *Lago de Petén Itzá* is a lovely body of water and you can tour the lake by boat from the Flores. A good vantage point is *King Canek's Lookout Point*, *El Mirador del Rey Canek* (Canek was an Itzá chief who ruled here in the early 1600s). If you'd like to view some indigenous animals, visit Isla Pentencito and the *Paraíso Escondido Wildlife Rescue Center and Zoo*.

If you are planning to visit the ruins at Tikal, some folks opt to stay at one of the hotels just outside the entrance to Tikal, but you will find better accommodations in El Remate or Flores and then you'll only have to deal with a short bus ride to Tikal. A couple of good side trips while in the area is the *Canopy Tarzan Tour* at the *Ixpanpajul Natural Park* or the *Actún Can Caves*.

Santa Lucia Cotzumalguapa

The town of Santa Lucia Cotzumalguapa lies on Guatemala's Pacific slope south of Antigua and is an important site for anybody that is interested in Mayan art and culture. As you pass through the countryside the first things you'll notice are the sugar cane *fincas* (plantations) interspersed with huge, carved stone

heads, all that remains of the *Pipils*, a non-Mayan Indian culture that was linked to the *Nahuatl*-speaking peoples of central Mexico (who have left similar heads in the state of Tabasco). *Finca Bilbao* has several ceremonial sites containing stone sculptures hidden among the cane fields while *Finca el Baúl* is still an active place of worship and *Finca Las Ilusiones* contains hundreds of objects collected from the fields over the centuries. The best time to visit the sites is in the morning and by taxi.

Montericco

Along Guatemala's southeastern Pacific coast is the small community of Montericco. Here the surrounding swamps are quite buggy but the long beach is quite picturesque (and the ferocious undertow very dangerous). There is one true attraction here, the *Biotopo Montericco-Hawaii*. Including the villages of Montericco and Hawaii, and the wetlands surrounding the two, and the long, lovely beach that edges the Pacific, the *Biotopo* is a reserve for nesting sea turtles (Leatherbacks, Olive Ridley's, and East Pacific Black Turtles), and although the area is protected, there is a great amount of turtle egg theft. The *Biotopo* maintains a small headquarters and visitor's center in Montericco next to the *Hotel Baule Beach* and has some baby turtles in tanks and exhibits of marine specimens. The staff, as well as volunteers, will often pick up turtle eggs from more remote places and rebury them next to their headquarters so that when they hatch *Biotopo* personnel can protect the baby turtles from predators by placing them in buckets and delivering them directly into the sea. The reserve is a good place to view turtles coming ashore at night to built a nest and lay their eggs. Leatherbacks usually nest here between October and December, while Olive Ridleys and East Pacific Black Turtles nest from July to December along this coast.

Gateway to the Caribbean

- 78 state-of-the-art floating docks
- Berthing for vessels up to 220 ft LOA, 8.5 ft draft (at mean low tide)
- Premium diesel and gasoline, water, pump-out facilities and multiple power types
- 24 hr security
- Five star customer service and concierge facilities
- Marina guests enjoy access to resort amenities including 3 restaurants and 2 bars, deli and café, gym, spa, pool and private beach
- Customs and immigration services
- Provisioning and yacht catering

BLUE HAVEN

marinareservations@bluehaventci.com | 649 946 9910

RESORT & MARINA | BLUEHAVENTCI.COM

A Little Basic Jamaican

Just enough to get you in trouble

Jamaicans have their own way of expressing themselves in everything they do and their speech is rich in variations of many common English words. Have no fear, the language spoken on Jamaica is English, but it is often spoken with the local dialect, *patois*. You'll hear a similar accent throughout the Caribbean, but in Jamaica it is thicker, fuller, and more colorful.

Two phrases that you'll hear on the island that have been vastly overused in the Caribbean are *Yeah mon* and *No Problem*. In Jamaica *Yeah mon* is not as drawled out as it is represented on TV and the pair are often used together as in "Yeah mon, no problem." They seem to complement each other that way and sound good together.

Television has also had another impact on Jamaican culture, today you'll find people dancing the *Jerry Springer,* yes that's right, a dance named after the famous (or is it infamous?) talk show host. The dance involves moving your arms and legs back and forth almost in a punching motion and then adding a left/right leg movement along with it. If you can't get the dance right it's said you're doing the *Sally* or the *Montel*, not the *Springer.*

One of the most popular words you'll hear in Jamaica is *Irie*. There really is no true English translation, *Irie* describes a state of being. For example, somebody might ask "How are you," and you might reply "Irie." You're telling the listener that you're feeling fine, cool, easy going, chilling…do you get the picture? *Irie* can also be used to describe a person or place that is pleasing or pleasant such as in "Dis ya Irie Mon." This roughly translates to "This is irie man."

One word that confused me at first was *Nyammings*. I saw it on signs of restaurants and I soon learned that *nyam* means to eat, so *Nyammings* were places to eat. If somebody tells you that they are going to "… *run a boat* at George's," it means that they are going to cook some food at George's and everyone contributes to the meal, sort of like a pot-luck.

As in most islands of the Caribbean and Bahamas, many folks tend to not pronounce "h" and "th" often becomes a "d" such as in *anadda*, which is nothing more than the word *another*, *dem*, which means *them*, or in *de*, which means *the*, and *nutten* which is *nothing*. *There* is usually pronounced as *deh*, and *down there* can be *dung deh*, while *father* can be *fahda*, and *lef* becomes *left*. The letter *a* has several different uses and is usually pronounced like a short *a* as in *I a going tomorrow…* or as in a *gwine*m meaning *I'm going to* or *gwaan* as in *go on*. Orange can become *arinj* in Jamaican, easily enough understood but maybe not when your ears first hear it.

This section is but a primer and is in no way meant to be a Jamaican dictionary. I will attempt to make you familiar with a few Jamaican phrases that you are likely to come across in your travels.

Jamaican Phrase	English Equivalent
A door	outdoors
Agony	sexual climax
Aks	ask
Alias	dangerous, violent
Asham	parched, ground, sweet corn
Babylon	the world outside, the "system," can even mean a policeman
Bald-head	someone without dreadlocks, one who works for Babylon
Bandulu	a criminal, conman
Bandulu bizness	a racket or con

Bankra	a large basket, may be hung on the sides of a donkey
Bashment	a party
Batty	backside, butt
Battybwoya	gay person
Beast	Policeman
Biscuit	an attractive woman
Boops	an older man who supports a younger woman
Boopsie	a kept woman
Black up	smoke ganga
Bredren	a Rasta's fellow Rastas, his brethren
Bud	bird
Cease and sekkle	stop everything you're doing and relax
Chatty Chatty	you talk too much
Chi Chi Man	a gay man
Deh	there
Duppy	ghost
Everyting Cook and Curry	Everything's fine
Ganga	marijuana
Hot-stepper	fugitive
Jah	God
Jah knows	God knows
Janga	shrimp or crayfish
Labalaba	to chat or gossip
Matey	mistress
More time	see you later
Nuh nuttin	not a big deal, no problem
Nuh true?	Isn't it so?
Nyam	to eat
Nyammings	places to eat
Ragga	a reggae style that uses digital rhythms exclusively
Running belly	diarrhea
Saal	bad luck
Seen	I understand or agree
Seen?	Do you understand or agree?
Tam	The often colorful woolen hat worn to cover dreadlocks
Teif	Thief
Tings saal	times are rough
Vexed	to be angry with
Wolf	A false Rasta, has the dreadlocks but not the beliefs
Zion	Ethiopia, the Rastafarian Holy Land

Dining

*Part of the secret of success in life
is to eat what you like
and let the food fight it out inside.*

Mark Twain

Food fight!
John Belushi

One of the simple joys of cruising, and traveling in general, is sampling the cuisine of different cultures. In this section I'll highlight what you will most likely find on the menu as you cruise the waters of the Northwest Caribbean. In general you can expect food to be a bit hotter, a bit spicier, in the Northwest Caribbean, and with the exception of the Cayman Islands and Jamaica (both of whom are heavily influenced by British cuisine), you'll find *huevos y frijoles* (eggs and beans) are a staple along with the *tortilla*, flat, round, unleavened bread made from corn. In the Spanish speaking countries of the Northwest Caribbean you'll delight in avoiding the tourist traps and finding a *comedor*, a local restaurant that serves up good local cuisine (*comida típico*) at prices far below those in the tourist haunts. Usually there is no menu at a *comedor* so you should inquire as to what's available or simply look at what's cooking on the stove. Occasionally you'll find what can best be described as a cross between a restaurant and a *comedor*, serving local food at low prices, and they have a menu. In general, you'll find the restaurants in the larger towns in hotels and tourist traps, while the *comedores* are usually found in the smaller settlements. This is not to say that you won't find a *comedor* in a large city, but in a large city you'll also find fast food take out restaurants such as you're used to in the United States (places like *Wendy's*, *Pizza Hut*, and even a *McDonald's* that delivers to your hotel in Guatemala City).

In the Spanish speaking countries breakfast is called *desayuno*, lunch, the midday meal, is called *almuerzo*, and dinner, or supper, is called *cena*. Normal routine calls for a light *desayuno*, with *almuerzo* being the largest meal of the day. You'll find that many restaurants offer a great midday meal, two or three courses for little money. This is of course for those who can afford it (and the turistas), much of the citizens of Mexico, Belize, Guatemala, and Honduras live below what we in the United States would call the poverty level and they would love to have three meals a day, and some would be thrilled to have two meals a day. Vegetarians will find just a few restaurants that cater to their needs, usually in the larger cities, however most restaurants have beans and eggs on their menus along with a variety of fruits and veggies.

When dining out you may find that an *IVA* (*Impuesto de Valor Agregado*) has been added to your bill. This is a tax, not a service charge or tip. If a tip has been added your bill should read *Servicio Incluido* or *Incluido Propina*. Expected tips range from 10%-15% in Honduras and Guatemala, and from 15-20% in Mexico. And one final note; you will find that few restaurants in the Northwest Caribbean have "no-smoking" areas.

One more warning, when traveling away from the more-touristy areas please be aware that cleanliness in food preparation may not be as thorough as what you are used to and what you expect. Fruit and vegetables are good sources of bacteria, especially those with a thin skin that gets eaten, such as lettuce or tomatoes. When cooking on your own vessel, all fresh produce should be washed in fresh water, not just some water from a stream mind you, and it would help to add 8-10 drops of bleach or iodine to the wash. Picking up a parasite this way and you can be sure of several weeks of misery at the very least. Be careful.

Now let's briefly discuss the value of some of the foods you'll encounter in the Northwest Caribbean and how they can affect your health. *Cassava*, also known as *manioc* or *yucca*, is used to make tapioca and can help prevent heart disease, reduce the risk of cancer, prevent cataracts, is loaded with *iron, magnesium*, and *Vitamin C*, and can help keep your sun and salt weathered skin smooth. Although not well known in the United States, *cassava* is the world's #2 vegetable crop after potatoes. Plantains can help lower your blood pressure, prevent and treat ulcers, prevent constipation, and decrease the risk of heart disease. Ounce for ounce, plantains contain more *potassium* than bananas. Coconut oil is rich in *lauric acid*, which research has shown raises your good cholesterol, HDL, while lowering the risk of heart disease. Lauric acid is also an anti-inflammatory, anti-bacterial, and anti-viral agent. *Callaloo* is a green leafy vegetable much like spinach, and in that regard *callaloo* offers similar benefits as spinach. *Callaloo* is rich in *Vitamin C*, has four times the amount of calcium, and over two times the amount of iron and *Vitamin A* as broccoli and other vegetables.

Mexico

The custom in Mexico is to eat the heaviest meal of the day between 1300-1600 and many restaurants serve a set lunch at this time. Don't forget the *Siesta* after lunch. Most tourist haunts serve a light supper between 2100-2300 as well. One thing I love about dining in Mexico is that the staff considers it rude to present you with your bill before you ask for it. Be sure to say *"La cuenta por favor"* when you're ready to settle.

Yucatán cuisine is unique indeed, not to mention hot, sometimes very, very hot. The heart of many meals is the *habanero* pepper (meaning *from Havana*), sometimes called a *Scotch Bonnet* in parts of the Caribbean. This lantern-shaped bit of hellfire, estimated to be 20-50 times hotter than the *jalapeño* of northern Mexico, comes in green, red, or yellow, and you should always ask if a dish of salsa contains *habanero* before dipping a chip in it (unless you like it really, really hot). On the whole, peppers are usually found on the side instead of cooked into the meal in the Yucatán, where many Yucateco sauces are fruit based. And another warning, some Mexican restaurants may serve mayonnaise on lobster, if you don't appreciate that particular taste then ask for the mayo on the side.

Besides the tacos and burritos that you would expect to find in Mexico, there are many other dishes that you'll never find in your typical Mexican restaurant back home. The *Antojito* is an entire class of dishes in Mexico, and are made from corn (similar to tortillas) and are a social food that should be enjoyed in company. For that reason *antojitos* are often served in bars as a happy-hour appetizer or snack. *Sopas* are like little tortillas, they are cooked on a griddle until brown and then the edge is pinched up and the *sopa* is put back on the griddle and piled high with cheese, onion, salsa, beans, and meat. The best place to find these treats is usually an open-air market, *mercado*, an important part of Mexican life that can be found bustling with activity in every community. Here you can see everything made on the spot, *tacos, enchiladas, burritos, quesadillas, antojitos, sopas*, and more.

If you'd like to try something different, pick up a *jicama* (pronounced *he-cama*), a delicious root whose taste lies somewhere between an apple and a potato. The *jicama* is usually eaten raw, peeled, sprinkled with lime juice or chili, and salted to taste.

You can usually pick this up at a vendor's booth along with a Yucatán orange, a *naranja*, which is served peeled and, if you'd like to try the local variety, served dusted with a red chili powder. Besides the items I've mentioned you'll find all manner of fruits-on-a-stick, candies, and grilled meats for your sampling pleasure. *Chareles* are tiny river fish that are fried until crisp; *pilconcillo* which is sugar cane candy often used to sweeten coffee; and watermelons which are said to be the source of the colors of the Mexican flag.

Each state in the Yucatán offers its own particular fare besides the standard *burritos* and *tacos*. *Poc Chuc* (Mayan for *charcoal grilled steak*) has been made famous by the restaurants of Los Almendros and consists of thinly sliced pork or beef marinated in sour orange and vinegar, then grilled and served with a topping of pickled onion. *Sopa de limon* is a chicken soup with lime juice and is served with tortillas. Any menu item served *a la Yucateca* is usually some form of grilled seafood or meat flavored with a spicy *anchiote* paste (*anchiote* is a fragrant red spice). *Pibil* features meat marinated in a rich *pibil* sauce and then steam-baked in banana leaves in an earthen pit, *Cochinita Pibil* is pork, and *Pollo Pibil* is chicken.

If a menu item is served *a la Veracruz* it is prepared using ripe tomatoes, green peppers, and onions. If the item is served *con ajo* it is sautéed in garlic and butter. If an item is served *al gusto*, it means it is cooked to your pleasure. *Tik n' chik* is a whole fish that is usually cooked on the beach in a wire rack and is seasoned with onions, peppers, and *anchiote*. You'll often find wild duck, *pato*, served in a variety of ways in Quintana Roo where hunting is almost a national pastime. In the Yucatán you'll often find the *annatto* seed, a triangular, rust-colored seed with a mild herbal-iodine flavor, pureed with garlic and the juice of a sour orange and used as a marinade for grilled meats.

If you're a beer drinker you'll be happy with the choices available in Quintana Roo. Besides the usual *Dos Equis, Sol*, and *Corona*, you can sample Mexican brewed *Bohemia, Superior, Tecate,* and *Victoria*, or you can try the Yucatán brewed *Montejo* or *Leon Negra*, a dark amber brew. When buying bottled beer you might have to pay a deposit for each bottle, so save your receipts and return your bottles for a refund and you'll quickly find yourself with enough money for another beer. A unique and light alcohol drink is *chelada*, a glass of lemon-lime soda with a little beer added. *Licuados* are fresh fruit juice drinks that are available plain or mixed with milk, *con leche*. *Horchata* is a tasty rice drink made from rice and milk and flavored with cane sugar and cinnamon while *Jamaica*, pronounced *ah-MY-ka*, is a juice drink made from flowers. In the Yucatán you can usually find a bottle of *Xtabentun*, a very sweet and warm liqueur made from honey that is said to have been around for centuries. It is claimed that *Xtabentun* was given to virgins just before the priests offered them as a sacrifice. Brandies are also made in Mexico with *San Marcos* and *Presidente* probably being the best known. For the more adventuresome *Pulque* is a thick, almost milky beer that is made from the maguey cactus and is served in special bars called *pulquerías*.

One cannot cruise Mexican waters without sampling the locally produced tequila (anything labeled *nacional* is produced in Mexico and if it's not *nacional*, it will cost more). In Mexico, tequila, by law, is made from the *blue agave* plant and Mexican tequila is often of a higher proof than that sold in the United States. As there are different types of rum, there are also different types of tequilas. *Anejo* is aged in oaken barrels for at least one year while *reposado* (rested) is aged from two months to a year. *Joven abocado* (gold) is not aged but has color and flavor added while *plata* (sometimes called *blanco*) is also not aged and is normally sold within two months of distilling. *Sauza Hornitos* is a very strong tequila while *Commemorativo* is quite smooth.

A worm does not come in bottles of tequila in Mexico, if you desire a bit of worm protein you'll have to pick up a bottle of *Mescal*, sometimes shown as *Mezcal*, which is basically the same drink as tequila except that it is made from a different type of *agave* cactus, the *maguey*. Both tequila and mescal are made from the same part of the plants, the "pineapple," but tequila is manufactured in ovens and pressure cookers while mescal is cooked underground over open fires which give the product a deeper, more smoky flavor. Most tequilas are produced in and around the state of Jalisco while most mescals are produced in and around Oaxaca, pronounced wah-ha-kuh. The worm found in bottles of mescal is a grub that lives on the maguey cactus and proves the bottle's authenticity. No, the worm is not hallucinogenic. That rumor is based on the fact that the peyote cactus is also called *mescal*, but if you're at the point that you're finishing off the worm you might not be able to tell anyway.

Belize

One difference between Mexican and Belizean cuisine is that the Mexican cooks like to make the entrees spicy hot (*muy caliente*), while Belizean cooks tend to add coconut milk to many dishes. Besides all the drinks with coconut milk in them, you might find chicken, fish, and even beef stewed in coconut milk, as well as rice and refried beans that are simmered in it (*Rice and Beanz*), and bananas that are mashed and boiled in it. But not all dining in Belize is centered on coconut milk, you'll also sample an unusual mixture called *recado* (sometimes shown as *rekaado*), a savory red *achiote* paste that smells of clove and peppers, is made from ground annatto seeds, cornmeal, spices, vinegar, salt, and is used almost exclusively as a rub for roasting chicken.

If you like your food spicy hot, you won't be disappointed. In 1983, Marie Sharp redefined the culinary landscape in Belize with her unique hot sauces that have become a cottage industry of sorts. Originally, Ms. Sharp only wished to use up more peppers from her farm, but now her sauces are akin to a national condiment ranging in heat from mild to "beware" and "no wimps allowed" and they can be found on nearly every table. Marie's shop is located in Dangriga in an unmarked building on a dirt road and she welcomes visitors and is happy to give tours and tastings.

And speaking of Dangriga, the town is famous for its *cassava*, a root vegetable that has been used since pre-Columbian times by Amerindians. *Cassava* is used as an addition to soups and meat dishes and cassava flour is made into cassava bread (*bami*), typically it is flat bread that is cooked on a large griddle. Belize is also known for its cashew wine as well as for fish cooked in coconut milk with a side dish of mashed or pounded plantain, a delicious dish called *hudut*. Another special "national dish" is the tailless *gibnut*, the *agouti paca*, a relative of the guinea pig. The *gibnut* is shown as the *Royal Rat* on many Belizean menus because the British press objected to its being served to Queen Elizabeth II in 1985. *Bambam* is another traditional Belizean dish made with cassava as is *Bail op*, which is usually served up with pig's tail or fish. *Chimoaleh* is a traditional dish of blackened chicken soup with rice, and *Dujunu* is another traditional dish, mashed and steamed corn wrapped in a leaf. *Eskabaycheh* is a pickled onion soup made with chicken or fish.

One of the things you'll come to notice in Belize is that there are no fast food restaurants, no *McDonalds*, no *KFCs*, no *Burger Kings* are to be found, but fast food CAN be found, just ask, but Belizean fast food restaurants won't look like the chain restaurants that you're used to seeing. The Belize version of fast food restaurants are generally small with no fancy marquees, usually have an area where you can stand or sit to eat, and the food is not akin to what you find back home, Belizean fast food is not fired chicken or burger and fry combos, but it is inexpensive all the same. Here the menu contains items, some of which you'll recognize, such as *burritos, tacos, panades, garnaches* (sometime shown as *garnaaches*), *salbutes, bolos* and *tamalitos. Panades* (sometimes shown as *panaades*) are corn turnovers stuffed with finely chopped meat, beans, or fish and deep-fried and served with a garnish of cabbage and you can usually pick up eight for US$1.

Garnaches are fried corn tortillas, similar to nacho chips, but round and about the size of small pancakes and topped with beans, cabbage, and cheese, you can usually pick up six for US$1. *Salbutes* are fried tortillas topped with chicken, tomatoes, beans, and cilantro, and you can usually get four *salbutes* for US$1. In the markets you'll find vendors selling *bolos*, plantain leaves wrapped around a filling of chicken, and *tamalitos*, grated corn steamed in corn-husks with chicken. A local favorite is *Cowfoot Soup*, it's considered a delicacy and can't be found just anywhere. For those of you with a sweet tooth don't miss *Strech-mi-gots*, a taffy like candy, and *tablayta*, a coconut based candy.

With almost all meals you'll usually find red beans and rice being served. Don't confuse this staple with the Cajun or Cuban variety as the beans in Belize are cooked first and the rice is then cooked in the beans with coconut milk. The dish is usually served with a meat and either coleslaw or potato salad. There is also a dish called beans and rice that is served with the beans either on top of the rice or in a separate bowl.

For those with a taste for spirits, *Rompopo* is a locally made alcoholic drink that is similar to eggnog, and if you're after Belizean brewed beer, try *Bilikin*, regular, premium, or stout (a deep, dark beer that's lighter than most stouts). I'm not much of a beer drinker myself, I much prefer rum, but I've noted that many people are split about *Belikin*, some love it, others hate with a passion.

The Cayman Islands

Due to the location of the Cayman Islands, the cuisine here has a heavy Cuban and Jamaican influence that's enlivened by jerk, curry, and other vibrant seasonings that add their best qualities to a variety of locally caught seafood dishes. Entrees (often turtlemeat) are usually complimented by coconut, plantains, breadfruit, yams, cassava, rice and peas, and a mixture of West Indian side dishes. In addition to the Caribbean and Central American influence you'll also find a mixture of European, Italian, Mexican, German, Thai, Chinese, Japanese, Indian, and authentic "Tex-Mex" dishes available at the many restaurants and fast food chains on the islands.

If you get a chance, try a *pattie*; these meat filled pastries are to Caymanians what hamburgers are to Americans. Rum connoisseurs will be happy to know that *Blackbeard's Liquors* (http://blackbeards.ky/) has several locations throughout the Caymans and besides carrying all the major lines of beverages, they also sell their own brand of spirits that are bottled in the Cayman Islands. The *Tortuga Rum* Company (http://www.tortugarumcakes.com/) not only sells fine 151-proof rum, but their famous chocolate rum cake must be sampled by all visitors to these islands (and be sure to take some with you when you go; by the way, *Blackbeard's* also manufactures rum cakes; rum cakes being the only Caymanian export). *The Tortuga Rum Company* also manufactures their own line of jams, jellies, sauces, and chutneys as does *Hawley Haven Farm*, while *Otto Watler's Savannah Farm* produces an excellent dark brown honey. There are two breweries in the islands, and one of the most popular is located at *Hammerhead's* on the George Town waterfront where Nelson Dilbert has been brewing *Old Dutch* beer for over 6 years. A favorite local brew is called *Stingray* and can be found everywhere on Grand Cayman.

To get a true taste of local Caymanian cuisine, try to be at Little Cayman in early May for their fabled *Little Cayman Cook-off*. The chef's submissions are eaten by all who attend! Cayman Brac has their own cook-off in September.

Guatemala

Like the cuisine of most nations, Guatemalan fare is a blend of influences, Spanish, Mayan, and European. There is even a bit of a Mexican influence on Guatemalan fare as you can find tacos and tortillas here and there, but the choices are fewer than those of Guatemala's northern neighbor. Color plays an important part in the Guatemalan kitchen and dishes such as *jocón*, chicken with a green sauce prepared from a base of fresh coriander, are unique and colorful gastronomic delights. The vivid green and red colors of some dishes are a reflection of Guatemalan landscapes.

The cuisine in Guatemala can be broken down into three primary groups, *Mayan* cuisine, the oldest style of cooking in the country, *Ladino* cuisine, which as you would guess has a hefty Spanish influence, and *Creole* cuisine such as you would find along the coast, particularly in the Garifuna settlement of Livingston.

Mayan cuisine is based on two staples, beans (*frijoles*) and corn (*maize*). *Frijoles* are black kidney beans and can be served in two ways. *Volteados* are boiled, mashed, and then refried, while *parados* are boiled whole with onion slices. For breakfast, *desayuno*, *frijoles* are served with eggs and cream while at other meals *frijoles* are served in a separate dish. *Maize* appears at almost every meal in the form of the tortilla, a flat, thin pancake made of ground corn and shaped by hand before being traditionally cooked on a *comal*, a flat clay griddle atop a fire. Tortillas are best when eaten warm, this is why they are served wrapped in a cloth. Sometimes a restaurateur will serve a Norte Americano bread instead of tortillas thinking that you won't like the local staple.

Maize is also an ingredient of several snacks that you can pick up from vendors all over the country. The *tamal* is basically the same as what you would call a *tamale*, and is usually cornmeal stuffed with meat and fried wrapped in a banana leaf. The *chuchito* is another meat filled pastry wrapped in a corn husk. You will also find a range of dishes from *Chili Rellenos* to *Frijoles Borrachos* (drunken beans), and *manchamanteles con arroz blanco* (*stew that stains the tablecloth*) to *Chicken Pepian*, chicken cooked in a spicy pumpkin and sesame seed sauce. The fearless palate might savor *tepezcuintle*, a Mayan specialty and a large member of the rodent family. Chili peppers are another Mayan staple and it's not unusual to find a bottle of them on your table. *Mosh*, oats served with honey and cinnamon, is often found on a Mayan breakfast menu.

Ladino food has a strong Mexican influence, but for the most part you'll find quite a bit of grilled or fried meat, perfect for those on a low-carb diet. There's even a noticeable French influence with such specialties as *mushroom quiche* and *profiteroles* with ice cream. You'll also find dishes such as *carne guisada* (stewed beef and sauce), *chirmol* (grilled steak served with a tomato/onion sauce), *fiambre* (a meat, fish, and cheese salad) For appetizers you might sample *boquitas*, small teasers that range from olives to peanuts or crackers, while for dessert you might try *flan de naranja* (orange-flavored flan) or hot bananas in a chili-chocolate sauce.

Along Guatemala's Caribbean coast you'll find food with a distinctive Creole (Caribbean/African) influence with seafood, coconuts, and bananas showing up on every menu along with fried plantains, *plátanos fritos*.

Guatemala grows a lot of coffee so you can find a cup of java everywhere although I'm told the best beans are exported (I must be the only person on the planet that does not drink coffee). Breakfast is usually served with a cup of hot coffee, tea, chocolate, or *atol*, a warm sweet beverage made with either rice or maize and sugar. In the larger cities you'll find a stronger grade of coffee while in the country the coffee may be a bit watered down and not as tasty. Soft drinks are usually referred to as *aquas* (which you would think would mean just water, but not so in some places), and *refrescos* are water-based fruit drinks with fruit flavoring. One of my favorites is the *Liquido*, a thick fruit-based frozen drink that is often served with either milk or water and can range from lemonade flavored to chocolate and banana.

Beer is readily available in Guatemala; you'll find *Cabra* and *Dorada* along with *Gallo* (pronounced guy-yo) and *Victoria* (two of the most popular beers), and the hard to find *Moza*, a darker brew with a caramel flavor. True beer lovers will appreciate *Montecarlo*, a bit more pricey, but worth it. Rum, *ron*, can be found everywhere in Guatemala, the country grows a lot of sugar cane. *Ron Botan Añejo* is a good rum that's not too expensive, while *Ron Zacapa Centenario* is a smoother rum that has won many international awards including *Super Premium* and the coveted *Platinum Award* (for five consecutive years) by the judges of *Caribbean Week's Rum Fest*. An *aquardiente* called *Quetzalteca* is often described as the nation's rocket fuel and comes in a deceptively tiny bottle. Another popular pot-liquor is *Venado* and both are available

Gibnut, the Belize Royal Rat

Baleada from Honduras

Ackee & Saltfish, Bammies & Plantains, Jamaica

Antojitos, Mexico

Salt beef rundown, Cayman Islands

Topado Olanchano from Honduras

almost everywhere. A locally brewed spirit called *Chicha* is made from almost anything and is so cheap it's practically given away.

Honduras

In Honduras you'll find many places to get a good meal, from hotel restaurants, which usually have the best food (and the highest prices), to *comedores*, small eateries offering the best in local cuisine at economical prices. In most large Honduran towns, and especially along well-traveled highways, you find *buffets*, which are just what their name implies. Here you can choose from a variety of dishes and pay only for what you get.

The cuisine of Honduras varies from region to region where corn and beans, which date to pre-Columbian times, and squash from Mexico, blend with the staple root crops of South America. Corn is the base for *tortillas*, which are served with most dishes as it is in Guatemala and Mexico too. In Honduras you can sample over 20 different types of *tamales* all made from steamed cornmeal and filled with meats, beans, veggies, and chilies. In the eastern lowlands you'll find cassava root and rice are important staples to be eaten along with seafood, plantains, and coconut.

Anafres are a fusion of beans, cheese, and *chorizo* (a sausage) and are cooked in small earthen ovens fueled by coal. *Tapados* are soups, and two of the most popular are *Tapado Costeno* and *Tapado Olanchano*, and both feature beef and plantains. *Tapadao Costeno* (from the coast) also features cassava, bananas, and coconut, while the more central *Olancho* region dish features pork ribs and corn.

The main Honduran dish is called *plato típico*, and is generally a piece of beef served with fried plantain, rice, beans, cheese, and sour cream. Beef, *bistec* or *carne*, is generally a staple of Honduran menus, but the best beef is usually exported. Pork, *cerdo*, is another popular meat that you'll find on most menus along with fried chicken, *pollo frito*. The northern coast of Honduras and the Bay Islands are known for their fried fish, *pescado frito*, while the Bay Islands are also known for their *bando*, a stew made with yucca and other veggies. In Garifuna settlements you might be served coconut bread, *pan de coco*.

Other Honduran dishes include *pinchos*, which is similar to a *shish kabob*, a skewered meat and vegetable dish. If you are so inclined you can try the *sopa de mondongo*, a tripe stew. *Candinga* is pork liver with onions and sweet peppers and *chanfaina de menudo de marrameo* is stewed pork heart and liver.

The Catholic Church has had its impact on the cuisine of Honduras. A popular dish on Fridays is dry fish cakes in soup, *sopa de tortas de pescado seco*. On any other day of the week you might try the delicious Copan-style pork roast, a whole pig stuffed with spiced corn dough and roasted in adobe ovens.

The typical Honduran snack is called a *baleada*, a tortilla that is usually filled with beans, cheese, and cream, and then heated over an open grill. Also popular are grilled ears of corn sprinkled with orange and salt and you'll see folks selling these on the roadside in many places. If you have a sweet tooth you can sample *Capirotada* which are small cheese and cornmeal balls served in a heavy cane syrup or *Rosquillas*, delicious bread rings that are even better when dunked in strong Honduran coffee.

When you're walking around the local markets be sure and pick up some *tajadas*, fried plantain slices served with lime juice or salsa, or some papaya slices sprinkled with hot sauce. Fruit treats are everywhere, and if you like pineapples, you must try the *Azucarrón* pineapple, a super sugary pineapple that is absolutely divine (and not exported). A specialty of the *Pava Bay Resort* on Roatán is a baked mango dessert. Several mangoes are sliced thinly to cover the bottom of a large baking pan, sprinkled with ground cinnamon, covered lightly with sugar and finally topped with butter. Baked at 400° until lightly browned, you must then drench the dessert with heavy cream and enjoy it to no end.

Honduras boasts five beers (*cerveza*), *Imperial*, *Polar*, *Nacional*, *Port Royal*, and *Salva Vida*, all manufactured by the same company, *Cervecría Nacional*. *Nacional* seems to be the most popular, though it is the most tasteless, while *Salva Vida*, the *Lifesaver*, has the most appeal for true beer aficionados. The country also produces an inexpensive rum, *Flora de Cana*. *El Buen Gusto* is a brand of Honduran produced liquor called *aguardiente*, which is sometimes called *Yuscarán* for the town in which it is distilled. *Rompopo* is eggnog blended with *aguardiente* (you'll probably remember *Rompopo* from the section on Belize- *rompopo* can also be found in Honduras). Another favorite libation here is *ponche de piña navideño*, a Christmas beverage made with pineapple pulp, cane syrup, and *aquardiente*. Beer in cans can be purchased and drunk anywhere, but bottles are another story. The government of Honduras has imposed a deposit fee on bottles so business establishments wishing to retain their bottles request that you drink bottled beer on their premises. This also means that bottled drinks are more expensive than canned drinks, even soft drinks (*frescas*), with this in mind some vendors will keep the bottle and pour your beverage in a clear plastic bag, a *bolsa*, and give you a straw, a *pajilla*, if you wish to walk around with your drink. One drink I suggest you try is called *Guifitty*, an aphrodisiac beverage that is usually prepared by the Garifunas on the mainland but can also be found in the Bay Islands.

As a final note, Honduras has a new industry, the cultivation of crocodiles for their meat. This burgeoning industry is currently producing 30,000 pounds of meat per year with much of it going to the Bay Islands and some being exported as far away as China.

Jamaica

Ackee, rice, salt fish are nice
And the rum is fine any time of year

Harry Belafonte
Jamaica Farewell

Jamaican cuisine fulfills this island's motto: Out of many, one people. Here you will find a unique and eclectic mix of Arawak, African, Maroon, British, Spanish, and Indian (originating with the indentured servants who came to the island after the abolition of slavery) influences. Vegetarians will love dining in Jamaica as there are Rastafarian *I-tal* restaurants all over the island (meatless fare that is, in theory, cooked without salt).

Curried foods are of Indian origin and are quite popular while such dishes as chickpeas and pita bread are Lebanese in origin. Popular sauces such as *Pickapeppa* or *Jamaican Hell Fire* will add a real zing to your meals, and *Mango Chutney*, of Indian origin, is a favorite of many, myself included.

Peas and rice are served with almost every meal and usually consists of red or *gungo* (brown) peas mixed with rice, coconut milk, and other spices.

But while peas and rice are the primary staple of Jamaican cooks, the national dish is saltfish and *ackee*, which is usually served for breakfast or eaten as a snack. The saltfish is usually salted cod and the dish is often served with green bananas, johnnycake, dumplings, and *bammies* (cassava cakes). *Ackee* came to Jamaica from West Africa and is a fruit that is always boiled before cooking in order to release the toxin (*hypoglycin*) that is inside. Because of this toxin *ackee* can only be picked after the pods have opened naturally revealing three glossy black seeds surrounded by a waxy, yellow pulp. Then the pulp or *aril* must be thoroughly cleaned of the red fiber and the cooking water discarded. There are two varieties of ackee, *butter ackee* and *cheese ackee*, and when cooked they resemble scrambled eggs and are often cooked with onions, peppers, and tomatoes.

If you're wondering about the saltfish, remember that during Jamaica's early years of isolation meat had to be dried, pickled or salted, and some of these same foods are still popular today.

Another typically Jamaican dish is jerk pork or chicken. The term jerk is the method of cooking and does not reflect the nature of the cook. Jerk pork or chicken is cooked over a pimento wood fire and was originated by the *Maroons* in the Portland Hills of eastern Jamaica who needed to cook a meal (usually wild boar), but did not need to create telltale smoke that would give away their location. The absolute best jerk pork or chicken is found on the east coast at *Boston Beach*, just east of Port Antonio, to find the best, head for the vendor with the longest line.

Another noteworthy Jamaica dish is an appetizer known as *Solomon Grundy*, which is a peppery pickled herring pâté served on crackers. Peppered crayfish, *janga*, are popular and are of the fresh water variety and usually come from the rivers and streams of Westmoreland and St. Elizabeth parishes. You'll find these delicious crayfish boiled with pepper and salt at a lot of local roadside stands along Jamaica's back roads.

These roadside stands are where you'll find true Jamaican cooking such as *Patties*, meat filled pastries, or *Stamp and Go*, fried fish fritters usually served as a cocktail time teaser or appetizer. Fried fish and *bammies* are Arawakan in origin and are very popular in Jamaica. A *Bammie* is a fried, pancake shaped bread with a texture akin to a sponge and was the staple food of the poorer folks on the island before flour became readily available. Also served with fried fish is *festival*, a sweet, fried cornmeal dumpling. *Bulla* is a molasses-flavored round cake and *bun* is a spicy, fruit bread that is served year round (usually with cheese), but is featured at Easter.

Other snacks you'll find along the road include plantains, fried yams, boiled and roasted corn, sugar cane, and *pepperpot*, a stew in most other countries, but in Jamaica it's a soup which usually consists of greens, okra, dasheen, and corned beef or pork. *Escovitched* fish is any large fish that has been cut into thin slices and sautéed in a peppery vinegar and onion sauce. *Run-dun*, sometimes called *Run Down*, is onions, scallions, and pickled fish, usually shad or cod, that has been stewed in coconut milk and often served with boiled green bananas. If you're a groom and it's your wedding night, you might find yourself served a traditional aphrodisiac called *mannish water*, goat soup that is made from the goat's testicles. Another potent aphrodisiac is *cow cod soup* made from a bull's testicles, they sure do like their testicles in Jamaica. And if you see a menu item called *seapuss*, it's octopus.

Earlier we discussed *ackee*, a popular fruit on the island, but there are others as well that are unique to Jamaica. The *Ortanique* is a hybrid, a cross between an orange and a tangerine that was created by Charles Jackson of *Manchester Parish*. Its name is a hybrid as well, composed of *orange*, tangerine, and *unique*. The pear-shaped, red *otaheite apple* was introduced to the island, along with *breadfruit* by Captain Bligh with his first shipment from the South Pacific, and offers a sweet white flesh surrounding a central seed. The breadfruit is a staple and is usually served boiled, roasted, fried like chips, or straight from the fire or oven with butter. *Naseberry* is the same as a sapodilla and the *ugli fruit* is a hybrid of a grapefruit and a tangerine and often seen in grocery stores all over the world.

After a spicy Jamaican meal you'll be ready for a tasty dessert such as *soursop* ice cream, baked bananas served with coconut cream sauce, *grizzada* (a spicy coconut tart), or the more exotic *matrimony*. *Matrimony* is a colorful blending of tropical fruits, including the purple skinned *starapple*, topped with a rich, creamy nutmeg sauce. A particularly tasty concoction is called *blue drawers*, or *duckanoo*, a mixture of cornmeal, coconut, spices, and brown sugar, all wrapped in banana leaves, boiled, and sometimes served with a rum sauce. If you like pudding you might want to try *Corn Pone,* made from cornmeal, coconut, sugar, and various spices. *Sweet potato pudding* is another popular dessert and is a mix of sweet potatoes, raisins, and coconut, and *totoes* are akin to gingerbread cookies that have had coconut added to the batter. And while you're on the island don't forget to pick up some locally made rum cake such as *Tortuga*.

Now let's discuss Jamaican libations, and most people equate the island of Jamaica with rum, which is plentiful and good, the most famous of which is *Appleton's*. *Wray and Nephew* manufacture a good white over-proof rum, cheap but strong. Jamaicans often manufacture a sort of moonshine, white rum, which is exceptionally strong and is often called *Cowneck* since only a cow's throat could tolerate the concoction. Similar is *John Crow Batty* which is said to be so rough that only the John Crow vultures can stomach it.

There are also several nice liqueurs to be found on the island, especially the well-known *Tia Maria*. Jamaica's local brews include *Dragon Stout* and *Red Stripe*, two good beers, which compete with locally brewed versions of *Guinness*, *McPherson*, and *Heineken*. Coffee connoisseurs are probably already salivating over the thought of Jamaican *Blue Mountain Coffee*, one of the finest and most sought after beans in the world. If you're in Jamaica around Christmas you must sample *Sorrel*, a bright red drink made by stewing and sweetening the petals of the Sudanese shrub. A nice side trip while in Jamaica is the tour of the *Appleton Estate Rum Factory*. For more information call the distillery 876-963-9215, or email them at appleton@infochan.com.

For liquid Viagra Jamaican men sometimes imbibe in certain "stamina potions" such as *tanpon-it-long*, which is said to carry a Jamaican man through marathon romantic bouts. The main ingredient in many of these drinks is *Irish moss*, a seaweed that is sold in tins or fresh in bags. *Irish moss* can be found in *Magnum* along with linseed, *Strong Back* along with *Dragon Stout* and peanuts, and *Pep-Up* where it's mixed with red wine and *Dragon Stout*. A very popular Rasta tonic is *roots wine*, which is made from a variety of herbs including ganga at times. These concoctions are time consuming and you can usually find a *juice man* in the markets in town to sell you a bottle or two, but they often won't sell to a woman since after all, it is a "man thing."

Busing Around

One of the best ways to get around Central America, from Panama to the United States is by bus. If you are like me and don't like flying, or perhaps I should say, if you don't like crashing, you will love getting around by bus, it's cheap, fairly reliable, and you can get just about anywhere in Central and North America with little effort. Bear in mind that while these buses may leave on time if they originate at a primary point such as Guatemala City in Guatemala, or Tapachula, Matamoros, Mexico City, or Cancun in Mexico, they may not always arrive on time. Add a minimum of 10% to your estimated travel time and pray that is enough. For instance, you will be told that the bus from Tapachula to Matamoros in Mexico takes 27 hours to run that route, sorry folks, but no way. I've ridden that bus 20 times and never made it in under 31 hours.

Now as we are discussing bussing around Central America, let me explain that there are several different classes of *autobusses* (pronounced *auto-boose*) that you can take. In this article I will focus on the upper end of the scale, the first class busses, *Primero* or *Ejecutivo* class. At the opposite end of the scale are the colorful and very lively chicken buses. These are usually old school buses, exactly like the ones in which you may have spent countless hours riding to and from school. They are very colorful, each one decorated by its owner, and always crowded (the standing joke being "How many people can you get on a chicken bus?" The answer being "Four more.").

Chicken buses are the basic mode of public transportation in Central America and extremely economical. It's not unusual to board a chicken bus and spend time talking to a woman who is taking her chickens, turkeys, or even a small pig to market, hence the name chicken buses. Often you'll find people riding on top along with the luggage, if you want to truly experience the culture of Central America, travel by chicken bus, if you prefer a bit of comfort and a bathroom aboard, go *primero* class.

One last tip on taking buses in Central America before we discuss particular buses and routes. You'll likely be taking taxis from the bus stations to hotels and back, and always, I repeat, ALWAYS, settle on a fare before you enter the cab, don't give the driver the opportunity to drive away with you in his cab without agreeing to a price or you'll find yourself paying 2-3 times what it should cost and more (unless of course you anger the driver by your refusal to pay and he plops you out in the middle of nowhere with all your luggage to find your way with your own two feet in the hot, humid, midday sun). Also, never, I repeat, NEVER, take any taxi that doesn't look like a taxi, don't take an illegal taxi, especially in the border towns, particularly along the Mexico/Guatemala border.

From the *Río Dulce* your first stop on a bus trip to anywhere in Central America, unless you're taking a pre-arranged trip to Copán, San Pedro Sula, or Tikal, will be Guatemala City. There are several buses a day leaving *Río Dulce* for Guatemala City, one, *Litegua* (pronounced *la-teeg-wa,* http://www.litegua.com/) even has one that leaves at 0300 from *Río Dulce*. *ADN* is the best of the bus lines servicing *Río Dulce*, but it only runs on the weekends and only if enough passengers have booked. The cost for an *ADN* ticket is around US $26-$35 one way and the buses are first class. *Litegua* and *Linea Dorada* (http://lineadorada.com.gt/) also offer daily service for a price of around US $13. You'll want to make sure you catch a nonstop from *Río Dulce* to Guatemala City. A nonstop bus is one that doesn't stop at every bus stop along the way, but does stop halfway to Guatemala City for lunch, this will save you a lot of time as sometimes it takes a bus 30-45 minutes to get through the traffic in Morales alone (the nonstop *Linea Dorada* bus leaves the *Río* daily at 1300).

There are other buses going from the *Río Dulce* to Guatemala City, such as *Fuente Del Norte*, but I cannot recommend them and will not attempt to entice anybody to board one (with the possible exception of the very nice buses that this line operates in the Flores area). Even with the *Litegua* and *Linea Dorada* buses you might get the occasional bus in which the air-conditioning does not work, but generally these buses are in good shape although they're often full so be sure to get your ticket early. You can pick up a ticket in *Río Dulce* at the bus stations which are located on the main highway north of the bridge, just up from *Bruno's* or *Río Bravo Pizza*.

When you arrive in Guatemala City take note that different bus lines go to different terminals, *Galgos* (pronounced *guy-gos*) goes to the *Galgos* terminal, and *Linea Dorada* goes to the *Linea Dorada* terminal. This is important when you go from your hotel to the bus terminal to board a bus headed back to the *Río Dulce* from Guatemala City. The *TICA Bus* terminal is located at 11a Calle 2-74, *Zona 9*; the

Galgos (*Transportes Galgos*) terminal is located at 7a Avenida 19-14, *Zone 1*, the *Linea Dorada* terminal is located at 16 Calle 10-03, *Zona 1*, and the *ADN* terminal is located at 15 Calle, 9-18, in *Zona 1*.

You can also catch a bus in *Río Dulce* for Honduras. Catch any bus in town to the Morales stop, there you can pick up the *Maya del Oro* bus to San Pedro Sula in Honduras. From there you can catch a bus to Copan, Tegucigalpa, or La Ceiba. For more information check with the travel agents (*Ottitrans*) in *Río Dulce* or with the bus lines. *Cotraipbal* (504-434-4932) operates ten buses a day from San Pedro Sula to Tela, La Ceiba, Tocoa, and Trujillo between 0100-1400, and two buses to Tegucigalpa between 0100-0430 daily. North of the *Río Dulce*, at Flores, *Mundo Maya* departs Santa Elena for Belize City and Chetumal in Mexico at 0500 daily. In Chetumal you can take a daily bus (0600 and 1400) to Xcalak, the trip takes about four hours.

In Guatemala City you can catch buses to take you into Mexico, for those headed there or to the United States, or you can opt for buses heading south to Honduras, Costa Rica, San Salvador, Nicaragua, and Panama. *TICA Bus* runs south to Panama and is one of the best while *Galgos* can also take you into Honduras.

Without a doubt *Galgos* is the best line in Guatemala and their buses and service cannot be beat, unfortunately their coverage area is limited (personally, I wish every bus were of the quality of the *Galgos* line). *Galgos* is also THE bus to take to the border crossing with Mexico and on into Tapachula to pick up one of the fine Mexican buses that will take you through that country and into the United States. From Tapachula you can even catch buses to the Yucatán Peninsula.

Galgos also services several locations inside Guatemala such as Xela, and even runs south to El Salvador, while *King* (502-2369-0404/0456) offers buses from Guatemala City to El Salvador, Honduras, Nicaragua, and Costa Rica. *Hedman Alas* is the best first class bus in Honduras, servicing San Pedro Sula, Copán Ruinas, La Ceiba, Tegucigalpa, Tela, departing Antigua, Guatemala at 0400, and Guatemala City at 0500 (it takes about 9½ hours to go from Guatemala City to La Ceiba in Honduras). You can contact *Hedman Alas* via email at info@hedmanalas.com, or by phone in Guatemala City at 502-2362-5072, or in La Ceiba, Honduras at 502-441-5347.

The *Galgos* bus from Guatemala City to Tapachula, Mexico, departs at 7:30 AM has two levels, the lower level is first class, *primero*, about US\$35 with larger, roomier seats (complete with a blanket and pillow), while the upper level tourist class, *turismo*, costs about US\$27, and while the *turismo* class seats are not as large as the *primero* class seats, they are still more comfortable than the normal U.S. *Greyhound* bus in my humble opinion. *Galgos* has a stewardess on board with breakfast, lunch, and soft drinks, and the trip to the border with Mexico takes about 6½ hours.

Just before the bus's arrival at the border with Mexico (*frontera*), the driver will allow a money changer to come onboard to change your *Quetzales* or US\$ into *Pesos*. The rate is as much as ½ *peso* less than the going rate. For example, if the official rate of exchange for *pesos* is in the neighborhood of 10.5 *pesos* = US \$1, the money changer will only gave you 10 *pesos* for US \$1, but he does save you the inconvenience of having to find a bank or *Casa de Cambio* for an exchange, so if you only need a small amount changed you might consider this form of exchange.

When you disembark at the border to clear out of Guatemala you will be swamped by children wanting to help you go in the right direction and many more money changers, men with huge wads of cash on them (and guns hidden nearby to protect themselves). If you need to change your *Quetzales* into *Pesos*, change your money on the Guatemalan side, NOT the Mexican side (you'll need Q10 to clear out of Guatemala). The *Galgos* bus crosses at the *Talisman Bridge* and the Guatemalan side of the border is NOT an area to wander around at night, especially if you're a *gringo*. I advise you to clear immediately, cross to the Mexican side (a much safer place), and get back on the bus to Tapachula as soon as you can.

Once you officially clear out of Guatemala you will walk a hundred yards or so across the *Talisman Bridge* to the Mexican *Immigration* office, the yellow building on the right, and here you will clear into Mexico. Make sure that the *Immigration* officer checks the *Turismo* box at the bottom of your tourist visa. When this is complete you will need to walk over to your bus, remove your luggage, take it to the guards by the *Immigration* office, let them check it, and then walk a hundred yards or so up the road where the *Galgos* bus will then pick you up for the final ten miles

Litegua Bus, Río Dulce to Guatemala City, Guatemala.

Galgos Bus, Guatemala City, Guatemala, to Tapachula, Mexico.

into Tapachula. Do not allow any children, *niños,* to assist you with your baggage, the Mexican officials do not permit this.

At the main bus terminal in Tapachula, the *Cristobal Colón* station, you can find a bus to anywhere in Mexico and even into the United States. Most take the bus from Tapachula to Matamoros for the crossover into Brownsville, Texas; this bus takes about 31 hours and costs around US$145 for the trip with stops for breakfast and dinner. After an early morning arrival in Matamoros you'll have a 4-5 hour wait for the first morning bus into Brownsville (US$10) at 0630 or you can take a taxi across at any time of the day or night for about US$35. Make sure you arrange with the driver that he will clear you out of the Mexican side, take you across the border and drop you off at a hotel or at the site of your choice.

At the border in Matamoros, and at the Matamoros bus terminal, you might get a chance to play the traffic light game. When clearing *Customs* you will see what looks like a traffic light and a small button. The agents will ask you to push the button and if the light comes up red, you must have your bags searched, if your light comes up green you can pass go, put your bags back on the button, and go on your way. I've played this game many times and have never seen a green light, so good luck.

For online information concerning Mexican buses and routes, a great website (in Spanish and English) is *Ticket Bus,* http://www.ticketbus.com.mx/wtbkd/index.jsp. Here you can check out routes, bus lines, schedules, and even make reservations and purchase tickets that you can pick up upon your arrival at the bus station. I've used this site and can testify to its quality. Another site with good links to Mexican bus lines is *The Bus Station,* www.busstation.net/main/busmex.htm.

You'll find that Mexican buses are very comfortable and the drivers very professional. As far as the Mexican buses themselves go, I prefer *UNO,* it is indeed first class, with three seats across instead of four, making for wider seats and more leg room. *ADOGL* is my second choice, but be aware that there is a difference between the *ADO* (http://www.ado.com.mx/ado/) and the *ADOGL* (http://www.adogl.com.mx/en/) buses even though they are owned by the same company. The *ADOGL* buses have two rear axles, they are larger, and they make fewer stops. *Transportpais* is a very nice line and certainly top quality. I don't like the *SUR* line as most of their buses don't have bathrooms aboard, but they rarely travel over two hours without a stop. And while we're on the subject, always take some toilet paper with you, bathrooms (*baños*) in Mexican bus stations (*Termino de Autobus*) often do not have toilet seats, and they rarely have toilet paper (for that matter some of the buses don't have toilet paper either). In some bus stations ladies sit outside the bathrooms selling you several folded up sheets of toilet paper for 2-5 pesos, it's best to carry a roll of toilet paper with you. Most bathrooms in Mexican bus stations will cost you 30 pesos to enter.

Nearly all Mexican bus stations have small snack counters or vending machines and often street vendors nearby, but the larger stations will usually have a small grill selling hot food, most of it pre-made. And be warned that Mexican bus stations are LOUD, and the station at Vera Cruz may be the loudest of them all.

When traveling on a bus in Central America it's a good idea to carry water, munchies, and a comfortable pillow with you. I also carry a good set of ear plugs as the buses usually have videos playing from four screens strategically placed throughout the bus. The sound is directed through speakers over every seat and is controlled by the driver. The videos begin about 0700-0900 and continue sometimes until 2200-2300 at night. Expect several stops for passport checks by the Mexican *Army, Police,* and *Immigration.* Between the troubles that the Mexican government is having with the rebels based in Chiapas, and the cartels all over the country, you may expect many stops as the authorities search for weapons, drugs, and cash.

References

Hart, J. C. & Stone, W. T. (1982). *A Cruising Guide to the Caribbean and the Bahamas.* New York, NY: Dodd, Mead & Co.

Bowditch, N..(1977). *American Practical Navigator.* DMA Hydrographic Center.

Huber, J. & J. (1998). *Best Dives of the Caribbean.* Edison, NJ: Hunter Publishing.

Stoll, D. (1993). *Between Two Armies in the Ixil Towns of Guatemala.* New York, NY: Columbia University Press.

Schlesinger, S. (1982). *Bitter Fruit : The Untold story of the American Coup in Guatemala.* New York, NY: Doubleday.

Davis, S. (1985). *Bob Marley.* New York, NY: Doubleday.

Sanford, V. (2003). *Buried Secrets: Truth and Human Rights in Guatemala.* New York, NY: Palgrave Macmillan.

Michener, J. (1989). *Caribbean.* New York, NY: Random House.

Gordon, A.L. *Circulation of the Caribbean Sea*; A. L. , *Journal of Geophysical Research*, 72, 6207-6223.

Paschke, B. & Volpendesta, D. *Clamor of Innocence: Central American Short Stories.*

Parker, C. *Coastal And Offshore Weather, The Essential Handbook.*r

Owens, J. (1976). *Dread, The Rastafarians of Jamaica.* Kingston: Sangsters.

Wouk, H. (1965). *Don't Stop The Carnival.* New York, NY: Doubleday.

Andrade, C. A. & Barton, E. D. *Eddy Development and Motion in the Caribbean Sea.* Journal of Geophysical Research, 105, 26191-26201.

Anfuso, J. (1984). *Efrain Rios Montt, Servant or Dictator? The Real Story of Guatemala's Controversial Born-again President.* Ventura, CA: Vision House.

Simon, J.M. (1983). *Guatemala, Eternal Spring, Eternal Tyranny.* New York, NY: W. W. Norton.

Fried, J.L. (1983) *Guatemala in Rebellion: Unfinished History.* New York, NY: Grove Press.

Simon, J.M. (2011). *Guatemala's Lost Photographs.* Guatemala: elPeriódico

Carmack, R.M. (1988). *Harvest of Violence: The Maya Indians and the Guatemalan Crisis.* Norman, OK: University of Oklahoma Press.

LeFeber, W. (1993). *Inevitable Revolutions: The United States in Central America.* New York, NY: WW. Norton & Co.

Menchu, Rigoberta. *I, Rigoberta Menchu.*

Falla, R. (1994). *Massacres in the Jungle: Ixcán, Guatemala, 1975-1982.* Boulder, CO: Westview Press.

Thompson, J.E. (1970). *Maya History and Religion.* Norman, OK: University of Oklahoma Press.

Pavlidis, S. J. (1997). *On And Off The Beaten Path*; Cocoa Beach, FL: Seaworthy Publications.

Popol Vuh (D. Tedlock, Trans). New York, NY: Simon & Schuster.

Nicholas, T. & Sparrow, B. (1979). *Rastafari, A Way of Life.* New York, NY: Anchor Press.

Reed's Nautical Almanac, Caribbean 2014

Sailing Directions For The Caribbean Sea; Pub. #147, Defense Mapping Agency, #SDPUB147

Fash, W. L. *Scribes, Warriors, and Kings: The City of Copán and the Ancient Maya.* out of print.

Secret History: The CIA's Classified Account of its Operations in Guatemala, 1952-1954; Nick Cullather, Stanford University Press 1999

Gleijeses, P. (1991). *Shattered Hope: The Guatemalan Revolution and the United States*; Piero, Princeton University Press

Parsons, K. (2000). *Spanish For Cruisers*; Hallettsville, TX: Aventuras Publishing Co.

Jones, D. (1969). *The Concise Guide to Caribbean Weather.*

The Doctor's Book of Food Remedies. (1998). Rodale, Inc.

Pavlidis, S. J. (2012). *The Exuma Guide, 3rd Edition.* Cocoa Beach, FL: Seaworthy Publications.

The First Primer on the People Called the Garifuna; Myrtle Palacio, Gelssima Research & Services, 1993

Pavlidis, S. J. (2012). *The Leeward Islands Guide, 2nd Edition.* Cocoa Beach, FL: Seaworthy Publications.

Harrison, P. (1999). *The Lords of Tikal: Rulers of an Ancient Mayan City.*

Coe, M.D. (1987). *The Maya, 4th rev. ed.*

Argüelles, J. (1987). *The Mayan Factor*; Santa Fe, NM: José, Bear & Co.

Hendrickson, R. (1984). *The Ocean Almanac.* New York, NY: Doubleday.

The Pirates Own Book. New York, NY: A. & C. B. & Philidelphia, PA: Thomas, Cowperthwait, & Co.

Pavlidis, S. J. (2011). *The Puerto Rico Guide, 2nd Edition.* Cocoa Beach, FL: Seaworthy Publications.

Barrett, L. (1977). *The Rastafarians.* Boston, MA: Beacon Press.

The Rise and Fall of Maya Civilization; J. Eric S. Thompson, 2nd enl. ed. 1966, reprinted 1977

The Separation of the Yucatán Current from the Campeche Bank and the intrusion of the loop current into the Gulf of Mexico; R. L. Molinari and J. Morrison, *Journal of Geophysical Research*, 93, 10645-10654.

Pavlidis, S. J. (2011). *The Virgin Islands Guide, 2nd Edition.* Cocoa Beach, FL: Seaworthy Publications.

de Lisser, H. *The White Witch of Rose Hall.* United Kingdom: Macmillan.

Pavlidis, S. J. (2013). *The Windward Islands Guide, 2nd Ed.* Cocoa Beach, FL: Seaworthy Publications.

The Yachtsman's Guide to Jamaica; John Lethbridge, out of print

Tedlock, B. *Time and the Highland Maya.*

Perera, V. (1993). *Unfinished Conquest: The Guatemalan Tragedy.* University of California Press.

Robinson, B. (1963). *Where the Trade Winds Blow.* New York, NY: Charles Scribner's Sons.

Appendices

Appendix A: Navigational Lights

Navigational light characteristics may differ from those published here and are subject to change without notice. Lights in this list must be considered as unreliable, especially those in Honduras and Mexico, it is not unusual for a light to be out of commission for long periods of time or for its characteristics to differ from those shown here.

All lights are listed from north to south and those in Jamaica are also listed from east to west. Please note that the lights listed for Honduras do not cover the eastern tip of the country where the low lying land borders with Nicaragua. Cruisers should give this area a berth of 10 miles and never sail in water less than ten fathoms in depth; this is a shallow, poorly charted area.

Light Abbreviations:

Aero: Aircraft beacon
G: Green
GP Fl: Group flashing, successive groups of flashes, specified in number, regularly repeated
Fl: Flashing with shorter periods of light than dark, less than 50 flashes per minute
Fl (*): Group flashing with the number inside the brackets
Fxd: Fixed light
Iso: Isophase, having equal periods of light and dark
L Fl: Long flashing, a flash of two or more seconds repeated
M: Distance in nautical miles that the light is supposed to be visible
Oc: Occulting with longer periods of light than dark
Q: Quick flashing, light is regularly repeated
Range-F: Front range light
Range-R: Rear range light
R: Red
VQ Fl: Very quick flashing, regularly repeated
W: White
Y: Yellow

LIGHT	LAT/LON	CHARACTERISTICS	HT.	RNG.
BELIZE				
Bahía de Chetumal				
Consejo Point Light	18° 27.0' N, 88° 20.0' W	Fxd W	50'	5 M
Corozal Light	18° 22.0' N, 88° 27.0' W	Fxd R		5 M
Belize City and Approaches				
Belize City Av. Light	17° 32.5' N, 88° 18.5' W	Q W	90'	30 M
North Drowned Cay Lt.	17° 29.8' N, 88° 08.8' W	Q W		
Fort George Light	17° 29.6' N, 88° 10.7' W	Fl R 5s	52'	8 M
Middle Ground Light	17° 28.0' N, 88° 10.5' W	Fl R 2.5s	26'	5 M
Sugar Berth A Light	17° 25.5' N, 88° 08.9' W	Fl G 2.5s	16'	5 M
Westward Patch Light	17° 25.5' N, 88° 11.3' W	Q R	16'	5 M
Frank Knoll Light	17° 23.8' N, 88° 11.7' W	Q W	16'	5 M
Sugar Berth B Ligh	17° 23.5' N, 88° 10.6' W	Fl R 2.5s	16'	5 M
Robinson Point Light	17° 22.0' N, 88° 11.7' W	Q W	38'	8 M
Three Triangles Light	17° 21.5' N, 88° 12.3' W	Fl G 5s	16'	5 M
Sittee Point to Mullins River				
Manatee River Light	17° 13.8' N, 88° 18.2' W	Fxd W	33'	2 M
Colson Point Light	17° 04.4' N, 88° 14.2' W	FL W 10s	39'	9 M
Sittee Point Light	16° 48.4' N, 88° 14.8' W	Fl W 5s	30'	8 M

LIGHT	LAT/LON	CHARACTERISTICS	HT.	RNG.
Punta Gorda to Sittee Point				
Placencia Lagoon Av. Lt.	16° 32.0' N, 88° 25.2' W	Fxd R	315'	35 M
Bugle Cays Light	16° 29.4' N, 88° 19.2' W	Fl (2) W 10s	61'	10 M
Monkey River Light	16° 22.0' N, 88° 29.1' W	Fxd W	52'	8 M
East Snake Cay Light	16° 12.5' N, 88° 30.4' W	Fl W 3s	65'	13
Punta Gorda Light	16° 06.3' N, 88° 47.9' W	Fxd W	56'	9 M
The Lights of Belize's Barrier Reef				
Northeast Spit Light	17° 22.8' N, 88° 05.3' W	Q G	16'	
White Grounds Spit Light	17° 22.7' N, 88° 07.0' W	Fl W 2.5s	16'	5 M
Spanish Cay Spit Light	17° 22.5' N, 88° 08.5' W	Q G	16'	5 M
Halfway Lt. (1-Man Cay)	17° 22.2' N, 88° 09.5' W	Q R	16'	5 M
Water Cay Spit Light	17° 21.4' N, 88° 04.4' W	Q R	16'	5 M
Goffs Cay, Sandbore Lt.	17° 20.4' N, 88° 02.0' W	Fl R 5s	16'	3 M
Southwest Side Light	17° 22.0' N, 88° 09.7' W	Q G	16'	5 M
Eastern Channel Range-F	17° 19.7' N, 88° 02.6' W	Q W	23'	9 M
Eastern Channel Range-R		Fl W 2.5s	62'	11 M
Hunting Cay Light	16° 06.6' N, 88° 15.8' W	Fl W 10s	57'	13 M
The Lights of Belize's Offshore Reefs				
Glover Reef				
Northeast Side/Reef Light	16° 54.6' N, 87° 42.0' W	Fl W 5s	36'	9 M
Southwest Cays Light	16° 42.9' N, 87° 50.6' W	Fl (2) W 5s	36'	9 M
Lighthouse Reef				
Sandbore Cay Light	17° 28.1' N, 87° 29.2' W	Fl W 10s	83'	17 M
Half Moon Cay Light	17° 12.3' N, 87° 31.6' W	Fl (4) W 15s	80'	14 M
Turneffe Islands				
Mauger Cay Light	17° 36.5' N, 87° 46.2' W	Fl (2) W 10s	61'	13 M
Cay Bokel Light	17° 09.8' N, 87° 54.4' W	Fl (3) W 15s	33'	8 M
THE CAYMAN ISLANDS				
Cayman Brac				
North East Point Light	19° 45.1' N, 79° 43.4' W	Fl W 20s	150'	12 M
Cayman Brac Light	19° 41.0' N, 79° 53.5' W	Fl (2) W 15s	41'	15 M
Little Cayman				
East Point Light	19° 42.4' N, 79° 58.2' W	Fl W 15s	36'	10 M
South West Point Light	19° 39.5' N, 80° 06.8' W	Fl W 5s	30'	10 M
Owen's Sound Channel E	Privately maintained	Fl R 5s		
Owen's Sound Channel W	Privately maintained	Fl G 5s		
Owen's Sound Range-F	Privately maintained	Q G		
Owen's Sound Range-R	Privately maintained	Q R		
Grand Cayman				
Boastwain Point Light	19° 23.1' N, 81° 24.6' W	Fl W 15s	90'	15 M
Gorling Bluff Light	19° 18.0' N, 81° 06.3' W	Fl (2) W 20s	72'	12 M
Grand Cayman Light	19° 17.8' N, 81° 23.0' W	Q R	41'	6 M
Hog Sty Bay Range-F	19° 17.7' N, 81° 23.1' W	Fxd G	13'	
Hog Sty Bay Range-R	090° from front at 100 meters.	Fxd G	33'	3 M
George Town Av. Light	19° 17.5' N, 81° 21.5' W	Fl W G	39'	20 M
Sand Cay Light	19° 15.7' N, 81° 23.2' W	Fl (2) W 10s	30'	15 M
GUATEMALA				
Cabo Tres Puntas				
Cabo Tres Punta Light	15° 57.4' N, 88° 36.2' W	Fl W 10s	132'	17 M

LIGHT	LAT/LON	CHARACTERISTICS	HT.	RNG.
Bahía de Amatique (Honduras Bay)				
Ox Tongue Shoal Light	15° 53.9' N, 88° 41.1' W	Fl W 3s	13'	12 M
Heredia Shoal Light	15° 50.8' N, 88° 40.4' W	Fl R 6s	20'	12 M
Bajo Villedo Light	15° 44.7' N, 88° 36.9' W	Fl W 2s	17'	
Puerto Barrios - Bahía de Santo Tomás de Castilla				
Head of Pier Light	15° 44.5' N, 88° 36.6' W	Oc W 4s		5 M
Punta Barrios Light	15° 43.8' N, 88° 35.8' W	Fl W 8s		25 M
Martias de Galves Rng.-F	15° 41.6' N, 88° 37.2' W	Q Y	35'	
Martias de Galves Rng.-R	15° 41.4' N, 88° 37.3' W	Oc Y 4s	80'	

HONDURAS
Mainland

LIGHT	LAT/LON	CHARACTERISTICS	HT.	RNG.
Punta Caxinas Light	16° 01.5' N, 86° 00.6' W	Fl W 7s	75'	19 M
Cabo Camaron Light	15° 59.2' N, 85° 01.9' W	Fl W 5s	73'	19 M
Cayos Vivorillo Light	15° 50.0' N, 83° 17.7' W	Fl W 10s		13 M
Punta Patuca Light	15° 49.0' N, 84° 18.2' W	Fl W 10s	73'	22 M
Cabo Falso Light	15° 15.2' N, 83° 23.7' W	Fl W 5s	75'	18 M
Puerto de Cabotaje				
E jetty light		Fl R		
W jetty light		Fl G		
Puerto la Ceiba				
La Ceiba Light	15° 47.5' N, 86° 47.8' W	Fl W 5s	16'	
Punta Obispo				
Punta Obispo Light	15° 50.9' N, 87° 22.5 W	Fl W 5s	132'	20 M
Punta Sal				
Punta Sal Light	15° 55.5' N, 87° 36.1' W	Fl (4) W 30s	275'	15 M
Punta Caballos				
Punta Cortes	15° 51.4' N, 87° 57.6' W	Fl W 5s	190'	20 M
#1 Light	15° 51.10' N, 87° 57.55' W	Fl G 5s		
#2 Light	15° 51.14' N, 87° 58.16' W	Fl R 4s		5 M
#3 Light	15° 50.67' N, 87° 58.00' W	Fl G 6s		5 M
#4 Light	15° 50.5' N, 87° 58.3' W	Q (3) R		

Las Islas Santanilla

LIGHT	LAT/LON	CHARACTERISTICS	HT.	RNG.
Isla del Cisne Av. light	17° 24.5' N, 83° 56.5' W	Fl W 5s	70'	28 M

Islas de la Bahía (The Bay Islands)
Isla de Guanaja

LIGHT	LAT/LON	CHARACTERISTICS	HT.	RNG.
Black Rock Point Light	16° 29.9' N, 85° 49.0' W	Fl W 10s	200'	25 M
Pond Cay Light	16° 26.3' N, 85° 52.8' W	Q G	29'	2 M
Isla de Roatán				
West End	16° 18.0' N, 86° 35.3' W	Fl W 20s		10 M
Coxen's Hole		Fxd W	25'	
Banco Becerro		Fl Y		
Punta Queste Light	16° 16.1' N, 86° 36.1' W	Fl W 5s	74'	19 M
Brick Bay Channel-W	Privately maintained	Fl G		
Brick Bay Channel- E	Privately maintained	Fl R		
French Harbour	16° 23.5' N, 86° 23.0' W	Q W	27'	15 M
Oakridge Harbour	16° 23.0' N, 86° 21.0' W	Fl W 5s	25'	4 M
Isla de Utila				
Cerro Pumpkin Light	16° 07.0' N, 86° 53.0' W	Fl W 10s	325'	20 M
Puerto Este Light	16° 05.0' N, 86° 55.0' W	Fl W		4 M

LIGHT	LAT/LON	CHARACTERISTICS	HT.	RNG.
Cayos Cochinos				
Cochino Grande Light	15° 58.5' N, 86° 28.6' W	Fl W 5s	516'	18 M
NORTHERN COAST OF JAMAICA				
Port Antonio				
Folly Point Light	18° 11.3' N, 76° 26.6' W	L Fl W 10s	54'	23 M
Folly Point Range F	18° 11.2' N, 76° 26.6' W	Fxd R beacon		
Folly Point Range R-068°		Fxd R beacon		
Titchfield Light	18° 11.0' N, 76° 27.1' W	Q G beacon		
W. Harbour Range F	18° 10.9' N, 76° 27.6' W	Fxd R	25'	
W. Harbour Range R-249°		Fxd R	277'	
Galina Point				
Galina Point	18° 25.2' N, 76° 55.1' W	Fl W 12s	62'	12 M
Ocho Rios				
Range F	18° 24.5' N, 77° 06.9' W	Oc R 5s	42'	10 M
Range R- 169°		Oc R 5s	150'	10 M
Beacon	18° 24.7' N, 77° 06.7' W	Fl G 5s	16'	
Beacon	18° 27.6' N, 77° 06.6' W	Fl G 1.5s	16'	
St. Ann's Bay				
Channel entrance W		Fl R 3s		
Channel entrance E		Fl G 3s		
Harbor Range F		Fxd R	122'	11 M
Harbor Range R- 193°		Fxd R	270'	11 M
Discovery Bay				
Entrance Channel outer W		Fl R 7.5s		
Entrance Channel outer E		Fl G 7.5s		
Entrance Channel inner W		Fl R 5s		
Entrance Channel inner E		Fl G 5s		
Discovery Bay Range F	18° 27.7' N, 77° 24.6' W	Fxd R	25'	
Discovery Bay Range R-193°		Fxd R	40'	
Falmouth Harbour				
Falmouth Harbour Light	18° 29.3' N, 77° 39.1' W	Fxd R	37'	
Rose Hall				
Rose Hall Lighthouse	18° 32.1' N, 77° 49.2' W	Fl (5) W 30s	106'	22 M
Montego Bay				
Upper Range F	18° 28.7' N, 77° 55.6' W	Fxd R	44'	5 M
Upper Range R-035.2°		Fxd R	113'	5 M
Lower Range F	18° 28.2' N, 77° 55.5' W	Fxd R	22'	7 M
Lower Range R-118.5°		Fxd R	57'	5 M
Montego Bay Light #1	18° 27.8' N, 77° 56.2' W	Fl R		
Montego Bay Light #2	18° 27.8' N, 77° 56.2' W	Fl R 5s	16'	
Montego Bay Light #3	18° 27.8' N, 77° 56.3' W	Fl R 3s	16'	
Montego Bay Light #4	18° 27.7' N, 77° 56.5' W	Fl R 5s	16'	
Montego Bay Light #5	18° 27.6' N, 77° 56.5' W	Fl R 3s	16'	
Montego Bay Light #6	18° 27.7' N, 77° 56.2' W	Fxd G	20'	
Ent. Ch. Range (front)	18° 27.6' N, 77° 56.3' W	Oc W 2s	26'	
Ent. Ch. Range (rear-201°)		Oc W 3s	43'	
Lucea				
Flagstaff Reef Light		Fl R 4s	23'	5 M
Negril				
Negril Point	18° 14.7' N, 78° 21.7' W	Fl W R 2s	100'	15 M

LIGHT	LAT/LON	CHARACTERISTICS	HT.	RNG.

THE YUCATÁN CHANNEL
Cuba

Cabo San Antonio	21° 52.0' N, 84° 57.2' W	Fl (2) W 10s	102'	18 M

QUINTANA ROO-THE YUCATÁN COAST OF MEXICO
Isla Mujeres to Cabo Catoche

Cabo Catoche	21° 36.3' N, 87° 06.1' W	Fl (4) W 20s	49'	25 M
Isla Contoy	21° 31.6' N, 86° 48.3' W	Fl W 7s	105'	21M
El Dormitorio	21° 22.5' N, 86° 48.3' W	Fl W 6s	10'	5 M
El Cabezo	21° 19.3' N, 86° 46.7' W	Fl (2) W 10s	10'	5 M

Isla Mujeres

Roca El Yunque (Yunke)	21° 15.9' N, 86° 45.4' W	Fl G 5s	16'	6 M
Piedra la Carbonera	21° 15.3' N, 86° 45.4' W	Fl (2) W 10s	62'	20 M
Roca la Carbonera	21° 14.8' N, 86° 45.4' W	Fl W 3s	20'	6 M
Bajo Pepito	21° 13.0' N, 86° 45.4' W	Fl R 4s		
El Meco	21° 12.7' N, 86° 48.4' W	Fl W 6s	26'	11 M
Southeast Light	21° 12.1' N, 86° 43.1' W	Fl (4) W 16s	75'	14 M
Roca de la Bandera	21° 09.9' N, 86° 44.0' W	Fl (2) W 10s	13'	11 M

Mainland: Isla Mujeres to Isla de Cozumel

Punta Cancún	21° 08.3' N, 86° 44.5' W	Fl (3) W 12s	49'	11 M
Punta Nizuk	21° 02.0' N, 86° 47.0' W	Fl (4) W 16s	33'	11 M
Puerto Morelos	20° 50.7' N, 86° 53.0' W	Fl W 6s	52'	18 M
Duque de Alba	20° 50.4' N, 86° 52.7' W	Iso W 2s	16'	11
Punta Brava	20° 48.6' N, 86° 54.8' W	Fl (4) W 16s	33'	11 M
Punta Maroma	20° 43.5' N, 86° 58.0' W	Fl (2) W 10s	36'	11 M
Playa del Carmen	20° 37.0' N, 87° 04.7' W	Fl (3) W 12s	39'	11 M
Xcaret Range-front	20° 35.0' N, 87° 06.0' W	Fl W 3s		
Xcaret Range-rear	20° 35.0' N, 87° 06.0' W	Iso W 2s		
Xcaret Jetty-north side	20° 35.0' N, 87° 06'.0 W	Fl G 5s		
Xcaret Jetty-south side	20° 35.0' N, 87° 06.0' W	Fl R 5s		
Xcaret Wharf-west side	20° 20.0' N, 87° 59.0' W	Fl G 3s		
Xcaret Wharf-east side	20° 20.0' N, 87° 59.0' W	Fl R 3s		
Caleta de Chachalet	20° 29.5' N, 87° 14.0' W	Fl (2) W 10s	33'	11 M
Caleta de Xel-Ha	20° 28.2' N, 87° 16.0' W	Fl W 6s	39'	11 M

Isla de Cozumel

Punta Molas	20° 35.2' N, 86° 43.9' W	Fl (3) W 12s	69'	16 M
Banco Playa- North	20° 31.6' N, 86° 56.4' W	Fl G 5s	26'	6 M
Banco Playa- South	20° 31.6' N, 86° 56.4' W	Fl R 5s	30'	6 M
Cozumel Aviation Light	20° 30.6' N, 86° 56.6' W	Fl W G 10s	82'	14 M
San Miguel de Cozumel	20° 30.4' N, 86° 57.3' W	Fl (2) W 5s	56'	15 M
Bahía Caleta- North	20° 28.0' N, 86° 59.0' W	Fl G 5s	30'	7 M
Bahía Caleta- South	20° 28.0' N, 86° 59.0' W	Fl R 5s	30'	7 M
Punta Celerain	20° 16.0' N, 86° 59.5' W	Fl W 5s	85'	20 M

Isla Cozumel to Bahía del Espíritu Santo

Tulum	20° 12.0' N, 87° 26.8' W	Fl W 6s	75'	15 M
Punta Allen	19° 46.9' N, 87° 28.0' W	Fl (4) W 16s	72'	16 M
Punta Vigia Chico	19° 46.3' N, 87° 35.1' W	Fl (4) W 16s	39'	11 M
Cayo Culebras	19° 42.0' N, 87° 28.0' W	Fl (3) W 12s	46'	11 M
Punta Nohku	19° 38.7' N, 87° 27.3' W	Fl (2) W 10s	39'	11 M
Punta Pajaros	19° 35.8' N, 87° 24.8' W	Fl W 6s	36'	10 M

LIGHT	LAT/LON	CHARACTERISTICS	HT.	RNG.
Bahía del Espirítu Santo				
Punta Owen	19° 19.7' N, 87° 26.6' W	Fl (3) W 12s	39'	11 M
Punta Herrero	19° 18.7' N, 87° 26.8' W	Fl (2) W 10s	75'	15 M
El Ubero	19° 04.5' N, 87° 33.5' W	Fl (3) W 12s	33'	11 M
Arrecife del Chinchorro (Banco Chinchorro) to Belize				
Cayo Norte	18° 45.8' N, 87° 18.9' W	Fl W 6s	52'	11 M
El Majahaul	18° 43.8' N, 87° 41.8' W	Fl (4) W 16s	33'	11 M
Cayo Centro	18° 35.5' N, 87° 19.9' W	Fl (2) W 10s	50'	11 M
Punta Gavilan	18° 25.2' N, 87° 46.1' W	Fl W 6s	36'	11 M
Cayo Lobos	18° 23.5' N, 87° 23.2' W	Fl (3) W 12s	46'	11 M
Xcalak	18° 15.8' N, 87° 50.2' W	Fl (3) W 12s	43'	17 M
Bahía de Chetumal				
Ciudad Chetumal	18° 31.2' N, 87° 16.5' W	Fl W 6s	59'	17 M
La Aguada	18° 14.0' N, 87° 55.0' W	Fl (2) W 10s	40'	11 M
Chetumal Bay Bulkhead	17° 56.0' N, 88° 08.0' W	Fl W 1.5s	30'	10 M

Appendix B: Marinas

Some of the marinas listed below may be untenable in certain winds and dockside depths listed may not reflect entrance channel depths at low water. Always check with the Dockmaster prior to arrival. All the marinas can handle your garbage disposal problems however some may levy a charge per bag for those who are not guests at their docks. For cruisers seeking services *Nearby* may mean either a walk or short taxi ride away.

MARINA	LOCATION	FUEL	GROC.	DINING	E-MAIL or WEBSITE
NORTHERN COAST OF JAMAICA					
Glistening Waters Marina	Falmouth	None	Nearby	Yes	info@glisteningwaters.com
Montego Bay Yacht Club*	Montego Bay	D & G	Nearby	Yes	mbyc@cwjamaica.com
Ocho Rios Marina	Ocho Rios	None	Nearby	Nearby	
Pier One	Montego Bay	None	Nearby	Yes	info@pieronejamaica.com
Errol Flynn Marina**	Port Antonio	D & G	Yes	Yes	info@errolflynnmarina.com
Fisherman's Inn	Falmouth	None	Nearby	Yes	
Royal Jamaica Y. C.***	Kingston	D & G	Nearby	Yes	rjycmanager@flowja.com

* The gas dock is shallow so you'll have to jerry can it by dinghy, and the diesel pump is located on the main dock where you'll have to drop a hook and come bow or stern to in order to fill your tank.

** The fuel dock is located on the western side of the harbor at the marina's haul-out yard.

*** Dockage is available for members of accredited yacht clubs.

CAYMAN ISLANDS					
Barcadere	Grand Cayman	D & G	Nearby	Yes	enquiries@barcadere.com
Cayman Islands Yacht Club	Grand Cayman	D & G	Nearby	Yes	info@ciyachtclub.ky
Harbour House Marina*	Grand Cayman	D & G	Nearby	Nearby	info@harbourhousemarina.com
Kaibo Yacht Club	Grand Cayman	D & G	Nearby	Yes	marina@kaibo.ky

* *Harbour House Marina* is a boatyard and chandlery, it has no transient facilities, but it does offer fuel.

HONDURAS					
Barefoot Cay Marina	Brick Bay, Roatán	None	Nearby	Nearby	info@barefootcay.com
Billares Marina*	Isla de Utila	None			
Brick Bay Marina	Brick Bay, Roatán	None	Nearby	Yes	
Brooksy Point Marina	French Hrb. Roatán	None**	Nearby	No	brooksypointyachtclub@gmail.com
CoCo View Resort	French Hrb. Roatán	None	Nearby	Nearby	ccv@cocoviewresort.com
Fantasy Island	French Hrb. Roatán	D & G	Nearby	Yes	info@fantasyislandresort.com

MARINA	LOCATION	FUEL	GROC.	DINING	E-MAIL or WEBSITE
Gibson Bight Marina	Roatán	None	Nearby	Nearby	info@gibsonbightmarina.com
La Ceiba Shipyard***	La Ceiba	Yes	Nearby	Nearby	laceibashipyard@gmail.com
Oak Ridge Marina****	Oak Ridge, Roatán	None	Nearby	Nearby	
Parrot Tree Plantation	2nd Bight, Roatán	None	Nearby	Yes	info@parrottree.com
Roatán Yacht Club	French Hrb.Roatán	None	Nearby	Yes	
Turtlegrass Marina	Calabash, Roatán	None	Nearby	Yes	info@turtlegrass.net
Utila Lodge	Isla de Utila	None	Nearby	Yes	

* *Billares Marina* is a private marina located in the small lagoon west/southwest of town
** Marina owners can make a fuel run for you by automobile
*** The *La Ceiba Shipyard* does not have a fuel dock but can arrange for a truck to arrive at your slip for fueling.
**** Also known as *Sandy Byrd's Marina*

GUATEMALA

Amatique Bay Marina	Puerto Barrios	D & G	Nearby	Yes	redessociales@amatiquebay.net
Bruno's Marina	Río Dulce	None	Nearby	Nearby	info@brunoshotel.com
Burnt Key Marina	Bahía de Tejano	None	Limited	Yes	
Calypso Marina	Laguna La Joya	Nearby	No	Soon	save196023@gmail.com
Capt. John's Marina	Río Dulce	None	No	No	
Catamaran Hotel Marina	Río Dulce	None	Nearby	Yes	hotelcatamaran@gmail.com
Crowbar Marina	Río Dulce	None	Nearby	Yes	
El Relleno	Río Dulce	None	Nearby	Nearby	
Freddie's Marina	Río Dulce	None	Nearby	Nearby	
Hacienda Tijax	Río Dulce	None	Nearby	Yes	info@tijax.com
La Joya del Rio Marina	Río Dulce	None	Nearby	Nearby	
Mango's Marina	Río Dulce	None	Nearby	Yes	mango@riodulcemangomarina.com
Mansion del Rio	Río Dulce	None	Nearby	Yes	turismo@hotelesdeguate.com
Mar Marine	Río Dulce	None	Nearby	Yes	info@marmarine.com
Monkey Bay Marina	Río Dulce	None	Nearby	Nearby	harbormaster@monkeybaymarina.com
Nana Juana Marina	Río Dulce	None	Nearby	Yes	info@hotelmarinananajuana.com
Ram Marina	Río Dulce	D & G	Yes	Yes	info@rammarina.com
Tortugal Marina	Río Dulce	None	Nearby	Yes	holatortugal@gmail.com
Xalaha Marina	Río Dulce	None	Nearby	Nearby	

Appendix C: Service Facilities

As with any place, businesses come and go, sometimes seemingly overnight. Certain entries on the following lists may no longer exist by the time this guide is published or may have changed their names or phone numbers.

Appendix C1: Jamaica

Driving is on the left in Jamaica.

FACILITY	LOCATION	TELEPHONE	E-MAIL ADDRESS OR WEBSITE
AUTO RENTALS			
Abe Car Rentals	Ocho Rios	876-974-1008	
Alex's Rent-A-Car	Montego Bay	876-940-6260	
Apex Rent-A-Car	Montego Bay	876-952-7587	http://www.apex-cars.com/
Avis	Montego Bay	876-952-0762	
Bamboo Jeep &Bike	Port Antonio	876-993-3209	

FACILITY	LOCATION	TELEPHONE	E-MAIL ADDRESS OR WEBSITE
Bargain Rent-A-Car	Montego Bay	876-952-0762	
Beaumont's Rentals	Montego Bay	876-926-0311	http://www.beaumontcarrentalja.com
Better Wheels	Ocho Rios	876-795-1937	
Budget	Montego Bay	876-952-9765	www.budgetjamaica.com
Budget (airport)	Montego Bay	876-952-3838	www.budgetjamaica.com
Budget	Ocho Rios	876-974-1288	www.budgetjamaica.com
Caribbean Rentals	Kingston	876-929-4817	http://www.caribbeancarrentals.net/
Caribbean Rentals	Montego Bay	876-952-0664	http://www.caribbeancarrentals.net/
Caribbean Rentals	Ocho Rios	876-974-2123	http://www.caribbeancarrentals.net/
Caribbean Rentals	Runaway Bay	876-973-5185	http://www.caribbeancarrentals.net/
Central Rent-A-Car	Montego Bay	876-952-3347	http://www.centralrentacar.com/
Chalis Car Rental	Montego Bay	876-952-9361	http://www.chaliscarrentaljamaica.com/
Champagne Tours	Montego Bay	876-952-7475	
Chrilmar Car Rental	Montego Bay	876-952-7621	
Coconut Car Rental	Negril	876-957-3100	
Demario's Rentals	Montego Bay	876-971-4051	
Discount Rent-A-Car	Montego Bay	876-952-1943	
Dollar Rent-A-Car	Negril	876-957-4110	tropical@cwjamaica.com
Dollar Rent-A-Car	Ocho Rios	876-953-9110	tropical@cwjamaica.com
Eastern Rent-A-Car	Port Antonio	876-993-3624	eastern@cwjamaica.com
Efficient Rent-A-Car	Montego Bay	876-952-7797	
EZ Rent A Car	Montego Bay	876-952-3793	www.e-zrentacar.com/
Fantasy Rent-A-Car	Montego Bay	876-940-6672	
Fiesta Car Rentals	Montego Bay	876-684-9388	http://www.fiestacarrentals.com/about.html
Island Car Rentals	Montego Bay	876-952-5771	http://www.islandcarrentals.com/
Island Car Rentals	Ocho Rios	876-974-2666	http://www.islandcarrentals.com/
Metro Car Rentals	Montego Bay	876-978-5468	http://metrocarrentals.com/
Payless Car Rental	Montego Bay	876-971-2760	
Payless Car Rental	Montego Bay	876-971-8003	
Port Antonio Car Rtl.	Port Antonio	876-993-3624	http://www.portantoniocarrentals.com/
Rite Car Rental.	Negril	876-957-4667	
Sunbird Car Rentals	Montego Bay	876-952-3015	
Sunshine Rentals	Ocho Rios	876-974-2980	
Thrifty Car Rental	Montego Bay	876-952-5825	
Triple A Rent-A-Car	Ocho Rios	876-974-2859	triplea30@hotmail.com
Vernon's Rentals	Negril	876-957-4354	http://vernonscarrental.com/
Wright's Car Rentals	Negril	876-957-4908	

DIESEL REPAIR/PARTS

Errol Flynn Boatyard	Port Antonio	876-715-6044	www.errolflynnmarina.com
PA Marine Services	Port Antonio	876-289-2890	admin@port-antonio-marine-services.com
Power & Tractor	Montego Bay	876-979-8711	

DIVING

Dive Seaworld	Montego Bay	876-953-2180	http://www.diveseaworld.com/
Dream Team Divers	Negril	876-957-0054	http://www.dreamteamdiversjamaica.com/
Lady G Diver	Port Antonio	876-715-5957	http://www.ladygdiver.com/html/
Marine Life Divers	Negril	876-957-3245	http://www.mldiversnegril.com/
Resort Divers	Runaway Bay	876-881-5760	http://www.resortdivers.com/
Sun Divers	Negril	876-957-4503	http://www.sundiversnegril.com/

ELECTRONICS/ELECTRICAL

DESMAC Elect.	Kingston	876-923-8835	
Errol Flynn Boatyard	Port Antonio	876-715-6044	www.errolflynnmarina.com

FACILITY	LOCATION	TELEPHONE	E-MAIL ADDRESS OR WEBSITE
PA Marine Services	Port Antonio	876-289-2890	admin@port-antonio-marine-services.com
Tony Shim	Kingston	876-924-1112	

FABRICATION AND WELDING

FACILITY	LOCATION	TELEPHONE	E-MAIL ADDRESS OR WEBSITE
Bell's Welding	Ocho Rios	876-974-1691	
HS Services	St. Ann, Discovery Bay	876-670-0379	
Mobile Welding	Montego Bay	876-952-0690	
Nunes Welding	St. Ann, Discovery Bay	876-973-0306	

HAUL OUT

FACILITY	LOCATION	TELEPHONE	E-MAIL ADDRESS OR WEBSITE
Barham's Wharf	Savanna-la-Mar	876-955-3171	
Errol Flynn Boatyard	Port Antonio	876-715-6044	www.errolflynnmarina.com
Kingston Drydock	Kingston	876-928-7281	
Black's Drydock*	Port Royal		
Royal Jamaica YC	Kingston	876-924-8685	

HULL REPAIR/PAINTING

FACILITY	LOCATION	TELEPHONE	E-MAIL ADDRESS OR WEBSITE
Errol Flynn Boatyard	Port Antonio	876-715-6044	www.errolflynnmarina.com
PA Marine Services	Port Antonio	876-289-2890	admin@port-antonio-marine-services.com

INTERNET ACCESS

FACILITY	LOCATION	TELEPHONE	E-MAIL ADDRESS OR WEBSITE
Computer Central	St. Ann's Bay	876-972-9963	sales@computercentralplus.com
Cyber Bar	Montego Bay	876-940-6020	
Cybershores	Montego Bay	876-971-1050	marlon@cybershorescafe.com
Ela Systems	Port Antonio	876-715-3180	
Errol Flynn Marina	Port Antonio	876-715-6044	www.errolflynnmarina.com
Game Zone Plus	Montego Bay	876-940-1840	
Global Courier	Montego Bay	876-971-2792	info@globalcourierja.com
Internet Jungle	Ocho Rios	876-675-8730	internetjungle@cwjamaica.com
Internet Zone	Montego Bay	876-940-7843	internetzone@cwjamaica.com
Irie Vibes	Negril	876-957-4731	jamaica@jamaicaconnection.com
Jack in the Box	Ocho Rios	876-795-4800	jackintheboxgames@yahoo.com
Montego Bay YC	Montego Bay	876-979-8038	mbyc@cwjamaica.com
Negril Calling Serv.	Negril	876-957-3212	
Taj Internet Café	Ocho Rios	876-974-7438	

MARINE SUPPLIES

FACILITY	LOCATION	TELEPHONE	E-MAIL ADDRESS OR WEBSITE
Boat Shop	Kingston	876-929-1775	*The Boat Shop*, VHF ch. 68
Commercial Marine	Kingston	876-923-6915	jtame@angel.com
Durae's	Kingston	876-925-7633	
Errol Flynn Boatyard	Port Antonio	876-715-6044	www.errolflynnmarina.com
Ocean Runner	Kingston	876-923-6915	
Sea Supply*	Montego Bay	876-940-2327	seasupplymbj@bellsouth.net

OUTBOARD REPAIR

FACILITY	LOCATION	TELEPHONE	E-MAIL ADDRESS OR WEBSITE
Commercial Marine	Kingston	876-923-6915	jtame@angel.com
Durae's	Kingston	876-925-7633	
Errol Flynn Boatyard	Port Antonio	876-715-6044	www.errolflynnmarina.com
Ocean Runner	Kingston	876-923-6915	
Yamaha Engines	Kingston	876-927-8700	

PROPANE

FACILITY	LOCATION	TELEPHONE	E-MAIL ADDRESS OR WEBSITE
Montego Bay YC**	Montego Bay	876-979-8038	mbyc@cwjamaica.com
Errol Flynn Marina	Port Antonio	876-715-6044	www.errolflynnmarina.com

REFRIGERATION AND AIR CONDITIONING

FACILITY	LOCATION	TELEPHONE	E-MAIL ADDRESS OR WEBSITE
Errol Flynn Boatyard	Port Antonio	876-715-6044	www.errolflynnmarina.com
PA Marine Services	Port Antonio	876-289-2890	admin@port-antonio-marine-services.com

* *Sea Supply* is primarily a tackle store, they have a minor selection of basic marine supplies.

** Ask the office at the *MBYC* to arrange a taxi for you to the propane fill station, they're happy to help.

Appendix C2: Cayman Islands

Please note that "GT" means George Town; "Cayman B." means Cayman Brac; "Little Cay." means Little Cayman Island, and "Grand Cay." means Grand Cayman Island.

FACILITY	LOCATION	TELEPHONE	E-MAIL ADDRESS OR WEBSITE
AUTO RENTALS			
Ace Hertz	GT, Grand Cayman	345-949-2280	acehertz@candw.ky
Andy's Rent-a-Car	Hell, Grand Cayman	345-949-8111	info@andys.ky
Avis	GT, Grand Cayman	345-949-2468	avisgcm@candw.ky
Brac Rent-a-Car	Stake Bay, Cayman B.	345-948-1840	scottaud@candw.ky
B&S Motor Ventures	South Side, Cayman B.	345-948-1646	the_rock@candw.ky
Budget	GT, Grand Cayman	345-949-5605	budgetgrandcayman@candw.ky
Cayman Rentals	GT, Grand Cayman	345-949-1013	cayauto@candy.ky
CB Rent-a-Car	West End, Cayman B.	345-948-2424	cbcars@candw.ky
Coconut Rentals	GT, Grand Cayman	345-949-6955	coconut@candw.ky
Conmac	GT, Grand Cayman	345-949-6955	
Dollar Rent-a-Car	GT, Grand Cayman	345-949-8484	dollar@candw.ky
Economy Rentals	GT, Grand Cayman	345-949-9550	economy@candw.ky
E. Scott Rent-a-Car	GT, Grand Cayman	345-949-8867	
Four D's Car Rental	Spot Bay, Cayman B.	345-948-1599	4-d@candw.ky
Hertz	GT, Grand Cayman	345-943-4378	rubio@hertzcayman.com
GT Leasing	GT, Grand Cayman	345-945-3415	bmwrent@candw.ky
Island Paradise	GT, Grand Cayman	345-945-5831	
Island Style	GT, Grand Cayman	345-949-3233	
Marshall's Rentals	GT, Grand Cayman	345-949-0550	mar_rac@candw.ky
McLaughlin Rentals	Village Sq., Little Cay.	345-948-1000	littlecay@candw.ky
McCurley's Tours	GT, Grand Cayman	345-947-9726	mccurley@cwhiptop.com
Payless Car Rental	GT, Grand Cayman	345-743-1270	www.paylesscar.com/
Scooten Scooters	Blossom Village, L.C.	345-916-4971	http://www.scootenscooters.com/
Scooters & Wheels	GT, Grand Cayman	345-949-0064	scooters50@weststartv.com
Soto's 4X4 Rentals	GT, Grand Cayman	345-945-2424	sotos4x4@candw.ky
Sunshine's Rentals	GT, Grand Cayman	345-949-3858	sales@sunshinecarrentals.com
Thrifty Car Rental	GT, Grand Cayman	345-949-6640	thrifty@candw.ky
DIESEL REPAIR/PARTS			
Atlantic Supply	GT, Grand Cayman	345-949-0333	atsupply@candw.ky
Compass Marine	GT, Grand Cayman	345-916-0660	bill@compassmarine.ky
Harbour House Mar.	GT, Grand Cayman	345-947-1307	http://www.harbourhousemarina.com/
Marine Diesel	Batabano, Grand Cay.	345-949-3555	mdcayman@candw.ky
Marine Power	GT, Grand Cayman	345-947-1945	http://www.marinepower.ky/
Moore Marine	GT, Grand Cayman	345-949-6672	http://www.mooremarineservices.ky/
Scott's Marine	GT, Grand Cayman	345-949-4186	info@scottsmarinecayman.com
DIVING			
Ambassador Divers	GT, Grand Cayman	345-925-7278	http://www.ambassadordivers.com/
Cayman Turtle Divers	Grand Cayman	345-938-0184	http://www.caymanturtledivers.com/
Deep Blue Divers	Grand Cayman	345-916-1293	http://www.deepbluediverscayman.com/
Dive Cayman Islands	Grand Cayman	345-949-0623	http://www.caymanislands.ky/
Divers Down	Grand Cayman	345-945-1611	https://www.diversdown.net/
Divetech	Lighthouse Point	345-946-5658	http://www.divetech.com/
Dive Cayman	Grand Cayman	345-945-5132	http://www.donfosters.com/
Indigo Divers	Grand Cayman	345-525-3932	https://indigodivers.com/
Reef Divers	Cayman Brac	855-439-6813	http://www.caymanbracbeachresort.com/
Wall to Wall Diving	Grand Cayman	345-916-6408	https://walltowalldiving.com/

FACILITY	LOCATION	TELEPHONE	E-MAIL ADDRESS OR WEBSITE
ELECTRONICS/ELECTRICAL			
Compass Marine	GT, Grand Cayman	345-945-0660	bill@compassmarine.ky
Harbour House Mar.	GT, Grand Cayman	345-947-1307	jcuff@candw.ky
Scott's Marine	GT, Grand Cayman	345-949-4186	scottind@candw.ky
FABRICATION/WELDING			
Caribbean Eng.	GT, Grand Cayman	345-946-5000	skippy@candw.ky
Casaban Welding	GT, Grand Cayman	345-916-0742	
Cayman Metal	GT, Grand Cayman	345-945-4066	
Compass Marine	GT, Grand Cayman	345-916-0660	mike@compassmarine.ky
Ghezzi Mechanical	GT, Grand Cayman	345-946-2790	bghezzi@candw.ky
Harbour House Mar.	GT, Grand Cayman	345-947-1307	jcuff@candw.ky
Scott's Marine	GT, Grand Cayman	345-949-4186	scottind@candw.ky
Tropical Metals	GT, Grand Cayman	345-949-4437	
HAUL OUT			
Barcadere (Scott's)	GT, Grand Cayman	345-949-3743	enquiries@barcadere.com
Harbour House Mar.	GT, Grand Cayman	345-947-1307	hhmrogen@candw.ky
ProYacht	GT, Grand Cayman	345-916-0697	proyacht@candw.ky
HULL REPAIR/PAINTING			
Compass Marine	GT, Grand Cayman	345-916-0660	mike@compassmarine.ky
Harbour House Mar.	GT, Grand Cayman	345-947-1307	hhmrogen@candw.ky
Pro Yacht	GT, Grand Cayman	345-945-4676	http://www.proyacht.ky/
Scott's Marine	GT, Grand Cayman	345-949-4186	scottind@candw.ky
INTERNET ACCESS			
Azzurro by Rayazzi	GT, Grand Cayman	345-946-7745	
Café del Sol	GT, Grand Cayman	345-946-2233	coffee@cafedelsol.ky
Geek's Internet	GT, Grand Cayman	345-943-4335	
My Computer	GT, Grand Cayman	345-325-0945	
PD's Pub	GT, Grand Cayman	345-949-7144	info@pdspub.com
The Thirsty Surfer	Reef Resort Grand Cay.	345-947-2337	sales@thirstysurfer.com
Olde English Bakery	GT, Grand Cayman	345-945-2420	
MARINE SUPPLIES			
Atlantic Supply	GT, Grand Cayman	345-949-0333	trucksandheavyequipmentpartscayman.com/
Brown's Marine	GT, Grand Cayman	345-949-4174	brownsmarine@candw.ky
Capt. Solomon	GT, Grand Cayman		
Harbour House Mar.	GT, Grand Cayman	345-947-1307	jcuff@candw.ky
Kirk Marine	GT, Grand Cayman	345-946-3575	http://kirkmarine.ky/
Melody Marine	GT, Grand Cayman	345-947-1093	chipchip@candw.ky
Scott's Marine	GT, Grand Cayman	345-949-4186	scottind@candw.ky
OUTBOARD REPAIR			
Brown's Marine	GT, Grand Cayman	345-949-4174	brownsmarine@candw.ky
Cayman Outboard	GT, Grand Cayman	345-945-0432	
Cayman Sports	GT, Grand Cayman	345-943-2005	http://www.cpsm.ky/
Compass Marine	GT, Grand Cayman	345-916-0660	mike@compassmarine.ky
Harbour House Mar.	GT, Grand Cayman	345-947-1307	jcuff@candw.ky
Marine Power	GT, Grand Cayman	345-947-1945	mpower@candw.ky
Kirk Marine	GT, Grand Cayman	345-946-3577	kirkboat@candw.ky
Scott's Marine	GT, Grand Cayman	345-949-4186	scottind@candw.ky
PROPANE			
Home Gas	GT, Grand Cayman	345-949-7474	http://www.homegas.net/
PROPELLER			
Harbour House Mar.	GT, Grand Cayman	345-947-1307	jcuff@candw.ky

FACILITY	LOCATION	TELEPHONE	E-MAIL ADDRESS OR WEBSITE
REFRIGERATION & AC			
Ghezzi Mechanical	GT, Grand Cayman		bghezzi@candw.ky
RIGGING			
Compass Marine	GT, Grand Cayman	345-916-0660	mike@compassmarine.ky
Harbour House Mar.	GT, Grand Cayman	345-947-1307	jcuff@candw.ky
SAIL/CANVAS REPAIR			
Windward Sailing	GT, Grand Cayman	345-947-2649	http://www.caymanwindsurf.ky/

Appendix C3: Honduras

In the case of 8-digit phone numbers (not counting the 504 country code), numbers beginning with 2 are landlines while those with 3 or 9 are cell phones.

FACILITY	LOCATION	TELEPHONE	E-MAIL ADDRESS OR WEBSITE
AUTO RENTALS			
A & G Rent-a-Car	Airport, Roatán	504-957-2374	yussef20roatan@yahoo.com
Arena	Airport, Roatán	504-445-1882	bessiefusa2001@yahoo.com
Autos Corporativos	Roatán	504-2216-4000	www.hondurasrentacar.com/localidades.asp
Autos Corporativos	San Pedro Sula	504-2252-0814	www.hondurasrentacar.com/localidades.asp
Autos Corporativos	Tegucigalpa (airport)	504-2234-3183	www.hondurasrentacar.com/localidades.asp
Avis	Coxen Hole, Roatán	504-445-0122	avishonduras@unete.com
Avis	La Ceiba	504-441-2802	avishonduras@unete.com
Avis	Puerto Cortés	504-665-0740	
Avis	San Pedro Sula	504-553-0888	avishonduras@unete.com
Avis (airport)	Tegucigalpa	504-2234-5724	avishonduras@unete.com
Best Car Rental	Airport, Roatán	504-445-2268	http://www.roatanbestcarrental.com/
Blitz Rent-a-Car	San Pedro Sula	504-2668-2471	
Budget	Comayagua	504-772-9212	covesa.brac@datum.hn
Budget	Coxen Hole, Roatán	504-2445-2290	
Budget	La Ceiba	504-441-1105	covesa.brac@datum.hn
Budget	San Pedro Sula	504-552-2295	covesa.brac@datum.hn
Budget	Tegucigalpa	504-2239-1244	
Budget (airport)	Tegucigalpa	504-2233-3030	
Carib. Rent A Car	Airport, Roatán	504-455-7351	http://www.caribbeanroatan.com/
Captain Van's	West End, Roatán	504-2445-5040	info@captainvans.com
Coral Reef Rentals	Roatán	504-445-1990	
Econo Rent-a-Car	La Ceiba	504-2442-8686	
Econo Rent-a-Car	La Ceiba (airport)	504-2442-1688	
Econo Rent-a-Car	San Pedro Sula (airport)	504-2668-1884	
Econo Rent-a-Car	Roatán	504-2445-2249	www.econorentacarhn.com
Econo Rent-a-Car	Tegucigalpa	504-2291-0107	
Euroamerican	San Pedro Sula (airport)	504-2580-9090	euroamerican@sulanet.net
Euroamerican	Tebucigalpa (airport)	504-2280-9195	euroamerican@sulanet.net
Express Rent-a-Car	San Pedro Sula	504-557-6383	
Fun in the Sun	Utila	504-2425-3245	www.utilaboddenrentals.com/index.html
Hertz (airport)	San Pedro Sula	504-2580-9191	
Hertz (airport)	Tegucigalpa	504-2280-9195	
Island Rentals	French Hrbr., Roatán	504-465-7740	islandrental2000@yahoo.com
Jeffries	Coxen Hole, Roatán	504-2445-1824	jeffresrent@hondusoft.com
Molinari Rent-a-Car	La Ceiba	504-2443-2391	
Molinari Rent-a-Car	San Pedro Sula	504-2552-2870	
Molinari Rent-a-Car	Tegucigalpa	504-2232-0682	

FACILITY	LOCATION	TELEPHONE	E-MAIL ADDRESS OR WEBSITE
Omega Rent-a-Car	San Pedro Sula	504-552-7626	info@omegarentacar.com
Parque Automotiz	La Ceiba	504-2442-4140	
Parque Automotiz	San Pedro Sula	504-2561-8600	
Parque Automotiz	Tegucigalpa	504-2216-4000	
Ramirez	Roatán	518-533-9800	www.ramirezrentacar.com
Roatán 4x4	Roatán	504-9811-2296	http://roatan4x4.com/
Roatán Rentals	West End, Roatán	504-445-1171	djackson@roatan-net.com
Sandy Bay Rentals	West End, Roatán	504-445-1710	
Thrifty (airport)	Roatán	504-445-1729	
Thrifty (airport)	San Pedro Sula	504-668-2427	
Thrifty (airport)	Tegucigalpa	504-234-3183	
Toyota Rent-a-Car	Coxen Hole, Roatán	504-445-1166	trac@floreshn.com
Toyota Rent-a-Car	La Ceiba	504-2443-1975	trac@floreshn.com
Toyota Rent-a-Car	San Pedro Sula	504-2557-2666	trac@floreshn.com
Toyota Rent-a-Car	Tegucigalpa	504 2443-1975	trac@floreshn.com
Tropical Rez	French Hrbr., Roatán	504-455-7841	info@tropicalrez.com

DIESEL REPAIR/PARTS

FACILITY	LOCATION	TELEPHONE	E-MAIL ADDRESS OR WEBSITE
Blue Seas Marine	Dixon Cove, Roatán	504-445-1510	blueseas@bitelnet.com
Clema	French Hrbr., Roatán	504-9580-7232	
Cross Creek Yanmar	Utila	504-425-3134	
Dixon's Marine	Mt. Pleasant, Roatán	504-2455-6897	daneikdixon@yahoo.com
Kelsa	French Hrbr., Roatán	504-9604-8441	
La Ceiba Shipyard	La Ceiba	504-2408-9813	http://laceibashipyard.com/
Luven	French Hrbr., Roatán	504-3310-3817	
Morel Bodden	French Hrbr., Roatán	504-9943-9856	
Smiley	French Hrbr., Roatán	504-9725-7299	
Sonny	French Hrbr., Roatán	504-9587-8944	
Willie Camay	French Hrbr., Roatán	504-9977-2790	
Separate Wilmont B,	Guanaja	504-2453-445	http://wilmontbay.com/

DIVING

FACILITY	LOCATION	TELEPHONE	E-MAIL ADDRESS OR WEBSITE
Alton's Dive Center	Utila	504-2425-3704	http://diveinutila.com/site/
Captain Morgan's	Utila	504-2425-3349	www.divingutila.com
Coconut Tree Divers	French Hrbr., Roatán		http://www.coconuttreedivers.com/
College of Diving	Utila	504-2425-3291	http://www.dive-utila.com/
SCUBA Roatan	Half Moon Bay	504-8963-6222	http://www.scubaroatanhonduras.com/
Sun Divers	Half Moon Bay	504-3335-7281	http://sundiversroatan.com/
Utila Dive Center	Utila	504-2425-3326	http://www.utiladivecenter.com/en
West End Divers	West End, Roatán	504-2425-3326	http://www.westenddivers.info/

ELECTRONICS/ELECTRICAL

FACILITY	LOCATION	TELEPHONE	E-MAIL ADDRESS OR WEBSITE
Dixon's Marine	Mt. Pleasant, Roatán	504-2455-6897	daneikdixon@yahoo.com
Eagle Marine Dry.	La Ceiba	504-2453-4457	eaglemarine@tevisat.net
La Ceiba Shipyard	La Ceiba	504-2408-9813	http://laceibashipyard.com/
Pedro Ortega	French Hrbr., Roatán	504-9535-3228	workortega@hotmail.com
Robert Turcios	French Hrbr., Roatán	504-9577-1190	

FABRICATION AND WELDING

FACILITY	LOCATION	TELEPHONE	E-MAIL ADDRESS OR WEBSITE
Bodden Rentals	Oak Ridge, Roatán	504-2425-3245	www.utilaboddenrentals.com/index.html
Darcy Martinez	French Hrbr., Roatán	504-9992-3902	
Eagle Marine Dry.	La Ceiba	504-2453-4457	eaglemarine@tevisat.net
Fremofer Taller	French Hrbr., Roatán	504-2455-6724	
Gasina Gases	French Hrbr., Roatán	504-455-7933	
La Ceiba Shipyard	La Ceiba	504-991-6175	http://laceibashipyard.com/

FACILITY	LOCATION	TELEPHONE	E-MAIL ADDRESS OR WEBSITE
Martinez Power Bts.	French Hrbr., Roatán	504-9992-3902	
Peter Schmitt	Port Royal, Roatán		Crazy Horse, VHF ch. 68 & 72
Rockie Dilbert	French Hrbr., Roatán	504-9720-3468	
Shipyard	Oak Ridge, Roatán	504-9995-5461	
Shipyard	Savannah Bight, Guanaja		
Torno Industrial	French Hrbr., Roatán	504-9929-2541	

HAUL OUT

Eagle Marine Dry.	La Ceiba	504-2453-4457	eaglemarine@tevisat.net
La Ceiba Shipyard	La Ceiba	504-991-6175	http://laceibashipyard.com/
FH Marine Railway	French Hrbr., Roatán	504-3382-2172	
Navy Base	Puerto Cortés		
Seth Archer's	French Hrbr., Roatán		
Shipyard*	Oak Ridge, Roatán		
Shipyard*	Savannah Bight, Guanaja		

HULL REPAIR/PAINTING

Eagle Marine Dry.	La Ceiba	504-2453-4457	eaglemarine@tevisat.net
La Ceiba Shipyard	La Ceiba	504-991-6175	http://laceibashipyard.com/
Martinez Power Bts.	French Hrbr., Roatán	504-9992-3902	
Sherman Boat Rep.	French Hrbr., Roatán	504-9778-2219	
Shipyard	Oak Ridge, Roatán		
Shipyard	Savannah Bight, Guanaja		

INFLATABLES/LIFERAFTS

La Ceiba Shipyard	La Ceiba	504-991-6175	shipyard@laceiba.com

INTERNET ACCESS

@cess Cyber Coffee	Tegucigalpa	504-220-5182	access@honduras.com
Atlantis Computers	Mt. Pleasant, Roatán	504-455-0382	
Bay Islands Resort	Sandy Bay, Roatán		bislands@hondutel.hn
Bayview Internet	Utila	504-425-3114	
BJ's Backyard	Oak Ridge, Roatán		http://www.roatanonline.com/bj_backyard/
Blue Channel Pub	West End, Roatán		
Budget Internet Café	Sandy Bay, Roatán		jtdesign@netscape.net
Café@Cafe	La Ceiba		
Chat Phone	La Ceiba		
Chessier Internet	Puerto Cortés		
Computeck	Tegucigalpa	504-441-3231	lcic@caribe.hn
Compu Pro	Trujillo	504-434-4517	
Copán Net	Copán		
Cyber Coffee	Tegucigalpa	504-220-5182	access@honduras.com
End of the World	Michael Rock, Guanaja	504-991-1257	
Expatriates	La Ceiba	504-440-3373	
French Harbor YC	French Hrbr., Roatán		
Hondutel Internet	Coxen Hole, Roatán	504-445-1415	
Hondusoft Internet	La Ceiba	504-443-4152	laceiba@hondusoft.com
Hondusoft Internet	San Pedro Sula	504-550-4975	sps@hondusoft.com
Hondusoft Internet	West End, Roatán	504-445-1548	roatan@hondusoft.com
Howell's Internet	Utila	504-425-3317	howells@utila-net.com
Intercon	La Ceiba	504-440-1430	intercon@honduras.com
Internet Café	Coxen Hole, Roatán	504-445-1241	internetcafe@roatanet.com
Internet Café	Utila	504-425-3124	bicomput@hondutel.hn
King's Café	West End, Roatán		
La Casa de Todo	Copán Ruinas	504-651-4186	info@casadetodo.com

FACILITY	LOCATION	TELEPHONE	E-MAIL ADDRESS OR WEBSITE
La Ceiba Internet	La Ceiba	504-440-1505	icic@caribe.hn
La Ceiba Shipyard	La Ceiba	504-991-6175	http://laceibashipyard.com/
Mango	Tela		
Mango's Tree House	Utila	504-425-3124	internetcafe@utila-net.com
Maya Connections	Copán Ruinas		
Mermaid's Corner	Utila		
Metronet	La Ceiba		
Paradise Computers	Coxen Hole, Roatán	504-445-1611	paradise@globalnet.hn
Paradise Computers	West End, Roatán	504-2445-4028	paradise@globalnet.hn
Plantation Beach	Cayo Cochinos	504-442-0974	pbr@laceiba.com
Precios Café	Yoro	504-647-3149	webmaster@progresonet.hn
Que Tal Café	Coxen Hole, Roatán	504-445-1007	quetal@globalnet.hn
Roatán Dive & YC	French Hrbr., Roatán	504-455-5407	reservat@roatanyachtclub.com
Roli's Place	Omoa	504-658-9082	RG@yaxpactours.com
Rudon's Cyber	Puerto Cortés		
Sandy Bay Internet	West End, Roatán	504-980-2403	
Sol Caribe	Coxen Hole, Roatán	504-445-0134	
Solef Cyber Café	La Esperanza	504-783-0726	
Trujillo Online	Trujillo		

MARINE SUPPLIES

FACILITY	LOCATION	TELEPHONE	E-MAIL ADDRESS OR WEBSITE
Blue Seas Marine	Dixon Cove, Roatán	504-445-1509	blueseas@bitelnet.com
Dixon's Marine	Mt. Pleasant, Roatán	504-2455-6897	daneikdixon@yahoo.com
Hybur Marine Supp.	Frenc Hrbr. Roatán	504-2455-7564	
La Ceiba Shipyard	La Ceiba	504-991-6175	http://laceibashipyard.com/
Marine & Bldg.	French Hrbr., Roatán	504-455-7571	mhybur@hondutel.hn
Martinez Powerboat	French Hrbr., Roatán	504-455-5489	
Motores Kawas**	La Ceiba	504-443-2161	
Naviera Hybur	French Hrbr., Roatán	504-2455-7564	navierahybur@globalnet.hn
Parker Store	French Hrbr., Roatán	504-2455-5156	esantos@cendema.com
Sunshine Shop	Coxen Hole, Roatán	504-445-5586	
Vegas Electric	French Hrbr., Roatán	504-455-1244	vegas@globalnet.hn

OUTBOARD REPAIR

FACILITY	LOCATION	TELEPHONE	E-MAIL ADDRESS OR WEBSITE
Extra Shine	Guanaja	504-453-4124	Extra Gas
Kelsa	French Hrbr., Roatán	504-9604-8441	
La Ceiba Shipyard	La Ceiba	504-991-6175	http://laceibashipyard.com/
Travis Kirkwood	French Hrbr., Roatán	504-8994-5606	
Wilmont Bay Serv.	Guanaja		
Ultra Motor	La Ceiba	504-2427-8510	
Ultra Motor	San Pedro Sula	504-2531-7600	
Ultra Motor	Tegucigalpa	504-2202-7000	
Wilmont Bay Serv.	Tegucigalpa	504-2453-4457	

PROPANE

FACILITY	LOCATION	TELEPHONE	E-MAIL ADDRESS OR WEBSITE
Derek	French Hrbr., Roatán	504-9795-7246	
Gasolinera Ron	Coxen Hole, Roatán	504-445-1921	
La Ceiba Shipyard	La Ceiba	504-991-6175	http://laceibashipyard.com/
Luven	French Hrbr., Roatán	504-3310-3817	
SolGas	French Hrbr., Roatán	504-2455-7507	
Texgas	Mt. Pleasant, Roatán	504-2455-7348	
Tropigas	French Hrbr., Roatán	504-2455-7669	
Tropigas	Mt. Pleasant, Roatán	504-2455-7498	
Venta Gas Butano	Jonesville, Roatán	504-435-2244	

FACILITY	LOCATION	TELEPHONE	E-MAIL ADDRESS OR WEBSITE
Wilmont Bay Serv.	Bonacca, Guanaja	504-2453-4457	
PROPELLER			
La Ceiba Shipyard	La Ceiba	504-991-6175	http://laceibashipyard.com/
REFRIGERATION & AC			
Anastacio Marin	French Hrbr., Roatán	504-9656-5230	
Cool Wind Supply	French Hrbr., Roatán	504-2445-7771	coolwind@globalnet.hn
Friopartes	French Hrbr., Roatán	504-2480-5263	geren_roatan@friopartes-hn.com
Gerald Bodden	French Hrbr., Roatán	504-3315-5132	
La Ceiba Shipyard	La Ceiba	504-991-6175	http://laceibashipyard.com/
Midence's Ref.	Coxen Hole, Roatán	504-2445-1013	
Tropical A/C	French Hrbr., Roatán	504-2455-7464	lelandwoods1@hotmail.com
RIGGING			
La Ceiba Shipyard	La Ceiba	504-991-6175	http://laceibashipyard.com/
SAIL/CANVAS REPAIR			
La Ceiba Shipyard	La Ceiba	504-991-6175	http://laceibashipyard.com/
Judy	Oak Ridge, Roatán	504-435-1501	
Roatán Awning	Brick Bay, Roatán	504-3385-7457	daveroatan@yahoo.com
Toni	French Hrbr., Roatán	504-9829-1216	
Valdina's	French Hrbr., Roatán	504-2455-5605	
WOODWORKING			
Jackson Errol	French Hrbr., Roatán	504-2455-7509	

* These shipyards are used primarily by the shrimping fleet, they can haul a yacht of large size but you'll have to make arrangements well beforehand.

** *Motores Kawas* is an auto supply outlet but they do carry a selection of marine supplies.

Appendix C4: Guatemala

You will notice that the phone numbers in Guatemala are 8-digit numbers (following the 502 country code). The first of the eight numbers tells you a lot about the number. If the first number is a 2, you know that number is a land line in Guatemala City, a prefix of 5 means the number is a cell phone, and a prefix of 7 means the number is local to the *Río Dulce* area.

FACILITY	LOCATION	TELEPHONE	E-MAIL ADDRESS OR WEBSITE
AUTO RENTALS			
Adaesa	Guatemala City	502-2220-2180	adaesa@itelgua.com
Ahorrent	Guatemala City		info@ahorrent.com
Budget	Guatemala City		contactenos@budget.com.gt
Ceiba Rent	Antigua	502-7832-4168	info@ceibarent.com
Chicken Truck	Río Dulce	502-5765-5424	monitors VHF ch. 68: *Chicken Truck*
Hertz	Guatemala City	502-3274-4424	info@rentautos.com.gt
Rental El Toque	Antigua	502-5523-9393	riotel@itelgua.com
Rental El Toque	Guatemala City	502-2473-1330	riotel@itelgua.com
Rental El Toque	Quetzaltenango	502-5202-3681	riotel@itelgua.com
Sahara Rent-a-Car	Antigua	502-7831-5500	
Tabarini	Antigua	502-7832-8107	tabarini@tabarini.com
Tabarini	Flores/Santa Elena	502-7926-0253	tabarini@tabarini.com
Tabarini	Guatemala City	502-2331-2643	tabarini@tabarini.com
DIESEL REPAIR/PARTS			
El Toque (The Shop)	Río Dulce	502-7930-5191	riotel@itelgua.com
Mar Marine	Río Dulce	502-7930-5089	
RAM Marina	Río Dulce	502-7930-5408	info@rammarina.com

FACILITY	LOCATION	TELEPHONE	E-MAIL ADDRESS OR WEBSITE
DIVING			
ATi Divers	Solola	502-5706-4117	http://www.atidivers.com/
Pana Divers	Guatemala City	502-2416-3300	http://panadivers.com/
Pro Divers	Guatemala City	502-2416-3300	http://www.prodiverstore.com/
ELECTRONICS/ELECTRICAL			
El Toque (The Shop)	Río Dulce	502-7930-5191	riotel@itelgua.com
Richard	Río Dulce	502-5687-0291	
Transmares S.A.	Guatemala City	502-2339-2990	
Transmares S.A.	Puerto Santo Tomás	502-7339-2990	
Windward Marine	Río Dulce	502-5732-2802	
FABRICATION			
Bruno's	Río Dulce	502-7930-5175	info@brunoshotel.com
Carlos' Welding	Río Dulce		
Don Abel's	Río Dulce	502-7930-5059	
El Toque (The Shop)	Río Dulce	502-7930-5191	riote@itelgua.com
HAUL OUT			
Astilleros Magdalena	Río Dulce	502-7930-5059	
Carlos Welding	Río Dulce		
Nana Juana	Río Dulce	502 7930 5230	info@hotelmarinananajuana.com
RAM Marina Río Dulce	502-7930-5408		info@rammarina.com
HULL REPAIR/PAINTING			
Don Abel's	Río Dulce	502-7930-5059	
El Toque (The Shop)	Río Dulce	502-7930-5191	riote@itelgua.com
Mar Marine	Río Dulce	502-7930-5089	http://marmarine.com/
RAM Marina Río Dulce	502-7930-5408		info@rammarina.com
INTERNET ACCESS			
Alternatives	Xela		
Amatique Bay Mar.	Puerto Barrios	502-7948-1800	info@amatiquebay.net
Atitlan Café	Panahachel		
Bagel Barn	Antigua		http://thebagelbarn.com/
Café Internet (5 loc.)	Guatemala City	502-2337-4004	cafeinternet@centramerica.com
Cyber Place	Guatemala City	502-2232-2660	ciberplace@intelnett.com
Caffé dei Fiori	Guatemala City		
Cafénet	Puerto Barrios		
Café Virtual	Guatemala City	502-2332-8029	
Captain Nemo's	Río Dulce	502-7930-5177	rio@guate.net
Chic Chicken (3 loc.)	Guatemala City	502-2385-4985	
Conexion	Antigua	502-2832-3768	users@conexion.com
Contacto	Río Dulce		
Cyber Center.Net	Puerto Barrios	502-7952-4892	
Cyber Mania	Antigua		
Cyber Mania	Guatemala City	502-2337-4060	usa@cybermania.com
Cyber Mania Tikal	Guatemala City	502-2440-2739	tf@cybermania.com
Cybermannia	Guatemala City		
Denny's Beach	Lago Izabal	502-4636-6156	http://dennysbeach.com/
E-Café	Guatemala City	502-2369-0180	ecafe@al123.com
Enet Café	Guatemala City	502-2332-1404	café@enet.com.gt
Global Net Café	Guatemala City	502-2253-0211	gnc@gdir.com
Hacienda Tijax	Río Dulce	502-7902-0858	tijax@guate.net
Happy Fish Rest.	Livingston	502-5510-3772	happyfishrest@hotmail.com
High Tech	Guatemala City	502-2440-2868	cafeinternetgua@hotmail.com

FACILITY	LOCATION	TELEPHONE	E-MAIL ADDRESS OR WEBSITE
Holiday Inn	Guatemala City		
Hoodie's Boliche	Río Dulce	502-4947-5677	
Hotel Puerto Libre	Puerto Barrios	502-7948-4738	puertolibre@direcway.com
J&M Internet Café	Quetzaltenango	502-761-1436	jmnetcafe@c.net.gt
Maya Com.	Xela		
Moccas Internet	Guatemala City	502-2332-0802	info@moccas.com
RAM Marina	Río Dulce	502-7930-5408	info@rammarina.com
Red Virtu@l	Puerto Barrios	502-5299-8168	rvirtual@intelnett.com
Supernet	Guatemala City	502-2232-6161	msovalle@intelnet.net.gt
Telecabina	Antigua		
Tortugal Marina	Río Dulce	502-7306-6432	info@tortugal.com
Uranus Café	Guatemala City	502-2251-8255	info@educomsa.com
Unais (6 locations)	Guatemala City	502-2385-8661	
Video City	Coatepeque		
Vista Hermosa	Guatemala City	502-2369-6463	vh@cybermannia.com
ZL Represent.	Quetzaltenango		

MARINE SUPPLIES

Agromar	Río Dulce	502-7930-5140	
Commecial Pesq.	Puerto Barrios		
El Toque (*The Shop*)	Río Dulce	502-7930-5191	riote@itelgua.com
Equipos del Rio	Río Dulce	502-7930-5615	equiposdelrio@yahoo.com
Mar Marnie	Río Dulce	502-7930-5089	
RAM Marina	Río Dulce	502-7930-5408	info@rammarina.com
Sistemas Solares	Antigua	502-7934-6754	info@solar.gt
Sistemas Solares	Guatemala City	502-2434-0825	info@solar.gt
Sistemas Solares	Río Dulce	502-7930-5249	info@solar.gt

OUTBOARD REPAIR

Agromar (*Johnson*)	Río Dulce	502-7930-5140	
Canella (*Yamaha*)	Río Dulce	502-7930-5094	
Commecial Pesq.	Puerto Barrios		
Mar Marine (*Suzuki*)	Río Dulce	502-7930-5089	http://marmarine.com/
Recopsa (*Honda*)	Río Dulce		

REFRIGERATION & AC

Hector	Río Dulce	502-5597-1705	
Sandusca Ref.	Puerto Barrios		
Seakist	Río Dulce	502-5027-2093	http://www.seakistservices.com/

RIGGING

El Toque Final	Río Dulce	502-7930-5191	riote@itelgua.com
Cayo Quemado	Río Dulce	502-5776-5856	http://www.quemadosails.com/

SAIL/ CANVAS REPAIR

El Toque Final	Río Dulce	502-7930-5191	riote@itelgua.com
Río Dulce Canvas	Río Dulce		*Río Dulce Canvas* on VHF ch. 68
Cayo Quemado	Río Dulce	502-5776-5856	http://www.quemadosails.com/

Appendix D: Waypoints

Caution: Waypoints are not to be used for navigational purposes. The waypoints in this guide are intended to place you in the general area of the described position. All routes, cuts, and anchorages must be negotiated by eyeball navigation. The author and publisher take no responsibility for the misuse of the following waypoints. Waypoints along any tight passage offer a false sense of security and any navigator who uses waypoints to negotiate a tricky passage instead of piloting by eye is, to be blunt, a fool and deserving of whatever fate befalls him or her. Waypoints are listed from north to south, except for the waypoints on the northern coast of Jamaica which are listed from east to west and then north to south in the Montego Bay and Oracabessa areas, and the waypoints for Honduras, which are listed from west to east and north to south for easy reference.

Latitude is "North" and longitude is "West;" "nm" means *nautical mile(s)*. Datum used is WGS84.

DESCRIPTION	LATITUDE	LONGITUDE
WINDWARD PASSAGE		
Windward Passage- approximately midway between Cuba and Haiti	20° 00.00'	74° 00.00'
NORTHERN COAST OF JAMAICA		
Port Antonio- ½ nm N of entrance channel	18° 11.75'	76° 26.80'
Foster's Cove- ¼ nm N of entrance	18° 21.50'	76° 50.50'
Port Maria- ¼ nm NE of Carabita Island	18° 22.50'	76° 53.00'
Galina Point- 1½ nm N of	18° 25.50'	76° 53.00'
Oracabessa Bay- ½ nm N of point E of bay	18° 25.50'	76° 56.40'
Oracabessa Bay- ¼ nm NW of entrance channel leading to old marina	18° 24.85'	76° 56.78'
Oracabessa Bay-.1 nm NW of entrance channel to anchorage	18° 24.50'	76° 57.05'
Frankfort Point- 1 nm N of	18° 26.30'	77° 02.40'
Ocho Rios- ¾ nm N of marked entrance channel	18° 25.50'	77° 07.00'
St. Ann's Point- 1 nm N of	18° 27.50'	77° 10.25'
St. Ann's Bay- ½ nm NNE of marked entrance channel	18° 27.40'	77° 11.75'
Flat Point- 1¾ nm N of	18° 30.00'	77° 18.50'
Discovery Bay- 1½ nm N of marked entrance channel	18° 28.90'	77° 24.28'
Río Bueno- clears point between Discovery Bay and Río Bueno	18° 29.00'	77° 26.35'
Río Bueno- ¾ nm N of harbor entrance	18° 29.00'	77° 27.35'
Falmouth Harbour- ½ nm NE of	18° 30.35'	77° 38.15'
Montego Bay Point- 1 nm N of	18° 32.00'	77° 53.70'
Montego Bay- ¼ nm N or marked entrance channel	18° 28.30'	77° 56.20'
Bogue Lagoon- ¼ nm NW of entrance channel through reefs	18° 27.28'	77° 57.70'
Bogue Lagoon- inner waypoint at entrance channel through reefs*	18° 27.205'	77° 57.548'
Bogue Lagoon- start of channel exiting lagoon*	18° 27.05'	77° 57.04'
Mosquito Cove- ¼ nm N of entrance	18° 28.00'	78° 06.50'
Lucea; outer waypoint- 1¼ nm NNW of entrance	18° 28.40'	78° 09.80'
Lucea; inner waypoint- 1¼ nm NNW of entrance	18° 27.65'	78° 09.75'
*Use this waypoint a reference, you MUST use your eyes when piloting this channel.		
THE CAYMAN ISLANDS		
Cayman Brac-1 nm NE of northeast tip	19° 46.00'	79° 43.00'
Cayman Brac- 200 yards NNW of town dock	19° 44.81'	79° 46.12'
Cayman Brac, Stake Bay- ¼ nm offshore	19° 43.80'	79° 51.00'
Cayman Brac, Scott's Anchorage- ¼ mile north of rock jetty	19° 41.82'	79° 52.75'
Cayman Brac, Dick Sesinger's Bay- ¼ nm S of entrance channel	19° 40.81'	79° 53.15'
Cayman Brac- 1 nm SW of West End Point	19° 40.00'	79° 54.00'
Little Cayman- 1 nm NE of East Point	19° 43.50'	79° 56.50'
Little Cayman, Main Channel- ¼ nm NE of break in reef	19° 42.73'	79° 57.65'
Little Cayman- ¼ S of entrance channel into Owen's Sound	19° 39.25'	80° 04.45'
Little Cayman- ½ nm SW of West End Point	19° 39.20'	80° 07.00'

DESCRIPTION	LATITUDE	LONGITUDE
Grand Cayman, NW tip- 2 nm N of Boatswain Point	19° 25.00'	81° 25.00'
Grand Cayman, North Sound, turning point to channels from west	19° 24.00'	81° 21.00'
Grand Cayman, North Sound, *Stingray Channel*- ¼ nm N of	19° 23.10'	81° 20.43'
Grand Cayman, North Sound, *Main Channel*- ¼ nm N of	19° 22.90'	81° 19.72'
Grand Cayman, North Sound, *Rum Point Channel*- ¼ nm N of	19° 22.80'	81° 17.50'
Grand Cayman, North Sound, Governor's Creek- ¼ nm ENE of	19° 21.55'	81° 21.90'
Grand Cayman, North Sound, *Kaibo Yacht Club*- ½ nm SW of	19° 21.00'	81° 17.00'
Grand Cayman, East Channel, ½ nm E of channel entrance	19° 18.80'	81° 04.00'
Grand Cayman, North Sound, *Harbour House Marina*, ¼ nm N of ch.	19° 18.10'	81° 19.50'
Grand Cayman, SE tip- 2nm S of eastern reefs	19° 15.00'	81° 05.00'
Grand Cayman, SW tip- 1 nm S of Sand Cay Light	19° 14.00'	81° 24.00'

HONDURAS

Las Islas Santanilla (The Swan Islands)

Las Islas Santanilla- 1 nm N of Isla Grande	17° 26.00'	83° 56.00'
Las Islas Santanilla, Isla Grande, James Bay- ¼ nm NW of	17° 25.00'	83° 56.40'

Islas de la Bahía (The Bay Islands)

Guanaja, Western and Northern Shore

Guanaja, NE tip, 1 nm SE of light at Black Rock Point	16° 29.30'	85° 48.15'
Guanaja, Mangrove Bight- ¼ nm NNW of channel entrance	16° 30.75'	85° 52.65'
Guanaja, Michael Rock Channel- ¼ nm NNW of entrance channel	16° 29.85'	85° 54.15'
Guanaja, Soldado Channel- ¼ nm NW of	16° 28.90'	85° 55.50'
Guanaja, Pine Ridge Channel- ¼ nm NW of entrance to channel	16° 28.85'	85° 55.90'
Guanaja, Pine Ridge Channel- ¼ nm NW of	16° 27.85'	85° 55.90'
Guanaja, Blue Rock Channel- NW waypoint	16° 26.22'	85° 57.13'
Guanaja, Blue Rock Channel- intermediate waypoint	16° 26.10'	85° 56.75'
Guanaja, Blue Rock Channel- ¼ nm SW of Blue Rock	16° 26.03'	85° 56.46'

Guanaja-Eastern and Southern Shore

Guanaja, Savannah Bight, North East Cay Channel- ¼ nm ESE of	16° 28.65'	85° 48.80'
Guanaja, Pond Cay Channel- ¼ nm SE of	16° 26.10'	85° 52.50'

Roatán-Southern Shore

Roatán, Morat- ¼ nm SSE of entrance channel	16° 25.20'	86° 10.90'
Roatán, Isla Barbareta, Pigeon Cay Channel- ¼ nm SSE of entrance	16° 24.60'	86° 07.35'
Roatán, Isla Barbareta, channel W of Pigeon Cays- ¼ nm S of	16° 24.45'	86° 08.60'
Roatán, Helene Harbour- ¼ nm S of entrance channel	16° 24.45'	86° 12.70'
Roatán, Mr. Field Bay- ¼ nm SSW of entrance channel	16° 24.40'	86° 13.95'
Roatán, Old Port Royal Harbor- ¼ nm SSE of entrance channel	16° 24.40'	86° 15.93'
Roatán, Port Royal Harbor- ¼ nm SSE of Fort Cay Channel	16° 23.90'	86° 17.45'
Roatán, shoals SE of Isla Barbaretta-1 nm S of SE tip	16° 23.50'	86° 05.90'
Roatán, Port Royal Harbor- ¼ nm SSE of Lime Cay Channel	16° 23.50'	86° 18.45'
Roatán, Calabash Bight- ¼ nm S of entrance channel	16° 23.00'	86° 20.00'
Roatán, Fiddlers Bight- ¼ nm SSE of entrance channel	16° 23.00'	86° 20.27'
Roatán, Hog Pen Bight- ¼ nm SSE of entrance channel	16° 23.05'	86° 21.75'
Roatán, Oak Ridge Harbor- ¼ nm SSE of entrance channel	16° 22.90'	86° 21.10'
Roatán, Jonesville Bight- ¼ nm S of entrance channel	16° 22.80'	86° 22.35'
Roatán, Carib Point Bight- ¼ nm SE of entrance channel	16° 22.45'	86° 22.90'
Roatán, Neverstain Bight, ¼ nm S of entrance channel	16° 21.90'	86° 23.74'
Roatán, Second Bight, *Parrot Tree Marina*- ¼ S of ent. ch.	16° 21.80'	86° 24.50'
Roatán, Big Cay Channel- ¼ nm SSE of entrance channel	16° 21.30'	86° 25.80'
Roatán, Old French Harbour- ¼ nm SSW of entrance channel	16° 20.85'	86° 27.00'
Roatán, French Harbour- ¼ nm SE of entrance channel	16° 20.80'	86° 27.50'
Roatán, Brick Bay Channel- ¼ nm SSE of entrance	16° 19.65'	86° 28.65'

DESCRIPTION	LATITUDE	LONGITUDE
Roatán, Dixon Cove- ¼ nm S of entrance	16° 19.00'	86° 29.90'
Roatán, Lower Dixon Cove- ¼ nm S of entrance	16° 18.97'	86° 30.35'
Roatán, Coxen Hole- harbor entrance, .4 nm N of *Seal Bank*	16° 18.70'	86° 32.80'
Roatán, Coxen Hole- ¼ nm E of *Seal Bank*	16° 18.30'	86° 32.10'
Roatán, Coxen Hole- ¼ nm W of *Seal Bank*	16° 18.20'	86° 33.20'
Roatán, West End- ¼ m W of channel entrance	16° 17.72'	86° 36.34'

Roatán-Northern Shore

Roatán, Pollytilly Bight Channel- ¼ nm NNW of entrance	16° 24.70'	86° 23.90'
Roatán, Milton Bight Channel- ¼ nm NNW of entrance	16° 24.50'	86° 24.80'
Roatán, Johnson Bight Channel- ¼ nm NNW of entrance	16° 24.20'	86° 25.50'
Roatán, Big Bight Channel- ¼ nm NNW of entrance	16° 23.50'	86° 27.40'
Roatán, Hottest Sparrow Channel- ¼ nm N of entrance	16° 22.20'	86° 30.65'
Roatán, Man O' War Channel- ¼ nm NNW of entrance	16° 21.80'	86° 31.45'
Roatán, Anthony's Key Channel- ¼ nm NNW of entrance	16° 19.80'	86° 34.50'
Roatán, Gibson Bight- ¼ nm NNW of entrance	16° 19.50'	86° 35.28'

Utila

Utila, Puerto Este- .1 SW of entrance channel	16° 05.15'	86° 54.10'
Utila, Diamond Cay- ½ nm E of	16° 03.90'	86° 57.25'

Cayos Cochinos

Cayos Cochinos, Cochino Grande- ½ nm W of NW tip of	15° 59.00'	86° 29.50'
Cayos Cochinos- ¾ nm E of Cochino Grande	15° 58.10'	86° 27.90'
Cayos Cochinos, Lower Monitor Cay- ½ nm S of entrance channel	15° 56.50'	86° 29.05'
Cayos Cochinos- 25' shoal on rhumb line to La Ceiba	15° 54.68'	86° 32.15'

The Mainland

Trujillo- 1½ nm NW of Punta Caxinas	16° 03.00'	86° 02.00'
Punta Sal- 3 nm WNW of	15° 56.00'	87° 39.00'
Puerto Escondido- ½ nm NW of entrance	15° 54.85'	87° 38.50'
Laguna el Diamante- ½ nm NW of entrance	15° 54.00'	87° 39.40'
Puerto Cortés- ¾ nm WNW of Punta Caballos	15° 51.20'	87° 58.60'
La Ceiba, Puerto de Cabotaje- ¼ nm NNW of entrance	15° 48.18'	86° 45.67'
Omoa- ½ nm NW of Punta de Omoa	15° 47.30'	88° 03.50'

GUATEMALA

Cabo Tres Puntas- 1 nm WNW of	15° 58.50'	88° 38.50'
Bahía de Graciosa- ½ nm WNW of entrance	15° 52.50'	88° 34.50'
Puerto Barrios- 1½ nm north of entrance to bay	15° 46.00'	88° 36.90'
Puerto Barrios, *Amatique Bay Marina*- ¼ nm NW of entrance	15° 45.00'	88° 35.00'
Livingston, Río Dulce- ¼ nm NE of sea buoy	15° 50.34'	88° 43.64'
Río Dulce- hot springs- 50' S of	15° 46.46'	88° 48.72'
El Golfete, N- 1.4 nm SW of Cayo Grande	15° 46.60'	88° 50.10'
El Golfete, Bahía de Tejano- ¼ nm NW of entrance	15° 46.30	88° 50.10'
El Golfete, Bahía Buenavista for inbound vessels- ¼ nm NW of ent.	15° 45.63'	88° 50.90'
El Golfete, Bahía Buenavista for outbound vessels- ¼ nm NW of ent.	15° 45.40'	88° 51.10'
El Golfete, Cayo Largo- ½ nm NE of	15° 42.25'	88° 55.27'
Lago Izabal, Finca Jocolo- ¼ nm SE of	15° 36.50'	89° 03.00'
Lago Izabal, Finca Paraiso- ¼ nm SE of	15° 33.50'	89° 12.50'
Lago Izabal, El Estor- ½ nm S of town	15° 31.20'	89° 20.30'
Lago Izabal, Bocas de Bujajal- ½ N of Río Polochic	15° 28.90'	89° 21.50'
Lago Izabal, Denny's Beach- ¼ nm NW of	15° 28.75'	89° 01.41'
Lago Izabal, Mariscos- ¼ nm NW of town	15° 25.69'	89° 05.97'
Lago Izabal, Puerto Refugio- ½ nm N of western tip	15° 24.65'	89° 16.30'

Appendix E: Metric Conversion

Visitors to the Northwest Caribbean, will find the metric system in use and many grocery items and fuel measured in liters and kilograms. As a rule of thumb, a meter is just a little longer than a yard and a liter is very close to a quart. If in doubt use the following table.

1 centimeter (cm) = 0.4 inch	1 inch = 2.54 centimeters
1 meter (m) = 3.28 feet	1 foot = 30.48 centimeters
1 meter = 0.55 fathoms	1 fathom = 1.83 meters
1 kilometer (km) = 0.62 miles	1 yard = 0.91 meters
1 kilometer = 0.54 nautical miles	1 nautical mile = 1.852 kilometers
1 liter (l) = 0.26 gallons	1 gallon = 3.75 liters
1 gram (g) = 0.035 ounces	1 ounce = 28.4 grams
1 metric ton = 1.1 tons	1 pound = 454 grams

Appendix F: A Little Spanish

A Little Basic Spanish

(Just enough to get you into trouble!)

While command of the Spanish language is not a prerequisite for happy cruising in the Northwest Caribbean, knowing a little will certainly help you get by better and everybody will love you for at least trying.

Buenos dias. Good morning.
Buenas tardes. Good afternoon.
Buenas noches. Good night.
¿Cómo está usted? How are you?
¿Muy bien gracias, y usted? I am fine thank you, and you?
¿Como se llama? What is your name?
Me llamo es . . . My name is. . .
¿Habla usted Inglés? Do you speak English?
¿Habla usted Español? Do you speak Spanish?
¿Hay alquien aqui que hable Ingles? Is there anybody here who speaks English?
No muy bien. Not very well.
Muy poco. Very little.
¿Cómo se dice. . . ? How do you say. . .?
¿Como? What did you say?
No entiendo. I don't understand.
No se. I don't know.
Escríbame por favor. Please write it down for me.
¿Donde está e. . .? Where is . . .?
　anclaje-anchorage
　arrecife-reef
　　Bahía-bay
　　bano- bathroom
　　bajo-shoal
　banco-bank
　Capitán de Puerto-Harbormaster
　caleta-cove

canal-channel
desembarcadero-landing
ducha-shower
embarcadero-wharf, quay
ferretería-hardware store
Immigración-Immigration
lavandería-laundry
mecánico-mechanic
médico-doctor
pasaje-passage
punta-point
radas-roadstead
supermercado-supermarket
telefono-telephone
¿Donde puedo comprar . . .? Where can I buy . . .?
Necesito. . . I need. . .?
¿Tiene usted . . .? Do you have. . . ?
   agua-water
   agua potable-drinking water
   arroz- rice
   azúcar-sugar
   café-coffee
   camarones-shrimp
   carne-meat
   cebolla- onions
   cerveza-beer
   chillo- snapper
   cigarillos-cigarettes
   ensalada- salad
   fósforos-matches
   fuego-a light
   gasoil-diesel
   gasolina-gasoline
   helado- ice cream
   hielo- ice
   huevos-eggs
   jamón-ham
   jugo-juice
   jugo de naranjas- orange juice
   langosta- lobster
   leche-milk
   limones-limes
   mantequilla-butter
   mero- sea bass
   narnaja- orange
   pan-bread
   patatas-potatoes
   pavo- turkey
   pina- pineapple
   plátanos-bananas
   pollo-chicken
   propano-propane

queso-cheese
setas- mushrooms
sopa- soup
té- te
tomate-tomato
vino-wine

Colors, Numbers, Directions, and Days:

blanco-white
negro-black
azul-blue
rojo-red
verde-green
amarillo-yellow
aquí-here
allí-there
la derecha-right
la izquierda-left
uno-1
dos-2
tres-3
quatro-4
cinco-5
seis-6
seite-7
ocho-8
nueve-9
diez-10
once-11
doce-12
trece-13
catorce-14
quince-15
diéz y seis-16
diéz y seite-17
diéz y ocho-18
diéz y nuevo-19
veinte-20
veinte y uno-21
treinta-30
cuarenta-40
cincuenta-50
sesenta-60
setenta-70
ochenta-80
noventa-90
cien-100
ciento y uno-101
mil-1,000
mil uno-1,001
lunes-Monday
martes-Tuesday

miércoles-Wednesday
juevos-Thursday
viernos-Friday
sábado-Saturday
domingo-Sunday
ahora-now
manana- tomorrow

¿Quién? Who?
¿Qué? What?
¿Cuando? When?
¿Donde? Where?
¿Por qué? Why?
¿Cómo? How?
¿Qué lejos? How far is it?
    Está lejos. It's far.
    Está cerca. It's near.
¿Qué hora es? What time is it?
¿A qué hora? At what time?
Tengo hambre. I'm hungry.
Perdóneme. Excuse me.
¿Puede ayudarme? Can you help me?
¿Qué es eso? What is this (that)?
¿Cuánto cuesta? What does it cost?
Por favor. Please.
Quisiera... I would like...
Quiero... I want...
    comer to eat
    lo mejor the best
    un habitacion a room
Dame éste. Give me this one.
Dame eso. Give me that one.
No tengo dinero. I have no money.
¡No se mueva! Don't move!
¡Manos arriba! Put your hands up!
¡Buena suerte! Good luck!

Appendix G: Flags

Belize

Honduras

Cayman Islands

Jamaica

Guatemala

Mexico

Index

About the Author

Photo Courtesy of Danielle Courteau

Stephen J. Pavlidis has been cruising and living aboard since 1989. First aboard his 40' cutter-rigged sloop, *IV Play,* and today he is cruising aboard his 31' Chris Craft, *Swan Song.*

Starting in the Exuma Cays, over 20 years ago, Steve began his writing career with guides to the many fascinating destinations he visited. Many of his books stand alone to this day as the quintessential guides to the areas he covers.

His books are different than most other cruising guides in some very significant ways. All of the charts in Steve's books were created using data personally collected while visiting each area using a computerized system that interfaces GPS and depth soundings.

Other books by Stephen J. Pavlidis:

Life at Sea Level, ISBN 978-1-892399-33-5
The Exuma Guide, 3rd Edition, ISBN 978-1-892399-31-1
A Cruising Guide to the Leeward Islands, 2nd Edition, ISBN 978-1-892399-36-6
The Puerto Rico Guide, 3rd Edition, ISBN 978-1-892399-39-7
A Cruising Guide to the Northern Bahamas, ISBN 978-1-892399-28-1
A Cruising Guide to the Turks and Caicos Islands, 3rd Edition, ISBN 978-1-892399-40-3
A Cruising Guide to the Virgin Islands, 2nd Edition, ISBN 978-1-892399-35-9
A Cruising Guide to the Windward Islands, 2nd Edition, ISBN 978-1-892399-37-3
A Cruising Guide to the Southern Bahamas, ISBN 978-1-892399-29-8

CPSIA information can be obtained
at www.ICGtesting.com
Printed in the USA
LVHW060130150922
728420LV00012B/657